NBC HANDBOOK OF PRONUNCIATION

NBC
Handbook of Pronunciation

THIRD EDITION

Originally Compiled by James F. Bender for the
National Broadcasting Company

Revised by Thomas Lee Crowell, Jr.

THOMAS Y. CROWELL COMPANY
New York   Established 1834

CONTENTS

PREFACE TO
THE THIRD EDITION

FIRST PUBLISHED IN 1943, the *NBC Handbook of Pronunciation* has established itself as the standard reference book on pronunciation in General American speech. This Third Edition contains more than 20,000 entries, a 30 per cent increase over the Second Edition. Outdated entries have been deleted, the core vocabulary has been checked, and many new words have been introduced. These include terms from all areas of space-age technology, international politics and diplomacy, medicine, sociology, the arts, economics, law, philosophy, psychology, and religion, as well as additional familiar but difficult-to-pronounce names of people and places.

Persons whose names have come to the attention of American audiences during the last decade have been listed in a special supplement of Names in the News, an international roster of statesmen, politicians, writers, scientists, artists, entertainers, sports figures, and socialites.

As it was of the Second Edition, the purpose of the present book has been to record the pronunciations used by educated persons in the greater part of the United States, rather than to insist upon arbitrary standards of pronunciation unrelated to those commonly heard. The criteria employed by the editor in choosing both the words to be listed and their pronunciations are explained in the following section of the book, Standards of American Pronunciation. The principles observed have been essentially those of the previous edition, except for a tendency toward simplification, as in the omission of most secondary accents and of certain sounds found in foreign words but not in the patterns of American speech, such as nasalized vowels in French.

The section on Standards of American Pronunciation also describes in detail the respelling system used in this book, including tables of sounds in American speech and the International Phonetic Alphabet.

The publishers record with deep regret the death of Dr. Thomas Lee Crowell, Jr., who prepared the revised manuscript for this edition. We are indebted to Mrs. Constance Taber Colby for advice and guidance during the late stages of the book's production, and to Jonathan Kaye, who, with the assistance of Miss Rochelle Braunstein, contributed most of the pronunciations for Names in the News.

STANDARDS OF
AMERICAN PRONUNCIATION

THAT PRONUNCIATION is best which is most readily understood, and that pronunciation is most readily understood which is used by most people. Thus a standard of pronunciation for the American radio and television broadcaster is reasonably based upon the speech heard and used by the audience that the broadcaster reaches. This means that the broadcaster would use the pronunciation that is spoken by the educated people of the area served by the station. If the station is a local one, the broadcaster would do well to pronounce words as the educated people of his community pronounce them. Otherwise he might be difficult to comprehend and might even alienate a part of his audience. On the other hand, when a broadcaster speaks over a powerful station or nation-wide hookup, he will be most readily understood by the majority of his listeners if he uses the pronunciation called by phoneticians "General American." That is the standard presented in this book.

It should be pointed out that this book does not pretend to prescribe how words *should* be pronounced according to some arbitrary standard; it merely records how they *are* pronounced by educated speakers across the greater part of the United States. Americans have never consented to have "correct" pronunciation laid down for them by a government academy, as is done in several European nations. It is not the purpose of this book to take the place of such an agency. This book is designed solely to present a convenient compilation of those pronunciations that will be immediately comprehensible to a great majority of Americans.

While there are many current varieties of British and American speech, the three main dialects used in the United States and Canada are frequently referred to as (*a*) New England, or Eastern, (*b*) Southern, (*c*) Western, Middle Western, or General American. According to the estimates made by Professor J. S. Kenyon, ten or eleven million Americans and Canadians speak the New England, or Eastern, dialect; twenty-six million the Southern variety; and at least ninety million speak General American. The fundamental differences among these three main dialects are few, but quite definite.

The words selected for listing in this book obviously represent only a small part of the rich vocabulary of contemporary American speech. This particular group of 20,000 words was chosen mainly from three classes:

1. Words, especially proper names, most frequently used by broadcasters.
2. Common words often mispronounced.
3. Perennially "difficult" names from history and the arts.

In those cases where variant pronunciations of a word are equally acceptable, an arbitrary decision has been made to include only one. For example, some excellent speakers prefer to pronounce the first vowel of *economics* as in the word *ell*, while others use the vowel as in *eel*; some say "nooz," others "nyooz," and still others use an intermediary vowel sound. Although there are thousands of words in everyday use that may be pronounced in alternate ways, the plan for this book called for one pronunciation for each word.

WAYS OF NOTING PRONUNCIATION

The spelling of the English language is highly inconsistent with its pronunciation. A letter such as *c* represents one sound in a word like *curtain* and an entirely different sound in *certain*. With this one exception, both words are pronounced alike despite the different spellings, i.e. *ur* and *er*, which represent the same vowel sound in the first syllable of each word. Words that are pronounced alike, such as meat–meet, pare–pear, two–too, etc., are known as homophones. Another source of inconsistency is the aphthong, or letter that is not pronounced in English words. There are many such letters: mus*c*le, plum*b*er, *gh*ost, has*t*en being representative.

In order to record pronunciation graphically, we must have some system that allows one symbol for each sound. Since there are twenty-six letters in the spelling alphabet and approximately forty sounds in American speech, it is obvious that more symbols are needed for recording pronunciation correctly. The need is met by at least three systems of notation, namely: diacritical markings, the International Phonetic Alphabet, and respelling.

A diacritical marking is attached to a letter to distinguish it in sound. A widely used system of diacritical markings of vowels in American speech is found in *Webster's New International Dictionary*.

The International Phonetic Alphabet, commonly referred to as the IPA, is perhaps less cumbersome than diacritical markings. Since many of the symbols are taken from the spelling alphabet, one may learn the IPA without a great expenditure of time. Within the last fifteen years it has become widely used in schools and colleges, and its present as well as future usefulness seems assured. There is a narrow version of the IPA and a broad one. The broad IPA has been selected for transcription in this book.

Many persons prefer respelling to the other two systems. Respelling has the advantage of making use of the symbols that comprise the spelling alphabet, so that it is not necessary to learn any new letters. On the other hand, respelling is likely to be less reliable than diacritical markings or the IPA, especially in regard to the unaccented vowel sound which occurs in words like lem*o*n, *a*bout, tak*e*n, penc*i*l, circ*u*s. Here, *uh* is used to record the unaccented vowel and also the accented vowel as in the word *up*, though, admittedly, it does not accurately represent the sound of the unaccented vowel.

Each word recorded in this book is transcribed twice. Thus, the demands of those who do not wish to learn new symbols as well as those who want to make use of the most modern system of pronunciation notation are met.

The problem of recording the pronunciation of foreign-language words is especially difficult because they involve many more sounds than are used in

American speech. Moreover, the average broadcaster cannot reproduce many of these sounds with any degree of faithfulness. A Russian *r*, for example, is different from an American *r*, and only after much practice under competent supervision can an American master a Russian *r* or, conversely, a Russian learn an American *r*.

While it is reasonable to expect an American announcer to master the sounds of one other language—usually French, Spanish, or German—it is obviously unfair to expect him to learn to produce correctly all the sounds of all the languages. What the announcer ordinarily does when confronted with new words of a foreign language is to approximate the native pronunciations in so far as the sounds of American speech will allow, unless, of course, the words have been anglicized, as in the case of *Florence, Italy*, for *Firenze, Italia*. This tendency conforms to what the layman does.

Thus, the pronunciations of foreign words recorded in this manual are only broadly approximate for the most part, yet they represent what broadcasters and educated listeners say. An example is the German word *Reich*. Here the final sound is a kind of prolonged *k* which is not found in the family of English or American speech sounds. The pronunciation most often heard in General American is *righk*. Similarly, the nasalization of vowels commonly found in French is not within the normal range of American speech; therefore, as in *pièce de résistance* (pyes duh ray zee STAHNS), it is not indicated in the pronouncing key. In the case of French words such as *chanteuse*, two approximations of the vowel sound in the final syllable are commonly heard: shahn TERZ and shahn TOO : Z. The former is included here as being somewhat closer to the actual French. In certain Oriental languages, no syllable is stressed more than another. This fact is indicated in the second column by printing all syllables in lower case letters: for example, *Keijo* is pronounced *kay joh*. However, in the case of familiar Oriental words that have become Americanized, such as *sukiyaki*, stresses are indicated as the word is normally pronounced in America.

The IPA and respelling systems used in this manual are as follows:

KEY WORD	RESPELLING	IPA
*a*t	*a*t	æt
ah	*ah*	ɑ
air	*air*	ɛər
*aw*ful	*AW* fuhl	ˈɔfəl
s*ay*	s*ay*	se
*b*ack	*b*ak	bæk
*ch*air	*ch*air	tʃɛər
d*o*	d*oo* :	du
*e*lm	*e*lm	ɛlm
*ee*l	*ee*l	il
*ser*ver	*SER* ver	ˈsɝvər
serv*er*	SER *ver*	ˈsɝvər
*f*it	*f*it	fɪt
*g*o	*g*oh	go
*h*urt	*h*ert	hɝt

KEY WORD	RESPELLING	IPA
*i*s	*i*z	ɪz
h*igh*	h*igh*	haɪ
*j*et	*j*et	dʒɛt
*k*iss	*k*is	kɪs
*l*amb	*l*am	læm
*m*y	*m*igh	maɪ
*n*ice	*n*ighs	naɪs
si*ng*	si*ng*	sɪŋ
oh	*oh*	o
*oi*l	*oi*l	ɔɪl
f*oo*t	f*oo*t	fʊt
f*oo*d	f*oo*:d	fud
ho*w*	ho*w*	haʊ
*p*ie	*p*igh	paɪ
*r*ay	*r*ay	re
*s*o	*s*oh	so
*sh*all	*sh*al	ʃæl
*t*o	*t*oo:	tu
*th*in	*th*in	θɪn
*th*en	*th*:en	ðɛn
*a*bove	*uh* BUHV	əˈbʌv
ab*o*ve	uh B*UH*V	əˈbʌv
*v*ine	*v*ighn	vaɪn
*w*ine	*w*ighn	waɪn
*wh*ine	*hw*ighn	hwaɪn
*y*ou	*y*oo:	ju
*z*oo	*z*oo:	zu
rou*ge*	roo:*zh*	ruʒ

NBC HANDBOOK OF PRONUNCIATION

A

Aachen	AH kuhn	ˈɑkən
Aalborg	AWL bawr	ˈɔlbɔr
Aalsmeer	AHLS mair	ˈɑlsmɛr
Aalten	AHL tuhn	ˈɑltən
Aaron	AI ruhn	ˈɛrən
Abaco	A buh koh	ˈæbəko
abacus	A buh kuhs	ˈæbəkəs
abandon	uh BAN duhn	əˈbændən
abattoir	a buh TWAHR	æbəˈtwar
Abaya, Hernando	ah BIGH ah, air NAHN doh	ɑˈbaɪɑ, ɛrˈnɑndo
Abbas	ah BAHS	ɑˈbas
abbé	A bay	ˈæbe
Abdallah	ahb DAH lah	ɑbˈdɑlɑ
abdomen	ab DOH muhn	æbˈdomən
abdominal	ab DAH mi nuhl	æbˈdɑmɪnəl
Abednego	a BED ni goh	æˈbɛdnɪgo
Abelard	A buh lahrd	ˈæbəlard
Abello	ah BE yaw	ɑˈbɛjɔ
Abercrombie, Abercromby	A ber kruhm bi	ˈæbərkrəmbɪ
Aberdeen (Scotland)	a ber DEEN	æbərˈdin
aberrant	a BAI ruhnt	æˈbɛrənt
aberration	a buh RAY shuhn	æbəˈreʃən
Aberystwyth	a buh RIST with	æbəˈrɪstwɪθ
abeyance	uh BAY uhns	əˈbeəns
abhor	uhb HAWR	əbˈhɔr
abhorrent	uhb HAW ruhnt	əbˈhɔrənt
Abidjan	AH bee jahn	ˈɑbidʒɑn
Abigail	A bi gayl	ˈæbɪgel
Abilene (Syria)	a buh LEE ni	æbəˈlinɪ
Abilene (U.S.)	A buh leen	ˈæbəlin
Abimelech	uh BI muh lek	əˈbɪmələk
Abinoam	uh BI noh am	əˈbɪnoæm
abject (a)	AB jekt	ˈæbdʒɛkt
ablation	a BLAY shuhn	æˈbleʃən
ablution	uh BLOO: shuhn	əˈbluʃən
aboriginal	a buh RI juh nuhl	æbəˈrɪdʒənəl
aborigines	a buh RI juh neez	æbəˈrɪdʒəniz
abort	uh BAWRT	əˈbɔrt
abortive	uh BAWR tiv	əˈbɔrtɪv
Abou ben Adhem	AH boo: ben AH dem	ˈɑbu bɛn ˈɑdɛm

at [æ]; ah [ɑ]; air [ɛ]; awful [ɔ]; say [e]; back [b]; chair [tʃ]; do [d]; elm [ɛ]; eel [i]; server [ˈɝ, ər]; fit [f]; go [g]; hurt [h]; is [ɪ]; high [aɪ]; jet [dʒ]; kiss [k]; lamb [l]; my [m]; nice [n]; sing [ŋ]; oh [o]; oil [ɔɪ]; foot [ʊ]; foo:d [u]; how [aʊ]; pie [p]; ray [r]; so [ ]; shall [ʃ]; to [t]; thin [θ]; th:en [ð]; above (uh BUHV) [ə, ˈʌ]; vine [v]; wine [w]; wh e [hw]; you [j]; zoo [z]; rouge (roo:zh) [ʒ].

H.P.—B

abracadabra	A bruh kuh DA bruh	ˈæbrəkəˈdæbrə
Abraham	AY bruh ham	ˈebrəhæm
Abram	AY bruhm	ˈebrəm
abrasion	uh BRAY zhuhn	əˈbreʒən
abrogate	A bruh gayt	ˈæbrəget
Abruzzi	a BROO : T si	æˈbrutsɪ
abscess	AB ses	ˈæbsɛs
abscissa	ab SI suh	æbˈsɪsə
abscond	ab SKAHND	æbˈskɑnd
absent (a)	AB suhnt	ˈæbsənt
absent (v)	ab SENT	æbˈsɛnt
absentee	AB suhn tee	ˈæbsənti
absinthe	AB sinth	ˈæbsɪnθ
absolute	AB suh loo : t	ˈæbsəlut
absolutely	AB suh loo : t li	ˈæbsəlutlɪ
absolve	uhb SAHLV	əbˈsɑlv
absorb	uhb SAWRB	əbˈsɔrb
abstemious	ab STEE mi uhs	æbˈstimɪəs
abstract (a, n)	AB strakt	ˈæbstrækt
abstract (v)	ab STRAKT	æbˈstrækt
abstruse	uhb STROO : S	əbˈstrus
absurd	uhb SERD	əbˈsɝd
absurdity	uhb SER duh ti	əbˈsɝdətɪ
abuse (n)	uh BYOO : S	əˈbjus
abuse (v)	uh BYOO : Z	əˈbjuz
abusive	uh BYOO : siv	əˈbjusɪv
Abydos (Egypt)	uh BIGH dahs	əˈbaɪdɑs
abyss	uh BIS	əˈbɪs
Abyssinia	a buh SI ni uh	æbəˈsɪnɪə
acacia	uh KAY shuh	əˈkeʃə
academe	a kuh DEEM	ækəˈdim
academician	uh ka duh MI shuhn	əkædəˈmɪʃən
académie (Fr.)	a ka day MEE	ækædeˈmi
academy	uh KA duh mi	əˈkædəmɪ
Acadia	uh KAY di uh	əˈkedɪə
acanthus	uh KAN thuhs	əˈkænθəs
a cappella	ah kuh PE luh	ɑkəˈpɛlə
a capriccio	ah kah PREE choh	ɑkɑˈpritʃo
accelerando	ak se luh RAHN doh	æksɛləˈrɑndo
accelerate	ak SE luh rayt	ækˈsɛləret
accelerator	ak SE luh ray ter	ækˈsɛləretər
accelerometer	ak se luh RAH muh ter	æksɛləˈrɑmətər
accent (n)	AK sent	ˈæksɛnt
accent (v)	ak SENT	ækˈsɛnt
accept	ak SEPT	ækˈsɛpt
acceptable	ak SEP tuh buhl	ækˈsɛptəbəl
acceptance	ak SEPT tuhns	ækˈsɛptəns
access (n)	AK ses	ˈæksɛs
accessary, accessory	ak SE suh ri	ækˈsɛsərɪ
acclamation	a kluh MAY shuhn	ækləˈmeʃən
acclimate	a KLIGH mit	æˈklaɪmɪt
acclimation	a kli MAY shuhn	æklɪˈmeʃən

---

at [æ]; ah [ɑ]; air [ɛ]; awful [ɔ]; say [e]; back [b]; chair [tʃ]; do [d]; elm [ɛ]; eel [i];
server [ˈɝ, ər]; fit [f]; go [g]; hurt [h]; is [ɪ]; high [aɪ]; jet [dʒ]; kiss [k]; lamb [l]; my [m];
nice [n];

acclimatization	uh KLIGH muh ti ZAY shuhn	əˈklaɪmətɪˈzeʃən
acclimatize	uh KLIGH muh tighz	əˈklaɪmətaɪz
accolade	A kuh layd	ˈækəled
accompaniment	uh KUHM puh ni muhnt	əˈkʌmpənɪmənt
accompanist	uh KUHM puh nist	əˈkʌmpənɪst
accomplish	uh KAHM plish	əˈkɑmplɪʃ
accouchement	uh KOO : SH muhnt	əˈkuʃmənt
accoucheur	a koo : SHER	æku'ʃɚ
accouter, accoutre	uh KOO : ter	əˈkutər
accouterment, accoutrement	uh KOO : ter muhnt	əˈkutərmənt
Accra	ah KRAH	ɑˈkrɑ
accredit	uh KRE dit	əˈkrɛdɪt
accrue	uh KROO :	əˈkru
accuracy	A kyuh ruh si	ˈækjərəsɪ
accurate	A kyuh rit	ˈækjərɪt
Aceldama	uh SEL duh muh	əˈsɛldəmə
acerbate	A ser bayt	ˈæsərbet
acerbity	uh SER bi ti	əˈsɚbɪtɪ
acervate	uh SER vit	əˈsɚvɪt
acetanilid, -e	a suh TA nuh lid	æsəˈtænəlɪd
acetate	A suh tayt	ˈæsətet
acetic	uh SEE tik	əˈsitɪk
acetylene	uh SE tuh leen	əˈsɛtəlin
Achaean	uh KEE uhn	əˈkiən
Achaia	uh KAY uh	əˈkeə
Achenbach	AH kuhn bahk	ˈɑkənbɑk
Acheron	A kuh ruhn	ˈækərən
Acheson, Dean	A chi suhn, deen	ˈætʃɪsən, din
Achilles	uh KI leez	əˈkɪliz
Achitophel	uh KI tuh fel	əˈkɪtəfɛl
achromatic	a kruh MA tik	ækrəˈmætɪk
acid	A sid	ˈæsɪd
acidity	uh SI duh ti	əˈsɪdətɪ
acidoid	A si doid	ˈæsɪdɔɪd
acidulous	uh SI juh luhs	əˈsɪdʒələs
acierate	A si uh rayt	ˈæsɪəret
acinus	A si nuhs	ˈæsɪnəs
acme	AK mi	ˈækmɪ
acne	AK ni	ˈæknɪ
acolyte	A kuh light	ˈækəlaɪt
aconite	A kuh night	ˈækənaɪt
acorn	AY kawrn	ˈekɔrn
Acosta	ah KAW stah	ɑˈkɔstɑ
acousticon, A-	uh KOO : sti kahn	əˈkustɪkɑn
acoustics	uh KOO : stiks	əˈkustɪks
acquaintance	uh KWAYN tuhns	əˈkwentəns
acquiesce	a kwi ES	ækwɪˈɛs
acquisitive	uh KWI zuh tiv	əˈkwɪzətɪv
acrimony	A kruh moh ni	ˈækrəmonɪ
acromegaly	a kroh ME guh li	ækroˈmɛgəli

sing [ŋ] ; *oh* [o] ; *oil* [ɔɪ] ; foot [ʊ] ; foo*d* [u] ; *how* [aʊ] ; *p*ie [p] ; *r*ay [r] ; *s*o [s] ; *sh*all [ʃ] ;
*t*o [t] ; *th*in [θ] ; *th:*en [ð] ; above (*uh* B*UH*V) [ə, ˈʌ] ; *v*ine [v] ; *w*ine [w] ; *wh*ine [hw] ;
*y*ou [j] ; *z*oo [z] ; rouge (roo:*zh*) [ʒ].

acronym	A kruh nim	ˈækrənɪm
acropolis	uh KRAH puh lis	əˈkrɑpəlɪs
across	uh KRAWS	əˈkrɔs
acrostic	uh KRAW stik	əˈkrɔstɪk
acrylic	uh KRI lik	əˈkrɪlɪk
Actaeon	ak TEE uhn	ækˈtiən
actin	AK tin	ˈæktɪn
Actium	AK ti uhm	ˈæktɪəm
actomyosin	ak tuh MIGH uh sin	æktəˈmaɪəsɪn
actor	AK ter	ˈæktər
acts	akts	ækts
actual	AK choo uhl	ˈæktʃʊəl
actually	AK choo uh li	ˈæktʃʊəlɪ
acumen	uh KYOO : muhn	əˈkjumən
acute	uh KYOO : T	əˈkjut
Ada, Adah	AY duh	ˈedə
adage	A dij	ˈædɪdʒ
adagio	uh DAH zhi oh	əˈdɑʒɪo
adamant	A duh muhnt	ˈædəmənt
adamantine	a duh MAN tin	ædəˈmæntɪn
Adamic, Louis	A duh mik	ˈædəmɪk
addict (n)	A dikt	ˈædɪkt
addict (v)	uh DIKT	əˈdɪkt
Addis Ababa	A dis AH buh buh	ˈædɪsˈɑbəbə
addle	A duhl	ˈædəl
address (n)	A dres	ˈædrɛs
address (v)	uh DRESS	əˈdrɛs
addressograph	uh DRE suh graf	əˈdrɛsəgræf
adduce	uh DYOO : S	əˈdjus
Adelaide	A duh layd	ˈædəled
Adelphi (college)	uh DEL figh	əˈdɛlfaɪ
Aden	AH duhn	ˈɑdən
Adenauer, Konrad	AH duh now er, KOHN raht	ˈɑdənauər, ˈkonrat
adenoid	A duh noid	ˈædənɔɪd
adenosine	uh DE nuh sin	əˈdɛnəsɪn
adept (a)	uh DEPT	əˈdɛpt
adept (n)	A dept	ˈædɛpt
adequate	A duh kwit	ˈædəkwɪt
adermin	uh DER min	əˈdɚmɪn
à deux	ah DER	ɑˈdɚ
adherence	ad HI ruhns	ædˈhɪrəns
adherent	ad HI ruhnt	ædˈhɪrənt
adhesion	ad HEE zhuhn	ædˈhiʒən
ad hoc	ad HAHK	ædˈhɑk
ad hominem	ad HAH mi nem	ædˈhɑmɪnɛm
adiantum	a di AN tuhm	ædɪˈæntəm
adieu, -x	uh DYOO :, -Z	əˈdju, -z
Adige	AH dee je	ˈɑdidʒe
ad infinitum	ad in fi NIGH tuhm	ædɪnfɪˈnaɪtəm
ad interim	ad IN tuh rim	ædˈɪntərɪm
adios	ah DYOHS	ɑˈdjos

at [æ]; ah [ɑ]; air [ɛ]; awful [ɔ]; say [e]; back [b]; chair [tʃ]; do [d]; elm [ɛ]; eel [i];
server [ˈɝ, ər]; fit [f]; go [g]; hurt [h]; is [ɪ]; high [aɪ]; jet [dʒ]; kiss [k]; lamb [l]; my [m];
nice [n];

adipose	A duh pohs	ˈædəpos
adjacent	uh JAY suhnt	əˈdʒesənt
adjective	A jik tiv	ˈædʒɪktɪv
adjourn	uh JERN	əˈdʒɜ˞n
adjudicate	uh JOO: di kayt	əˈdʒudɪket
adjunct	A juhngkt	ˈædʒəŋkt
adjure	uh JOOR	əˈdʒʊr
adjust	uh JUHST	əˈdʒʌst
adjutant	A juh tuhnt	ˈædʒətənt
Adlai	AD lay	ˈædle
ad libitum	ad LI bi tuhm	ædˈlɪbɪtəm
admirable	AD muh ruh buhl	ˈædmərəbəl
admiralty, A-	AD muh ruhl ti	ˈædmərəltɪ
admit	ad MIT	ædˈmɪt
admittance	ad MIT ns	ædˈmɪtns
admonish	ad MAH nish	ædˈmɑnɪʃ
ad nauseam	ad NAW zi uhm	ædˈnɔzɪəm
adobe	uh DOH bi	əˈdobɪ
adolescence	a duh LE suhns	ædəˈlɛsəns
Adonais	a duh NAY is	ædəˈneɪs
Adonijah	a duh NIGH juh	ædəˈnaɪdʒə
Adonis	uh DAH nis	əˈdɑnɪs
adorable	uh DOH ruh buhl	əˈdorəbəl
adoration	a duh RAY shuhn	ædəˈreʃən
adrenal	uh DREE nuhl	əˈdrinəl
adrenalin, -e	uh DRE nuh lin	əˈdrɛnəlɪn
adrenergic	a dre NER jik	ædrɛˈnɜ˞dʒɪk
Adriatic	ay dri A tik	edrɪˈætɪk
adroit	uh DROIT	əˈdrɔɪt
adtevac	AD tuh vak	ˈædtəvæk
adulatory	A juh luh taw ri	ˈædʒələtɔrɪ
Adullum	uh DUH luhm	əˈdʌləm
adult	uh DUHLT	əˈdʌlt
adumbrate	uh DUHM brayt	əˈdʌmbret
ad valorem	ad vuh LOH ruhm	æd vəˈlorəm
advance	uhd VANS	ədˈvæns
advantage	uhd VAN tij	ədˈvæntɪdʒ
advantageous	ad vuhn TAY juhs	ædvənˈtedʒəs
advent	AD vent	ˈædvɛnt
adventure	uhd VEN cher	ədˈvɛntʃər
adversary	AD ver se ri	ˈædvərsɛrɪ
adverse	uhd VERS	ədˈvɜ˞s
advertise	AD ver tighz	ˈædvərtaɪz
advertisement	ad ver TIGHZ muhnt	ædvərˈtaɪzmənt
advertiser	AD ver tigh zer	ˈædvərtaɪzər
advice (n)	uhd VIGHS	ədˈvaɪs
advise (v)	uhd VIGHZ	ədˈvaɪz
advocacy	AD vuh kuh si	ˈædvəkəsɪ
advocate (n)	AD vuh kit	ˈædvəkɪt
advocate (v)	AD vuh kayt	ˈædvəket
Aegean	uh JEE uhn	əˈdʒiən
Aegeus	EE ji uhs	ˈidʒɪəs

si*ng* [ŋ]; *oh* [o]; *oil* [ɔɪ]; *foot* [ʊ]; *foo:*d [u]; *how* [aʊ]; *p*ie [p]; *r*ay [r]; *s*o [s]; s*h*all [ʃ];
*t*o [t]; *th*in [θ]; *th:*en [ð]; *a*bove (*uh* B*U*HV) [ə, ˈʌ]; *v*ine [v]; *w*ine [w]; *wh*ine [hw];
*y*ou [j]; *z*oo [z]; rouge (roo:*zh*) [ʒ].

aegis	EE jis	ˈidʒɪs
Aegisthus	ee JIS thuhs	iˈdʒɪsθəs
Aeneas	i NEE uhs	ɪˈniəs
Aeneid	i NEE id	ɪˈniɪd
Aeolian	ee OH li uhn	iˈoliən
Aeolus	EE uh luhs	ˈiələs
aeon	EE uhn	ˈiən
aerate	AI rayt	ˈɛret
aerial (a)	ay I ri uhl	eˈɪriəl
aerial (n)	AI ri uhl	ˈɛriəl
aerie	AI ri	ˈɛri
aerodrome	AI ruh drohm	ˈɛrədrom
aerodyne	AI ruh dighn	ˈɛrədaɪn
aeronaut	AI ruh nawt	ˈɛrənɔt
aeronautics	ai ruh NAW tiks	ɛrəˈnɔtɪks
Aerovias	igh roh VEE ahs	aɪroˈvias
aery	AI ri	ˈɛri
Aeschines	E ski neez	ˈɛskɪniz
Aeschylus	E skuh luhs	ˈɛskələs
Aesculapius	e skyuh LAY pi uhs	ɛskjəˈlepiəs
Aesop	EE sahp	ˈisɑp
aesthete	ES theet	ˈɛsθit
aesthetic	es THE tik	ɛsˈθɛtɪk
Aetna	ET nuh	ˈɛtnə
affair	uh FAIR	əˈfɛr
affaire	a FAIR	æˈfɛr
affenpinscher	AH fuhn pin sher	ˈɑfənpɪnʃər
afferent	A fuh ruhnt	ˈæfərənt
affirm	uh FERM	əˈfɝm
affirmation	a fer MAY shuhn	æfərˈmeʃən
affix (n)	A fiks	ˈæfɪks
affix (v)	uh FIKS	əˈfɪks
affluence	A floo uhns	ˈæfluəns
affluent	A floo uhnt	ˈæfluənt
affront	uh FRUHNT	əˈfrʌnt
afghan, A-	AF gan	ˈæfgæn
Afghanistan	af GA nuh stan	æfˈgænəstæn
aficionado	a fee syuh NAH do	æfisjəˈnɑdo
a fortiori	ay fawr shi O ri	e fɔrʃiˈori
Africa	A fri kuh	ˈæfrɪkə
Africaine	a free KEN	æfriˈkɛn
Africana	a fri KAH nah	æfrɪˈkɑnɑ
Africanthropus	a fri KAN thruh puhs	æfrɪˈkænθrəpəs
Afrikaans	a fri KAHNZ	æfrɪˈkɑnz
Afro-	A froh	ˈæfro
aft	aft	æft
after	AF ter	ˈæftər
aftosa	af TOH suh	æfˈtosə
Agag	AY gag	ˈegæg
again	uh GEN	əˈgɛn
against	uh GENST	əˈgɛnst
Aga Khan	AH guh KAHN	ˈɑgə ˈkɑn

at [æ]; ah [ɑ]; air [ɛ]; awful [ɔ]; say [e]; back [b]; chair [tʃ]; do [d]; elm [ɛ]; eel [i];
server [ˈɝ, ər]; fit [f]; go [g]; hurt [h]; is [ɪ]; high [aɪ]; jet [dʒ]; kiss [k]; lamb [l]; my [m];
nice [n];

Agamemnon	a guh MEM nuhn	ægəˈmɛmnən
agape (" love ")	uh GAH pay	əˈgɑpe
agape (" wide open ")	uh GAYP	əˈgep
agar, A-	AY gahr	ˈegɑr
agaric	uh GA rik	əˈgærɪk
Agassiz	A guh si	ˈægəsɪ
agate	A git	ˈægɪt
agave	uh GAY vi	əˈgevɪ
Agee	uh GEE	əˈgi
agenda	uh JEN duh	əˈdʒɛndə
ageratum	a juh RAY tuhm	ædʒəˈretəm
aggrandize	A gruhn dighz	ˈægrəndaɪz
aggrandizement	uh GRAN diz muhnt	əˈgrændɪzmənt
aggravate	A gruh vayt	ˈægrəvet
aggregate (a, n)	A gruh git	ˈægrəgɪt
aggregate (v)	A gruh gayt	ˈægrəget
aggressor	uh GRE ser	əˈgrɛsər
aghast	uh GAST	əˈgæst
agile	A jil	ˈædʒɪl
agility	uh JI luh ti	əˈdʒɪlətɪ
Agincourt	A jin kawrt	ˈædʒɪnkɔrt
agitato	ah ji TAH toh	ɑdʒɪˈtɑto
agnostic	ag NAH stik	ægˈnɑstɪk
Agnus Dei	AG nuhs DEE igh	ˈægnəs ˈdiaɪ
agoraphobia	a guh ruh FOH bi uh	ægərəˈfobɪə
Agrado	ah GRAH doh	ɑˈgrado
agrarian	a GRAI ri uhn	æˈgrɛrɪən
agravic	uh GRA vik	əˈgrævɪk
agreeable	uh GREE uh buhl	əˈgriəbəl
agriculture	A gri kuhl cher	ˈægrɪkəltʃər
agriculturist	A gri kuhl chuh rist	ˈægrɪkəltʃərɪst
agronomist	uh GRAH nuh mist	əˈgrɑnəmɪst
ague	AY gyoo :	ˈegju
Aguecheek	AY gyoo cheek	ˈegjʊtʃik
Aguilar	ah gi LAHR	ɑgɪˈlɑr
Aguinaldo	ah gi NAHL doh	ɑgɪˈnaldo
Aguirre	ah GEE ray	ɑˈgire
Ahab	AY hab	ˈehæb
Ahasuerus	uh haz yoo EE ruhs	əhæzjʊˈirəs
Ahaz	AY haz	ˈehæz
Aherne, Brian	uh HERN, BRIGH uhn	əˈhɜn, ˈbraɪən
Ahitophel	uh HI tuh fel	əˈhɪtəfɛl
Ahmed	AH med	ˈɑmɛd
aide-de-camp	AYD duh KAMP	ˈed dəˈkæmp
aigrette	AY gret	ˈegrɛt
aiguillette	ay gwi LET	egwɪˈlɛt
Aiken	AY kuhn	ˈekən
ailurophobia	ay loo ruh FOH bi uh	elʊrəˈfobɪə
aîné	ay NAY	eˈne
Ainsworth	AYNS werth	ˈenswərθ
airplane	AIR playn	ˈɛrplen
aisle	ighl	aɪl

---

sing [ŋ] ; *oh* [o] ; *oil* [ɔɪ] ; *foot* [ʊ] ; *foo:d* [u] ; *how* [aʊ] ; *pie* [p] ; *ray* [r] ; *so* [s] ; *shall* [ʃ] ; *to* [t] ; *thin* [θ] ; *th:en* [ð] ; *above* (*uh* B*UH*V) [ə, ˈʌ] ; *vine* [v] ; *wine* [w] ; *whine* [hw] ; *you* [j] ; *zoo* [z] ; *rouge* (roo:*zh*) [ʒ].

Aisne	ayn	en
Aix-la-Chapelle	AYKS lah shah PEL	ˈekslaʃaˈpɛl
Ajaccio	ah YAH choh	aˈjatʃo
Ajax	AY jaks	ˈedʒæks
Akeley	AY kli	ˈeklɪ
Akihito	ah ki HEE toh	akɪˈhito
akin	uh KIN	əˈkɪn
Akintola	a keen TAW lah	ækinˈtɔla
Akyab	ahk YAHB	akˈyab
à la	ah lah	ala
Alabama	a luh BA muh	æləˈbæmə
alabaster	A luh ba ster	ˈæləbæstər
Aladdin	uh LA din	əˈlædɪn
Alamo	A luh moh	ˈæləmo
Aland	AH luhnd	ˈalənd
Alaric	A luh rik	ˈælərɪk
Alarie	ah lah REE	alaˈri
alas	uh LAS	əˈlæs
Alaska	uh LA skuh	əˈlæskə
Alban	AWL buhn	ˈɔlbən
Albanese, Licia	ahl bah NAY say, LEE chah	albaˈnese, ˈlitʃa
Albania	al BAY ni uh	ælˈbenɪə
Albany	AWL buh ni	ˈɔlbənɪ
albatross	AL buh traws	ˈælbətrɔs
albedo	al BEE doh	ælˈbido
albeit	awl BEE it	ɔlˈbiɪt
Albemarle	AL buh mahrl	ˈælbəmɑrl
Albéniz	ahl BAY nith	alˈbenɪθ
Alberich	AHL be rik	ˈalberɪk
Alberoni	ahl bay ROH nee	albeˈroni
Albert (French)	al BAIR	ælˈbɛr
Alberta	al BER tuh	ælˈbɝtə
Alberti	ahl BAIR tee	alˈbɛrti
Albertina	al ber TEE nuh	ælbərˈtinə
Albertinelli	al bair ti NE li	ælbɛrtɪˈnɛlɪ
Albigenses	al bi JEN seez	ælbɪˈdʒɛnsiz
Albigensian	al bi JEN si uhn	ælbɪˈdʒɛnsɪən
albino	al BIGH noh	ælˈbaɪno
Albion	AL bi uhn	ˈælbɪən
Albrecht	AHL brekt	ˈalbrɛkt
Albricht	AWL brikt	ˈɔlbrɪkt
album	AL buhm	ˈælbəm
albumen	al BYOO: muhn	ælˈbjumən
Albuquerque	al buh KER ki	ælbəˈkɝkɪ
alcaide	al KAYD	ælˈked
alcalde	al KAHL day	alˈkalde
alcántara, A-	ahl KAHN tah rah	alˈkantara
Alcatraz	AL kuh traz	ˈælkətræz
alcazar, A-	al KA zer	ælˈkæzər
Alceste	al SEST	ælˈsɛst
Alcestis	al SE stis	ælˈsɛstɪs
alchemist	Al kuh mist	ˈælkəmɪst

at [æ]; ah [ɑ]; air [ɛ]; awful [ɔ]; say [e]; back [b]; chair [tʃ]; do [d]; elm [ɛ]; eel [i]; server [ˈɝ, ər]; fit [f]; go [g]; hurt [h]; is [ɪ]; high [aɪ]; jet [dʒ]; kiss [k]; lamb [l]; my [m]; nice [n];

alchemy	Al kuh mi	ˈælkəmɪ
Alcibiades	al suh BIGH uh deez	ælsəˈbaɪədiz
Alcinoüs	al SI noo uhs	ælˈsɪnʊəs
alclad	AL klad	ˈælklæd
Alcmene	alk MEE ni	ælkˈminɪ
Alcoa	al KOH uh	ælˈkoə
Alcott	AWL kuht	ˈɔlkət
alcove	AL kohv	ˈælkov
Aldebaran	al DE buh ruhn	ælˈdɛbərən
alder	AWL der	ˈɔldər
alderman	AWL der muhn	ˈɔldərmən
Aldernay	AWL der ni	ˈɔldərnɪ
Aldershot	AWL der shaht	ˈɔldərʃɑt
Aldine	AWL dighn	ˈɔldaɪn
Aldrich	AWL drich	ˈɔldrɪtʃ
Aleichem, Sholem	ah LAY kem, SHOH lem	ɑˈlekɛm, ˈʃolɛm
Alemán, Miguel	ah lay MAHN, mee GEL	ɑleˈmɑn, miˈgɛl
alert	uh LERT	əˈlɝt
Aleut	A li oo:t	ˈælɪut
Aleutian	uh LOO: shuhn	əˈluʃən
Alexander	a lig ZAN der	ælɪgˈzændər
Alexandretta	a lig zan DRE tuh	ælɪgzænˈdrɛtə
Alexandria	a lig ZAN dri uh	ælɪgˈzændrɪə
Alexis	uh LEK sis	əˈlɛksɪs
Al-Faquih	al fah KEE	ælfɑˈki
Alfaro	ahl FAH roh	ɑlˈfɑro
Alfonso	al FAWN soh	ælˈfɔnso
Alfreda	al FREE duh	ælˈfridə
alfresco	al FRE skoh	ælˈfrɛsko
alga	AL guh	ˈælgə
algae	AL jee	ˈældʒi
Alger	AL jer	ˈældʒər
Algeria	al JI ri uh	ælˈdʒɪrɪə
Algerian	al JI ri uhn	ælˈdʒɪrɪən
Algernon	AL jer nahn	ˈældʒərnɑn
Algol	AL gahl	ˈælgɑl
Algonquin	al GAHNG kwin	ælˈgɑŋkwɪn
Algren	AWL grin	ˈɔlgrɪn
Alhambra	al HAM bruh	ælˈhæmbrə
Ali	AH lee	ˈɑli
alias	AY li uhs	ˈelɪəs
aliases	AY li uh siz	ˈelɪəsɪz
Ali Baba	A li BA buh	ˈælɪ ˈbæbə
alibi	A li bigh	ˈælɪbaɪ
alien	AY li uhn	ˈelɪən
alienate	AY li uh nayt	ˈelɪənet
alienation	ay li uh NAY shuhn	elɪəˈneʃən
Alighieri	ah lee gi E ri	ɑligɪˈɛrɪ
alignment	uh LIGHN muhnt	əˈlaɪnmənt
alimentary	a luh MEN tuh ri	æləˈmɛntərɪ
alimony	A luh moh ni	ˈæləmonɪ
Alison	A li suhn	ˈælɪsən

sing [ŋ] ; *oh* [o] ; *oi*l [ɔɪ] ; *foo*t [ʊ] ; *foo:*d [u] ; *how* [aʊ] ; *p*ie [p] ; *r*ay [r] ; *s*o [s] ; *sh*all [ʃ] ;
*t*o [t] ; *th*in [θ] ; *th:*en [ð] ; above (*uh* B*UH*V) [ə, ˈʌ] ; *v*ine [v] ; *w*ine [w] ; *wh*ine [hw] ;
*y*ou [j] ; *z*oo [z] ; *r*ouge (roo:*zh*) [ʒ].

Alitalia	ah li TAHL yuh	alɪˈtaljə
alkali	AL kuh ligh	ˈælkəlaɪ
alkaline	AL kuh lin	ˈælkəlɪn
alla breve	ah lah BRAY vay	ɑla ˈbreve
Allah	AH lah	ˈɑla
Allais	a LAY	æˈle
allargando	ah lahr GAHN doh	ɑlarˈgando
Allegany	A luh gay ni	ˈæləgenɪ
allege	uh LEJ	əˈlɛdʒ
Alleghany	A luh gay ni	ˈæləgenɪ
Allegheny	A luh gay ni	ˈæləgenɪ
allegiance	uh LEE juhns	əˈlidʒəns
allegory	A luh gaw ri	ˈæləgɔrɪ
allegretto	a luh GRE toh	æləˈgreto
allegro	uh LAY groh	əˈlegro
allele	uh LEEL	əˈlil
alleluia, -h	a luh LOO : yuh	æləˈlujə
allemande	a luh MAND	æləˈmænd
allentando	ah len TAHN doh	ɑlɛnˈtando
allergic	uh LER jik	əˈlɜˑdʒɪk
allergy	A ler ji	ˈælədʒɪ
allerhöchst	ah ler HERKST	ɑlərˈhɜˑkst
alleviate	uh LEE vi ayt	əˈliviet
alliance	uh LIGH uhns	əˈlaɪəns
allied (a)	A lighd	ˈælaɪd
alligator	A luh gay ter	ˈæləgetər
allineation	uh li ni AY shuhn	əlɪnɪˈeʃən
alliteration	uh li tuh RAY shuhn	əlɪtəˈreʃən
alliterative	uh LI tuh ray tiv	əˈlɪtəretɪv
allium	A li uhm	ˈælɪəm
allocate	A luh kayt	ˈæləket
allometry	uh LAH muh tri	əˈlɑmətrɪ
allomorph	A luh mawrf	ˈæləmɔrf
allopatric	a luh PA trik	æləˈpætrik
allophone	A luh fohn	ˈæləfon
allosyndesis	a luh SIN duh sis	æləˈsɪndəsɪs
alloy (n)	A loi	ˈælɔɪ
alloy (v)	uh LOI	əˈlɔɪ
allspice	AWL spighs	ˈɔlspaɪs
allude	uh LOO : D	əˈlud
allure	uh LOOR	əˈlʊr
allusion	uh LOO : zhuhn	əˈluʒən
allusive	uh LOO : siv	əˈlusɪv
alluvial	uh LOO : vi uhl	əˈluvɪəl
ally (n)	A ligh	ˈælaɪ
ally (v)	uh LIGH	əˈlaɪ
Allyson	A li suhn	ˈælɪsən
Alma Mater	AL muh MAH ter	ˈælmə ˈmatər
almanac	AWL muh nak	ˈɔlmənæk
Alma-Tadema	AL muh TA di muh	ˈælmə ˈtædɪmə
Almaviva	ahl mah VEE vah	ɑlmaˈviva
almond	AH muhnd	ˈamənd

---

at [æ]; *ah* [ɑ]; *air* [ɛ]; *aw*ful [ɔ]; *say* [e]; *back* [b]; *ch*air [tʃ]; *do* [d]; *elm* [ɛ]; *eel* [i];
server [ˈɜˑ, ər]; *f*it [f]; *go* [g]; *h*urt [h]; *is* [ɪ]; *high* [aɪ]; *jet* [dʒ]; *kiss* [k]; *l*amb [l]; *my* [m];
nice [n];

almoner	AL muh ner	ˈælmənər
almost	AWL mohst	ˈɔlmost
alms	ahmz	ɑmz
alnico	AL ni koh	ˈælnɪko
aloe	A loh	ˈælo
aloha	ah LOH hah	ɑˈlohɑ
Alois	uh LOIS	əˈlɔɪs
Alonzo	ah LAWN soh	ɑˈlɔnso
aloof	uh LOO : F	əˈluf
alopecia	a luh PEE shi uh	æləˈpiʃɪə
Aloys	uh LOIS	əˈlɔɪs
Aloysius	a loh I shuhs	æloˈɪʃəs
alpaca	al PA kuh	ælˈpækə
alpenstock	AL pin stahk	ˈælpɪnstɑk
alphabetize	AL fuh buh tighz	ˈælfəbətaɪz
alpine, A-	AL pighn	ˈælpaɪn
Alpujarras, Alpuxaras	ahl poo : HAH rahs	ɑlpuˈhɑrɑs
Alsace	AL sas	ˈælsæs
alsike	AL sighk	ˈælsaɪk
Altaic	al TAY ik	ælˈteɪk
Altair	al TAH ir	ælˈtɑɪr
Altamira	ahl tah MEE rah	ɑltɑˈmirɑ
altazimuth	al TA zi muhth	ælˈtæzɪməθ
alter	AWL ter	ˈɔltər
altercation	awl ter KAY shuhn	ɔltərˈkeʃən
alter ego	Al ter EE goh	ˈæltər ˈigo
alternate (a, n)	AWL ter nit	ˈɔltərnɪt
alternate (v)	AWL ter nayt	ˈɔltərnet
alternately	AWL ter nit li	ˈɔltərnɪtlɪ
alternation	awl ter NAY shuhn	ɔltərˈneʃən
alternative	awl TER nuh tiv	ɔlˈtɜnətɪv
alterne	AWL tern	ˈɔltərn
althaea, althea, A-	al THEE uh	ælˈθiə
altimeter	al TI muh ter	ælˈtɪmətər
altitude	AL ti too : d	ˈæltɪtud
alto	AL toh	ˈælto
Alto Adige	AHL taw AH dee je	ˈɑltɔ ˈɑdidʒɛ
Altrocchi	ahl TRAW ki	ɑlˈtrɔkɪ
altruism	AL troo i zuhm	ˈæltruɪzəm
aluminium (British)	a loo MI ni uhm	ælʊˈmɪnɪəm
aluminum	uh LOO : mi nuhm	əˈlumɪnəm
alumna (fem. sing.)	uh LUHM nuh	əˈlʌmnə
alumnae (fem. pl.)	uh LUHM nee	əˈlʌmni
alumni (masc. pl.)	uh LUHM nigh	əˈlʌmnaɪ
alumnus (masc. sing.)	uh LUHM nuhs	əˈlʌmnəs
Alvarado	ahl vah RAH doh	ɑlvɑˈrado
alveolar	al VEE uh ler	ælˈviələr
always	AWL wiz	ˈɔlwɪz
Aly Khan	AH lee KAHN	ˈɑli ˈkɑn
alyssum	uh LI suhm	əˈlɪsəm
amabile	ah MAH bi lay	ɑˈmɑbɪle
Amadeus	ah mah DAY uhs	ɑmɑˈdeəs

sing [ŋ]; *oh* [o]; *oil* [ɔɪ]; *foot* [ʊ]; *foo:d* [u]; *how* [aʊ]; *pie* [p]; *ray* [r]; *so* [s]; *shall* [ʃ]; *to* [t]; *thin* [θ]; *th:en* [ð]; *above* (*uh BUH*V) [ə, ˈʌ]; *vine* [v]; *wine* [w]; *whine* [hw]; *you* [j]; *zoo* [z]; *rouge* (*roo:zh*) [ʒ].

Amadis	A muh dis	ˈæmədɪs
Amalek	A muh lek	ˈæmələk
Amalekite	A muh luh kight	ˈæmələkaɪt
Amalfi	ah MAHL fee	aˈmɑlfi
amalgam	uh MAL guhm	əˈmælgəm
amalgamate (a, n)	uh MAL guh mit	əˈmælgəmɪt
amalgamate (v)	uh MAL guh mayt	əˈmælgəmet
Amalthea, Amalthaea	a muhl THEE uh	æməlˈθiə
Amara, Lucine	ah MAH ruh,	aˈmɑrə, luˈtʃinə
	loo : CHEE nuh	
amaranth	A muh ranth	ˈæmərænθ
amaranthine	a muh RAN thin	æməˈrænθɪn
Amarillo	a muh RI loh	æməˈrɪlo
amaryllis, A-	a muh RI lis	æməˈrɪlɪs
amass	uh MAS	əˈmæs
amateur	A muh choor	ˈæmətʃur
amateurish	a muh CHOO rish	æməˈtʃurɪʃ
Amati	ah MAH tee	aˈmɑti
Amato	ah MAH toh	aˈmɑto
amatory	A muh taw ri	ˈæmətɔrɪ
Amaya	ah MIGH ah	aˈmaɪa
amazon, A-	A muh zahn	ˈæməzɑn
ambassador	am BA suh der	æmˈbæsədər
ambassadorial	am ba suh DAW ri uhl	æmbæsəˈdɔrɪəl
ambergris	AM ber grees	ˈæmbərgris
ambidexterity	am buh dek STE ruh ti	æmbədɛkˈstɛrətɪ
ambidextrous	am buh DEK struhs	æmbəˈdɛkstrəs
ambient	AM bi uhnt	ˈæmbɪənt
ambiguity	am bi GYOO : uh ti	æmbɪˈgjuətɪ
ambiguous	am BI gyoo uhs	æmˈbɪgjuəs
ambition	am BI shuhn	æmˈbɪʃən
ambitious	am BI shuhs	æmˈbɪʃəs
ambivalence	am BI vuh luhns	amˈbɪvələns
ambiversion	am bi VER zhuhn	æmbɪˈvɚʒən
ambivert	AM bi vert	ˈæmbɪvərt
Amboina	am BOI nuh	æmˈbɔɪnə
Ambrose	AM brohz	ˈæmbroz
ambrosia	am BROH zhuh	æmˈbroʒə
ambulance	AM byuh luhns	ˈæmbjələns
ambulatory	AM byuh luh taw ri	ˈæmbjələtɔrɪ
ambuscade	am buh SKAYD	æmbəˈsked
ambush	AM boosh	ˈæmbuʃ
Ameche, Don	uh MEE chi	əˈmitʃɪ
ameer	uh MIR	əˈmɪr
Amelia	uh MEE lyuh	əˈmiljə
ameliorate	uh MEE lyuh rayt	əˈmiljəret
ameliorative	uh MEE lyuh ray tiv	əˈmiljəretɪv
amen (singing)	AH MEN	ˈɑˈmɛn
amen (speaking)	AY MEN	ˈeˈmɛn
amenable	uh MEE nuh buhl	əˈminəbəl
amend	uh MEND	əˈmɛnd
amendatory	uh MEN duh taw ri	əˈmɛndətɔrɪ

---

at [æ]; *ah* [ɑ]; *air* [ɛ]; *awful* [ɔ]; *say* [e]; *back* [b]; *chair* [tʃ]; *do* [d]; *elm* [ɛ]; *eel* [i]; *server* [ˈɝ, ər]; *f*it [f]; *go* [g]; *h*urt [h]; *is* [ɪ]; *high* [aɪ]; *jet* [dʒ]; *kiss* [k]; *lamb* [l]; *my* [m]; *nice* [n];

amende honorable	uh MEND AH nuh ruh buhl	əˈmɛnd ˈɑnərəbəl
amendment	uh MEND muhnt	əˈmɛndmənt
amenity	uh ME nuh ti	əˈmɛnətɪ
America	uh ME ri kuh	əˈmɛrɪkə
américaine	ah may ree KEN	ɑmeriˈkɛn
American	uh ME ri kuhn	əˈmɛrɪkən
Americana	uh me ri KA nuh	əmɛrɪˈkænə
Amery	AY muh ri	ˈemərɪ
amethyst	A muh thist	ˈæməθɪst
Amfortas	ahm FAWR tahs	ɑmˈfɔrtɑs
Amherst	A merst	ˈæmərst
amiability	ay mi uh BI luh ti	emɪəˈbɪlətɪ
amiable	AY mi uh buhl	ˈemɪəbəl
amicability	a mi kuh BI luh ti	æmɪkəˈbɪlətɪ
amicable	A mi kuh buhl	ˈæmɪkəbəl
amidol	A muh dohl	ˈæmədol
amidon	A muh dahn	ˈæmədɑn
Amiens	A mi uhnz	ˈæmɪənz
amiga	ah MEE gah	ɑˈmigɑ
amigo	ah MEE goh	ɑˈmigo
amino	uh MEE noh	əˈmino
amir	uh MIR	əˈmɪr
Amish	A mish	ˈæmɪʃ
amiss	uh MIS	əˈmɪs
amity, A-	A muh ti	ˈæmətɪ
Amman	AH mahn	ˈɑmɑn
Ammon	A muhn	ˈæmən
ammonia	uh MOH nyuh	əˈmonjə
ammoniac	uh MOH ni ak	əˈmonɪæk
ammonium	uh MOH ni uhm	əˈmonɪəm
ammunition	a myoo NI shuhn	æmjuˈnɪʃən
Amneris	am NE ris	æmˈnɛrɪs
amnesia	am NEE zhuh	æmˈniʒə
amnesty	AM nuh sti	ˈæmnəstɪ
amoeba	uh MEE buh	əˈmibə
amok	uh MUHK	əˈmʌk
among	uh MUHNG	əˈmʌŋ
amoral	ay MAW ruhl	eˈmɔrəl
Amorite	A muh right	ˈæmərait
amoroso	ah muh ROH soh	ɑməˈroso
amorous	A muh ruhs	ˈæmərəs
amorphous	uh MAWR fuhs	əˈmɔrfəs
amortization	A mer ti ZAY shuhn	ˈæmərtɪˈzeʃən
amortize	A mer tighz	ˈæmərtaɪz
Amory	AY muh ri	ˈemərɪ
Amos	AY muhs	ˈeməs
amour	uh MOOR	əˈmur
Amoy	uh MOI	əˈmɔɪ
amperage	am PI rij	æmˈpɪrɪdʒ
ampere	AM pir	ˈæmpɪr
ampersand	AM per sand	ˈæmpərsænd

sing [ŋ] ; *oh* [o] ; *oil* [ɔɪ] ; *foot* [ʊ] ; *foo:d* [u] ; *how* [aʊ] ; *pie* [p] ; *ray* [r] ; *so* [s] ; *shall* [ʃ] ; *to* [t] ; *thin* [θ] ; *th:en* [ð] ; *above* (*uh BUHV*) [ə, ˈʌ] ; *vine* [v] ; *wine* [w] ; *whine* [hw] ; *you* [j] ; *zoo* [z] ; *rouge* (roo:*zh*) [ʒ].

amphibian	am FI bi uhn	æmˈfɪbɪən
amphibious	am FI bi uhs	æmˈfɪbɪəs
Amphion	am FIGH uhn	æmˈfaɪən
amphitheater, -re	AM fi thee uh ter	ˈæmfɪθiətər
Amphitrite	am fi TRIGH ti	amfɪˈtraɪtɪ
Amphitryon	am FI tri uhn	æmˈfɪtrɪən
amplifier	AM pli figh er	ˈæmplɪfaɪər
amplify	AM pli figh	ˈæmplɪfaɪ
amplitude	AM pli tyoo : d	ˈæmplɪtjud
amrita	uhm REE tuh	əmˈritə
Amritsar	uhm RIT ser	əmˈrɪtsər
Amsterdam	AM ster dam	ˈæmstərdæm
Amtorg	AM tawrg	ˈæmtɔrg
amuck	uh MUHK	əˈmʌk
amulet	A myoo lit	ˈæmjʊlɪt
Amundsen	AH muhn suhn	ˈɑmənsən
Amur	ah MOOR	ɑˈmʊr
amusement	uh MYOO : Z muhnt	əˈmjuzmənt
Amy	AY mi	ˈemɪ
Amytal	A mi tal	ˈæmɪtæl
anabiosis	a nuh bigh OH sis	ænəbaɪˈosɪs
anachronism	uh NA kruh ni zuhm	əˈnækrənɪzəm
anaconda, A-	a nuh KAHN duh	ænəˈkɑndə
anacoustic	a nuh KOO : stik	ænəˈkustɪk
Anacreon	uh NA kri uhn	əˈnækrɪən
anaculture	A nuh kuhl cher	ˈænəkəltʃər
anaemia	uh NEE mi uh	əˈnimɪə
anaesthesia	a nuhs THEE zhuh	ænəsˈθiʒə
anaesthetic	a nuhs THE tik	ænəsˈθɛtɪk
anaesthetist	uh NES thuh tist	əˈnɛsθətɪst
anagram	A nuh gram	ˈænəgræm
Anak	AY nak	ˈenæk
analgesia	a nal JEE zi uh	ænælˈdʒizɪə
analgesic	a nal JEE zik	ænælˈdʒizɪk
analine	A nuh lin	ˈænəlɪn
analog, -ue	A nuh lawg	ˈænəlɔg
analogous	uh NA luh guhs	əˈnæləgəs
analogy	uh NA luh ji	əˈnælədʒɪ
analyser	A nuh ligh zer	ˈænəlaɪzər
analyses	uh NA luh seez	əˈnæləsiz
analysis	uh NA luh sis	əˈnæləsɪs
analyst	A nuh list	ˈænəlɪst
analytic	a nuh LI tik	ænəˈlɪtɪk
analyze	A nuh lighz	ˈænəlaɪz
Ananias	a nuh NIGH uhs	ænəˈnaɪəs
anankastic	a nang KAS tik	ænæŋˈkæstɪk
anapest	A nuh pest	ˈænəpɛst
anarchism	A ner ki zuhm	ˈænərkɪzəm
anarchist	A ner kist	ˈænərkɪst
anarchy	A ner ki	ˈænərkɪ
Anasazi	a nuh SAH zi	ænəˈsɑzɪ
Anastasia	a nuh STAY zhuh	ænəˈsteʒə

at [æ] ; ah [ɑ] ; air [ɛ] ; awful [ɔ] ; say [e] ; back [b] ; chair [tʃ] ; do [d] ; elm [ɛ] ; eel [i] ; server [ˈɝ, ər] ; fit [f] ; go [g] ; hurt [h] ; is [ɪ] ; high [aɪ] ; jet [dʒ] ; kiss [k] ; lamb [l] ; my [m] ; nice [n] ;

Anastasius	a nuh STAY shuhs	ænəˈsteʃəs
anathema	uh NA thuh muh	əˈnæθəmə
Anatole	A nuh tohl	ˈænətol
Anatolia	a nuh TOH li uh	ænəˈtolɪə
anatomical	a nuh TAH mi kuhl	ænəˈtɑmɪkəl
anatomy	uh NA tuh mi	əˈnætəmɪ
Anaxagoras	a nak SA guh ruhs	ænækˈsægərəs
ancestor	AN ses ter	ˈænsɛstər
ancestral	an SE struhl	ænˈsɛstrəl
ancestry	AN se stri	ˈænsɛstrɪ
anchor	ANG ker	ˈæŋkər
anchorage, A-	ANG kuh rij	ˈæŋkərɪdʒ
anchorite	ANG kuh right	ˈæŋkəraɪt
anchovy	AN choh vi	ˈæntʃovɪ
ancienne noblesse	ahn SYEN noh BLES	ɑnˈsjɛn noˈblɛs
ancien régime	ahn SYEN ray ZHEEM	ɑnˈsjɛn reˈʒim
ancient	AYN shuhnt	ˈenʃənt
ancillary	AN si le ri	ˈænsɪlɛrɪ
Ancona	ahng KOH nuh	ɑŋˈkonə
Andalusia	an duh LOO : zhuh	ændəˈluʒə
Andaman	AN duh muhn	ˈændəmən
andante	ahn DAHN tay	ɑnˈdɑnte
andantino	ahn dahn TEE noh	ɑndɑnˈtino
Andean	AN di uhn	ˈændɪən
Andes	AN deez	ˈændiz
Andorra	an DAW ruh	ænˈdɔrə
Andover	AN doh ver	ˈændovər
Andrade	ahn DRAH day	ɑnˈdrɑde
Andrassy	AHN drah shi	ˈɑndrɑʃɪ
André	AHN dray	ˈɑndre
Andreef, Andreev	ahn DRAY yef	ɑnˈdrejɛf
Andrew	AN droo :	ˈændru
Andreyev	ahn DRAY yef	ɑnˈdrejɛf
andric	AN drik	ˈændrɪk
Androcles	AN druh kleez	ˈændrəkliz
Androclus	AN druh kluhs	ˈændrəkləs
androgen	AN druh juhn	ˈændrədʒən
androgenous	an DRAH juh nuhs	ænˈdrɑdʒənəs
Andromache	an DRAH muh ki	ænˈdrɑməkɪ
Andromaque	ahn droh MAHK	ɑndroˈmɑk
Andromeda	an DRAH mi duh	ænˈdrɑmɪdə
Andronicus	an druh NIGH kuhs	ændrəˈnaɪkəs
Andronicus (Shakespeare)	an DRAH ni kuhs	ænˈdrɑnɪkəs
androsterone	an DRAH stuh rohn	ænˈdrɑstəron
Andvari, Andwari	AHN dwah ri	ˈɑndwarɪ
anecdotal	A nik doht l	ˈænɪkdotl
anecdote	A nik doht	ˈænɪkdot
anecdotist	A nik doh tist	ˈænɪkdotɪst
anemia	uh NEE mi uh	əˈnimɪə
anemone, A-	uh NE muh ni	əˈnɛmənɪ
anent	uh NENT	əˈnɛnt

sing [ŋ]; oh [o]; oil [ɔɪ]; foot [ʊ]; foo:d [u]; how [aʊ]; pie [p]; ray [r]; so [s]; shall [ʃ];
to [t]; thin [θ]; th:en [ð]; above (uh BUHV) [ə, ˈʌ]; vine [v]; wine [w]; whine [hw];
you [j]; zoo [z]; rouge (roo:zh) [ʒ].

anesthesia	a nuhs THEE zhuh	ænəsˈθiʒə
anesthetic	a nuhs THE tik	ænəsˈθɛtɪk
anesthetist	uh NES thuh tist	əˈnɛsθətɪst
aneurin	A nyuh rin	ˈænjərɪn
aneurysm, aneurism	A nyoo ri zuhm	ˈænjʊrɪzəm
anew	uh NYOO :	əˈnju
angel	AYN juhl	ˈendʒəl
ángel, Á- (Spanish)	AHN hel	ˈɑnhɛl
Angela	AN juh luh	ˈændʒələ
Angelica	an JE li kuh	ænˈdʒɛlɪkə
Angelici	ahng GE lee chee	ɑŋˈgelitʃi
Angell, James Rowland	AYN juhl, jaymz ROH lund	ˈendʒəl, dʒemz ˈrolənd
Angelus, a-	AN juh luhs	ˈændʒələs
anger	ANG ger	ˈæŋgər
Angevin	AN juh vin	ˈændʒəvɪn
angina pectoris	an JIGH nuh PEK tuh ris	ænˈdʒaɪnə ˈpɛktərɪs
angiosperm	AN ji oh sperm	ˈændʒɪospərm
angiotonin	an ji AH tuh nin	ændʒɪˈɑtənɪn
anglaise	ahng GLEZ	ɑŋˈglɛz
angle	ANG guhl	ˈæŋgəl
angler	ANG gler	ˈæŋglər
Anglican	ANG gli kuhn	ˈæŋglɪkən
Anglicanism	ANG gli kuh ni zuhm	ˈæŋglɪkənɪzəm
Anglo-	ANG gloh	ˈæŋglo
Anglophile	ANG gloh fighl	ˈæŋglofaɪl
Anglophobe	ANG gloh fohb	ˈæŋglofob
Anglo-Saxon	ANG gloh SAK suhn	ˈæŋgloˈsæksən
Angola	ang GOH luh	æŋˈgolə
Angora	ang GAW ruh	æŋˈgorə
angostura	ang guh STYOO ruh	æŋgəˈstjurə
angry	ANG gri	ˈæŋgrɪ
angst	ahngst	ɑŋst
angstrom, A-	ANG struhm	ˈæŋstrəm
anguish	ANG gwish	ˈæŋgwɪʃ
angular	ANG gyoo ler	ˈæŋgjulər
Angus	ANG guhs	ˈæŋgəs
Anhalt	AHN hahlt	ˈɑnhɑlt
anilin, -e	A nuh lin	ˈænəlɪn
animadversion	a nuh mad VER zhuhn	ænəmædˈvɜʒən
animal	A nuh muhl	ˈænəməl
animalcule	a nuh MAL kyool	ænəˈmælkjul
animando	ah ni MAHN doh	ɑnɪˈmɑndo
animate (a)	A nuh mit	ˈænəmɪt
animate (v)	A nuh mayt	ˈænəmet
animato	ah ni MAH toh	ɑnɪˈmɑto
animism	A nuh mi zuhm	ˈænəmɪzəm
animus	A nuh muhs	ˈænəməs
anise	A nis	ˈænɪs
aniseed	A ni seed	ˈænɪsid
anisotropic	a nigh suh TRAH pik	ænaɪsəˈtrɑpɪk
Anita	uh NEE tuh	əˈnitə
Anjou	AHN joo :	ˈɑndʒu

at [æ] ; ah [ɑ] ; air [ɛ] ; awful [ɔ] ;· say [e] ; back [b] ; chair [tʃ] ; do [d] ; elm [ɛ] ; eel [i] ;
server [ˈɜ, ər] ; fit [f] ; go [g] ; hurt [h] ; is [ɪ] ; high [aɪ] ; jet [dʒ] ; kiss [k] ; lamb [l] ; my [m] ;
nice [n] ;

Ankara	ANG kuh ruh	ˈæŋkərə
ankle	ANG kuhl	ˈæŋkəl
ankus	ANG kuhs	ˈæŋkəs
Ann	an	æn
Anna	A nuh	ˈænə
annalist	A nuh list	ˈænəlɪst
annals	A nuhlz	ˈænəlz
Annapolis	uh NA puh lis	əˈnæpəlɪs
Anne	an	æn
anneal	uh NEEL	əˈnil
annex (n)	A neks	ˈænɛks
annex (v)	uh NEKS	əˈnɛks
annexation	a nek SAY shuhn	ænɛkˈseʃən
Annie	A ni	ˈænɪ
annihilate	uh NIGH uh layt	əˈnaɪəlet
annihilation	uh nigh uh LAY shuhn	ənaɪəˈleʃən
anniversary	a nuh VER suh ri	ænəˈvɝsərɪ
anno Christi	A noh KRI sti	ˈæno ˈkrɪstɪ
anno Domini	A noh DAH muh ni	ˈæno ˈdɑmənɪ
anno hebraico	A noh hi BRAY i koh	ˈæno hɪˈbreɪko
anno mundi	A noh MOON di	ˈæno ˈmʊndɪ
annotate	A nuh tayt	ˈænətet
annotation	a nuh TAY shuhn	ænəˈteʃən
annotator	A nuh tay ter	ˈænətetər
announcer	uh NOWN ser	əˈnaʊnsər
annoyance	uh NOI uhns	əˈnɔɪəns
annual	A nyoo uhl	ˈænjʊəl
annuity	uh NYOO : uh ti	əˈnjuətɪ
annul	uh NUHL	əˈnʌl
annunciation	uh nuhn si AY shuhn	ənʌnsɪˈeʃən
Annunzio, Gabriele d'	duh NOON zi oh, gah bri E lay	dəˈnʊnzɪo, gɑbrɪˈele
annus mirabilis	A nuhs mi RA bi lis	ˈænəs mɪˈræbɪlɪs
anode	A nohd	ˈænod
anodyne	A nuh dighn	ˈænədaɪn
anomalistic	uh nah muh LI stik	ənɑməˈlɪstɪk
anomalous	uh NAH muh luhs	əˈnɑmələs
anomaly	uh NAH muh li	əˈnɑməlɪ
another	uh NUH th : er	əˈnʌðər
Anouilh, Jean	ah NOOyah zhahn	ɑˈnujɑ ʒɑn
anoxia	uh NAHK si uh	əˈnɑksɪə
Anschluss	AHN shloos	ˈɑnʃlʊs
Ansermet	AHN zer may	ˈɑnzərme
answer	AN ser	ˈænsər
answerable	AN suh ruh buhl	ˈænsərəbəl
ant	ant	ænt
antacid	ant A sid	æntˈæsɪd
antagonism	an TA guh ni zuhm	ænˈtægənɪzəm
antarctic, A-	ant AHRK tik	æntˈɑrktɪk
Antarctica	ant AHRK ti kuh	æntˈɑrktɪkə
Antares	an TAI reez	ænˈtɛriz
ante	AN ti	ˈæntɪ

---

sing [ŋ] ; *oh* [o] ; *oil* [ɔɪ] ; *foot* [ʊ] ; *foo*:d [u] ; *how* [aʊ] ; *pie* [p] ; *ray* [r] ; *so* [s] ; *shall* [ʃ] ; *to* [t] ; *thin* [θ] ; *th*:en [ð] ; *above* (*uh BUH*V) [ə, ˈʌ] ; *vine* [v] ; *wine* [w] ; *whine* [hw] ; *you* [j] ; *zoo* [z] ; *rouge* (roo:*zh*) [ʒ].

H.P.—C

ante bellum	AN ti BE luhm	ˈæntɪ ˈbɛləm
antecede	an tuh SEED	æntəˈsid
antecedence	an tuh SEE duhns	æntəˈsidəns
antecedent	an tuh SEE duhnt	æntəˈsidənt
antechamber	AN ti chaym ber	ˈæntɪtʃembər
antedate (n)	AN ti dayt	ˈæntɪdet
antedate (v)	an ti DAYT	æntɪˈdet
antediluvian	an ti di LOO: vi uhn	æntɪdɪˈluviən
antelope	AN tuh lohp	ˈæntəlop
ante meridiem	AN ti muh RI di em	ˈæntɪ məˈrɪdiəm
antenna	an TE nuh	ænˈtɛnə
antennae	an TE nee	ænˈtɛni
antepenultimate	AN ti pi NUHL tuh mit	ˈæntɪpɪˈnʌltəmɪt
anterior	an TI ri er	ænˈtɪriər
Antheil	AN tighl	ˈæntaɪl
anthelion	ant HEE li uhn	æntˈhiliən
anthem	AN thuhm	ˈænθəm
anthill	ANT hil	ˈænthɪl
Anthony	AN thuh ni	ˈænθəni
anthracite	AN thruh sight	ˈænθrəsaɪt
anthrax	AN thraks	ˈænθræks
anthropoid	AN thruh poid	ˈænθrəpɔɪd
anthropologist	an thruh PAH luh jist	ænθrəˈpɑlədʒɪst
anthropology	an thruh PAH luh ji	ænθrəˈpɑlədʒɪ
anthropomorphism	AN thruh puh MAWR fi zuhm	ˈænθrəpəˈmɔrfɪzəm
anthropophagi	an thruh PAH fuh jigh	ænθrəˈpɑfədʒaɪ
antiaircraft	an ti AIR kraft	æntɪˈɛrkræft
antibiotic	an ti bigh AH tik	æntɪbaɪˈɑtɪk
antic	AN tik	ˈæntɪk
antichrist, A-	AN ti krighst	ˈæntɪkraɪst
anticipate	an TI suh payt	ænˈtɪsəpet
anticipation	an ti suh PAY shuhn	æntɪsəˈpeʃən
anticipatory	an TI suh puh taw ri	ænˈtɪsəpətɔrɪ
anticlimax	an ti KLIGH maks	æntɪˈklaɪmæks
antidote	AN ti doht	ˈæntɪdot
Antietam	an TEE tuhm	ænˈtitəm
Antigone	an TI guh ni	ænˈtɪgəni
Antigua	an TEE gwuh	ænˈtigwə
antihistamine	an ti HI stuh min	æntɪˈhɪstəmɪn
Antillean	an TI li uhn	ænˈtɪliən
Antilles	an TI leez	ænˈtɪliz
antimacassar	AN ti muh KA ser	ˈæntɪməˈkæsər
antimony	AN tuh moh ni	ˈæntəmoni
antinode	AN ti nohd	ˈæntɪnod
Antioch	AN ti ahk	ˈæntɪɑk
antipasto	an ti PA stoh	æntɪˈpæsto
antipathy	an TI puh thi	ænˈtɪpəθɪ
antiphonal	an TI fuh nuhl	ænˈtɪfənəl
antiphony	an TI fuh ni	ænˈtɪfəni
antipodal	an TI puh duhl	ænˈtɪpədəl
antipodean	an ti puh DEE uhn	æntɪpəˈdiən

at [æ]; ah [ɑ]; air [ɛ]; awful [ɔ]; say [e]; back [b]; chair [tʃ]; do [d]; elm [ɛ]; eel [i]; server [ˈɜ, ər]; fit [f]; go [g]; hurt [h]; is [ɪ]; high [aɪ]; jet [dʒ]; kiss [k]; lamb [l]; my [m]; nice [n];

antipodes	an TI puh deez	ænˈtɪpədiz
antiquarian	an ti KWAI ri uhn	æntɪˈkwɛrɪən
antiquary	AN ti kwai ri	ˈæntɪkwɛrɪ
antiquated	AN ti kway tid	ˈæntɪkwetɪd
antique	an TEEK	ænˈtik
antiquity	an TI kwuh ti	ænˈtɪkwətɪ
antirrhinum	an ti RIGH nuhm	æntɪˈraɪnəm
antiseptic	an ti SEP tik	æntɪˈsɛptɪk
antisocial	an ti SOH shuhl	æntɪˈsoʃəl
antistrophe	an TI struh fi	ænˈtɪstrəfɪ
antithesis	an TI thuh sis	ænˈtɪθəsɪs
antithetic	an ti THE tik	æntɪˈθɛtɪk
antitoxin	an ti TAHK sin	æntɪˈtɑksɪn
antler	ANT ler	ˈæntlər
Antoinette	an twuh NET	æntwəˈnɛt
Antonicelli	an taw ni CHE li	æntɒnɪˈtʃɛlɪ
Antony	AN tuh ni	ˈæntənɪ
antonym	AN tuh nim	ˈæntənɪm
antrum	AN truhm	ˈæntrəm
Antwerp	ANT werp	ˈæntwərp
anxiety	ang ZIGH uh ti	æŋˈzaɪətɪ
anxious	ANGK shuhs	ˈæŋkʃəs
any	E ni	ɛnɪ
anybody	E ni bah di	ˈɛnɪbɑdɪ
Anzac	AN zak	ˈænzæk
A-OK, A-okay	AY oh kay	ˈeoke
aoodad	AH oo dad	ˈɑʊdæd
aorta	ay AWR tuh	eˈɔrtə
Aosta	ah AW stah	ɑˈɔstɑ
à outrance	ah oo TRAHNS	ɑ ʊˈtrɑns
Apache	uh PA chi	əˈpætʃɪ
apache (French)	uh PAHSH	əˈpɑʃ
Apalachicola	a puh la chuh KOH luh	æpəlætʃəˈkolə
Aparri	ah PAH ree	ɑˈpɑrɪ
apart	uh PAHRT	əˈpɑrt
apartheid	uh PAHRT hight	əˈpɑrthaɪt
apathetic	a puh THE tik	æpəˈθɛtɪk
apathy	A puh thi	ˈæpəθɪ
Apel	AH pel	ˈɑpɛl
Apennines	A puh nighnz	ˈæpənaɪnz
aperçu	ah pair SOO	ɑpɛrˈsʊ
apéritif	a pay ree TEEF	æperiˈtif
aperitive	uh PAI ruh tiv	əˈpɛrətɪv
aperture	A per cher	ˈæpərtʃər
apex	AY peks	ˈepɛks
aphasia	uh FAY zhuh	əˈfeʒə
aphasic	uh FAY zik	əˈfezɪk
aphelion	uh FEE li uhn	əˈfilɪən
aphid	AY fid	ˈefɪd
aphonia	uh FOH ni uh	əˈfonɪə
aphorism	A fuh ri zuhm	ˈæfərɪzəm
aphoristic	a fuh RI stik	æfəˈrɪstɪk

sing [ŋ]; oh [o]; oil [ɔɪ]; foot [ʊ]; foo:d [u]; how [aʊ]; pie [p]; ray [r]; so [s]; shall [ʃ]; to [t]; thin [θ]; th:en [ð]; above (uh BUHV) [ə, ˈʌ]; vine [v]; wine [w]; whine [hw]; you [j]; zoo [z]; rouge (roo:zh) [ʒ].

Aphrodite	a fruh DIGH ti	æfrə'daɪtɪ
Apia	AH pee ah	'ɑpiɑ
apian	AY pi uhn	'epɪən
apiary	AY pi ai ri	'epɪɛrɪ
apiculture	AY pi kuhl cher	'epɪkəltʃər
apish	AY pish	'epɪʃ
aplomb	uh PLAHM	ə'plɑm
apocalypse, A-	uh PAH kuh lips	ə'pɑkəlɪps
apocalyptic	uh pah kuh LIP tik	əpɑkə'lɪptɪk
apochromatic	a puh kroh MA tik	æpəkro'mætɪk
apocope	uh PAH kuh pi	ə'pɑkəpɪ
apocrypha, A-	uh PAH kruh fuh	ə'pɑkrəfə
apocryphal, A-	uh PAH kruh fuhl	ə'pɑkrəfəl
apogee	A puh jee	'æpədʒi
Apollinaris	uh pah luh NAI ris	əpɑlə'nɛrɪs
Apollo	uh PAH loh	ə'pɑlo
Apollyon	uh PAH lyuhn	ə'pɑljən
apologetic	uh pah luh JE tik	əpɑlə'dʒɛtɪk
apologia	a puh LOH ji uh	æpə'lodʒɪə
apoplectic	a puh PLEK tik	æpə'plɛktɪk
apoplexy	A puh plek si	'æpəplɛksɪ
apostasy	uh PAH stuh si	ə'pɑstəsɪ
apostate	uh PAH stit	ə'pɑstɪt
apostatize	uh PAH stuh tighz	ə'pɑstətaɪz
a posteriori	ay pah sti ri AW righ	e pɑstɪrɪ'ɔraɪ
apostil, -le	uh PAH stil	ə'pɑstɪl
apostle, A-	uh PAH suhl	ə'pɑsəl
apostolic	a puh STAH lik	æpə'stɑlɪk
apothegm, apothem	A puh them	'æpəθɛm
apotheosis	uh pah thi OH sis	əpɑθɪ'osɪs
appal, -l	uh PAWL	ə'pɔl
Appalachian	a puh LA chuhn	æpə'lætʃən
apparatus	a puh RA tuhs	æpə'rætəs
apparel	uh PÁ ruhl	ə'pærəl
apparent	uh PA ruhnt	ə'pærənt
apparition	a puh RI shuhn	æpə'rɪʃən
appeal	uh PEEL	ə'pil
appearance	uh PI ruhns	ə'pɪrəns
appel	ah PEL	ɑ'pɛl
appellant	uh PE luhnt	ə'pɛlənt
appellate	uh PE lit	ə'pɛlɪt
appendage	uh PEN dij	ə'pɛndɪdʒ
appendectomist	a puhn DEK tuh mist	æpən'dɛktəmɪst
appendectomy	a puhn DEK tuh mi	æpən'dɛktəmɪ
appendices	uh PEN duh seez	ə'pɛndəsiz
appendicitis	uh pen duh SIGH tis	əpɛndə'saɪtɪs
appendix	uh PEN diks	ə'pɛndɪks
appertain	a per TAYN	æpər'ten
appetite	A puh tight	'æpətaɪt
Appian	A pi uhn	'æpɪən
applause	uh PLAWZ	ə'plɔz
appliance	uh PLIGH uhns	ə'plaɪəns

at [æ] ; ah [ɑ] ; air [ɛ] ; awful [ɔ] ; say [e] ; back [b] ; chair [tʃ] ; do [d] ; elm [ɛ] ; eel [i] ;
server ['ɝ, ər] ; fit [f] ; go [g] ; hurt [h] ; is [ɪ] ; high [aɪ] ; jet [dʒ] ; kiss [k] ; lamb [l] ; my [m] ;
nice [n] ;

applicable	A pli kuh buhl	ˈæplɪkəbəl
applicant	A pli kuhnt	ˈæplɪkənt
application	a pli KAY shuhn	æplɪˈkeʃən
applicator	A pli kay ter	ˈæplɪketər
applicatory	A pli kuh taw ri	ˈæplɪkətɔrɪ
appliqué	a pli KAY	æplɪˈke
appoggiatura	uh pah juh TOO : ruh	əpɑdʒəˈturə
appointee	uh POIN ti	əˈpɔɪntɪ
Appomattox	a puh MA tuhks	æpəˈmætəks
apportion	uh PAWR shuhn	əˈpɔrʃən
apportionment	uh PAWR shuhn muhnt	əˈpɔrʃənmənt
apposable	uh POH zuh buhl	əˈpozəbəl
apposite	A puh zit	ˈæpəzɪt
apposition	a puh ZI shuhn	æpəˈzɪʃən
appositive	uh PAH zuh tiv	əˈpɑzətɪv
appraisal	uh PRAY zuhl	əˈprezəl
appreciable	uh PREE shuh buhl	əˈpriʃəbəl
appreciate	uh PREE shi ayt	əˈpriʃɪet
appreciation	uh pree shi AY shuhn	əˈpriʃɪˈeʃən
appreciative	uh PREE shuh tiv	əˈpriʃətɪv
apprehensible	a pri HEN suh buhl	æprɪˈhɛnsəbəl
apprentice	uh PREN tis	əˈprɛntɪs
approbation	a pruh BAY shuhn	æprəˈbeʃən
appropriate (a)	uh PROH pri it	əˈproprɪɪt
appropriate (v)	uh PROH pri ayt	əˈpropriet
approximate (a)	uh PRAHK suh mit	əˈprɑksəmɪt
approximate (v)	uh PRAHK suh mayt	əˈprɑksəmet
appurtenance	uh PER tuh nuhns	əˈpɝtənəns
apricot	AY pri kaht	ˈeprɪkɑt
April	AY pruhl	ˈeprəl
a priori	ay pree OH righ	e priˈorɑɪ
apron	AY pruhn	ˈeprən
à propos	a pruh POH	æ prəˈpo
apse	aps	æps
apt	apt	æpt
aptitude	AP ti tyoo : d	ˈæptɪtjud
Apuleius	a pyoo LEE uhs	æpjʊˈliəs
aqua	A kwuh	ˈækwə
aquacade	A kwuh kayd	ˈækwəked
aquamarine	a kwuh muh REEN	ækwəməˈrin
aquarium	uh KWAI ri uhm	əˈkwɛrɪəm
Aquarius	uh KWAI ri uhs	əˈkwɛrɪəs
aquatic	uh KWA tik	əˈkwætɪk
aquatint	A kwuh tint	ˈækwətɪnt
aquavit	A kwuh veet	ˈækwəvit
aqua vitae	A kwuh VIGH ti	ˈækwəˈvaɪtɪ
aqueduct	A kwi duhkt	ˈækwɪdəkt
aqueous	AY kwi uhs	ˈekwɪəs
Aquila	A kwi luh	ˈækwɪlə
aquilegia	a kwi LEE ji uh	ækwɪˈlidʒɪə
aquiline	A kwuh lighn	ˈækwəlaɪn
Aquinas	uh KWIGH nuhs	əˈkwaɪnəs

sing [ŋ] ; oh [o] ; oil [ɔɪ] ; foot [ʊ] ; foo :d [u] ; how [aʊ] ; pie [p] ; ray [r] ; so [s] ; shall [ʃ] ;
to [t] ; thin [θ] ; th :en [ð] ; above (uh BUHV) [ə, ˈʌ] ; vine [v] ; wine [w] ; whine [hw] ;
you [j] ; zoo [z] ; rouge (roo :zh) [ʒ].

Arab	A ruhb	ˈærəb
arabesque	a ruh BESK	ærəˈbɛsk
Arabia	uh RAY bi uh	əˈrebɪə
Arabic	A ruh bik	ˈærəbɪk
arable	A ruh buhl	ˈærəbəl
Araby	A ruh bi	ˈærəbɪ
Aral	AI ruhl	ˈɛrəl
Aramaic	a ruh MAY ik	ærəˈmeɪk
Aranda	ah RAHN dah	aˈrɑndɑ
Aranha	ah RAH nyah	aˈrɑnjɑ
Arapaho, -e	uh RA puh hoh	əˈræpəho
Ararat	A ruh rat	ˈærəræt
Arawak	AH rah wahk	ˈɑrɑwɑk
Arawakan	ah rah WAH kuhn	ɑrɑˈwɑkən
arbiter	AHR bi ter	ˈɑrbɪtər
arbitrage	AHR buh trij	ˈɑrbətrɪdʒ
arbitrament	ahr BI truh muhnt	ɑrˈbɪtrəmənt
arbitrary	AHR buh trai ri	ˈɑrbətrɛrɪ
arbitrate	AHR buh trayt	ˈɑrbətret
arbitration	ahr bi TRAY shuhn	ɑrbɪˈtreʃən
arbitrator	AHR buh tray ter	ˈɑrbətretər
arbor, arbour, A-	AHR ber	ˈɑrbər
arboreal	ahr BAW ri uhl	ɑrˈbɔrɪəl
arboretum	ahr buh REE tuhm	ɑrbəˈritəm
arbor vitae	AHR ber VIGH ti	ˈɑrbər ˈvaɪtɪ
arbutus	ahr BYOO : tuhs	ɑrˈbjutəs
arc	ahrk	ɑrk
Arc, Jeanne d'	dahrk, zhahn	dɑrk, ʒɑn
arcade	ahr KAYD	ɑrˈked
Arcadia	ahr KAY di uh	ɑrˈkedɪə
Arcady	AHR kuh di	ˈɑrkədɪ
arcanum	ahr KAY nuhm	ɑrˈkenəm
Arcaro, Eddie	ahr KAI roh	ɑrˈkɛro
Arc de Triomphe	ahrk duh tree OHMF	ɑrk də triˈomf
Arce, José	AHR say, hoh SAY	ˈɑrse, hoˈse
arch	ahrch	ɑrtʃ
archaeologist	ahr ki AH luh jist	ɑrkɪˈɑlədʒɪst
archaeology	ahr ki AH luh ji	ɑrkɪˈɑlədʒɪ
archaic	ahr KAY ik	ɑrˈkeɪk
archangel	AHRK ayn juhl	ˈɑrkendʒəl
archbishop	AHRCH bi shuhp	ˈɑrtʃbɪʃəp
archdeacon	AHRCH dee kuhn	ˈɑrtʃdikən
archdiocese	AHRCH digh uh seez	ˈɑrtʃdaɪəsiz
archduke	AHRCH doo : k	ˈɑrtʃduk
arch enemy	AHRCH e nuh mi	ˈɑrtʃ ɛnəmɪ
archeologist	ahr ki AH luh jist	ɑrkɪˈɑlədʒɪst
archeology	ahr ki AH luh ji	ɑrkɪˈɑlədʒɪ
archer, A-	AHR cher	ˈɑrtʃər
archetype	AHR kuh tighp	ˈærkətaɪp
archfiend	AHRCH feend	ˈɑrtʃfind
archiepiscopal	ahr ki uh PI skuh puhl	ɑrkɪəˈpɪskəpəl
archimandrite	ahr ki MAN dright	ɑrkɪˈmændraɪt

at [æ]; ah [ɑ]; air [ɛ]; awful [ɔ]; say [e]; back [b]; chair [tʃ]; do [d]; elm [ɛ]; eel [i];
server [ˈɜ, ər]; fit [f]; go [g]; hurt [h]; is [ɪ]; high [aɪ]; jet [dʒ]; kiss [k]; lamb [l]; my [m];
nice [n];

Archimedean	ahr ki MEE di uhn	ɑrkɪˈmidɪən
Archimedes	ahr ki MEE deez	ɑrkɪˈmidiz
arching	AHR ching	ˈɑrtʃɪŋ
archipelago	ahr kuh PE luh goh	ɑrkəˈpɛləgo
architect	AHR kuh tekt	ˈɑrkətɛkt
architectonic	ahr ki tek TAH nik	ɑrkɪtɛkˈtɑnɪk
architecture	AHR kuh tek cher	ˈɑrkətɛktʃər
architrave	AHR kuh trayv	ˈɑrkətrev
archive	AHR kighv	ˈɑrkaɪv
archivist	AHR kuh vist	ˈɑrkəvɪst
archly	AHRCH li	ˈɑrtʃlɪ
archon	AHR kahn	ˈɑrkɑn
archpriest	AHRCH preest	ˈɑrtʃprist
Arciniegas, Germán	ahr si NYAY gahs, hair MAHN	ɑrsɪˈnjegɑs, hɛrˈmɑn
arctic, A-	AHRK tik	ˈɑrktɪk
Arcturus	ahrk TYOO ruhs	ɑrkˈtjʊrəs
Ardennes	ahr DENZ	ɑrˈdɛnz
Arditi	ahr DEE tee	ɑrˈditi
ardor, ardour	AHR der	ˈɑrdər
arduous	AHR joo uhs	ˈɑrdʒʊəs
area	AI ri uh	ˈɛrɪə
arena	uh REE nuh	əˈrinə
Arensky	uh REN ski	əˈrɛnskɪ
Areopagus	a ri AH puh guhs	ærɪˈɑpəgəs
Arethusa	a ri THOO: zuh	ærɪˈθuzə
Arévalo	ah RAY vah loh	ɑˈrevɑlo
Arezzo	ah RET soh	ɑˈrɛtso
Argana	ahr GAH nah	ɑrˈgɑnɑ
argent	AHR juhnt	ˈɑrdʒənt
Argentina	ahr juhn TEE nuh	ɑrdʒənˈtinə
argentine, A-	AHR juhn tighn	ˈɑrdʒəntaɪn
Argive	AHR jighv	ˈɑrdʒaɪv
Argonaut	AHR guh nawt	ˈɑrgənɔt
Argonne	AHR gahn	ˈɑrgɑn
argosy	AHR guh si	ˈɑrgəsɪ
argue	AHR gyoo	ˈɑrgjʊ
argument	AHR gyoo muhnt	ˈɑrgjʊmənt
argumentative	ahr gyoo MEN tuh tiv	ɑrgjʊˈmɛntətɪv
Argus	AHR guhs	ˈɑrgəs
argyle	ARH gighl	ˈɑrgaɪl
Argyll	ahr GIGHL	ɑrˈgaɪl
argyrol, A-	AHR juh rawl	ˈɑrdʒərɔl
aria	AH ri uh	ˈɑrɪə
Ariadne	a ri AD ni	ærɪˈædnɪ
Arian	AI ri uhn	ˈɛrɪən
Arias	AH ri ahs	ˈɑrɪɑs
arid	A rid	ˈærɪd
Ariel, a-	AI ri uhl	ˈɛrɪəl
Aries	AI reez	ˈɛriz
ariose	AI ri ohs	ˈɛrɪos
arioso	ah ri OH soh	ɑrɪˈoso

sing [ŋ] ; oh [o] ; oil [ɔɪ] ; foot [ʊ] ; foo:d [u] ; how [aʊ] ; pie [p] ; ray [r] ; so [s] ; shall [ʃ] ; to [t] ; thin [θ] ; th:en [ð] ; above (uh BUHV) [ə, ˈʌ] ; vine [v] ; wine [w] ; whine [hw] ; you [j] ; zoo [z] ; rouge (roo:zh) [ʒ].

Aristarchus	a ri STAHR kuhs	ærɪˈstɑrkəs
Aristides	a ri STIGH deez	ærɪˈstaɪdiz
aristocracy	a ri STAH kruh si	ærɪˈstɑkrəsɪ
aristocrat	uh RI stuh krat	əˈrɪstəkræt
Aristophanes	a ri STAH fuh neez	ærɪˈstɑfəniz
Aristotelian	a ri stuh TEE li uhn	ærɪstəˈtiliən
Aristotle	A ri stah tuhl	ˈærɪstɑtəl
arithmetic (a)	a rith ME tik	ærɪθˈmɛtɪk
arithmetic (n)	uh RITH muh tik	əˈrɪθmətɪk
a rivederci	ah ree vay DAIR chi	ɑriveˈdɛrtʃi
Arizona	a ri ZOH nuh	ærɪˈzonə
Arkansan	ahr KAN zuhn	arˈkænzən
Arkansas	AHR kuhn saw	ˈarkənsɔ
Arliss	AHR lis	ˈarlɪs
armada	ahr MAH duh	arˈmɑdə
armadillo	ahr muh DI loh	arməˈdɪlo
Armageddon	ahr muh GE duhn	arməˈgɛdən
armament	AHR muh muhnt	ˈarməmənt
Armas	AHR mahs	ˈarmas
Armbruster	AHRM broo : ster	ˈarmbrustər
Armenia	ahr MEE ni uh	arˈminiə
armistice	AHR muh stis	ˈarməstɪs
armor, armour, A-	AHR mer	ˈarmər
armory	AHR muh ri	ˈarmərɪ
Arnaz, Desi	ahr NAHZ, DAY see	arˈnaz, ˈdesi
Arnhem	AHRN hem	ˈarnhɛm
arnica	AHR ni kuh	ˈarnɪkə
Arnold	AHR nuhld	ˈarnəld
aroma	uh ROH muh	əˈromə
aromatic	a ruh MA tik	ærəˈmætɪk
arouse	uh ROWZ	əˈrauz
arpeggio	ahr PE joh	arˈpɛdʒo
arraign	uh RAYN	əˈren
arrant	A ruhnt	ˈærənt
arras, A-	A ruhs	ˈærəs
Arrau, Claudio	uh ROW, KLAW dee oh	əˈrau, ˈklɔdio
array	uh RAY	əˈre
arrayal	uh RAY uhl	əˈreəl
arrear	uh RIR	əˈrɪr
arrière pensée	ah ri AIR pahn SAY	arɪˈɛr panˈse
arrogance	AI ruh guhns	ˈɛrəgəns
arrogant	AI ruh guhnt	ˈɛrəgənt
arrondissement	ah rawn dees MAHN	arɔndisˈman
arrow	AI roh	ˈɛro
arrowroot	AI roh roo : t	ˈɛrorut
arsenal	AHR suh nuhl	ˈarsənəl
arsenic(n)	AHR suh nik	ˈarsənɪk
arsenic (a)	ahr SE nik	arˈsɛnɪk
arson	AHR suhn	ˈarsən
Artaxerxes	AHR tuh ZERK seez	ˈartəˈzɝksiz
Artemis	AHR tuh mis	ˈartəmɪs
arterial	ahr TI ri uhl	arˈtɪriəl

at [æ] ; ah [ɑ] ; air [ɛ] ; awful [ɔ] ; say [e] ; back [b] ; chair [tʃ] ; do [d] ; elm [ɛ] ; eel [i] ; server [ˈɝ, ər] ; fit [f] ; go [g] ; hurt [h] ; is [ɪ] ; high [aɪ] ; jet [dʒ] ; kiss [k] ; lamb [l] ; my [m] ; nice [n] ;

arteriosclerosis	ahr TI ri oh skli ROH sis	ɑrˈtɪrɪoskliˈrosɪs
artery	AHR tuh ri	ˈɑrtərɪ
artesian	ahr TEE zhuhn	ɑrˈtiʒən
arthritis	ahr THRIGH tis	ɑrˈθraɪtɪs
Arthurian	ahr THOO ri uhn	ɑrˈθʊrɪən
artichoke	AHR ti chohk	ˈɑrtɪtʃok
articulate (a)	ahr TI kyuh lit	ɑrˈtɪkjəlɪt
articulate (v)	ahr TI kyuh layt	ɑrˈtɪkjəlet
artifice	AHR tuh fis	ˈɑrtəfɪs
artificer	ahr TI fuh ser	ɑrˈtɪfəsər
artillery	ahr TI luh ri	ɑrˈtɪlərɪ
artisan	AHR tuh zuhn	ˈɑrtəzən
artist	AHR tist	ˈɑrtɪst
artiste	ahr TEEST	ɑrˈtist
artistic	ahr TI stik	ɑrˈtɪstɪk
artistry	AHR ti stri	ˈɑrtɪstrɪ
Artsibashev	ahrt si BAH shef	ɑrtsɪˈbɑʃɛf
Artzybasheff	ahrt si BAH shef	ɑrtsɪˈbɑʃɛf
Aruba	uh ROO: buh	əˈrubə
Arundel (England)	A ruhn duhl	ˈærəndəl
Arundel (Maryland)	uh RUHN duhl	əˈrʌndəl
aryan, A-	AI ri uhn	ˈɛrɪən
Arze	AHR say	ˈɑrse
Asa	AY suh	ˈesə
Asad	ah SAHD	ɑˈsad
asafetida, asafoetida	a suh FE ti duh	æsəˈfɛtɪdə
Asaph	A suhf	ˈæsəf
asbestos	as BE stuhs	æsˈbɛstəs
Ascanius	as KAY ni uhs	æsˈkenɪəs
ascend	uh SEND	əˈsɛnd
ascendancy, ascendency	uh SEN duhn si	əˈsɛndənsɪ
ascension	uh SEN shuhn	əˈsɛnʃən
ascent	uh SENT	əˈsɛnt
asceptic	uh SEP tik	əˈsɛptɪk
ascertain	a ser TAYN	æsərˈten
ascetic	uh SE tik	əˈsɛtɪk
Asch, Sholem	ash, SHOH luhm	æʃ, ˈʃoləm
Ascham	A skuhm	ˈæskəm
Asclepius	a SKLEE pi uhs	æˈsklipɪəs
ascorbic	uh SKAWR bik	əˈskɔrbɪk
ascot, A-	A skuht	ˈæskət
ascribe	uh SKRIGHB	əˈskraɪb
ashamed	uh SHAYMD	əˈʃemd
Ashanti	uh SHAN ti	əˈʃæntɪ
Ashdod	ASH dahd	ˈæʃdad
Ashe	ash	æʃ
ashen	A shuhn	ˈæʃən
Asher	A sher	ˈæʃər
ashore	uh SHAWR	əˈʃɔr
Ashtoreth	ASH tuh rith	ˈæʃtərɪθ
Ashur	AH shoor	ˈɑʃʊr
Asia	AY zhuh	ˈeʒə

---

sing [ŋ] ; *oh* [o] ; *oil* [ɔɪ] ; *foot* [ʊ] ; *foo*:d [u] ; *how* [aʊ] ; *pie* [p] ; *ray* [r] ; *so* [s] ; *shall* [ʃ] ; *to* [t] ; *thin* [θ] ; *th:*en [ð] ; *above (uh BUHV)* [ə, ˈʌ] ; *vine* [v] ; *wine* [w] ; *whine* [hw] ; *you* [j] ; *zoo* [z] ; *rouge (roo:zh)* [ʒ].

Asiatic	ay zhi A tik	eʒɪˈætɪk
aside	uh SIGHD	əˈsaɪd
asinine	A si nighn	ˈæsɪnaɪn
ask	ask	æsk
askance	uh SKANS	əˈskæns
Askelon	A skuh lahn	ˈæskəlɑn
askew	uh SKYOO:	əˈskju
aslant	uh SLANT	əˈslænt
Asmara	ah SMAH ruh	ɑˈsmɑrə
asocial	ay SO shuhl	eˈsoʃəl
asp	asp	æsp
asparagus	uh SPA ruh guhs	əˈspærəgəs
Aspasia	uh SPAY zhuh	əˈspeʒə
aspect	A spekt	ˈæspɛkt
aspen	A spuhn	ˈæspən
asperity	uh SPAI ruh ti	əˈspɛrətɪ
aspersion	uh SPER zhuhn	əˈspɚʒən
asphalt	AS fawlt	ˈæsfɔlt
asphodel	AS fuh del	ˈæsfədɛl
asphyxiate	as FIK si ayt	æsˈfɪksɪet
asphyxiation	as fik si AY shuhn	æsfɪksɪˈeʃən
aspic	A spik	ˈæspɪk
aspidistra, A-	a spi DI struh	æspɪˈdɪstrə
aspirant	uh SPIGH ruhnt	əˈspaɪrənt
aspirate (a, n)	A spuh rit	ˈæspərɪt
aspirate (v)	A spuh rayt	ˈæspəret
aspire	uh SPIGHR	əˈspaɪr
aspirin	A spuh rin	ˈæspərɪn
Asquith	A skwith	ˈæskwɪθ
ass	as	æs
assail	uh SAYL	əˈsel
assailant	uh SAY luhnt	əˈselənt
Assam	a SAM	æˈsæm
Assamese	a suh MEEZ	æsəˈmiz
assassin	uh SA sin	əˈsæsɪn
assassinate	uh SA si nayt	əˈsæsɪnet
assassination	uh sa si NAY shuhn	əsæsɪˈneʃən
assault	uh SAWLT	əˈsɔlt
assay (n)	A say	ˈæse
assay (v)	uh SAY	əˈse
assemblage	uh SEM blij	əˈsɛmblɪdʒ
assembly	uh SEM bli	əˈsɛmblɪ
assent	uh SENT	əˈsɛnt
assert	uh SERT	əˈsɚt
assertion	uh SER shuhn	əˈsɚʃən
assess	uh SES	əˈsɛs
assessment	uh SES muhnt	əˈsɛsmənt
assessor	uh SE ser	əˈsɛsər
asset	A set	ˈæsɛt
assiduous	uh SI joo uhs	əˈsɪdʒʊəs
assign	uh SIGHN	əˈsaɪn
assignable	uh SIGH nuh buhl	əˈsaɪnəbəl

at [æ]; ah [ɑ]; air [ɛ]; awful [ɔ]; say [e]; back [b]; chair [tʃ]; do [d]; elm [ɛ]; eel [i];
server [ˈɝ, ər]; fit [f]; go [g]; hurt [h]; is [ɪ]; high [aɪ]; jet [dʒ]; kiss [k]; lamb [l]; my [m];
nice [n];

assignat	A sig nat	ˈæsɪgnæt
assignation	a sig NAY shuhn	æsɪgˈneʃən
assignee	uh SIGH ni	əˈsaɪnɪ
assimilable	uh SI muh luh buhl	əˈsɪmələbəl
assimilate	uh SI muh layt	əˈsɪmələt
assimilation	uh si muh LAY shuhn	əsɪməˈleʃən
assist	uh SIST	əˈsɪst
assistance	uh SI stuhns	əˈsɪstəns
assistant	uh SI stuhnt	əˈsɪstənt
assize	uh SIGHZ	əˈsaɪz
associate (a, n)	uh SOH shi it	əˈsoʃɪt
associate (v)	uh SOH shi ayt	əˈsoʃɪet
association	uh soh shi AY shuhn	əsoʃɪˈeʃən
associative	uh SOH shi ay tiv	əˈsoʃɪetɪv
assonance	A suh nuhns	ˈæsənəns
assortment	uh SAWRT muhnt	əˈsɔrtmənt
assuage	uh SWAYJ	əˈswedʒ
assume	uh SOO : M	əˈsum
assumption	uh SUHMP shuhn	əˈsʌmpʃən
assurance	uh SHOO ruhns	əˈʃurəns
assure	uh SHOOR	əˈʃur
Assyrian	uh SI ri uhn	əˈsɪrɪən
Assyriology	uh si ri AH luh ji	əsɪrɪˈɑlədʒɪ
aster	A ster	ˈæstər
asterisk	A stuh risk	ˈæstərɪsk
astern	uh STERN	əˈstɝn
asteroid	A stuh roid	ˈæstərɔɪd
asthma	AZ muh	ˈæzmə
asthmatic	az MA tik	æzˈmætɪk
astigmatism	uh STIG muh ti zuhm	əˈstɪgmətɪzəm
astir	uh STER	əˈstɝ
astonish	uh STAH nish	əˈstɑnɪʃ
Astor	A ster	ˈæstər
astound	uh STOWND	əˈstaund
astrachan, A-, astrakhan	A struh kuhn	ˈæstrəkən
Astraea	a STREE uh	æˈstriə
Astrakhan (Russia)	a struh KAN	æstrəˈkæn
astral	A struhl	ˈæstrəl
astray	uh STRAY	əˈstre
astride	uh STRIGHD	əˈstraɪd
astringent	uh STRIN juhnt	əˈstrɪndʒənt
astrionics	a stri AH niks	æstrɪˈɑnɪks
astrodome	A struh dohm	ˈæstrədom
astrogation	a struh GAY shuhn	æstrəˈgeʃən
astrolabe	A struh layb	ˈæstrəleb
astrologer	uh STRA luh jer	əˈstrɑlədʒər
astrology	uh STRAH luh ji	əˈstrɑlədʒɪ
astronaut	A struh nawt	ˈæstrənɔt
astronautics	a struh NAW tiks	æstrəˈnɔtɪks
astronomer	uh STRAH nuh mer	əˈstrɑnəmər
astronomical	a struh NAH mi kuhl	æstrəˈnɑmɪkəl
astronomy	uh STRAH nuh mi	əˈstrɑnəmɪ

sing [ŋ] ; *oh* [o] ; *oil* [ɔɪ] ; *foot* [ʊ] ; *foo:*d [u] ; *how* [aʊ] ; *pie* [p] ; *ray* [r] ; *so* [s] ; *shall* [ʃ] ; *to* [t] ; *thin* [θ] ; *th:*en [ð] ; *above* (*uh BUH*V) [ə, ˈʌ] ; *vine* [v] ; *wine* [w] ; *whine* [hw] ; *you* [j] ; *zoo* [z] ; *rouge* (roo:*zh*) [ʒ].

astrophysics	a struh FI ziks	æstrəˈfɪzɪks
astute	uh STOO : T	əˈstut
Asunción	ah soo : n see OHN	ɑsunsiˈon
asunder	uh SUHN der	əˈsʌndər
Aswan, Assuan	ah SWAHN	ɑˈswɑn
asylum	uh SIGH luhm	əˈsailəm
asymmetry	uh SI muh tri	əˈsɪmətrɪ
atabrin, -e, A-,	A tuh brin	ˈætəbrɪn
Atalanta	a tuh LAN tuh	ætəˈlæntə
Ataturk, Kemal	ah tah TERK, ke MAHL	ɑtɑˈtɝk, kɛˈmɑl
atavism	A tuh vi zuhm	ˈætəvɪzəm
Ate	AY ti	ˈetɪ
atelier	A tuhl yay	ˈætəlje
a tempo	ah TEM poh	ɑˈtɛmpo
Athanasian	a thuh NAY zhuhn	æθəˈneʒən
atheism	AY thi i zuhm	ˈeθɪɪzəm
atheist	AY thi ist	ˈeθɪɪst
atheling	A thuh ling	ˈæθəlɪŋ
Athena	uh THEE nuh	əˈθinə
athenaeum, atheneum, A-	a thuh NEE uhm	æθəˈniəm
Athenagoras	ah the nuh GAW ruhs	ɑθenəˈgɔrəs
Athenian	uh THEE ni uhn	əˈθiniən
Athens	A thinz	ˈæθɪnz
athirst	uh THERST	əˈθɝst
athlete	ATH leet	ˈæθlit
athletic	ath LE tik	æθˈlɛtɪk
athodyd	A thuh did	ˈæθədɪd
athrocyte	A thruh sight	ˈæθrəsaɪt
athwart	uh THWAWRT	əˈθwɔrt
Atlanta	at LAN tuh	ætˈlæntə
atlantean, A-	at lan TEE uhn	ætlænˈtiən
Atlantic	at LAN tik	ætˈlæntɪk
Atlantis	at LAN tis	ætˈlæntɪs
atlas, A-	AT luhs	ˈætləs
atmosphere	AT muhs fir	ˈætməsfɪr
atmospheric	at muhs FAI rik	ætməsˈfɛrɪk
atoll	A tawl	ˈætɔl
atom	A tuhm	ˈætəm
atomic	uh TAH mik	əˈtɑmɪk
atomizer	A tuh migh zer	ˈætəmaɪzər
atonal	ay TOH nuhl	eˈtonəl
atonality	ay toh NA luh ti	etoˈnælətɪ
atone	uh TOHN	əˈton
atonemen	uh TOHN muhnt	əˈtonmənt
atonic	uh TAH nik	əˈtɑnɪk
atony	A tuh ni	ˈætənɪ
Atreus	AY troo : s	ˈetrus
atrium	AY tri uhm	ˈetrɪəm
atrociou	uh TROH shuhs	əˈtroʃəs
atrocity	uh TRAH suh ti	əˈtrɑsətɪ
atrophy	A truh fi	ˈætrəfɪ

at [æ] ; *ah* [ɑ] ; *air* [ɛ] ; *awful* [ɔ] ; *say* [e] ; *back* [b] ; *chair* [tʃ] ; *do* [d] ; *elm* [ɛ] ; *eel* [i] ; *server* [ˈɝ, ər] ; *f*it [f] ; *go* [g] ; *hurt* [h] ; *is* [ɪ] ; *high* [aɪ] ; *jet* [dʒ] ; *kiss* [k] ; *lamb* [l] ; *my* [m] ; *nice* [n] ;

atropine, A-	A truh peen	ˈætrəpin
attach	uh TACH	əˈtætʃ
attaché	a tuh SHAY	ætəˈʃe
attacked	uh TAKT	əˈtækt
attain	uh TAYN	əˈten
attainable	uh TAY nuh buhl	əˈtenəbəl
attainment	uh TAYN muhnt	əˈtenmənt
attar	A ter	ˈætər
attempt	uh TEMPT	əˈtɛmpt
attention	uh TEN shuhn	əˈtɛnʃən
attenuate (a)	uh TE nyoo it	əˈtɛnjuɪt
attenuate (v)	uh TE nyoo ayt	əˈtɛnjuet
attenuation	uh te nyoo AY shuhn	ətɛnjuˈeʃən
attic, A-	A tik	ˈætɪk
atticism, A-	A ti si zuhm	ˈætɪsɪzəm
Attila	A tuh luh	ˈætələ
attire	uh TIGHR	əˈtaɪr
attirement	uh TIGHR muhnt	əˈtaɪrmənt
attitude	A tuh tyoo:d	ˈætətjud
Attlee	AT lee	ˈætli
attorney	uh TER ni	əˈtɝnɪ
attract	uh TRAKT	əˈtrækt
attraction	uh TRAK shuhn	əˈtrækʃən
attribute (n)	A truh byoo:t	ˈætrəbjut
attribute (v)	uh TRI byoot	əˈtrɪbjut
attribution	a tri BYOO: shuhn	ætrɪˈbjuʃən
attributive	uh TRI byoo tiv	əˈtrɪbjutɪv
attrition	uh TRI shuhn	əˈtrɪʃən
Attu	a TOO:	æˈtu
attune	uh TOO:N	əˈtun
atypical	ay TI pi kuhl	eˈtɪpɪkəl
aubade	oh BAHD	oˈbad
auberge	oh BAIRZH	oˈbɛrʒ
Aubrey	AW bri	ˈɔbrɪ
auburn, A-	AW bern	ˈɔbərn
Aubusson	oh boo SAWN	obuˈsɔn
Aucassin	oh kah SAN	okɑˈsæn
Auchincloss	AW kin klaws	ˈɔkɪnklɔs
Auchinleck	AW kin lek	ˈɔkɪnlɛk
Auckland	AW kluhnd	ˈɔklənd
au courant	oh koo RAHN	o kuˈrɑn
auction	AWK shuhn	ˈɔkʃən
audacious	aw DAY shuhs	ɔˈdeʃəs
audacity	aw DA suh ti	ɔˈdæsətɪ
Auden	AW duhn	ˈɔdən
audible	AW du buhl	ˈɔdəbəl
audience	AW di uhns	ˈɔdɪəns
audiology	aw di AH luh ji	ɔdɪˈɑlədʒɪ
audiophile	AW di uh fighl	ˈɔdɪəfaɪl
audit	AW dit	ˈɔdɪt
audition	aw DI shuhn	ɔˈdɪʃən
auditor	AW di ter	ˈɔdɪtər

sing [ŋ] ; *oh* [o] ; *oil* [ɔɪ] ; *foot* [ʊ] ; *foo:d* [u] ; *how* [aʊ] ; *pie* [p] ; *ray* [r] ; *so* [s] ; *shall* [ʃ] ; *to* [t] ; *thin* [θ] ; *th:en* [ð] ; *above* (*uh BUHV*) [ə, ˈʌ] ; *vine* [v] ; *wine* [w] ; *whine* [hw] ; *you* [j] ; *zoo* [z] ; *rouge* (*roo:zh*) [ʒ].

auditorium	aw di TAW ri uhm	ɔdɪˈtɔrɪəm
Audubon	AW duh bahn	ˈɔdəbɑn
Auer	OW er	ˈauər
au fait	oh FAY	oˈfe
au fond	oh FAWN	oˈfɔn
auf Wiedersehen	owf VEE der zay uhn	auf ˈvidərzeən
Augean	aw JEE uhn	ɔˈdʒiən
auger	AW ger	ˈɔgər
aught	awt	ɔt
augment	awg MENT	ɔgˈmɛnt
au gratin	oh GRA tuhn	oˈgrætən
augur	AW ger	ˈɔgər
augury	AW gyuh ri	ˈɔgjərɪ
August	AW guhst	ˈɔgəst
august	aw GUHST	ɔˈgʌst
Augustan	aw GUH stuhn	ɔˈgʌstən
Augustine	AW guh steen	ˈɔgəstin
Augustus	aw GUH stuhs	ɔˈgʌstəs
au jus	oh ZHOO	oˈʒu
auk	awk	ɔk
au lait	oh LAY	oˈle
auld lang syne	awld lang SIGHN	ɔld læŋ ˈsaɪn
aulic	AW lik	ˈɔlɪk
Aumont	oh MOHN	oˈmon
au naturel	oh na too REL	o nætuˈrɛl
Aunos	ah oo NOHS	auˈnos
aunt	ant	ænt
aura	AW ruh	ˈɔrə
aural	AW ruhl	ˈɔrəl
aureole	AW ri ohl	ˈɔrɪol
aureomycin	aw ri oh MIGH sin	ɔrɪoˈmaɪsɪn
au revoir	oh ruh VWAHR	o rəˈvwɑr
auricular	aw RI kyuh ler	ɔˈrɪkjələr
auriferous	aw RI fuh ruhs	ɔˈrɪfərəs
Auriga	aw RIGH guh	ɔˈraɪgə
Auriol	oh ri AWL	orɪˈɔl
aurora, A-	aw RAW ruh	ɔˈrɔrə
auscultation	aw skuhl TAY shuhn	ɔskəlˈteʃən
Ausgleich	OWS glighk	ˈausglaɪk
auspice	AW spis	ˈɔspɪs
auspices	AW spi siz	ˈɔspɪsɪz
auspicious	aw SPI shuhs	ɔˈspɪʃəs
Auster	AW ster	ˈɔstər
austere	aw STIR	ɔˈstɪr
austerity	aw STAI ruh ti	ɔˈstɛrətɪ
Austerlitz	AW ster lits	ˈɔstərlɪts
Australasia	aw struh LAY zhuh	ɔstrəˈleʒə
Australia	aw STRAY lyuh	ɔˈstreljə
Australian	aw STRAY lyuhn	ɔˈstreljən
australis	aw STRAY lis	ɔˈstrelɪs
Australopithecinae	aw stray luh pi thuh SIGH nee	ɔstreləpɪθəˈsaɪni

---

at [æ] ; ah [ɑ] ; air [ɛ] ; awful [ɔ] ; say [e] ; back [b] ; chair [tʃ] ; do [d] ; elm [ɛ] ; eel [i] ; server [ˈɜ, ər] ; fit [f] ; go [g] ; hurt [h] ; is [ɪ] ; high [aɪ] ; jet [dʒ] ; kiss [k] ; lamb [l] ; my [m] ; nice [n] ;

Austria	AW stri uh	ˈɔstriə
austro-, A-	AW stroh	ˈɔstro
Ausubel	OW suh bel	ˈaʊsəbɛl
autarchic, autarkic	aw TAHR kik	ɔˈtɑrkɪk
autarchist, autarkist	AW tahr kist	ˈɔtɑrkɪst
autarchy, autarky	AW tahr ki	ˈɔtɑrkɪ
authentic	aw THEN tik	ɔˈθɛntɪk
authenticate	aw THEN ti kayt	ɔˈθɛntɪket
authenticity	aw thuhn TI suh ti	ɔθənˈtɪsətɪ
author	AW ther	ˈɔθər
authoritative	uh THAW ruh tay tiv	əˈθɔrətetɪv
authority	uh THAW ruh ti	əˈθɔrətɪ
authorization	aw thuh ri ZAY shuhn	ɔθərɪˈzeʃən
authorize	AW thuh righz	ˈɔθəraɪz
autism	AW ti zuhm	ˈɔtɪzəm
autistic	aw TI stik	ɔˈtɪstɪk
auto	AW toh	ˈɔto
autobahn	AW tuh bahn	ˈɔtəbɑn
autobiographical	aw tuh bigh uh GRA fi kuhl	ɔtəbaɪəˈgræfɪkəl
autobiography	aw tuh bigh AH gruh fi	ɔtəbaɪˈɑgrəfɪ
autocracy	aw TAH kruh si	ɔˈtɑkrəsɪ
autocrat	AW tuh krat	ˈɔtəkræt
auto-da-fé	aw toh duh FAY	ɔtodəˈfe
autogiro, autogyro, A-	aw tuh JIGH roh	ɔtəˈdʒaɪro
automat	AW tuh mat	ˈɔtəmæt
automatic	aw tuh MA tik	ɔtəˈmætɪk
automation	aw tuh MAY shuhn	ɔtəˈmeʃən
automatism	aw TAH muh ti zuhm	ɔˈtɑmətɪzəm
automaton	aw TAH muh tahn	ɔˈtɑmətɑn
automobile	AW tuh muh beel	ˈɔtəməbil
autonomous	aw TAH nuh muhs	ɔˈtɑnəməs
autonomy	aw TAH nuh mi	ɔˈtɑnəmɪ
autopsy	AW tahp si	ˈɔtɑpsɪ
autumn	AW tuhm	ˈɔtəm
autumnal	aw TUHM nuhl	ɔˈtʌmnəl
auxiliary	awg ZI lyuh ri	ɔgˈzɪljərɪ
avail	uh VAYL	əˈvel
availability	uh vay luh BI luh ti	əveləˈbɪlətɪ
avalanche	A vuh lanch	ˈævəlæntʃ
Avalon	A vuh lahn	ˈævəlɑn
avant-garde	ah vahnt GAHRD	ɑvɑntˈgɑrd
avarice	A vuh ris	ˈævərɪs
avaricious	a vuh RI shuhs	ævəˈrɪʃəs
avast	uh VAST	əˈvæst
avatar	a vuh TAHR	ævəˈtɑr
avaunt	uh VAWNT	əˈvɔnt
ave, A-	AH vay	ˈave
Ave Maria	AH vay muh REE uh	ˈave məˈrɪə
avenge	uh VENJ	əˈvɛndʒ
avenue	A vuh noo:	ˈævənu
average	A vrij	ˈævrɪdʒ

sing [ŋ] ; *oh* [o] ; *oil* [ɔɪ] ; *foot* [ʊ] ; *foo:*d [u] ; *how* [aʊ] ; *pie* [p] ; *ray* [r] ; *so* [s] ; *shall* [ʃ] ;
to [t] ; *thin* [θ] ; *th:*en [ð] ; *above* (*uh BUH*V) [ə, ˈʌ] ; *vine* [v] ; *wine* [w] ; *whine* [hw] ;
you [j] ; *zoo* [z] ; *rouge* (roo:*zh*) [ʒ].

averse	uh VERS	əˈvɝs
aversion	uh VER zhuhn	əˈvɝʒən
avert	uh VERT	əˈvɝt
aviary	AY vi ai ri	ˈevɪɛrɪ
aviation	ay vi AY shuhn	evɪˈeʃən
aviator	Ay vi ay ter	ˈevɪetər
aviatrix	ay vi AY triks	evɪˈetrɪks
avid	A vid	ˈævɪd
avidity	uh VI duh ti	əˈvɪdətɪ
Avignon	a vee NYAHN	æviˈnjɑn
Ávila	AH vee lah	ˈɑvilɑ
aviso	uh VIGH zoh	əˈvaɪzo
avocado	a vuh KAH doh	ævəˈkɑdo
avocation	a vuh KAY shuhn	ævəˈkeʃən
avoid	uh VOID	əˈvɔɪd
avoidance	uh VOI duhns	əˈvɔɪdəns
avoirdupois	a ver duh POIZ	ævərdəˈpɔɪz
Avon	AY vuhn	ˈevən
avow	uh VOW	əˈvaʊ
avowal	uh VOW uhl	əˈvaʊəl
awaken	uh WAY kuhn	əˈwekən
aware	uh WAIR	əˈwɛr
awe	aw	ɔ
aweigh	uh WAY	əˈwe
awesome	AW suhm	ˈɔsəm
awful	AW fuhl	ˈɔfəl
awfully	AW fli	ˈɔflɪ
awhile	uh HWIGHL	əˈhwaɪl
awkward	AW kwerd	ˈɔkwərd
awl	awl	ɔl
awning	AW ning	ˈɔnɪŋ
awry	uh RIGH	əˈraɪ
ax, -e	aks	æks
axes (pl. of *ax*)	AK siz	ˈæksɪz
axes (pl. of *axis*)	AK seez	ˈæksiz
axiom	AK si uhm	ˈæksɪəm
axiomatic	ak si uh MA tik	æksɪəˈmætɪk
axis	AK sis	ˈæksɪs
axle	AK suhl	ˈæksəl
Axminster	AKS min ster	ˈæksmɪnstər
ay (alas)	ay	e
ay, -e (always)	ay	e
ay, -e (yes)	igh	aɪ
Ayling	AY ling	ˈelɪŋ
Ayr	air	ɛr
Ayres	airz	ɛrz
Ayrshire	AIR shir	ˈɛrʃɪr
Azad	ah ZAHD	ɑˈzɑd
azalea, A-	uh ZAY lyuh	əˈzeljə
Azcárate	ahs KAH rah tay	ɑsˈkɑrate
Azerbaijan, Azerbaidzhan	ah zer bigh JAHN	ɑzərbaɪˈdʒɑn

at [æ] ; *ah* [ɑ] ; *air* [ɛ] ; *awful* [ɔ] ; s*ay* [e] ; *b*ack [b] ; *ch*air [tʃ] ; *d*o [d] ; *e*lm [ɛ] ; *ee*l [i] ; s*er*ver [ˈɝ, ər] ; *f*it [f] ; *g*o [g] ; *h*urt [h] ; *i*s [ɪ] ; *h*igh [aɪ] ; *j*et [dʒ] ; *k*iss [k] ; *l*amb [l] ; *m*y [m] ; *n*ice [n] ;

azimuth	A zuh muhth	ˈæzəməθ
Azmi	AHZ mee	ˈɑzmi
Azores	AY zohrz	ˈezorz
Azov	AH zahf	ˈɑzɑf
Aztec	AZ tek	ˈæztɛk
Aztecan	AZ te kuhn	ˈæztɛkən
azure	A zher	ˈæʒər

B

baa	ba	bæ
Baal	BAY uhl	ˈbeəl
Baalim	BAY uh lim	ˈbeəlɪm
Baba	BAH bah	ˈbɑbɑ
babbitt, B-	BA bit	ˈbæbɪt
babbittry, B-	BA bi tri	ˈbæbɪtrɪ
babel, B-	BA buhl	ˈbæbəl
Babel, Isaac	BAH bil, ee SAHK	ˈbɑbɪl, iˈsak
Babilée	bah bee LAY	bɑbiˈle
Babism	BAH bi zuhm	ˈbɑbɪzəm
Babist	BAH bist	ˈbɑbɪst
Babite	BAH bight	ˈbɑbaɪt
babka	BAHP kah	ˈbɑpkɑ
baboo, B-	BAH boo :	ˈbɑbu
baboon	ba BOO : N	bæˈbun
babu, B-	BAH boo :	ˈbɑbu
babushka	buh BOOSH kuh	bəˈbuʃkə
Babylon	BA buh luhn	ˈbæbələn
Babylonia	ba buh LOH ni uh	bæbəˈloniə
Bacall	buh KAWL	bəˈkɔl
baccalaureate	ba kuh LAW ri it	bækəˈlɔrɪt
baccarat, baccara	BA kuh rah	ˈbækərɑ
Bacchae	BA kee	ˈbæki
bacchanal	BA kuh nuhl	ˈbækənəl
bacchanalia, B-	ba kuh NAY li uh	bækəˈneliə
bacchanalian, B-	ba kuh NAY li uhn	bækəˈneliən
bacchant	BA kuhnt	ˈbækənt
Bacchus	BA kuhs	ˈbækəs
Bach	bahk	bɑk
Bache (& Co.)	baych	betʃ
bachelor	BA chuh ler	ˈbætʃələr
bacilli	buh SI ligh	bəˈsɪlaɪ
bacillus	buh SI luhs	bəˈsɪləs
backgammon	BAK ga muhn	ˈbækgæmən
background	BAK grownd	ˈbækgraʊnd
Backhaus	BAH kows	ˈbɑkaʊs
Backhouse	BA kuhs	ˈbækəs
Baconian	bay KOH ni uhn	beˈkoniən

sing [ŋ] ; oh [o] ; oil [ɔɪ] ; foot [ʊ] ; foo:d [u] ; how [aʊ] ; pie [p] ; ray [r] ; so [s] ; shall [ʃ] ;
to [t] ; thin [θ] ; th:en [ð] ; above (uh BUHV) [ə, ˈʌ] ; vine [v] ; wine [w] ; whine [hw] ;
you [j] ; zoo [z] ; rouge (roo:zh) [ʒ].

bacteria	bak TI ri uh	bæk'tırıə
bacterid	BAK tuh rid	'bæktərıd
bacteriology	bak ti ri AH luh ji	bæktırı'alədʒı
bacteriophage	bak TI ri uh fayj	bæk'tırıəfedʒ
bacteriostasis	bak ti ri uh STAY sis	bæktırıə'stesıs
Bactrian	BAK tri uhn	'bæktrıən
bade	bad	bæd
Baden (Germany)	BAH duhn	'badən
Baden (U.S.)	BAY duhn	'bedən
Baden-Powell	BAY duhn POH uhl	'bedən 'poəl
badinage	BA duh nij	'bædənıdʒ
badlands, B-	BAD landz	'bædlændz
badminton	BAD min tuhn	'bædmıntən
Badoglio, Pietro	bah DOH lyoh, PYE troh	ba'doljo, 'pjɛtro
Badura-Skoda	buh DOO : ruh SKOH duh	bə'durə-'skodə
baedeker, B-	BAY di ker	'bedıkər
Baffin	BA fin	'bæfın
bagatelle	BA guh tel	'bægətɛl
Bagdad	BAG dad	'bægdæd
Bagehot	BA juht	'bædʒət
bagel	BAY guhl	'begəl
baggage	BA gij	'bægıdʒ
Baghdad	BAG dad	'bægdæd
bagnio	BA nyoh	'bænjo
Bagnold, Enid	BAG nohld, EE nid	'bægnold, 'inıd
bagpipe	BAG pighp	'bægpaıp
baguet, -te	ba GET	bæ'gɛt
bah	bah	ba
Bahai	buh HAH ee	bə'hai
Bahaism	buh HAH i zuhm	bə'haızəm
Bahaist	buh HAH ist	bə'haıst
Bahama	buh HAH muh	bə'hamə
Bahia	buh HEE uh	bə'hiə
Bahrein	bah RAYN	ba'ren
Baikal	bigh KAHL	baı'kal
bailee	BAY lee	'beli
bailey, B-	BAY li	'belı
bailiwick	BAY luh wik	'beləwık
bairn	bairn	bern
baize	bayz	bez
bakelite, B-	BAYK light	'beklaıt
baksheesh, bakshish	BAK sheesh	'bækʃiʃ
Baku	bah KOO :	ba'ku
Balaam	BAY luhm	'beləm
balaclava, Balaklava	ba luh KLAH vuh	bælə'klavə
balalaika	ba luh LIGH kuh	bælə'laıkə
Balanchine	ba lan SHEEN	bælæn'ʃin
Balaton	BAH lah tawn	'balatən
Balbo	BAHL boh	'balbo
Balboa	bal BOH uh	bæl'boə
balbriggan	bal BRI guhn	bæl'brıgən
balcony	BAL kuh ni	'bælkənı

at [æ]; ah [a]; air [ɛ]; awful [ɔ]; say [e]; back [b]; chair [tʃ]; do [d]; elm [ɛ]; eel [i];
server ['ɝ, ər]; fit [f]; go [g]; hurt [h]; is [ı]; high [aı]; jet [dʒ]; kiss [k]; lamb [l]; my [m];
nice [n];

bald	bawld	bɔld
baldachin, baldaquin	BAL duh kin	ˈbældəkɪn
Balder	BAWL der	ˈbɔldər
balderdash	BAWL der dash	ˈbɔldərdæʃ
baldpate	BAWLD payt	ˈbɔldpet
baldric	BAWL drik	ˈbɔldrɪk
Baldwin	BAWL dwin	ˈbɔldwɪn
Bâle	bahl	bɑl
bale	bayl	bel
Balearic	ba li A rik	bælɪˈærɪk
baleen	buh LEEN	bəˈlin
Balenciaga	bah len see AH gah	bɑlɛnsiˈɑgɑ
Balfour	BAL foor	ˈbælfʊr
Bali	BAH li	ˈbɑlɪ
Balikpapan	BAH leek PAH pahn	ˈbɑlikˈpɑpɑn
Balinese	bah li NEEZ	bɑlɪˈniz
balk	bawk	bɔk
Balkan	BAWL kuhn	ˈbɔlkən
ball	bawl	bɔl
ballad	BA luhd	ˈbæləd
ballade	buh LAHD	bəˈlɑd
balladry	BA luh dri	ˈbælədrɪ
Ballantine	BA luhn tighn	ˈbæləntaɪn
ballast	BA luhst	ˈbæləst
ballerina	ba luh REE nuh	bæləˈrinə
ballet	BA lay	ˈbæle
Balliol	BAY lyuhl	ˈbeljəl
ballistic	buh LI stik	bəˈlɪstɪk
Ballo in Maschera	BAH loh een MAH skay rah	ˈbɑlo in ˈmɑskerɑ
ballonet	ba loh NET	bæloˈnɛt
balloon	buh LOO : N	bəˈlun
ballroom	BAWL room	ˈbɔlrʊm
ballyhoo (n)	BA li hoo :	ˈbælɪhu
ballyhoo (v)	ba li HOO :	bælɪˈhu
balm	bahm	bɑm
Balmain	bahl MAIN	bɑlˈmɛn
Balmoral	bal MAW ruhl	bælˈmɔrəl
balsam	BAWL suhm	ˈbɔlsəm
balsamic	bawl SA mik	bɔlˈsæmɪk
Balthasar	bal THA zer	bælˈθæzər
Baltic	BAWL tik	ˈbɔltɪk
Baltimore	BAWL tuh mawr	ˈbɔltəmɔr
Baluchistan	buh LOO : chi stan	bəˈlutʃɪstæn
baluster	BA luh ster	ˈbæləstər
balustrade	ba luh STRAYD	bæləˈstred
Balzac	BAL zak	ˈbælzæk
Bamako	bah MAH koh	bɑˈmɑko
bambino	bam BEE noh	bæmˈbino
bamboo	bam BOO :	bæmˈbu
bamboozle	bam BOO : zuhl	bæmˈbuzəl
banal	BAY nuhl	ˈbenəl
banana	buh NA nuh	bəˈnænə

sing [ŋ] ; oh [o] ; oil [ɔɪ] ; foot [ʊ] ; foo:d [u] ; how [aʊ] ; pie [p] ; ray [r] ; so [s] ; shall [ʃ] ; to [t] ; thin [θ] ; th:en [ð] ; above (uh BUHV) [ə, ˈʌ] ; vine [v] ; wine [w] ; whine [hw] ; you [j] ; zoo [z] ; rouge (roo:zh) [ʒ].

bandage	BAN dij	ˈbændɪdʒ
bandana, bandanna	ban DA nuh	bænˈdænə
bandeau	BAN doh	ˈbændo
Bandoeng, Bandung	BAHN doong	ˈbɑnduŋ
bandy-legged	BAN di le gid	ˈbændɪlɛgɪd
bane	bayn	ben
baneberry	BAYN bai ri	ˈbenbɛrɪ
baneful	BAYN fuhl	ˈbenfəl
Banff	bamf	bæmf
bangalore, B-	BANG guh lawr	ˈbæŋgəlɔr
Bangkok	BANG kahk	ˈbæŋkɑk
bangle	BANG guhl	ˈbæŋgəl
banish	BA nish	ˈbænɪʃ
banister, bannister	BA ni ster	ˈbænɪstər
Banjermasin	bahn jer MAH sin	bɑndʒərˈmɑsɪn
bankruptcy	BANG kruhpt si	ˈbæŋkrəptsɪ
banner	BA ner	ˈbænər
bannock	BA nuhk	ˈbænək
banns, bans	banz	bænz
banquet	BANG kwit	ˈbæŋkwɪt
Banquo	BANG kwoh	ˈbæŋkwo
banshee, banshie	BAN shee	ˈbænʃi
bantam, B-	BAN tuhm	ˈbæntəm
banter	BAN ter	ˈbæntər
bantling	BANT ling	ˈbæntlɪŋ
Bantu	BAN too:	ˈbæntu
banyan, banian	BA nyuhn	ˈbænjən
Banyuwangi	bahn yoo WAHNG i	bɑnyuˈwɑŋɪ
banzai	BAHN zah ee	ˈbɑnzɑi
Bao Dai	bow DIGH	bau ˈdaɪ
baptism	BAP ti zuhm	ˈbæptɪzəm
baptismal	bap TIZ muhl	bæpˈtɪzməl
baptist, B-	BAP tist	ˈbæptɪst
baptistery, baptistry	BAP ti stri	ˈbæptɪstrɪ
baptize	BAP tighz	ˈbæptaɪz
Barabas	BA ruh buhs	ˈbærəbəs
Barabbas (Bible)	buh RA buhs	bəˈræbəs
Barabbas (Shakespeare)	BA ruh buhs	ˈbærəbəs
Baraca	buh RA kuh	bəˈrækə
Baranowicze	bah rah naw VEE che	bɑrɑnɔˈvitʃɛ
Barbados	bahr BAY dohz	bɑrˈbedoz
barbarian	bahr BAI ri uhn	bɑrˈbɛrɪən
barbaric	bahr BAI rik	bɑrˈbɛrɪk
barbarism	BAHR buh ri zuhm	ˈbɑrbərɪzəm
barbarity	bahr BAI ruh ti	bɑrˈbɛrətɪ
Barbarossa	bahr buh RAW suh	bɑrbəˈrɔsə
barbarous	BAHR buh ruhs	ˈbɑrbərəs
Barbary	BAHR buh ri	ˈbɑrbərɪ
barbed	bahrbd	bɑrbd
barberry	BAHR bai ri	ˈbɑrbɛrɪ
barbet	BAHR bit	ˈbɑrbɪt
barbette	bahr BET	bɑrˈbɛt

at [æ]; *ah* [ɑ]; *air* [ɛ]; *awful* [ɔ]; *say* [e]; *back* [b]; *chair* [tʃ]; *do* [d]; *elm* [ɛ]; *eel* [i]; *server* [ˈɜ, ər]; *fit* [f]; *go* [g]; *hurt* [h]; *is* [ɪ]; *high* [aɪ]; *jet* [dʒ]; *kiss* [k]; *lamb* [l]; *my* [m]; *nice* [n];

Barbiere di Siviglia	bahr BYE ray dee see VEEL yah	bɑr'bjɛre di si'viljɑ
Barbirolli	bahr bi ROH li	bɑrbɪ'rolɪ
barbiturate	bahr BI chuh rit	bɑr'bɪtʃərɪt
barbituric	bahr buh TYOO rik	bɑrbə'tjʊrɪk
barcarole, barcarolle	BAHR kuh rohl	'bɑrkərol
Barcelona	bahr suh LOH nuh	bɑrsə'lonə
Bardot, Brigitte	bahr DOH, bri JEET	bɑr'do, brɪ'dʒit
barefaced	BAIR fayst	'bɛrfest
bareheaded	BAIR he did	'bɛrhɛdɪd
Barents	BAH rents	'bɑrɛnts
bargain	BAHR guhn	'bɑrgən
barge	bahrj	bɑrdʒ
bargeman	BAHRJ muhn	'bɑrdʒmən
baritone	BA ruh tohn	'bærəton
barium	BAI ri uhm	'bɛrɪəm
barkentine	BAHR kuhn teen	'bɑrkəntin
barker	BAHR ker	'bɑrkər
Bar-le-Duc	bahr luh DOOK	bɑr lə 'dʊk
barley	BAHR li	'bɑrlɪ
barleycorn, B-	BAHR li kawrn	'bɑrlɪkɔrn
Barmecide	BAHR muh sighd	'bɑrməsaid
bar mitzvah, bar mizvah, B-	bahr MITS vuh	bɑr'mɪtsvə
barmy	BAHR mi	'bɑrmɪ
Barnabas	BAHR nuh buhs	'bɑrnəbəs
barnacle	BAHR nuh kuhl	'bɑrnəkəl
Barnard	BAHR nerd	'bɑrnərd
Barnouw	BAHR noh	'bɑrno
barnstorm	BAHRN stawrm	'bɑrnstɔrm
barnyard	BAHRN yahrd	'bɑrnjɑrd
barometer	buh RAH muh ter	bə'rɑmətər
barometric	ba ruh ME trik	bærə'mɛtrɪk
baron	BA ruhn	'bærən
baroness	BA ruh nis	'bærənɪs
baronet	BA ruh net	'bærənɛt
baronetcy	BA ruh net si	'bærənɛtsɪ
baroque	buh ROHK	bə'rok
barouche	buh ROO:SH	bə'ruʃ
barque	bahrk	bɑrk
barquentine	BAHR kuhn teen	'bɑrkəntin
barracks	BA ruhks	'bærəks
barracuda	ba ruh KOO:duh	bærə'kudə
barrage	buh RAHZH	bə'rɑʒ
barranca, B-	bah RAHNG kuh	bɑ'rɑŋkə
Barrault	bah ROH	bɑ'ro
barred	bahrd	bɑrd
barrel	BA ruhl	'bærəl
barren	BA ruhn	'bærən
barricade (n)	BA ruh kayd	'bærəked
barricade (v)	ba ruh KAYD	bærə'ked
barrier	BA ri er	'bærɪər

---

sing [ŋ]; oh [o]; oil [ɔɪ]; foot [ʊ]; foo:d [u]; how [aʊ]; pie [p]; ray [r]; so [s]; shall [ʃ]; to [t]; thin [θ]; th:en [ð]; above (uh BUHV) [ə, 'ʌ]; vine [v]; wine [w]; whine [hw]; you [j]; zoo [z]; rouge (roo:zh) [ʒ].

barrister	BA ri ster	ˈbærɪstər
Barro	BAH roh	ˈbɑro
barroom	BAHR roo:m	ˈbɑrrum
Bartholdi	bahr tawl DEE	bɑrtɔlˈdi
Bartholomew	bahr THAH luh myoo:	bɑrˈθɑləmju
Bartlett	BAHRT lit	ˈbɑrtlɪt
Bartók, Béla	bahr TAWK, BAY lah	bɑrˈtɔk, ˈbelɑ
Baruch (Bible)	BAI ruhk	ˈbɛrək
Baruch, Andre	buh ROO:SH, AHN dray	bəˈruʃ, ˈɑndre
Baruch, Bernard	buh ROO:K, ber NAHRD	bəˈruk, bərˈnɑrd
barytone	BA ruh tohn	ˈbærəton
Barzun, Jacques	BAHR zuhn, zhahk	ˈbɑrzən, ʒak
basal	BAY suhl	ˈbesəl
basalt	buh SAWLT	bəˈsɔlt
base	bays	bes
baseball	BAYS bawl	ˈbesbɔl
Basel	BAH zuhl	ˈbɑzəl
basement	BAYS muhnt	ˈbesmənt
baseness	BAYS nis	ˈbesnɪs
basenji, B-	buh SEN ji	bəˈsɛndʒɪ
bases (pl. of *base*)	BAY siz	ˈbesɪz
bases (pl. of *basis*)	BAY seez	ˈbesiz
Bashkir	bahsh KIR	bɑʃˈkɪr
Bashkirov, Dimitri	bahsh KEER uhf, dee MEE tree	bɑʃˈkirʌf, diˈmitri
basic	BAY sik	ˈbesɪk
basil, B-	BA zuhl	ˈbæzəl
basilar	BA suh ler	ˈbæsələr
basilic	buh SI lik	bəˈsɪlɪk
basilica	buh SI li kuh	bəˈsɪlɪkə
basilisk	BA suh lisk	ˈbæsəlɪsk
basin	BAY suhn	ˈbesən
basis	BAY sis	ˈbesɪs
bask	bask	bæsk
basket	BA skit	ˈbæskɪt
basketball	BA skit bawl	ˈbæskɪtbɔl
basoid	BAY soid	ˈbesɔɪd
basque, B-	bask	bæsk
Basra	BUHS ruh	ˈbʌsrə
bas-relief	bah ruh LEEF	bɑrəˈlif
bass (fish)	bas	bæs
bass (sound)	bays	bes
basso	BA soh	ˈbæso
bassoon	buh SOO:N	bəˈsun
basso profundo	BA soh pruh FOON doh	ˈbæso prəˈfundo
Bastar	bah STAHR	bɑˈstar
bastard	BA sterd	ˈbæstərd
bastardy	BA ster di	ˈbæstərdɪ
baste	bayst	best
bastile, bastille, B-	ba STEEL	bæˈstil
bastinado	ba stuh NAY doh	bæstəˈnedo
bastion	BAS chuhn	ˈbæstʃən

---

at [æ]; *ah* [ɑ]; *air* [ɛ]; *awful* [ɔ]; *say* [e]; *back* [b]; *chair* [tʃ]; *do* [d]; *elm* [ɛ]; *eel* [i];
server [ˈɝ, ər]; *f* it [f]; *go* [g]; *hurt* [h]; *is* [ɪ]; *high* [aɪ]; *jet* [dʒ]; *kiss* [k]; *lamb* [l]; *my* [m];
nice [n];

Bataan	buh TAHN	bəˈtɑn
Batang	bah tahng	bɑ tɑŋ
Batavia	buh TAY vi uh	bəˈtevɪə
bateau	ba TOH	bæˈto
bath	bath	bæθ
bathe	bayth :	beð
batholith	BA thuh lith	ˈbæθəlɪθ
bathos	BAY thahs	ˈbeθɑs
Bathsheba	bath SHEE buh	bæθˈʃibə
bathyscaphe	BA thi skayf	ˈbæθɪskef
bathysphere	BA thi sfir	ˈbæθɪsfɪr
batik	bah TEEK	bɑˈtik
Batista, Fulgencio	bah TEE stah, fool HEN syoh	bɑˈtistɑ, fulˈhɛnsjo
batiste	buh TEEST	bəˈtist
baton	ba TAHN	bæˈtɑn
Baton Rouge	BA tuhn ROO : ZH	ˈbætənˈruʒ
batrachian, B-	buh TRAY ki uhn	bəˈtrekɪən
battalion	buh TA lyuhn	bəˈtæljən
batten	BA tuhn	ˈbætən
battik	BA tik	ˈbætɪk
battledore	BA tuhl dawr	ˈbætəldɔr
battue	ba TOO :	bæˈtu
Batum	bah TOOM	bɑˈtum
bauble	BAW buhl	ˈbɔbəl
Baudelaire	boh duh LAIR	bodəˈlɛər
Baudouin	BOH dwan	ˈbodwæn
Bauhaus	BOW hows	ˈbauhaus
baulk	bawk	bɔk
bauxite	BAWK sight	ˈbɔksaɪt
Bavaria	buh VAI ri uh	bəˈvɛrɪə
Bavarian	buh VAI ri uhn	bəˈvɛrɪən
Bayard	BAY erd	ˈbeərd
bayberry	BAY bai ri	ˈbebɛrɪ
Bayeux	bay YOO :	beˈju
bayonet	BAY uh net	ˈbeənɛt
Bayonne (France)	bah YAWN	bɑˈjɔn
Bayonne (U.S.)	BAY ohn	ˈbeon
bayou	BIGH oo :	ˈbaɪu
Bayreuth	bigh ROIT	baɪˈrɔɪt
bazaar, bazar	buh ZAHR	bəˈzɑr
bazooka	buh ZOO : kuh	bəˈzukə
bdellium	DE li uhm	ˈdɛlɪəm
beach-la-mar	beech lah MAHR	bitʃlɑˈmɑr
beacon, B-	BEE kuhn	ˈbikən
Beaconsfield	BEE kuhnz feeld	ˈbikənzfild
beagle	BEE guhl	ˈbigəl
bear	bair	bɛr
beard	bird	bɪrd
bearing	BAI ring	ˈbɛrɪŋ
béarnaise	bay ahr NEZ	beɑrˈnɛz
beatific	bee uh TI fik	biəˈtɪfɪk

sing [ŋ] ; *oh* [o] ; *oil* [ɔɪ] ; *foot* [ʊ] ; *foo :*d [u] ; *how* [aʊ] ; *pie* [p] ; *ray* [r] ; *so* [s] ; *shall* [ʃ] ;
to [t] ; *thin* [θ] ; *th :*en [ð] ; *above* (*uh* B*UH*V) [ə, ˈʌ] ; *vine* [v] ; *wine* [w] ; *whine* [hw] ;
you [j] ; *zoo* [z] ; *rouge* (roo :*zh*) [ʒ].

beatify	bee A tuh figh	bi'ætəfaɪ
beatitude	bee A tuh too : d	bi'ætətud
beatnik	BEET nik	'bitnɪk
Beatrice	BEE uh tris	'biətrɪs
Beatty, David	BEE ti	'bitɪ
beau	boh	bo
Beau Brummel	boh BRUH muhl	bo'brʌməl
Beauchamp	BEE chuhm	'bitʃəm
Beaufort	boh FAWR	bo'fɔr
beau geste	boh ZHEST	bo'ʒɛst
Beauharnais	boh ahr NAY	boɑr'ne
beau ideal	boh igh DEE uhl	bo aɪ'dɪəl
Beaulac	BOH lak	'bolæk
Beaulieu (England)	BYOO : li	'bjulɪ
beau monde	boh MAWND	bo'mɔnd
Beaumont	BOH mahnt	'bomɑnt
beauteous	BYOO : ti uhs	'bjutɪəs
beautification	byoo : tuh fuh KAY shuhn	bjutəfə'keʃən
beautiful	BYOO : tuh fuhl	'bjutəfəl
beauty	BYOO : ti	'bjutɪ
Beauvoir, Simone de	boh VWAH, see MOHN duh	bo'vwɑ, si'mon də
beaux	bohz	boz
beaux-arts	boh ZAHR	bo'zɑr
beaux-yeux	boh ZYER	bo'zjɝ
Beaverbrook	BEE ver brook	'bivɝbrʊk
Bebler	BE bler	'bɛblər
bebop	BEE bahp	'bibɑp
becalm	bi KAHM	bɪ'kɑm
béchamel	bay shah MEL	beʃɑ'mɛl
becharm	bi CHAHRM	bɪ'tʃɑrm
bêche-de-mer	besh duh MAIR	bɛʃdə'mɛr
Bechuana	be choo AH nuh	bɛtʃu'ɑnə
Bechuanaland	be choo : AH nah land	bɛtʃu'ɑnɑlænd
Becke	BE kuh	'bɛkə
Becket	BE kit	'bɛkɪt
become	bi KUHM	bɪ'kʌm
Becquerel	be KREL	be'krɛl
bedaub	bi DAWB	bɪ'dɔb
Bedaux	buh DOH	bə'do
bedclothes	BED klohz	'bɛdkloz
bedeck	bi DEK	bɪ'dɛk
bedevil	bi DE vuhl	bɪ'dɛvəl
Bedford	BED ferd	'bɛdfərd
Bedivere	BE duh vir	'bɛdəvir
bedizen	bi DI zuhn	bɪ'dɪzən
bedlam	BED luhm	'bɛdləm
Bedloe	BED loh	'bɛdlo
Bedouin	BE doo in	'bɛduɪn
beefeater	BEEF ee ter	'bifitər
Beelzebub	bi EL zuh buhb	bɪ'ɛlzəbəb
been	bin	bɪn
beer	bir	bɪr

at [æ] ; *ah* [ɑ] ; *air* [ɛ] ; *aw*ful [ɔ] ; *say* [e] ; *b*ack [b] ; *ch*air [tʃ] ; *d*o [d] ; *e*lm [ɛ] ; *ee*l [i] ;
server ['ɝ, ər] ; *f*it [f] ; *g*o [g] ; *h*urt [h] ; *is* [ɪ] ; *high* [aɪ] ; *j*et [dʒ] ; *k*iss [k] ; *l*amb [l] ; *m*y [m] ;
*n*ice [n] ;

Beersheba	bir SHEE buh	bɪrˈʃibə
beestings, biestings	BEE stingz	ˈbistɪŋz
Beethoven	BAY toh vuhn	ˈbetovən
beetle-browed	BEE tuhl browd	ˈbitəlbraʊd
befall	bi FAWL	bɪˈfɔl
befog	bi FAHG	bɪˈfɑg
beforehand	bi FAWR hand	biˈfɔrhænd
beginning	bi GI ning	bɪˈgɪnɪŋ
begone	bi GAWN	bɪˈgɔn
begonia	bi GOH ni uh	bɪˈgonɪə
begot	bi GAHT	bɪˈgɑt
beguile	bi GIGHL	biˈgaɪl
beguine	bi GEEN	bɪˈgin
begum	BEE guhm	ˈbigəm
behalf	bi HAF	bɪˈhæf
behavior, behaviour	bi HAY vyer	bɪˈhevjər
behaviorism	bi HAY vyuh ri zuhm	bɪˈhevjərɪzəm
behemoth	bi HEE muhth	bɪˈhiməθ
Behn	bayn	ben
behoove	bi HOO : V	bɪˈhuv
behove	bi HOHV	bɪˈhov
Behrman	BAIR muhn	ˈbeərmən
beige	bayzh	beʒ
Beirut	BAY roo : t	ˈberut
bejel	BE juhl	ˈbɛdʒəl
belabor, belabour	bi LAY ber	bɪˈlebər
Belafonte	bel uh FAHN tee	bɛləˈfɑnti
Belasco	buh LA skoh	bəˈlæsko
bel canto	bel KAHN toh	bɛlˈkɑnto
belch	belch	bɛltʃ
beldam, beldame	BEL duhm	ˈbɛldəm
bel-esprit	be le SPREE	bɛlɛˈspri
Belfast	BEL fast	ˈbɛlfæst
belfry	BEL fri	ˈbɛlfrɪ
belga	BEL guh	ˈbɛlgə
Belgian	BEL juhn	ˈbɛldʒən
Belgic	BEL jik	ˈbɛldʒɪk
Belgium	BEL juhm	ˈbɛldʒəm
Belgrade	bel GRAYD	bɛlˈgred
Belgravia	bel GRAY vi uh	bɛlˈgrevɪə
Belial	BEE li uhl	ˈbilɪəl
belie	bi LIGH	bɪˈlaɪ
belief	bi LEEF	bɪˈlif
believe	bi LEEV	bɪˈliv
belladonna	be luh DAH nuh	bɛləˈdɑnə
Bellamy	BE luh mi	ˈbɛləmɪ
belle	bel	bɛl
Belleau	be LOH	bɛˈlo
Belleek	buh LEEK	bəˈlik
Bellerophon	buh LE ruh fuhn	bəˈlɛrəfən
belles-lettres	bel LE truh	bɛlˈlɛtrə
bellicose	BE luh kohs	ˈbɛləkos

sing [ŋ] ; oh [o] ; oil [ɔɪ] ; foot [ʊ] ; foo:d [u] ; how [aʊ] ; pie [p] ; ray [r] ; so [s] ; shall [ʃ] ;
to [t] ; thin [θ] ; th:en [ð] ; above (uh BUHV) [ə, ˈʌ] ; vine [v] ; wine [w] ; whine [hw] ;
you [j] ; zoo [z] ; rouge (roo:zh) [ʒ].

belligerence	buh LI juh ruhns	bəˈlɪdʒərəns
belligerent	buh LI juh ruhnt	bəˈlɪdʒərənt
Bellini	be LEE ni	beˈlinɪ
bellman	BEL muhn	ˈbɛlmən
bellmouthed	BEL mowth : d	ˈbɛlmaʊðd
Belloise	bel WOIZ	bɛlˈwɔɪz
bellows	BE lohz	ˈbɛloz
bellwether	BEL we th : er	ˈbɛlwɛðər
bellwort	BEL wert	ˈbɛlwərt
beloved	bi LUH vid	bɪˈlʌvɪd
below	bi LOH	bɪˈlo
Belshazzar	bel SHA zer	bɛlˈʃæzər
beluga	buh LOO : guh	bəˈlugə
belvedere, B-	bel vuh DIR	bɛlvəˈdɪr
Belvoir (castle)	BEE ver	ˈbivər
Belvoir (U.S.)	BEL vwahr	ˈbɛlvwar
Bemelmans, Ludwig	BE muhl muhnz, LUHD wig	ˈbɛməlmənz, ˈlʌdwɪg
bemuse	bi MYOO : Z	bɪˈmjuz
Benares	buh NAH riz	bəˈnarɪz
bench	bench	bɛntʃ
beneath	bi NEETH	bɪˈniθ
benedicite, B-	be nuh DI suh ti	bɛnəˈdɪsəti
benedick, B-	BE nuh dik	ˈbɛnədɪk
benedict, B-	BE nuh dikt	ˈbɛnədɪkt
benedictine, B-	be nuh DIK tin	bɛnəˈdɪktɪn
benediction	be nuh DIK shuhn	bɛnəˈdɪkʃən
benedictory	be nuh DIK tuh ri	bɛnəˈdɪktərɪ
Benedictus	be nuh DIK tuhs	bɛnəˈdɪktəs
benefaction	be nuh FAK shuhn	bɛnəˈfækʃən
benefactor	BE nuh fak ter	ˈbɛnəfæktər
benefice	BE nuh fis	ˈbɛnəfɪs
beneficence	buh NE fuh suhns	bəˈnɛfəsəns
beneficent	buh NE fuh suhnt	bəˈnɛfəsənt
beneficial	be nuh FI shuhl	bɛnəˈfɪʃəl
beneficiary	be nuh FI shuh ri	bɛnəˈfɪʃərɪ
benefit	BE nuh fit	ˈbɛnəfɪt
Benelux	BE ni luhks	ˈbɛnɪləks
Beneš	BE nesh	ˈbɛnɛʃ
Benét	be NAY	bɛˈne
benevolence	buh NE vuh luhns	bəˈnɛvələns
benevolent	buh NE vuh luhnt	bəˈnɛvələnt
Bengal	ben GAWL	bɛnˈgɔl
Bengalese	ben guh LEEZ	bɛngəˈliz
Bengali	ben GAW li	bɛnˈgɔlɪ
Bengaline	BENG guh lin	ˈbɛŋgəlɪn
Bengasi, Benghazi	ben GAH zi	bɛnˈgazɪ
Ben-Gurion	ben GOO ri uhn	bɛn ˈgurɪən
benighted	bi NIGH tid	bɪˈnaɪtɪd
benign	bi NIGHN	bɪˈnaɪn
benignant	bi NIG nuhnt	bɪˈnɪgnənt
benignity	bi NIG nu ti	bɪˈnɪgnətɪ

at [æ] ; ah [ɑ] ; air [ɛ] ; awful [ɔ] ; say [e] ; back [b] ; chair [tʃ] ; do [d] ; elm [ɛ] ; eel [i] ; server [ˈɜ, ər] ; fit [f] ; go [g] ; hurt [h] ; is [ɪ] ; high [aɪ] ; jet [dʒ] ; kiss [k] ; lamb [l] ; my [m] ; nice [n] ;

benison	BE nuh zuhn	ˈbɛnəzən
Benjamin	BEN juh muhn	ˈbɛndʒəmən
Benoni	buh NOH nigh	bəˈnonaɪ
Bentham	BEN thuhm	ˈbɛnθəm
benthoscope	BEN thuh skohp	ˈbɛnθəskop
ben trovato	ben troh VAH toh	bɛn troˈvato
benumb	bi NUHM	bɪˈnʌm
benzedrine, B-	BEN zuh dreen	ˈbɛnzədrin
benzene	BEN zeen	ˈbɛnzin
benzine	BEN zeen	ˈbɛnzin
benzoate	BEN zoh it	ˈbɛnzoɪt
benzoin	BEN zoh in	ˈbɛnzoɪn
benzol	BEN zohl	ˈbɛnzol
Ben-Zvi, Yitzhak	ben-tsvee, yits HAHK	bɛn-tsvi, jɪtsˈhɑk
benzyl	BEN zil	ˈbɛnzɪl
Beowulf	BAY uh woolf	ˈbeəwʊlf
bequeath	bi KWEETH :	bɪˈkwið
bequeathal	bi KWEE th : uhl	bɪˈkwiðəl
bequest	bi KWEST	bɪˈkwɛst
berate	bi RAYT	bɪˈret
Berber	BER ber	ˈbɝbər
berceuse	bair SERZ	bɛrˈsɝz
Berchtesgaden	BAIRK tes gah duhn	ˈbɛrktɛsgɑdən
Bercovici	bair koh VEE chee	bɛrkoˈvitʃi
Berdyaev	ber dee IGH ef	bɝdiˈæɪɛf
Berea	ber EE uh	bərˈiə
bereave	bi REEV	bɪˈriv
Berenson, Bernard	BE ren suhn, ber NAHRD	ˈbɛrɛnsən, bərˈnɑrd
beret	buh RAY	bəˈre
Bergen (Norway)	BAIR guhn	ˈbɛrgən
Bergen (U.S.)	BER guhn	ˈbɝgən
Bergerac	BER juh rak	ˈbɝdʒəræk
Berggrav	BAIR grahv	ˈbɛrgrɑv
Bergman (Ingrid, Ingmar)	BAIRG mahn (ING rid, ING mahr)	ˈbɛrgmɑn, (ˈɪŋrid, ˈɪŋmɑr)
Bergson, Henri	BAIRG suhn, AHN ree	ˈbɛrgsən, ˈɑnri
Beria	BE ri yah	ˈbɛrjɑ
beriberi	BAI ri BAI ri	ˈbɛrɪˈbɛrɪ
Bering	BI ring	ˈbɪrɪŋ
Berkeley (California)	BERK li	ˈbɝklɪ
Berkeley (London)	BARK li	ˈbɑrklɪ
Berkshire	BERK shir	ˈbɝkʃɪr
Berle, A. A.	BER li	ˈbɝlɪ
Berlin (Germany)	ber LIN	bərˈlɪn
Berlin (U.S.)	BER lin	ˈbɝlɪn
Berlioz	BAIR li ohz	ˈbɛrlɪoz
Bermuda	ber MYOO : duh	bərˈmjudə
Bermúdez	bair MOO : des	bɛrˈmudɛs
Bern, Berne	bairn	bɛrn
Bernadotte	BER nuh daht	ˈbɝnədɑt
Bernardine	BER ner din	ˈbɝnərdɪn
Bernhardt	BERN hahrt	ˈbɝnhɑrt

sing [ŋ]; *oh* [o]; *oil* [ɔɪ]; *foot* [ʊ]; *foo:d* [u]; *how* [aʊ]; *pie* [p]; *ray* [r]; *so* [s]; *shall* [ʃ]; *to* [t]; *thin* [θ]; *th:en* [ð]; above (*uh* B*UH*V) [ə, ˈʌ]; *vine* [v]; *wine* [w]; *whine* [hw]; *you* [j]; *zoo* [z]; *rouge* (roo:*zh*) [ʒ].

Bernice	ber NEES	bərˈnis
Bernstein	BERN steen	ˈbɚnstin
Berreta	be RE tah	bɛˈrɛtɑ
berserk	BER serk	ˈbɚsərk
Bertha	BER thuh	ˈbɚθə
Bertillon	BER tuh lahn	ˈbɚtəlɑn
beryl	BAI ril	ˈbɛrɪl
beryllium	buh RI li uhm	bəˈrɪliəm
beseech	bi SEECH	bɪˈsitʃ
beshrew	bi SHROO :	bɪˈʃru
besides	bi SIGHDZ	bɪˈsaɪdz
besique	buh ZEEK	bəˈzik
besom	BEE zuhm	ˈbizəm
Bessarabia	be suh RAY bi uh	bɛsəˈrebiə
Bessemer	BE suh mer	ˈbɛsəmər
bestial	BES chuhl	ˈbɛstʃəl
bestiality	bes chi A luh ti	bɛstʃɪˈælətɪ
bestiary	BE sti ai ri	ˈbɛstɪɛrɪ
bestir	bi STER	bɪˈstɚ
bestow	bi STOH	bɪˈsto
beta	BAY tuh	ˈbetə
Betancourt	be tahn KOORT	betɑnˈkʊrt
betatron	BAY tuh trahn	ˈbetətrɑn
Betelguese	BEE tuhl joo : z	ˈbitəldʒuz
bête noire	bayt NWAHR	betˈnwɑr
Bethany	BE thuh ni	ˈbɛθənɪ
Bethel	BE thuhl	ˈbɛθəl
Bethesda	buh THEZ duh	bəˈθɛzdə
Bethlehem	BETH li hem	ˈbɛθlɪhɛm
Bethmann-Hollweg	BAYT mahn HOHL vek	ˈbetmɑn ˈholvɛk
Bethsaida	beth SAY uh duh	bɛθˈseədə
betimes	bi TIGHMZ	bɪˈtaɪmz
bêtise	be TEEZ	bɛˈtiz
betroth	bi TROHTH :	bɪˈtroð
betrothal	bi TROH th : uhl	bɪˈtroðəl
betrothed (a, n)	bi TRAWTHT	bɪˈtroθt
better, bettor	BE ter	ˈbɛtər
Beulah	BYOO : luh	ˈbjulə
bevatron	BE vuh trahn	ˈbɛvətrɑn
beverage	BE vrij	ˈbɛvrɪdʒ
Beverwijk	BAY ver wighk	ˈbevərwaɪk
bevy	BE vi	ˈbɛvɪ
beware	bi WAIR	bɪˈwɛr
bewildered	bi WIL derd	bɪˈwɪldərd
bey	bay	be
Beyle	bayl	bel
beyond	bi YAHND	bɪˈjɑnd
Beyrouth	BAY roo : t	ˈberut
bezique	buh ZEEK	bəˈzik
Bhagavad-Gita	BUH guh vuhd GEE tah	ˈbʌɡəvəd ˈgitɑ
Bhopal, Bhopol	boh PAHL	boˈpɑl
Bhutan	boo : TAHN	buˈtɑn

at [æ] ; ah [ɑ] ; air [ɛ] ; awful [ɔ] ; say [e] ; back [b] ; chair [tʃ] ; do [d] ; elm [ɛ] ; eel [i] ;
server [ˈɚ, ər] ; fit [f] ; go [g] ; hurt [h] ; is [ɪ] ; high [aɪ] ; jet [dʒ] ; kiss [k] ; lamb [l] ; my [m] ;
nice [n] ;

bi-	bigh	baɪ
Bialystok	byah LI stawk	bjɑˈlɪstɔk
Biancolli	bi an KAW lee	bɪænˈkɔli
biannual	bigh A nyoo uhl	baɪˈænjʊəl
Biarritz	BEE uh rits	ˈbiərɪts
bias	BIGH uhs	ˈbaɪəs
bibelot	BI bloh	ˈbɪblo
Bible	BIGH buhl	ˈbaɪbəl
biblical, B-	BI bli kuhl	ˈbɪblɪkəl
Biblicist	BI bli sist	ˈbɪblɪsɪst
bibliographer	bi bli AH gruh fer	bɪblɪˈɑgrəfər
bibliography	bi bli AH gruh fi	bɪblɪˈɑgrəfɪ
bibliophile	BI bli uh fighl	ˈbɪblɪəfaɪl
bibliothèque	bee bli oh TEK	biblɪoˈtɛk
bibliotics	bi bli AH tiks	bɪblɪˈɑtɪks
bibulous	BI byuh luhs	ˈbɪbjələs
bicameral	bigh KA muh ruhl	baɪˈkæmərəl
bicarbonate	bigh KAHR buh nit	baɪˈkɑrbənɪt
bicentenary	bigh SEN tuh nai ri	baɪˈsɛntənɛrɪ
bicentennial	bigh sen TE ni uhl	baɪsɛnˈtɛnɪəl
biceps	BIGH seps	ˈbaɪsɛps
bichloride	bigh KLOH righd	baɪˈkloraɪd
bichromate (n)	bigh KROH mit	baɪˈkromɪt
bichromate (v)	bigh KROH mayt	baɪˈkromet
bicker	BI ker	ˈbɪkər
bicuspid	bigh KUH spid	baɪˈkʌspɪd
bicycle	BIGH si kuhl	ˈbaɪsɪkəl
bicycling	BIGH si kling	ˈbaɪsɪklɪŋ
bicyclist	BIGH si klist	ˈbaɪsɪklɪst
Bidault	bee DOH	biˈdo
biddable	BI duh buhl	ˈbɪdəbəl
Biddle	BI duhl	ˈbɪdəl
bide	bighd	baɪd
biennial	bigh E ni uhl	baɪˈɛnɪəl
bier	bir	bɪr
bifilar	bigh FIGH ler	baɪˈfaɪlər
bifocal	bigh FOH kuhl	baɪˈfokəl
bifurcate (a)	bigh FER kit	baɪˈfɝkɪt
bifurcate (v)	BIGH fer kayt	ˈbaɪfɝket
bigamist	BI guh mist	ˈbɪgəmɪst
bigamy	BI guh mi	ˈbɪgəmɪ
bight	bight	baɪt
bignonia	big NOH ni uh	bɪgˈnonɪə
bigot	BI guht	ˈbɪgət
bigoted	BI guh tid	ˈbɪgətɪd
bigotry	BI guh tri	ˈbɪgətrɪ
bigwig	BIG wig	ˈbɪgwɪg
Bihac	BEE hahch	ˈbihɑtʃ
bijou	BEE zhoo:	ˈbiʒu
Bikaner	BEE kuh ner	ˈbikənər
bikini, B-	buh KEE ni	bəˈkinɪ
bilabial	bigh LAY bi uhl	baɪˈlebɪəl

sing [ŋ] ; *oh* [o] ; *oil* [ɔɪ] ; *foot* [ʊ] ; *foo*:d [u] ; *how* [aʊ] ; *pie* [p] ; *ray* [r] ; *so* [s] ; *shall* [ʃ] ; *to* [t] ; *thin* [θ] ; *th*:en [ð] ; above (*uh* BUHV) [ə, ˈʌ] ; *vine* [v] ; *wine* [w] ; *whine* [hw] ; *you* [j] ; *zoo* [z] ; rouge (roo:*zh*) [ʒ].

bilateral	bigh LA tuh ruhl	baɪˈlætərəl
Bilbao	bil BAH oh	bɪlˈbɑo
Bildad	BIL dad	ˈbɪldæd
bilge	bilj	bɪldʒ
bilgy	BIL ji	ˈbɪldʒɪ
bilingual	bigh LING gwuhl	baɪˈlɪŋgwəl
bilious	BI lyuhs	ˈbɪljəs
bilk	bilk	bɪlk
billet	BI lit	ˈbɪlɪt
billet-doux	bi li DOO:	bɪlɪˈdu
billiard	BI lyerd	ˈbɪljərd
billingsgate, B-	BI lingz gayt	ˈbɪlɪŋzget
billion	BI lyuhn	ˈbɪljən
billionaire	BI lyuh nair	ˈbɪljənɛr
bimetalism	bih ME tuh li zuhm	baɪˈmɛtəlɪzəm
binary	BIGH nuh ri	ˈbaɪnərɪ
binaural	bigh NAW ruhl	baɪˈnɔrəl
binder	BIGHN der	ˈbaɪndər
bindery	BIGHN duh ri	ˈbaɪndərɪ
Binet	bi NAY	bɪˈne
Bingen	BING guhn	ˈbɪŋgən
bingo	BING goh	ˈbɪŋgo
binnacle	BI nuh kuhl	ˈbɪnəkəl
binocle	BI nuh kuhl	ˈbɪnəkəl
binocular	bigh NAH kyuh ler	baɪˈnɑkjələr
binomial	bigh NOH mi uhl	baɪˈnomɪəl
bioclimatics	bigh oh kligh MA tiks	baɪoklaɪˈmætɪks
biodyne	BIGH uh dighn	ˈbaɪədaɪn
biogenesis	bigh oh JE nuh sis	baɪoˈdʒɛnəsɪs
biographer	bigh AH gruh fer	baɪˈɑgrəfər
biography	bigh AH gruh fi	baɪˈɑgrəfɪ
biological	bigh uh LAH ji kuhl	baɪəˈlɑdʒɪkəl
biology	bigh AH luh ji	baɪˈɑlədʒɪ
bionomics	bigh uh NAH miks	baɪəˈnɑmɪks
bio-pak	BIGH uh pak	ˈbaɪəpæk
biosynthesis	bigh oh SIN thuh sis	baɪoˈsɪnθəsɪs
biotin	BIGH uh tin	ˈbaɪətɪn
biparous	BI puh ruhs	ˈbɪpərəs
bipartite	bigh PAHR tight	baɪˈpartaɪt
biped	BIGH ped	ˈbaɪpɛd
biplane	BIGH playn	ˈbaɪplen
bipod	BIGH pahd	ˈbaɪpɑd
birch	berch	bɝtʃ
bird's-eye, birdseye, B-	BERD zigh	ˈbɝdzaɪ
bireme	BIGH reem	ˈbaɪrim
biretta	bi RE tuh	bɪˈrɛtə
Birmingham (Alabama)	BER ming ham	ˈbɝmɪŋhæm
Birmingham (England)	BER ming uhm	ˈbɝmɪŋəm
Bisayas	bi SAH yahs	bɪˈsɑjɑs
Biscay	BI skay	ˈbɪske
biscuit	BI skit	ˈbɪskɪt
bisect	bigh SEKT	baɪˈsɛkt

---

at [æ]; ah [ɑ]; air [ɛ]; awful [ɔ]; say [e]; back [b]; chair [tʃ]; do [d]; elm [ɛ]; eel [i]; server [ˈɝ, ər]; fit [f]; go [g]; hurt [h]; is [ɪ]; high [aɪ]; jet [dʒ]; kiss [k]; lamb [l]; my [m]; nice [n];

bishop	BI shuhp	ˈbɪʃəp
bishopric	BI shuh prik	ˈbɪʃəprɪk
Bismarck	BIZ mahrk	ˈbɪzmɑrk
bismuth	BIZ muhth	ˈbɪzməθ
bison	BIGH suhn	ˈbaɪsən
bisque	bisk	bɪsk
bister, bistre	BI ster	ˈbɪstər
bittern	BI tern	ˈbɪtərn
bitumen	bi TYOO : muhn	bɪˈtjumən
bituminous	bi TYOO : muh nuhs	bɪˈtjumənəs
bivalence	bigh VAY luhns	baɪˈveləns
bivalent	bigh VAY luhnt	baɪˈvelənt
bivalve	BIGH valv	ˈbaɪvælv
bivouac	BIV wak	ˈbɪvwæk
bizarre	bi ZAHR	bɪˈzɑr
Bizerte	bi ZER tuh	bɪˈzɜtə
Bizet	bi ZAY	bɪˈze
Bjoerling, Jussi	bi ER ling, YOO si	bɪˈɜlɪŋ, ˈjusɪ
Björnson, Björnsson	BYAWRN suhn	ˈbjɔrnsən
blab	blab	blæb
blackamoor	BLA kuh moor	ˈblækəmʊr
blackguard	BLA gerd	ˈblægərd
blamable	BLAY muh buhl	ˈbleməbəl
blanch, -e, B-	blanch	blæntʃ
blanc-mange	bluh MAHNZH	bləˈmɑnʒ
bland	bland	blænd
blanket	BLANG kit	ˈblæŋkɪt
Blasco-Ibáñez, Vicente	BLAH skoh ee BAH nyeth, vee THEN te	ˈblɑsko iˈbɑnjeθ, viˈθɛntɛ
blasé	blah ZAY	blɑˈze
blaspheme	blas FEEM	blæsˈfim
blasphemous	BLAS fi muhs	ˈblæsfɪməs
blasphemy	BLAS fi mi	ˈblæsfɪmɪ
blastoderm	BLA stuh derm	ˈblæstədərm
blastula	BLAS choo luh	ˈblæstʃulə
blatancy	BLAY tuhn si	ˈbletənsɪ
blatant	BLAY t ʌnt	ˈbletənt
blatherskite	BLA th : er skight	ˈblæðərskaɪt
Blavatsky	bluh VAHT ski	bləˈvɑtskɪ
blazon	BLAY zuhn	ˈblezən
bleary	BLI ri	ˈblɪrɪ
bleat	bleet	blit
blemish	BLE mish	ˈblɛmɪʃ
Blenheim	BLE nʌhm	ˈblɛnəm
Blériot	BLE ri ʌ	ˈblɛrɪo
blessed (a)	BLE sid	ˈblɛsɪd
blessed (v)	blest	blɛst
blew	bloo :	blu
blindman's buff	BLIGHND manz buhf	ˈblaɪnd mænz bʌf
blissful	BLIS fuhl	ˈblɪsfəl
blithe	blighth :	blaɪð
blitz	blits	blɪts

---

sing [ŋ]; *oh* [o]; *oil* [ɔɪ]; *foot* [ʊ]; *foo*:d [u]; *how* [aʊ]; *p*ie [p]; *r*ay [r]; *s*o [s]; *sh*all [ʃ]; *t*o [t]; *th*in [θ]; *th*:en [ð]; above (*uh* B*UH*V) [ə, ˈʌ]; *v*ine [v]; *w*ine [w]; *wh*ine [hw]; *y*ou [j]; *z*oo [z]; rouge (roo:*zh*) [ʒ].

blitzkrieg, B-	BLITS kreeg	ˈblɪtskrig
Bliven	BLI vuhn	ˈblɪvən
Bloch	blahk	blɑk
blockade (n)	BLAH kayd	ˈblɑked
blockade (v)	blah KAYD	blɑˈked
Bloemfontein	BLOO : M fahn tayn	ˈblumfɑnten
Blois	blwah	blwɑ
blond, blonde	blahnd	blɑnd
bloomer, B-	bloo : mer	ˈblumər
blossom	BLAH suhm	ˈblɑsəm
blotter	BLAH ter	ˈblɑtər
blouse	blowz	blauz
blowoff	BLOH awf	ˈbloɔf
blowzy	BLOW zi	ˈblauzɪ
blubber	BLUH ber	ˈblʌbər
Blucher	BLOO : ker	ˈblukər
blücher	BLOO : cher	ˈblutʃər
bludgeon	BLUH juhn	ˈblʌdʒən
blue	bloo :	blu
Bluebeard	BLOO : bird	ˈblubərd
bluestocking	BLOO : stah king	ˈblustɑkɪŋ
blunderbuss	BLUHN der buhs	ˈblʌndərbʌs
bluster	BLUH ster	ˈblʌstər
Blut und Eisen	BLOO : T oont IGH zuhn	ˈblut unt ˈaɪzən
B'nai B'rith	buh NAY BRITH	bəˈne ˈbrɪθ
boa	BOH uh	ˈboə
boar	bohr	bor
board	bawrd	bɔrd
boarish	BOH rish	ˈborɪʃ
Boas	BOH az	ˈboæz
boatswain	BOH suhn	ˈbosən
Boaz	BOH az	ˈboæz
bobbin	BAH bin	ˈbɑbɪn
bobeche	buh BESH	bəˈbɛʃ
bobolink	BAH buh lingk	ˈbɑbəlɪŋk
bobsled	BAHB sled	ˈbɑbslɛd
bobsleigh	BAHB slay	ˈbɑbsle
Boca Raton	BOH kuh ruh TAHN	ˈbokə rəˈtan
Boccaccio, Giovanni	boh KAH chi oh, joh VAH ni	boˈkatʃio, dʒoˈvanɪ
boche, B-	bahsh	bɑʃ
bock	bahk	bɑk
bode	bohd	bod
Bodensee	BOH duhn zay	ˈbodənze
bodkin	BAHD kin	ˈbɑdkɪn
Bodleian	bahd LEE uhn	badˈliən
Boeing	BOH ing	ˈboɪŋ
Boeotia	bi OH shi uh	bɪˈoʃɪə
Boeotian	bi OH shuhn	bɪˈoʃən
Boer	bohr	bor
Boethius	boh EE thi uhs	boˈiθɪəs
Boettiger	BE ti ger	ˈbɛtɪgər

at [æ]; ah [ɑ]; air [ɛ]; awful [ɔ]; say [e]; back [b]; chair [tʃ]; do [d]; elm [ɛ]; eel [i]; server [ˈɝ, ər]; fit [f]; go [g]; hurt [h]; is [ɪ]; high [aɪ]; jet [dʒ]; kiss [k]; lamb [l]; my [m]; nice [n];

Bogan	BOH guhn	ˈbogən
bogey	BOH gi	ˈbogɪ
boggle	BAH guhl	ˈbagəl
bogie	BOH gi	ˈbogɪ
Bogotá	boh goh TAH	bogoˈta
bogy	BOH gi	ˈbogɪ
bohème	boh EM	boˈɛm
Bohemia	boh HEE mi uh	boˈhimɪə
Böhm	berm	bɜm
Bohol	buh HAWL	bəˈhɔl
Bohr	bohr	bor
Boise	BOI si	ˈbɔɪsɪ
Boisson	bwah SAWN	bwaˈsɔn
boisterous	BOI stuh ruhs	ˈbɔɪstərəs
Bokhara	boh KAH ruh	boˈkarə
bola	BOH luh	ˈbolə
bolero	boh LAI roh	boˈlɛro
Boleyn	BOO lin	ˈbʊlɪn
Bolivar	BAH luh ver	ˈbaləvər
Bolivia, b-	buh LI vi uh	bəˈlɪvɪə
Bolivian	buh LI vi uhn	bəˈlɪvɪən
bollard, B-	BAH lerd	ˈbalərd
bolo	BOH loh	ˈbolo
Bologna (Italy)	buh LOH nyuh	bəˈlonjə
bologna, B- (sausage)	buh LOH ni	bəˈlonɪ
Bolognese	bah luh NYEEZ	baləˈnjiz
bolometer	boh LAH muh ter	boˈlamətər
bolshevik, B-	BAHL shuh vik	ˈbalʃəvɪk
bolsheviki, B-	bahl shuh VEE ki	balʃəˈvikɪ
Bolshoi	BOHL shoi	ˈbolʃɔɪ
bolster	BOHL ster	ˈbolstər
bolus	BOH luhs	ˈboləs
Bolzano	bawlt SAH naw	bɔltˈsano
bomb	bahm	bam
bombard (n)	BAHM bahrd	ˈbambard
bombard (v)	bahm BAHRD	bamˈbard
bombardier	bahm ber DIR	bambərˈdɪr
bombardon	BAHM ber duhn	ˈbambərdən
bombasine	bahm buh ZEEN	bambəˈzin
bombast	BAHM bast	ˈbambæst
bombastic	bahm BA stik	bamˈbæstɪk
Bombay	bahm BAY	bamˈbe
bombazine	bahm buh ZEEN	bambəˈzin
bombe	bawmb	bɔmb
bomber	BAH mer	ˈbamər
Bombois	bohm BWAH	bomˈbwa
bombproof	BAHM proo:f	ˈbampruf
bombshell	BAHM shel	ˈbamʃɛl
bona fide	BOH nuh FIGHD	ˈbonəˈfaɪd
bonanza	buh NAN zuh	bəˈnænzə
Bonaparte	BOH nuh pahrt	ˈbonəpart
Bonapartist	BOH nuh pahr tist	ˈbonəpartɪst

sing [ŋ]; oh [o]; oil [ɔɪ]; foot [ʊ]; foo:d [u]; how [aʊ]; pie [p]; ray [r]; so [s]; shall [ʃ];
to [t]; thin [θ]; th:en [ð]; above (uh BUHV) [ə, ˈʌ]; vine [v]; wine [w]; whine [hw];
you [j]; zoo [z]; rouge (roo:zh) [ʒ].

Bonaventura	bah nuh ven TYOO ruh	banəvɛnˈtjurə
bonbon	BAHN bahn	ˈbanban
bondage	BAHN dij	ˈbandɪdʒ
bonfire	BAHN fighr	ˈbanfaɪr
bongo	BAHNG goh	ˈbaŋgo
Bonheur	baw NER	bɔˈnɝ
bonhomie, bonhommie	bah nuh MEE	banəˈmi
bonito	buh NEE toh	bəˈnito
bon jour	bohn ZHOO : R	bonˈʒur
bon mot	bohn MOH	bonˈmo
Bonn	bahn	ˈban
Bonnard	baw NAHR	bɔˈnar
bonne femme	buhn FAM	bənˈfæm
bonne heure	buhn ER	bənˈɝ
Bonnet	baw NAY	bɔˈne
bonnet	BAH nit	ˈbanɪt
bonsai	BAHN sigh	ˈbansaɪ
bon soir	bohn SWAHR	bonˈswar
Bon Ton (shop)	BAHN tahn	ˈban tan
bon ton	bohn TOHN	bonˈton
bonus	BOH nuhs	ˈbonəs
bon vivant	bohn vee VAHN	bonviˈvan
bon voyage	bohn vwah YAHZH	bon vwaˈjaʒ
booby	BOO : bi	ˈbubɪ
boogie-woogie	BOO gi WOO gi	ˈbugɪ ˈwʊgɪ
boohoo	BOO : hoo :	ˈbuhu
boondock	BOO : N dahk	ˈbundak
boondoggle	BOO : N dah guhl	ˈbundagəl
boor, B-	boor	bʊr
Boötes	boh OH teez	boˈotiz
booth, B-	boo : th	buθ
booths	boo : th : z	buðz
bootless	BOO : T lis	ˈbutlɪs
boracic	boh RA sik	boˈræsɪk
Borah	BOH ruh	ˈborə
borate	BOH rayt	ˈboret
Bordeaux	bawr DOH	bɔrˈdo
bordelaise	bawrd LEZ	bɔrdˈlɛz
bore	bohr	bor
borealis	boh ri A lis	borɪˈælɪs
Boreas	BOH ri uhs	ˈborɪəs
Borghese	bawr GAY zay	bɔrˈgeze
Borgia	BAWR juh	ˈbɔrdʒə
Borglum	BAWR gluhm	ˈbɔrgləm
boric	BOH rik	ˈborɪk
Boris	BOH ris	ˈborɪs
Borisoglebsk	baw ree saw GLEPSK	bɔrɪsɔˈglɛpsk
Borkh, Inge	bawrk, ING guh	bɔrk, ˈɪŋgə
Borneo	BAWR ni oh	ˈbɔrnɪo
borough	BUH roh	ˈbʌro
borrow, B-	BAW roh	ˈbɔro
borsch	bawrsh	bɔrʃ

at [æ] ; *ah* [ɑ] ; *air* [ɛ] ; *awful* [ɔ] ; *say* [e] ; *back* [b] ; *chair* [tʃ] ; *do* [d] ; *elm* [ɛ] ; *eel* [i] ; *server* [ˈɝ, ər] ; *fit* [f] ; *go* [g] ; *hurt* [h] ; *is* [ɪ] ; *high* [aɪ] ; *jet* [dʒ] ; *kiss* [k] ; *lamb* [l] ; *my* [m] ; *nice* [n] ;

borscht, borsht	bawrsht	bɔrʃt
borzoi, B-	BAWR zoi	ˈbɔrzɔɪ
boscage	BAH skij	ˈbɑskɪdʒ
Bose	bohs	bos
bosh	bahsh	bɑʃ
boskage	BAH skij	ˈbɑskɪdʒ
Bosnia	BAHZ ni uh	ˈbɑznɪə
bosom	BOO zuhm	ˈbʊzəm
Bosphorus	BAHS fuh ruhs	ˈbɑsfərəs
Bosporus	BAH spuh ruhs	ˈbɑspərəs
Bossuet	bah SWAY	bɑˈswe
Boston, b-	BAW stuhn	ˈbɔstən
bosun	BOH suhn	ˈbosən
botanical	buh TA ni kuhl	bəˈtænɪkəl
botany	BAH tuh ni	ˈbɑtənɪ
botch	bahch	bɑtʃ
bother	BAH th : er	ˈbɑðər
Bottegari	boh tuh GAH ree	botəˈgɑri
Botticelli	bah ti CHE li	bɑtɪˈtʃɛlɪ
Botticini	bah ti CHEE ni	bɑtɪˈtʃini
botulism	BAH chuh li zuhm	ˈbɑtʃəlɪzəm
Botvinnik, Mikhail	baht VEE nyik, mi KIGHL	bɑtˈvinjɪk, mɪˈkaɪl
bouclé	boo : KLAY	buˈkle
boudoir	BOO : dwahr	ˈbudwɑr
bougainvillaea	boo : guhn VI li uh	bugənˈvɪlɪə
Bougainville	boo : gahn VEEL	bugɑnˈvil
bough	bow	baʊ
bought	bawt	bɔt
bougie	boo : ZHEE	buˈʒi
Bouguereau	boo : GROH	buˈgro
bouillabaisse	boo : lyuh BAYS	bulyəˈbes
bouillon	BOO lyuhn	ˈbʊljən
Boulanger	boo lahn ZHAY	bʊlɑnˈʒe
boulevard	BOO luh vahrd	ˈbʊləvɑrd
Boulogne	boo LOHN	buˈlon
Boult	bohlt	ˈbolt
Boun Oum	boo : n oo : m	bun um
bounteous	BOWN ti uhs	ˈbaʊntɪəs
bouquet (aroma)	boo : KAY	buˈke
bouquet (flowers)	boh KAY	boˈke
Bourbon (European)	BOOR buhn	ˈbʊrbən
Bourbon, b- (U.S. ; whisky)	BER buhn	ˈbɝbən
bourgeois (middle class)	boor ZHWAH	bʊrˈʒwɑ
bourgeois (type)	ber JOIS	bərˈdʒɔɪs
bourgeoise	boor ZHWAHZ	bʊrˈʒwɑz
bourgeoisie	boor zhwah ZEE	bʊrʒwɑˈzi
Bourget	boor ZHAY	bʊrˈʒe
Bourke	berk	bɝk
bourn, -e	bawrn	bɔrn
Bournemouth	BAWRN muhth	ˈbɔrnməθ
bourse	boors	bʊrs

sing [ŋ] ; oh [o] ; oil [ɔɪ] ; foot [ʊ] ; foo:d [u] ; how [aʊ] ; pie [p] ; ray [r] ; so [s] ; shall [ʃ] ; to [t] ; thin [θ] ; th:en [ð] ; above (uh BUHV) [ə, ˈʌ] ; vine [v] ; wine [w] ; whine [hw] ; you [j] ; zoo [z] ; rouge (roo:zh) [ʒ].

boutonnière	boo tuh NYAIR	butəˈnjɛr
Bovary	BOH vah ri	ˈbovɑrɪ
bovine	BOH vighn	ˈbovaɪn
bow (prow; nod)	bow	baʊ
bow (weapon; curve(d); knot)	bo	bo
Bowdich, Bowditch	BOW dich	ˈbaʊdɪtʃ
Bowdler	BOWD ler	ˈbaʊdlər
bowdlerize	BOWD luh righz	ˈbaʊdləraɪz
Bowdoin	BOH duhn	ˈbodən
bower (arbor; cards; anchor)	BOW er	ˈbaʊər
bower (violinist)	BO er	ˈboər
bowery, B-	BOW ri	ˈbaʊrɪ
bowie, B-	BOO i	ˈbuɪ
bowl	bohl	bol
bowlegged	BO le gid	ˈbolɛgɪd
bowler	BOH ler	ˈbolər
bowline	BOH lighn	ˈbolaɪn
bowman (archer)	BOH muhn	ˈbomən
bowman (oarsman)	BOW muhn	ˈbaʊmən
bowshot	BOH shaht	ˈboʃɑt
bowsprit	BOW sprit	ˈbaʊsprɪt
bowstring	BOH string	ˈbostrɪŋ
bowyer	BOH yer	ˈbojər
boxer	BAHK ser	ˈbɑksər
boycott	BOI kaht	ˈbɔɪkɑt
Boyer	BOI yer	ˈbɔɪjər
Boyer, Charles	bwah YAY	bwɑˈje
boysenberry	BOI suhn be ri	ˈbɔɪsənbɛrɪ
bra	brah	brɑ
Brabant	bruh BANT	brəˈbænt
brace	brays	bres
bracelet	BRAY slit	ˈbreslɪt
bracero	bra SE roh	bræˈsɛro
brach	brach	brætʃ
brachet	BRA chit	ˈbrætʃɪt
brachial	BRAY ki uhl	ˈbrekɪəl
brachiopod	BRAY ki uh pahd	ˈbrekɪəpɑd
brachium	BRAY ki uhm	ˈbrekɪəm
brachycephalic	bra ki suh FA lik	brækɪsəˈfælɪk
brackish	BRA kish	ˈbrækɪʃ
brae	bray	bre
Braganca	brah GAHN suh	brɑˈgɑnsə
braggadocio	bra guh DOH shi oh	brægəˈdoʃɪo
braggart	BRA gert	ˈbrægərt
Brahe	brah	brɑ
Brahma, b-	BRAH muh	ˈbrɑmə
Brahman	BRAH muhn	ˈbrɑmən
Brahmaputra	brah muh POO: truh	brɑməˈputrə
Brahmin	BRAH min	ˈbrɑmɪn
Brahms	brahmz	brɑmz

*a*t [æ]; *ah* [ɑ]; *air* [ɛ]; *aw*ful [ɔ]; *say* [e]; *b*ack [b]; *ch*air [tʃ]; *do* [d]; *elm* [ɛ]; *eel* [i]; *server* [ˈɝ, ər]; *f*it [f]; *go* [g]; *h*urt [h]; *is* [ɪ]; *high* [aɪ]; *jet* [dʒ]; *kiss* [k]; *l*amb [l]; *my* [m]; *n*ice [n];

braid	brayd	bred
braille, B-	brayl	brel
Brailowsky	brigh LOHV skee	braɪˈlovski
brainpan	BRAYN pan	ˈbrenpæn
braise	brayz	brez
brakeage	BRAY kij	ˈbrekɪdʒ
Bramante	brah MAHN tay	brɑˈmɑnte
Braña	BRAH nyah	ˈbrɑnjɑ
branch	branch	bræntʃ
Brancusi	brahn KOO : see	brɑnˈkusi
Brandeis	BRAN dighs	ˈbrændaɪs
brandied	BRAN did	ˈbrændɪd
brand-new	BRAND nyoo :	ˈbrænd nju
Brandt, Willy	BRAHNT, VI li	ˈbrɑnt, ˈvɪlɪ
Braniff	BRA nif	ˈbrænɪf
brant	brant	brænt
Braque, Georges	brahk, zhawrzh	brɑk, ʒɔrʒ
brash	brash	bræʃ
brasier	BRAY zher	ˈbreʒər
Brasilia	bruh SI li uh	brəˈsɪlɪə
brass	bras	bræs
brassard	BRA serd	ˈbræsərd
brassie	BRA si	ˈbræsɪ
brassiere	bruh ZIR	brəˈzɪr
brass winds	BRAS windz	ˈbræs wɪndz
Bratislava	BRAH ti slah vuh	ˈbrɑtɪslɑvə
Braun	brawn	ˈbrɔn
bravado	bruh VAH doh	brəˈvɑdo
bravo	BRAH voh	ˈbrɑvo
bravura	bruh VYOO ruh	brəˈvjʊrə
brawny	BRAW ni	ˈbrɔnɪ
brazier	BRAY zher	ˈbreʒər
Brazil, b-	bruh ZIL	brəˈzɪl
Brazzaville	brah zah VEEL	brɑzɑˈvil
breach	breech	britʃ
breadstuff	BRED stuhf	ˈbredstʌf
breadth	bredth	bredθ
breadthways	BREDTH wayz	ˈbredθ wez
breadthwise	BREDTH wighz	ˈbredθ waɪz
breakage	BRAY kij	ˈbrekɪdʒ
breakfast	BREK fuhst	ˈbrekfəst
breast	brest	brest
breastbone	BREST bohn	ˈbrest bon
breath	breth	breθ
breathe	breeth :	brið
breathed	breeth : d	brið d
breathing	BREE th : ing	ˈbriðɪŋ
breathy	BRE thi	ˈbreθɪ
breccia	BRE chi uh	ˈbretʃɪə
Brecht, Bertolt	brekt, BER tawlt	ˈbrekt, ˈbɝtɔlt
breech	breech	britʃ
breeches	BRI chiz	ˈbrɪtʃɪz

sing [ŋ] ; *oh* [o] ; *oil* [ɔɪ] ; *foot* [ʊ] ; *foo:*d [u] ; *how* [aʊ] ; *pie* [p] ; *ray* [r] ; *so* [s] ; *sh*all [ʃ] ;
to [t] ; *thin* [θ] ; *th:*en [ð] ; *above* (*uh* B*UH*V) [ə, ˈʌ] ; *vine* [v] ; *wine* [w] ; *wh*ine [hw] ;
you [j] ; *zoo* [z] ; *rouge* (roo:*zh*) [ʒ].

breechloader	BREECH loh der	ˈbritʃlodər
Bremen (Germany)	BRAY muhn	ˈbremən
Bremen (U.S.)	BREE muhn	ˈbrimən
Brenner	BRE ner	ˈbrɛnər
Brescia	BRE shah	ˈbrɛʃɑ
Breslau	BRES law	ˈbrɛslɔ
Brest	brest	brɛst
Brest-Litovsk	brest li TAWFSK	brɛst lɪˈtɔfsk
brethren	BRE th : ruhn	ˈbrɛðrən
Breton	BRE tuhn	ˈbrɛtən
Bretton	BRE tuhn	ˈbrɛtən
breve	breev	briv
brevet	bruh VET	brəˈvɛt
brevetcy	bruh VET si	brəˈvɛtsɪ
breviary	BREE vi ai ri	ˈbrivɪɛrɪ
brevier	bruh VIR	brəˈvɪr
brevity	BRE vuh ti	ˈbrɛvətɪ
brew	broo :	bru
brewery	BROO : uh ri	ˈbruərɪ
brewis	BROO : is	ˈbruɪs
Briand, Aristide	bree AHN, ah ree STEED	briˈɑn, ɑriˈstid
Briareus	brigh AI ri uhs	braɪˈɛrɪəs
bribery	BRIGH buh ri	ˈbraɪbərɪ
bric-a-brac	BRIK uh brak	ˈbrɪkəbræk
brickkiln	BRIK kil	ˈbrɪk kɪl
bricole	bri KOHL	brɪˈkol
bridegroom	BRIGHD groo : m	ˈbraɪdgrum
bridesmaid	BRIGHDZ mayd	ˈbraɪdzmed
bridle	BRIGH duhl	ˈbraɪdəl
bridoon	bri DOO : N	brɪˈdun
bridwell	BRIGHD wel	ˈbraɪdwɛl
Brie	bree	bri
brigade	bri GAYD	brɪˈged
brigadier	bri guh DIR	brɪgəˈdɪr
brigand	BRI guhnd	ˈbrɪgənd
brigantine	BRI guhn teen	ˈbrɪgəntin
brilliance	BRI lyuhns	ˈbrɪljəns
brilliancy	BRI lyuhn si	ˈbrɪljənsɪ
brilliant	BRI lyuhnt	ˈbrɪljənt
brilliantine	BRI lyuhn teen	ˈbrɪljəntin
Brindisi	BRIN duh zi	ˈbrɪndəzɪ
brindled	BRIN duhld	ˈbrɪndəld
brink	brink	brɪŋk
brioche	BREE ohsh	ˈbrioʃ
briolette	bree uh LET	briəˈlɛt
briquet, -te	bri KET	brɪˈkɛt
Brisbane	BRIZ bayn	ˈbrɪzben
Briseis	brigh SEE is	braɪˈsiɪs
brisket	BRI skit	ˈbrɪskɪt
bristle	BRI suhl	ˈbrɪsəl
Britannia, b-	bri TA ni uh	brɪˈtænɪə
Britannic	bri TA nik	brɪˈtænɪk

at [æ] ; *ah* [ɑ] ; *air* [ɛ] ; *awful* [ɔ] ; *say* [e] ; *back* [b] ; *chair* [tʃ] ; *do* [d] ; *elm* [ɛ] ; *eel* [i] ; *server* [ˈɜ, ər] ; *fit* [f] ; *go* [g] ; *hurt* [h] ; *is* [ɪ] ; *high* [aɪ] ; *jet* [dʒ] ; *kiss* [k] ; *lamb* [l] ; *my* [m] ; *nice* [n] ;

Briticism	BRI tuh si zuhm	ˈbrɪtəsɪzəm
Britisher	BRI ti sher	ˈbrɪtɪʃər
Briton	BRI tuhn	ˈbrɪtən
Brno	BER noh	ˈbɝno
broach	brohch	brotʃ
broadbill	BRAWD bil	ˈbrɔdbɪl
broadbrim	BRAWD brim	ˈbrɔdbrɪm
broadcast	BRAWD kast	ˈbrɔdkæst
broad gauge	BRAWD gayj	ˈbrɔdgedʒ
Brobdingnag	BRAHB ding nag	ˈbrɑbdɪŋnæg
Brobdingnagian	brahb ding NA gi uhn	brɑbdɪŋˈnægɪən
brocade	broh KAYD	broˈked
brocatel, -le	brah kuh TEL	brɑkəˈtɛl
broccoli	BRAH kuh li	ˈbrɑkəlɪ
broché	broh SHAY	broˈʃe
brochette	broh SHET	broˈʃɛt
brochure	broh SHOOR	broˈʃʊr
brogan	BROH guhn	ˈbrogən
brogue	brohg	brog
broider	BROI der	ˈbrɔɪdər
brokerage	BROH kuh rij	ˈbrokərɪdʒ
brome	brohm	brom
bromide	BROH mighd	ˈbromaɪd
bromine	BROH meen	ˈbromin
bronchial	BRAHNG ki uhl	ˈbrɑŋkɪəl
bronchitis	brahn KIGH tis	brɑnˈkaɪtɪs
broncho	BRAHNG koh	ˈbrɑŋko
bronchoscope	BRAHNG kuh skohp	ˈbrɑŋkəskop
bronco	BRAHNG koh	ˈbrɑŋko
Bronte	BRAHN ti	ˈbrɑntɪ
brontosaurus	brahn tuh SAW ruhs	brɑntəˈsɔrəs
Bronx, b-	brahngks	brɑŋks
bronze	brahnz	brɑnz
brooch	brohch	brotʃ
brood	broo : d	brud
Brooks, Van Wyck	brooks, van WIK	brʊks, væn ˈwɪk
broom	broo : m	brum
brothel	BRAW thuhl	ˈbrɔθəl
brotherhood	BRUH th : er hood	ˈbrʌðərhʊd
Brou	broo :	bru
brougham	broo : m	brum
Broun	broo : n	brun
browbeat	BROW beet	ˈbraʊbit
brown	brown	braʊn
browse	browz	braʊz
Broz	brawz	brɔz
brucellosis	broo : suh LOH sis	brusəˈlosɪs
Bruckner	BROOK ner	ˈbrʊknər
Bruges	BROO : jiz	ˈbrudʒɪz
bruin	BROO : in	ˈbruɪn
bruise	broo : z	bruz
bruiser	BROO : zer	ˈbruzər

si*ng* [ŋ] ; *oh* [o] ; *oil* [ɔɪ] ; *foot* [ʊ] ; foo:d [u] ; *how* [aʊ] ; *pie* [p] ; ray [r] ; *so* [s] ; *sh*all [ʃ] ; *to* [t] ; *thin* [θ] ; *th:*en [ð] ; above (*uh* B*UH*V) [ə, ˈʌ] ; *vine* [v] ; *wine* [w] ; *wh*ine [hw] ; *you* [j] ; *zoo* [z] ; rouge (roo:*zh*) [ʒ].

bruit	broo : t	brut
Brumaire	broo MAIR	bruˈmɛr
brumal	BROO : muhl	ˈbruməl
brume	broo : m	brum
Brunei	broo NAY	bruˈne
brunet, -te	broo : NET	bruˈnɛt
Brunetière	broon TYAIR	brʊnˈtjɛr
Brunhild	BROO : N hild	ˈbrunhɪld
Brunnhilde	broon HIL duh	brʊnˈhɪldə
brusque	bruhsk	brʌsk
Brussels	BRUH suhlz	ˈbrʌsəlz
brut	brit	brɪt
brute	broo : t	brut
Bruxelles	broo SEL	bruˈsɛl
Bruyère	broo YAIR	bruˈjɛr
Bryansk	bri AHNSK	brɪˈɑnsk
Brynhild	BRIN hild	ˈbrɪnhɪld
Bryn Mawr	brin mahr	ˈbrɪn ˈmɑr
bryophyte	BRIGH uh fight	ˈbraɪəfaɪt
Brython	BRI thuhn	ˈbrɪθən
Brythonic	bri THAH nik	brɪˈθɑnɪk
Buber, Martin	BOO : ber, MAHR tin	ˈbubər, ˈmɑrtɪn
bubo	BYOO : boh	ˈbjubo
bubonic	byoo : BAH nik	bjuˈbɑnɪk
buccal	BUH kuhl	ˈbʌkəl
buccaneer	buh kuh NIR	bəkəˈnɪr
buccinator	BUHK si nay ter	ˈbʌksɪnetər
Bucephalus	byoo : SE fuh luhs	bjuˈsɛfələs
Buchan, John	BUH kuhn	ˈbʌkən
Buchanan	byoo : KA nuhn	bjuˈkænən
Bucharest	byoo : kuh REST	bjukəˈrɛst
Buchenwald	BOO : kuhn vahlt	ˈbukənvɑlt
Buchman	BUHK muhn	ˈbʌkmən
Buchmanism	BUHK muh ni zuhm	ˈbʌkmənɪzəm
Buchmanite	BUHK muh night	ˈbʌkmənaɪt
buckaroo	BUH kuh roo :	ˈbʌkəru
Buckeye	BUH kigh	ˈbʌkaɪ
Buckingham	BUH king uhm	ˈbʌkɪŋəm
bucko	BUH koh	ˈbʌko
buckram	BUH kruhm	ˈbʌkrəm
buckwheat	BUHK hweet	ˈbʌkhwit
bucolic	byoo : KAH lik	bjuˈkɑlɪk
Budapest	BOO duh pest	ˈbudəpɛst
Buddha	BOO duh	ˈbudə
Buddhism	BOO di zuhm	ˈbudɪzəm
buddleia	buhd LEE uh	bədˈliə
Budenny	boo : DE ni	buˈdɛni
budgerigar	buh juh ri GAHR	bədʒərɪˈgɑr
Budweiser	BUHD wigh zer	ˈbʌdwaɪzər
Buell	BYOO : uhl	ˈbjuəl
Buenaventura	BWAY nah ven TOO ruh	ˈbwenɑvɛnˈturə
Buenos Aires	BWAY nohs IGH rays	ˈbwenosˈaɪrez

at [æ] ; ah [ɑ] ; air [ɛ] ; awful [ɔ] ; say [e] ; back [b] ; chair [tʃ] ; do [d] ; elm [ɛ] ; eel [i] ;
server [ˈɜ, ər] ; fit [f] ; go [g] ; hurt [h] ; is [ɪ] ; high [aɪ] ; jet [dʒ] ; kiss [k] ; lamb [l] ; my [m] ;
nice [n] ;

buffalo, B-	BUH fuh loh	ˈbʌfəlo
buffet (blow)	BUH fit	ˈbʌfɪt
buffet (sideboard)	boo FAY	buˈfe
buffo	BOO : foh	ˈbufo
buffoon	buh FOO : N	bəˈfun
buffoonery	buh FOO : nuh ri	bəˈfunərɪ
Bug (river)	boog	bʊg
Buganda	boo : GAHN duh	buˈgɑndə
bugle	BYOO : guhl	ˈbjugəl
Buitenzorg	BWI tuhn zawrk	ˈbwɪtənzɔrk
Bukharin	boo : k HAH rin	bukˈhɑrɪn
bulbil	BUHL bil	ˈbʌlbɪl
bulbous	BUHL buhs	ˈbʌlbəs
bulbul	BOOL bool	ˈbulbʊl
Bulganin	boo : l GAH nin	bulˈgɑnɪn
Bulgar	BUHL ger	ˈbʌlgər
Bulgaria	buhl GAI ri uh	bəlˈgɛrɪə
bulger	BUHL jer	ˈbʌldʒər
bulimia	byoo : LI mi uh	bjuˈlɪmɪə
bulkhead	BUHLK hed	ˈbʌlkhɛd
Bull, Ole	BOO : L, OH luh	bul, ˈolə
bulldoze	BOOL dohz	ˈbuldoz
bullet	BOO lit	ˈbulɪt
bulletin	BOO luh tin	ˈbulətɪn
bullion	BOO lyuhn	ˈbuljən
Bull Moose	bool moo : s	bul mus
bullock	BOO luhk	ˈbulək
bulwark	BOOL werk	ˈbulwərk
bumpkin	BUHMP kin	ˈbʌmpkɪn
bumptious	BUHMP shuhs	ˈbʌmpʃəs
buna, B-	BOO : nuh	ˈbunə
Bunche	buhnch	bʌntʃ
bunco	BUHNG koh	ˈbʌŋko
buncombe, B-	BUHNG kuhm	ˈbʌŋkəm
Bund	boond	bund
Bundestag	BOON duhs tahk	ˈbundəstɑk
Bundeswehr	BOON des vair	ˈbundɛsvɛər
bungalow	BUHNG guh loh	ˈbʌŋgəlo
bunghole	BUHNG hohl	ˈbʌŋhol
bunion	BUH nyuhn	ˈbʌnjən
Bunsen	BUHN suhn	ˈbʌnsən
bunting	BUHN ting	ˈbʌntɪŋ
buoy	boi	bɔɪ
buoyancy	BOI uhn si	ˈbɔɪənsɪ
buoyant	BOI uhnt	ˈbɔɪənt
Burbage	BER bij	ˈbɝbɪdʒ
Burbank	BER bangk	ˈbɝbæŋk
burberry	BER bai ri	ˈbɝberɪ
burdock	BER dahk	ˈbɝdɑk
bureau	BYOO : roh	ˈbjuro
bureaucracy	byoo RAH kruh si	bjuˈrɑkrəsɪ
buret, burette	byoo RET	bjuˈrɛt

sing [ŋ] ; *oh* [o] ; *oil* [ɔɪ] ; *foot* [ʊ] ; *foo :*d [u] ; *how* [aʊ] ; *pie* [p] ; *ray* [r] ; *so* [s] ; *shall* [ʃ] ;
to [t] ; *thin* [θ] ; *th :*en [ð] ; *above* (*uh* BUHV) [ə, ˈʌ] ; *vine* [v] ; *wine* [w] ; *whine* [hw] ;
you [j] ; *zoo* [z] ; *rouge* (roo :*zh*) [ʒ].

burgeon	BER juhn	ˈbɝdʒən
burgher	BER ger	ˈbɝgər
Burghley	BER li	ˈbɝlɪ
burglar	BER gler	ˈbɝglər
burglarize	BER gluh righz	ˈbɝgləraɪz
burglary	BER gluh ri	ˈbɝglərɪ
burgomaster	BER guh ma ster	ˈbɝgəmæstər
burgrave	BER grayv	ˈbɝgrev
Burgundian	ber GUHN di uhn	bərˈgʌndɪən
Burgundy	BER guhn di	ˈbɝgəndɪ
burial	BAI ri uhl	ˈbɛrɪəl
burin	BYOO rin	ˈbjʊrɪn
burl	berl	bɝl
burlap	BER lap	ˈbɝlæp
Burleigh	BER li	ˈbɝlɪ
burlesque	ber LESK	bərˈlɛsk
burley, B-	BER li	ˈbɝlɪ
burly	BER li	ˈbɝlɪ
Burma	BER muh	ˈbɝmə
Burmese	ber MEEZ	bərˈmiz
burnoose	ber NOO : S	bərˈnus
burnsides	BERN sighdz	ˈbɝnsaɪdz
burro	BUH roh	ˈbʌro
burrow	BUH roh	ˈbʌro
bursar	BER ser	ˈbɝsər
burse	bers	bɝs
bursitis	ber SIGH tis	bərˈsaɪtɪs
burthen	BER th : uhn	ˈbɝðən
Burundi	boo : ROON dee	buˈrʊndi
bury	BAI ri	ˈbɛrɪ
busby	BUHZ bi	ˈbʌzbɪ
bushel	BOO shuhl	ˈbʊʃəl
bushido, B-	BOO : shee doh	ˈbʊʃido
bushwhacker	BOOSH hwaker	ˈbʊʃhwækər
business	BIZ nis	ˈbɪznɪs
businessman	BIZ nis man	ˈbɪznɪsmæn
buskin	BUH skin	ˈbʌskɪn
Busra, Busrah	BUHS ruh	ˈbʌsrə
Bustamante	boo stah MAHN tay	bustaˈmɑnte
bustard	BUH sterd	ˈbʌstərd
bustle	BUH suhl	ˈbʌsəl
Busuanga	boo : SWAHNG gah	buˈswɑŋgɑ
busy	BI zi	ˈbɪzɪ
busyness	BI zi nis	ˈbɪzɪnɪs
butadiene	byoo : tuh DIGH een	bjutəˈdaɪin
butane	BYOO : tayn	ˈbjuten
butchery	BOO chuh ri	ˈbʊtʃərɪ
butlery	BUHT luh ri	ˈbʌtlərɪ
butt	buht	bʌt
butte, B-	byoo : t	bjut
butterine	BUH tuh reen	ˈbʌtərin
butterwort	BUH ter wert	ˈbʌtərwərt

buttock	BUH tuhk	ˈbʌtək
buttress	BUH tris	ˈbʌtrɪs
butyl	BYOO : til	ˈbjutɪl
butyrate	BYOO : tuh rayt	ˈbjutəret
butyric	byoo : TI rik	bjuˈtɪrɪk
buxom	BUHK suhm	ˈbʌksəm
buzzard	BUH zerd	ˈbʌzərd
bye	bigh	baɪ
bye-low	BIGH loh	ˈbaɪlo
bylaw, byelaw	BIGH law	ˈbaɪlɔ
byline	BIGH lighn	ˈbaɪlaɪn
byre	bighr	baɪr
byrnie	BER ni	ˈbɝnɪ
Byron	BIGH ruhn	ˈbaɪrən
Bysshe	bish	bɪʃ
byssinosis	bi suh NOH sis	bɪsəˈnosɪs
bystander	BIGH stan der	ˈbaɪstændər
Byzantine	bi ZAN tin	bɪˈzæntɪn
Byzantium	bi ZAN ti uhm	bɪˈzæntɪəm

C

cabal	kuh BAL	kəˈbæl
cabala	KA buh luh	ˈkæbələ
caballero	ka buh LAI roh	kæbəlˈlero
cabana	kuh BA nuh	kəˈbænə
cabaret	ka buh RAY	kæbəˈre
cabbala	KA buh luh	ˈkæbələ
Cabell	KA buhl	ˈkæbəl
cabinet	KA buh nit	ˈkæbənɪt
cabob	kuh BAHB	kəˈbɑb
caboose	kuh BOO : S	kəˈbus
Cabot	KA buht	ˈkæbət
Cabrera	ka BRAY ruh	kæˈbrerə
cabriole	KA bri ohl	ˈkæbrɪol
cabriolet	ka bri uh LAY	kabrɪəˈle
cacao	kuh KAY oh	kəˈkeo
Caccia	KAH chah	ˈkɑtʃɑ
cache	kash	kæʃ
cachet	ka SHAY	kæˈʃe
cachou	kuh SHOO :	kəˈʃu
cachucha	kuh CHOO : chuh	kəˈtʃutʃə
cacique	kuh SEEK	kəˈsik
cacodyl	KA kuh dil	ˈkækədɪl
cacophonous	kuh KAH fuh nuhs	kəˈkɑfənəs
cacophony	kuh KAH fuh ni	kəˈkɑfənɪ
cadaver	kuh DA ver	kəˈdævər
cadaverous	kuh DA vuh ruhs	kəˈdævərəs
cadence	KAY duhns	ˈkedəns

---

sing [ŋ] ; *oh* [o] ; *oil* [ɔɪ] ; *foot* [ʊ] ; *foo:*d [u] ; *how* [aʊ] ; *pie* [p] ; *ray* [r] ; *so* [s] ; *shall* [ʃ] ; *to* [t] ; *thin* [θ] ; *th:*en [ð] ; *above* (*uh BUH*V) [ə, ˈʌ] ; *vine* [v] ; *wine* [w] ; *whine* [hw] ; *you* [j] ; *zoo* [z] ; *rouge* (roo:*zh*) [ʒ].

cadenza	kuh DEN zuh	kəˈdɛnzə
cadet	kuh DET	kəˈdɛt
cadgy	KA ji	ˈkædʒɪ
cadi	KAH di	ˈkɑdɪ
Cádiz	KAY diz	ˈkedɪz
Cadmean	kad MEE uhn	kædˈmiən
cadmium	KAD mi uhm	ˈkædmɪəm
Cadmus	KAD muhs	ˈkædməs
Cadogan	kuh DUH guhn	kəˈdʌgən
cadre	KA druh	ˈkædrə
caduceus	kuh DOO: si uhs	kəˈdusɪəs
Caedmon	KAD muhn	ˈkædmən
Caedmonian	kad MOH ni uhn	kædˈmonɪən
Caen	kahn	kɑn
Caerleon	kahr LEE uhn	kɑrˈliən
Caesar	SEE zer	ˈsizər
Caesarean, Caesarian	si ZAI ri uhn	sɪˈzɛrɪən
caesura	si ZHOO ruh	sɪˈʒurə
café	kuh FAY	kəˈfé
café au lait	ka FAY oh LAY	kæˈfe oˈle
café noir	ka fay NWAHR	kæfeˈnwɑr
cafeteria	ka fuh TI ri uh	kæfəˈtɪrɪə
caffein, -e	KA feen	ˈkæfin
Cafritz	KA frits	ˈkæfrɪts
caftan	KAF tuhn	ˈkæftən
cagey, cagy	KAY ji	ˈkedʒɪ
cahier	kah YAY	kɑˈye
cahoots	kuh HOO: TS	kəˈhuts
cairn	kairn	kɛrn
Cairo (Egypt)	KIGH roh	ˈkaɪro
Cairo (Illinois)	KAY roh	ˈkero
caisson	KAY suhn	ˈkesən
caitiff	KAY tif	ˈketɪf
Caius	KAY uhs	ˈkeəs
Caius (college)	keez	kiz
cajole	kuh JOHL	kəˈdʒol
cajolery	kuh JOH luh ri	kəˈdʒolərɪ
Cajun	KAY juhn	ˈkedʒən
calabash	KA luh bash	ˈkæləbæʃ
calaboose	KA luh boo: s	ˈkæləbus
caladium	kuh LAY di uhm	kəˈledɪəm
Calais (France)	KA lay	ˈkæle
Calais (U.S.)	KA lis	ˈkælɪs
calamine	KA luh mighn	ˈkæləmaɪn
calamitous	kuh LA muh tuhs	kəˈlæmətəs
calamity	kuh LA muh ti	kəˈlæmətɪ
calamus	KA luh muhs	ˈkæləməs
calash	kuh LASH	kəˈlæʃ
calcaneus	kal KAY ni uhs	kælˈkenɪəs
calcareus	kal KAI ri uhs	kælˈkɛrɪəs
calceolaria	kal si uh LAI ri uh	kælsɪəˈlɛrɪə
calcimine	KAL suh mighn	ˈkælsəmaɪn

at [æ] ; ah [ɑ] ; air [ɛ] ; awful [ɔ] ; say [e] ; back [b] ; chair [tʃ] ; do [d] ; elm [ɛ] ; eel [i] ; server [ˈɝ, ər] ; fit [f] ; go [g] ; hurt [h] ; is [ɪ] ; high [aɪ] ; jet [dʒ] ; kiss [k] ; lamb [l] ; my [m] ; nice [n] ;

calcine	KAL sighn	ˈkælsaɪn
calcium	KAL si uhm	ˈkælsɪəm
calculable	KAL kyuh luh buhl	ˈkælkjələbəl
calculate	KAL kyuh layt	ˈkælkjəlet
calculation	kal kyuh LAY shuhn	kælkjəˈleʃən
calculator	KAL kyuh lay ter	ˈkælkjəletər
calculus	KAL kyuh luhs	ˈkælkjələs
Calcutta	kal KUH tuh	kælˈkʌtə
Calderon (English)	KAWL duh ruhn	ˈkɔldərən
Calderón (Spanish)	kahl de RAWN	kɑldɛˈrɔn
caldron	KAWL druhn	ˈkɔldrən
Caleb	KAY luhb	ˈkeləb
calèche	kah LESH	kɑˈlɛʃ
Caledonia	ka luh DOH ni uh	kæləˈdonɪə
calendar	KA luhn der	ˈkæləndər
calender	KA luhn der	ˈkæləndər
calendula	kuh LEN dyuh luh	kəˈlɛndjələ
calf	kaf	kæf
Cali	KAH li	ˈkɑlɪ
Caliban	KA luh ban	ˈkæləbæn
caliber, calibre	KA luh ber	ˈkæləbər
calibrate	KA luh brayt	ˈkæləbret
calico	KA luh koh	ˈkæləko
calif	KAY lif	ˈkelɪf
California	ka luh FAWR nyuh	kæləˈfɔrnjə
caliper	KA luh per	ˈkæləpər
caliph	KAY lif	ˈkelɪf
caliphate	KA luh fayt	ˈkæləfet
calisthenic	ka luhs THE nik	kæləsˈθɛnɪk
calix	KAY liks	ˈkelɪks
calk	kawk	kɔk
calla	KA luh	ˈkælə
Callao	kah YAH oh	kɑˈjao
Callas	KAH lahs	ˈkɑlɑs
calligraphy	kuh LI gruh fi	kəˈlɪgrəfɪ
calliope, C-	kuh LIGH uh pi	kəˈlaɪəpɪ
calliopsis	ka li AHP sis	kælɪˈɑpsɪs
calliper	KA luh per	ˈkæləpər
callisthenics	ka luhs THE niks	kæləsˈθɛnɪks
Callisto	kuh LI stoh	kəˈlɪsto
callow	KA loh	ˈkælo
calm	kahm	kɑm
calomel	KA luh muhl	ˈkæləməl
caloric	kuh LAW rik	kəˈlɔrɪk
calorie, calory	KA luh ri	ˈkælərɪ
calumet	KA lyoo met	ˈkæljʊmɛt
calumniate	kuh LUHM ni ayt	kəˈlʌmnɪet
calumniator	kuh LUHM ni ay ter	kəˈlʌmnɪetər
calumny	KA luhm ni	ˈkæləmnɪ
calvaria	kal VAI ri uh	kælˈvɛrɪə
Calvary	KAL vuh ri	ˈkælvərɪ
Calvin	KAL vin	ˈkælvɪn

sing [ŋ]; oh [o]; oil [ɔɪ]; foot [ʊ]; foo:d [u]; how [aʊ]; pie [p]; ray [r]; so [s]; shall [ʃ]; to [t]; thin [θ]; th:en [ð]; above (uh BUHV) [ə, ˈʌ]; vine [v]; wine [w]; whine [hw]; you [j]; zoo [z]; rouge (roo:zh) [ʒ].

Calvinism	KAL vi ni zuhm	ˈkælvɪnɪzəm
Calvinist	KAL vi nist	ˈkælvɪnɪst
calycle	KA li kuhl	ˈkælɪkəl
Calydon	KA luh duhn	ˈkælədən
Calypso, c-	kuh LIP soh	kəˈlɪpso
calyx	KAY liks	ˈkelɪks
Camacho	kah MAH choh	kɑˈmatʃo
Camaguey	kah mah GWAY	kɑmɑˈgwe
camaraderie	kah muh RAH duh ri	kɑməˈrɑdərɪ
Camargo	kah MAHR goh	kɑˈmɑrgo
camarilla	kah muh RI luh	kɑməˈrɪlə
cambium	KAM bi uhm	ˈkæmbɪəm
Cambodia	kam BOH di uh	kæmˈbodɪə
Cambrai	kahm BRAY	kɑmˈbre
Cambrian	KAM bri uhn	ˈkæmbrɪən
cambric	KAYM brik	ˈkembrɪk
Cambridge	KAYM brij	ˈkembrɪdʒ
camellia	kuh MEE li uh	kəˈmilɪə
camelopard, C-	kuh ME luh pahrd	kəˈmɛləpard
Camelot	KA muh laht	ˈkæməlɑt
Camembert	KA muhm bair	ˈkæməmbɛr
cameo	KA mi oh	ˈkæmɪo
camera	KA muh ruh	ˈkæmərə
camisole	KA muh sohl	ˈkæməsol
camomile	KA muh mighl	ˈkæməmaɪl
Camorra	kuh MAW ruh	kəˈmɔrə
camouflage	KA muh flahj	ˈkæməflɑdʒ
campagna, C-	kahm PAH nyuh	kɑmˈpɑnjə
Campania	kam PAY ni uh	kæmˈpenɪə
campanile	kam puh NEE li	kæmpəˈnilɪ
campanula	kam PA nyoo luh	kæmˈpænjʊlə
Campbellite	KA muh light	ˈkæməlaɪt
Campden	KAM duhn	ˈkæmdən
camphor	KAM fer	ˈkæmfər
campo	KAM poh	ˈkæmpo
Campora	kahm PAW rah	kɑmˈpɔrɑ
Camus	kah MOO	kɑˈmu
Cana	KAY nuh	ˈkenə
Canaan	KAY nuhn	ˈkenən
Canada	KA nuh duh	ˈkænədə
Canadian	kuh NAY di uhn	kəˈnedɪən
canaille	kuh NAYL	kəˈnel
Canakkale Bogazi	chah NAH kah le baw AH zi	tʃɑˈnakɑlɛ bɔˈɑzɪ
canalization	kuh na li ZAY shuhn	kənælɪˈzeʃən
canapé	KA nuh pi	ˈkænəpɪ
canard	kuh NAHRD	kəˈnard
Canary, c-	kuh NAI ri	kəˈnɛrɪ
Cañas	KAH nyahs	ˈkɑnjɑs
canasta	kuh NA stuh	kəˈnæstə
Canaveral	kuh NA vuh ruhl	kəˈnævərəl
Canberra	KAN bai ruh	ˈkænbɛrə

at [æ]; *ah* [ɑ]; *air* [ɛ]; *awful* [ɔ]; *say* [e]; *back* [b]; *chair* [tʃ]; *do* [d]; *elm* [ɛ]; *eel* [i]; *server* [ˈɝ, ər]; *f*it [f]; *go* [g]; *h*urt [h]; *is* [ɪ]; *high* [aɪ]; *jet* [dʒ]; *k*iss [k]; *l*amb [l]; *my* [m]; *nice* [n];

cancan	KAN kan	ˈkænkæn
cancellation	kan suh LAY shuhn	kænsəˈleʃən
candelabra	kan duh LAH bruh	kændəˈlabrə
candelabrum	kan duh LAH bruhm	kændəˈlabrəm
candescent	kan DE suhnt	kænˈdɛsənt
Candia	KAN di uh	ˈkændiə
candid	KAND did	ˈkændɪd
Candida	KAN di duh	ˈkændɪdə
candidacy	KAN duh duh si	ˈkændədəsɪ
candidate	KAN duh dit	ˈkændədɪt
Candlemas	KAN duhl muhs	ˈkændəlməs
candor, candour	KAN der	ˈkændər
Canham	KAN uhm	ˈkænəm
Caniff	kuh NIF	kəˈnɪf
canine	KAY nighn	ˈkenaɪn
Canis	KAY nis	ˈkenɪs
canister	KA ni ster	ˈkænɪstər
canker	KANG ker	ˈkæŋkər
canna	KA nuh	ˈkænə
Cannes	kan	kæn
cannibal	KA nuh buhl	ˈkænəbəl
cannon	KA nuhn	ˈkænən
cannoneer	ka nuh NIR	kænəˈnɪr
canoe	kuh NOO:	kəˈnu
canon	KA nuhn	ˈkænən
cañon	KA nyuhn	ˈkænjən
canonical	kuh NAH ni kuhl	kəˈnɑnɪkəl
canonize	KA nuh nighz	ˈkænənaɪz
Canopus	kuh NOH puhs	kəˈnopəs
Canossa	kuh NAH suh	kəˈnɑsə
can't	kant	kænt
cant	kant	kænt
cantabile	kahn TAH bi lay	kɑnˈtɑbɪle
Cantabrigian	kan tuh BRI ji uhn	kæntəˈbrɪdʒɪən
cantalever	KAN tuh le ver	ˈkæntəlɛvər
cantaloup, -e	KAN tuh lohp	ˈkæntəlop
cantata	kuhn TAH tuh	kənˈtɑtə
canteen	kan TEEN	kæˈtin
Cantelli	kahn TE li	kɑnˈtɛlɪ
canter	KAN ter	ˈkæntər
Canterbury	KAN ter bai ri	ˈkæntərbɛrɪ
canticle	KAN ti kuhl	ˈkæntɪkəl
cantilever	KAN tuh le ver	ˈkæntəlɛvər
cantina	kan TEE nuh	kænˈtinə
Cantinflas	kahn TEEN flahs	kɑnˈtinflɑs
canto	KAN toh	ˈkænto
Canton (China)	kan TAHN	kænˈtɑn
canton, C- (U.S.)	KAN tuhn	ˈkæntən
cantonment	kan TAHN muhnt	kænˈtɑnmənt
cantor	KAN ter	ˈkæntər
Canuck	kuh NUHK	kəˈnʌk
canyon	KA nyuhn	ˈkænjən

---

sing [ŋ]; *oh* [o]; *oil* [ɔɪ]; *foot* [ʊ]; *foo*:d [u]; *how* [aʊ]; *pie* [p]; *ray* [r]; *so* [s]; *shall* [ʃ]; *to* [t]; *thin* [θ]; *th*:en [ð]; *above* (*uh* BUHV) [ə, ˈʌ]; *vine* [v]; *wine* [w]; *whine* [hw]; *you* [j]; *zoo* [z]; *rouge* (roo:*zh*) [ʒ].

canzone	kahnt SOH nay	kɑnt'sone
Caodaism	KOW digh i zuhm	'kaʊdaɪɪzəm
caoutchouc	KOO : chook	'kuchʊk
capacious	kuh PAY shuhs	kə'peʃəs
cap-a-pie	ka puh PEE	kæpə'pi
caparison	kuh PA ruh suhn	kə'pærəsən
capcom	KAP kahm	'kæpkɑm
Čapek, Karel	CHAH pek, KAH rel	'tʃapɛk, 'kɑrɛl
Capella	kuh PE luh	kə'pɛlə
caper	KAY per	'kepər
Capernaum	kuh PER ni uhm	kə'pɜˈnɪəm
Capetian	kuh PEE shuhn	kə'piʃən
Cape Verde	kayp VERD	kep 'vɜˈd
Capezio	kuh PEE zee oh	kə'pizio
caph	kahf	kɑf
capillary	KA puh lai ri	'kæpəlɛrɪ
capital	KA puh tuhl	'kæpətəl
capitalism	KA puh tuh li zuhm	'kæpətəlɪzəm
capitalist	KA puh tuh list	'kæpətəlɪst
capitol	KA puh tuhl	'kæpətəl
capitulate	kuh PI chyuh layt	kə'pɪtʃjəlet
capon	KAY puhn	'kepən
caporal	ka puh RAL	kæpə'ræl
Caporetto	ka puh RE toh	kæpə'rɛto
Capote, c-	kuh POH tee	kə'poti
capriccio	kuh PREE chi oh	kə'pritʃɪo
caprice	kuh PREES	kə'pris
capricious	kuh PRI shuhs	kə'prɪʃəs
Capricorn	KA pri kawrn	'kæprɪkɔrn
capsize	kap SIGHZ	kæp'saɪz
capsule	KAP suhl	'kæpsəl
captain	KAP tin	'kæptɪn
caption	KAP shuhn	'kæpʃən
captious	KAP shuhs	'kæpʃəs
captivate	KAP tuh vayt	'kæptəvet
captor	KAP ter	'kæptər
capture	KAP cher	'kæptʃər
capuchin, C-	KA pyoo chin	'kæpjʊtʃɪn
Capulet	KA pyoo let	'kæpjʊlɛt
caput	KAY puht	'kepət
carabao	kah ruh BAH oh	kɑrə'bɑo
Caracas	kuh RAH kuhs	kə'rɑkəs
caracul	KA ruh kuhl	'kærəkəl
carafe	kuh RAF	kə'ræf
caramel	KA ruh muhl	'kærəməl
carat	KA ruht	'kærət
caravan	KA ruh van	'kærəvæn
caravansary	ka ruh VAN suh ri	kærə'vænsərɪ
caravanserai	ka ruh VAN suh righ	kærə'vænsəraɪ
caravel	KA ruh vel	'kærəvɛl
caraway	KA ruh way	'kærəwe
carbide	KAHR bighd	'kɑrbaɪd

at [æ]; *ah* [ɑ]; *air* [ɛ]; *awful* [ɔ]; *say* [e]; *back* [b]; *chair* [tʃ]; *do* [d]; *elm* [ɛ]; *eel* [i]; *server* ['ɝ, ər]; *fit* [f]; *go* [g]; *hurt* [h]; *is* [ɪ]; *high* [aɪ]; *jet* [dʒ]; *kiss* [k]; *lamb* [l]; *my* [m]; *nice* [n];

carbine	KAHR bighn	ˈkɑrbaɪn
carbohydrate	kahr buh HIGH drayt	kɑrbəˈhaɪdret
carbolic	kahr BAH lik	kɑrˈbɑlɪk
carbon	KAHR buhn	ˈkɑrbən
Carbonari	kahr buh NAH ree	kɑrbəˈnɑri
carborundum, C-	kahr buh RUHN duhm	kɑrbəˈrʌndəm
carbuncle	KAHR buhng kuhl	ˈkɑrbəŋkəl
carburetor	KAHR buh ray ter	ˈkɑrbəretər
carcass	KAHR kuhs	ˈkɑrkəs
Carcassonne	kahr kah SAWN	kɑrkɑˈsɔn
carcinogen	kahr SI nuh juhn	kɑrˈsɪnədʒən
carcinoma	kahr suh NOH muh	kɑrsəˈnomə
cardamom	KAHR duh muhm	ˈkɑrdəməm
Cárdenas	KAHR de nahs	ˈkɑrdɛnɑs
cardiac	KAHR di ak	ˈkɑrdɪæk
cardiacal	kahr DIGH uh kuhl	kɑrˈdaɪəkəl
Cardiff	KAHR dif	ˈkɑrdɪf
cardigan, C-	KAHR di guhn	ˈkɑrdɪgən
Cardin	kahr DAN	kɑrˈdæn
cardinal	KAHR duh nuhl	ˈkɑrdənəl
Cardozo	kahr DOH zoh	kɑrˈdozo
Carducci	kahr DOO : chee	kɑrˈdutʃi
care, C-	kair	kɛr
careen	kuh REEN	kəˈrin
career	kuh RIR	kəˈrɪr
caress	kuh RES	kəˈrɛs
caret	KA rit	ˈkærɪt
Carew	kuh ROO :	kəˈru
Caria	KAH ri uh	ˈkɑrɪə
Carías	kah REE ahs	kɑˈriɑs
Caribbean	ka ri BEE uhn	kærɪˈbiən
caribou	KA ruh boo :	ˈkærəbu
caricature	KA ri kuh cher	ˈkærɪkətʃər
caricaturist	KA ri kuh chuh rist	ˈkærɪkətʃərɪst
caries	KAI reez	ˈkɛriz
carillon	KA ruh lahn	ˈkærəlɑn
Carlos	KAHR lohs	ˈkɑrlos
Carlovingian	kahr luh VIN ji uhn	kɑrləˈvɪndʒɪən
Carlsbad	KAHRLZ bad	ˈkɑrlzbæd
Carlsruhe	KAHRLZ roo : uh	ˈkɑrlzruə
carmagnole	KAHR muh nyohl	ˈkɑrmənjol
Carmel	kahr MEL	kɑrˈmɛl
Carmelite	KAHR muh light	ˈkɑrməlaɪt
Carmen	KAHR muhn	ˈkɑrmən
Carmichael	KAHR migh kuhl	ˈkɑrmaɪkəl
carmine	KAHR min	ˈkɑrmɪn
Carmona	kahr MOH nuh	kɑrˈmonə
carnage	KAHR nij	ˈkɑrnɪdʒ
carnation	kahr NAY shuhn	kɑrˈneʃən
Carnegie, Andrew	kahr NAY gi	kɑrˈnegɪ
Carnegie Hall	KAHR nuh gi	ˈkɑrnəgɪ
Carneiro	kahr NAY roh	kɑrˈnero

sing [ŋ] ; *oh* [o] ; *oil* [ɔɪ] ; *foot* [ʊ] ; *foo*:d [u] ; *how* [aʊ] ; *pie* [p] ; *ray* [r] ; *so* [s] ; *shall* [ʃ] ;
to [t] ; *thin* [θ] ; *th*:en [ð] ; above (*uh* B*UH*V) [ə, ˈʌ] ; *vine* [v] ; *wine* [w] ; *whine* [hw] ;
you [j] ; *zoo* [z] ; rouge (roo:*zh*) [ʒ].

Carnera	kahr NAI ruh	kɑrˈnɛrə
carnival	KAHR nuh vuhl	ˈkɑrnəvəl
Carnivora	kahr NI vuh ruh	kɑrˈnɪvərə
carnivorous	kahr NI vuh ruhs	kɑrˈnɪvərəs
carol, C-	KA ruhl	ˈkærəl
Carolina	ka ruh LIGH nuh	kærəˈlaɪnə
Caroline	KA ruh lighn	ˈkærəlaɪn
Carolingian	ka ruh LIN ji uhn	kærəˈlɪndʒɪən
Carolinian	ka ruh LI ni uhn	kærəˈlɪnɪən
carom	KA ruhm	ˈkærəm
Caron	kah ROHN	kɑˈron
carotid	kuh RAH tid	kəˈrɑtɪd
carousal	kuh ROW zuhl	kəˈraʊzəl
carouse	kuh ROWZ	kəˈraʊz
carousel	KA ruh sel	ˈkærəsɛl
Carpathia	kahr PAY thi uh	kɑrˈpeɪθɪə
Carpathian	kahr PAY thi uhn	kɑrˈpeɪθɪən
Carpatho-Ukraine	kahr PAY thoh yoo : KRAYN	kɑrˈpeɪθo juˈkren
carpe diem	KAHR pi DIGH em	ˈkɑrpɪ ˈdaɪɛm
Carradine	KA ruh deen	ˈkærədin
Carrara	kuh RAH ruh	kəˈrɑrə
carriage	KA rij	ˈkærɪdʒ
carrier	KA ri er	ˈkærɪər
carrot	KA ruht	ˈkærət
carrousel	KA ruh sel	ˈkærəsɛl
carry	KA ri	ˈkærɪ
Cartagena	kahr tuh JEE nuh	kɑrtəˈdʒinə
carte	kahrt	kɑrt
carte blanche	kahrt BLAHNSH	kɑrt ˈblɑnʃ
carte de visite	kahrt duh vee ZEET	kɑrt də viˈzit
carte du jour	kahrt doo ZHOOR	kɑrt du ˈʒur
cartel	kahr TEL	kɑrˈtɛl
Cartesian	kahr TEE zhuhn	kɑrˈtiʒən
Carthage	KAHR thij	ˈkɑrθɪdʒ
Carthaginian	kahr thuh JI ni uhn	kɑrθəˈdʒɪnɪən
Carthusian	kahr THOO : zhuhn	kɑrˈθuʒən
Cartier	kahr TYAY	kɑrˈtje
cartilage	KAHR tuh lij	ˈkɑrtəlɪdʒ
cartilaginous	kahr tuh LA juh nuhs	kɑrtəˈlædʒənəs
cartographer	kahr TAH gruh fer	kɑrˈtɑgrəfər
cartography	kahr TAH gruh fi	kɑrˈtɑgrəfɪ
carton	KAHR tuhn	ˈkɑrtən
cartoon	kahr TOO : N	kɑrˈtun
cartouch, -e	kahr TOO : SH	kɑrˈtuʃ
cartridge	KAHR trij	ˈkɑrtrɪdʒ
Caruso	kuh ROO : soh	kəˈruso
caryatid	ka ri A tid	kærɪˈætɪd
casaba	kuh SAH buh	kəˈsɑbə
Casabianca	ka suh bi ANG kuh	kæsəbɪˈæŋkə
Casablanca	ka suh BLANG kuh	kæsəˈblæŋkə
Casadesus	ka sat SOO	kæsætˈsu

at [æ]; *ah* [ɑ]; *air* [ɛ]; *awful* [ɔ]; *say* [e]; *back* [b]; *chair* [tʃ]; *do* [d]; *elm* [ɛ]; *eel* [i]; *server* [ˈɝ, ər]; *f*it [f]; *go* [g]; *h*urt [h]; *is* [ɪ]; *high* [aɪ]; *jet* [dʒ]; *kiss* [k]; *l*amb [l]; *my* [m]; *n*ice [n];

Casals	kah SAHLS	kɑˈsɑls
Casanova	ka zuh NOH vuh	kæzəˈnovə
casba, -h, K-	KAHZ bah	ˈkɑzbɑ
cascade	ka SKAYD	kæˈsked
cascara	ka SKAI ruh	kæˈskɛrə
casein	KAY seen	ˈkesin
casement	KAYS muhnt	ˈkesmənt
cashew	KA shoo :	ˈkæʃu
cashier	ka SHIR	kæˈʃɪr
cashmere	KASH mir	ˈkæʃmɪr
Cashmere (India)	kash MIR	kæʃˈmɪr
Casimir	KA suh mir	ˈkæsəmɪr
casing	KAY sing	ˈkesɪŋ
casino	kuh SEE noh	kəˈsino
cask	kask	kæsk
casque	kask	kæsk
casket	KA skit	ˈkæskɪt
Caspian	KA spi uhn	ˈkæspɪən
cassaba	kuh SAH buh	kəˈsɑbə
Cassandra	kuh SAN druh	kəˈsændrə
cassava	kah SAH vuh	kɑˈsɑvə
casserole	KA suh rohl	ˈkæsərol
cassia	KA shuh	ˈkæʃə
cassimere	KA suh mir	ˈkæsəmɪr
Cassini	kah SEE ni	kɑˈsini
cassino	kuh SEE noh	kəˈsino
Cassiopeia	ka si uh PEE uh	kæsɪəˈpiə
cassock	KA suhk	ˈkæsək
cassowary	KA suh wai ri	ˈkæsəwɛri
cast	kast	kæst
castanet	ka stuh NET	kæstəˈnɛt
castaway	KA stuh way	ˈkæstəwe
caste	kast	kæst
castigate	KA stuh gayt	ˈkæstəget
Castiglione	kah stee LYAW ne	kɑstiˈljɔnɛ
Castiglioni	kah stee LYAW nee	kɑstiˈljoni
castile, C-	ka STEEL	kæˈstil
Castile (N.Y.)	ka STIGHL	kæˈstaɪl
Castilian	ka STI lyuhn	kæˈstɪljən
Castillo	ka STEE yoh	kæˈstijo
castle	KA suhl	ˈkæsəl
castor, C-	KA ster	ˈkæstər
castrate	KA strayt	ˈkæstret
Castro	KA stroh	ˈkæstro
casual	KA zhoo uhl	ˈkæʒuəl
casualty	KA zhool ti	ˈkæʒʊltɪ
casuist	KA zhoo ist	ˈkæʒuɪst
casuistry	KA zhoo i stri	ˈkæʒuɪstrɪ
casus belli	KAY suhs BE ligh	ˈkesəs ˈbɛlaɪ
catabolism	kuh TA buh li zuhm	kəˈtæbəlɪzəm
catachresis	ka tuh KREE sis	kætəˈkrisɪs
cataclysm	KA tuh kli zuhm	ˈkætəklɪzəm

sing [ŋ] ; oh [o] ; oil [ɔɪ] ; foot [ʊ] ; foo:d [u] ; how [aʊ] ; pie [p] ; ray [r] ; so [s] ; shall [ʃ] ;
to [t] ; thin [θ] ; th:en [ð] ; above (uh BUHV) [ə, ˈʌ] ; vine [v] ; wine [w] ; whine [hw] ;
you [j] ; zoo [z] ; rouge (roo:zh) [ʒ].

catacomb	KA tuh kohm	ˈkætəkom
catafalque	KA tuh falk	ˈkætəfælk
Catalan	KA tuh lan	ˈkætəlæn
catalepsy	KA tuh lep si	ˈkætəlɛpsɪ
catalog, -ue	KA tuh lawg	ˈkætəlɔg
catalpa	kuh TAL puh	kəˈtælpə
catalysis	kuh TA luh sis	kəˈtæləsɪs
catalyst	KA tuh list	ˈkætəlɪst
catamaran	ka tuh muh RAN	kætəməˈræn
catamite	KA tuh might	ˈkætəmaɪt
catapult	KA tuh puhlt	ˈkætəpʌlt
cataract	KA tuh rakt	ˈkætərækt
catarrh	kuh TAHR	kəˈtɑr
catastrophe	kuh TA struh fi	kəˈtæstrəfɪ
catastrophic	ka tuh STRAH fik	kætəˈstrɑfɪk
Catawba, c-	kuh TAW buh	kəˈtɔbə
catcall	KAT kawl	ˈkætkɔl
catch	kach	kætʃ
catchup	KA chuhp	ˈkætʃəp
categorical	ka tuh GAW ri kuhl	kætəˈgɔrɪkəl
categorize	KA tuh guh righz	ˈkætəgəraɪz
category	KA tuh gaw ri	ˈkætəgɔrɪ
cater	KAY ter	ˈketər
cater-corner	KA ter kawr ner	ˈkætərkɔrnər
caterer	KAY tuh rer	ˈketərər
caterpillar	KA ter pi ler	ˈkætərpɪlər
caterwaul	KA ter wawl	ˈkætərwɔl
catharsis	kuh THAHR sis	kəˈθɑrsɪs
cathartic	kuh THAHR tik	kəˈθɑrtɪk
Cathay	kuh THAY	kəˈθe
cathect	kuh THEKT	kəˈθɛkt
cathedral	kuh THEE druhl	kəˈθidrəl
cathepsin	kuh THEP sin	kəˈθɛpsɪn
Cather, Willa	KA th : er, WI luh	ˈkæðər, ˈwɪlə
catheter	KA thuh ter	ˈkæθətər
cathode	KA thohd	ˈkæθod
catholic, C-	KA thuh lik	ˈkæθəlɪk
catholicism, C-	kuh THAH luh si zuhm	kəˈθɑləsɪzəm
catholicity	ka thuh LI suh ti	kæθəˈlɪsətɪ
Cato	KAY toh	ˈketo
Catroux	ka TROO :	kæˈtru
catsup	KA chup	ˈkætʃəp
Catullus	kuh TUH luhs	kəˈtʌləs
Caucasia	kaw KAY zhuh	kɔˈkeʒə
Caucasian	kaw KAY zhuhn	kɔˈkeʒən
Caucasus	KAW kuh suhs	ˈkɔkəsəs
caucus	KAW kuhs	ˈkɔkəs
caudal	KAW duhl	ˈkɔdəl
caudillo, C-	kaw DEE lyoh	kɔˈdiljo
caudle	KAW duhl	ˈkɔdəl
caught	kawt	kɔt
cauldron	KAWL druhn	ˈkɔldrən

at [æ] ; ah [ɑ] ; air [ɛ] ; awful [ɔ] ; say [e] ; back [b] ; chair [tʃ] ; do [d] ; elm [ɛ] ; eel [i] ; server [ˈɜ, ər] ; fit [f] ; go [g] ; hurt [h] ; is [ɪ] ; high [aɪ] ; jet [dʒ] ; kiss [k] ; lamb [l] ; my [m] ; nice [n] ;

cauliflower	KAW luh flow er	ˈkɔləflauər
caulk	kawk	kɔk
causal	KAW zuhl	ˈkɔzəl
causality	kaw ZA luh ti	kɔˈzælətɪ
causative	KAW zuh tiv	ˈkɔzətɪv
cause	kawz	kɔz
cause célèbre	kohz say LE bruh	koz seˈlɛbrə
causerie	koh zuh REE	kozəˈri
causeway	KAWZ way	ˈkɔzwe
caustic	KAW stik	ˈkɔstɪk
cauterize	KAW tuh righz	ˈkɔtəraɪz
caution	KAW shuhn	ˈkɔʃən
cautionary	KAW shuh nai ri	ˈkɔʃənɛrɪ
cavalcade	ka vuhl KAYD	kævəlˈked
cavalier, C-	ka vuh LIR	kævəˈlɪr
Cavalleria Rusticana	kah vah lay REE uh roo : sti KAH nuh	kavaleˈriə rustɪˈkanə
cavatina	ka vuh TEE nuh	kævəˈtinə
caveat	KAY vi at	ˈkevɪæt
caveat emptor	KAY vi at EMP tawr	ˈkevɪæt ˈɛmptɔr
cave canem	KAY vi KAY nem	ˈkevɪ ˈkenɛm
Cavell	KA vuhl	ˈkævəl
Cavendish	KA vuhn dish	ˈkævəndɪʃ
cavern	KA vern	ˈkævərn
cavernous	KA ver nuhs	ˈkævərnəs
cavetto	kuh VE toh	kəˈvɛto
caviar, -e	KA vi ahr	ˈkævɪɑr
cavil	KA vuhl	ˈkævəl
cavitation	ka vi TAY shuhn	kævɪˈteʃən
Cavite	kah VEE tay	kɑˈvite
cavort	kuh VAWRT	kəˈvɔrt
Cavour	kah VOOR	kɑˈvur
Cawnpore	kawn POHR	kɔnˈpor
Caxton	KAK stuhn	ˈkækstən
cayenne, C-	kigh EN	kaɪˈɛn
cayman	KAY muhn	ˈkemən
Cayman (islands)	kigh MAHN	kaɪˈman
Cayuga	kigh YOO : guh	kaɪˈyugə
cayuse, C-	kigh YOO : S	kaɪˈyus
Cebu	say BOO :	seˈbu
Cecil (U.S.)	SEE sil	ˈsisɪl
Cecil (British)	SE suhl	ˈsɛsəl
cedar	SEE der	ˈsidər
cede	seed	sid
cedilla	si DI luh	sɪˈdɪlə
ceiling	SEE ling	ˈsilɪŋ
celandine	SE luhn dighn	ˈsɛləndaɪn
celanese, C-	SE luh neez	ˈsɛləniz
Celebes	SE luh beez	ˈsɛləbiz
celebrant	SE luh bruhnt	ˈsɛləbrənt
celebrate	SE luh brayt	ˈsɛləbret
celebrity	suh LE bruh ti	səˈlɛbrətɪ

sing [ŋ]; oh [o]; oil [ɔɪ]; foot [ʊ]; foo:d [u]; how [au]; pie [p]; ray [r]; so [s]; shall [ʃ]; to [t]; thin [θ]; th:en [ð]; above (uh BUHV) [ə, ˈʌ]; vine [v]; wine [w]; whine [hw]; you [j]; zoo [z]; rouge (roo:zh) [ʒ].

celerity	suh LE ruh ti	səˈlɛrətɪ
celery	SE luh ri	ˈsɛlərɪ
celesta	suh LE stuh	səˈlɛstə
celestial	suh LES chuhl	səˈlɛstʃəl
celiac	SEE li ak	ˈsilɪæk
celibacy	SE luh buh si	ˈsɛləbəsɪ
celibate	SE luh bit	ˈsɛləbɪt
Cellini	chuh LEE ni	tʃəˈlinɪ
cellist	CHE list	ˈtʃɛlɪst
cello	CHE loh	ˈtʃɛlo
cellophane	SE luh fayn	ˈsɛləfen
cellular	SE lyoo ler	ˈsɛljʊlər
celluloid, C-	SE lyoo loid	ˈsɛljʊlɔɪd
cellulose	SE lyoo lohs	ˈsɛljʊlos
celotex, C-	SE luh teks	ˈsɛlətɛks
Celt	selt	sɛlt
Celtic	SEL tik	ˈsɛltɪk
celtuce	SEL tis	ˈsɛltɪs
cement	si MENT	sɪˈmɛnt
cemetery	SE muh tai ri	ˈsɛmətɛrɪ
Cenci	CHEN chi	ˈtʃɛntʃɪ
Cenis	suh NEE	səˈni
cenotaph	SE nuh taf	ˈsɛnətæf
censer	SEN ser	ˈsɛnsər
censor	SEN ser	ˈsɛnsər
censorious	sen SAW ri uhs	sɛnˈsɔrɪəs
censorship	SEN ser ship	ˈsɛnsərʃɪp
censure	SEN sher	ˈsɛnʃər
census	SEN suhs	ˈsɛnsəs
centaur, C-	SEN tawr	ˈsɛntɔr
Centaurus	sen TAW ruhs	sɛnˈtɔrəs
centavo	sen TAH voh	sɛnˈtɑvo
centenary	SEN tuh nai ri	ˈsɛntənɛrɪ
centennial	sen TE ni uhl	sɛnˈtɛnɪəl
centigrade	SEN tuh grayd	ˈsɛntəgred
centime	SAHN teem	ˈsɑntim
centimeter	SEN tuh mee ter	ˈsɛntəmitər
centipede	SEN tuh peed	ˈsɛntəpid
cento	SEN toh	ˈsɛnto
centrifugal	sen TRI fyoo guhl	sɛnˈtrɪfjʊgəl
centrifuge	SEN truh fyoo:j	ˈsɛntrəfjudʒ
centripetal	sen TRI puh tuhl	sɛnˈtrɪpətəl
century	SEN chuh ri	ˈsɛntʃərɪ
cephalic	suh FA lik	səˈfælɪk
cephalopod	SE fuh luh pahd	ˈsɛfələpɑd
Cephalus	SE fuh luhs	ˈsɛfələs
Cephas	SEE fuhs	ˈsifəs
Cepheid	SE fi id	ˈsefɪd
Cepheus	SEE fyoo:s	ˈsifjus
Ceram	si RAM	sɪˈræm
ceramic	suh RA mik	səˈræmɪk
ceramist	SE ruh mist	ˈsɛrəmɪst

at [æ]; ah [ɑ]; air [ɛ]; awful [ɔ]; say [e]; back [b]; chair [tʃ]; do [d]; elm [ɛ]; eel [i]; server [ˈɜ, ər]; fit [f]; go [g]; hurt [h]; is [ɪ]; high [aɪ]; jet [dʒ]; kiss [k]; lamb [l]; my [m]; nice [n];

Cerberus	SER buh ruhs	ˈsɚbərəs
cere	sir	sɪr
cerebellum	se ruh BE luhm	sɛrəˈbɛləm
cerebral	SE ruh bruhl	ˈsɛrəbrəl
cerebrate	SE ruh brayt	ˈsɛrəbret
cerebrum	SE ruh bruhm	ˈsɛrəbrəm
cerement	SIR muhnt	ˈsɪrmənt
ceremonial	se ruh MOH ni uhl	sɛrəˈmonɪəl
ceremony	SE ruh moh ni	ˈsɛrəmonɪ
Ceres	SI reez	ˈsɪriz
Cerf	serf	ˈsɚf
cerise	suh REEZ	səˈriz
certain	SER tuhn	ˈsɚtən
certificate	ser TI fuh kit	sərˈtɪfəkɪt
certification	ser tuh fi KAY shuhn	sɚtəfɪˈkeʃən
certify	SER tuh figh	ˈsɚtəfaɪ
certiorari	ser shi uh RAI ri	sɚʃɪəˈrɛrɪ
certitude	SER tuh too:d	ˈsɚtətud
cerumen	suh ROO: muhn	səˈrumən
Cervantes	ser VAN teez	sərˈvæntiz
cervical	SER vi kuhl	ˈsɚvɪkəl
cervix	SER viks	ˈsɚvɪks
Cesarea	se suh REE uh	sɛsəˈriə
cessation	se SAY shuhn	sɛˈseʃən
cestus	SE stuhs	ˈsɛstəs
cetane	SEE tayn	ˈsiten
ceteris paribus	SE tuh ris PA ri buhs	ˈsɛtərɪs ˈpærɪbəs
Cetus	SEE tuhs	ˈsitəs
Ceylon	si LAHN	sɪˈlɑn
Ceylonese	see luh NEEZ	sɪləˈniz
Ceyx	SEE iks	ˈsiɪks
Cézanne	say ZAHN	seˈzɑn
cha-cha	CHAH chah	ˈtʃɑtʃɑ
Chaco	CHAH koh	ˈtʃɑko
chaconne	shah KAWN	ʃɑˈkɔn
Chad	chad	tʃæd
chafe	chayf	tʃef
chaff	chaf	tʃæf
chaffinch	CHA finch	ˈtʃæfɪntʃ
Chagall	shah GAHL	ʃɑˈgɑl
Chagres	CHAH gres	ˈtʃɑgrɛs
chagrin	shuh GRIN	ʃəˈgrɪn
Chahar	CHAH hahr	ˈtʃɑhɑr
chaise	shayz	ʃez
chaise longue	shayz LAWNG	ʃez ˈlɔŋ
Chaikovsky	chigh KAWF ski	tʃaɪˈkɔfskɪ
Chalcedon	KAL si duhn	ˈkælsɪdən
chalcedony	kal SE duh ni	kælˈsɛdənɪ
Chaldea	kal DEE uh	kælˈdiə
Chaldean	kal DEE uhn	kælˈdiən
Chaldee	kal DEE	kælˈdi
chalet	sha LAY	ʃæˈle

sing [ŋ]; oh [o]; oil [ɔɪ]; foot [ʊ]; foo:d [u]; how [aʊ]; pie [p]; ray [r]; so [s]; shall [ʃ]; to [t]; thin [θ]; th:en [ð]; above (uh BUHV) [ə, ˈʌ]; vine [v]; wine [w]; whine [hw]; you [j]; zoo [z]; rouge (roo:zh) [ʒ].

Chaliapin	shah li AH pin	ʃɑlɪˈɑpɪn
chalice	CHA lis	ˈtʃælɪs
chalk	chawk	tʃɔk
challis	SHA li	ˈʃælɪ
cham, C-	kam	kæm
chamberlain, C-	CHAYM ber lin	ˈtʃembərlɪn
chambray	SHAM bray	ˈʃæmbre
chameleon	kuh MEE li uhn	kəˈmilɪən
chamois	SHA mi	ˈʃæmɪ
chamomile	KA muh mighl	ˈkæməmaɪl
Chamorro	chah MAW roh	tʃɑmˈmɔro
champagne, C-	sham PAYN	ʃæmˈpen
champaign, C-	sham PAYN	ʃæmˈpen
champion	CHAM pi uhn	ˈtʃæmpɪən
Champlain	sham PLAYN	ʃæmˈplen
Champs Elysées	shahn zay lee ZAY	ʃɑnzeliˈze
Chanaka	chuh NAH kuh	tʃəˈnɑkə
chancel	CHAN suhl	ˈtʃænsəl
chancellery	CHAN suh luh ri	ˈtʃænsələrɪ
chancellor	CHAN suh ler	ˈtʃænsələr
chancery	CHAN suh ri	ˈtʃænsərɪ
chancre	SHANG ker	ˈʃæŋkər
chandelier	shan duh LIR	ʃændəˈlɪr
Chanel	shuh NEL	ʃəˈnɛl
Changchow	chang chow	tʃæŋ tʃau
Changchun	chahng choon	tʃæŋ tʃun
changeling	CHAYNJ ling	ˈtʃendʒlɪŋ
Changsha	chahng shah	tʃɑŋ ʃɑ
Changteh	chahng te	tʃɑŋ tɛ
chanson	shahn SAWN	ʃɑnˈsɔn
chanteuse	shahn TERZ	ʃɑnˈtɝz
chantey	CHAN ti	ˈtʃæntɪ
chanticleer	CHAN ti klir	ˈtʃæntɪklɪr
Chantilly, c-	shan TI li	ʃænˈtɪlɪ
chanty	CHAN ti	ˈtʃæntɪ
Chanukah	HAH noo kuh	ˈhɑnʊkə
Chaochow	chow joh	tʃau dʒo
chaos	KAY ahs	ˈkeɑs
chaotic	kay AH tik	keˈɑtɪk
chap	chap	tʃæp
chaparajos	chah puh RAH hohs	tʃɑpəˈrɑhos
chaparral	cha puh RAL	tʃæpəˈræl
chapeau	sha POH	ʃæˈpo
chaperon, -e	SHA puh rohn	ˈʃæpəron
chapfallen	CHAP faw luhn	ˈtʃæpfɔlən
chaplain	CHA plin	ˈtʃæplɪn
Chaplin	CHA plin	ˈtʃæplɪn
Chapultepec	chuh POOL tuh pek	tʃəˈpʊltəpɛk
chaqueta	chah KAY tuh	tʃɑˈketə
char	chahr	tʃɑr
char-a-banc	SHA ruh bangk	ˈʃærəbæŋk
character	KA ruhk ter	ˈkærəktər

at [æ]; ah [ɑ]; air [ɛ]; awful [ɔ]; say [e]; back [b]; chair [tʃ]; do [d]; elm [ɛ]; eel [i];
server [ˈɝ, ər]; fit [f]; go [g]; hurt [h]; is [ɪ]; high [aɪ]; jet [dʒ]; kiss [k]; lamb [l]; my [m];
nice [n];

characteristic	ka ruhk tuh RI stik	kærəktə'rɪstɪk
charade	shuh RAYD	ʃə'red
charcoal	CHAHR kohl	'tʃɑrkol
chargeable	CHAHR juh buhl	'tʃɑrdʒəbəl
chargé d'affaires	shahr ZHAY da FAIR	ʃɑr'ʒe dæ'fɛr
charily	CHAI ruh li	'tʃɛrəlɪ
chariot	CHA ri uht	'tʃærɪət
charioteer	cha ri uh TIR	tʃærɪə'tɪr
charisma	kuh RIZ muh	kə'rɪzmə
charismatic	ka riz MA tik	kærɪz'mætɪk
charitable	CHA ruh tuh buhl	'tʃærətəbəl
charity	CHA ruh ti	'tʃærətɪ
charivari	shuh ri vuh REE	ʃərɪvə'ri
charlatan	SHAHR luh tuhn	'ʃɑrlətən
Charlemagne	SHAHR luh mayn	'ʃɑrləmen
Charles (French)	shahrl	ʃɑrl
Charleston	CHAHRLZ tuhn	'tʃɑrlztən
Charlotte, c-	SHAHR luht	'ʃɑrlət
Charon	KAY ruhn	'kerən
Chartism	CHAHR ti zuhm	'tʃɑrtɪzəm
Chartres	SHAHR truh	'ʃɑrtrə
chartreuse, C-	shahr TRERZ	ʃɑr'trɝz
chary	CHAI ri	'tʃɛrɪ
Charybdis	kuh RIB dis	kə'rɪbdɪs
Chasins	CHAY sinz	'tʃesɪnz
chasm	KA zuhm	'kæzəm
chassé	sha SAY	ʃæ'se
chasseur	sha SER	ʃæ'sɝ
chassis	SHA si	'ʃæsɪ
chaste	chayst	tʃest
chasten	CHAY suhn	'tʃesən
chastise	CHA stighz	'tʃæstaɪz
chastisement	cha STIGHZ muhnt	tʃæ'staɪzmənt
chastity	CHA stuh ti	'tʃæstətɪ
chasuble	CHA zyoo buhl	'tʃæzjʊbəl
château	sha TOH	ʃæ'to
Chateaubriand	sha toh bree AHN	ʃætobri'ɑn
Château-Thierry	sha toh tye REE	ʃætotje'ri
châtelaine	SHA tuh layn	'ʃætəlen
Chatham	CHA tuhm	'tʃætəm
Chattanooga	cha tuh NOO : guh	tʃætə'nugə
chattel	CHA tuhl	'tʃætəl
Chaucer	CHAW ser	'tʃɔsər
Chaucerian	chaw SI ri uhn	tʃɔ'sɪrɪən
chauffeur	SHOH fer	'ʃofər
chaulmoogra	chawl MOO : gruh	tʃɔl'mugrə
chaussure	shoh SOOR	ʃo'sʊr
Chautauqua	shuh TAW kwuh	ʃə'tɔkwə
chauvinism	SHOH vi ni zuhm	'ʃovɪnɪzəm
chauvinistic	shoh vi NI stik	ʃovɪ'nɪstɪk
Chaves	CHAH ves	'tʃɑvɛs
Chavez	CHAH ves	'tʃɑvɛs

---

sing [ŋ] ; *oh* [o] ; *oi*l [ɔɪ] ; foot [ʊ] ; foo:d [u] ; how [aʊ] ; *p*ie [p] ; ray [r] ; so [s] ; *sh*all [ʃ] ;
to [t] ; *th*in [θ] ; *th*:en [ð] ; above (*uh* B*UH*V) [ə, 'ʌ] ; *v*ine [v] ; *w*ine [w] ; *wh*ine [hw] ;
*y*ou [j] ; *z*oo [z] ; rouge (roo:*zh*) [ʒ].

Chayefsky	chigh EF skee	tʃaɪˈɛfski
Cheddar	CHE der	ˈtʃɛdər
cheese	cheez	tʃiz
cheetah	CHEE tuh	ˈtʃitə
chef	shef	ʃɛf
chef-d'oeuvre	she DER vruh	ʃɛˈdɝvrə
Chefoo	chee foo :	tʃi fu
Chekhov	CHE kawf	ˈtʃɛkɔf
Chelsea	CHEL si	ˈtʃɛlsɪ
chemical	KE mi kuhl	ˈkɛmɪkəl
chemise	shuh MEEZ	ʃəˈmiz
chemistry	KE mi stri	ˈkɛmɪstrɪ
Chemnitz	KEM nits	ˈkɛmnɪts
chemurgy	KE mer ji	ˈkɛmərdʒɪ
Chengtu	cheng too :	tʃɛŋ tu
Chenier	shay NYAY	ʃeˈnje
chenille	shuh NEEL	ʃəˈnil
Chennault	shuh NAWLT	ʃəˈnɔlt
Cheops	KEE ahps	ˈkiɑps
cheque	chek	tʃɛk
chequer	CHE ker	ˈtʃɛkər
Cherbourg	SHAIR boorg	ˈʃɛrburg
cherchez la femme	shair shay luh FAM	ʃɛrʃeləˈfæm
Cherith	KI rith	ˈkɪrɪθ
Cherne	chern	tʃɝn
Cherokee	CHE ruh kee	ˈtʃɛrəki
cheroot	shuh ROO : T	ʃəˈrut
cherub	CHE ruhb	ˈtʃɛrəb
cherubic	chuh ROO : bik	tʃəˈrubɪk
chervil	CHER vil	ˈtʃɝvɪl
Chesapeake	CHE suh peek	ˈtʃɛsəpik
Cheshire	CHE sher	ˈtʃɛʃər
chestnut	CHES nuht	ˈtʃɛsnət
cheval-de-frise	shuh VAL duh FREEZ	ʃəˈvældəˈfriz
chevalier	she vuh LIR	ʃɛvəˈlɪr
Chevalier	shuh val YAY	ʃəvælˈye
cheviot (cloth)	SHE vi uht	ˈʃɛvɪət
cheviot, C- (sheep ; hills)	CHE vi uht	ˈtʃɛvɪət
Chevrolet	SHE vruh lay	ˈʃɛvrəle
chevron	SHE vruhn	ˈʃɛvrən
chevy	CHE vi	ˈtʃɛvɪ
chew	choo :	tʃu
Cheyenne	shigh EN	ʃaɪˈɛn
Chiang Kai-shek	chi AHNG KIGH SHEK	tʃɪˈɑŋ ˈkaɪ ˈʃɛk
Chianti	ki AN ti	kɪˈæntɪ
chiaroscuro	ki ah ruh SKYOO roh	kɪɑrəˈskjuro
chiasma	kigh AZ muh	kaɪˈæzmə
chic	sheek	ʃik
Chicago	shuh KAH goh	ʃəˈkɑgo
chicane	shi KAYN	ʃɪˈken
chicanery	shi KAY nuh ri	ʃɪˈkenərɪ

at [æ]; ah [ɑ]; air [ɛ]; awful [ɔ]; say [e]; back [b]; chair [tʃ]; do [d]; elm [ɛ]; eel [i]; server [ˈɝ, ər]; fit [f]; go [g]; hurt [h]; is [ɪ]; high [aɪ]; jet [dʒ]; kiss [k]; lamb [l]; my [m]; nice [n];

chichi	SHEE shee	ˈʃiʃi
Chichibu	chee chee BOO:	tʃitʃiˈbu
chicle	CHI kuhl	ˈtʃɪkəl
Chico, c-	CHEE koh	ˈtʃiko
chicory	CHI kuh ri	ˈtʃɪkərɪ
chieftain	CHEEF tuhn	ˈtʃiftən
Chiesa	ki AY zuh	kɪˈezə
chiffon	shi FAHN	ʃɪˈfɑn
chiffonier	shi fuh NIR	ʃɪfəˈnɪr
chigger	CHI ger	ˈtʃɪgər
chignon	SHEE nyahn	ˈʃinjɑn
Chihuahua	chi WAH wah	tʃɪˈwɑwɑ
chilblain	CHIL blayn	ˈtʃɪlblen
Chile	CHI li	ˈtʃɪlɪ
chile con carne	CHI li kahn KAHR ni	ˈtʃɪlɪ kɑn ˈkɑrnɪ
chili	CHI li	ˈtʃɪlɪ
Chillon	shuh LAHN	ʃəˈlɑn
chimera, chimaera	kuh MI ruh	kəˈmɪrə
chimerical	kuh MI ri kuhl	kəˈmɪrɪkəl
chimpanzee	chim pan ZEE	tʃɪmpænˈzi
China	CHIGH nuh	ˈtʃaɪnə
chinchilla	chin CHI luh	tʃɪnˈtʃɪlə
Chindwin	CHIN dwin	ˈtʃɪndwɪn
chine	chighn	tʃaɪn
Chinese	chigh NEEZ	tʃaɪˈniz
Chino-	CHIGH noh	ˈtʃaɪno
chino	CHEE noh	ˈtʃino
Chinook	chi NOO: K	tʃɪˈnuk
Chios	KIGH ahs	ˈkaɪɑs
Chippendale	CHI puhn dayl	ˈtʃɪpəndel
Chippewa	CHI puh wah	ˈtʃɪpəwɑ
Chiriboga	chee ree BAW gah	tʃiriˈbɔgɑ
Chirico, Giorgio de	kee REE koh, JAWR joh duh	kiˈriko, ˈdʒɔrdʒo də
chiromancy	KIGH ruh man si	ˈkaɪrəmænsɪ
Chiron	KIGH rahn	ˈkaɪrɑn
chiropodist	kigh RAH puh dist	kaɪˈrɑpədɪst
chiropody	kigh RAH puh di	kaɪˈrɑpədɪ
chiropractor	KIGH ruh prak ter	ˈkaɪrəpræktər
chirrup	CHI ruhp	ˈtʃɪrəp
chisel	CHI zuhl	ˈtʃɪzəl
Chisholm	CHI zuhm	ˈtʃɪzəm
chitterling	CHI ter ling	ˈtʃɪtərlɪŋ
chivalric	shi VAL rik	ʃɪˈvælrɪk
chivalrous	SHI vuhl ruhs	ˈʃɪvəlrəs
chivalry	SHI vuhl ri	ˈʃɪvəlrɪ
chive	chighv	tʃaɪv
chivy, chivvy	CHI vi	ˈtʃɪvɪ
chlamys	KLAY mis	ˈklemɪs
Chloe, Chloë	KLOH i	ˈkloɪ
chlorate (n)	KLAW rit	ˈklɔrɪt
chlorate (v)	KLAW rayt	ˈklɔret
chloride	KLOH righd	ˈkloraɪd

---

sing [ŋ] ; *oh* [o] ; *oil* [ɔɪ] ; *foot* [ʊ] ; *foo:d* [u] ; *how* [aʊ] ; *pie* [p] ; *ray* [r] ; *so* [s] ; *shall* [ʃ] ;
to [t] ; *thin* [θ] ; *th:en* [ð] ; *above* (*uh* B*UH*V) [ə, ˈʌ] ; *vine* [v] ; *wine* [w] ; *whine* [hw] ;
ou [j] ; *zoo* [z] ; *rouge* (roo:zh) [ʒ].

chlorinate	KLOH ri nayt	ˈklorɪnet
chlorine	KLOH reen	ˈklorin
chloroform	KLOH ruh fawrm	ˈklorəfɔrm
chloromycetin	kloh ruh migh SEE tin	klorəmaɪˈsitɪn
chlorophyl, -l	KLOH ruh fil	ˈklorəfɪl
chloroquine	KLOH ruh kwin	ˈklorəkwɪn
Choate	choht	tʃot
chock	chahk	tʃɑk
chock-full	chahk fool	tʃɑk fʊl
chocolate	CHAH klit	ˈtʃɑklɪt
Choctaw	CHAKH taw	ˈtʃɑktɔ
choir	kwighr	kwaɪr
Choiseul	shwah ZERL	ʃwaˈzɝl
choler	KAH ler	ˈkɑlər
cholera	KAH luh ruh	ˈkɑlərə
choleric	KAH luh rik	ˈkɑlərɪk
cholesterol	kuh LE stuh rohl	kəˈlɛstərol
Cholmondeley	CHUHM li	ˈtʃʌmlɪ
Chopin	SHOH pan	ˈʃopæn
chop suey	chahp SOO : i	tʃɑp ˈsuɪ
choral (a)	KAW ruhl	ˈkɔrəl
choral, -e (n)	kuh RAL	kəˈræl
Chorazin	koh RAY zin	koˈrezɪn
chord	kawrd	kɔrd
chore	chawr	tʃɔr
chorea	kaw REE uh	kɔˈriə
choreographer	kaw ri AH gruh fer	kɔrɪˈɑgrəfər
choreography	kaw ri AH gruh fi	kɔrɪˈɑgrəfɪ
choric	KAW rik	ˈkɔrɪk
chorine	KAW reen	ˈkɔrin
chorister	KAW ri ster	ˈkɔrɪstər
chorography	kaw RAH gruh fi	kəˈrɑgrəfɪ
chortle	CHAWR tuhl	ˈtʃɔrtəl
Chosen	choh sen	tʃo sɛn
Chou En-lai	joh en LIGH	dʒo ɛn ˈlaɪ
chough	chuhf	tʃʌf
chow	chow	tʃaʊ
chowchow	CHOW chow	ˈtʃaʊtʃaʊ
chowder	CHOW der	ˈtʃaʊdər
chow mein	chow MAYN	tʃaʊˈmen
chrestomathy	kre STAH muh thi	krɛˈstɑməθɪ
christen	KRI suhn	ˈkrɪsən
Christendom	KRI suhn duhm	ˈkrɪsəndəm
Christian	KRIS chuhn	ˈkrɪstʃən
Christiania	kris chi A ni uh	krɪstʃɪˈænɪə
Christianity	kris chi A nuh ti	krɪstʃɪˈænətɪ
Christmas	KRIS muhs	ˈkrɪsməs
Christoff, Boris	kris TAWF, baw REES	krɪsˈtɔf, bɔˈris
Christophe	kree STAWF	kriˈstɔf
Christopher	KRI stuh fer	ˈkrɪstəfər
chromatic	kroh MA tik	kroˈmætɪk
chrome	krohm	krom

at [æ] ; ah [ɑ] ; air [ɛ] ; awful [ɔ] ; say [e] ; back [b] ; chair [tʃ] ; do [d] ; elm [ɛ] ; eel [i] ; server [ˈɝ, ər] ; fit [f] ; go [g] ; hurt [h] ; is [ɪ] ; high [aɪ] ; jet [dʒ] ; kiss [k] ; lamb [l] ; my [m] ; nice [n] ;

chromosome	KROH muh sohm	ˈkroməsom
chromosphere	KROH muh sfir	ˈkroməsfɪr
chronic	KRAH nik	ˈkrɑnɪk
chronicle	KRAH ni kuhl	ˈkrɑnɪkəl
chronological	krah nuh LAH ji kuhl	krɑnəˈlɑdʒɪkəl
chronology	kruh NAH luh ji	krəˈnɑlədʒɪ
chronometer	kruh NAH muh ter	krəˈnɑmətər
chrysalis	KRI suh lis	ˈkrɪsəlɪs
chrysanthemum	kri SAN thuh muhm	krɪˈsænθəməm
Chryseis	krigh SEE is	kraɪˈsiɪs
Chrysler	KRIGH sler	ˈkraɪslər
Chrysostom	KRI suh stuhm	ˈkrɪsəstəm
chukker	CHUH ker	ˈtʃʌkər
Chungking	choong king	tʃʊŋ kɪŋ
Churchill	CHER chil	ˈtʃɝtʃɪl
churchman	CHERCH muhn	ˈtʃɝtʃmən
Chust	hoo : st	hust
chute	shoo : t	ʃut
chutney	CHUHT ni	ˈtʃʌtnɪ
cianfarra	chahn FAH rah	tʃɑnˈfɑrɑ
Ciano	CHAH noh	ˈtʃɑno
Ciardi	CHAHR dee	ˈtʃɑrdi
Cibber	SI ber	ˈsɪbər
cicada	si KAY duh	sɪˈkedə
cicala	si KAH luh	sɪˈkɑlə
cicatrix	SI kuh triks	ˈsɪkətrɪks
Cicero	SI suh roh	ˈsɪsəro
cicerone	si suh ROH ni	sɪsəˈronɪ
Ciceronian	si suh ROH ni uhn	sɪsəˈronɪən
Cid	sid	sɪd
ci-devant	see duh VAHN	sidəˈvɑn
Ciechanowski	che hah NAWF ski	tʃɛhɑˈnɔfskɪ
Cienfuegos	syen FWAY gohs	sjɛnˈfwegos
cigar	si GAHR	sɪˈgɑr
cigaret, -te	SI guh ret	ˈsɪgərɛt
Cilicia	si LI shuh	sɪˈlɪʃə
Cimabue	chee mah BOO : ay	tʃimɑˈbue
Cimarron	SI muh rahn	ˈsɪmərɑn
Cimbri	SIM bri	ˈsɪmbrɪ
Cimmerian	si MI ri uhn	sɪˈmɪrɪən
cinchona	sin KOH nuh	sɪnˈkonə
Cincinnati	sin suh NA ti	sɪnsəˈnætɪ
Cincinnatus	sin suh NA tuhs	sɪnsəˈnætəs
cincture	SINGK cher	ˈsɪŋktʃər
Cinderella	sin duh RE luh	sɪndəˈrɛlə
Ciné	si NAY	sɪˈne
cinema	SI nuh muh	ˈsɪnəmə
Cinemascope	SIN nuh muh skohp	ˈsɪnəməskop
Cinerama	si nuh RA muh	sɪnəˈræmə
cinerator	SI nuh ray ter	ˈsɪnəretər
cinnamon	SI nuh muhn	ˈsɪnəmən
Cinque Ports	singk pawrts	sɪŋk pɔrts

sing [ŋ] ; *oh* [o] ; *oil* [ɔɪ] ; *foot* [ʊ] ; *foo:*d [u] ; *how* [aʊ] ; *pie* [p] ; *ray* [r] ; *so* [s] ; *shall* [ʃ] ;
to [t] ; *thin* [θ] ; *th:*en [ð] ; *above* (*uh* BUH*V*) [ə, ˈʌ] ; *vine* [v] ; *wine* [w] ; *whine* [hw] ;
you [j] ; *zoo* [z] ; *rouge* (roo:*zh*) [ʒ].

Cinzano	chin ZAH noh	tʃɪnˈzɑno
cipher	SIGH fer	ˈsaɪfər
circa	SER kuh	ˈsɚkə
Circassian	ser KA shi uhn	sərˈkæʃɪən
Circe	SER si	ˈsɚsɪ
circuit	SER kit	ˈsɚkɪt
circuitous	ser KYOO : i tuhs	sərˈkjuɪtəs
circuitry	SER ki tri	ˈsɚkɪtrɪ
circular	SER kyuh ler	ˈsɚkjələr
circulation	ser kyuh LAY shuhn	sɚkjəˈleʃən
circulatory	SER kyuh luh tawri	ˈsɚkjələtɔrɪ
circumference	ser KUHM fuh ruhns	sərˈkʌmfərəns
circumflex	SER kuhm fleks	ˈsɚkəmflɛks
circumlocution	ser kuhm loh KYOO : shuhn	sɚkəmloˈkjuʃən
circumspect	SER kuhm spekt	ˈsɚkəmspɛkt
circumstance	SER kuhm stans	ˈsɚkəmstæns
circumstantial	ser kuhm STAN shuhl	sɚkəmˈstænʃəl
circus	SER kuhs	ˈsɚkəs
cirque	serk	sɚk
cirrhosis	si ROH sis	sɪˈrosɪs
cisalpine	sis AL pighn	sɪsˈælpaɪn
Cistercian	si STER shuhn	sɪˈstɚʃən
cistern	SI stern	ˈsɪstərn
citable	SIGH tuh buhl	ˈsaɪtəbəl
citadel	SI tuh duhl	ˈsɪtədəl
citation	sigh TAY shuhn	saɪˈteʃən
citatory	SIGH tuh taw ri	ˈsaɪtətɔrɪ
citeable	SIGH tuh buhl	ˈsaɪtəbəl
citizen	SI tuh zuhn	ˈsɪtəzən
citizenry	SI tuh zuhn ri	ˈsɪtəzənrɪ
citrate	SI trayt	ˈsɪtret
citreous	SI tri uhs	ˈsɪtrɪəs
citric	SI trik	ˈsɪtrɪk
citrine	SI trin	ˈsɪtrɪn
Citroen	SI troh en	ˈsɪtroən
citron	SI truhn	ˈsɪtrən
Città Vecchia	chee TAH VE ki ah	tʃiˈtɑ ˈvɛkɪɑ
ciudad	syoo DAHD	sjuˈdad
civet	SI vit	ˈsɪvɪt
civilian	suh VI lyuhn	səˈvɪljən
civility	suh VI luh ti	səˈvɪlətɪ
civilization	si vuh li ZAY shuhn	sɪvəlɪˈzeʃən
claimant	KLAY muhnt	ˈklemənt
clairvoyance	klair VOI uhns	klɛrˈvɔɪəns
clairvoyant	klair VOI uhnt	klɛrˈvɔɪənt
clamant	KLAY muhnt	ˈklemənt
clambake	KLAM bayk	ˈklæmbek
clamber	KLAM ber	ˈklæmbər
clamor, clamour	KLA mer	ˈklæmər
clandestine	klan DE stin	klænˈdɛstɪn
clangor, clangour	KLANG ger	ˈklæŋgər
clansman	KLANZ muhn	ˈklænzmən

at [æ] ; ah [ɑ] ; air [ɛ] ; awful [ɔ] ; say [e] ; back [b] ; chair [tʃ] ; do [d] ; elm [ɛ] ; eel [i] ;
server [ˈɜ, ər] ; fit [f] ; go [g] ; hurt [h] ; is [ɪ] ; high [aɪ] ; jet [dʒ] ; kiss [k] ; lamb [l] ; my [m] ;
nice [n] ;

clapboard	KLA berd	ˈklæbərd
claque	klak	klæk
claret	KLA ruht	ˈklærət
Claretian	kluh REE shuhn	kləˈriʃən
clarification	kla ruh fi KAY shuhn	klærəfɪˈkeʃən
clarinet	KLA ruh net	ˈklærənɛt
clarion	KLA ri uhn	ˈklærɪən
clarionet	KLA ri uh net	ˈklærɪənɛt
clarity	KLA ruh ti	ˈklærətɪ
clasp	klasp	klæsp
class	klas	klæs
classic	KLA sik	ˈklæsɪk
classify	KLA suh figh	ˈklæsəfaɪ
Claudel	kloh DEL	kloˈdɛl
Clausewitz, von	KLOW zuh vits, fawn	ˈklaʊzəvɪts, fɒn
claustrophobia	klaw struh FOH bi uh	klɒstrəˈfobɪə
clavichord	KLA vuh kawrd	ˈklævəkɔrd
clavicle	KLA vuh kuhl	ˈklævəkəl
clavier	KLAY vi er	ˈklevɪər
Clayhanger	KLAY hang er	ˈklehæŋgər
cleanly (a)	KLEN li	ˈklɛnlɪ
cleanly (adv.)	KLEEN li	ˈklinlɪ
cleanse	klenz	klɛnz
cleavage	KLEE vij	ˈklivɪdʒ
clef	klef	klɛf
clematis	KLE muh tis	ˈklɛmətɪs
Clemenceau	kle muhn SOH	klɛmənˈso
clemency	KLE muhn si	ˈklɛmənsɪ
Clemens	KLE muhnz	ˈklɛmənz
clement, C-	KLE muhnt	ˈklɛmənt
Cleon	KLEE ahn	ˈkliɑn
Cleopatra	klee uh PA truh	kliəˈpætrə
clergy	KLER ji	ˈklɜˈdʒɪ
clerical	KLAI ri kuhl	ˈklɛrɪkəl
clerihew	KLE ri hyoo :	ˈklɛrɪhju
clerk	klerk	klɜˈk
Cleva, Fausto	KLAY vah, FOW stoh	ˈkleva, ˈfaʊsto
Cleveland	KLEEV luhnd	ˈklivlənd
clew	kloo :	klu
Cliburn	KLIGH bern	ˈklaɪbərn
cliché	klee SHAY	kliˈʃe
Clichy	klee SHEE	kliˈʃi
Clicquot	KLEE koh	ˈkliko
client	KLIGH uhnt	ˈklaɪənt
clientele	kligh uhn TEL	klaɪənˈtɛl
climacteric	kligh MAK tuh rik	klaɪˈmæktərɪk
climactic	kligh MAK tik	klaɪˈmæktɪk
climatology	kligh muh TAH luh ji	klaɪməˈtɑlədʒɪ
climax	KLIGH maks	ˈklaɪmæks
clingy	KLING i	ˈklɪŋɪ
clinician	kli NI shuhn	klɪˈnɪʃən
Clio	KLIGH oh	ˈklaɪo

sing [ŋ]; *oh* [o]; *oil* [ɔɪ]; *foot* [ʊ]; *foo:*d [u]; *how* [aʊ]; *p*ie [p]; *ray* [r]; *so* [s]; *sh*all [ʃ];
*t*o [t]; *th*in [θ]; *th:*en [ð]; above (*uh* B*UH*V) [ə, ˈʌ]; *v*ine [v]; *w*ine [w]; *wh*ine [hw];
*y*ou [j]; *z*oo [z]; rouge (roo:*zh*) [ʒ].

clique	kleek	klik
clobber	KLAH ber	ˈklɑbər
clod	klahd	klɑd
Cloete	KLOO : tee	ˈkluti
cloisonné	kloi zuh NAY	klɔɪzəˈne
cloister	KLOI ster	ˈklɔɪstər
clonus	KLOH nuhs	ˈklonəs
Clooney, Cloony	KLOO : ni	ˈkluni
close (a, n)	klohs	klos
close (v)	klohz	kloz
closure	KLOH zher	ˈkloʒər
clot	klaht	klɑt
cloth	klawth	klɔθ
clothe	klohth :	kloð
clothes	klohz	kloz
clothier	KLOH th : yer	ˈkloðjər
cloture	KLOH cher	ˈklotʃər
clough, C-	kluhf	klʌf
clout	klowt	klaut
Clouzot	kloo : ZOH	kluˈzo
cloven	KLOH vuhn	ˈklovən
Clovis	KLOH vis	ˈklovɪs
clubable, clubbable	KLUH buh buhl	ˈklʌbəbəl
clue	kloo :	klu
Cluj	kloozh	kluʒ
Cluny	KLOO : ni	ˈkluni
Cluytens	klee TAHNS	kliˈtɑns
Clydesdale	KLIGHDZ dayl	ˈklaɪdzdel
Clytemnestra, Clytaemnestra	kligh tuhm NE struh	klaɪtəmˈnɛstrə
coach	kohch	kotʃ
coadjutant	koh A juh tuhnt	koˈædʒətənt
coadjutor	koh A juh ter	koˈædʒətər
coagulate	koh A gyoo layt	koˈægjʊlet
Coahuila	koh uh WEE luh	koəˈwilə
coalesce	koh uh LES	koəˈlɛs
coarse	kawrs	kɔrs
coauthor	koh AW ther	koˈɔθər
coaxial	koh AK si uhl	koˈæksɪəl
cobalt	KOH bawlt	ˈkobɔlt
cobbler	KAH bler	ˈkɑblər
Cóbh	kohv	kov
Coblenz	KOH blents	ˈkoblɛnts
cobra	KOH bruh	ˈkobrə
coca	KOH kuh	ˈkokə
cocain, -e	koh KAYN	koˈken
coccidiosis	kahk si di OH sis	kɑksɪdɪˈosɪs
coccus	KAH kuhs	ˈkɑkəs
coccyx	KAHK siks	ˈkɑksɪks
Cochin, c-	KOH chin	ˈkotʃɪn
cochineal	kah chuh NEEL	kɑtʃəˈnil
cochlea	KAH kli uh	ˈkɑklɪə

at [æ] ; ah [ɑ] ; air [ɛ] ; awful [ɔ] ; say [e] ; back [b] ; chair [tʃ] ; do [d] ; elm [ɛ] ; eel [i] ; server [ˈɝ, ər] ; fit [f] ; go [g] ; hurt [h] ; is [ɪ] ; high [aɪ] ; jet [dʒ] ; kiss [k] ; lamb [l] ; my [m] ; nice [n] ;

Cockaigne	kah KAYN	kɑˈken
cockalorum	kah kuh LAW ruhm	kɑkəˈlɔrəm
cockatoo	KAH kuh too :	ˈkɑkətu
cockatrice	KAH kuh tris	ˈkɑkətrɪs
Cockburn	KOH bern	ˈkobərn
cocker	KAH ker	ˈkɑkər
cockerel	KAH kuh ruhl	ˈkɑkərəl
cocklebur	KAH kuhl ber	ˈkɑkəlbər
cockney, C-	KAHK ni	ˈkɑknɪ
cockswain	KAHK suhn	ˈkɑksən
coco	KOH koh	ˈkoko
cocoa	KOH koh	ˈkoko
coconut	KOH kuh nuht	ˈkokənʌt
cocoon	kuh KOO : N	kəˈkun
cocotte	koh KAHT	koˈkɑt
Cocteau	kawk TOH	kɔkˈto
Cocytus	koh SIGH tuhs	koˈsaɪtəs
coda	KOH duh	ˈkodə
code	kohd	kod
codex	KOH deks	ˈkodɛks
Codex Juris Canonici	KOH deks JOO ris kuh NAH ni sigh	ˈkodɛks ˈdʒʊrɪs kəˈnɑnɪsaɪ
codger	KAH jer	ˈkɑdʒər
codicil	KAH duh sil	ˈkɑdəsɪl
codify	KAH duh figh	ˈkɑdəfaɪ
codling	KAHD ling	ˈkɑdlɪŋ
Coe	koh	ko
coeducation	koh e joo KAY shuhn	koɛdʒuˈkeʃən
coefficient	koh uh FI shuhnt	koəˈfɪʃənt
coeliac	SEE li ak	ˈsilɪæk
coerce	koh ERS	koˈɝs
Coeur de Lion	ker duh LEE uhn	kɜrdəˈliən
coeval	koh EE vuhl	koˈivəl
coexist	koh ih ZIST	koɪgˈzɪst
coffee	KAW fi	ˈkɔfɪ
cog	kahg	kɑg
cogency	KOH juhn si	ˈkodʒənsɪ
cogent	KOH juhnt	ˈkodʒənt
cogitate	KAH juh tayt	ˈkɑdʒətet
cogitation	kah juh TAY shuhn	kɑdʒəˈteʃən
cognac	KOH nyak	ˈkonjæk
cognate	KAHG nit	ˈkɑgnɪt
cognition	kahg NI shuhn	kɑgˈnɪʃən
cognizable	KAHG ni zuh buhl	ˈkɑgnɪzəbəl
cognizance	KAHG ni zuhns	ˈkɑgnɪzəns
cognizant	KAHG ni zuhnt	ˈkɑgnɪzənt
cognomen	kahg NOH muhn	kɑgˈnomən
cognoscible	kahg NAH suh buhl	kɑgˈnɑsəbəl
Cohan, George	koh HAN	koˈhæn
Cohen	KOH en	ˈkoɛn
coherent	koh HI ruhnt	koˈhɪrənt
cohesion	koh HEE zhuhn	koˈhiʒən

sing [ŋ] ; *oh* [o] ; *oil* [ɔɪ] ; *foot* [ʊ] ; *foo:d* [u] ; *how* [aʊ] ; *pie* [p] ; *ray* [r] ; *so* [s] ; *shall* [ʃ] ; *to* [t] ; *thin* [θ] ; *th:en* [ð] ; *above* (*uh BUH*V) [ə, ˈʌ] ; *vine* [v] ; *wine* [w] ; *whine* [hw] ; *you* [j] ; *zoo* [z] ; *rouge* (*roo:zh*) [ʒ].

H.P.—G

cohesive	koh HEE ziv	koˈhizɪv
Cohoes	koh HOHZ	koˈhoz
coif	koif	kɔif
coiffeur	kwah FER	kwɑˈfɝ
coiffure	kwah FYOOR	kwɑˈfjʊr
coign, -e	koin	kɔin
coinage	KOI nij	ˈkɔinɪdʒ
coincidentally	koh in suh DEN tuh li	koɪnsəˈdɛntəlɪ
coincidently	koh IN suh duhnt li	koˈɪnsədəntlɪ
Coke, Sir Edward	kook	kʊk
colander	KUH luhn der	ˈkʌləndər
Colbert, Claudette	kawl BAIR, kloh DET	kɔlˈbɛr, kloˈdɛt
Colchester	KOHL che ster	ˈkoltʃɛstər
colchicene	KAHL ki sin	ˈkɑlkɪsɪn
colchicum	KAHL ki kuhm	ˈkɑlkɪkəm
Colchis	KAHL kis	ˈkɑlkɪs
Coleridge	KOHL rij	ˈkolrɪdʒ
coleslaw	KOHL slaw	ˈkolslɔ
coleus	KOH li uhs	ˈkolɪəs
colic	KAH lik	ˈkɑlɪk
Coligny	kaw lee NYEE	kɔliˈnji
colitis	koh LIGH tis	koˈlaɪtɪs
collaborator	kuh LA buh ray ter	kəˈlæbəretər
collage	kuh LAHZH	kəˈlɑʒ
collapse	kuh LAPS	kəˈlæps
collard	KAH lerd	ˈkɑlərd
collate (compare)	kah LAYT	kɑˈlet
collate (combine)	KOH layt	ˈkolet
collateral	kuh LA tuh ruhl	kəˈlætərəl
collation	kah LA shuhn	kɑˈleʃən
collect	kuh LEKT	kəˈlɛkt
collectivist	kuh LEK ti vist	kəˈlɛktɪvɪst
collector	kuh LEK ter	kəˈlɛktər
colleen	KAH leen	ˈkɑlin
college	KAH lij	ˈkɑlɪdʒ
collegian	kuh LEE juhn	kəˈlidʒən
collegiate	kuh LEE jit	kəˈlidʒɪt
collie	KAH li	ˈkɑlɪ
colliery	KAH lyuh ri	ˈkɑljərɪ
collimate	KAH luh mayt	ˈkɑləmet
collimator	KAH luh may ter	ˈkɑləmetər
collins, C-	KAH linz	ˈkɑlɪnz
collision	kuh LI zhuhn	kəˈlɪʒən
collodion	kuh LOH di uhn	kəˈlodɪən
colloid	KAH loid	ˈkɑlɔɪd
colloquial	kuh LOH kwi uhl	kəˈlokwɪəl
colloquium	kuh LOH kwi uhm	kəˈlokwɪəm
colloquy	KAH luh kwi	ˈkɑləkwɪ
collude	kuh LOO : D	kəˈlud
collusion	kuh LOO : zhuhn	kəˈluʒən
cologne, C-	kuh LOHN	kəˈlon
Colombia	kuh LUHM bi uh	kəˈlʌmbɪə

at [æ] ; ah [ɑ] ; air [ɛ] ; awful [ɔ] ; say [e] ; back [b] ; chair [tʃ] ; do [d] ; elm [ɛ] ; eel [i] ;
server [ˈɝ, ər] ; fit [f] ; go [g] ; hurt [h] ; is [ɪ] ; high [aɪ] ; jet [dʒ] ; kiss [k] ; lamb [l] ; my [m] ;
nice [n] ;

Colombo	kuh LUHM boh	kəˈlʌmbo
colon	KOH luhn	ˈkolən
Colón	koh LOHN	koˈlon
colonel	KER nuhl	ˈkɝnəl
colonelcy	KER nuhl si	ˈkɝnəlsɪ
colonnade	kah luh NAYD	kɑləˈned
colony	KAH luh ni	ˈkɑlənɪ
colophon	KAH luh fuhn	ˈkɑləfən
coloquintida	kah luh KWIN ti duh	kɑləˈkwɪntɪdə
color, colour	KUH ler	ˈkʌlər
Colorado	kah luh RA doh	kɑləˈrædo
coloratura	kuh luh ruh TYOO ruh	kələrəˈtjʊrə
colossal	kuh LAH suhl	kəˈlɑsəl
Colosseum	kah luh SEE uhm	kɑləˈsiəm
colossus	kuh LAH suhs	kəˈlɑsəs
Colum, Padraic	KAH luhm, PAH drik	ˈkɑləm, ˈpɑdrɪk
Columba	kuh LUHM buh	kəˈlʌmbə
Columbia	kuh LUHM bi uh	kəˈlʌmbɪə
columbine, C-	KAH luhm bighn	ˈkɑləmbaɪn
Columbus	kuh LUHM buhs	kəˈlʌmbəs
column	KAH luhm	ˈkɑləm
columnar	kuh LUHM ner	kəˈlʌmnər
columnist	KAH luhm nist	ˈkɑləmnɪst
colure	kuh LYOOR	kəˈljʊr
colza	KAHL zuh	ˈkɑlzə
Coma Berenices	KOH muh bai ruh NIGH seez	ˈkomə bɛrəˈnaɪsiz
Comanche	koh MAN chi	koˈmæntʃɪ
comatose	KAH muh tohs	ˈkɑmətos
comb	kohm	kom
combat (n)	KAHM bat	ˈkɑmbæt
combat (v)	kuhm BAT	kəmˈbæt
combatant	KAHM buh tuhnt	ˈkɑmbətənt
combative	kuhm BA tiv	kɑmˈbætɪv
combe	koo : m	kum
combine (n)	KAHM bighn	ˈkɑmbaɪn
combine (v)	kuhm BIGHN	kəmˈbaɪn
combings	KOH mingz	ˈkomɪŋz
combustible	kuhm BUH stuh buhl	kəmˈbʌstəbəl
combustion	kuhm BUHS chuhn	kəmˈbʌstʃən
comedian	kuh MEE di uhn	kəˈmidɪən
comedienne	kuh mee di EN	kəmidɪˈɛn
comedy	KAH muh di	ˈkɑmədɪ
comely	KUHM li	ˈkʌmlɪ
Comenius	koh MEE ni uhs	koˈminɪəs
comestible	kuh ME stuh buhl	kəˈmɛstəbəl
comet	KAH mit	ˈkɑmɪt
comfit	KUHM fit	ˈkʌmfɪt
comfort	KUHM fert	ˈkʌmfərt
comfortable	KUHM fer tuh buhl	ˈkʌmfərtəbəl
comforter	KUHM fer ter	ˈkʌmfərtər
comic	KAH mik	ˈkɑmɪk

---

sing [ŋ] ; *oh* [o] ; *oil* [ɔɪ] ; *foot* [ʊ] ; *foo:d* [u] ; *how* [aʊ] ; *pie* [p] ; *ray* [r] ; *so* [s] ; *shall* [ʃ] ;
to [t] ; *thin* [θ] ; *th:en* [ð] ; *above* (*uh BUH*V) [ə, ˈʌ] ; *vine* [v] ; *wine* [w] ; *whine* [hw] ;
you [j] ; *zoo* [z] ; *rouge* (*roo:zh*) [ʒ].

Comines	kaw MEEN	kəˈmin
Cominform	KAH min fawrm	ˈkɑmɪnfɔrm
Comintern	KAH min tern	ˈkɑmɪntərn
comity	KAH muh ti	ˈkɑmətɪ
comma	KAH muh	ˈkɑmə
command	kuh MAND	kəˈmænd
commandant	kah muhn DANT	kɑmənˈdænt
commandment	kuh MAND muhnt	kəˈmændmənt
commando	kuh MAN doh	kəˈmændo
comme il faut	kaw meel FOH	kɔmilˈfo
commemorate	kuh ME muh rayt	kəˈmɛməret
commemorative	kuh ME muh ray tiv	kəˈmɛməretɪv
commencement	kuh MENS muhnt	kəˈmɛnsmənt
commendable	kuh MEN duh buhl	kəˈmɛndəbəl
commendation	kah muhn DAY shuhn	kɑmənˈdeʃən
commendatory	kuh MEN duh taw ri	kəˈmɛndətɔrɪ
commensurable	kuh MEN shoo ruh buhl	kəˈmɛnʃurəbəl
commensurate	kuh MEN shoo rit	kəˈmɛnʃurɪt
comment	KAH ment	ˈkɑmɛnt
commentary	KAH muhn tai ri	ˈkɑməntɛrɪ
commentator	KAH muhn tay ter	ˈkɑməntetər
commerce (n)	KAH mers	ˈkɑmərs
commercial	kuh MER shuhl	kəˈmɝʃəl
Commines	kaw MEEN	kəˈmin
commingle	kuh MING guhl	kəˈmɪŋgəl
commiserate	kuh MI zuh rayt	kəˈmɪzəret
commiseration	kuh mi zuh RAY shuhn	kəmɪzəˈreʃən
commissar	kah muh SAHR	kɑməˈsɑr
commissariat	kah muh SAH ri uht	kɑməˈsɑrɪət
commissary	KAH muh sai ri	ˈkɑməsɛrɪ
commissionaire	kuh mi shuh NAIR	kəmɪʃəˈnɛr
commissioned	kuh MI shuhnd	kəˈmɪʃənd
commit	kuh MIT	kəˈmɪt
commode	kuh MOHD	kəˈmod
commodious	kuh MOH di uhs	kəˈmodɪəs
commodity	kuh MAH duh ti	kəˈmɑdətɪ
commodore	KAH muh dawr	ˈkɑmədɔr
common	KAH muhn	ˈkɑmən
commonalty	KAH muh nuhl ti	ˈkɑmənəltɪ
commons	KAH muhnz	ˈkɑmənz
commonweal	KAH muhn weel	ˈkɑmənwil
communal	KAH myoo nuhl	ˈkɑmjunəl
commune (n)	KAH myoo : n	ˈkɑmjun
commune (v)	kuh MYOO : N	kəˈmjun
communicable	kuh MYOO : ni kuh buhl	kəˈmjunɪkəbəl
communicant	kuh MYOO : ni kuhnt	kəˈmjunɪkənt
communicate	kuh MYOO : nuh kayt	kəˈmjunəket
communication	kuh myoo : nuh KAY shuhn	kəmjunəˈkeʃən
communicative	kuh MYOO : nuh kay tiv	kəˈmjunəketɪv
communion	kuh MYOO : nyuhn	kəˈmjunjən
communiqué	kuh myoo : nuh KAY	kəmjunəˈke
communism, C-	KAH myoo ni zuhm	ˈkɑmjunɪzəm

at [æ]; *ah* [ɑ]; *air* [ɛ]; *awful* [ɔ]; *say* [e]; *back* [b]; *chair* [tʃ]; *do* [d]; *elm* [ɛ]; *eel* [i]; *server* [ˈɝ, ər]; *fit* [f]; *go* [g]; *hurt* [h]; *is* [ɪ]; *high* [aɪ]; *jet* [dʒ]; *kiss* [k]; *lamb* [l]; *my* [m]; *nice* [n];

communist, C-	KAH myoo nist	ˈkɑmjʊnɪst
commutable	kuh MYOO : tuh buhl	kəˈmjutəbəl
commutation	kah myoo TAY shuhn	kɑmjuˈteʃən
commute	kuh MYOO : T	kəˈmjut
Como	KOH moh	ˈkomo
Comoro	KAH muh roh	ˈkɑməro
compact (a, v)	kuhm PAKT	kəmˈpækt
compact (n)	KAHM pakt	ˈkɑmpækt
comparable	KAHM puh ruh buhl	ˈkɑmpərəbəl
comparative	kuhm PA ruh tiv	kəmˈpærətɪv
compare	kuhm PAIR	kəmˈpɛr
compass	KUHM puhs	ˈkʌmpəs
compatibility	kuhm pa tuh BI luh ti	kəmpætəˈbɪləti
compatible	kuhm PA tuh buhl	kəmˈpætəbəl
compatriot	kuhm PAY tri uht	kəmˈpetrɪət
compeer	kuhm PIR	kəmˈpɪr
compel	kuhm PEL	kəmˈpɛl
compendium	kuhm PEN di uhm	kəmˈpɛndɪəm
compensate	KAHM puhn sayt	ˈkɑmpənset
compensatory	kuhm PEN suh taw ri	kəmˈpɛnsətɔri
compete	kuhm PEET	kəmˈpit
competence	KAHM puh tuhns	ˈkɑmpətəns
competitor	kuhm PE tuh ter	kəmˈpɛtətər
compilation	kahm puh LAY shuhn	kɑmpəˈleʃən
complacence	kuhm PLAY suhns	kəmˈplesəns
complacent	kuhm PLAY suhnt	kəmˈplesənt
complaisance	kuhm PLAY zuhns	kəmˈplezəns
complaisant	kuhm PLAY zuhnt	kəmˈplezənt
complement (n)	KAHM pluh muhnt	ˈkɑmpləmənt
complement (v)	KAHM pluh ment	ˈkɑmpləmɛnt
complete	kuhm PLEET	kəmˈplit
complex (a)	kuhm PLEKS	kəmˈplɛks
complex (n)	KAHM pleks	ˈkɑmplɛks
complexion	kuhm PLEK shuhn	kəmˈplɛkʃən
compliance	kuhm PLIGH uhns	kəmˈplaɪəns
compliant	kuhm PLIGH uhnt	kəmˈplaɪənt
complicacy	KAHM pluh kuh si	ˈkɑmpləkəsɪ
complicate	KAHM pluh kayt	ˈkɑmpləket
complicity	kuhm PLI suh ti	kəmˈplɪsəti
compliment (n)	KAHM pluh muhnt	ˈkɑmpləmənt
compliment (v)	KAHM pluh ment	ˈkɑmpləmɛnt
complimentary	kahm pluh MEN tuh ri	kɑmpləˈmɛntəri
comply	kuhm PLIGH	kəmˈplaɪ
component	kuhm POH nuhnt	kəmˈponənt
comport	kuhm PAWRT	kəmˈpɔrt
compose	kuhm POHZ	kəmˈpoz
composite	kuhm PAH zit	kəmˈpɑzɪt
composition	kahm puh ZI shuhn	kɑmpəˈzɪʃən
compositor	kuhm PAH zi ter	kəmˈpɑzɪtər
compos mentis	KAHM puhs MEN tis	ˈkɑmpəs ˈmɛntɪs
composure	kuhm POH zher	kəmˈpoʒər
compote	KAHM poht	ˈkɑmpot

---

sing [ŋ] ; *oh* [o] ; *oil* [ɔɪ] ; *foot* [ʊ] ; *foo:d* [u] ; *how* [aʊ] ; *pie* [p] ; *ray* [r] ; *so* [s] ; *shall* [ʃ] ;
to [t] ; *thin* [θ] ; *th:en* [ð] ; *above* (*uh* B*UH*V) [ə, ˈʌ] ; *vine* [v] ; *wine* [w] ; *whine* ; [hw]
you [j] ; *zoo* [z] ; *rouge* (roo:*zh*) [ʒ].

compound (a, n)	KAHM pownd	ˈkɑmpaʊnd
compound (v)	kahm POWND	kɑmˈpaʊnd
comprehend	kahm pri HEND	kɑmprɪˈhɛnd
comprehensible	kahm pri HEN suh buhl	kɑmprɪˈhɛnsəbəl
comprehension	kahm pri HEN shuhn	kɑmprɪˈhɛnʃən
comprehensive	kahm pri HEN siv	kɑmprɪˈhɛnsɪv
compress (n)	KAHM pres	ˈkɑmprɛs
compress (v)	kuhm PRES	kəmˈprɛs
compressor	kuhm PRE ser	kəmˈprɛsər
comprise, comprize	kuhm PRIGHZ	kəmˈpraɪz
compromise	KAHM pruh mighz	ˈkɑmprəmaɪz
comptometer, C-	kahmp TAH muh ter	kɑmpˈtɑmətər
Compton	KAHMP tuhn	ˈkɑmptən
comptroller	kuhn TROH ler	kənˈtrolər
compulsion	kuhm PUHL shuhn	kəmˈpʌlʃən
compulsory	kuhm PUHL suh ri	kəmˈpʌlsərɪ
compunction	kuhm PUHNGK shuhn	kəmˈpʌŋkʃən
computable	kuhm PYOO : tuh buhl	kəmˈpjutəbəl
comrade	KAHM rad	ˈkɑmræd
Comus	KOH muhs	ˈkoməs
Conakry	KOH nah kree	ˈkonɑkri
con amore	kawn ah MAW rai	kɔn ɑˈmorɛ
Conant	KOH nuhnt	ˈkonənt
conative	KAH nuh tiv	ˈkɑnətɪv
concatenation	kahn ka tuh NAY shuhn	kɑnkætəˈneʃən
concave	KAHN kayv	ˈkɑnkev
concavity	kahn KA vuh ti	kɑnˈkævətɪ
conceal	kuhn SEEL	kənˈsil
concede	kuhn SEED	kənˈsid
conceit	kuhn SEET	kənˈsit
conceive	kuhn SEEV	kənˈsiv
concentrate	KAHN suhn trayt	ˈkɑnsəntret
concentration	kahn suhn TRAY shuhn	kɑnsənˈtreʃən
concentrative	KAHN suhn tray tiv	ˈkɑnsəntretɪv
concept	KAHN sept	ˈkɑnsɛpt
concern	kuhn SERN	kənˈsɝn
concert (n)	KAHN sert	ˈkɑnsərt
concert (v)	kuhn SERT	kənˈsɝt
Concertgebouw	kuhn SERT huh bow	kʌnˈsɝthəbaʊ
concertina	kahn ser TEE nuh	kɑnsərˈtinə
concertino	kahn cher TEE noh	kɑntʃərˈtino
concertmaster	KAHN sert MA ster	ˈkɑnsərtˈmæstər
concertmeister	KAHN sert MIGH ster	ˈkɑnsərtˈmaɪstər
concerto	kuhn CHAIR toh	kənˈtʃɛrto
concessionnaire	kuhn se shuh NAIR	kənsɛʃəˈnɛr
conch	kahngk	kɑŋk
Concha	KAWN chah	ˈkɔntʃɑ
Concheso	kawn CHE saw	kɔnˈtʃɛsɔ
concierge	kawn si ERZH	kɔnsɪˈɝʒ
conciliate	kuhn SI li ayt	kənˈsɪliet
conciliatory	kuhn SI li uh taw ri	kənˈsɪliətɔrɪ
concise	kuhn SIGHS	kənˈsaɪs

at [æ] ; *ah* [ɑ] ; *air* [ɛ] ; *awful* [ɔ] ; *say* [e] ; *back* [b] ; *chair* [tʃ] ; *do* [d] ; *elm* [ɛ] ; *eel* [i] ; *server* [ˈɝ, ər] ; *fit* [f] ; *go* [g] ; *hurt* [h] ; *is* [ɪ] ; *high* [aɪ] ; *jet* [dʒ] ; *kiss* [k] ; *lamb* [l] ; *my* [m] ; *nice* [n] ;

conclave	KAHN klayv	ˈkɑnklev
conclude	kuhn KLOO : D	kənˈklud
conclusion	kuhn KLOO : zhuhn	kənˈkluʒən
conclusive	kuhn KLOO : siv	kənˈklusɪv
concoct	kahn KAHKT	kɑnˈkɑkt
concomitant	kahn KAH muh tuhnt	kɑnˈkɑmətənt
concord, C- (U.S. other than Mass.)	KAHN kawrd	ˈkɑnkɔrd
Concord (Mass.)	KAHNG kerd	ˈkɑŋkərd
concordance	kuhn KAWR duhns	kənˈkɔrdəns
concordat	kuhn KAWR dat	kənˈkɔrdæt
concordia, C-	kuhn KAWR di uh	kənˈkɔrdɪə
concourse	KAHN kawrs	ˈkɑnkɔrs
concrete (a)	kahn KREET	kɑnˈkrit
concrete (n)	KAHN kreet	ˈkɑnkrit
concubinage	kahn KYOO : buh nij	kɑnˈkjubənɪdʒ
concubine	KAHNG kyoo bighn	ˈkɑŋkjʊbaɪn
concupiscence	kahn KYOO : puh suhns	kɑnˈkjupəsəns
concur	kuhn KER	kənˈkɚ
concurrence	kuhn KER uhns	kənˈkɚəns
concurrent	kuhn KER uhnt	kənˈkɚənt
concussion	kuhn KUH shuhn	kənˈkʌʃən
condemn	kuhn DEM	kənˈdɛm
condemnatory	kuhn DEM nuh taw ri	kənˈdɛmnətɔrɪ
condensation	kahn den SAY shuhn	kɑndɛnˈseʃən
condescend	kahn duh SEND	kɑndəˈsɛnd
condign	kuhn DIGHN	kənˈdaɪn
condiment	KAHN duh muhnt	ˈkɑndəmənt
condole	kuhn DOHL	kənˈdol
condolence	kuhn DOH luhns	kənˈdoləns
condone	kuhn DOHN	kənˈdon
condor	KAHN der	ˈkɑndər
condottiere	kahn dah TYAI ri	kɑndɑˈtjɛrɪ
conduce	kuhn DOO : S	kənˈdus
conducive	kuhn DOO : siv	kənˈdusɪv
conduct (n)	KAHN duhkt	ˈkɑndəkt
conduct (v)	kuhn DUHKT	kənˈdʌkt
conductor	kuhn DUHK ter	kənˈdʌktər
conduit	KAHN doo it	ˈkɑndʊɪt
Conelrad	KAH nuhl rad	ˈkɑnəlræd
Conestoga	kah nuh STOH guh	kɑnəˈstogə
coney, C-	KOH ni	ˈkonɪ
confabulate	kuhn FA byoo layt	kənˈfæbjʊlet
confectionary	kuhn FEK shuh nai ri	kənˈfɛkʃənɛrɪ
confederate, C- (a, n)	kuhn FE duh rit	kənˈfɛdərɪt
confederate (v)	kuhn FE duh rayt	kənˈfɛdəret
confederation	kuhn fe duh RAY shuhn	kənfɛdəˈreʃən
confer	kuhn FER	kənˈfɚ
conference	KAHN fuh ruhns	ˈkɑnfərəns
Confesor	kawn fe SAWR	kɔnfɛˈsor
confess	kuhn FES	kənˈfɛs
confessor	kuhn FE ser	kənˈfɛsər

sing [ŋ] ; *oh* [o] ; *oil* [ɔɪ] ; *foot* [ʊ] ; *foo:d* [u] ; *how* [aʊ] ; *pie* [p] ; *ray* [r] ; *so* [s] ; *shall* [ʃ] ; *to* [t] ; *thin* [θ] ; *th:en* [ð] ; *above* (*uh BUHV*) [ə, ˈʌ] ; *vine* [v] ; *wine* [w] ; *whine* [hw] ; *you* [j] ; *zoo* [z] ; *rouge* (*roo:zh*) [ʒ].

confetti	kuhn FE ti	kənˈfɛtɪ
confidant, -e	KAHN fuh dant	ˈkɑnfədænt
confident	KAHN fuh duhnt	ˈkɑnfədənt
confidential	kahn fuh DEN shuhl	kɑnfəˈdɛnʃəl
confine (n)	KAHN fighn	ˈkɑnfaɪn
confine (v)	kuhn FIGHN	kənˈfaɪn
confirm	kuhn FERM	kənˈfɝm
confirmation	kahn fer MAY shuhn	kɑnfərˈmeʃən
confirmatory	kuhn FER muh taw ri	kənˈfɝmətɔrɪ
confiscable	kuhn FI skuh buhl	kənˈfɪskəbəl
confiscate	KAHN fi skayt	ˈkɑnfɪsket
confiscator	KAHN fi skay ter	ˈkɑnfɪsketər
confiscatory	kuhn FI skuh taw ri	kənˈfɪskətɔrɪ
conflagration	kahn fluh GRAY shuhn	kɑnfləˈgreʃən
conflict (n)	KAHN flikt	ˈkɑnflɪkt
conflict (v)	kuhn FLIKT	kənˈflɪkt
confluence	KAHN floo : uhns	ˈkɑnfluəns
confound	kuhn FOWND	kənˈfaʊnd
confraternity	kahn fruh TER nuh ti	kɑnfrəˈtɝnətɪ
confrere	KAHN frair	ˈkɑnfrɛr
confront	kuhn FRUHNT	kənˈfrʌnt
Confucius	kuhn FYOO : shus	kənˈfjuʃəs
confusion	kuhn FYOO : zhuhn	kənˈfjuʒən
confutation	kahn fyoo TAY shuhn	kɑnfjuˈteʃən
confute	kuhn FYOO : T	kənˈfjut
conga	KAHNG guh	ˈkɑŋgə
congé	KAHN zhay	ˈkɑnʒe
congeal	kuhn JEEL	kənˈdʒil
congenial	kuhn JEE nyuhl	kənˈdʒinjəl
congenital	kuhn JE nuh tuhl	kənˈdʒɛnətəl
conger	KAHNG ger	ˈkɑŋgər
congeries	kahn JI reez	kɑnˈdʒɪriz
conglomerate (a, n)	kuhn GLAH muh rit	kənˈglɑmərɪt
conglomerate (v)	kuhn GLAH muh rayt	kənˈglɑməret
Congo	KAHNG goh	ˈkɑŋgo
Congolese	KAHNG guh leez	ˈkɑŋgəliz
congratulate	kuhn GRA chuh layt	kənˈgrætʃəlet
congratulatory	kuhn GRA chuh luh taw ri	kənˈgrætʃələtɔrɪ
congregate (a)	KAHNG gruh git	ˈkɑŋgrəgɪt
congregate (v)	KAHNG gruh gayt	ˈkɑŋgrəget
congregation	kahn gruh GAY shuhn	kɑŋgrəˈgeʃən
congress, C-	KAHNG gruhs	ˈkɑŋgrəs
congressional	kuhn GRE shuh nuhl	kənˈgrɛʃənəl
Congreve	KAHN greev	ˈkɑngriv
congruent	KAHNG groo uhnt	ˈkɑŋgruənt
congruity	kuhn GROO : uh ti	kənˈgruətɪ
conic	KAH nik	ˈkɑnɪk
conical	KAH ni kuhl	ˈkɑnɪkəl
conifer	KOH nuh fer	ˈkonəfər
conjecture	kuhn JEK cher	kənˈdʒɛktʃər
conjoin	kuhn JOIN	kənˈdʒɔɪn
conjugal	KAHN joo guhl	ˈkɑndʒʊgəl

at [æ] ; *ah* [ɑ] ; *air* [ɛ] ; *aw*ful [ɔ] ; *say* [e] ; *b*ack [b] ; *ch*air [tʃ] ; *d*o [d] ; *e*lm [ɛ] ; *ee*l [i] ; *ser*ver [ˈɝ, ər] ; *f*it [f] ; *g*o [g] ; *h*urt [h] ; *is* [ɪ] ; *high* [aɪ] ; *j*et [dʒ] ; *k*iss [k] ; *l*amb [l] ; *m*y [m] ; *n*ice [n] ;

conjugate (a, n)	KAHN joo git	ˈkɑndʒʊgɪt
conjugate (v)	KAHN joo gayt	ˈkɑndʒʊget
conjugation	kahn joo GAY shuhn	kɑndʒʊˈgeʃən
conjunction	kuhn JUHNGK shuhn	kənˈdʒʌnkʃən
conjure (entreat)	kuhn JOOR	kənˈdʒʊr
conjure (summon)	KAHN jer	ˈkɑndʒər
Connacht	KAH nuht	ˈkɑnət
Connaught	KAH nawt	ˈkɑnɔt
Connecticut	kuh NE ti kuht	kəˈnɛtɪkət
conning	KAH ning	ˈkɑnɪŋ
connivance	kuh NIGH vuhns	kəˈnaɪvəns
connoisseur	kah nuh SER	kɑnəˈsɝ
connotation	kah nuh TAY shuhn	kɑnəˈteʃən
connotative	KAH nuh tay tiv	ˈkɑnətetɪv
connubial	kuh NOO : bi uhl	kəˈnubɪəl
conquer	KAHNG ker	ˈkɑŋkər
conqueror	KAHNG kuh rer	ˈkɑŋkərər
conquest	KAHNG kwest	ˈkɑŋkwɛst
conquistador	kahn KWI stuh dawr	kɑnˈkwɪstədɔr
consanguinity	kahn sang GWI nuh ti	kɑnsæŋˈgwɪnətɪ
conscience	KAHN shuhns	ˈkɑnʃəns
conscientious	kahn shi EN shuhs	kɑnʃɪˈɛnʃəs
conscionable	KAHN shuh nuh buhl	ˈkɑnʃənəbəl
conscious	KAHN shuhs	ˈkɑnʃəs
consciousness	KAHN shuhs nis	ˈkɑnʃəsnɪs
consecrate	KAHN suh krayt	ˈkɑnsəkret
consensus	kuhn SEN suhs	kənˈsɛnsəs
consent	kuhn SENT	kənˈsɛnt
consequence	KAHN si kwens	ˈkɑnsɪkwɛns
consequently	KAHN si kwent li	ˈkɑnsɪkwɛntlɪ
conservatoire	kuhn ser vuh TWAHR	kənsɝvəˈtwɑr
conservatory	kuhn SER vuh taw ri	kənˈsɝvətɔrɪ
conserve (n)	KAHN serv	ˈkɑnsɝv
conserve (v)	kuhn SERV	kənˈsɝv
considerable	kuhn SI duh ruh buhl	kənˈsɪdərəbəl
Considine	KAHN si deen	ˈkɑnsɪdin
consign	kuhn SIGHN	kənˈsaɪn
consignee	kahn SIGH nee	kɑnˈsaɪni
consignor	kuhn SIGH ner	kənˈsaɪnər
consistory	kuhn SI stuh ri	kənˈsɪstərɪ
consol	KAHN sahl	ˈkɑnsɑl
consolation	kahn suh LAY shuhn	kɑnsəˈleʃən
consolatory	kuhn SAH luh taw ri	kənˈsɑlətɔrɪ
console (n)	KAHN sohl	ˈkɑnsol
console (v)	kuhn SOHL	kənˈsol
consommé	kahn suh MAY	kɑnsəˈme
consonant	KAHN suh nuhnt	ˈkɑnsənənt
consort (n)	KAHN sawrt	ˈkɑnsɔrt
consort (v)	kuhn SAWRT	kənˈsɔrt
conspiracy	kuhn SPI ruh si	kənˈspɪrəsɪ
conspirator	kuhn SPI ruh ter	kənˈspɪrətər
conspire	kuhn SPIGHR	kənˈspaɪr

sing [ŋ] ; *oh* [o] ; *oil* [ɔɪ] ; *foot* [ʊ] ; *foo*:d [u] ; *how* [aʊ] ; *pie* [p] ; *ray* [r] ; *so* [s] ; *shall* [ʃ] ; *to* [t] ; *thin* [θ] ; *th*:en [ð] ; *above* (*uh* BUHV) [ə, ˈʌ] ; *vine* [v] ; *wine* [w] ; *whine* [hw] ; *you* [j] ; *zoo* [z] ; *rouge* (roo:zh) [ʒ].

constable	KAHN stuh buhl	ˈkɑnstəbəl
Constable, John	KUHN stuh buhl	ˈkʌnstəbəl
constabulary	kuhn STA byoor lai ri	kənˈstæbjurlɛrɪ
constancy	KAHN stuhn si	ˈkɑnstənsɪ
Constantinople	kahn stan tuh NOH puhl	kɑnstæntəˈnopəl
consternation	kahn ster NAY shuhn	kɑnstərˈneʃən
constituency	kuhn STI choo : uhn si	kənˈstɪtʃuənsɪ
constituent	kuhn STI choo : uhnt	kənˈstɪtʃuənt
constrictor	kuhn STRIK ter	kənˈstrɪktər
construe	kuhn STROO :	kənˈstru
consul	KAHN suhl	ˈkɑnsəl
consular	KAHN suh ler	ˈkɑnsələr
consulate	KAHN suh lit	ˈkɑnsəlɪt
consultant	kuhn SUHL tuhnt	kənˈsʌltənt
consume	kuhn SOO : M	kənˈsum
consummate (a)	KAHN suh mit	ˈkɑnsəmɪt
consummate (v)	KAHN suh mayt	ˈkɑnsəmet
consumption	kuhn SUHMP shuhn	kənˈsʌmpʃən
consumptive	kuhn SUHMP tiv	kənˈsʌmptɪv
contagion	kuhn TAY juhn	kənˈtedʒən
contagious	kuhn TAY juhs	kənˈtedʒəs
contaminate	kuhn TA muhn nayt	kənˈtæmənet
contamination	kuhn ta muh NAY shuhn	kəntæməˈneʃən
contemn	kuhn TEM	kənˈtɛm
contemplate	KAHN tuhm playt	ˈkɑntəmplet
contemplation	kahn tuhm PLAY shuhn	kɑntəmˈpleʃən
contemplative	kuhn TEM pluh tiv	kənˈtɛmplətɪv
contemporaneous	kuhn tem puh RAY ni uhs	kəntɛmpəˈrenɪəs
contempt	kuhn TEMPT	kənˈtɛmpt
contemptible	kuhn TEMP tuh buhl	kənˈtɛmptəbəl
contemptuous	kuhn TEMP choo uhs	kənˈtɛmptʃuəs
contend	kuhn TEND	kənˈtɛnd
content (except " what is contained ")	kuhn TENT	kənˈtɛnt
content (" what is contained ")	KAHN tent	ˈkɑntɛnt
contest (n)	KAHN test	ˈkɑntɛst
contest (v)	kuhn TEST	kənˈtɛst
context	KAHN tekst	ˈkɑntɛkst
contextual	kuhn TEKS choo uhl	kənˈtɛkstʃuəl
contiguity	kahn ti GYOO : uh ti	kɑntɪˈgjuətɪ
contiguous	kuhn TI gyoo uhs	kənˈtɪgjuəs
continent	KAHN tuh nuhnt	ˈkɑntənənt
contingency	kuhn TIN juhn si	kənˈtɪndʒənsɪ
contingent	kuhn TIN juhnt	kənˈtɪndʒənt
continuance	kuhn TI nyoo uhns	kənˈtɪnjuəns
continuation	kuhn ti nyoo AY shuhn	kəntɪnjuˈeʃən
continue	kuhn TI nyoo	kənˈtɪnju
continuity	kahn tuh NOO : uh ti	kɑntəˈnuətɪ
contort	kuhn TAWRT	kənˈtɔrt
contour	KAHN toor	ˈkɑntur
contra	KAHN truh	ˈkɑntrə

at [æ] ; *ah* [ɑ] ; *air* [ɛ] ; *awful* [ɔ] ; *say* [e] ; *back* [b] ; *chair* [tʃ] ; *do* [d] ; *elm* [ɛ] ; *eel* [i] ; *server* [ˈɝ, ər] ; *f*it [f] ; *go* [g] ; *h*urt [h] ; *is* [ɪ] ; *high* [aɪ] ; *jet* [dʒ] ; *kiss* [k] ; *l*amb [l] ; *my* [m] ; *n*ice [n] ;

contraband	KAHN truh band	ˈkɑntrəbænd
contrabass	KAHN truh bays	ˈkɑntrəbes
contract (n)	KAHN trakt	ˈkɑntrækt
contract (v)	kuhn TRAKT	kənˈtrækt
contradictory	kahn truh DIK tuh ri	kɑntrəˈdɪktərɪ
contradistinction	kahn truh di STINGK shuhn	kɑntrədɪˈstɪŋkʃən
contrail	KAHN trayl	ˈkɑntrel
contralto	kuhn TRAL toh	kənˈtrælto
contrapuntal	kahn truh PUHN tuhl	kɑntrəˈpʌntəl
contrariwise	KAHN trai ri wighz	ˈkɑntrɛrɪwaɪz
contrary	KAHN trai ri	ˈkɑntrɛrɪ
contrast (n)	KAHN trast	ˈkɑntræst
contrast (v)	kuhn TRAST	kənˈtræst
contravene	kahn truh VEEN	kɑntrəˈvin
contretemps	KAHN truh tahn	ˈkɑntrətɑn
contribute	kuhn TRI byoot	kənˈtrɪbjʊt
contributory	kuhn TRI byoo taw ri	kənˈtrɪbjʊtərɪ
contrite	KAHN tright	ˈkɑntraɪt
control	kuhn TROHL	kənˈtrol
controller	kuhn TROH ler	kənˈtrolər
controversial	kahn truh VER shuhl	kɑntrəˈvɝʃəl
controversy	KAHN truh ver si	ˈkɑntrəvərsɪ
controvert	KAHN truh vert	ˈkɑntrəvərt
contumacious	kahn too MAY shuhs	kɑntʊˈmeʃəs
contumacy	KAHN too muh si	ˈkɑntʊməsɪ
contumely	KAHN too muh li	ˈkɑntʊməlɪ
contusion	kuhn TOO: zhuhn	kənˈtuʒən
conundrum	kuh NUHN druhm	kəˈnʌndrəm
convalescence	kahn vuh LE suhns	kɑnvəˈlɛsəns
convalescent	kahn vuh LE suhnt	kɑnvəˈlɛsənt
convene	kuhn VEEN	kənˈvin
convenience	kuhn VEE nyuhns	kənˈvinjəns
convenient	kuhn VEE nyuhnt	kənˈvinjənt
converge	kuhn VERJ	kənˈvɝdʒ
conversant	KAHN ver suhnt	ˈkɑnvərsənt
conversantly	KAHN ver suhnt li	ˈkɑnvərsəntlɪ
conversazione	kahn ver saht si OH ni	kɑnvərsɑtsɪˈonɪ
converse (a, v)	kuhn VERS	kənˈvɝs
converse (n)	KAHN vers	ˈkɑnvərs
conversely	kuhn VERS li	kənˈvɝslɪ
conversion	kuhn VER zhuhn	kənˈvɝʒən
convert (n)	KAHN vert	ˈkɑnvərt
convert (v)	kuhn VERT	kənˈvɝt
converter	kuhn VER ter	kənˈvɝtər
convertible	kuhn VER tuh buhl	kənˈvɝtəbəl
convertor	kuhn VER ter	kənˈvɝtər
convex	KAHN veks	ˈkɑnvɛks
convey	kuhn VAY	kənˈve
conveyance	kuhn VAY uhns	kənˈveəns
convict (n)	KAHN vikt	ˈkɑnvɪkt
convict (v)	kuhn VIKT	kənˈvɪkt

---

sing [ŋ]; *oh* [o]; *oil* [ɔɪ]; *foot* [ʊ]; *foo:*d [u]; *how* [aʊ]; *pie* [p]; *ray* [r]; *so* [s]; *shall* [ʃ]; *to* [t]; *thin* [θ]; *th:*en [ð]; *above* (*uh* B*UH*V) [ə, ˈʌ]; *vine* [v]; *wine* [w]; *whine* [hw]; *you* [j]; *zoo* [z]; *rouge* (roo:*zh*) [ʒ].

conviction	kuhn VIK shuhn	kənˈvɪkʃən
convince	kuhn VINS	kənˈvɪns
convivial	kuhn VI vi uhl	kənˈvɪvɪəl
convocation	kahn vuh KAY shuhn	kɑnvəˈkeʃən
convoke	kuhn VOHK	kənˈvok
convolution	kahn vuh LOO : shuhn	kɑnvəˈluʃən
convoy (n)	KAHN voi	ˈkɑnvɔɪ
convoy (v)	kuhn VOI	kənˈvɔɪ
convulsion	kuhn VUHL shuhn	kənˈvʌlʃən
cony	KOH ni	ˈkonɪ
coolie, cooly	KOO : li	ˈkulɪ
cooper, C-	KOO : per	ˈkupər
cooperate	koh AH puh rayt	koˈɑpəret
cooperative	koh AH puh ruh tiv	koˈɑpərətɪv
coordination	koh awr duh NAY shuhn	koordəˈneʃən
cootie	KOO : ti	ˈkutɪ
Copacabana	koh puh kuh BA nuh	kopəkəˈbænə
copal	KOH puhl	ˈkopəl
cope	kohp	kop
copeck	KOH pek	ˈkopɛk
Copenhagen	koh puhn HAY guhn	kopənˈhegən
Copernican	koh PER ni kuhn	koˈpɝnɪkən
Copernicus	koh PER ni kuhs	koˈpɝnɪkəs
coping	KOH ping	ˈkopɪŋ
copious	KOH pi uhs	ˈkopɪəs
Copland	KOH pluhnd	ˈkoplənd
Copley	KAH pli	ˈkɑplɪ
coppice	KAH pis	ˈkɑpɪs
copra	KAH pruh	ˈkɑprə
copse	kahps	kɑps
Copt	kahpt	kɑpt
Coptic	KAHP tik	ˈkɑptɪk
copula	KAH pyuh luh	ˈkɑpjələ
copulate (a, n)	KAH pyuh lit	ˈkɑpjəlɪt
copulate (v)	KAH pyuh layt	ˈkɑpjəlet
copulative	KAH pyuh lay tiv	ˈkɑpjəletɪv
copyist	KAH pi ist	ˈkɑpɪɪst
coquet, -te	koh KET	koˈkɛt
coquetry	KOH kuh tri	ˈkokətrɪ
coquilla	kuh KEE lyuh	kəˈkiljə
coquina	kuh KEE nuh	kəˈkinə
coquito	kuh KEE toh	kəˈkito
coral	KAH ruhl	ˈkɑrəl
coram populo	KOH ruhm PAH pyuh loh	ˈkorəm ˈpɑpjəlo
Corbett	KAWR bit	ˈkɔrbɪt
cordage	KAWR dij	ˈkɔrdɪdʒ
Corday	kawr DAY	kɔrˈde
Cordelia	kawr DEE lyuh	kɔrˈdiljə
Cordelier	kawr duh LIR	kɔrdəˈlɪr
cordial	KAWR juhl	ˈkɔrdʒəl
cordiality	kawr JA luh ti	kɔrˈdʒælətɪ
Cordier	KAWR dyer	ˈkɔrdjər

at [æ] ; *ah* [ɑ] ; *air* [ɛ] ; *awful* [ɔ] ; *say* [e] ; *back* [b] ; *chair* [tʃ] ; *do* [d] ; *elm* [ɛ] ; *eel* [i] ; *server* [ˈɝ, ər] ; *fit* [f] ; *go* [g] ; *hurt* [h] ; *is* [ɪ] ; *high* [aɪ] ; *jet* [dʒ] ; *kiss* [k] ; *lamb* [l] ; *my* [m] ; *nice* [n] ;

Cordiner	KAWR di ner	ˈkɔrdɪnər
cordoba	KAWR duh buh	ˈkɔrdəbə
Córdoba	KAWR duh vuh	ˈkɔrdəvə
cordon	KAWR duhn	ˈkɔrdən
cordon bleu	kawr DOHN BLER	kɔrˈdon ˈblɜ
Cordova	KAWR duh vuh	ˈkɔrdəvə
corduroy	KAWR duh roi	ˈkɔrdərɔɪ
Corelli	kaw RE lee	cɔˈrɛli
Corena, Fernando	koh RAY nah, fer NAHN doh	koˈrenɑ, fərˈnɑndo
coreopsis	kaw ri AHP sis	kɔrɪˈɑpsɪs
corespondent	koh ri SPAHN duhnt	kɔrɪˈspɑndənt
Corfu	KAWR fyoo :	ˈkɔrfju
corgi	KAWR gi	ˈkɔrgɪ
coriander	kaw ri AN der	kɔrɪˈændər
Corinth	KAW rinth	ˈkɔrɪnθ
Corinthian	kuh RIN thi uhn	kəˈrɪnθɪən
Coriolanus	kaw ri uh LAY nuhs	kɔrɪəˈlenəs
Corioles	kuh RIGH uh leez	kəˈraɪəliz
Coriolis, c-	kaw ri OH lis	kɔrɪˈolɪs
cork, C-	kawrk	kɔrk
cormorant	KAWR muh ruhnt	ˈkɔrmərənt
cornea	KAWR ni uh	ˈkɔrnɪə
Corneille	kawr NAY	kɔrˈne
Cornelius	kawr NEE lyuhs	kərˈniljəs
cornet	kawr NET	kɔrˈnɛt
cornice	KAWR nis	ˈkɔrnɪs
Cornish	KAWR nish	ˈkɔrnɪʃ
cornucopia	kawr nuh KOH pi uh	kɔrnəˈkopɪə
corollary	KAW ruh lai ri	ˈkɔrəlɛri
corona	kuh ROH nuh	kəˈronə
coronal (a)	kuh ROH nuhl	kəˈronəl
coronal (n)	KAW ruh nuhl	ˈkɔrənəl
coronary	KAW ruh nai ri	ˈkɔrənɛri
coroner	KAW ruh ner	ˈkɔrənər
coronet	KAW ruh net	ˈkɔrənɛt
Corot	kuh ROH	kəˈro
corporal	KAWR puh ruhl	ˈkɔrpərəl
corporate	KAWR puh rit	ˈkɔrpərɪt
corporeal	kawr PAW ri uhl	kɔrˈporɪəl
corps (sing.)	kawr	kɔr
corps (pl.)	kawrz	kɔrz
corpse	kawrps	kɔrps
corpulence	KAWR pyuh luhns	ˈkɔrpjələns
corpulent	KAWR pyuh luhnt	ˈkɔrpjələnt
Corpus Christi	KAWR puhs KRI sti	ˈkɔrpəs ˈkrɪstɪ
corpuscle	KAWR puh suhl	ˈkɔrpəsəl
corpus delicti	KAWR puhs di LIK tigh	ˈkɔrpəs dɪˈlɪktaɪ
Corpus Juris Civilis	KAWR puhs JOO ris si VIGH lis	ˈkɔrpəs ˈdʒurɪs sɪˈvaɪlɪs
corral	kuh RAL	kəˈræl
Correggio	kuh RE joh	kəˈredʒo

sing [ŋ]; *oh* [o]; *oil* [ɔɪ]; *foot* [ʊ]; *foo*:d [u]; *how* [aʊ]; *pie* [p]; *ray* [r]; *so* [s]; *shall* [ʃ]; *to* [t]; *thin* [θ]; *th*:en [ð]; *above* (*uh* B*UH*V) [ə, ˈʌ]; *vine* [v]; *wine* [w]; *whine* [hw]; *you* [j]; *zoo* [z]; *rouge* (roo:*zh*) [ʒ].

Corregidor	kuh RE guh dawr	kəˈrɛgədɔr
correlate	KAW ruh layt	ˈkɔrəlet
correlation	kaw ruh LAY shuhn	kɔrəˈleʃən
correlative	kuh RE luh tiv	kəˈrɛlətɪv
correspond	kaw ruh SPAHND	kɔrəˈspɑnd
correspondent	kaw ruh SPAHN duhnt	kɔrəˈspɑndənt
corridor	KAW ruh dawr	ˈkɔrədɔr
corrigible	KAW ruh juh buhl	ˈkɔrədʒəbəl
corroborate	kuh RAH buh rayt	kəˈrɑbəret
corroborative	kuh RAH buh ray tiv	kəˈrɑbəretɪv
corrode	kuh ROHD	kəˈrod
corrosion	kuh ROH zhuhn	kəˈroʒən
corrosive	kuh ROH siv	kəˈrosɪv
corrugate (a)	KAW ruh git	ˈkɔrəgɪt
corrugate (v)	KAW ruh gayt	ˈkɔrəget
corrugated	KAW ruh gay tid	ˈkɔrəgetɪd
corrugation	kaw ruh GAY shuhn	kɔrəˈgeʃən
corrupt	kuh RUHPT	kəˈrʌpt
corruptible	kuh RUHP tuh buhl	kəˈrʌptəbəl
corsage	kawr SAHZH	kɔrˈsɑʒ
corsair, C-	KAWR sair	ˈkɔrsɛr
Corsica	KAWR si kuh	ˈkɔrsɪkə
Corsican	KAW si kuhn	ˈkɔrsɪkən
cortege	kawr TAYZH	kɔrˈteʒ
Cortes	KAWR tez	ˈkɔrtɛz
Cortesa	kawr TAY sah	kɔrˈtesɑ
cortex	KAWR teks	ˈkɔrtɛks
cortical	KAWR ti kuhl	ˈkɔrtɪkəl
Cortines	kawr TEE nes	kɔrˈtines
cortisone	KAWR tuh sohn	ˈkɔrtəson
coruscate	KAW ruh skayt	ˈkɔrəsket
coruscation	kaw ruh SKAY shuhn	kɔrəˈskeʃən
corvée	kawr VAY	kɔrˈve
corvet, -te, C-	kawr VET	kɔrˈvɛt
Corvus	KAWR vuhs	ˈkɔrvəs
corybant, C-	KAW ruh bant	ˈkɔrəbænt
Corydon	KAW ruh duhn	ˈkɔrədən
Cos, c-	kahs	kɑs
Cosgrave	KAHZ grayv	ˈkɑzgrev
cosignatory	koh SIG nuh taw ri	koˈsɪgnətɔrɪ
cosine	KOH sign	ˈkosaɪn
cosmetic	kahz ME tik	kɑzˈmɛtɪk
cosmic	KAHZ mik	ˈkɑzmɪk
cosmogony	kahz MAH guh ni	kɑzˈmɑgənɪ
cosmology	kahz MAH luh ji	kɑzˈmɑlədʒɪ
cosmonaut	KAHZ muh nawt	ˈkɑzmənɔt
cosmopolitan	kahz muh PAH luh tuhn	kɑzməˈpɑlətən
cosmopolite	kahz MAH puh light	kɑzˈmɑpəlaɪt
cosmos	KAHZ muhs	ˈkɑzməs
cosmotron	KAHZ muh trahn	ˈkɑzmətrɑn
Cossack	KAH sak	ˈkɑsæk
costal	KAH stuhl	ˈkɑstəl

at [æ]; ah [ɑ]; air [ɛ]; awful [ɔ]; say [e]; back [b]; chair [tʃ]; do [d]; elm [ɛ]; eel [i]; server [ˈɝ, ər]; fit [f]; go [g]; hurt [h]; is [ɪ]; high [aɪ]; jet [dʒ]; kiss [k]; lamb [l]; my [m]; nice [n];

costard	KAH sterd	ˈkɑstərd
Costa Rica	KAH stuh REE kuh	ˈkɑstə ˈrikə
Costello	kah STE loh	kɑˈstɛlo
costermonger	KAH ster muhng ger	ˈkɑstərməŋgər
costume (n)	KAH stoo : m	ˈkɑstum
costume (v)	kah STOO : M	kɑˈstum
costumer	kah STOO : mer	kɑˈstumər
Côte d'Azur	koht da ZHOOR	kot dæˈʒur
coterie	KOH tuh ri	ˈkotərɪ
cotillion	koh TI lyuhn	koˈtɪljən
Cotswold	KAHTS wohld	ˈkɑtswold
cottage	KAH tij	ˈkɑtɪdʒ
couchant	KOW chuhnt	ˈkautʃənt
Coué	koo : AY	kuˈe
cougar	KOO : ger	ˈkugər
cough	kawf	kɔf
coulee	KOO : li	ˈkulɪ
coulisse	koo : LEES	kuˈlis
council	KOWN suhl	ˈkaunsəl
councilor, councillor	KOWN suh ler	ˈkaunsələr
counsel	KOWN suhl	ˈkaunsəl
counselor, counsellor	KOWN suh ler	ˈkaunsələr
countenance	KOWN tuh nuhns	ˈkauntənəns
counterfeit	KOWN ter fit	ˈkauntərfɪt
coup	koo :	ku
coup de grâce	koo : duh GRAHS	ku də ˈgrɑs
coup d'état	koo : day TAH	ku deˈtɑ
coup de théâtre	koo : duh tay AH truh	ku də teˈɑtrə
coupe	koo : p	kup
coupé	koo : PAY	kuˈpe
coupon	KOO : pahn	ˈkupɑn
courage	KER ij	ˈkɝɪdʒ
courant, -e	koo : RAHNT	kuˈrɑnt
Courbet	KOO : R bay	ˈkurbe
Cour Carrée	KOO : R kah RAY	ˈkurkɑ ˈre
courier	KOO ri er	ˈkurɪər
courteous	KER ti uhs	ˈkɝtɪəs
courtesan, courtezan	KAWR tuh zuhn	ˈkɔrtəzən
courtesy	KER tuh si	ˈkɝtəsɪ
courtier	KAWR ti er	ˈkɔrtɪər
courtly	KAWRT li	ˈkɔrtlɪ
Cousteau	koo : STOH	kuˈsto
couturier	koo : too RYAY	kutuˈrje
couvade	koo : VAHD	kuˈvɑd
Couve de Murville	koo : v duh moor VEEL	kuv də murˈvil
Covarrubias	koh vah ROO : bi ahs	kovɑˈrubɪɑs
covenant	KUH vuh nuhnt	ˈkʌvənənt
covenanter, covenantor, C-	KUH vuh nuhn ter	ˈkʌvənəntər
Coventry	KUH vuhn tri	ˈkʌvəntrɪ
covert	KUH vert	ˈkʌvərt
covet	KUH vit	ˈkʌvɪt

sing [ŋ] ; *oh* [o] ; *oil* [ɔɪ] ; *foot* [ʊ] ; *foo:d* [u] ; *how* [au] ; *pie* [p] ; *ray* [r] ; *so* [s] ; *shall* [ʃ] ; *to* [t] ; *thin* [θ] ; *th:en* [ð] ; *above* (*uh BUHV*) [ə, ˈʌ] ; *vine* [v] ; *wine* [w] ; *whine* [hw] ; *you* [j] ; *zoo* [z] ; *rouge* (roo:*zh*) [ʒ].

covetous	KUH vi tuhs	ˈkʌvɪtəs
covey	KUH vi	ˈkʌvɪ
coward	KOW erd	ˈkauərd
cowardice	KOW er dis	ˈkauərdɪs
Cowell	COW uhl	ˈcauəl
cowl	kowl	kaul
Cowley	KOW li	ˈkaulɪ
Cowper	KOO : per	ˈkupər
Coxey	KAHK si	ˈkɑksɪ
Coxsackie	kook SAH ki	kukˈsɑkɪ
coxswain	KAHK suhn	ˈkɑksən
coyote	KIGH oht	ˈkaɪot
cozen	KUH zuhn	ˈkʌzən
cozenage	KUH zuh nij	ˈkʌzənɪdʒ
Cracow	KRA kow	ˈkrækau
craft	kraft	kræft
cranium	KRAY ni uhm	ˈkrenɪəm
crape	krayp	krep
crash	krash	kræʃ
Crashaw	KRA shaw	ˈkræʃɔ
crater, C-	KRAY ter	ˈkretər
cravat	kruh VAT	krəˈvæt
craven	KRAY vuhn	ˈkrevən
crawfish	KRAW fish	ˈkrɔfɪʃ
crayfish	KRAY fish	ˈkrefɪʃ
crayon	KRAY uhn	ˈkreən
crease	krees	kris
creative	kree AY tiv	kriˈetɪv
creator, C-	kree AY ter	kriˈetər
creature	KREE cher	ˈkritʃər
crèche	kresh	krɛʃ
Crécy	KRE si	ˈkrɛsɪ
credence	KREE duhns	ˈkridəns
credential	kri DEN shuhl	krɪˈdɛnʃəl
credible	KRE duh buhl	ˈkrɛdəbəl
creditable	KRE di tuh buhl	ˈkrɛdɪtəbəl
creditor	KRE di ter	ˈkrɛdɪtər
credo	KREE doh	ˈkrido
credulity	kruh DOO : luh ti	krəˈdulətɪ
credulous	KRE joo luhs	ˈkrɛdʒuləs
creek, C-	kreek	krik
creel	kreel	kril
creese	krees	kris
cremate	KREE mayt	ˈkrimet
crematory	KREE muh taw ri̇	ˈkrimətɔrɪ
crème de menthe	krem duh MAHNT	krɛm də ˈmɑnt
Cremona	kri MOH nuh	krɪˈmonə
creole, C-	KREE ohl	ˈkriol
créole	kray AWL	kreˈɔl
Creon	KREE ahn	ˈkriɑn
creosol	KREE uh sohl	ˈkriəsol
creosote	KREE uh soht	ˈkriəsot

at [æ]; ah [ɑ]; air [ɛ]; awful [ɔ]; say [e]; back [b]; chair [tʃ]; do [d]; elm [ɛ]; eel [i]; server [ˈɝ, ər]; fit [f]; go [g]; hurt [h]; is [ɪ]; high [aɪ]; jet [dʒ]; kiss [k]; lamb [l]; my [m]; nice [n];

crepe de Chine	krayp duh SHEEN	krep də ˈʃin
crêpes suzette	krayp soo : ZET	krep suˈzɛt
crepuscle	kri PUH suhl	krɪˈpʌsəl
crepuscule	kri PUH skyool	krɪˈpʌskjʊl
crescendo	kruh SHEN doh	krəˈʃɛndo
crescent	KRE suhnt	ˈkrɛsənt
Cressida	KRE si duh	ˈkrɛsɪdə
Cressy	KRE si	ˈkrɛsɪ
cretaceous, C-	kri TAY shuhs	krɪˈteʃəs
Cretan	KREE tuhn	ˈkritən
Crete	kreet	krit
cretin	KREE tin	ˈkritɪn
cretinism	KREE ti ni zuhm	ˈkritɪnɪzəm
cretonne	kri TAHN	krɪˈtɑn
Creüsa	kree OO : suh	kriˈusə
crevasse	kruh VAS	krəˈvæs
crevice	KRE vis	ˈkrɛvɪs
cribbage	KRI bij	ˈkrɪbɪdʒ
Crichton	KRIGH tuhn	ˈkraɪtən
cricoid	KRIGH koid	ˈkraɪkɔɪd
Crimea	krigh MEE uh	kraɪˈmiə
criminal	KRI muh nuhl	ˈkrɪmənəl
crimson	KRIM zuhn	ˈkrɪmzən
crinoline	KRI nuh lin	ˈkrɪnəlɪn
Cripps	krips	krɪps
crises	KRIGH seez	ˈkraɪsiz
Criseyde	kri SAY duh	krɪˈsedə
crisis	KRIGH sis	ˈkraɪsɪs
Crispin	KRI spin	ˈkrɪspɪn
criteria	krigh TI ri uh	kraɪˈtɪrɪə
criterion	krigh TI ri uhn	kraɪˈtɪrɪən
criticism	KRI tuh si zuhm	ˈkrɪtəsɪzəm
critique	kri TEEK	krɪˈtik
croak	krohk	krok
Croat	KROH at	ˈkroæt
Croatia	kroh AY shuh	kroˈeʃə
Croatian	kroh AY shuhn	kroˈeʃən
Croce, Benedetto	KROH chi, be ne DE toh	ˈkrotʃɪ, bɛnɛˈdɛto
crochet	kroh SHAY	kroˈʃe
Crockett	KRAH kit	ˈkrakɪt
crocodile	KRAH kuh dighl	ˈkrakədaɪl
Croesus	KREE suhs	ˈkrisəs
croissant	krwah SAHN	krwɑˈsɑn
croix de feu	krwah duh FER	krwɑ də ˈfɝ
croix de guerre	krwah duh GAIR	krwɑ də ˈgɛr
Cro-Magnon	kroh MAG nahn	kroˈmægnɑn
Cromwell	KRAHM wuhl	ˈkrɑmwəl
Cronin	KROH nin	ˈkronɪn
croquet	kroh KAY	kroˈke
croquette	kroh KET	kroˈkɛt
crosier	KROH zher	ˈkroʒər
crotch	krahch	krɑtʃ

sing [ŋ] ; *oh* [o] ; *oil* [ɔɪ] ; *foot* [ʊ] ; *foo*:d [u] ; *how* [aʊ] ; *pie* [p] ; *ray* [r] ; *so* [s] ; *sh*all [ʃ] ;
to [t] ; *th*in [θ] ; *th*:en [ð] ; *above* (*uh* B*UH*V) [ə, ˈʌ] ; *vine* [v] ; *wine* [w] ; *wh*ine [hw] ;
you [j] ; *zoo* [z] ; *rouge* (roo:*zh*) [ʒ].

H.P.—H

crotchet	KRAH chit	ˈkrɑtʃɪt
croup	kroo : p	krup
croupier	KROO : pi er	ˈkrupɪər
crouton	kroo : TAHN	kruˈtɑn
Crowell	KROH uhl	ˈkroəl
crozier	KROH zher	ˈkroʒər
crucial	KROO : shuhl	ˈkruʃəl
crucify	KROO : suh figh	ˈkrusəfaɪ
cruel	KROO : uhl	ˈkruəl
cruelty	KROO : uhl ti	ˈkruəltɪ
cruet	KROO : it	ˈkruɪt
Cruikshank	KROOK shangk	ˈkrʊkʃæŋk
cruise	kroo : z	kruz
cruiser	KROO : zer	ˈkruzər
cruller	KRUH ler	ˈkrʌlər
crumpet	KRUHM pit	ˈkrʌmpɪt
crusade	kroo : SAYD	kruˈsed
crustacean	kruh STAY shuhn	krəˈsteʃən
crustaceous	kruh STAY shuhs	krəˈsteʃəs
crux	kruhks	krʌks
cryogenics	krigh uh JE niks	kraɪəˈdʒɛnɪks
cryophilic	krigh uh FI lik	kraɪəˈfɪlɪk
crypt	kript	krɪpt
cryptic	KRIP tik	ˈkrɪptɪk
cryptogram	KRIP tuh gram	ˈkrɪptəgræm
crystalline	KRI stuh lin	ˈkrɪstəlɪn
crystallization	kri stuh li ZAY shuhn	krɪstəlɪˈzeʃən
csardas	CHAHR dahsh	ˈtʃɑrdaʃ
Csongrád	CHAWNG grahd	ˈtʃɔŋɡrɑd
Cuba	KYOO : buh	ˈkjubə
Cuba libre	KYOO : buh LEE bruh	ˈkjubə ˈlibrə
Cuban	KYOO : buhn	ˈkjubən
cubicle	KYOO : bi kuhl	ˈkjubɪkəl
Cuchulainn, Cuchullin	koo KUH lin	kʊˈkʌlɪn
cuckold	KUH kuhld	ˈkʌkəld
cuckoo	KOO koo :	ˈkʊku
cucumber	KYOO : kuhm ber	ˈkjukəmbər
cucurbitaceous	kyoo ker bi TAY shuhs	kjukərbɪˈteʃəs
cue	kyoo :	kju
Cuénod, Hugues	koo : ay NOH, OO : guh	kueˈno, ˈuɡə
Cugat	KOO : gaht	ˈkuɡɑt
cui bono	KWEE BOH noh	ˈkwi ˈbono
cuirass	kwi RAS	kwɪˈræs
cuirassier	kwi ruh SIR	kwɪrəˈsɪr
cuisine	kwi ZEEN	kwɪˈzin
Culbertson	KUHL bert suhn	ˈkʌlbərtsən
cul-de-sac	kuhl duh SAK	kəl də ˈsæk
Culebra	KOO : LAY bruh	kuˈlebrə
culex	KYOO : leks	ˈkjulɛks
culinary	KYOO : luh nai ri	ˈkjulənɛrɪ
culminate	KUHL muh nayt	ˈkʌlmənet
culottes	koo LAHTS	kuˈlɑts

at [æ]; ah [ɑ]; air [ɛ]; awful [ɔ]; say [e]; back [b]; chair [tʃ]; do [d]; elm [ɛ]; eel [i]; server [ˈɝ, ər]; fit [f]; go [g]; hurt [h]; is [ɪ]; high [aɪ]; jet [dʒ]; kiss [k]; lamb [l]; my [m]; nice [n];

culprit	KUHL prit	ˈkʌlprɪt
cultivator	KUHL tuh vay ter	ˈkʌltəvetər
cultural	KUHL chuh ruhl	ˈkʌltʃərəl
culture	KUHL cher	ˈkʌltʃər
culvert	KUHL vert	ˈkʌlvərt
Cumae	KYOO : mee	ˈkjumi
Cumaean	kyoo MEE uhn	kjuˈmiən
cumbersome	KUHM ber suhm	ˈkʌmbərsəm
cumin	KUH min	ˈkʌmɪn
cum laude	koom LOW de	kʊm ˈlaʊdɛ
cumulative	KYOO : muh lay tiv	ˈkjuməletɪv
Cunard	kyoo NAHRD	kjuˈnɑrd
cuneiform	kyoo NEE uh fawrm	kjuˈniəfɔrm
cupboard	KUH berd	ˈkʌbərd
Cupid	KYOO : pid	ˈkjupɪd
cupidity	kyoo PI duh ti	kjuˈpɪdəti
cupola	KYOO : puh luh	ˈkjupələ
Curaçao	kyoo ruh SOH	kjurəˈso
curare	kyoo RAH ri	kjuˈrɑri
curate	KYOO rit	ˈkjʊrɪt
curative	KYOO ruh tiv	ˈkjʊrətɪv
curator	kyoo RAY ter	kjuˈretər
curé	kyoo RAY	kjuˈre
curette	kyoo RET	kjuˈrɛt
curfew	KER fyoo :	ˈkɝfju
curia, C-	KYOO ri uh	ˈkjʊriə
curie, C-	KYOO ri	ˈkjʊri
curious	KYOO ri uhs	ˈkjʊriəs
curium	KYOO ri uhm	ˈkjʊriəm
curmudgeon	ker MUH juhn	kərˈmʌdʒən
currant	KER uhnt	ˈkɝənt
current	KER uhnt	ˈkɝənt
curricle	KER i kuhl	ˈkɝɪkəl
curriculum	kuh RI · kyoo luhm	kəˈrɪkjʊləm
curry	KER i	ˈkɝi
cursive	KER siv	ˈkɝsɪv
cursorily	KER suh ri li	ˈkɝsərɪli
cursory	KER suh ri	ˈkɝsəri
curtail	ker TAYL	kərˈtel
curtsy, curtsey	KERT si	ˈkɝtsi
curvaceous	ker VAY shuhs	kərˈveʃəs
curvature	KER vuh cher	ˈkɝvətʃər
curvet	KER vit	ˈkɝvɪt
Curzon	KER zuhn	ˈkɝzən
cushion	KOO shuhn	ˈkʊʃən
cuspid	KUH spid	ˈkʌspɪd
cuspidor	KUH spi dawr	ˈkʌspɪdɔr
cussed	KUH sid	ˈkʌsɪd
custodian	kuhˈSTOH di uhn	kəˈstodɪən
custody	KUH stuh di	ˈkʌstədɪ
custom	KUH stuhm	ˈkʌstəm
customary	KUH stuh mai ri	ˈkʌstəmɛrɪ

sing [ŋ]; oh [o]; oil [ɔɪ]; foot [ʊ]; foo:d [u]; how [aʊ]; pie [p]; ray [r]; so [s]; shall [ʃ];
to [t]; thin [θ]; th:en [ð]; above (uh BUHV) [ə, ˈʌ]; vine [v]; wine [w]; whine [hw];
you [j]; zoo [z]; rouge (roo:zh) [ʒ].

cutaneous	kyoo : TAY ni uhs	kjuˈtenɪəs
cuticle	KYOO : ti kuhl	ˈkjutɪkəl
Cuticura	kyoo : ti KYOO ruh	kjutɪˈkjʊrə
cutlass	KUHT luhs	ˈkʌtləs
cutty, C-	KUH ti	ˈkʌtɪ
Cuvier	KOO : vi ay	ˈkuvɪe
Cuyp	koip	kɔɪp
Cuzco	KOO : skoh	ˈkusko
cyanide	SIGH uh nighd	ˈsaɪənaɪd
Cybele	SI buh lee	ˈsɪbəli
cybernetics	sigh ber NE tiks	saɪbərˈnɛtɪks
cyclamen	SI kluh muhn	ˈsɪkləmən
cycle	SIGH kuhl	ˈsaɪkəl
cyclic	SIGH klik	ˈsaɪklɪk
cyclical	SIGH kli kuhl	ˈsaɪklɪkəl
cyclone	SIGH klohn	ˈsaɪklon
cyclonic	sigh KLAH nik	saɪˈklɑnɪk
cyclonite	SIGH kluh night	ˈsaɪklənaɪt
cyclopaedia, cyclopedia	sigh kluh PEE di uh	saɪkləˈpidɪə
cyclopaedist, cyclopedist	sigh kluh PEE dist	saɪkləˈpidɪst
Cyclopean	sigh kluh PEE uhn	saɪkləˈpiən
Cyclops	SIGH klahps	ˈsaɪklɑps
cyclorama	sigh kluh RA muh	saɪkləˈræmə
cyclotron	SIGH kluh trahn	ˈsaɪklətrɑn
cygnet	SIG nit	ˈsɪgnɪt
Cygnus	SIG nuhs	ˈsɪgnəs
cylinder	SI lin der	ˈsɪlɪndər
cymbal	SIM buhl	ˈsɪmbəl
Cymbeline	SIM buh leen	ˈsɪmbəlin
Cymric	SIM rik	ˈsɪmrɪk
Cynewulf	KI nuh woolf	ˈkɪnəwulf
cynic	SI nik	ˈsɪnɪk
cynical	SI ni kuhl	ˈsɪnɪkəl
cynicism	SI nuh si zuhm	ˈsɪnəsɪzəm
cynophobia	si nuh FOH bi uh	sɪnəˈfobɪə
cynosure, C-	SIGH nuh shoor	ˈsaɪnəʃur
Cynthia	SIN thi uh	ˈsɪnθɪə
cypress	SIGH pruhs	ˈsaɪprəs
Cyprian	SI pri uhn	ˈsɪprɪən
Cyprus	SIGH pruhs	ˈsaɪprəs
Cyrano	SI ruh noh	ˈsɪrəno
Cyrenaica	si ruh NAY i kuh	sɪrəˈneɪkə
Cyrus	SIGH ruhs	ˈsaɪrəs
cyst	sist	sɪst
cystitis	si STIGH tis	sɪˈstaɪtɪs
Cytherea	si thuh REE uh	sɪθəˈriə
cytogenetics	sigh tuh juh NE tiks	saɪtədʒəˈnɛtɪks
cytology	sigh TAH luh ji	saɪˈtɑlədʒɪ
czar	zahr	zɑr
czardas	CHAHR dahsh	ˈtʃɑrdɑʃ
czarevitch	ZAH ruh vich	ˈzɑrəvɪtʃ
czarevna	zah REV nuh	zɑˈrɛvnə

at [æ] ; *ah* [ɑ] ; *air* [ɛ] ; *awful* [ɔ] ; *say* [e] ; *back* [b] ; *chair* [tʃ] ; *do* [d] ; *elm* [ɛ] ; *eel* [i] ; *server* [ˈɝ, ər] ; *f*it [f] ; *go* [g] ; *hurt* [h] ; *is* [ɪ] ; *high* [aɪ] ; *jet* [dʒ] ; *kiss* [k] ; *lamb* [l] ; *my* [m] ; *nice* [n] ;

czarina	zah REE nuh	zɑˈrinə
czarism	ZAH ri zuhm	ˈzɑrɪzəm
Czech	chek	tʃɛk
Czechoslovak	che kuh SLOH vak	tʃɛkəˈslovæk
Czechoslovakia	che kuh sloh VAH ki uh	tʃɛkəsloˈvɑkɪə
Czeladź	CHE lahj	ˈtʃɛlɑdʒ
Czerny	CHER ni	ˈtʃɝnɪ
Czestochowa	chan stuh KAW vah	tʃænstəˈkɔvɑ
Cziffra, György	CHEE frah, DYAWR dy	ˈtʃifrɑ, ˈdjɔrdj
Czortkow	CHAWRT koof	ˈtʃɔrtkʊf

D

Dabrowa Gornicza	dawn BRAW vah goor NEE chah	dɔnˈbrɔvɑ gʊrˈnitʃɑ
da capo	dah KAH poh	dɑˈkɑpo
Dachau	DAH kow	ˈdɑkaʊ
Daché, Lilly	dah SHAY	dɑˈʃe
dachshund	DAHKS hoond	ˈdɑkshʊnd
dactyl	DAK til	ˈdæktɪl
dactylology	dak ti LAH luh ji	dæktɪˈlɑlədʒɪ
Daedalus	DE duh luhs	ˈdɛdələs
Dagon	DAY guhn	ˈdegən
daguerreotype	duh GE ruh tighp	dəˈgɛrətaɪp
dahlia	DA lyuh	ˈdælyə
Dahomey	dah HOH may	dɑˈhome
Dail Eireann	DAWL AI ruhn	ˈdɔl ˈɛrən
Dai Nippon	DIGH ni PAHN	ˈdaɪ nɪˈpɑn
Daiquiri, d-	DIGH kuh ri	ˈdaɪkərɪ
Dairen	digh ren	daɪrɛn
dais	DAY is	ˈdeɪs
Dakar	da KAHR	dæˈkɑr
Daladier	dah lah DYAY	dɑlɑˈdje
Dalai Lama	dah LIGH LAH muh	dɑˈlaɪ ˈlɑmə
Dalhousie	dal HOO : zi	dælˈhuzɪ
Dali, Salvador	DAH li, sal vuh DAWR	ˈdɑlɪ, sælvəˈdɔr
Dallapiccola, Luigi	dah lah PEE koh lah, loo : EE jee	dɑlɑˈpikolɑ, luˈidʒi
Dallas	DA luhs	ˈdæləs
dalliance	DA li uhns	ˈdælɪəns
Damascus	duh MA skuhs	dəˈmæskəs
Dambovita	DUHM baw veet sah	ˈdʌmbɔvitsɑ
Damietta	da mi E tuh	dæmɪˈɛtə
Damocles	DA muh kleez	ˈdæməkliz
Dampier	DAM pir	ˈdæmpɪr
Danaus	DA ni uhs	ˈdænɪəs
dance	dans	dæns
Daniell	DA nyuhl	ˈdænjəl

sing [ŋ] ; oh [o] ; oil [ɔɪ] ; foot [ʊ] ; foo:d [u] ; how [aʊ] ; pie [p] ; ray [r] ; so [s] ; shall [ʃ] ; to [t] ; thin [θ] ; th:en [ð] ; above (uh BUHV) [ə, ˈʌ] ; vine [v] ; wine [w] ; whine [hw] ; you [j] ; zoo [z] ; rouge (roo:zh) [ʒ].

danio, D-	DAY ni oh	ˈdenɪo
Danish	DAY nish	ˈdenɪʃ
d'Annunzio, Gabriele	duh NOON zi oh, gah bri E lay	dəˈnʊnzɪo, gɑbrɪˈɛle
Dante	DAN ti	ˈdæntɪ
Danube	DA nyoo : b	ˈdænjub
Danzig	DAN sig	ˈdænsɪg
Daphne	DAF ni	ˈdæfnɪ
Daphnis	DAF nis	ˈdæfnɪs
d'Arc	dahrk	dɑrk
Dardanelles	dahr duh NELZ	dɑrdəˈnɛlz
Darien	DAI ri uhn	ˈdɛrɪən
Darius	duh RIGH uhs	dəˈraɪəs
Darlan	dahr LAHN	dɑrˈlɑn
Darmstadt	DAHRM shtaht	ˈdɑrmʃtɑt
Darrieux	da ri ER	dærɪˈɝ
Darwin	DAHR win	ˈdɑrwɪn
Darwinian	dahr WI ni uhn	dɑrˈwɪnɪən
dasheen	da SHEEN	dæˈʃin
Dassin, Jules	dah SAN, zhoo : l	dɑˈsæn, ʒul
data	DAY tuh	ˈdetə
datum	DAY tuhm	ˈdetəm
datura	duh TYOO ruh	dəˈtjʊrə
Daudet	doh DAY	doˈde
Daumier	doh MYAY	doˈmje
daunt	dawnt	dɔnt
dauphin	DAW fin	ˈdɔfɪn
Dauphin, Claude	doh FAN, klohd	doˈfæn, klod
dauphine	doh FEEN	doˈfin
Dauphiné	doh fee NAY	dofiˈne
dauphinoise	doh fee NWAHZ	dofiˈnwɑz
David (European)	dah VEED	dɑˈvid
da Vinci	duh VIN chi	dəˈvɪntʃɪ
Davis	DAY vis	ˈdevɪs
davit	DA vit	ˈdævɪt
deaf	def	dɛf
Deauville	DOH vil	ˈdovɪl
debacle	day BAH kuhl	deˈbɑkəl
debar	di BAHR	dɪˈbɑr
debark	di BAHRK	dɪˈbɑrk
debase	di BAYS	dɪˈbes
debate	di BAYT	dɪˈbet
debauch	di BAWCH	dɪˈbɔtʃ
debenture	di BEN cher	dɪˈbɛntʃer
debit	DE bit	ˈdɛbɪt
debonair, -e	de buh NAIR	dɛbəˈnɛr
Deborah	DE buh ruh	ˈdɛbərə
debouch	di BOO : SH	dɪˈbuʃ
Debré	duh BRAY	dəˈbre
Debrecen	DE bret sen	ˈdɛbrɛtsɛn
debris	duh BREE	dəˈbri
Debs	debz	dɛbz

at [æ]; ah [ɑ]; air [ɛ]; awful [ɔ]; say [e]; back [b]; chair [tʃ]; do [d]; elm [ɛ]; eel [i]; server [ˈɝ, ər]; fit [f]; go [g]; hurt [h]; is [ɪ]; high [aɪ]; jet [dʒ]; kiss [k]; lamb [l]; my [m]; nice [n];

Debussy	duh BYOO : si	dəˈbjusɪ
debut	di BYOO :	dɪˈbju
debutante	de byoo TAHNT	dɛbjuˈtɑnt
decade	DE kayd	ˈdɛked
decadence	DE kuh duhns	ˈdɛkədəns
decadent	DE kuh duhnt	ˈdɛkədənt
decal	DEE kal	ˈdikæl
decant	di KANT	dɪˈkænt
decapitate	di KA puh tayt	dɪˈkæpətet
decathlon	di KATH lahn	dɪˈkæθlɑn
Decatur	di KAY ter	dɪˈketər
Deccan	DE kuhn	ˈdɛkən
December	di SEM ber	dɪˈsɛmbər
decentralization	dee sen truh li ZAY shuhn	disɛntrəlɪˈzeʃən
decibel	DE suh bel	ˈdɛsəbɛl
decide	di SIGHD	dɪˈsaɪd
deciduous	di SI joo uhs	dɪˈsɪdʒʊəs
Decies	DEE sheez	ˈdiʃiz
decisive	di SIGH siv	dɪˈsaɪsɪv
declamatory	di KLA muh taw ri	dɪˈklæmətɔrɪ
declaration	de kluh RAY shuhn	dɛkləˈreʃən
déclassé	day kla SAY	deklæˈse
decline	di KLIGHN	dɪˈklaɪn
décolleté	day kahl TAY	dekɑlˈte
decompose	dee kuhm POHZ	dikəmˈpoz
décor	day KAWR	deˈkɔr
decorative	DE kuh ray tiv	ˈdɛkəretɪv
decorous	DE kuh ruhs	ˈdɛkərəs
decrease (n)	DEE krees	ˈdikris
decrease (v)	di KREES	dɪˈkris
decrepitude	di KRE puh too : d	dɪˈkrɛpətud
decrescendo	dee kruh SHEN doh	dikrəˈʃendo
dedicate	DE duh kayt	ˈdɛdəket
dedicatory	DE duh kuh taw ri	ˈdɛdəkətɔrɪ
deduce	di DOO : S	dɪˈdus
de facto	dee FAK toh	diˈfækto
defalcate	di FAL kayt	dɪˈfælket
defamatory	di FA muh taw ri	dɪˈfæmətɔrɪ
defense	di FENS	dɪˈfɛns
deference	DE fuh ruhns	ˈdɛfərəns
deficient	di FI shuhnt	dɪˈfɪʃənt
deficit	DE fuh sit	ˈdɛfəsɪt
defile	di FIGHL	dɪˈfaɪl
definite	DE fuh nit	ˈdɛfənɪt
Defoe	di FOH	dɪˈfo
dégagé	day gah ZHAY	degɑˈʒe
Degas	duh GAH	dəˈgɑ
De Gaulle	duh GOHL	dəˈgol
degenerate (a, n)	di JE nuh rit	dɪˈdʒɛnərɪt
degenerate (v)	di JE nuh rayt	dɪˈdʒɛnəret
Deianira	DEE uh NIGH ruh	ˈdiəˈnaɪrə
deign	dayn	den

si*ng* [ŋ] ; *oh* [o] ; *oil* [ɔɪ] ; *foot* [ʊ] ; *foo*:d [u] ; *how* [aʊ] ; *pie* [p] ; *ray* [r] ; *so* [s] ; *shall* [ʃ] ; *to* [t] ; *thin* [θ] ; *th*:en [ð] ; *above* (*uh* B*UH*V) [ə, ˈʌ] ; *v*ine [v] ; *w*ine [w] ; *wh*ine [hw] ; *y*ou [j] ; *z*oo [z] ; *rouge* (roo:*zh*) [ʒ].

Deimos	DIGH muhs	ˈdaɪməs
Deiphobus	dee I fuh buhs	diˈɪfəbəs
Deirdre	DIR dri	ˈdɪrdrɪ
déjeuner	day zher NAY	deʒərˈne
De Jong	duh YAWNG	dəˈjɔŋ
de jure	dee JOO ri	di ˈdʒʊrɪ
de Kooning, Willem	duh KOHN ing, VI lem	də konɪŋ, ˈvɪlɛm
De Koven	di KOH vuhn	dɪˈkovən
de Kruif	duh KRIGHF	də kraɪf
Delacroix	duh la KRWAH	dəlæˈkrwɑ
de la Mare	duh luh MAIR	dələˈmɛr
de la Roche, Mazo	duh lah RUHSH, ma ZOH	də lɑ ˈrʌʃ, mæˈzo
Delaware	DE luh wair	ˈdɛləwɛr
delectation	dee lek TAY shuhn	dilɛkˈteʃən
delegate (n)	DE luh git	ˈdɛləgɪt
delegate (v)	DE luh gayt	ˈdɛləget
deleterious	de luh TI ri uhs	dɛləˈtɪrɪəs
Delgado	del GAH doh	dɛlˈgɑdo
Delhi	DE li	ˈdɛlɪ
deliberate (a)	di LI buh rit	dɪˈlɪbərɪt
deliberate (v)	di LI buh rayt	dɪˈlɪbəret
deliberative	di LI buh ray tiv	dɪˈlɪbəretɪv
Delibes	duh LEEB	dəˈlib
Delilah	di LIGH luh	dɪˈlaɪlə
Della Casa, Lisa	de luh KAH suh, LEE suh	dɛlə ˈkɑsə, ˈlisə
Della Chiesa	DE luh ki AY zuh	ˈdɛlə kɪˈezə
Dello Joio	de luh JOI oh	dɛlə ˈdʒɔɪo
Delmar	del MAHR	dɛlˈmɑr
Del Monaco, Mario	del MOH nah koh, MAH ree oh	dɛl ˈmonɑko, ˈmɑrio
delphinium	del FI ni uhm	dɛlˈfɪnɪəm
Delphinus	del FIGH nuhs	dɛlˈfaɪnəs
delude	di LOO : D	dɪˈlud
delusion	di LOO : zhuhn	dɪˈluʒən
delusive	di LOO : siv	dɪˈlusɪv
de luxe	di LOOKS	dɪˈlʊks
demagogue	DE muh gahg	ˈdɛməgɑg
demand	di MAND	dɪˈmænd
demarcation	dee mahr KAY shuhn	dimɑrˈkeʃən
Demarest	DE muh ruhst	ˈdɛmərəst
dementia praecox	di MEN shuh PREE kahks	dɪˈmɛnʃə ˈprikɑks
Demerol	DE muh rohl	ˈdɛmərol
demesne	di MAYN	dɪˈmen
Demeter	di MEE ter	dɪˈmitər
Demetrius	di MEE tri uhs	dɪˈmitrɪəs
DeMille (Cecil B.)	duh MIL	dəˈmɪl
demi-monde	DE mi mahnd	ˈdɛmɪmɑnd
demise	di MIGHZ	dɪˈmaɪz
demi-tasse	DE mi tas	ˈdɛmɪtæs
demoiselle	de mwah ZEL	dɛmwɑˈzɛl
demoniac	di MOH ni ak	dɪˈmonɪæk
demoniacal	dee muh NIGH uh kuhl	dimməˈnaɪəkəl

at [æ] ; *ah* [ɑ] ; *air* [ɛ] ; *awful* [ɔ] ; *say* [e] ; *back* [b] ; *chair* [tʃ] ; *do* [d] ; *elm* [ɛ] ; *eel* [i] ; *server* [ˈɜ, ər] ; *f* it [f] ; *go* [g] ; *h*urt [h] ; *is* [ɪ] ; *high* [aɪ] ; *jet* [dʒ] ; *kiss* [k] ; *lamb* [l] ; *my* [m] ; *nice* [n] ;

demonology	dee muh NAH luh ji	dimə'nɑlədʒɪ
demonstrable	di MAHN struh buhl	dɪ'mɑnstrəbəl
demonstrate	DE muhn strayt	'dɛmənstret
demonstrative	di MAHN struh tiv	dɪ'mɑnstrətɪv
Demosthenes	di MAHS thuh neez	dɪ'mɑsθəniz
demur	di MER	dɪ'mɚ
demure	di MYOOR	dɪ'mjʊr
demurrer	di MER er	dɪ'mɚər
Demus, Jeorg	DAY moos, GAY awrg	'demʊs, 'geɔrg
demy	di MIGH	dɪ'maɪ
Deneb	DE neb	'dɛnɛb
dengue	DENG gi	'dɛŋgɪ
denier	duh NIR	də'nɪr
denigrate	DE nuh grayt	'dɛnəgret
Denmark	DEN mahrk	'dɛnmɑrk
denotation	dee noh TAY shuhn	dino'teʃən
denote	di NOHT	dɪ'not
denouement	day NOO : mahn	de'numɑn
de novo	dee NOH voh	di'novo
denunciate	di NUHN si ayt	dɪ'nʌnsiet
denunciation	di nuhn si AY shuhn	dɪnənsɪ'eʃən
depletion	di PLEE shuhn	dɪ'pliʃən
deposition	de puh ZI shuhn	dɛpə'zɪʃən
depot (military)	DE poh	'dɛpo
depot (railroad)	DEE poh	'dipo
deprecate	DE pruh kayt	'dɛprəket
depreciate	di PREE shi ayt	dɪ'priʃiet
depreciation	di pree shi AY shuhn	dɪpriʃɪ'eʃən
depredate	DE pri dayt	'dɛprɪdet
depredation	de pri DAY shuhn	dɛprɪ'deʃən
deprivation	de pruh VAY shuhn	dɛprə'veʃən
deprive	di PRIGHV	dɪ'praɪv
de profundis	dee proh FUHN dis	di pro'fʌndɪs
depute	di PYOO : T	dɪ'pjut
deputy	DE pyoo ti	'dɛpjʊtɪ
derby, D-	DER bi	'dɚbɪ
derby, D- (British)	DAHR bi	'dɑrbɪ
derelict	DE ruh likt	'dɛrəlɪkt
Deressa	de RE sah	dɛ'rɛsɑ
de rigueur	duh ree GER	də ri'gɛr
derivation	de ruh VAY shuhn	dɛrə'veʃən
dermatologist	der muh TAH luh jist	dɚmə'tɑlədʒɪst
dermatology	der muh TAH luh ji	dɚmə'tɑlədʒɪ
de Rochemont, Louis	duh rohsh MOHN, loo : EE	də roʃ'mon, lu'i
derogatory	di RAH guh taw.ri	dɪ'rɑgətɔrɪ
Dervaux	DAIR voh	'dɛərvo
De Sapio	duh SA pee oh	də 'sæpio
Desarzens	day zahr ZENZ	dezɑr'zɛnz
descant (n)	DE skant	'dɛskænt
descant (v)	de SKANT	dɛ'skænt
Descartes	day KAHRT	de'kɑrt
Desdemona	dez duh MOH nuh	dɛzdə'monə

sing [ŋ] ; *oh* [o] ; *oil* [ɔɪ] ; *foot* [ʊ] ; *foo:*d [u] ; *how* [aʊ] ; *pie* [p] ; *ray* [r] ; *so* [s] ; *sh*all [ʃ] ;
*t*o [t] ; *th*in [θ] ; *th:*en [ð] ; *above (uh BUHV)* [ə, 'ʌ] ; *v*ine [v] ; *w*ine [w] ; *wh*ine [hw] ;
*y*ou [j] ; *z*oo [z] ; *rouge (roo:zh)* [ʒ].

desert (n)	DE zert	ˈdɛzərt
desert (v)	di ZERT	dɪˈzɝt
deshabille	de zuh BEEL	dɛzəˈbil
De Sica, Vittorio	duh SEE kuh, vee TAWR yoh	də ˈsikə, viˈtɔrjo
desiccate	DE si kayt	ˈdɛsɪket
desideratum	di si duh RAY tuhm	dɪsɪdəˈretəm
designate (a)	DE zig nit	ˈdɛzɪgnɪt
designate (v)	DE zig nayt	ˈdɛzɪgnet
Des Moines	di MOIN	dɪˈmɔɪn
desolate (a)	DE suh lit	ˈdɛsəlɪt
desolate (v)	DE suh layt	ˈdɛsəlet
Désormière	day zawr MYAIR	dezɔrˈmjɛər
De Soto, de Soto	di SOH toh	dɪ ˈsoto
despatch	di SPACH	dɪˈspætʃ
desperado	de spuh RAH do	dɛspəˈrɑdo
despicable	DE spi kuh buhl	ˈdɛspɪkəbəl
Dessau	DE sow	ˈdɛsau
dessert	di ZERT	dɪˈzɝt
de Stijl, D-	duh STIGHL	də ˈstaɪl
destine	DE stin	ˈdɛstɪn
destiny	DE stuh ni	ˈdɛstənɪ
destruct	di STRUHKT	dɪˈstrʌkt
desuetude	DE swi too:d	ˈdɛswɪtud
desultory	DE suhl taw ri	ˈdɛsəltɔrɪ
detail (n)	DEE tayl	ˈditel
detail (v)	di TAYL	dɪˈtel
détente	day TAHNT	deˈtɑnt
deter	di TER	dɪˈtɝ
detergent	di TER juhnt	dɪˈtɝdʒənt
deteriorate	di TI ri uh rayt	dɪˈtɪrɪəret
determinism	di TER mi ni zuhm	dɪˈtɝmɪnɪzəm
deterrent	di TER uhnt	dɪˈtɝənt
de Tocqueville	di TAHK vil	dɪ ˈtɑkvɪl
detonate	DE tuh nayt	ˈdɛtənet
detour	DEE toor	ˈditʊr
Detroit	di TROIT	dɪˈtrɔɪt
de trop	duh TROH	dəˈtro
deuce	doo:s	dus
deucedly	DOO:sid li	ˈdusɪdlɪ
deus ex machina	DEE uhs eks MA ki nuh	ˈdiəs ɛks ˈmækɪnə
Deuteronomy	doo:tuh RAH nuh mi	dutəˈrɑnəmɪ
Deutschland	DOICH lahnt	ˈdɔɪtʃlɑnt
De Valera, Eamon	de vuh LAI ruh, AY muhn	dɛ vəˈlɛrə, ˈemən
devastate	DE vuh stayt	ˈdɛvəstet
deviant	DEE vi uhnt	ˈdiviənt
deviate (a, n)	DEE vi it	ˈdivɪɪt
deviate (v)	DEE vi ayt	ˈdiviet
deviationism	dee vi AY shuh ni zuhm	divɪˈeʃənɪzəm
Devonshire	DE vuhn shir	ˈdɛvənʃɪr
devotee	de vuh TEE	dɛvəˈti
De Vries	duh VREES	dəˈvris

at [æ]; ah [ɑ]; air [ɛ]; awful [ɔ]; say [e]; back [b]; chair [tʃ]; do [d]; elm [ɛ]; eel [i]; server [ˈɝ, ər]; fit [f]; go [g]; hurt [h]; is [ɪ]; high [aɪ]; jet [dʒ]; kiss [k]; lamb [l]; my [m]; nice [n];

diabetes	digh uh BEE tis	daɪəˈbitɪs
diable	di AH bluh	dɪˈɑblə
diabolic	digh uh BAH lik	daɪəˈbɑlɪk
diacritic	digh uh KRI tik	daɪəˈkrɪtɪk
diadem	DIGH uh dem	ˈdaɪədɛm
diagnose	digh uhg NOHS	daɪəgˈnos
diagnosis	digh uhg NOH sis	daɪəgˈnosɪs
diagram	DIGH uh gram	ˈdaɪəgræm
diagrammatic	digh uh gruh MA tik	daɪəgrəˈmætɪk
dialect	DIGH uh lekt	ˈdaɪəlɛkt
dialectics	digh uh LEK tiks	daɪəˈlɛtɪks
dialog, -ue	DIGH uh lawg	ˈdaɪəlɔg
diameter	digh A muh ter	daɪˈæməter
diamond	DIGH uh muhnd	ˈdaɪəmənd
Diana	digh A nuh	daɪˈænə
dianthus	digh AN thuhs	daɪˈænθəs
diapason	digh uh PAY zuhn	daɪəˈpezən
diaphragm	DIGH uh fram	ˈdaɪəfræm
diarrhea, diarrhoea	digh uh REE uh	daɪəˈriə
diary	DIGH uh ri	ˈdaɪərɪ
diastole	digh A stuh lee	daɪˈæstəli
diastolic	digh uh STAH lik	daɪəˈstɑlɪk
diatom	DIGH uh tuhm	ˈdaɪətəm
diatonic	digh uh TAH nik	daɪəˈtɑnɪk
diatribe	DIGH uh trighb	ˈdaɪətraɪb
Diaz	DEE ahs	ˈdiɑs
Dichter	DISH tuhr	ˈdɪʃtər
dictate	DIK tayt	ˈdɪktet
dictator	DIK tay ter	ˈdɪktetər
dictionary	DIK shuh nai ri	ˈdɪkʃənɛrɪ
dicumarol, D-	digh KOO : muh rawl	daɪˈku:mərɔl
didactic	digh DAK tik	daɪˈdæktɪk
Diderot	DEE duh roh	ˈdidəro
Dido	DIGH doh	ˈdaɪdo
Diefenbaker	DEE fuhn bay ker	ˈdifənbekər
Diego	dee AY goh	diˈego
Diem	dyem	djɛm
diene	DIGH een	ˈdaɪin
Dieppe	di EP	dɪˈɛp
Dies, Martin	dighz	daɪz
diesel, D-	DEE zuhl	ˈdizəl
Dies Irae	DIGH eez IGH ree	ˈdaɪiz ˈaɪri
diet	DIGH uht	ˈdaɪət
dietary	DIGH uh tai ri	ˈdaɪətɛrɪ
dietetic	digh uh TE tik	daɪəˈtɛtɪk
dictician, dietitian	digh uh TI shuhn	daɪəˈtɪʃən
Dietrich, Marlene	DEE trik, mahr LAY nuh	ˈditrɪk, mɑrˈlenə
dieu, D-	dyer	djɝ
differentiate	di fuh REN shi ayt	dɪfəˈrɛnʃɪet
differentiation	di fuh ren shi AY shuhn	dɪfərɛnʃɪˈeʃən
difficile (French)	di fuh SEEL	dɪfəˈsil
diffraction	di FRAK shuhn	dɪˈfrækʃən

---

sing [ŋ]; *oh* [o]; *oil* [ɔɪ]; *foot* [ʊ]; *foo*:d [u]; *how* [aʊ]; *pie* [p]; *ray* [r]; *so* [s]; *shall* [ʃ];
to [t]; *thin* [θ]; *th*:en [ð]; *above* (*uh* B*UH*V) [ə, ˈʌ]; *vine* [v]; *wine* [w]; *whine* [hw];
you [j]; *zoo* [z]; *rouge* (roo:*zh*) [ʒ].

diffuse (a)	di FYOO : S	dɪˈfjus
diffuse (v)	di FYOO : Z	dɪˈfjuz
digest (n)	DIGH jest	ˈdaɪdʒɛst
digest (v)	di JEST	dɪˈdʒɛst
digestion	di JES chuhn	dɪˈdʒɛstʃən
digital	DI ji tuhl	ˈdɪdʒɪtəl
digitalis	di ji TA lis	dɪdʒɪˈtælɪs
digress	duh GRES	dəˈgrɛs
dilapidated	di LA puh day tid	dɪˈlæpədetɪd
dilate	digh LAYT	daɪˈlet
dilatory	DI luh taw ri	ˈdɪlətɔrɪ
dilemma	di LE muh	dɪˈlɛmə
dilettante	DI luh tahnt	ˈdɪlətɑnt
dilettanti	di luh TAHN ti	dɪləˈtɑntɪ
Dillon	DI luhn	ˈdɪlən
dilute	di LOO : T	dɪˈlut
Di Maggio, Joe	di MA ji oh	dɪˈmædʒɪo
dimension	duh MEN shuhn	dəˈmɛnʃən
diminish	duh MI nish	dəˈmɪnɪʃ
diminuendo	duh mi nyoo EN doh	dəmɪnjuˈɛndo
Dimitrov	di MEE trawf	dɪˈmitrɔf
dimity	DI muh ti	ˈdɪmətɪ
Dinard	dee NAHR	diˈnɑr
Dinbergs	DEEN bairgs	ˈdinbɛrgs
Dinesen, Isak	DEE nuh suhn, EE sahk	ˈdinəsən, ˈisɑk
dinghy	DING gi	ˈdɪŋgɪ
dinosaur	DIGH nuh sawr	ˈdaɪnəsɔr
diocesan	digh AH suh suhn	daɪˈɑsəsən
diocese	DIGH uh sees	ˈdaɪəsis
Diogenes	digh AH juh neez	daɪˈɑdʒəniz
Diomede	DIGH uh meed	ˈdaɪəmid
Diomedes	digh uh MEE deez	daɪəˈmidiz
Dione	digh OH ni	daɪˈonɪ
Dionne	di UHN	dɪˈʌn
Dionysius	digh uh NI shi uhs	daɪəˈnɪʃɪəs
Dionysus	digh uh NIGH suhs	daɪəˈnaɪsəs
Dior	di AWR	dɪˈɔr
diorama	digh uh RA muh	daɪəˈræmə
Dioscuri	digh uh SKYOO righ	daɪəˈskjʊraɪ
diphtheria	dif THI ri uh	dɪfˈθɪrɪə
diphthong	DIF thawng	ˈdɪfθɔŋ
diphthongal	dif THAWNG guhl	dɪfˈθɔŋgəl
diplomacy	di PLOH muh si	dɪˈploməsɪ
diplomat	DI pluh mat	ˈdɪpləmæt
diplomate	DI pluh mayt	ˈdɪpləmet
diplomatist	di PLOH muh tist	dɪˈplomətɪst
dipsomania	dip suh MAY ni uh	dɪpsəˈmenɪə
diptych	DIP tik	ˈdɪptɪk
direct	duh REKT	dəˈrɛkt
direction	duh REK shuhn	dəˈrɛkʃən
directly	duh REKT li	dəˈrɛktlɪ
dirigible	DI ri juh buhl	ˈdɪrɪdʒəbəl

at [æ] ; *ah* [ɑ] ; *air* [ɛ] ; *awful* [ɔ] ; *say* [e] ; *back* [b] ; *chair* [tʃ] ; *do* [d] ; *elm* [ɛ] ; *eel* [i] ; *server* [ˈɝ, ər] ; *f*it [f] ; *go* [g] ; *hurt* [h] ; *is* [ɪ] ; *high* [aɪ] ; *jet* [dʒ] ; *kiss* [k] ; *lamb* [l] ; *my* [m] ; *nice* [n] ;

Dirksen	DERK suhn	ˈdɚksən
dirndl	DERN duhl	ˈdɚndəl
disable	dis AY buhl	dɪsˈebəl
DiSalle	di SAL	dɪˈsæl
disarm	dis AHRM	dɪsˈɑrm
disaster	di ZA ster	dɪˈzæstər
disburse	dis BERS	dɪsˈbɚs
discern	di SERN	dɪˈsɚn
discernible	di SER nuh buhl	dɪˈsɚnəbəl
discernment	di SERN muhnt	dɪˈsɚnmənt
discharge (n)	DIS chahrj	ˈdɪstʃɑrdʒ
discharge (v)	dis CHAHRJ	dɪsˈtʃɑrdʒ
disciplinary	DI suh pli nai ri	ˈdɪsəplɪnɛrɪ
discipline	DI suh plin	ˈdɪsəplɪn
disclosure	dis KLOH zher	dɪsˈkloʒər
discount (n)	DIS kownt	ˈdɪskaʊnt
discount (v)	dis KOWNT	dɪsˈkaʊnt
discourse (n)	DIS kawrs	ˈdɪskɔrs
discourse (v)	dis KAWRS	dɪsˈkɔrs
discourteous	dis KER ti uhs	dɪsˈkɚtɪəs
discrepancy	dis KRE puhn si	dɪsˈkrɛpənsɪ
discrepant	dis KRE puhnt	dɪsˈkrɛpənt
discretionary	di SKRE shuh nai ri	dɪˈskrɛʃənɛrɪ
discursive	dis KER siv	dɪsˈkɚsɪv
disdain	dis DAYN	dɪsˈden
disease	di ZEEZ	dɪˈziz
diseased	di ZEEZD	dɪˈzizd
disenfranchise	dis in FRAN chighz	dɪsɪnˈfræntʃaɪz
disfranchise	dis FRAN chighz	dɪsˈfræntʃaɪz
disfranchisement	dis FRAN chiz muhnt	dɪsˈfræntʃɪzmənt
disgorge	dis GAWRJ	dɪsˈgɔrdʒ
disguise	dis GIGHZ	dɪsˈgaɪz
dishabille	di suh BEEL	dɪsəˈbil
disheveled	di SHE vuhld	dɪˈʃɛvəld
dishonest	dis AH nist	dɪsˈɑnɪst
dishonor, dishonour	dis AH ner	dɪsˈɑnər
disillusion	di si LOO : zhuhn	dɪsɪˈluʒən
disintegrate	dis IN tuh grayt	dɪsˈɪntəgret
disinterested	dis IN tri stid	dɪsˈɪntrɪstɪd
disjunctive	dis JUHNGK tiv	dɪsˈdʒʌŋktɪv
dislike	dis LIGHK	dɪsˈlaɪk
dismantle	dis MAN tuhl	dɪsˈmæntəl
dismay	dis MAY	dɪsˈme
dismember	dis MEM ber	dɪsˈmɛmbər
Disney	DIZ ni	ˈdɪznɪ
disoblige	di suh BLIGHJ	dɪsəˈblaɪdʒ
disorder	dis AWR der	dɪsˈɔrdər
disorganize	dis AWR guh nighz	dɪsˈɔrgənaɪz
disown	dis OHN	dɪsˈon
disparage	di SPA rij	dɪˈspærɪdʒ
disparate	DI spuh rit	ˈdɪspərɪt
dispatch	di SPACH	dɪˈspætʃ

dispersion	di SPER zhuhn	dɪˈspɜˈʒən
display	di SPLAY	dɪˈsple
dispossess	di spuh ZES	dɪspəˈzɛs
disputable	di SPYOO : tuh buhl	dɪˈspjutəbəl
disputant	DI spyoo tuhnt	ˈdɪspjʊtənt
disputatious	di spyoo TAY shuhs	dɪspjuˈteʃəs
disputative	di SPYOO : tuh tiv	dɪˈsputətɪv
dispute	di SPYOO : T	dɪˈspjut
Disraeli	diz RAY li	dɪzˈrelɪ
disreputable	dis RE pyoo tuh buhl	dɪsˈrɛpjutəbəl
dissemble	di SEM buhl	dɪˈsɛmbəl
disseminate	di SE muh nayt	dɪˈsɛmənet
dissent	di SENT	dɪˈsɛnt
dissidence	DI suh duhns	ˈdɪsədəns
dissident	DI suh duhnt	ˈdɪsədənt
dissociate	di SOH shi ayt	dɪˈsoʃiet
dissociation	di soh si AY shuhn	dɪsosiˈeʃən
dissoluble	di SAH lyoo buhl	dɪˈsɑljʊbəl
dissolute	DI suh loo : t	ˈdɪsəlut
dissolution	di suh LOO : shuhn	dɪsəˈluʃən
dissolve	di ZAHLV	dɪˈzɑlv
dissolvent	di ZAHL vuhnt	dɪˈzɑlvənt
dissuade	di SWAYD	dɪˈswed
dissyllabic	di si LA bik	dɪsɪˈlæbɪk
Di Stefano	dee STE fah noh	di ˈstɛfɑno
distich	DI stik	ˈdɪstɪk
distillate	DI stuh lit	ˈdɪstəlɪt
distinct	di STINGKT	dɪˈstɪŋkt
distingué	di stang GAY	dɪstæŋˈge
distrait	di STRAY	dɪˈstre
distraught	di STRAWT	dɪˈstrɔt
dither	DI th : er	ˈdɪðər
dithyramb	DI thuh ram	ˈdɪθəræm
dithyrambic	di thuh RAM bik	dɪθəˈræmbɪk
diuresis	digh yoo REE sis	daɪjuˈrisɪs
diuretic	digh yoo RE tik	daɪjuˈrɛtɪk
diva	DEE vuh	ˈdivə
divagation	digh vuh GAY shuhn	daɪvəˈgeʃən
divan	DIGH van	ˈdaɪvæn
diverge	duh VERJ	dəˈvɜˈdʒ
divergence	duh VER juhns	dəˈvɜˈdʒəns
divers	DIGH verz	ˈdaɪvərz
diverse	duh VERS	dəˈvɜˈs
diversion	duh VER zhuhn	dəˈvɜˈʒən
divert	duh VERT	dəˈvɜˈt
Dives	DIGH veez	ˈdaɪviz
divest	duh VEST	dəˈvɛst
divide	duh VIGHD	dəˈvaɪd
dividend	DI vuh dend	ˈdɪvədɛnd
divorcee	duh VAWR say	dəˈvɔrse
divulge	duh VUHLJ	dəˈvʌldʒ
Dixiecrat	DIK si krat	ˈdɪksɪkræt

Djakarta	jah KAHR tuh	dʒaˈkɑrtə
Djakovica	DYAH kaw vit sah	ˈdjɑkɔvɪtsɑ
Djanet	JA net	ˈdʒænɛt
djebel, D-	JE buhl	ˈdʒɛbəl
Djibouti	ji BOO: ti	dʒɪˈbutɪ
Djilas, Milovan	JEE lahs, MEE loh vahn	ˈdʒilɑs, ˈmilovɑn
Dnepr	NEE per	ˈnipər
Dnepropetrovsk	nye praw pye TRAWFSK	njɛprɔpjeˈtrɔfsk
Dnestr	NEE ster	ˈnistər
Dnieper	NEE per	ˈnipər
Dniester	NEE ster	ˈnistər
Dobrudja, Dobruja	DOH broo juh	ˈdobrʊdʒə
docent	DOH suhnt	ˈdosənt
docile	DAH suhl	ˈdɑsəl
doctrinaire	dahk tri NAIR	dɑktrɪˈnɛr
doctrinal	DAHK tri nuhl	ˈdɑktrɪnəl
Dodecanese	doh DE kuh neez	doˈdɛkəniz
Dodgson	DAHJ suhn	ˈdɑdʒsən
dog	dawg	dɔg
doge	dohj	dodʒ
dogged (a)	DAW gid	ˈdɔgɪd
dogged (v)	dawgd	dɔgd
Dogger	DAW ger	ˈdɔgər
doggerel	DAW gu ruhl	ˈdɔgərəl
dogma	DAWG muh	ˈdɔgmə
Dohnányi	doh NAHN yee	doˈnɑnji
dolce far niente	DAWL che fahr NYEN te	ˈdɔltʃɛ fɑr ˈnjɛntɛ
doldrums	DAHL druhms	ˈdɑldrəms
doll	dahl	dɑl
dollar	DAH ler	ˈdɑlər
Dollfuss	DAHL fuhs	ˈdɑlfəs
dolman	DAHL muhn	ˈdɑlmən
dolomite	DAH luh might	ˈdɑləmaɪt
Dolores	duh LAW ris	dəˈlɔrɪs
doloroso	doh luh ROH soh	doləˈroso
dolorous	DAH luh ruhs	ˈdɑlərəs
Domei	doh MAY	doˈme
domicile	DAH muh sil	ˈdɑməsɪl
Dominican	duh MI ni kuhn	dəˈmɪnɪkən
Domremy	dohn ruh MEE	donrəˈmi
Don	dahn	dɑn
Donat	DOH nat	ˈdonæt
Donau	DOH now	ˈdonaʊ
Donegal	DAH ni gawl	ˈdɑnɪgɔl
Donets	dah NETS	dɑˈnɛts
Don Giovanni	dahn joh VAH ni	dɑn dʒoˈvɑnɪ
Donizetti	dah nuh ZE ti	dɑnəˈzɛtɪ
donjon	DUHN juhn	ˈdʌndʒən
Don Juan (Byron)	dahn JOO: uhn	dɑn ˈdʒuən
Don Juan (Spanish)	dawn HWAHN	dɔn ˈhwɑn
donkey	DAHNG ki	ˈdɑŋkɪ
Donna, d-	DAH nuh	ˈdɑnə

si*ng* [ŋ] ; *oh* [o] ; *oil* [ɔɪ] ; *foot* [ʊ] ; *foo*:d [u] ; *how* [aʊ] ; *p*ie [p] ; *r*ay [r] ; *s*o [s] ; *sh*all [ʃ] ; *t*o [t] ; *th*in [θ] ; *th*:en [ð] ; above (*uh* B*UH*V) [ə, ˈʌ] ; *v*ine [v] ; *w*ine [w] ; *wh*ine [hw] ; *y*ou [j] ; *z*oo [z] ; rouge (roo:*zh*) [ʒ].

Donne	duhn	dʌn
Donnybrook	DAH ni brook	ˈdɑnɪbrʊk
Don Pasquale	dahn pa SKWAH li	dɑn pæˈskwɑlɪ
Don Quijote, Don Quixote (Spanish)	dawn kee HOH tay	dɔn kiˈhote
Don Quixote	dahn KWIK suht	dɑn ˈkwɪksət
doodle	DOO : duhl	ˈdudəl
dopey	DOH pi	ˈdopɪ
Doppelgänger, d-	DAW puhl gayng ger	ˈdɔpəlgeŋər
doppler, D-	DAH pler	ˈdɑplər
Dorati	daw RAH ti	dɔˈrɑtɪ
Dorcas	DAWR kuhs	ˈdɔrkəs
Doré	daw RAY	dɔˈre
Doremus	duh REE muhs	dəˈriməs
dormitory	DAWR muh taw ri	ˈdɔrmətɔrɪ
Dorothea	dah ruh THEE uh	dɑrəˈθiə
Dorothy	DAH ruh thi	ˈdɑrəθɪ
Dórticos	DAWR ti kaws	ˈdɔrtɪkɔs
Dos Passos	dahs PA sohs	dɑs ˈpæsos
Dostoevski	daw staw YEF ski	dɔstɔˈyɛfskɪ
dotage	DOH tij	ˈdotɪdʒ
dotard	DOH terd	ˈdotərd
doth	duhth	dʌθ
Douai, Douay	doo : AY	duˈe
douane	dwahn	dwɑn
douanier	dwah NYAY	dwɑˈnje
double entendre	DOO : bluh ahn TAHN druh	ˈdublə ɑnˈtɑndrə
doublet	DUH blit	ˈdʌblɪt
doubloon	duh BLOO : N	dəˈblun
douceur	doo : SER	duˈsɝ
douche	doo : sh	duʃ
doughty	DOW ti	ˈdautɪ
Douglas	DUH gluhs	ˈdʌgləs
Doukhobors	DOO : kuh bawrz	ˈdukəbɔrz
dour	door	dʊr
Dover	DOH ver	ˈdovər
Dow	dow	dau
Dowson	DOW suhn	ˈdausən
doxology	dahk SAH luh ji	dɑkˈsɑlədʒɪ
doxy	DAHK si	ˈdɑksɪ
D'Oyly Carte	DOI li KAHRT	ˈdɔɪlɪ ˈkɑrt
dracaena	druh SEE nuh	drəˈsinə
drachm	dram	dræm
drachma	DRAK muh	ˈdrækmə
Draco	DRAY koh	ˈdreko
Draconian, d-	dray KOH ni uhn	dreˈkonɪən
draconic, D-	dray KAH nik	dreˈkɑnɪk
draegerman	DRAY ger muhn	ˈdregərmən
draft	draft	dræft
dragoon	druh GOO : N	drəˈgun
drama	DRAH muh	ˈdrɑmə
dramamine, D-	DRA muh meen	ˈdræməmin

at [æ] ; ah [ɑ] ; air [ɛ] ; awful [ɔ] ; say [e] ; back [b] ; chair [tʃ] ; do [d] ; elm [ɛ] ; eel [i] ; server [ˈɝ, ər] ; fit [f] ; go [g] ; hurt [h] ; is [ɪ] ; high [aɪ] ; jet [dʒ] ; kiss [k] ; lamb [l] ; my [m] ; nice [n] ;

dramatic	druh MA tik	ˈdrəˈmætɪk
dramatis personae	DRA muh tis per SOH nee	ˈdræmətɪs pərˈsoni
dramatist	DRA muh tist	ˈdræmətɪst
dramaturgy	DRA muh ter ji	ˈdræmətərdʒɪ
Drammen	DRAH muhn	ˈdrɑmən
draught	draft	dræft
draughts	drafts	dræfts
Drava	DRAH vah	ˈdrɑvɑ
Dravidian	druh VI di uhn	drəˈvɪdɪən
Dravidic	druh VI dik	drəˈvɪdɪk
Drees	drays	dres
Dreifuss	DRIGH fuhs	ˈdraɪfəs
Dreigroschenoper	DRIGH grohsh uhn OH puhr	ˈdraɪgroʃənˈopər
Dreiser	DRIGH ser	ˈdraɪsər
Dresden	DREZ duhn	ˈdrɛzdən
dressage	dre SAHZH	drɛˈsɑʒ
Dreyfus	DRAY fuhs	ˈdrefəs
drogue	drohg	drog
droll	drohl	drol
drollery	DROH luh ri	ˈdrolərɪ
dromedary	DRAH muh dai ri	ˈdrɑmədɛrɪ
Dromio	DROH mi oh	ˈdromɪo
droshky	DRAHSH ki	ˈdrɑʃkɪ
drought	drowt	draʊt
drouth	drowth	draʊθ
drowned	drownd	draʊnd
druid, D-	DROO : id	ˈdruɪd
Drusilla	droo : SI luh	druˈsɪlə
dryad, D-	DRIGH uhd	ˈdraɪəd
dual	DOO : uhl	ˈduəl
dualism	DOO : uh li zuhm	ˈduəlɪzəm
dub	duhb	dʌb
dubiety	doo : BIGH uh ti	duˈbaɪətɪ
dubious	DOO : bi uhs	ˈdubɪəs
Dublin	DUH blin	ˈdʌblɪn
Dubois	doo : BOIS	duˈbɔɪs
dubonnet, D-	doo : buh NAY	dubəˈne
Dubuque	duh BYOO : K	dəˈbjuk
ducat	DUH kuht	ˈdʌkət
duce, D-	DOO : che	ˈdutʃɛ
Duchamp, Marcel	doo : SHAHM, Mahr SEL	duˈʃɑm, mɑrˈsɛl
Duclos	doo KLOH	duˈklo
ductile	DUHK tuhl	ˈdʌktəl
dude	doo : d	dud
due	doo :	du
due (Italian)	DOO : ay	ˈdue
duel	DOO : uhl	ˈduəl
duenna	doo : E nuh	duˈɛnə
duet	doo : ET	duˈɛt
Duisburg-Hamborn	DEEs boork HAHM bawrn	ˈdisbʊrk ˈhɑmbɔrn
duke	doo : k	duk

sing [ŋ] ; *oh* [o] ; *oil* [ɔɪ] ; *foot* [ʊ] ; *foo:d* [u] ; *how* [aʊ] ; *pie* [p] ; *ray* [r] ; *so* [s] ; *shall* [ʃ] ; *to* [t] ; *thin* [θ] ; *th:en* [ð] ; above (*uh* B*UH*V) [ə, ˈʌ] ; *vine* [v] ; *wine* [w] ; *whine* [hw] ; *you* [j] ; *zoo* [z] ; rouge (roo:*zh*) [ʒ].

H.P.—I

Dukhobors	DOO : kuh bawrz	ˈdukəbɔrz
dulcimer	DUHL suh mer	ˈdʌlsəmər
Dulcinea	duhl SI ni uh	dəlˈsɪnɪə
Dulles	DUH luhs	ˈdʌləs
Duluth	duh LOO : TH	dəˈluθ
Dumas	doo : MAH	duˈmɑ
Du Maurier	duh MAW ree ay	də ˈmɔrie
Dunkirk	DUHN kerk	ˈdʌnkərk
Dunsany	duhn SAY ni	dənˈsenɪ
Duns Scotus	DUHNZ SKOH tuhs	ˈdʌnz ˈskotəs
duodenal	doo : uh DEE nuhl	duəˈdinəl
duodenum	doo : uh DEE nuhm	duəˈdinəm
duomo	DWAW maw	ˈdwɔmɔ
duopoly	dyoo AH puh li	djuˈɑpəlɪ
duopsony	dyoo AHP suh ni	djuˈɑpsənɪ
Duplessis	doo ple SEE	dupleˈsi
duplicate (a, n)	DOO : pluh kit	ˈdupləkɪt
duplicate (v)	DOO : pluh kayt	ˈdupləket
Du Pont	DOO : pahnt	ˈdupɑnt
Duquesne	doo : KAYN	duˈken
dural	DYOO ruhl	ˈdjurəl
duralumin, D-	doo RA loo min	duˈrælumɪn
duration	doo : RAY shuhn	duˈreʃən
durbar	DER bahr	ˈdɚbɑr
Durbin	DER buhn	ˈdɚbən
Dürer, Albrecht	DOO rer, AHL brekt	ˈdurər, ˈalbrɛkt
duress	DOO ris	ˈdurɪs
Durham	DER uhm	ˈdɚəm
during	DOO : ring	ˈdurɪŋ
Durocher	duh ROH sher	dəˈroʃər
Durrell	DER uhl	ˈdɚəl
Düsseldorf	DUH suhl dawrf	ˈdʌsəldorf
duteous	DOO : ti uhs	ˈdutɪəs
Dutra	DOO : trah	ˈdutrɑ
duty	DOO : ti	ˈdutɪ
Dvina	vi NAH	vɪˈnɑ
Dvinsk	veensk	vinsk
Dvořák	VAWR zhak	ˈvɔrʒæk
Dyak	DIGH ak	ˈdaɪæk
Dylan	DI luhn	ˈdɪlən
dynamic	digh NA mik	daɪˈnæmɪk
dynamite	DIGH nuh might	ˈdaɪnəmaɪt
dynamo	DIGH nuh moh	ˈdaɪnəmo
dynast	DIGH nast	ˈdaɪnæst
dynastic	digh NA stik	daɪˈnæstɪk
dynasty	DIGH nuh sti	ˈdaɪnəstɪ
dynatron	DIGH nuh trahn	ˈdaɪnətrɑn
dysbarism	dis BA ri zuhm	dɪsˈbærɪzəm
dysentery	DI suhn tai ri	ˈdɪsəntɛrɪ
dyslexia	dis LEK si uh	dɪsˈlɛksɪə
dysmenorrhea	dis me nuh REE uh	dɪsmɛnəˈriə
dysmetria	dis ME tri uh	dɪsˈmɛtrɪə

at [æ] ; ah [ɑ] ; air [ɛ] ; awful [ɔ] ; say [e] ; back [b] ; chair [tʃ] ; do [d] ; elm [ɛ] ; eel [i] ;
server [ˈɚ, ər] ; fit [f] ; go [g] ; hurt [h] ; is [ɪ] ; high [aɪ] ; jet [dʒ] ; kiss [k] ; lamb [l] ; my [m] ;
nice [n] ;

| dyspepsia | dis PEP shuh | dɪsˈpɛpʃə |
| dysphemia | dis FEE mi uh | dɪsˈfimɪə |

E

eager	EE ger	ˈigər
Eaker	AY ker	ˈekər
Eakins	AY kinz	ˈekɪnz
Earhart	AIR hahrt	ˈɛrhɑrt
early	ER li	ˈɝlɪ
earnest, E-	ER nist	ˈɝnɪst
earthquake	ERTH kwayk	ˈɝθkwek
eastward	EEST werd	ˈistwərd
easy	EE zi	ˈizɪ
eau	oh	o
Eban, Abba	E buhn, AH buh	ˈɛbən, ˈɑbə
ebon	E buhn	ˈɛbən
ebony	E buh ni	ˈɛbənɪ
Ebro	EE broh	ˈibro
ebulition	e buh LI shuhn	ɛbəˈlɪʃən
ebullient	i BUH lyuhnt	ɪˈbʌljənt
ecce homo	EK si HOH moh	ˈɛksɪ ˈhomo
eccentric	ik SEN trik	ɪkˈsɛntrɪk
eccentricity	ek suhn TRI suh ti	ɛksənˈtrɪsətɪ
Eccles	E kuhlz	ˈɛkəlz
Ecclesiastes	i klee zi A steez	ɪklizɪˈæstiz
ecclesiastical	i klee zi A sti kuhl	ɪklizɪˈæstɪkəl
Ecclesiasticus	i klee zi A sti kuhs	ɪklizɪˈæstɪkəs
ecdysiast	ek DI zi ast	ɛkˈdɪzɪæst
echelon	E shuh lahn	ˈɛʃəlɑn
echidna	i KID nuh	ɪˈkɪdnə
echinate	E ki nit	ˈɛkɪnɪt
echo, E-	E koh	ˈɛko
echoic	e KOH ik	ɛˈkoɪk
ecize	EE sighz	ˈisaɪz
éclair	AY klair	ˈeklɛr
éclat	ay KLAH	eˈklɑ
eclectic	i KLEK tik	ɪˈklɛktɪk
eclecticism	i KLEK tuh si zuhm	ɪˈklɛktəsɪzəm
eclipse	i KLIPS	ɪˈklɪps
ecliptic	i KLIP tik	ɪˈklɪptɪk
ecliptical	i KLIP ti kuhl	ɪˈklɪptɪkəl
eclog, -ue	E klawg	ˈɛklɔg
Ecole des Beaux Arts	ay KUHL day boh ZAHR	eˈkʌl de bo ˈzɑr
ecology	ee KAH luh ji	iˈkɑlədʒɪ
economic	ee kuh NAH mik	ikəˈnɑmɪk
economical	ee kuh NAH mi kuhl	ikəˈnɑmɪkəl
economics	ee kuh NAH miks	ikəˈnɑmɪks

sing [ŋ] ; *oh* [o] ; *oil* [ɔɪ] ; *foot* [ʊ] ; *foo*:d [u] ; *how* [aʊ] ; *pie* [p] ; *ray* [r] ; *so* [s] ; *shall* [ʃ] ;
to [t] ; *thin* |θ] ; *th*:en [ð] ; *above* (*uh* B*U*HV) [ə, ˈʌ] ; *vine* [v] ; *wine* [w] ; *whine* [hw] ;
you [j] ; *zoo* [z] ; *rouge* (roo:*zh*) [ʒ].

economist	i KAH nuh mist	ɪˈkɑnəmɪst
economy	i KAH nuh mi	ɪˈkɑnəmɪ
ecotone	EE kuh tohn	ˈikəton
ecotype	EE kuh tighp	ˈikətaɪp
écraseur	ay kra ZER	ekræˈzɝ
ecru	E kroo :	ˈɛkru
ecstasy	EK stuh si	ˈɛkstəsɪ
ecstatic	ik STA tik	ɪkˈstætɪk
ectoplasm	EK tuh pla zuhm	ˈɛktəplæzəm
Ecuador	E kwuh dawr	ˈɛkwədɔr
ecumenical	e kyoo : ME nuh kuhl	ɛkjuˈmɛnəkəl
eczema	EK suh muh	ˈɛksəmə
Edam	EE duhm	ˈidəm
Edda	E duh	ˈɛdə
eddy, E-	E di	ˈɛdɪ
edelweiss	AY duhl vighs	ˈedəlvaɪs
edema	i DEE muh	ɪˈdimə
Eden	EE duhn	ˈidən
edible	E duh buhl	ˈɛdəbəl
edict	EE dikt	ˈidɪkt
edifice	E duh fis	ˈɛdəfɪs
Edinburg (U.S.)	E duhn berg	ˈɛdənbɝg
Edinburgh (Scotland)	E duhn buh roh	ˈɛdənbəro
edition	i DI shuhn	ɪˈdɪʃən
editor	E di ter	ˈɛdɪtər
editorial	e duh TAW ri uhl	ɛdəˈtɔrɪəl
Edom	EE duhm	ˈidəm
educate	E joo kayt	ˈɛdʒʊket
education	e joo KAY shuhn	ɛdʒʊˈkeʃən
eerie, eery	I ri	ˈɪrɪ
effect	uh FEKT	əˈfɛkt
effectual	uh FEK choo uhl	əˈfɛktʃʊəl
effeminacy	uh FEE muh nuh si	əˈfɛmənəsɪ
effeminate	uh FE muh nit	əˈfɛmənɪt
efferent	E fuh ruhnt	ˈɛfərənt
effete	e FEET	ɛˈfit
efficacious	e fuh KAY shuhs	ɛfəˈkeʃəs
efficacy	E fi kuh si	ˈɛfɪkəsɪ
efficient	uh FI shuhnt	əˈfɪʃənt
effigy	E fuh ji	ˈɛfədʒɪ
efflorescence	e flaw RE suhns	ɛflɔˈrɛsəns
effort	E fert	ˈɛfərt
effrontery	e FRUHN tuh ri	ɛˈfrʌntərɪ
effulgence	e FUHL juhns	ɛˈfʌldʒəns
effulgent	e FUHL juhnt	ɛˈfʌldʒənt
effusion	e FYOO : zhuhn	ɛˈfjuʒən
effusive	e FYOO : siv	ɛˈfjusɪv
Efremov	E fruh mawf	ˈɛfrəmɔf
egad	i GAD	ɪˈgæd
Eger	AY ger	ˈegər
Egeria	i JI ri uh	ɪˈdʒɪrɪə
egg	eg	ɛg

at [æ]; ah [ɑ]; air [ɛ]; awful [ɔ]; say [e]; back [b]; chair [tʃ]; do [d]; elm [ɛ]; eel [i];
server [ˈɝ, ər]; fit [f]; go [g]; hurt [h]; is [ɪ]; high [aɪ]; jet [dʒ]; kiss [k]; lamb [l]; my [m];
nice [n];

egis	EE jis	ˈidʒɪs
eglantine	E gluhn tighn	ˈɛgləntaɪn
ego	EE goh	ˈigo
egoism	EE goh i zuhm	ˈigoɪzəm
egoist	EE goh ist	ˈigoɪst
egotism	EE guh ti zuhm	ˈigətɪzəm
egotist	EE guh tist	ˈigətɪst
egregious	i GREE juhs	ɪˈgridʒəs
egregiously	i GREE juhs li	ɪˈgridʒəslɪ
egress	EE gres	ˈigrɛs
egret	EE grit	ˈigrɪt
Egypt	EE jipt	ˈidʒɪpt
Egyptian	i JIP shuhn	ɪˈdʒɪpʃən
Egyptology	ee jip TAH luh ji	idʒɪpˈtalədʒɪ
eh	ay	e
Ehrenburg	e ren BOO : RK	ɛrɛnˈburk
Ehrlich	AIR lik	ˈɛrlɪk
Eichmann	IGHK mahn	ˈaɪkmɑn
eider	IGH der	ˈaɪdər
eidolon	igh DOH luhn	aɪˈdolən
Eiffel	IGH fuhl	ˈaɪfəl
Eiger	IGH ger	ˈaɪgər
eighth	aytth	etθ
eikon	IGH kahn	ˈaɪkɑn
Einstein	IGHN stighn	ˈaɪnstaɪn
Eire	AI ruh	ˈɛrə
Eisenhower	IGH zuhn how er	ˈaɪzənhauər
either	EE th : er	ˈiðər
ejaculation	i ja kyoo LAY shuhn	ɪdʒækjuˈleʃən
eject	i JEKT	ɪˈdʒɛkt
eke	eek	ik
elaborate (a)	i LA buh rit	ɪˈlæbərɪt
elaborate (v)	i LA buh rayt	ɪˈlæbəret
Elaine	i LAYN	ɪˈlen
El Al	el al	ˈɛl ˈæl
El Alamein	el a luh MAYN	ɛl æləˈmen
Elamite	EE luh might	ˈiləmaɪt
élan	ay LAHN	eˈlɑn
elastic	i LA stik	ɪˈlæstɪk
Elberfeld	EL ber felt	ˈɛlbərfɛlt
El Dorado, Eldorado	el doh RAH doh	ɛl doˈrado
Eleazar, Eleazer	e li AY zer	ɛlɪˈezər
elect	i LEKT	ɪˈlɛkt
elector	i LEK ter	ɪˈlɛktər
electoral	i LEK tuh ruhl	ɪˈlɛktərəl
electorate	i LEK tuh rit	ɪˈlɛktərɪt
Electra	i LEK truh	ɪˈlɛktrə
electrically	i LEK tri kuh li	ɪˈlɛktrɪkəlɪ
electricity	i lek TRI suh ti	ɪlɛkˈtrɪsətɪ
electrify	i LEK truh figh	ɪˈlɛktrəfaɪ
electrocardiogram	i lek troh KAHR di uh gram	ɪlɛktroˈkɑrdɪəgræm

---

sing [ŋ] ; *oh* [o] ; *oil* [ɔɪ] ; *foot* [ʊ] ; *foo:*d [u] ; *how* [aʊ] ; *p*ie [p] ; *r*ay [r] ; *s*o [s] ; *sh*all [ʃ] ;
*t*o [t] ; *th*in [θ] ; *th:*en [ð] ; above (*uh* B*UH*V) [ə, ˈʌ] ; *v*ine [v] ; *w*ine [w] ; *wh*ine [hw] ;
*y*ou [j] ; *z*oo [z] ; rouge (roo:*zh*) [ʒ].

electrocute	i LEK truh kyoo : t	ɪˈlɛktrəkjut
electrode	i LEK trohd	ɪˈlɛktrod
electrodynamometer	i lek troh digh nuh MAH muh ter	ɪlɛktrodaɪnəˈmɑmətər
electrolier	i lek troh LIR	ɪlɛktroˈlɪr
electrolysis	i lek TRAH luh sis	ɪlɛkˈtrɑləsɪs
electrolyte	i LEK truh light	ɪˈlɛktrəlaɪt
electromagnetic	i lek troh mag NE tik	ɪlɛktromægˈnɛtɪk
electrometer	i lek TRAH muh ter	ɪlɛkˈtrɑmətər
electromotor	i lek truh MOH ter	ɪlɛktrəˈmotər
electron	i LEK trahn	ɪˈlɛktrɑn
electronic	i lek TRAH nik	ɪlɛkˈtrɑnɪk
electrostatics	i lek truh STA tiks	ɪlɛktrəˈstætɪks
electrotype	i LEK truh tighp	ɪˈlɛktrətaɪp
electrotypy	i LEK truh tigh pi	ɪˈlɛktrətaɪpɪ
electuary	i LEK choo ai ri	ɪˈlɛktʃʊɛrɪ
eleemosynary	e luh MAH suh nai ri	ɛləˈmɑsənɛrɪ
elegance	E luh guhns	ˈɛləgəns
elegant	E luh guhnt	ˈɛləgənt
elegiac	e luh JIGH uhk	ɛləˈdʒaɪək
elegize	e luh JIGHZ	ɛləˈdʒaɪz
element	E luh muhnt	ˈɛləmənt
elemental	e luh MEN tuhl	ɛləˈmɛntəl
elementary	e luh MEN tuh ri	ɛləˈmɛntərɪ
elephant	E luh fuhnt	ˈɛləfənt
elephantiasis	e luh fuhn TIGH uh sis	ɛləfənˈtaɪəsɪs
elephantine	e luh FAN teen	ɛləˈfæntin
Eleusinian	e lyoo SI ni uhn	ɛljuˈsɪnɪən
Eleusis	e LOO : sis	ɛˈlusɪs
elevate	E luh vayt	ˈɛləvet
elevator	E luh vay ter	ˈɛləvetər
eleven	i LE vuhn	ɪˈlɛvən
elevon	E luh vahn	ˈɛləvɑn
Elgin	El jin	ˈɛldʒɪn
Elgin (British)	EL gin	ˈɛlgɪn
El Greco	el GRE koh	ɛl ˈgrɛko
Eli	EE ligh	ˈilaɪ
Elia	EE li uh	ˈilɪə
Elias	i LIGH uhs	ɪˈlaɪəs
elicit	i LI sit	ɪˈlɪsɪt
elide	i LIGHD	ɪˈlaɪd
eligibility	e li juh BI luh ti	ɛlɪdʒəˈbɪlətɪ
eligible	E li juh buhl	ˈɛlɪdʒəbəl
Elihu	E luh hyoo :	ˈɛləhju
Elihu (Bible)	i LIGH hyoo :	ɪˈlaɪhju
Elijah	i LIGH juh	ɪˈlaɪdʒə
Elisha	i LIGH shuh	ɪˈlaɪʃə
elision	i LI zhuhn	ɪˈlɪʒən
Elisir d'Amore	ay lee ZIR da MAW ray	eliˈzɪr dæˈmɔre
elite	i LEET	ɪˈlit
elixir	i LIK ser	ɪˈlɪksər
Eliza	i LIGH zuh	ɪˈlaɪzə

Elizabethan	i li zuh BEE thuhn	ɪlɪzə'biθən
Elizalde	e lee SAHL de	ɛli'sɑldɛ
Elkanah	EL kuh nuh	'ɛlkənə
Ellice	E lis	'ɛlɪs
ellipse	i LIPS	ɪ'lɪps
ellipsis	i LIP sis	ɪ'lɪpsɪs
Ellsworth	ELZ werth	'ɛlzwərθ
elm	elm	ɛlm
Elmira	el MIGH ruh	ɛl'maɪrə
elocution	e luh KYOO : shuhn	ɛlə'kjuʃən
Elohim	e LOH him	ɛ'lohɪm
Elohistic	e loh HI stik	ɛlo'hɪstɪk
eloign, eloin	i LOIN	ɪ'lɔɪn
elongate	i LAWNG gayt	ɪ'lɔŋget
elope	i LOHP	ɪ'lop
eloquence	E luh kwuhns	'ɛləkwəns
El Paso	el PA soh	ɛl 'pæso
Elsa	EL suh	'ɛlsə
El Salvador	el SAL vuh dawr	ɛl'sælvədɔr
elsewhere	ELS hwair	'ɛlshwɛr
Elsie	EL si	ɛlsɪ
Éluard, Paul	ay loo : AHR, pawl	elu'ɑr, pɔl
elucidate	i LOO : suh dayt	ɪ'lusədet
elude	i LOO : D	ɪ'lud
elusion	i LOO : zhuhn	ɪ'luʒən
elusive	i LOO : siv	ɪ'lusɪv
elusory	i LOO : suh ri	ɪ'lusərɪ
elves	elvz	ɛlvz
Elvira	el VIGH ruh	ɛl'vaɪrə
Ely	EE li	'ilɪ
Elysian	i LI zhuhn	ɪ'lɪʒən
Elysium	i LI zhi uhm	ɪ'lɪʒɪəm
emaciate	i MAY shi ayt	ɪ'meʃɪet
emaciation	i may shi AY shuhn	ɪmeʃɪ'eʃən
emanate	E muh nayt	'ɛmənet
emanation	e muh NAY shuhn	ɛmə'neʃən
emanative	E muh nay tiv	'ɛmənetɪv
emancipate	i MAN suh payt	ɪ'mænsəpet
emancipation	i man suh PAY shuhn	ɪmænsə'peʃən
emancipator	i MAN suh pay ter	ɪ'mænsəpetər
emasculate (a)	i MA skyoo lit	ɪ'mæskjʊlɪt
emasculate (v)	i MA skyoo layt	ɪ'mæskjʊlet
embalm	im BAHM	ɪm'bɑm
embarcation	em bahr KAY shuhn	ɛmbɑr'keʃən
embargo	im BAHR goh	ɪm'bɑrgo
embark	im BAHRK	ɪm'bɑrk
embarkation	em bahr KAY shuhn	ɛmbɑr'keʃən
embarras	ahn ba RAH	ɑnbæ'rɑ
embarrass	im BA ruhs	ɪm'bærəs
embassy	EM buh si	'ɛmbəsɪ
embellish	im BE lish	ɪm'bɛlɪʃ
ember	EM ber	'ɛmbər

---

sing [ŋ] ; oh [o] ; oil [ɔɪ] ; foot [ʊ] ; foo:d [u] ; how [aʊ] ; pie [p] ; ray [r] ; so [s] ; shall [ʃ] ; to [t] ; thin [θ] ; th:en [ð] ; above (uh BUHV) [ə, 'ʌ] ; vine [v] ; wine [w] ; whine [hw] ; you [j] ; zoo [z] ; rouge (roo:zh) [ʒ].

emblazon	em BLAY zuhn	ɛmˈblezən
emblematic	em bluh MA tik	ɛmbləˈmætɪk
emblematize	em BLE muh tighz	ɛmˈblɛmətaɪz
embodiment	im BAH di muhnt	ɪmˈbɑdɪmənt
embolism	EM buh li zuhm	ˈɛmbəlɪzəm
embolus	EM buh luhs	ˈɛmbələs
emboss	im BAWS	ɪmˈbɔs
embrasure	em BRAY zher	ɛmˈbreʒər
embrocate	EM broh kayt	ˈɛmbroket
embroidery	im BROI duh ri	ɪmˈbrɔɪdərɪ
embryo	EM bri oh	ˈɛmbrɪo
embryology	em bri AH luh ji	ɛmbrɪˈɑlədʒɪ
embryonic	em bri AH nik	ɛmbrɪˈɑnɪk
emeer	uh MIR	əˈmɪr
emendation	ee men DAY shuhn	imɛnˈdeʃən
emerald	E muh ruhld	ˈɛmərəld
emergency	i MER juhn si	ɪˈmɝdʒənsɪ
emeritus	i MAI ruh tuhs	ɪˈmɛrətəs
emersed	i MERST	ɪˈmɝst
emersion	ee MER shuhn	iˈmɝʃən
emetic	i ME tik	ɪˈmɛtɪk
émeute	i MYOO : T	ɪˈmjut
emigrant	E muh gruhnt	ˈɛməgrənt
emigrate	E muh grayt	ˈɛməgret
émigré	E muh gray	ˈɛməgre
Emilio	ay MEE lyoh	eˈmiljo
eminence	E muh nuhns	ˈɛmənəns
emir	uh MIR	əˈmɪr
emissary	E muh sai ri	ˈɛməsɛrɪ
emission	i MI shuhn	ɪˈmɪʃən
emissivity	e muh SI vuh ti	ɛməˈsɪvətɪ
Emmaus	e MAY uhs	ɛˈmeəs
emollient	i MAH lyuhnt	ɪˈmɑljənt
emolument	i MAH lyoo muhnt	ɪˈmɑljʊmənt
emperor	EM puh rer	ˈɛmpərər
empery	EM puh ri	ˈɛmpərɪ
emphasis	EM fuh sis	ˈɛmfəsɪs
emphatic	im FA tik	ɪmˈfætɪk
empiric	em PI rik	ɛmˈpɪrɪk
empirical	em PI ri kuhl	ɛmˈpɪrɪkəl
empiricism	em PI ruh si zuhm	ɛmˈpɪrəsɪzəm
employe, -e	im PLOI ee	ɪmˈplɔii
Emporia	em PAW ri uh	ɛmˈpɔrɪə
emporium	em PAW ri uhm	ɛmˈpɔrɪəm
empyrean	em puh REE uhn	ɛmpəˈrɪən
emu	EE myoo :	ˈimju
emulate	E myoo layt	ˈɛmjʊlet
emulation	e myoo LAY shuhn	ɛmjʊˈleʃən
emulsify	i MUHL suh figh	ɪˈmʌlsəfaɪ
emulsion	i MUHL shuhn	ɪˈmʌlʃən
enamor, enamour	i NA mer	ɪˈnæmər
en casserole	en KA suh rohl	ɛn ˈkæsərol

at [æ] ; *ah* [ɑ] ; *air* [ɛ] ; *awful* [ɔ] ; *say* [e] ; *back* [b] ; *chair* [tʃ] ; *do* [d] ; *elm* [ɛ] ; *eel* [i] ; *server* [ˈɝ, ər] ; *f*it [f] ; *go* [g] ; *hurt* [h] ; *is* [ɪ] ; *high* [aɪ] ; *jet* [dʒ] ; *kiss* [k] ; *lamb* [l] ; *my* [m] ; *nice* [n] ;

enceinte	en SAYNT	ɛnˈsent
Enceladus	en SE luh duhs	ɛnˈsɛlədəs
encephalic	en suh FA lik	ɛnsəˈfælɪk
encephalitis	en se fuh LIGH tis	ɛnsɛfəˈlaɪtɪs
encephalon	en SE fuh lahn	ɛnˈsɛfəlɑn
enchiridion	en kigh RI di uhn	ɛnkaɪˈrɪdɪən
encina	en SEE nuh	ɛnˈsinə
enclave	EN klayv	ˈɛnklev
enclitic	en KLI tik	ɛnˈklɪtɪk
enclosure	in KLOH zher	ɪnˈkloʒər
encomium	en KOH mi uhm	ɛnˈkomɪəm
encompass	in KUHM puhs	ɪnˈkʌmpəs
encore	AHNG kawr	ˈɑŋkɔr
encourage	in KER ij	ɪnˈkɝɪdʒ
encroach	in KROHCH	ɪnˈkrotʃ
encumbrance	in KUHM bruhns	ɪnˈkʌmbrəns
encyclical	en SI kli kuhl	ɛnˈsɪklɪkəl
encyclopedia, encyclopaedia	in sigh kluh PEE di uh	ɪnsaɪkləˈpidɪə
encyclopedist, encyclopaedist, E-	in sigh kluh PEE dist	ɪnsaɪkləˈpidɪst
endeavor, endeavour	in DE ver	ɪnˈdɛvər
endemic	en DE mik	ɛnˈdɛmɪk
endive	EN dighv	ˈɛndaɪv
endocrin	EN duh krin	ˈɛndəkrɪn
endocrine	EN duh krighn	ˈɛndəkraɪn
endocrinology	en doh krigh NAH luh ji	ɛndokraɪˈnɑlədʒɪ
endodontia	en duh DAHN shi uh	ɛndəˈdɑnʃɪə
Endor	EN der	ˈɛndər
endorse	in DAWRS	ɪnˈdɔrs
endowment	in DOW muhnt	ɪnˈdaʊmənt
endure	in DOOR	ɪnˈdʊr
Endymion	en DI mi uhn	ɛnˈdɪmɪən
energy	E ner ji	ˈɛnərdʒɪ
enervate	E ner vayt	ˈɛnərvet
Enesco	e NE skoh	ɛˈnɛsko
enfilade	en fuh LAYD	ɛnfəˈled
enfranchise	en FRAN chighz	ɛnˈfræntʃaɪz
enfranchisement	en FRAN chiz muhnt	ɛnˈfræntʃɪzmənt
Engedi	en GEE digh	ɛnˈgidaɪ
Engels	ENG uhls	ˈɛŋəls
engine	EN juhn	ˈɛndʒən
engineer	en juh NIR	ɛndʒəˈnɪr
England	ING gluhnd	ˈɪŋglənd
English	ING glish	ˈɪŋglɪʃ
engross	in GROHS	ɪnˈgros
enhance	in HANS	ɪnˈhæns
eniac	E ni ak	ˈɛnɪæk
Enid	EE nid	ˈinɪd
enigma	i NIG muh	ɪˈnɪgmə
enigmatic	e nig MA tik	ɛnɪgˈmætɪk
Eniwetok	e nuh WEE tahk	ɛnəˈwitɑk

sing [ŋ] ; *oh* [o] ; *oil* [ɔɪ] ; f*oo*t [ʊ] ; f*oo*:d [u] ; h*ow* [aʊ] ; *p*ie [p] ; ray [r] ; *s*o [s] ; *sh*all [ʃ] ; *t*o [t] ; *th*in [θ] ; *th*:en [ð] ; above (*uh* B*U*HV) [ə, ˈʌ] ; *v*ine [v] ; *w*ine [w] ; *wh*ine [hw] ; *y*ou [j] ; *z*oo [z] ; rouge (roo:*zh*) [ʒ].

enjambement	in JAM muhnt	ɪn'dʒæmmənt
enlightenment	in LIGHT uhn muhnt	ɪn'laɪtənmənt
enliven	in LIGH vuhn	ɪn'laɪvən
enmesh	en MESH	ɛn'mɛʃ
enmity	EN muh ti	'ɛnmətɪ
ennui	AHN wee	'ɑnwi
Enoch	EE nuhk	'inək
enormity	i NAWR muh ti	ɪ'nɔrmətɪ
enormous	i NAWR muhs	ɪ'nɔrməs
Enos	EE nuhs	'inəs
enough	i NUHF	ɪ'nʌf
enow	i NOW	ɪ'naʊ
en route	ahn ROO : T	ɑn'rut
ensconce	en SKAHNS	ɛn'skɑns
ensemble	ahn SAHM buhl	ɑn'sɑmbəl
ensign (banner)	EN sighn	'ɛnsaɪn
ensign (officer)	EN suhn	'ɛnsən
ensilage	EN suh lij	'ɛnsəlɪdʒ
ensue	en SOO :	ɛn'su
ensure	in SHOOR	ɪn'ʃʊr
entablature	en TA bluh cher	ɛn'tæblətʃər
Entebbe	en TE be	ɛn'tɛbe
entente	ahn TAHNT	ɑn'tɑnt
entente cordiale	ahn TAHNT kawr DYAL	ɑn'tɑnt kɔr'djæl
enthral, -l	in THRAWL	ɪn'θrɔl
enthusiasm	in THOO : zi a zuhm	ɪn'θuzɪæzəm
enthusiast	in THOO : zi ast	ɪn'θuzɪæst
enthusiastic	in thoo : zi A stik	ɪnθuzɪ'æstɪk
enthymeme	EN thuh meem	'ɛnθəmim
entire	in TIGHR	ɪn'taɪr
entirety	in TIGHR ti	ɪn'taɪrtɪ
entomb	in TOO : M	ɪn'tum
entomology	en tuh MAH luh ji	ɛntə'mɑlədʒɪ
entourage	ahn too RAHZH	ɑntu'rɑʒ
entr'acte	ahn TRAKT	ɑn'trækt
entrails	EN truhlz	'ɛntrəlz
entrance (n)	EN truhns	'ɛntrəns
entrance (v)	in TRANS	ɪn'træns
entree	AHN tray	'ɑntre
entremets	AHN truh may	'ɑntrəme
entre nous	ahn truh NOO :	ɑntrə'nu
entresol	EN ter sahl	'ɛntərsɑl
entropy	EN truh pi	'ɛntrəpɪ
enunciate	i NUHN si ayt	ɪ'nʌnsɪet
enuresis	e nyoo REE sis	ɛnju'risɪs
envelop (v)	in VE luhp	ɪn'vɛləp
envelope (n)	EN vuh lohp	'ɛnvəlop
enviable	EN vi uh buhl	'ɛnvɪəbəl
environ	in VIGH ruhn	ɪn'vaɪrən
environment	in VIGH ruhn muhnt	ɪn'vaɪrənmənt
envisage	en VI zij	ɛn'vɪzɪdʒ
envoy	EN voi	'ɛnvɔɪ

at [æ] ; *ah* [ɑ] ; *air* [ɛ] ; *aw*ful [ɔ] ; s*ay* [e] ; *b*ack [b] ; *ch*air [tʃ] ; *d*o [d] ; *e*lm [ɛ] ; *ee*l [i] ; *ser*ver ['ɜ, ər] ; *f*it [f] ; *g*o [g] ; *h*urt [h] ; *i*s [ɪ] ; *high* [aɪ] ; *j*et [dʒ] ; *k*iss [k] ; *l*amb [l] ; *m*y [m] ; *n*ice [n] ;

enzyme	EN zighm	ˈɛnzaɪm
Eolian	ee OH li uhn	iˈolɪən
epaulet, -te	E puh let	ˈɛpəlɛt
epee	e PAY	ɛˈpe
ephebic, E-	e FEE bik	ɛˈfibɪk
ephedrine	e FE drin	ɛˈfɛdrɪn
ephemeral	uh FE muh ruhl	əˈfɛmərəl
ephemeris	uh FE muh ris	əˈfɛmərɪs
Ephesian	i FEE zhuhn	ɪˈfiʒən
Ephesus	E fuh suhs	ˈɛfəsəs
ephor	E fawr	ˈɛfɔr
Ephraim	EE fri uhm	ˈifrɪəm
epic	E pik	ˈɛpɪk
epicene	E puh seen	ˈɛpəsin
Epictetus	e pik TEE tuhs	ɛpɪkˈtitəs
epicure	E pi kyoor	ˈɛpɪkjʊr
epicurean, E-	e pi kyoo REE uhn	ɛpɪkjuˈriən
Epicurus	e pi KYOO ruhs	ɛpɪˈkjʊrəs
epidemiology	e puh de mi AH luh ji	ɛpədɛmɪˈɑlədʒɪ
epidermis	e puh DER mis	ɛpəˈdɝmɪs
epiglottis	e puh GLAH tis	ɛpəˈglɑtɪs
epigram	E puh gram	ˈɛpəgræm
epilepsy	E puh lep si	ˈɛpəlɛpsɪ
epilog, -ue	E puh lawg	ˈɛpəlɔg
epinephrine	e pi NE frin	ɛpɪˈnɛfrɪn
Epiphany	i PI fuh ni	ɪˈpɪfənɪ
episcopacy	i PI skuh puh si	ɪˈpɪskəpəsɪ
episcopal, E-	i PI skuh puhl	ɪˈpɪskəpəl
episcopate	i PI skuh pit	ɪˈpɪskəpɪt
episode	E puh sohd	ˈɛpəsod
episodic	e puh SAH dik	ɛpəˈsɑdɪk
epistemology	i pi stuh MAH luh ji	ɪpɪstəˈmɑlədʒɪ
epistle, E-	i PI suhl	ɪˈpɪsəl
epistolary	i PI stuh lai ri	ɪˈpɪstəlɛrɪ
epitaph	E puh taf	ˈɛpətæf
epithet	E puh thet	ˈɛpəθɛt
epitome	i PI tuh mi	ɪˈpɪtəmɪ
epizootic	e pi zoh AH tik	ɛpɪzoˈɑtɪk
e pluribus unum	ee PLOO ruh buhs YOO : nuhm	iˈplʊrəbəsˈjunəm
epoch	E puhk	ˈɛpək
epochal	E puh kuhl	ˈɛpəkəl
epode	E pohd	ˈɛpod
eponym	E puh nim	ˈɛpənɪm
eponymous	e PAH nuh muhs	ɛˈpɑnəməs
epopee	E puh pay	ˈɛpəpe
epos	E pahs	ˈɛpɑs
epsilon	EP suh lahn	ˈɛpsəlɑn
Epsom	EP suhm	ˈɛpsəm
Epstein	EP stighn	ˈɛpstaɪn
Epworth	EP werth	ˈɛpwərθ
equability	e kwuh BI luh ti	ɛkwəˈbɪlətɪ

sing [ŋ] ; *oh* [o] ; *oi*l [ɔɪ] ; *foo*t [ʊ] ; *foo*:d [u] ; *how* [aʊ] ; *pie* [p] ; *ray* [r] ; *so* [s] ; *shall* [ʃ] ; *to* [t] ; *thin* [θ] ; *th*:en [ð] ; above (*uh* B*UH*V) [ə, ˈʌ] ; *vine* [v] ; *wine* [w] ; *whine* [hw] ; *you* [j] ; *zoo* [z] ; rouge (roo:*zh*) [ʒ].

equable	E kwuh buhl	ˈɛkwəbəl
equal	EE kwuhl	ˈikwəl
equality	i KWAH luh ti	ɪˈkwɑlətɪ
equalization	ee kwuh luh ZAY shuhn	ikwələˈzeʃən
equanimity	ee kwuh NI muh ti	ikwəˈnɪmətɪ
equate	i KWAYT	ɪˈkwet
equation	i KWAY zhuhn	ɪˈkweʒən
equator	i KWAY ter	ɪˈkwetər
equatorial	ee kwuh TAW ri uhl	ikwəˈtɔrɪəl
equerry	E kwuh ri	ˈɛkwərɪ
equestrian	i KWE stri uhn	ɪˈkwɛstrɪən
equestrienne	i kwe stri EN	ɪkwɛstrɪˈɛn
equidistant	ee kwuh DI stuhnt	ikwəˈdɪstənt
equilateral	ee kwuh LA tuh ruhl	ikwəˈlætərəl
equilibrium	ee kwuh LI bri uhm	ikwəˈlɪbrɪəm
equine	EE kwighn	ˈikwaɪn
equinoctial	ee kwuh NAHK shuhl	ikwəˈnɑkʃəl
equinox	EE kwuh nahks	ˈikwənɑks
equip	i KWIP	ɪˈkwɪp
equipage	E kwuh pij	ˈɛkwəpɪdʒ
equipoise	E kwuh poiz	ˈɛkwəpɔɪz
equipotential	ee kwi poh TEN shuhl	ikwɪpoˈtɛnʃəl
equitable	E kwi tuh buhl	ˈɛkwɪtəbəl
equity	E kwuh ti	ˈɛkwətɪ
equivalent	i KWI vuh luhnt	ɪˈkwɪvələnt
equivocal	i KWI vuh kuhl	ɪˈkwɪvəkəl
equivocate	i KWI vuh kayt	ɪˈkwɪvəket
equivocation	i kwi vuh KAY shuhn	ɪkwɪvəˈkeʃən
equivoke, equivoque	E kwi vohk	ˈɛkwɪvok
Equuleus	i KWOO : li uhs	ɪˈkwulɪəs
era	I ruh	ˈɪrə
eradiate	ee RAY di ayt	iˈredɪet
eradicant	i RA di kuhnt	ɪˈrædɪkənt
eradicate	i RA di kayt	ɪˈrædɪket
erase	i RAYS	ɪˈres
eraser	i RAY ser	ɪˈresər
Erasmus	i RAZ muhs	ɪˈræzməs
erasure	i RAY sher	ɪˈreʃer
Erato	E ruh toh	ˈɛrəto
ere	air	ɛr
Erebus	E ruh buhs	ˈɛrəbəs
Erechtheum	e rik THEE uhm	ɛrɪkˈθiəm
erectile	i REK tuhl	ɪˈrɛktəl
Erede, Alberto	e RAY day, ahl BER toh	ɛˈrede, ɑlˈbɝto
eremite	E ruh might	ˈɛrəmaɪt
Erewhon	E ruh hwuhn	ˈɛrəhwən
Erfurt	AIR foort	ˈɛrfurt
erg	erg	ɝg
ergot	ER guht	ˈɝgət
Eric	AI rik	ˈɛrɪk
Eridanus	i RI duh nuhs	ɪˈrɪdənəs
Erie	I ri	ˈɪrɪ

Erin	AI rin	ˈɛrɪn
Erinyes	i RI ni eez	ɪˈrɪnɪiz
Eritrea	e ri TREE uh	ɛrɪˈtriə
Erivan	e ri VAHN	ɛrɪˈvɑn
erlking	ERL king	ˈɝˈlkɪŋ
ermine	ER min	ˈɝmɪn
Ernani	air NAH ni	ɛrˈnɑnɪ
Eros, e-	I rahs	ˈɪrɑs
erosion	i ROH zhuhn	ɪˈroʒən
erosive	i ROH siv	ɪˈrosɪv
erotic	i RAH tik	ɪˈrɑtɪk
err	er	ɝ
errand	AI ruhnd	ˈɛrənd
errant	AI ruhnt	ˈɛrənt
errata	i RAH tuh	ɪˈrɑtə
erratic	i RA tik	ɪˈrætɪk
erratum	i RAY tuhm	ɪˈretəm
error	AI rer	ˈɛrər
ersatz	air ZAHTS	ɛrˈzɑts
Erse	ers	ɝs
Érsekújvár	AYR she KOO: i vahr	ˈɛrʃɛˈkuɪvɑr
Erskine	ER skin	ˈɝˈskɪn
erubescent	e roo BE suhnt	ɛruˈbesənt
erudite	AI ryoo dight	ˈɛrjʊdaɪt
Ervine	ER vin	ˈɝvɪn
erysipelas	ai ruh SI puh luhs	ɛrəˈsɪpələs
erythroblastosis	i ri throh bla STO sis	ɪrɪθroblæˈstosɪs
erythrocyte	i RI throh sight	ɪˈrɪθrosaɪt
Esau	EE saw	ˈisɔ
escadrille	e skuh DRIL	ɛskəˈdrɪl
escalade	e skuh LAYD	ɛskəˈled
escalator	E skuh lay ter	ˈɛskəletər
escapade	E skuh payd	ˈɛskəped
escargot	e skahr GOH	ɛskɑrˈgo
escarole	E skuh rohl	ˈɛskərol
escarpment	e SKAHRP muhnt	ɛˈskɑrpmənt
eschatology	e skuh TAH luh ji	ɛskəˈtalədʒɪ
escheat	es CHEET	ɛsˈtʃit
eschew	es CHOO:	ɛsˈtʃu
Escorial	e SKAW ri uhl	ɛˈskɔrɪəl
escort (n)	E skawrt	ˈɛskɔrt
escort (v)	e SKAWRT	ɛˈskɔrt
escritoire	e skri TWAHR	ɛskrɪˈtwɑr
Escurial	e SKYOO ri uhl	ɛˈskjʊrɪəl
escutcheon	i SKUH chuhn	ɪˈskʌtʃən
Esdraelon	es dri EE luhn	ɛsdrɪˈilən
Esdras	EZ druhs	ˈɛzdrəs
Eskimo	E skuh moh	ˈɛskəmo
Esmeralda	ez muh RAL duh	ɛzməˈrældə
esophagus	i SAH fuh guhs	ɪˈsɑfəgəs
esoteric	e suh TE rik	ɛsəˈtɛrɪk
espagnol, -e	e spa NYOHL	ɛspæˈnjol

sing [ŋ] ; *oh* [o] ; *oil* [ɔɪ] ; *foot* [ʊ] ; *foo:d* [u] ; *how* [aʊ] ; *pie* [p] ; *ray* [r] ; *so* [s] ; *shall* [ʃ] ; *to* [t] ; *thin* [θ] ; *th:en* [ð] ; *above* (*uh BUHV*) [ə, ˈʌ] ; *vine* [v] ; *wine* [w] ; *whine* [hw] ; *you* [j] ; *zoo* [z] ; *rouge* (*roo:zh*) [ʒ].

espalier	e SPAL yer	ɛˈspæljər
Esperanto	e spuh RAHN toh	ɛspəˈrɑnto
espial	e SPIGH uhl	ɛˈspaɪəl
espionage	E spi uh nij	ˈɛspɪənɪdʒ
esplanade	e spluh NAYD	ɛspləˈned
espousal	i SPOW zuhl	ɪˈspaʊzəl
espouse	i SPOWZ	ɪˈspaʊz
esprit	e SPREE	ɛˈspri
esprit de corps	e SPREE duh KAWR	ɛˈspri də ˈkɔr
esquire, E-	uh SKWIGHR	əˈskwaɪr
essay (n)	E say	ˈɛse
essay (v)	uh SAY	əˈse
essayist	E say ist	ˈɛseɪst
Essen	E suhn	ˈɛsən
essence	E suhns	ˈɛsəns
Essene	E seen	ˈɛsin
essential	uh SEN shuhl	əˈsɛnʃəl
Essex	E siks	ˈɛsɪks
Este	E ste	ˈɛstɛ
Esther	E ster	ˈɛstər
esthete	ES theet	ˈɛsθit
estimate (n)	E stuh mit	ˈɛstəmɪt
estimate (v)	E stuh mayt	ˈɛstəmet
Estonia	e STOH ni uh	ɛˈstoniə
estovers	e STOH verz	ɛˈstovərz
estrange	uh STRAYNJ	əˈstrendʒ
estreat	e STREET	ɛˈstrit
Estremadura	e stre mah TH:OO: rah	ɛstrɛmɑˈðurɑ
estrogen	E struh juhn	ˈɛstrədʒən
estrogenic	e struh JE nik	ɛstrəˈdʒɛnɪk
estrone	E strohn	ˈɛstron
estrus	E struhs	ˈɛstrəs
estuary	ES choo ai ri	ˈɛstʃuɛri
etamine	E tuh meen	ˈɛtəmin
Étaples	e TAH pluh	ɛˈtɑplə
et cetera	et SE tuh ruh	ɛtˈsɛtərə
Eteocles	i TEE uh kleez	ɪˈtiəkliz
Ethan	EE thuhn	ˈiθən
ether	EE ther	ˈiθər
ethereal	i THI ri uhl	ɪˈθɪrɪəl
Ethiopia	ee thi OH pi uh	iθɪˈopɪə
Ethiopian	ee thi OH pi uhn	iθɪˈopɪən
ethmoid	ETH moid	ˈɛθmɔɪd
ethnic	ETH nik	ˈɛθnɪk
ethnology	eth NAH luh ji	ɛθˈnɑlədʒɪ
ethos	EE thahs	ˈiθɑs
etiolate	EE ti uh layt	ˈitɪəlet
etiology	ee ti AH luh ji	itɪˈɑlədʒɪ
etiquette	E ti ket	ˈɛtɪkɛt
Etna	ET nuh	ˈɛtnə
Eton	EE tuhn	ˈitən
étouffé	ay too FAY	etuˈfe

at [æ]; ah [ɑ]; air [ɛ]; awful [ɔ]; say [e]; back [b]; chair [tʃ]; do [d]; elm [ɛ]; eel [i]; server [ˈɝ, ər]; fit [f]; go [g]; hurt [h]; is [ɪ]; high [aɪ]; jet [dʒ]; kiss [k]; lamb [l]; my [m]; nice [n];

Etruria	i TROO ri uh	ɪˈtrʊrɪə
Etrurian	i TROO ri uhn	ɪˈtrʊrɪən
Etruscan	i TRUH skuhn	ɪˈtrʌskən
et tu, Brute	et too: BROO: te	ɛt tu ˈbrutɛ
étude	AY too:d	ˈetud
etui	ay TWEE	eˈtwi
etymology	e tuh MAH luh ji	ɛtəˈmɑlədʒɪ
Euboea	yoo BEE uh	juˈbiə
eucaine	yoo: KAYN	juˈken
eucalyptus	yoo: kuh LIP tuhs	jukəˈlɪptəs
Eucharist	YOO: kuh rist	ˈjukərɪst
euchre	YOO: ker	ˈjukər
Euclid	YOO: klid	ˈjuklɪd
Euclidean, Euclidian	yoo: KLI di uhn	juˈklɪdɪən
eudaemonia	yoo: di MOH ni uh	judɪˈmonɪə
eugenic	yoo JE nik	juˈdʒɛnɪk
eulogia	yoo LOH ji uh	juˈlodʒɪə
eulogium	yoo LOH ji uhm	juˈlodʒɪəm
eulogy	YOO: luh ji	ˈjulədʒɪ
Eumenides	yoo: ME nuh deez	juˈmɛnədiz
Eunice	YOO: nis	ˈjunɪs
Eunomia	yoo: NOH mi uh	juˈnomɪə
eunuch	YOO: nuhk	ˈjunək
eupepsia	yoo PEP shuh	juˈpɛpʃə
euphemism	YOO: fuh mi zuhm	ˈjufəmɪzəm
euphonic	yoo FAH nik	juˈfɑnɪk
euphony	YOO: fuh ni	ˈjufənɪ
euphorbia	yoo FAWR bi uh	juˈfɔrbɪə
euphoria	yoo FAW ri uh	juˈfɔrɪə
Euphrates	yoo: FRAY teez	juˈfretiz
Euphrosyne	yoo: FRAH suh nee	juˈfrɑsəni
euphuism	YOO: fyoo: i zuhm	ˈjufjuɪzəm
Eurasia	yoo RAY zhuh	juˈreʒə
eureka	yoo REE kuh	juˈrikə
eurhythmic	yoo RITH: mik	juˈrɪðmɪk
Euripides	yoo RI puh deez	juˈrɪpədiz
Euroclydon	yoo RAH kli dahn	juˈrɑklɪdɑn
Europa	yoo ROH puh	juˈropə
Europe	YOO ruhp	ˈjurəp
European	yoo ruh PEE uhn	jurəˈpiən
Eurydice	yoo RI duh see	juˈrɪdəsi
eurythmic	yoo RITH: mik	juˈrɪðmɪk
Eustachian	yoo STAY ki uhn	juˈstekɪən
Euterpe	yoo: TER pi	juˈtɝpɪ
euthanasia	yoo thuh NAY zhuh	juθəˈneʒə
evacuate	i VA kyoo: ayt	ɪˈvækjuet
evanescent	e vuh NE suhnt	ɛvəˈnɛsənt
evangelical	ee van JE li kuhl	ivænˈdʒɛlɪkəl
Evangeline	i VAN juh lin	ɪˈvændʒəlɪn
evangelism	i VAN juh li zuhm	ɪˈvændʒəlɪzəm
evaporate	i VA puh rayt	ɪˈvæpəret
Evarts	E verts	ˈɛvərts

sing [ŋ] ; oh [o] ; oil [ɔɪ] ; foot [ʊ] ; foo:d [u] ; how [aʊ] ; pie [p] ; ray [r] ; so [s] ; shall [ʃ] ; to [t] ; thin [θ] ; th:en [ð] ; above (uh BUHV) [ə, ˈʌ] ; vine [v] ; wine [w] ; whine [hw] ; ou [j] ; zoo [z] ; rouge (roo:zh) [ʒ].

evasion	i VAY zhuhn	ɪˈveʒən
evasive	i VAY siv	ɪˈvesɪv
Eve	eev	iv
Evelyn, John	EEV lin	ˈivlɪn
evening (n)	EEV ning	ˈivnɪŋ
evening (v)	EE vuh ning	ˈivənɪŋ
event	i VENT	ɪˈvɛnt
eventual	i VEN choo uhl	ɪˈvɛntʃʊəl
everglade, -s, E-	E ver glayd	ˈɛvərgled
everyone	E vri wuhn	ˈɛvrɪwən
evict	i VIKT	ɪˈvɪkt
evidential	e vuh DEN shuhl	ɛvəˈdɛnʃəl
evidently	E vuh duhnt li	ˈɛvədəntlɪ
evil	EE vuhl	ˈivəl
evince	i VINS	ɪˈvɪns
eviscerate	i VI suh rayt	ɪˈvɪsəret
evocative	i VAH kuh tiv	ɪˈvɑkətɪv
evoke	i VOHK	ɪˈvok
evolution	e vuh LOO : shuhn	ɛvəˈluʃən
evolve	i VAHLV	ɪˈvɑlv
ewe	yoo :	ju
Ewell	YOO : uhl	ˈjuəl
Ewigkeit	E vik kight	ˈɛvɪkkaɪt
ewig-weibliche	E vik VIGH bli kuh	ˈɛvɪk ˈvaɪblɪkə
Ewing	YOO : ing	ˈjuɪŋ
exacerbate	ig ZA ser bayt	ɪgˈzæsərbet
exact	ig ZAKT	ɪgˈzækt
exactitude	ig ZAK tuh too : d	ɪgˈzæktətud
exactly	ig ZAKT li	ɪgˈzæktlɪ
exaggerate	ig ZA juh rayt	ɪgˈzædʒəret
exalt	ig ZAWLT	ɪgˈzɔlt
examination	ig za muh NAY shuhn	ɪgzæməˈneʃən
examine	ig ZA min	ɪgˈzæmɪn
example	ig ZAM puhl	ɪgˈzæmpəl
exarch	EK sahrk	ˈɛksɑrk
exasperate	ig ZA spuh rayt	ɪgˈzæspəret
Excalibur	ek SKA luh ber	ɛkˈskæləbər
ex cathedra	eks kuh THEE druh	ɛks kəˈθidrə
excavate	EK skuh vayt	ˈɛkskəvet
excavator	EK skuh vay ter	ˈɛkskəvetər
exceed	ik SEED	ɪkˈsid
excel	ik SEL	ɪkˈsɛl
excellency, E-	EK suh luhn si	ˈɛksələnsɪ
excellent	EK suh luhnt	ˈɛksələnt
excelsior	ik SEL si er	ɪkˈsɛlsɪər
except	ik SEPT	ɪkˈsɛpt
excerpt (n)	EK serpt	ˈɛksərpt
excerpt (v)	ik SERPT	ɪkˈsɝpt
excess (adj)	EK ses	ˈɛksɛs
excess (n)	ik SES	ɪkˈsɛs
exchange	iks CHAYNJ	ɪksˈtʃendʒ
exchequer, E-	iks CHE ker	ɪksˈtʃɛkər

at [æ] ; ah [ɑ] ; air [ɛ] ; awful [ɔ] ; say [e] ; back [b] ; chair [tʃ] ; do [d] ; elm [ɛ] ; eel [i] ;
server [ˈɝ, ər] ; fit [f] ; go [g] ; hurt [h] ; is [ɪ] ; high [aɪ] ; jet [dʒ] ; kiss [k] ; lamb [l] ; my [m] ;
nice [n] ;

excise (n)	EK sighz	ˈɛksaɪz
excise (v)	ik SIGHZ	ɪkˈsaɪz
excitant	ik SIGH tuhnt	ɪkˈsaɪtənt
excitatory	ik SIGH tuh taw ri	ɪkˈsaɪtətɔrɪ
excite	ik SIGHT	ɪkˈsaɪt
exciter, excitor	ik SIGH ter	ɪkˈsaɪtər
exclamation	ek skluh MAY shuhn	ɛkskləˈmeʃən
exclamatory	ik SKLA muh taw ri	ɪkˈsklæmətɔrɪ
exclusive	ik SKLOO : siv	ɪkˈsklusɪv
excommunicate	ek skuh MYOO : nuh kayt	ɛkskəˈmjunəket
excoriate	ik SKAW ri ayt	ɪkˈskɔrɪet
excrescence	ik SKRE suhns	ɪkˈskrɛsəns
excretive	ik SKREE tiv	ɪkˈskritɪv
excretory	EK skri taw ri	ˈɛkskrɪtɔrɪ
excruciate	ik SKROO : shi ayt	ɪkˈskruʃɪet
exculpate	EK skuhl payt	ˈɛkskəlpet
excursion	ik SKER zhuhn	ɪkˈskɝʒən
excusatory	ik SKYOO : zuh taw ri	ɪkˈskyuzətɔrɪ
execrable	EK si kruh buhl	ˈɛksɪkrəbəl
executant	ig ZE kyoo tuhnt	ɪgˈzɛkyutənt
execute	EK si kyoo : t	ˈɛksɪkyut
executive	ig ZE kyoo tiv	ɪgˈzɛkyutɪv
executor (performer)	EK si kyoo : ter	ˈɛksɪkyutər
executor (of a will)	ig ZE kyoo ter	ɪgˈzɛkyutər
exegesis	ek suh JEE sis	ɛksəˈdʒisɪs
exegetic	ek suh JE tik	ɛksəˈdʒɛtɪk
exemplar	ig ZEM pler	ɪgˈzɛmplər
exemplary	ig ZEM pluh ri	ɪgˈzɛmplərɪ
exemplify	ig ZEM pluh figh	ɪgˈzɛmpləfaɪ
exempli gratia	eg ZEM pligh GRAY shi uh	ɛgˈzɛmplaɪ ˈgreʃɪə
exempt	ig ZEMPT	ɪgˈzɛmpt
exercise	EK ser sighz	ˈɛksərsaɪz
exert	ig ZERT	ɪgˈzɝt
exertion	ig ZER shuhn	ɪgˈzɝʃən
exeunt	EK si uhnt	ˈɛksɪənt
exeunt omnes	EK si uhnt AHM neez	ˈɛksɪənt ˈɑmniz
exfoliate	eks FOH li ayt	ɛksˈfolɪet
exhalant	eks HAY luhnt	ɛksˈhelənt
exhalation	eks huh LAY shuhn	ɛkshəˈleʃən
exhale	eks HAYL	ɛksˈhel
exhaust	ig ZAWST	ɪgˈzɔst
exhaustion	ig ZAWS chuhn	ɪgˈzɔstʃən
exhibit	ig ZI bit	ɪgˈzɪbɪt
exhibition	ek suh BI shuhn	ɛksəˈbɪʃən
exhibitive	ig ZI buh tiv	ɪgˈzɪbətɪv
exhilarate	ig ZI luh rayt	ɪgˈzɪləret
exhort	ig ZAWRT	ɪgˈzɔrt
exhortation	eg zawr TAY shuhn	ɛgzɔrˈteʃən
exhortative	ig ZAWR tuh tiv	ɪgˈzɔrtətɪv
exhume	ig ZYOO : M	ɪgˈzjum
exigence	EK suh juhns	ˈɛksədʒəns
exigency	EK suh juhn si	ˈɛksədʒənsɪ

sing [ŋ]; *oh* [o]; *oil* [ɔɪ]; *foot* [ʊ]; *foo*:d [u]; *how* [aʊ]; *pie* [p]; *ray* [r]; *so* [s]; *shall* [ʃ]
to [t]; *thin* [θ]; *th*:en [ð]; *above* (*uh BUH*V) [ə, ˈʌ]; *vine* [v]; *wine* [w]; *whine* [hw];
you [j]; *zoo* [z]; *rouge* (roo:*zh*) [ʒ].

H.P.—K

exigent	EK suh juhnt	ˈɛksədʒənt
exiguous	ig ZI gyoo : uhs	ɪgˈzɪgjʊəs
exile	EG zighl	ˈɛgzaɪl
exist	ig ZIST	ɪgˈzɪst
existential	eg zi STEN shuhl	ɛgzɪˈstɛnʃəl
existentialism, E-	eg zi STEN shuh li zuhm	ɛgzɪˈstɛnʃəlɪzəm
existentialist, E-	eg zi STEN shuh list	ɛgzɪˈstɛnʃəlɪst
exit	EG zit	ˈɛgzɪt
ex libris	eks LIGH bris	ɛks ˈlaɪbrɪs
exodus, E-	EK suh duhs	ˈɛksədəs
ex officio	eks uh FI shi oh	ɛks əˈfɪʃɪo
exonerate	ig ZAH nuh rayt	ɪgˈzɑnəret
exophthalmic	ek sahf THAL mik	ɛksɑfˈθælmɪk
exorable	EK suh ruh buhl	ˈɛksərəbəl
exorbitance	ig ZAWR buh tuhns	ɪgˈzɔrbətəns
exorbitant	ig ZAWR buh tuhnt	ɪgˈzɔrbətənt
exorcise	EK sawr sighz	ˈɛksɔrsaɪz
exorcism	EK sawr si zuhm	ˈɛksɔrsɪzəm
exorcist	EK sawr sist	ˈɛksɔrsɪst
exorcize	EK sawr sighz	ˈɛksɔrsaɪz
exordium	ig ZAWR di uhm	ɪgˈzɔrdɪəm
exosphere	EK suhs fir	ˈɛksəsfɪr
exoteric	ek suh TE rik	ɛksəˈtɛrɪk
exotic	ig ZAH tik	ɪgˈzɑtɪk
expand	ik SPAND	ɪkˈspænd
ex parte	eks PAHR ti	ɛks ˈpɑrtɪ
expatiate	ik SPAY shi ayt	ɪkˈspeʃɪet
expatriate (a, n)	eks PAY tri it	ɛksˈpetrɪt
expatriate (v)	eks PAY tri ayt	ɛksˈpetrɪet
expectorant	ik SPEK tuh ruhnt	ɪkˈspɛktərənt
expectorate	ik SPEK tuh rayt	ɪkˈspɛktəret
expedient	ik SPEE di uhnt	ɪkˈspidɪənt
expedite	EK spi dight	ˈɛkspɪdaɪt
experience	ik SPI ri uhns	ɪkˈspɪrɪəns
experiment	ik SPE ruh muhnt	ɪkˈspɛrəmənt
expert	EK spert	ˈɛkspərt
expiable	EK spi uh buhl	ˈɛkspɪəbəl
expiate	EK spi ayt	ˈɛkspɪet
expiation	ek spi AY shuhn	ɛkspɪˈeʃən
expiatory	EK spi uh taw ri	ˈɛkspɪətɔrɪ
expiration	ek spuh RAY shuhn	ɛkspəˈreʃən
expiratory	ik SPIGH ruh taw ri	ɪkˈspaɪrətɔrɪ
expire	ik SPIGHR	ɪkˈspaɪr
expletive	EK spli tiv	ˈɛksplɪtɪv
explicable	EK spli kuh buhl	ˈɛksplɪkəbəl
explicative	EK spli kay tiv	ˈɛksplɪketɪv
explicit	ik SPLI sit	ɪkˈsplɪsɪt
exploit (n)	EK sploit	ˈɛksplɔɪt
exploit (v)	ik SPLOIT	ɪkˈsplɔɪt
exploratory	ik SPLAW ruh taw ri	ɪkˈsplɔrətɔrɪ
explosive	ik SPLOH siv	ɪkˈsplosɪv
exponent	ik SPOH nuhnt	ɪkˈsponənt

at [æ]; ah [ɑ]; air [ɛ]; awful [ɔ]; say [e]; back [b]; chair [tʃ]; do [d]; elm [ɛ]; eel [i]; server [ˈɝ, ər]; fit [f]; go [g]; hurt [h]; is [ɪ]; high [aɪ]; jet [dʒ]; kiss [k]; lamb [l]; my [m]; nice [n];

export (n)	EK spawrt	ˈɛkspɔrt
export (v)	ik SPAWRT	ɪkˈspɔrt
expose	ik SPOHZ	ɪkˈspoz
exposé	ek spoh ZAY	ɛkspoˈze
exposition	ek spuh ZI shuhn	ɛkspəˈzɪʃən
expository	ik SPAH zuh taw ri	ɪkˈspɑzətɔri
ex post facto	eks pohst FAK toh	ɛks post ˈfækto
expostulate	ik SPAHS chuh layt	ɪkˈspɑstʃəlet
exposure	ik SPOH zher	ɪkˈspoʒər
expropriate	eks PROH pri ayt	ɛksˈproprɪet
expulsion	ik SPUHL shuhn	ɪkˈspʌlʃən
expunge	ik SPUHNJ	ɪkˈspʌndʒ
expurgate	EK sper gayt	ˈɛkspərget
exquisite	EK skwi zit	ˈɛkskwɪzɪt
extant	EK stuhnt	ˈɛkstənt
extemporaneity	ek stem puh ruh NEE uh ti	ɛkstɛmpərəˈniətɪ
extemporary	ik STEM puh rai ri	ɪkˈstɛmpərɛrɪ
extempore	ik STEM puh ri	ɪkˈstɛmpərɪ
extend	ik STEND	ɪkˈstɛnd
extenuate	ik STE nyoo ayt	ɪkˈstɛnjʊet
extinct	ik STINGKT	ɪkˈstɪŋkt
extirpate	EK ster payt	ˈɛkstərpet
extol, -l	ik STOHL	ɪkˈstol
extort	ik STAWRT	ɪkˈstɔrt
extortion	ik STAWR shuhn	ɪkˈstɔrʃən
extortionary	ik STAWR shuh nai ri	ɪkˈstɔrʃənɛrɪ
extra	EK struh	ˈɛkstrə
extract (n)	EK strakt	ˈɛkstrækt
extract (v)	ik STRAKT	ɪkˈstrækt
extradite	EK struh dight	ˈɛkstrədaɪt
extradition	ik struh DI shuhn	ɪkstrəˈdɪʃən
extramural	ik struh MYOO ruhl	ɪkstrəˈmjʊrəl
extraneous	ik STRAY ni uhs	ɪkˈstrenɪəs
extraordinary	ik STRAWR duh nai ri	ɪkˈstrɔrdənɛrɪ
extrasensory	ek struh SEN suh ri	ɛkstrəˈsɛnsərɪ
extravagance	ik STRA vuh guhns	ɪkˈstrævəgəns
extravagancy	ik STRA vuh guhn si	ɪkˈstrævəgənsɪ
extravagant	ik STRA vuh guhnt	ɪkˈstrævəgənt
extravaganza	ik stra vuh GAN zuh	ɪkstrævəˈgænzə
extravert	EK struh vert	ˈɛkstrəvərt
extremity	ik STRE muh ti	ɪkˈstrɛmətɪ
extricate	EK stri kayt	ˈɛkstrɪket
extrinsic	ek STRIN sik	ɛkˈstrɪnsɪk
extroversion	ek stroh VER zhuhn	ɛkstroˈvɜʒən
extrovert	EK stroh vert	ˈɛkstrovərt
exuberance	ig ZOO : buh ruhns	ɪgˈzubərəns
exuberant	ig ZOO : buh ruhnt	ɪgˈzubərənt
exude	ig ZOO : D	ɪgˈzud
exult	ig ZUHLT	ɪgˈzʌlt
exultation	eg zuhl TAY shuhn	ɛgzəlˈteʃən
Eyck, van	IGHK, van	ˈaɪk, væn
eyre, E-	air	ɛr

sing [ŋ] ; oh [o] ; oil [ɔɪ] ; foot [ʊ] ; foo:d [u] ; how [aʊ] ; pie [p] ; ray [r] ; so [s] ; shall [ʃ] ;
to [t] ; thin [θ] ; th:en [ð] ; above (uh BUHV) [ə, ˈʌ] ; vine [v] ; wine [w] ; whine [hw] ;
you [j] ; zoo [z] ; rouge (roo:zh) [ʒ].

eyrie, eyry	AI ri	ˈɛrɪ
Ezekiel	i ZEE ki uhl	ɪˈzikɪəl
Ezra	EZ ruh	ˈɛzrə

F

Faber	FAY ber	ˈfebər
Fabian	FAY bi uhn	ˈfebɪən
Fabianism	FAY bi uh ni zuhm	ˈfebɪənɪzəm
Fabiola	fah bee OH lah	fɑbiˈolɑ
Fabius	FAY bi uhs	ˈfebɪəs
fabliau	FA bli oh	ˈfæblɪo
Fabre	FA bruh	ˈfæbrə
fabric	FA brik	ˈfæbrɪk
fabricate	FA bri kayt	ˈfæbrɪket
fabulous	FA byoo luhs	ˈfæbjʊləs
façade	fuh SAHD	fəˈsɑd
facet	FA sit	ˈfæsɪt
facetious	fuh SEE shuhs	fəˈsiʃəs
facial	FAY shuhl	ˈfeʃəl
faciend	FAY shi end	ˈfeʃɪend
facile	FA suhl	ˈfæsəl
facilitate	fuh SI luh tayt	fəˈsɪlətet
facility	fuh SI luh ti	fəˈsɪlətɪ
facsimile	fak SI muh li	fækˈsɪməlɪ
faction	FAK shuhn	ˈfækʃən
factious	FAK shuhs	ˈfækʃəs
factitious	fak TI shuhs	fækˈtɪʃəs
factor	FAK ter	ˈfæktər
factory	FAK tuh ri	ˈfæktərɪ
factotum	fak TOH tuhm	fækˈtotəm
factual	FAK choo uhl	ˈfæktʃʊəl
faculty	FA kuhl ti	ˈfækəltɪ
faerie, faery	FAY uh ri	ˈfeərɪ
Faeroe	FAI roh	ˈfɛro
Fafnir	FAHV nir	ˈfɑvnɪr
Fagin	FAY gin	ˈfegɪn
fagot, faggot	FA guht	ˈfægət
Fahrenheit	FA ruhn hight	ˈfærənhaɪt
fairy	FAI ri	ˈfɛrɪ
Faisal	FIGH suhl	ˈfaɪsəl
fait accompli	FAY ta kohn PLEE	ˈfe tækonˈpli
Faiyum	figh YOO : M	faɪˈjum
faker	FAY ker	ˈfekər
fakir	fuh KIR	fəˈkɪr
Falange	FAY lanj	ˈfelændʒ
Falangist	fuh LAN jist	fəˈlændʒɪst
falchion	FAWL chuhn	ˈfɔltʃən

---

at [æ]; *ah* [ɑ]; *air* [ɛ]; *awful* [ɔ]; *say* [e]; *back* [b]; *chair* [tʃ]; *do* [d]; *elm* [ɛ]; *eel* [i];
server [ˈɝ, ər]; *f*it [f]; *go* [g]; *hurt* [h]; *is* [ɪ]; *high* [aɪ]; *jet* [dʒ]; *kiss* [k]; *lamb* [l]; *my* [m];
nice [n];

falcon	FAWL kuhn	ˈfɔlkən
falconer	FAWL kuh ner	ˈfɔlkənər
falconry	FAWL kuhn ri	ˈfɔlkənrɪ
falderal	FAL duh ral	ˈfældəræl
Falkland	FAWK luhnd	ˈfɔklənd
fallacious	fuh LAY shuhs	fəˈleʃəs
fallacy	FA luh si	ˈfæləsɪ
fallible	FA luh buhl	ˈfæləbəl
Fallopian	fuh LOH pi uhn	fəˈlopɪən
fallow	FA loh	ˈfælo
falsehood	FAWLS hood	ˈfɔlshʊd
falsetto	fawl SE toh	fɔlˈseto
falsify	FAWL suh figh	ˈfɔlsəfaɪ
Falstaff	FAWL staf	ˈfɔlstæf
faltboat	FAHLT boht	ˈfɑltbot
Fameuse	fuh MYOO : Z	fəˈmjuz
familiar	fuh MI lyer	fəˈmɪljər
familiarity	fuh mi li AI ruh ti	fəmɪlɪˈerətɪ
familiarize	fuh MIL yuh righz	fəˈmɪljəraɪz
family	FAM li	ˈfæmlɪ
famine	FA min	ˈfæmɪn
fanatic	fuh NA tik	fəˈnætɪk
fanaticism	fuh NA tuh si zuhm	fəˈnætəsɪzəm
fancier	FAN si er	ˈfænsɪər
fancy	FAN si	ˈfænsɪ
fandango	fan DANG goh	fænˈdæŋgo
Faneuil	FA nuhl	ˈfænəl
fanfare	FAN fair	ˈfænfɛr
fanfaronade	fan fuh ruh NAYD	fænfərəˈned
fantasm	FAN ta zuhm	ˈfæntæzəm
fantasy	FAN tuh si	ˈfæntəsɪ
far	fahr	fɑr
farad	FA ruhd	ˈfærəd
faraday, F-	FA ruh day	ˈfærəde
Farah	fuh RAH	fəˈrɑ
farandole	FA ruhn dohl	ˈfærəndol
farce	fahrs	fɑrs
farci	fahr SEE	fɑrˈsi
fardel	FAHR duhl	ˈfɑrdəl
farina, F-	fuh REE nuh	fəˈrinə
Farnadi	fahr NAH dee	fɑrˈnɑdi
Faroe	FAI roh	ˈfero
Farouk	fa ROO : K	fæˈruk
farrago	fuh RAY goh	fəˈrego
Farragut	FA ruh guht	ˈfærəgət
Farrar	fuh RAHR	fəˈrɑr
farrier	FA ri er	ˈfærɪər
farrow	FA roh	ˈfæro
farthing	FAHR th : ing	ˈfɑrðɪŋ
farthingale	FAHR th : ing gayl	ˈfɑrðɪŋgel
fasces	FA seez	ˈfæsiz
fascinate	FA suh nayt	ˈfæsənet

sing [ŋ] ; *oh* [o] ; *oil* [ɔɪ] ; *foot* [ʊ] ; *foo:*d [u] ; *how* [aʊ] ; *pie* [p] ; *ray* [r] ; *so* [s] ; *shall* [ʃ] ;
to [t] ; *thin* [θ] ; *th:*en [ð] ; *above* (*uh* B*UH*V) [ə, ˈʌ] ; *vine* [v] ; *wine* [w] ; *whine* [hw] ;
you [j] ; *zoo* [z] ; *rouge* (roo:*zh*) [ʒ].

fascism, F-	FA shi zuhm	ˈfæʃɪzəm
fascist	FA shist	ˈfæʃɪst
Fascisti	fuh SHI sti	fəˈʃɪstɪ
fashion	FA shuhn	ˈfæʃən
fashioner	FA shuh ner	ˈfæʃənər
fasten	FA suhn	ˈfæsən
fastidious	fa STI di uhs	fæˈstɪdɪəs
fatal	FAY tuhl	ˈfetəl
Fata Morgana, f- m-	FAH tuh mawr GAH nuh	ˈfɑtə mɔrˈgɑnə
Fath, Jacques	faht, zhahk	fɑt, ʒɑk
fathom	FA th:uhm	ˈfæðəm
fatigue	fuh TEEG	fəˈtig
Fatima	FA ti muh	ˈfætɪmə
Fatima (cigarets)	fuh TEE muh	fəˈtimə
fatuity	fuh TOO: uh ti	fəˈtuətɪ
fatuous	FA choo uhs	ˈfætʃuəs
Faubus	FAW buhs	ˈfɔbəs
faucet	FAW sit	ˈfɔsɪt
Faulkner	FAWK ner	ˈfɔknər
fault	fawlt	fɔlt
faun	fawn	fɔn
fauna	FAW nuh	ˈfɔnə
Faure	fohr	for
Fauré	foh RAY	foˈre
Faust	fowst	faʊst
Faustus	FAW stuhs	faʊstəs
faute de mieux	foht duh MYER	fot də ˈmjɝ
fauteuil	foh TER yuh	foˈtɝyə
fauve, F-	fohv	fov
Fauvist	FOH vist	ˈfovɪst
faux pas	foh PAH	foˈpɑ
favor, favour	FAY ver	ˈfevər
favorite, favourite	FAY vuh rit	ˈfevərɪt
Fawcett	FAW set	ˈfɔsɛt
Fawkes	fawks	fɔks
fealty	FEE uhl ti	ˈfiəltɪ
feasible	FEE zuh buhl	ˈfizəbəl
feat	feet	fit
feature	FEE cher	ˈfitʃər
febrile	FEE bruhl	ˈfibrəl
February	FE broo ai ri	ˈfɛbrʊɛrɪ
fecal	FEE kuhl	ˈfikəl
feces	FEE seez	ˈfisiz
Fechner	FEK ner	ˈfɛknər
fecund	FEE kuhnd	ˈfikənd
fecundity	fi KUHN duh ti	fɪˈkʌndətɪ
federal, F-	FE duh ruhl	ˈfɛdərəl
federalist, F-	FE duh ruh list	ˈfɛdərəlɪst
federation	fe duh RAY shuhn	fɛdəˈreʃən
Federigo	fe de REE goh	fɛdɛˈrigo
fedora	fi DAW ruh	fɪˈdɔrə
feign	fayn	fen

at [æ]; ah [ɑ]; air [ɛ]; awful [ɔ]; say [e]; back [b]; chair [tʃ]; do [d]; elm [ɛ]; eel [i]; server [ˈɝ, ər]; fit [f]; go [g]; hurt [h]; is [ɪ]; high [aɪ]; jet [dʒ]; kiss [k]; lamb [l]; my [m]; nice [n];

Feikema, Feike	FIGH kuh muh, FIGH ki	ˈfaɪkəmə, ˈfaɪkɪ
Feisal	FIGH suhl	ˈfaɪsəl
felicitous	fuh LI suh tuhs	fəˈlɪsətəs
felicity	fuh LI suh ti	fəˈlɪsətɪ
feline	FEE lighn	ˈfilaɪn
Felix	FEE liks	ˈfilɪks
fellah	FE luh	ˈfɛlə
fellatio	fuh LAY shi oh	fəˈleʃɪo
fellow	FE loh	ˈfɛlo
felon	FE luhn	ˈfɛlən
felonious	fuh LOH ni uhs	fəlˈonɪəs
felony	FE luh ni	ˈfɛlənɪ
femineity	fe muh NEE uh ti	fɛməˈniətɪ
feminine	FE muh nin	ˈfɛmənɪn
femininity	fe muh NI nuh ti	fɛməˈnɪnətɪ
feminism	FE muh ni zuhm	ˈfɛmənɪzəm
femme fatale	fem fa TAL	fɛm fæˈtæl
femoral	FE muh ruhl	ˈfɛmərəl
femur	FEE mer	ˈfimər
Fénelon	FE nuh lahn	ˈfɛnəlɑn
Fenian	FEE ni uhn	ˈfinɪən
fennel	FE nuhl	ˈfɛnəl
Fenrir	FEN rer	ˈfɛnrər
fenugreek	FE nyoo greek	ˈfɛnjʊgrik
feodal	FYOO duhl	ˈfjʊdəl
feoff	fef	fɛf
ferment (n)	FER muhnt	ˈfɝmənt
ferment (v)	fer MENT	fərˈmɛnt
Fermi	FAIR mee	ˈfɛrmi
fermium	FER mi uhm	ˈfɝmɪəm
fern	fern	fɝn
Fernandel	fair nahn DEL	fɛrnɑnˈdɛl
Fernandes	fair NAHN des	fɛrˈnɑndɛs
Fernandez	fer NAN diz	fərˈnændɪz
ferocious	fuh ROH shuhs	fəˈroʃəs
ferocity	fuh RAH suh ti	fəˈrɑsətɪ
Ferrara	fuh RAH ruh	fəˈrɑrə
Ferrer	fuh RAIR	fəˈrɛr
ferret	FE rit	ˈfɛrɪt
ferriage	FE ri ij	ˈfɛrɪɪdʒ
ferrule	FE ruhl	ˈfɛrəl
ferry	FE ri	ˈfɛrɪ
fertile	FER tuhl	ˈfɝtəl
ferule	FE ruhl	ˈfɛrəl
fervent	FER vuhnt	ˈfɝvənt
fervid	FER vid	ˈfɝvɪd
fervor, fervour	FER ver	ˈfɝvər
Fescennine	FE suh nighn	ˈfɛsənaɪn
festoon	fe STOO : N	fɛˈstun
Festung	FE stoong	ˈfɛstʊŋ
Festus	FE stuhs	ˈfɛstəs
fetal	FEE tuhl	ˈfitəl

sing [ŋ] ; *oh* [o] ; *oil* [ɔɪ] ; *foot* [ʊ] ; *foo:*d [u] ; *how* [aʊ] ; *p*ie [p] ; *ray* [r] ; *so* [s] ; *sh*all [ʃ] ;
to [t] ; *th*in [θ] ; *th:*en [ð] ; above (*uh BUH*V) [ə, ˈʌ] ; *v*ine [v] ; *w*ine [w] ; *wh*ine [hw] ;
*y*ou [j] ; *z*oo [z] ; rouge (roo:*zh*) [ʒ].

fete	fayt	fet
fête champêtre	fet shahn PE truh	fɛt ʃɑn'pɛtrə
fetich	FEE tish	'fitɪʃ
fetid	FE tid	'fɛtɪd
fetish	FEE tish	'fitɪʃ
fetus	FEE tuhs	'fitəs
Feuchtwanger	FOIKT vahng ger	'fɔɪktvɑŋgər
feud	fyoo : d	fjud
feudal	FYOO : duhl	'fjudəl
fever	FEE ver	'fivər
fey	fay	fe
fez, F-	fez	fɛz
fiacre	fi AH ker	fɪ'ɑkər
fiancé, fiancée	fee ahn SAY	fiɑn'se
Fianna	FEE uh nuh	'fiənə
fiasco	fi A skoh	fɪ'æsko
fiat	FIGH uht	'faɪət
fibrin	FIGH brin	'faɪbrɪn
fibula	FI byoo luh	'fɪbjʊlə
Fichte	FIK tuh	'fɪktə
fichu	FI shoo :	'fɪʃu
fictitious	fik TI shuhs	fɪk'tɪʃəs
Fidelio (opera)	fi DAY li oh	fɪ'delɪo
Fidelio (brewery)	fi DE lyoh	fɪ'dɛljo
fidelity	figh DE luh ti	faɪ'dɛlətɪ
fiducial	fi DOO : shuhl	fɪ'duʃəl
fiduciary	fi DOO : shi ai ri	fɪ'duʃɪɛrɪ
fief	feef	fif
fiery	FIGH ri	'faɪrɪ
Fiesole	FYE zaw le	'fjɛzɔlɛ
fiesta	fi E stuh	fɪ'ɛstə
fife	fighf	faɪf
fifth	fifth	fɪfθ
figaro	FI guh roh	'fɪgəro
Figl	FI guhl	'fɪgəl
figment	FIG muhnt	'fɪgmənt
Figuerola	fee guh ROH lah	figə'rolɑ
figurative	FI gyoo ruh tiv	'fɪgjʊrətɪv
figure	FI gyer	'fɪgjər
figurine	fi gyoo REEN	fɪgjʊ'rin
Fiji	FEE jee	'fidʒi
Fijian	FEE jee uhn	'fidʒɪən
filament	FI luh muhnt	'fɪləmənt
filariasis	fi luh RIGH uh sis	filə'raɪəsɪs
filch	filch	fɪltʃ
filet	fi LAY	fɪ'le
Filho	FEE lyoo	'filjʊ
filial	FI li uhl	'fɪlɪəl
filibuster	fi luh BUH ster	filə'bʌstər
Filipino	fi luh PEE noh	filə'pino
fille de joie	fee duh ZHWAH	fi də 'ʒwɑ
fillet (band)	FI lit	'fɪlɪt

at [æ] ; ah [ɑ] ; air [ɛ] ; awful [ɔ] ; say [e] ; back [b] ; chair [tʃ] ; do [d] ; elm [ɛ] ; eel [i] ; server ['ɝ, ər] ; fit [f] ; go [g] ; hurt [h] ; is [ɪ] ; high [aɪ] ; jet [dʒ] ; kiss [k] ; lamb [l] ; my [m] ; nice [n] ;

fillet (slice)	FI lay	ˈfɪle
fillip	FI lup	ˈfɪləp
film	film	fɪlm
finagle	fi NAY guhl	fɪˈnegəl
finale	fi NAH li	fɪˈnɑlɪ
finalist	FIGH nuh list	ˈfaɪnəlɪst
finality	figh NA luh ti	faɪˈnælətɪ
finance (n)	FIGH nans	ˈfaɪnæns
finance (v)	fi NANS	fɪˈnæns
financier	fi nuhn SIR	fɪnənˈsɪr
finesse	fi NES	fɪˈnɛs
finger	FING ger	ˈfɪŋgər
finis	FIGH nis	ˈfaɪnɪs
Finisterre	fi ni STAIR	fɪnɪˈstɛr
finite	FIGH night	ˈfaɪnaɪt
fink	fingk	fɪŋk
Finland	FIN luhnd	ˈfɪnlənd
Finlandia	fin LAN di uh	fɪnˈlændɪə
finnan haddie	FI nuhn HA di	ˈfɪnən ˈhædɪ
Finno-	FI noh	ˈfɪno
Finsteraarhorn	fin ster AHR hawrn	fɪnstərˈɑrhɔrn
fiord	fyawrd	fjɔrd
Fiorello	fee uh RE loh	fiəˈrɛlo
Firenze	fi REND ze	fɪˈrɛndzɛ
firing	FIGH ring	ˈfaɪrɪŋ
Firkusny	fir KOOSH ni	fɪrˈkuʃnɪ
firn	firn	fɪrn
fiscal	FI skuhl	ˈfɪskəl
fission	FI shuhn	ˈfɪʃən
fissionable	FI shuh nuh buhl	ˈfɪʃənəbəl
fissure	FI sher	ˈfɪʃər
Fistoulari, Anatol	fi stoo: LAH ree, AH nuh tohl	fɪstuˈlɑri, ˈɑnətol
fistula	FIS choo luh	ˈfɪstʃʊlə
fitchew	FI choo:	ˈfɪtʃu
Fiume	FYOO: me	ˈfjumɛ
fizgig	FIZ gig	ˈfɪzgɪg
fjeld	fyeld	fjɛld
fjord	fjawrd	fjɔrd
flabellum	fluh BE luhm	fləˈbɛləm
flaccid	FLAK sid	ˈflæksɪd
flagellant	FLA juh luhnt	ˈflædʒələnt
flageolet	FLA juh let	ˈflædʒəlɛt
flagitious	fluh JI shuhs	fləˈdʒɪʃəs
flagon	FLA guhn	ˈflægən
flagrant	FLAY gruhnt	ˈflegrənt
Flagstad	FLAG stad	ˈflægstæd
flair	flair	flɛr
flak	flak	flæk
flam	flam	flæm
flamboyant	flam BOI uhnt	flæmˈbɔɪənt
flamen	FLAY men	ˈflemɛn

flamenco	flah MENG koh	flɑˈmɛŋko
flamingo	fluh MING goh	fləˈmɪŋgo
Flanagan, Flanigan	FLA nuh guhn	ˈflænəgən
flaneur	flah NER	flɑˈnɛr
flange	flanj	flændʒ
flank	flangk	flæŋk
flannel	FLA nuhl	ˈflænəl
flatulence	FLA chuh luhns	ˈflætʃələns
flatus	FLAY tuhs	ˈfletəs
Flaubert	floh BAIR	floˈbɛr
flaunt	flawnt	flɔnt
flautist	FLAW tist	ˈflɔtɪst
flavor, flavour	FLAY ver	ˈflevər
fleur-de-lis (sing.)	fler duh LEE	fler də ˈli
fleurs-de-lis (pl.)	fler duh LEEZ	flər də liz
flew	floo:	flu
flexile	FLEK sil	ˈflɛksɪl
Flexner	FLEK sner	ˈflɛksnər
flexuous	FLEK shoo uhs	ˈflɛkʃuəs
flexure	FLEK sher	ˈflɛkʃər
flibbertigibbet	FLI ber ti ji bit	ˈflɪbərtɪdʒɪbɪt
Fliegende Holländer, der	FLEE gen duh HOH layn dair, dair	ˈfligəndə ˈholendɛr, dɛr
flier	FLIGH er	ˈflaɪər
flimsy	FLIM zi	ˈflɪmzɪ
flippancy	FLI puhn si	ˈflɪpənsɪ
flippant	FLI punt	ˈflɪpənt
flirtatious	fler TAY shuhs	flərˈteʃəs
flitch	flich	flɪtʃ
floe	floh	flo
floozy	FLOO: zi	ˈfluzɪ
Flora, f-	FLAW ruh	ˈflɔrə
floral	FLAW ruhl	ˈflɔrəl
Florence	FLAW ruhns	ˈflɔrəns
Florentine	FLAW ruh teen	ˈflɔrəntin
Flores	FLAW res	ˈflɔrɛs
florescence	flaw RE suhns	floˈrɛsəns
florid	FLAW rid	ˈflɔrɪd
Florida	FLAW ruh duh	ˈflɔrədə
Floridian	fluh RI di uhn	fləˈrɪdɪən
florin	FLAW rin	ˈflɔrɪn
florist	FLAW rist	ˈflɔrɪst
flotage	FLOH tij	ˈflotɪdʒ
flotation	floh TAY shuhn	floˈteʃən
flotilla	floh TI luh	floˈtɪlə
Flotow	FLOH toh	ˈfloto
flotsam	FLAHT suhm	ˈflɑtsəm
flounce	flowns	flauns
flour	flowr	flaur
flourish	FLER ish	ˈflɜrɪʃ
flower	flowr	flaur
fluctuate	FLUHK choo ayt	ˈflʌktʃuet

at [æ]; ah [ɑ]; air [ɛ]; awful [ɔ]; say [e]; back [b]; chair [tʃ]; do [d]; elm [ɛ]; eel [i]; server [ˈɜ, ər]; fit [f]; go [g]; hurt [h]; is [ɪ]; high [aɪ]; jet [dʒ]; kiss [k]; lamb [l]; my [m]; nice [n];

fluctuation	fluhk choo AY shuhn	fləktʃuˈeʃən
flue	floo :	flu
fluent	FLOO : uhnt	ˈfluənt
fluid	FLOO : id	ˈfluɪd
fluke	floo : k	fluk
flume	floo : m	flum
flummery	FLUH muh ri	ˈflʌmərɪ
flunk	fluhngk	flʌŋk
fluorescent	floo : uh RE suhnt	fluəˈrɛsənt
fluoridate	FLOO : uh ri dayt	ˈfluərɪdet
fluoride	FLOO : uh righd	ˈfluəraɪd
fluoridize	FLOO : uh ri dighz	ˈfluərɪdaɪz
fluorine	FLOO : uh reen	ˈfluərin
fluoroscope	FLOO ruh skohp	ˈfluʊrəskop
fluoroscopy	floo RAH skuh pi	fluʊˈrɑskəpɪ
fluorosis	floo : uh ROH sis	fluəˈrosɪs
flurry	FLER i	ˈflɝɪ
flute	floo : t	flut
flutist	FLOO : tist	ˈflutɪst
fluvial	FLOO : vi uhl	ˈfluvɪəl
flux	fluhks	flʌks
flyer	FLIGH er	ˈflaɪər
foal	fohl	fol
fob	fahb	fɑb
focal	FOH kuhl	ˈfokəl
Foch	fawsh	fɔʃ
focus	FOH kuhs	ˈfokəs
foetal	FEE tuhl	ˈfitəl
foetus	FEE tuhs	ˈfitəs
fogey, fogy	FOH gi	ˈfogɪ
Fogg	fahg	ˈfɑg
foible	FOI buhl	ˈfɔɪbəl
foie gras	fwah GRAH	fwa ˈgrɑ
foist	foist	fɔɪst
Fokine	faw KEEN	fɔˈkin
fokker, F-	FAH ker	ˈfɑkər
folderol	FAHL duh rahl	ˈfɑldərɑl
Foldes, Andor	FOHL desh, AHN dawr	ˈfoldɛʃ, ˈɑndɔr
foliage	FOH li ij	ˈfolɪɪdʒ
foliation	foh li AY shuhn	folɪˈeʃən
Folies Bergères	foh LEE bair ZHAIR	foˈli bɛrˈʒɛr
folk	fohk	fok
Folkestone	FOHK stuhn	ˈfokstən
Folketing	FAHL ke ting	ˈfɑlkɛtɪŋ
folklore	FOHK lawr	ˈfoklɔr
follicle	FAH li kuhl	ˈfɑlɪkəl
Fomalhaut	FOH muhl hawt	ˈfoməlhɔt
foment	foh MENT	foˈmɛnt
fomentation	foh muhn TAY shuhn	fomənˈteʃən
fond	fahnd	fɑnd
fondant	FAHN duhnt	ˈfɑndənt
fondue	FAHN doo :	ˈfɑndu

---

sing [ŋ] ; oh [o] ; oil [ɔɪ] ; foot [ʊ] ; foo:d [u] ; how [aʊ] ; pie [p] ; ray [r] ; so [s] ; shall [ʃ] ;
to [t] ; thin [θ] ; th:en [ð] ; above (uh BUHV) [ə, ˈʌ] ; vine [v] ; wine [w] ; whine [hw] ;
you [j] ; zoo [z] ; rouge (roo:zh) [ʒ].

Fontainebleau	FAHN tin bloh	ˈfɑntɪnblo
Fontanne	fawn TAN	fɔnˈtæn
Fontéchevade	fawn taysh VAHD	fɔnteʃˈvɑd
Fonteyn	FAWN ten	ˈfɔntɛn
Foochow	foo : chow	fu tʃau
food	foo : d	fud
forage	FAW rij	ˈfɔrɪdʒ
forbad, forbade	fer BAD	fərˈbæd
forbear (n)	FAWR bair	ˈfɔrbɛr
forbear (v)	fawr BAIR	fɔrˈbɛr
force majeure	fawrs ma ZHER	fɔrs mæˈʒɜ
forcemeat	FAWRS meet	ˈfɔrsmit
forceps	FAWR suhps	ˈfɔrsəps
forebear	FAWR bair	ˈfɔrbɛr
forecastle	FOHK suhl	ˈfoksəl
forehead	FAW rid	ˈfɔrɪd
foreign	FAW rin	ˈfɔrɪn
forest	FAW rist	ˈfɔrɪst
forestation	faw ri STAY shuhn	fɔrɪˈsteʃən
forfeit	FAWR fit	ˈfɔrfɪt
forge	fawrj	fɔrdʒ
forgery	FAWR juh ri	ˈfɔrdʒərɪ
forint	FAW rint	ˈfɔrɪnt
formagen	FAWR muh juhn	ˈfɔrmədʒən
formaldehyde	fawr MAL duh highd	fɔrˈmældəhaɪd
format	FAWR mat	ˈfɔrmæt
formative	FAWR muh tiv	ˈfɔmətɪv
formidable	FAWR mi duh buhl	ˈfɔrmɪdəbəl
Formidable (British ship)	faw MI duh buhl	fɔˈmɪdəbəl
Formosa	fawr MOH suh	fɔrˈmosə
formula	FAWR myuh luh	ˈfɔrmjələ
formulae	FAWR myuh lee	ˈfɔrmjəli
forsooth	fer SOO : TH	fərˈsuθ
forsythia	fer SI thi uh	fərˈsɪθɪə
Fortaleza	fawr tuh LAY zuh	fɔrtəˈlezə
fortalice	FAWR tuh lis	ˈfɔrtəlɪs
forte (a, adv)	FAWR ti	ˈfɔrtɪ
forte (n)	fawrt	fɔrt
forthwith	fawrth WITH	fɔrθˈwɪθ
fortissimo	fawr TI suh moh	fɔrˈtɪsəmo
fortitude	FAWR tuh too : d	ˈfɔrtətud
fortuitous	fawr TOO : uh tuhs	fɔrˈtuətəs
Fortuna	fawr TYOO : nuh	fɔrˈtjunə
fortune	FAWR chuhn	ˈfɔrtʃən
forum	FAW ruhm	ˈfɔrəm
forward	FAWR werd	ˈfɔrwərd
Forza del Destino	FAWRT sah del de STEE noh	ˈfɔrtsɑ dɛl dɛˈstino
Foss	faws	fɔs
fossa	FAH suh	ˈfɑsə
Foucault	foo : KOH	fuˈko

at [æ] ; *ah* [ɑ] ; *air* [ɛ] ; *awful* [ɔ] ; *say* [e] ; *back* [b] ; *chair* [tʃ] ; *do* [d] ; *elm* [ɛ] ; *eel* [i] ; *server* [ˈɜ, ər] ; *f*it [f] ; *go* [g] ; *hurt* [h] ; *is* [ɪ] ; *high* [aɪ] ; *jet* [dʒ] ; *kiss* [k] ; *lamb* [l] ; *my* [m] ; *nice* [n] ;

Fouché	foo : SHAY	fuˈʃe
fought	fawt	fɔt
foulard	foo : LAHRD	fuˈlɑrd
foulmouthed	FOWL mowth : d	ˈfaʊlmaʊðd
Fournet	foo : r NAY	furˈne
Fournier (French)	foor ni AY	fʊrnɪˈe
Fournier (Spanish)	foo : r NEER	furˈnir
foy	foi	fɔɪ
foyer	FOI er	ˈfɔɪər
fracas	FRAY kuhs	ˈfrekəs
fracture	FRAK cher	ˈfræktʃər
Fra Diavolo	frah DYAH voh loh	fra ˈdjɑvolo
fraenum	FREE nuhm	ˈfrinəm
fragile	FRA juhl	ˈfrædʒəl
fragmentary	FRAG muhn tai ri	ˈfrægɪrɔnterɪ
Fragonard	fra gaw NAHR	frægoˈnɑr
fragrant	FRAY gruhnt	ˈfregrənt
frailty	FRAYL ti	ˈfreltɪ
franc	frangk	fræŋk
française (Fr.)	frahn SEZ	franˈsɛz
Françaix	frahn SAY	franˈse
France	frans	fræns
Francesca	frahn CHES kuh	franˈtʃeskə
Franceschi	frahn CHE skee	franˈtʃeski
Francescatti	frahn che SKAH ti	frantʃɛˈskatɪ
franchise	FRAN chighz	ˈfræntʃaɪz
Franciscan	fran SIS kuhn	frænˈsɪskən
Franck, César	frahngk, say ZAHR	fraŋk, seˈzɑr
Franco, Francisco	FRANG koh, fran SIS koh	ˈfræŋko, frænˈsɪsko
Franco-	FRANG koh	ˈfræŋko
Franconia	frang KOH ni uh	fræŋˈkonɪə
Francophile	FRANG kuh fighl	ˈfræŋkəfaɪl
Francophobe	FRANG kuh fohb	ˈfræŋkəfob
franc-tireur	frahn tee RER	fræntiˈrɝ
frangible	FRAN juh buhl	ˈfrændʒəbəl
Frankenstein	FRANG kuhn stighn	ˈfræŋkənstaɪn
Frankfurt am Main	FRAHNGK foort ahm MIGHN	ˈfraŋkfurt ɑm ˈmaɪn
frankfurter, F-	FRANGK fer ter	ˈfræŋkfərtər
frankincense	FRANG kin sens	ˈfræŋkɪnsɛns
franklin, F-	FRANGK lin	ˈfræŋklɪn
Franz (American)	franz	frænz
Franz (European)	frahnts	frants
frap	frap	fræp
frappé	fra PAY	fræˈpe
fraternize	FRA ter nighz	ˈfrætərnaɪz
fratricide	FRA truh sighd	ˈfrætrəsaɪd
Frau	frow	frau
fraud	frawd	frɔd
fraudulent	FRAW juh luhnt	ˈfrɔdʒələnt
fraught	frawt	frɔt
Fräulein	FROI lighn	ˈfrɔɪlaɪn

sing [ŋ] ; *oh* [o] ; *oil* [ɔɪ] ; *foot* [ʊ] ; *foo* :d [u] ; *how* [aʊ] ; *pie* [p] ; *ray* [r] ; *so* [s] ; *shall* [ʃ] ; *to* [t] ; *thin* [θ] ; *th*:en [ð] ; *above* (*uh* B*UH*V) [ə, ˈʌ] ; *vine* [v] ; *wine* [w] ; *whine* [hw] ; *you* [j] ; *zoo* [z] ; *rouge* (roo:*zh*) [ʒ].

Fraunhofer	FROWN hoh fer	ˈfraʊnhofər
freak	freek	frik
Fredericton	FRE duh rik tuhn	ˈfrɛdərɪktən
Fredrikstad	FRE dreek stah	ˈfrɛdrɪkstɑ
freesia	FREE zhuh	ˈfriʒə
Freetown	FREE town	ˈfritaʊn
Freiburg	FRIGH berg	ˈfraɪbərg
Freneau	fri NOH	frɪˈno
frenetic	fruh NE tik	frəˈnɛtɪk
frenum	FREE nuhm	ˈfrinəm
freon, F-	FREE ahn	ˈfriɑn
frequence	FREE kwuhns	ˈfrikwəns
frequency	FREE kwuhn si	ˈfrikwənsɪ
frequent (a)	FREE kwuhnt	ˈfrikwənt
frequent (v)	fri KWENT	frɪˈkwɛnt
frère	frair	frɛr
fresco	FRE skoh	ˈfrɛsko
Fresno	FREZ noh	ˈfrɛzno
Freud	froid	frɔɪd
Freudian	FROI di uhn	ˈfrɔɪdɪən
Freundlich	FROIND lik	ˈfrɔɪndlɪk
Frey	fray	fre
Freya, Freyja	FRAY uh	ˈfreə
friable	FRIGH uh buhl	ˈfraɪəbəl
friar	FRIGH er	ˈfraɪər
fricandeau, fricando	fri kuhn DOH	frɪkənˈdo
fricassee	fri kuh SEE	frɪkəˈsi
Frick	frik	frɪk
Fricsay, Ferenc	FREE chigh, FE rents	ˈfritʃaɪ, ˈfɛrɛnts
Fridtjof Nansen	FREET yawf NAHN suhn	ˈfritjof ˈnɑnsən
Friedberg	FREED berg	ˈfridbərg
Fries	freez	friz
Friesian	FREE zhuhn	ˈfriʒən
frieze	freez	friz
frigate	FRI git	ˈfrɪgɪt
Frigg	frig	frɪg
Frigga	FRI guh	ˈfrɪgə
frigid	FRI jid	ˈfrɪdʒɪd
frijol	FREE hohl	ˈfrihol
frijole	free HOH li	friˈholɪ
Friml	FRI muhl	ˈfrɪməl
frisé	fri ZAY	frɪˈze
frisette	fri ZET	frɪˈzɛt
friseur	free ZER	friˈzɝ
Frisian	FRI zhuhn	ˈfrɪʒən
frivolity	fri VAH luh ti	frɪˈvɑlətɪ
frivolous	FRI vuh luhs	ˈfrɪvələs
frizette	fri ZET	frɪˈzɛt
Fröbel	FRER buhl	ˈfrɝbəl
Frobisher	FROH bi sher	ˈfrobɪʃər
Frohman	FROH muhn	ˈfromən
Froissart	FROI sahrt	ˈfrɔɪsɑrt

at [æ]; *ah* [ɑ]; *air* [ɛ]; *awful* [ɔ]; *say* [e]; *back* [b]; *chair* [tʃ]; *do* [d]; *elm* [ɛ]; *eel* [i];
server [ˈɝ, ər]; *f*it [f]; *go* [g]; *h*urt [h]; *is* [ɪ]; *high* [aɪ]; *jet* [dʒ]; *kiss* [k]; *lamb* [l]; *my* [m];
nice [n];

Fromm	frohm	from
Fronde	frohnd	frond
Frondizi	frahn DEE zee	frɑn'dizi
frontage	FRUHN tij	'frʌntɪdʒ
Frontenac	FRAHN tuh nak	'frɑntənæk
frontier	fruhn TIR	frən'tɪr
frontispiece	FRUHN tis pees	'frʌntɪspis
frottage	fruh TAHZH	frə'tɑʒ
Froude	froo : d	frud
froufrou	FROO : froo :	'frufru
frow	frow	frɑʊ
fructify	FRUHK tuh figh	'frʌktəfɑɪ
frugal	FROO : guhl	'frugəl
fruition	froo : I shuhn	fru'ɪʃən
frumentaceous	froo : men TAY shuhs	frumɛn'teʃəs
frumenty	FROO : muhn ti	'fruməntɪ
Frunze	FROO : N ze	'frunzɛ
frustrate	FRUH strayt	'frʌstret
fry	frigh	frɑɪ
Fuad	foo : AHD	fu'ɑd
Fuchs	fyoo : ks	'fjuks
fuchsia	FYOO : shuh	'fjuʃə
fuchsin, -e	FOOK sin	'fʊksɪn
Fuegian	fyoo : EE ji uhn	fju'idʒɪən
fuehrer, F-	FYOO rer	'fjʊrər
fuel	FYOO : uhl	'fjuəl
Fuente	FWEN tuh	'fwɛntə
fugacious	fyoo : GAY shuhs	fju'geʃəs
fugitive	FYOO : juh tiv	'fjudʒətɪv
fugle	FYOO : guhl	'fjugəl
fugue	fyoo : g	fjug
führer, F-	FYOO rer	'fjʊrər
Fuji	FOO : jee	'fudʒi
Fujiyama	foo : jee YAH mah	fudʒi'jɑmɑ
Fukien	foo : kyen	fu kjɛn
Fukui	foo : koo : ee	fu ku i
Fukuoka	FOO : koo : AW kah	'fuku'ɔkɑ
Fula, -h	FOO : lah	'fulɑ
fulcrum	FUHL kruhm	'fʌlkrəm
fulgent	FUHL juhnt	'fʌldʒənt
fulminant	FUHL muh nuhnt	'fʌlmənənt
fulminate	FUHL muh nayt	'fʌlmənet
fulsome	FOOL suhm	'fʊlsəm
fumatory	FYOO : muh taw ri	'fjumətɔrɪ
fumigate	FYOO : muh gayt	'fjuməget
funambulist	fyoo NAM byoo list	fjʊ'næmbjʊlɪst
Funchal	foon SHAHL	fʊn'ʃɑl
function	FUHNGK shuhn	'fʌŋkʃən
functionary	FUHNGK shuh nai ri	'fʌŋkʃənɛrɪ
Fundy	FUHN di	'fʌndɪ
funeral	FYOO : nuh ruhl	'fjunərəl
funereal	fyoo : NI ri uhl	fju'nɪrɪəl

---

sing [ŋ] ; *oh* [o] ; *oil* [ɔɪ] ; *foot* [ʊ] ; *foo:*d [u] ; *how* [aʊ] ; *p*ie [p] ; *ray* [r] ; *so* [s] ; *sh*all [ʃ] ;
to [t] ; *thin* [θ] ; *th*:en [ð] ; *above* (*uh* B*UH*V) [ə, 'ʌ] ; *v*ine [v] ; *w*ine [w] ; *wh*ine [hw] ;
you [j] ; *zoo* [z] ; *rouge* (roo:*zh*) [ʒ].

fungi	FUHN jigh	ˈfʌndʒaɪ
fungicide	FUHN juh sighd	ˈfʌndʒəsaɪd
fungus	FUHNG guhs	ˈfʌŋgəs
funicular	fyoo : NI kyoo ler	fjuˈnɪkjʊlər
furbelow	FER buh loh	ˈfɝbəlo
furcate (a)	FER kit	ˈfɝkɪt
furcate (v)	FER kayt	ˈfɝket
furious	FYOO ri uhs	ˈfjʊrɪəs
furlough	FER loh	ˈfɝlo
furor, furore	FYOO rawr	ˈfjʊrɔr
furrier	FER i er	ˈfɝɪər
furrow	FER oh	ˈfɝo
furry	FER i	ˈfɝɪ
Furtwängler	FIRT veng ler	ˈfɪrtvɛŋlər
fury	FYOO ri	ˈfjʊrɪ
furze	ferz	fɝz
fusel	FYOO : zuhl	ˈfjuzəl
fuselage	FYOO : zuh lij	ˈfjuzəlɪdʒ
fusil	FYOO : zuhl	ˈfjuzəl
fusilier, fusileer	fyoo : zuh LIR	fjuzəˈlɪr
fusillade	FYOO : zuh layd	ˈfjuzəled
fusion	FYOO : zhuhn	ˈfjuʒən
fustian	FUHS chuhn	ˈfʌstʃən
futile	FYOO : tuhl	ˈfjutəl
future	FYOO : cher	ˈfjutʃər
futurist	FYOO : chuh rist	ˈfjutʃərɪst
futurity	fyoo : TYOO ruh ti	fjuˈtjʊrətɪ
fyke	fighk	faɪk
fylfot	FIL faht	ˈfɪlfɑt

G

gabardine	GA ber deen	ˈgæbərdin
Gabin, Jean	gah BAN, zhahn	gɑˈbæn, ʒɑn
gabion	GAY bi uhn	ˈgebɪən
Gabon	ga BOHN	gæˈbon
Gabor	guh BAWR	gəˈbɔr
Gaboriau	ga baw RYOH	gæbɔˈrjo
Gabriel	GAY bri uhl	ˈgebrɪəl
Gabrilowitsch	gah bri LUH vich	gɑbrɪˈlʌvɪtʃ
Gaea	JEE uh	ˈdʒiə
Gaekwar	GIGHK wahr	ˈgaɪkwɑr
Gaelic	GAY lik	ˈgelɪk
Gaetano	gah e TAH noh	gɑɛˈtɑno
gage	gayj	gedʒ
Gagliano	gah LYAH noh	gɑˈljɑno
Gaillard	GAY lahrd	ˈgelɑrd
gaillardia	gay LAHR di uh	geˈlɑrdɪə

at [æ] ; ah [ɑ] ; air [ɛ] ; awful [ɔ] ; say [e] ; back [b] ; chair [tʃ] ; do [d] ; elm [ɛ] ; eel [i] ; server [ˈɝ, ər] ; fit [f] ; go [g] ; hurt [h] ; is [ɪ] ; high [aɪ] ; jet [dʒ] : kiss [k] ; lamb [l] ; my [m] ; nice [n] ;

gainsay	gayn SAY	genّse
Gainsborough	GAYNZ buh roh	ّgenzbərə
Gaitskell	GAYT skuhl	ّgetskəl
Gaius	GAY uhs	ّgeəs
gala	GAY luh	ّgelə
galactic	guh LAK tik	gəّlæktık
Galahad	GA luh had	ّgæləhæd
Galápagos	guh LAH puh gohs	gəّlɑpəgos
Galatea	ga luh TEE uh	gæləّtiə
Galatia	guh LAY shuh	gəّleʃə
galaxy, G-	GA luhk si	ّgæləksı
Galbraith	GAWL brayth	ّgɔlbreθ
Galen	GAY luhn	ّgelən
Galicia	guh LI shuh	gəّlıʃə
Galilee	GA luh lee	ّgæləli
Galileo	ga luh LEE oh	gæləّlio
gallant (a)	GA luhnt	ّgælənt
gallant (n, v)	guh LANT	gəّlænt
gallantly	GA luhnt li	ّgæləntlı
gallantry	GA luhn tri	ّgæləntrı
Gallegos	gah YAY gohs	gɑّyegos
galleon	GA li uhn	ّgælıən
gallery	GA luh ri	ّgælərı
Gallic	GA lik	ّgælık
gallicism, G-	GA luh si zuhm	ّgæləsızəm
Galli-Curci	ga li KER chi	gælıّkɝtʃı
galligaskins	ga li GA skinz	gælıّgæskınz
gallimaufry	ga luh MAW fri	gæləّmɔfrı
Gallipoli	guh LI puh li	gəّlıpəlı
Gallipolis	ga luh puh LEES	gæləpəّlis
gallivant	GA luh vant	ّgæləvænt
Gallo	GA loh	ّgælo
galloon	guh LOO : N	gəّlun
gallop	GA luhp	ّgæləp
gallopade	ga luh PAYD	gæləّped
Galloway	GA luh way	ّgæləwe
gallows	GA lohz	ّgæloz
galop	GA luhp	ّgæləp
galore	guh LAWR	gəّlɔr
galosh, -e	guh LAHSH	gəّlɑʃ
Galsworthy	GAWLZ wer th : i	ّgɔlzwərðı
Galton	GAWL tuhn	ّgɔltən
Galuppi	gah LOO : pee	gɑّlupi
Galvani	gal VAH ni	gælّvɑnı
galvanic	gal VA nik	gælّvænık
Galveston	GAL vi stuhn	ّgælvıstən
Galvez	gahl VES	gɑlّvɛs
Galway	GAWL way	ّgɔlwe
galyak, galyac	GAL yak	ّgælyæk
Gama	GA muh	ّgæmə
Gamaliel	guh MAY li uhl	gəّmelıəl
Gamarra	gah MAH rah	gɑّmɑrɑ

---

sing [ŋ] ; *oh* [o] ; *oil* [ɔɪ] ; *foot* [ʊ] ; *foo:d* [u] ; *how* [aʊ] ; *pie* [p] ; *ray* [r] ; *so* [s] ; *shall* [ʃ] ; *to* [t] ; *thin* [θ] ; *th:en* [ð] ; *above* (*uh* B*UH*V) [ə, ّʌ] ; *vine* [v] ; *wine* [w] ; *whine* [hw] ; *you* [j] ; *zoo* [z] ; *rouge* (roo:*zh*) [ʒ].

H.P.—L

gamb, -e	gamb	gæmb
gambado	gam BAY doh	ˈgæmˈbedo
gambeson	GAM bi suhn	ˈgæmbɪsən
Gambetta	gam BE tuh	gæmˈbɛtə
Gambia	GAM bi uh	ˈgæmbɪə
gambier, G-	GAM ber	ˈgæmbər
gambit	GAM bit	ˈgæmbɪt
gamble	GAM buhl	ˈgæmbəl
gamboge	gam BOHJ	gæmˈboʒ
gambol	GAM buhl	ˈgæmbəl
gambrel	GAM bruhl	ˈgæmbrəl
Gambrell	gam BREL	gæmˈbrɛl
Gambrinus	gam BRIGH nuhs	gæmˈbraɪnəs
gamete	GA meet	ˈgæmit
gamin	GA min	ˈgæmɪn
gamma	GA muh	ˈgæmə
gamut	GA muht	ˈgæmət
gamy	GAY mi	ˈgemɪ
Gandhi	GAHN di	ˈgɑndɪ
ganef	GAH nuhf	ˈgɑnəf
Ganges	GAN jeez	ˈgændʒiz
ganglion	GANG gli uhn	ˈgæŋglɪən
gangrene	GANG green	ˈgæŋgrin
gangrenous	GANG gri nuhs	ˈgæŋgrɪnəs
gangue	gang	gæŋ
Gannett	GA net	ˈgænɛt
ganov	GAH nuhf	ˈgɑnəf
gantlet	GAWNT lit	ˈgɔntlɪt
gantry, G-	GAN tri	ˈgæntrɪ
Ganymede	GA nuh meed	ˈgænəmid
gaol	jayl	dʒel
gaoler	JAY ler	ˈdʒelər
gape	gayp	gep
garage	guh RAHZH	gəˈrɑʒ
Garamond	GA ruh mahnd	ˈgærəmɑnd
Garand	GA ruhnd	ˈgærənd
Garcia	gahr SEE uh	gɑrˈsiə
garçon	gar SOHN	gærˈson
gardener	GAHRD ner	ˈgɑrdnər
gardenia	gahr DEE nyuh	gɑrˈdinjə
Gareth	GA rith	ˈgærɪθ
Garfield	GAHR feeld	ˈgɑrfild
Gargantua	gahr GAN choo uh	gɑrˈgæntʃuə
gargoyle	GAHR goil	ˈgɑrgɔɪl
Garibaldi	ga ruh BAWL di	gærəˈbɔldɪ
garish	GAI rish	ˈgɛrɪʃ
Garner	GAHR ner	ˈgɑrnər
garnishee	gahr ni SHEE	gɑrnɪˈʃi
garniture	GAHR ni cher	ˈgɑrnɪtʃər
Garonne	ga RAWN	gæˈrɔn
garret	GA rit	ˈgærɪt
Garret, -t	GA rit	ˈgærɪt

at [æ] ; ah [ɑ] ; air [ɛ] ; awful [ɔ] ; say [e] ; back [b] ; chair [tʃ] ; do [d] ; elm [ɛ] ; eel [i] ; server [ˈɝ, ər] ; fit [f] ; go [g] ; hurt [h] ; is [ɪ] ; high [aɪ] ; jet [dʒ] ; kiss [k] ; lamb [l] ; my [m] ; nice [n] ;

Garrick	GA rik	ˈgærɪk
garrison, G-	GA ri suhn	ˈgærɪsən
garrote, garrotte	guh RAHT	gəˈrɑt
garrulity	guh ROO : luh ti	gəˈrulətɪ
garrulous	GA roo luhs	ˈgærʊləs
Gary, Romain	gah REE, roh MAN	gɑˈri, roˈmæn
Garźon	gahr SOHN	gɑrˈson
gas	gas	gæs
Gascon	GA skuhn	ˈgæskən
gasconade	ga skuh NAYD	gæskəˈned
Gascony	GA skuh ni	ˈgæskənɪ
gaseous	GA shuhs	ˈgæʃəs
gasoline	GA suh leen	ˈgæsəlin
gasometer	ga SAH muh ter	gæˈsɑmətər
gasp	gasp	gæsp
Gaspé	ga SPAY	gæˈspe
Gasperi	ga SPAI ri	gæˈspɛrɪ
Gastonia	ga STOH ni uh	gæˈstonɪə
gastric	GA strik	ˈgæstrɪk
gastritis	ga STRIGH tis	gæˈstraɪtɪs
Gath	gath	gæθ
gather	GA th : er	ˈgæðər
Gatling	GAT ling	ˈgætlɪŋ
Gatti-Casazza	GAH ti kah SAHT sah	ˈgɑtɪ kɑˈsɑtsɑ
Gatun	gah TOO : N	gɑˈtun
gauche	gohsh	goʃ
gaucho, G-	GOW choh	ˈgautʃo
gauge	gayj	gedʒ
Gaugin	goh GAN	goˈgæn
Gaul	gawl	gɔl
gauleiter, G-	GOW ligh ter	ˈgaʊlaɪtər
gaunt	gawnt	gɔnt
gauntlet	GAWNT lit	ˈgɔntlɪt
Gautama	GOW tuh muh	ˈgautəmə
Gautier	goh TYAY	goˈtje
gavot, -te	guh VAHT	gəˈvɑt
Gawain	GAH win	ˈgawɪn
Gaza	GAY zuh	ˈgezə
gazebo	guh ZEE boh	gəˈzibo
gazelle	guh ZEL	gəˈzɛl
gazette	guh ZET	gəˈzɛt
gazetteer	ga zuh TIR	gæzəˈtɪr
Gdynia	guh DEE nyah	gəˈdinjɑ
gear	gir	gɪr
Gedda	GE duh	ˈgɛdə
Geddes, Bel	bel GE diz	bɛlˈgɛdɪz
Geehern	GEE ern	ˈgiərn
gefilte, gefüllte	ge FIL tuh	gɛˈfɪltə
gegenschein	GAY guhn shighn	ˈgegənʃaɪn
Gehenna	gi HE nuh	gɪˈhɛnə
Gehlen, Reinhard	GAY luhn, RIGHN hahrt	ˈgelən, ˈraɪnhɑrt
Geiger	GIGH ger	ˈgaɪgər

geisha	GAY shuh	ˈgeʃə
Geissler	GIGH sler	ˈgaɪslər
gelatin, -e	JE luh tuhn	ˈdʒelətən
gelatinous	ji LAY tuh nuhs	dʒɪˈletənəs
gelding	GEL ding	ˈgeldɪŋ
gelid	JE lid	ˈdʒelɪd
Gemini	JE muh nigh	ˈdʒemənaɪ
gemutlich	guh MOOT lik	gəˈmʊtlɪk
gendarme	ZHAHN dahrm	ˈʒɑndɑrm
genealogy	jee ni A luh ji	dʒinɪˈælədʒɪ
generic	juh NE rik	dʒəˈnerɪk
Genesee	JE nuh see	ˈdʒenəsi
genesis, G-	JE nuh sis	ˈdʒenəsɪs
genet	JE nit	ˈdʒenɪt
geneticist	juh NE tuh sist	dʒəˈnetəsɪst
Geneva	juh NEE vuh	dʒəˈnivə
Genghis Khan	JEN giz KAHN	ˈdʒeŋgɪs ˈkɑn
genial	JEE nyuhl	ˈdʒinjəl
genie	JEE ni	ˈdʒinɪ
genii	JEE ni igh	ˈdʒinɪaɪ
genius	JEE nyuhs	ˈdʒinjəs
genius loci	JEE ni uhs LOH sigh	ˈdʒinɪəs ˈlosaɪ
Genoa	JE noh uh	ˈdʒenoə
genocide	JE nuh sighd	ˈdʒenəsaɪd
genre	ZHAHN ruh	ˈʒɑnrə
gens	jenz	dʒenz
gentian	JEN shuhn	ˈdʒenʃən
gentile, G-	JEN tighl	ˈdʒentaɪl
gentleman	JEN tuhl muhn	ˈdʒentəlmən
Gentoo	jen TOO:	dʒenˈtu
gentry	JEN tri	ˈdʒentrɪ
genuflection	je nyoo FLEK shuhn	dʒenjuˈflekʃən
genuine	JE nyoo: in	ˈdʒenjuɪn
genus	JEE nuhs	ˈdʒinəs
geocentric	jee oh SEN trik	dʒioˈsentrɪk
geocentricity	jee uh sen TRI suh ti	dʒiəsenˈtrɪsətɪ
geodetic	jee uh DE tik	dʒiəˈdetɪk
geoduck	JEE uh duhk	ˈdʒiədək
Geoffrey	JE free	ˈdʒefri
geography	jee AH gruh fi	dʒiˈɑgrəfɪ
geology	jee AH luh ji	dʒiˈɑlədʒɪ
geometric	jee uh ME trik	dʒiəˈmetrɪk
geometry	jee AH muh tri	dʒiˈɑmətrɪ
geophysical	jee oh FI zi kuhl	dʒioˈfɪzɪkəl
geophysics	jee oh FI ziks	dʒioˈfɪzɪks
geopolitics	jee oh PAH luh tiks	dʒioˈpɑlətɪks
geoponic	jee uh PAH nik	dʒiəˈpɑnɪk
Georgetown	JAWRJ town	ˈdʒɔrdʒtaun
georgette	jawr JET	dʒɔrˈdʒet
Georgia	JAWR juh	ˈdʒɔrdʒə
Georgian	JAWR juhn	ˈdʒɔrdʒən
geoscope	JEE uh skohp	ˈdʒiəskop

at [æ]; ah [ɑ]; air [ɛ]; awful [ɔ]; say [e]; back [b]; chair [tʃ]; do [d]; elm [ɛ]; eel [i];
server [ˈɝ, ər]; fit [f]; go [g]; hurt [h]; is [ɪ]; high [aɪ]; jet [dʒ]; kiss [k]; lamb [l]; my [m];
nice [n];

Geraint	juh RAYNT	dʒəˈrent
Geraldine	JE ruhl deen	ˈdʒerəldin
geranium	ji RAY ni uhm	dʒɪˈreniəm
Gerard	ji RAHRD	dʒɪˈrɑrd
Gergesenes	GER guh seenz	ˈgɝgəsinz
geriatrics	je ri A triks	dʒerɪˈætrɪks
germane	jer MAYN	dʒərˈmen
germanium	jer MAY ni uhm	dʒərˈmeniəm
Germano-	JER muh noh	ˈdʒɝməno
Germany	JER muh ni	ˈdʒɝməni
germicide	JER muh sighd	ˈdʒɝməsaɪd
Geronimo	juh RAH nuh moh	dʒəˈrɑnəmo
gerontocracy	je ruhn TAH kruh si	dʒerənˈtɑkrəsɪ
gerontology	je ruhn TAH luh ji	dʒerənˈtɑlədʒɪ
Gerry	GE ri	ˈgerɪ
gerrymander	GE ri man der	ˈgerɪmændər
Gershwin	GER shwin	ˈgɝʃwɪn
Geryon	JI ri uhn	ˈdʒɪrɪən
gest, -e	jest	dʒest
Gestalt	guh SHTAHLT	gəˈʃtɑlt
Gestapo	guh STAH poh	gəˈstɑpo
Gesta Romanorum	JE stuh roh muh NAW ruhm	ˈdʒestə roməˈnɔrəm
gestation	je STAY shuhn	dʒeˈsteʃən
gesture	JES cher	ˈdʒestʃər
gesundheit, G-	guh ZOONT hight	gəˈzunthaɪt
Gethsemane, g-	geth SE muh ni	geθˈsemənɪ
Gettysburg	GE tiz berg	ˈgetɪzbɔrg
gewgaw	GYOO: gaw	ˈgjugɔ
geyser	GIGH zer	ˈgaɪzər
geyser (" heater," British)	GEE zer	ˈgizər
Gezira	juh ZEE ruh	dʒəˈzirə
Ghana	GAH nuh	ˈgɑnə
ghastly	GAST li	ˈgæstlɪ
ghat, ghaut, G-	gawt	gɔt
Gheber, Ghebre	GAY ber	ˈgebər
ghee	gee	gi
Ghent	gent	gent
gherkin	GER kin	ˈgɝkɪn
ghetto	GE toh	ˈgeto
Ghibelline	GI buh lin	ˈgɪbəlɪn
Ghiberti	gee BAIR tee	giˈberti
Ghirlandajo	gir lahn DAH jaw	gɪrlɑnˈdɑjɔ
ghoul	goo: l	gul
Giannini	zhah NEE nee	ʒɑˈnini
giantism	JIGH uhn ti zuhm	ˈdʒaɪəntɪzəm
giaour	jowr	dʒaʊr
Giarabub	jah rah BOO: B	dʒɑrɑˈbub
gibber	JI ber	ˈdʒɪbər
gibberish	JI buh rish	ˈdʒɪbərɪʃ
gibbet	JI bit	ˈdʒɪbɪt

gibbon, G-	GI buhn	ˈgɪbən
gibbous	GI buhs	ˈgɪbəs
gibe	jighb	dʒaɪb
Gibeon	GI bi uhn	ˈgɪbɪən
giblet	JI blit	ˈdʒɪblɪt
Gibraltar	ji BRAWL ter	dʒɪˈbrɔltər
Gide	zheed	ʒid
Gideon	GI di uhn	ˈgɪdɪən
Gideonse	GI di uhnz	ˈgɪdɪənz
Gielgud	GEEL good	ˈgilgud
Gieseking	GEE zuh king	ˈgizəkɪŋ
gigantean	jigh gan TEE uhn	dʒaɪgænˈtiən
gigantic	jigh GAN tik	dʒaɪˈgæntɪk
gigantomachy	jigh gan TAH muh ki	dʒaɪgænˈtɑməkɪ
Gigli	JEE yee	ˈdʒiyi
gigolo	JI guh loh	ˈdʒɪgəlo
gigot	JI guht	ˈdʒɪgət
gigue	zheeg	ʒig
Gila	HEE luh	ˈhilə
Gilboa	gil BOH uh	gɪlˈboə
Gilchrist	GIL krist	ˈgɪlkrɪst
Gilead	GI li uhd	ˈgɪlɪəd
Gilels	gi LELZ	gɪˈlɛlz
Giles	jighlz	dʒaɪlz
Gilgamesh	GIL guh mesh	ˈgɪlgəmɛʃ
gill (anatomy ; ravine)	gil	gɪl
gill (measure)	jil	dʒɪl
Gillespie	gi LE spi	gɪˈlɛspɪ
Gillette	ji LET	dʒɪˈlɛt
gillie	GI li	ˈgɪlɪ
gillyflower	JI li flow er	ˈdʒɪlɪflauər
gimbals	JIM buhlz	ˈdʒɪmbəlz
gimcrack	JIM krak	ˈdʒɪmkræk
gimlet	GIM lit	ˈgɪmlɪt
gimmick	GI mik	ˈgɪmɪk
gimp	gimp	gɪmp
gin	jin	dʒɪn
gingham	GING uhm	ˈgɪŋəm
Gingold, Hermione	GING gohld, her MIGH uh nee	ˈgɪŋgold, hərˈmaɪəni
Ginn	gin	gɪn
ginseng	JIN seng	ˈdʒɪnsɛŋ
Gioconda, la	joh KAHN duh, lah	dʒoˈkɑndə, lɑ
giocoso	jaw KAW saw	dʒɔˈkɔsɔ
Giorgione	jawr JAW ne	dʒɔrˈdʒɔnɛ
Giotto	JAH toh	ˈdʒɑto
giovanezza	jaw vah NET sah	dʒɔvaˈnɛtsa
Giovanni	joh VAH ni	dʒoˈvɑnɪ
giraffe, G-	juh RAF	dʒəˈræf
Giral	hee RAHL	hiˈrɑl
Girard	juh RAHRD	dʒəˈrɑrd
Giraudoux	zhee roh DOO :	ʒiroˈdu

at [æ]; ah [ɑ]; air [ɛ]; awful [ɔ]; say [e]; back [b]; chair [tʃ]; do [d]; elm [ɛ]; eel [i];
server [ˈɝ, ər]; fit [f]; go [g]; hurt [h]; is [ɪ]; high [aɪ]; jet [dʒ]; kiss [k]; lamb [l]; my [m];
nice [n];

151   **gnaw**

girl	gerl	gɜˈl
Gironde	juh RAHND	dʒəˈrɑnd
Girondist	juh RAHN dist	dʒəˈrɑndɪst
Girosi	ji RAW see	dʒɪˈrɔsi
Gissing	GI sing	ˈgɪsɪŋ
Giulini, Carlo-Maria	joo: LEE nee, KAHR loh mah REE ah	dʒuˈlini, ˈkɑrlo mɑˈriɑ
Giuseppe	jee: oo: ZE pee	dʒiuˈzɛpi
Givenchy	ZHEE vahn shee	ˈʒivɑnʃi
Gjellerup	YE luh roop	ˈjɛlərup
glabrous	GLAY bruhs	ˈglebrəs
glacé	gla SAY	glæˈse
glacial	GLAY shuhl	ˈgleʃəl
glacier	GLAY sher	ˈgleʃər
glacis	GLAY sis	ˈglesɪs
gladiator	GLA di ay ter	ˈglædɪetər
gladiolus	gla di OH luhs	glædɪˈoləs
Gladstone	GLAD stohn	ˈglædston
Glamis (Scotland)	glahmz	glɑmz
Glamis (Shakespeare)	GLAH mis	ˈglɑmɪs
glamor, glamour	GLA mer	ˈglæmər
glance	glans	glæns
Glarus (Switzerland)	GLAH ruhs	ˈglɑrəs
Glarus (Wisconsin)	GLA ruhs	ˈglærəs
Glasgow	GLAS goh	ˈglæsgo
Glaspell	GLA spel	ˈglæspɛl
glass, G-	glas	glæs
glaucoma	glaw KOH muh	glɔˈkomə
glaze	glayz	glez
glazier	GLAY zher	ˈgleʒər
Glazunov	gla zoo: NAWF	glæzuˈnɔf
Glengarry, g-	glen GA ri	glɛnˈgærɪ
Glinka	GLING kuh	ˈglɪŋkə
global	GLOH buhl	ˈglobəl
globin	GLOH bin	ˈglobɪn
globule	GLAH byool	ˈglɑbjʊl
glockenspiel	GLAH kuhn speel	ˈglɑkənspil
Gloucester (England, Massachusetts)	GLAH ster	ˈglɑstər
Gloucester (Ohio)	GLOW ster	ˈglaʊstər
glower	GLOW er	ˈglaʊər
Gluck	glook	glʊk
glucose	GLOO: kohs	ˈglukos
glue	gloo:	glu
Glueck	gloo: k	gluk
gluten	GLOO: tuhn	ˈglutən
glutinous	GLOO: ti nuhs	ˈglutɪnəs
glycerin, -e	GLI suh rin	ˈglɪsərɪn
gnarled	nahrld	nɑrld
gnash	nash	næʃ
gnat	nat	næt
gnaw	naw	nɔ

Gneisenau	guh NIGH zuh now	gəˈnaɪzənaʊ
gneiss	nighs	naɪs
gnome	nohm	nom
gnomic	NOH mik	ˈnomɪk
gnostic, G-	NAH stik	ˈnɑstɪk
gnu	noo :	nu
Goa	GOH uh	ˈgoə
Gobbi, Tito	GOH bee, TEE toh	ˈgobi, ˈtito
gobbledygook	GAH buhl di gook	ˈgabəldɪguk
Gobelin	GAH buh lin	ˈgabəlɪn
Gobi	GOH bi	ˈgobɪ
god, G-	gahd	gɑd
Godfrey	GAHD fri	ˈgɑdfrɪ
Godiva	guh DIGH vuh	gəˈdaɪvə
godiveau	gaw dee VOH	gɔdiˈvo
Godowsky	goh DAWF ski	goˈdɔfskɪ
Godunov	gaw doo NAWF	gɔduˈnɔf
Goebbels	GER belz	ˈgɜbɛlz
Goering	GER ing	ˈgɜɪŋ
Goethals	GOH thuhlz	ˈgoθəlz
Goethe	GER tuh	ˈgɜtə
Gog	gahg	gɑg
Gogh, van	van GOH	væn ˈgo
Gogol	GOH guhl	ˈgogəl
Goidelic	goi DE lik	gɔɪˈdɛlɪk
goiter, goitre	GOI ter	ˈgɔɪtər
Golconda	gahl KAHN duh	galˈkɑndə
Goldmark	GOHLD mahrk	ˈgoldmɑrk
Goldoni	gawl DAW ni	gɔlˈdɔnɪ
golem, G-	GOH lim	ˈgolɪm
golf	gahlf	gɑlf
Golgotha	GAHL guh thuh	ˈgɑlgəθə
goliard	GOH lyerd	ˈgoljərd
goliardic	goh LYAHR dik	goˈljɑrdɪk
Goliath	guh LIGH uth	gəˈlaɪəθ
Golschmann, Vladimir	GOHLSH mahn, VLAH duh meer	ˈgolʃman, ˈvladəmir
Gómez	GOH mez	ˈgomɛz
Gomorrah, Gomorrha	guh MAW ruh	gəˈmɔrə
Gompers	GAHM perz	ˈgɑmpərz
Gomulka	goh MOO : L kuh	goˈmulkə
Goncourt	gohn KOO : R	gonˈkur
Gond	gahnd	gɑnd
Gondi	GAHN di	ˈgɑndɪ
gondola	GAHN duh luh	ˈgɑndələ
gondolier	gahn duh LIR	gandəˈlɪr
Goneril	GAH nuh ril	ˈgɑnərɪl
gonfalon	GAHN fuh luhn	ˈgɑnfələn
gonorrhea, gonorrhoea	gah nuh REE uh	ganəˈriə
Gonsalez, Gonzalez	gawn SAH les	gɔnˈsalɛs
googol	GOO : gahl	ˈgugɑl
gook	gook	guk

at [æ]; ah [ɑ]; air [ɛ]; awful [ɔ]; say [e]; back [b]; chair [tʃ]; do [d]; elm [ɛ]; eel [i]; server [ˈɜ, ər]; fit [f]; go [g]; hurt [h]; is [ɪ]; high [aɪ]; jet [dʒ]; kiss [k]; lamb [l]; my [m]; nice [n];

goon	goo : n	gun
gooseberry	GOO : S bai ri	ˈgʊsbɛrɪ
Goosens	GOO : suhns	ˈgusəns
gopher	GOH fer	ˈgofər
Gorgas	GAWR guhs	ˈgɔrgəs
gorget	GAWR jit	ˈgɔrdʒɪt
Gorgon	GAWR guhn	ˈgɔrgən
Gorgonzola	gawr guhn ZOH luh	gɔrgənˈzolə
Gorki, Gorky	GAWR ki	ˈgɔrkɪ
gormand	GAWR muhnd	ˈgɔrmənd
Gorno-Badakhshan	GAWR noh ba dak SHAHN	ˈgɔrno bædækˈʃɑn
Goshen	GOH shuhn	ˈgoʃən
gosling	GAHZ ling	ˈgɑzlɪŋ
Gosplan	gaws PLAHN	gɔsˈplɑn
gospodin	gaw spaw DEEN	gɔspɔˈdin
gosport, G-	GAH spohrt	ˈgɑsport
gossamer	GAH suh mer	ˈgɑsəmər
Gosse	gaws	gɔs
Göteborg	JAY tuh bawrg	ˈdʒetəbɔrg
Goth	gahth	gɑθ
Gotham (England)	GOH thuhm	ˈgoθəm
Gotham (New York City)	GAH thuhm	ˈgɑθəm
Gothenburg	GAH tuhn berg	ˈgɑtənbərg
Gothic	GAH thik	ˈgɑθɪk
Götterdämmerung	ger ter DE muh roong	gərtərˈdɛmərʊŋ
Göttingen	GER ting uhn	ˈgɝtɪŋən
Gottwald	GAWT vahld	ˈgɔtvɑlt
gouache	gwash	gwæʃ
Goucher	GOW cher	ˈgautʃər
Gouda	GOW duh	ˈgaudə
Goudge	goo : j	gudʒ
Goudy	GOW di	ˈgaudɪ
gouge	gowj	gaudʒ
goujon	GOO : juhn	ˈgudʒən
goulash	GOO : lash	ˈgulæʃ
Gould	goo : ld	guld
Gounod	GOO : noh	ˈguno
gourd	gawrd	gɔrd
gourmand	GOOR muhnd	ˈgʊrmənd
gourmet	GOOR may	ˈgʊrme
government	GUH vern muhnt	ˈgʌvərnmənt
governor	GUH ver ner	ˈgʌvərnər
Govorov	GAW vaw rawf	ˈgɔvɔrɔf
Gower	GOW er	ˈgauər
gox	gahks	gɑks
Goya	GAW yuh	ˈgɔjə
Gracchus	GRA kuhs	ˈgrækəs
gracious	GRAY shuhs	ˈgreʃəs
gradual	GRA joo uhl	ˈgrædʒʊəl
graduate (a, n)	GRA joo it	ˈgrædʒʊɪt
graduate (v)	GRA joo ayt	ˈgrædʒʊet

sing [ŋ] ; oh [o] ; oil [ɔɪ] ; foot [ʊ] ; foo:d [u] ; how [aʊ] ; pie [p] ; ray [r] ; so [s] ; shall [ʃ] ; to [t] ; thin [θ] ; th:en [ð] ; above (uh BUHV) [ə, ˈʌ] ; vine [v] ; wine [w] ; whine [hw] ; you [j] ; zoo [z] ; rouge (roo:zh) [ʒ].

Graf	grahf	grɑf
graft	graft	græft
graham, G-	GRAY uhm	ˈgreəm
Grail	grayl	grel
Grainger	GRAYN jer	ˈgrendʒər
gramercy (interjection)	gruh MER si	grəˈmɝsɪ
Gramercy	GRA mer si	ˈgræmərsɪ
Granada	gruh NAH duh	grəˈnɑdə
granary	GRA nuh ri	ˈgrænərɪ
Gran Chaco	grahn CHAH koh	grɑn ˈtʃɑko
Grand Coulee	grand KOO : li	grænd ˈkulɪ
grandee	GRAN dee	ˈgrændi
grandeur	GRAN jer	ˈgrændʒər
grandfather	GRAND fah th : er	ˈgrændfɑðər
grandiloquent	gran DI luh kwuhnt	grænˈdɪləkwənt
grandiose	GRAN di ohs	ˈgrændɪos
Grandjany, Marcel	grahnd zha NEE, mahr SEL	grɑndʒæˈni, mɑrˈsɛl
grandma	GRAND mah	ˈgrændmɑ
grandmother	GRAND muh th : er	ˈgrændməðər
Grand Pré	gran pray	græn pre
Grand Teton	grand TEE tahn	grænd ˈtitɑn
grant, G-	grant	grænt
granule	GRA nyool	ˈgrænjʊl
grappa	GRAH pah	ˈgrɑpɑ
grasp	grasp	græsp
grass	gras	græs
Gratian	GRAY shuhn	ˈgreʃən
Gratiano	gra shi AH noh	græʃɪˈɑno
gratis	GRAY tis	ˈgretɪs
gratitude	GRA ti too : d	ˈgrætɪtud
Grattan	GRA tuhn	ˈgrætən
gratuitous	gruh TOO : uh tuhs	grəˈtuətəs
gratuity	gruh TOO : uh ti	grəˈtuətɪ
Grau San Martin	grow san mahr TEEN	grau sæn mɑrˈtin
gravamen	gruh VAY men	grəˈvemɛn
grave	grayv	grev
gravity	GRA vuh ti	ˈgrævətɪ
Graziano	grat si AH noh	grætsɪˈɑno
grazier	GRAY zher	ˈgreʒər
grease	grees	gris
greasy	GREE si	ˈgrisɪ
Grecian	GREE shuhn	ˈgriʃən
Greco-	GREE koh	ˈgriko
Greece	grees	gris
Greeley	GREE li	ˈgrilɪ
Greenland	GREEN luhnd	ˈgrinlənd
Greenock	GREE nuhk	ˈgrinək
greenockite	GREE nuh kight	ˈgrinəkaɪt
Greenough	GREE noh	ˈgrino
Greensboro	GREENZ ber oh	ˈgrinzbəro
Greenwich (England)	GRI nij	ˈgrɪnɪdʒ
Greenwich Village	GRE nich VI lij	ˈgrɛnɪtʃ ˈvɪlɪdʒ

at [æ]; ah [ɑ]; air [ɛ]; awful [ɔ]; say [e]; back [b]; chair [tʃ]; do [d]; elm [ɛ]; eel [i]; server [ˈɝ, ər]; fit [f]; go [g]; hurt [h]; is [ɪ]; high [aɪ]; jet [dʒ]; kiss [k]; lamb [l]; my [m]; nice [n];

greet, G-	greet	grit
gregarious	gri GAI ri uhs	grɪˈgɛrɪəs
Gregorian	gri GAW ri uhn	grɪˈgɔrɪən
Gregory	GRE guh ri	ˈgrɛgərɪ
gremlin	GREM lin	ˈgrɛmlɪn
Grenada	gri NAH duh	grɪˈnɑdə
grenade	gri NAYD	grɪˈned
grenadier	gre nuh DIR	grɛnəˈdɪr
grenadine, G-	gre nuh DEEN	grɛnəˈdin
Grendel	GREN duhl	ˈgrɛndəl
Grenoble	gruh NOH buhl	grəˈnobəl
Grenville	GREN vil	ˈgrɛnvɪl
Gresham	GRE shuhm	ˈgrɛʃəm
Gretna	GRET nuh	ˈgrɛtnə
Greuze	grerz	grɜz
grew	groo :	gru
gridiron	GRID igh ern	ˈgrɪdaɪərn
Grieg	greeg	grig
grievance	GREE vuhns	ˈgrivəns
grievous	GREE vuhs	ˈgrivəs
griffin, G-	GRI fin	ˈgrɪfɪn
griffon	GRI fuhn	ˈgrɪfən
grim	grim	grɪm
grimace	gri MAYS	grɪˈmes
Grimes	grighmz	graɪmz
grimly	GRIM li	ˈgrɪmlɪ
Grimm	grim	grɪm
Grimsby	GRIMZ bi	ˈgrɪmzbɪ
grimy	GRIGH mi	ˈgraɪmɪ
gringo	GRING goh	ˈgrɪŋgo
gripe	grighp	graɪp
grippe	grip	grɪp
Griselda	gri ZEL duh	grɪˈzɛldə
grisette	gri ZET	grɪˈzɛt
grisly	GRIZ li	ˈgrɪzlɪ
gristle	GRI suhl	ˈgrɪsəl
Griva	GREE vah	ˈgrivɑ
Griz Nez	gree NAY	gri ˈne
grizzly	GRIZ li	ˈgrɪzlɪ
groat	groht	grot
grocery	GROH suh ri	ˈgrosərɪ
grog	grahg	grɑg
grogram	GRAH gruhm	ˈgrɑgrəm
groin	groin	grɔɪn
Grolier	GROH li er	ˈgrolɪər
Gromyko	gruh MEE koh	grəˈmiko
Gronchi	GRAWN ki	ˈgrɔnkɪ
Groningen	GROH ning uhn	ˈgronɪŋən
groschen	GROH shuhn	ˈgroʃən
grosgrain	GROH grayn	ˈgrogren
gross	grohs	gros
Grosvenor	GROHV ner	ˈgrovnər

sing [ŋ] ; *oh* [o] ; *oil* [ɔɪ] ; *foot* [ʊ] ; *foo*:d [u] ; *how* [aʊ] ; *p*ie [p] ; *r*ay [r] ; *s*o [s] ; *sh*all [ʃ] ;
*t*o [t] ; *thin* [θ] ; *th:*en [ð] ; *above* (*uh BUHV*) [ə, ˈʌ] ; *v*ine [v] ; *w*ine [w] ; *wh*ine [hw] ;
*y*ou [j] ; *z*oo [z] ; *rouge* (roo:*zh*) [ʒ].

Grosz	grohs	grɔs
grot	graht	grɑt
grotesque	groh TESK	groˈtɛsk
Grotewohl	GRAW tuh vohl	ˈgrɔtəvol
Grotius	GROH shi uhs	ˈgroʃɪəs
Groton	GRAH tuhn	ˈgrɑtən
grotto	GRAH toh	ˈgrɑto
groundsel	GROWND suhl	ˈgraʊndsəl
grovel	GRUH vuhl	ˈgrʌvəl
Grozny	GRAWZ ni	ˈgrɔznɪ
Grudziadz	GROO jawnts	ˈgrʊdʒɔnts
Gruen	GROO: uhn	ˈgruən
Grundy	GRUHN di	ˈgrʌndɪ
Grus	gruhs	grʌs
Gruyère	gree YAIR	griˈjɛr
guacharo	GWAH chah roh	ˈgwatʃaro
Guadalajara	gwah dah lah HAHR rah	gwadalaˈhɑrɑ
Guadalcanal	gwah duhl kuh NAL	gwadəlkəˈnæl
Guadalquivir	gwah duhl KWI ver	gwadəlˈkwɪvər
Guadalupe	gwah duh LOO: P	gwadəˈlup
Guadeloupe	gwah duh LOO: P	gwadəˈlup
Guadiana	gwah di AH nuh	gwadɪˈɑnə
Guadix	gwah TH: EESH	gwaˈðiʃ
Guam	gwahm	gwɑm
Guanajuato	gwah nah HWAH taw	gwanɑˈhwɑtɔ
guano	GWAH noh	ˈgwano
Guantánamo	gwahn TAH nah maw	gwɑnˈtɑnɑmɔ
Guaporé	gwah paw RAY	gwapɔˈre
Guarani	gwah rah NEE	gwarɑˈni
guarantee	ga ruhn TEE	gærənˈti
guarantor	GA ruhn ter	ˈgærəntər
guaranty	GA ruhn ti	ˈgærəntɪ
guard	gahrd	gɑrd
guardian	GAHR di uhn	ˈgɑrdɪən
Guarneri	gwahr NE ree	gwɑrˈnɛri
Guarnerius	gwahr NAI ri uhs	gwɑrˈnɛrɪəs
Guatemala	gwah tuh MAH luh	gwatəˈmalə
guava	GWAH vuh	ˈgwavə
Guayaquil	gwigh ah KEEL	gwaɪɑˈkil
guayule	gwah YOO: lay	gwaˈjule
gubernatorial	goo: ber nuh TAW ri uhl	gubərnəˈtɔrɪəl
guberniya	goo BAIR ni yah	guˈbɛrnɪja
Gudrun	GOOD roo: n	ˈgʊdrun
Gueden, Hilde	GOO: duhn, HIL duh	ˈgudən, ˈhɪldə
Guelich	GYOO: lik	ˈgjulɪk
Guelph, Guelf	gwelf	gwɛlf
Guerard	gay RAHRD	geˈrɑrd
guerdon	GER duhn	ˈgɝdən
Guernsey	GERN zi	ˈgɝnzɪ
guerre	gair	gɛr
Guerrero	gay RAI roh	geˈrɛro
guerrilla, guerilla	guh RI luh	gəˈrɪlə

*a*t [æ] ; *ah* [ɑ] ; *air* [ɛ] ; *aw*ful [ɔ] ; s*ay* [e] ; *b*ack [b] ; *ch*air [tʃ] ; *d*o [d] ; *e*lm [ɛ] ; *ee*l [i] ;
s*er*ver [ˈɝ, ər] ; *f*it [f] ; *g*o [g] ; *h*urt [h] ; *i*s [ɪ] ; h*igh* [aɪ] ; *j*et [dʒ] ; *k*iss [k] ; *l*amb [l] ; *m*y [m] ;
*n*ice [n] ;

Guevara	ge VAH rah	geˈvɑrɑ
Guggenheim	GOO guhn highm	ˈgʊgənhaɪm
Guglielmo	goo YEL moh	gʊˈjɛlmo
Guiana	gi A nuh	gɪˈænə
guide	gighd	gaɪd
Guido	GWEE doh	ˈgwido
guidon	GIGH duhn	ˈgaɪdən
guild	gild	gɪld
guilder	GIL der	ˈgɪldər
guile	gighl	gaɪl
Guilford	GIL ferd	ˈgɪlfərd
Guillaume	gee YOHM	giˈjom
guillemot	GI luh maht	ˈgɪləmɑt
guillotine	GI luh teen	ˈgɪlətin
guimpe	gimp	gɪmp
Guinea, g-	GI ni	ˈgɪnɪ
Guinevere	GWI nuh vir	ˈgwɪnəvɪr
Guipuzcoa	gee POO : TH kaw ah	giˈpuθkɔɑ
guise	gighz	gaɪz
Guise	geez	giz
guitar	gi TAHR	gɪˈtɑr
Guitry	GEE tri	ˈgitrɪ
Guizot	gee ZOH	giˈzo
Gujarat	goo jah RAHT	gʊdʒɑˈrɑt
Gujarati	goo jah RAH ti	gʊdʒɑˈrɑtɪ
gulch	guhlch	gʌltʃ
gulden	GOOL duhn	ˈgʊldən
gules	gyoo : lz	gjulz
gulf	guhlf	gʌlf
Gullah	GUH luh	ˈgʌlə
gullet	GUH lit	ˈgʌlɪt
gullible	GUH luh buhl	ˈgʌləbəl
Gulliver	GUH luh ver	ˈgʌləvər
gumbo	GUHM boh	ˈgʌmbo
Gunnar	GOO nahr	ˈgʊnɑr
gunsel	GUHN suhl	ˈgʌnsəl
Gunther	GUHN ther	ˈgʌnθər
gunwale	GUH nuhl	ˈgʌnəl
guppy	GUH pi	ˈgʌpɪ
Gurev, Guriev	GOOR yef	ˈgʊrjɛf
Gurkha	GOOR kuh	ˈgʊrkə
Gurko	GER koh	ˈgɝko
Gusev, Gussev	GOO : sef	ˈgusɛf
gusset	GUH sit	ˈgʌsɪt
Gustaf	GOO stahf	ˈgʊstɑf
gustatory	GUH stuh taw ri	ˈgʌstətɔrɪ
Gustavus	guh STAY vuhs	gəˈstevəs
Gutenberg	GOO : tuhn berg	ˈgutənbɝg
Guthrie, Tyrone	GUH three, tigh ROHN	ˈgʌθri, taɪˈron
Gutierrez	goo TYE res	gʊˈtjɛrɛs
gutta percha	GUH tuh PER chuh	ˈgʌtə ˈpɝtʃə
Gwinnett	gwi NET	gwɪˈnɛt

sing [ŋ] ; *oh* [o] ; *oil* [ɔɪ] ; *foot* [ʊ] ; *foo*:d [u] ; *how* [aʊ] ; *pie* [p] ; *ray* [r] ; *so* [s] ; *shall* [ʃ] ;
to [t] ; *thin* [θ] ; *th*:en [ð] ; *above* (*uh* BUHV) [ə, ˈʌ] ; *vine* [v] ; *wine* [w] ; *whine* [hw] ;
you [j] ; *zoo* [z] ; *rouge* (roo:zh) [ʒ].

Gwyn	gwin	gwɪn
gymnasium (school)	gim NAH zi uhm	gɪmˈnɑzɪəm
gymnasium (sports)	jim NAY zi uhm	dʒɪmˈnezɪəm
gymnast	JIM nast	ˈdʒɪmnæst
gymnastics	jim NA stiks	dʒɪmˈnæstɪks
gymnosophist	jim NAH suh fist	dʒɪmˈnɑsəfist
gymnosperm	JIM nuh sperm	ˈdʒɪmnəspərm
gynandrous	jigh NAN druhs	dʒaɪˈnændrəs
gynarchy	JIGH nahr ki	ˈdʒaɪnɑrkɪ
gynecology	jigh ni KAH luh ji	dʒaɪnɪˈkɑlədʒɪ
gyniatrics	jigh ni A triks	dʒaɪnɪˈætrɪks
Gyöngyös	DYUHN dyuhsh	ˈdjʌndjəʃ
Györ	dyuhr	djʌr
gypsophila	jip SAH fuh luh	dʒɪpˈsɑfələ
gypsum	JIP suhm	ˈdʒɪpsəm
gypsy	JIP si	ˈdʒɪpsɪ
gyrate	JIGH rayt	ˈdʒaɪret
gyrene	jigh REEN	dʒaɪˈrin
gyrfalcon	JER fawl kuhn	ˈdʒɝfɔlkən
gyroscope	JIGH ruh skohp	ˈdʒaɪrəskop
gyve	jighv	dʒaɪv

H

Haakon	HAW koon	ˈhɔkʊn
Haapsalu	HAHP sah loo	ˈhɑpsalʊ
Haarlem	HAHR luhm	ˈhɑrləm
Habakkuk	huh BA kuhk	həˈbækək
habanera	hah buh NAY ruh	hɑbəˈnerə
habeas corpus	HAY bi uhs KAWR puhs	ˈhebɪəs ˈkɔrpəs
habergeon	HA ber juhn	ˈhæbərdʒən
habiliment	huh BI luh muhnt	həˈbɪləmənt
habitat	HA buh tat	ˈhæbətæt
habitué	huh BI choo ay	həˈbɪtʃue
Habsburg	HAPS berg	ˈhæpsbɝg
hacienda	hah si EN duh	hɑsɪˈɛndə
hackney	HAK ni	ˈhæknɪ
Hadassah	hah DAH suh	hɑˈdɑsə
hadj	haj	hædʒ
hadji	HA jee	ˈhædʒi
Hadrian	HAY dree uhn	ˈhedrɪən
Haeckel	HE kuhl	ˈhɛkəl
haematite	HE muh tight	ˈhɛmətaɪt
haemoglobin	HEE muh gloh bin	ˈhiməglobɪn
Haganah	HAH gah nah	ˈhɑgɑnɑ
Hagar	HAY ger	ˈhegər
Hagen, Uta	HAH guhn, OO: tuh	ˈhɑgən, ˈutə
Haggada, -h, h-	huh GAH duh	həˈgɑdə

Haggai	HA gi igh	ˈhægɪɑɪ
haggard, H-	HA gerd	ˈhægərd
haggis	HA gis	ˈhægɪs
hagiarchy	HA gi ahr ki	ˈhægɪɑrkɪ
hagiocracy	ha gi AH kruh si	hægɪˈɑkrəsɪ
Hagiographa	ha gi AH gruh fuh	hægɪˈɑgrəfə
hagiography	ha gi AH gruh fi	hægɪˈɑgrəfɪ
Hague	hayg	heg
ha-ha (interjection)	hah HAH	hɑˈhɑ
ha-ha (fence)	HAH hah	ˈhɑhɑ
Hahnemann	HAH nuh muhn	ˈhɑnəmən
Haifa	HIGH fuh	ˈhaɪfə
Haig	hayg	heg
haiku	HIGH koo :	ˈhaɪku
Haile Selassie	HIGH li suh LA si	ˈhaɪlɪ səˈlæsɪ
Hainan	high nahn	haɪ nɑn
Hainaut	ay NOH	eˈno
Haiti	HAY ti	ˈhetɪ
Hakluyt	HA kloo : t	ˈhæklut
Halakah, Halacha	hah lah KAH	hɑlɑˈkɑ
halakist, halachist	HAH luh kist	ˈhɑləkɪst
Halasz	HAH lahsh	ˈhɑlɑʃ
halberd	HAL berd	ˈhælbərd
halcyon	HAL si uhn	ˈhælsɪən
Haldane	HAWL dayn	ˈhɔlden
Haleakala	hah lay ah kah LAH	hɑleɑkɑˈlɑ
half	haf	hæf
halfpenny	HAY puh ni	ˈhepənɪ
halibut	HA luh buht	ˈhæləbət
Halifax	HA luh faks	ˈhæləfæks
halite	HA light	ˈhælaɪt
halitosis	ha luh TOH sis	hæləˈtosɪs
hall	hawl	hɔl
Halle	HA li	ˈhælɪ
Halleck	HA luhk	ˈhælək
hallelujah, halleluiah	ha luh LOO : yuh	hæləˈlujə
Halley	HA li	ˈhælɪ
hallo	huh LOH	həˈlo
halloo	huh LOO :	həˈlu
hallucination	huh loo : suh NAY shuhn	həlusəˈneʃən
Halmahera, Halmaheira	hahl mah HAY rah	hɑlmɑˈherɑ
halogen	HA luh juhn	ˈhælədʒən
Hals	hals	hæls
Halsey	HAWL zi	ˈhɔlzɪ
halvah	hahl VAH	hɑlˈvɑ
halve	hav	hæv
Hamadan	HA muh dan	ˈhæmədæn
hamadryad	ha muh DRIGH uhd	hæməˈdraɪəd
hamal	huh MAHL	həˈmɑl
Haman	HAY muhn	ˈhemən
Hambletonian	ham buhl TOH ni uhn	hæmbəlˈtonɪən
Hambro, Leonid	HAM broh, LEE uh nid	ˈhæmbro, ˈliənɪd

sing [ŋ] ; *oh* [o] ; *oi*l [ɔɪ] ; *foot* [ʊ] ; *foo:*d [u] ; *how* [aʊ] ; *pie* [p] ; *ray* [r] ; *so* [s] ; *sh*all [ʃ] ;
to [t] ; *th*in [θ] ; *th:*en [ð] ; above (*uh* B*UH*V) [ə, ˈʌ] ; *vine* [v] ; *wine* [w] ; *wh*ine [hw] ;
you [j] ; *zoo* [z] ; rouge (roo:*zh*) [ʒ].

hamburg, H-	HAM berg	ˈhæmbərg
Hämeenlinna	HA mayn li nah	ˈhæmenlɪnɑ
Hamelin	HA muh lin	ˈhæməlɪn
Hamilcar	huh MIL kahr	həˈmɪlkɑr
Hamilton	HA muhl tuhn	ˈhæməltən
Hamitic	ha MI tik	hæˈmɪtɪk
hamlet, H-	HAM lit	ˈhæmlɪt
Hammarskjöld, Dag	HA mair shoold, dag YAL	ˈhæmɛrʃʊld, dæg
Hjalmar	mair	ˈjælmɛr
Hammerfest	HA mer fest	ˈhæmərfɛst
Hammerstein	HA mer stighn	ˈhæmərstaɪn
Hammurabi	hah moo RAH bi	hɑmʊˈrɑbɪ
Hampden	HAM duhn	ˈhæmdən
Hampshire	HAMP sher	ˈhæmpʃər
Hamsun	HAM suhn	ˈhæmsən
Hamtramck	ham TRA mik	hæmˈtræmɪk
Han	hahn	hɑn
handbook	HAND book	ˈhændbʊk
handcuff	HAND kuhf	ˈhændkəf
Handel	HAN duhl	ˈhændəl
handful	HAND fool	ˈhændfʊl
handkerchief	HANG ker chif	ˈhæŋkərtʃɪf
handsel	HAN suhl	ˈhænsəl
handsome	HAN suhm	ˈhænsəm
hangar	HANG er	ˈhæŋər
Hangchow	hang chow	hæŋ tʃaʊ
hanger	HANG er	ˈhæŋər
Hangkow	hang kow	hæŋ kaʊ
Hannibal	HA nuh buhl	ˈhænəbəl
Hanoi	hah NOI	hɑˈnɔɪ
Hanover	HA noh ver	ˈhænovər
Hansard	HAN serd	ˈhænsərd
hanse, H-	hans	hæns
Hanseatic	han si A tik	hænsɪˈætɪk
Hänsel and Gretel	HEN suhl uhn GRE tuhl	ˈhɛnsəl ən ˈgrɛtəl
Hansen	HAHN suhn	ˈhɑnsən
hansom	HAN suhm	ˈhænsəm
Hanson	HAN suhn	ˈhænsən
Hanukka, -h	HAH noo kah	ˈhɑnʊkɑ
haphtarah	hahf tah RAH	hɑftɑˈrɑ
Hapsburg	HAPS berg	ˈhæpsbərg
hara-kiri	HAH ruh KI ri	ˈhɑrə ˈkɪrɪ
harangue	huh RANG	həˈræŋ
harass	HA ruhs	ˈhærəs
harbinger	HAHR bin jer	ˈhɑrbɪndʒər
Hardelot, d'	dahr duh LOH	dɑrdəˈlo
Hardwicke	HAHRD wik	ˈhɑrdwɪk
harebell	HAIR bel	ˈhɛrbɛl
harem	HAI ruhm	ˈhɛrəm
Hargreaves	HAHR greevz	ˈhɑrgrivz
haricot	HA ri koh	ˈhærɪko
hari-kari	HAH ri KAH ri	ˈhɑrɪ ˈkɑrɪ

at [æ] ; *ah* [ɑ] ; *air* [ɛ] ; *aw*ful [ɔ] ; *say* [e] ; *b*ack [b] ; *ch*air [tʃ] ; *do* [d] ; *elm* [ɛ] ; *eel* [i] ; *server* [ˈɝ, ər] ; *f*it [f] ; *go* [g] ; *h*urt [h] ; *is* [ɪ] ; *high* [aɪ] ; *jet* [dʒ] ; *k*iss [k] ; *l*amb [l] ; *my* [m] ; *n*ice [n] ;

Harleian	HAHR li uhn	ˈhɑrlɪən
Harlem	HAHR luhm	ˈhɑrləm
harlequin, H-	HAHR luh kwin	ˈhɑrləkwɪn
harlequinade	hahr luh kwi NAYD	hɑrləkwɪˈned
harlot	HAHR luht	ˈhɑrlət
harmonic	hahr MAH nik	hɑrˈmɑnɪk
harmonica	hahr MAH ni kuh	hɑrˈmɑnɪkə
harmonious	hahr MOH ni uhs	hɑrˈmonɪəs
harpsichord	HAHRP si kawrd	ˈhɑrpsɪkɔrd
Harrovian	ha ROH vi uhn	hæˈrovɪən
Harrow, h-	HA roh	ˈhæro
Harte, Bret	hahrt, bret	hɑrt, brɛt
hartebeest	HAHR tuh beest	ˈhɑrtəbist
Harz	hahrts	hɑrts
Hasdrubal	HAZ droo buhl	ˈhæzdrubəl
hasenpfeffer	HAH suhn FE fer	ˈhɑsənˈfɛfər
Hashemite	HAH shuh might	ˈhɑʃəmaɪt
hashish, hasheesh	HA sheesh	ˈhæʃiʃ
Hassan	HAH sahn	ˈhɑsɑn
hasta la vista	AH stah lah VEE stah	ˈɑstɑ lɑ ˈvista
hasta mañana	AH stah mah NYAH nah	ˈɑstɑ mɑˈnjɑnɑ
hasten	HAY suhn	ˈhesən
Hastings	HAY stingz	ˈhestɪŋz
Hathor	HA thawr	ˈhæθɔr
Hatoyama	hah toh YAH mah	hɑtoˈyɑmɑ
Hatteras	HA tuh ruhs	ˈhætərəs
Hatvan	HAHT vahn	ˈhɑtvɑn
hauberk	HAW berk	ˈhɔbərk
Haugesund	HOW guh soon	ˈhaʊgəsʊn
haul	hawl	hɔl
haunch	hawnch	hɔntʃ
haunt	hawnt	hɔnt
Hauptmann	HOWPT mahn	ˈhaʊptmɑn
Hausa, Haussa	HOW sah	ˈhaʊsɑ
Hausfrau	HOWS frow	ˈhaʊsfraʊ
hautboy	HOH boi	ˈhobɔɪ
hauteur	hoh TER	hoˈtɝ
haut monde	oh MOHND	o ˈmond
Havana	huh VA nuh	həˈvænə
havelock, H-	HAV lahk	ˈhævlɑk
Haverford	HA ver ferd	ˈhævərfərd
havoc	HA vuhk	ˈhævək
Havre	HAH ver	ˈhɑvər
Hawaii	huh WAH ee	həˈwai
Hawaiian	huh WAH yuhn	həˈwɑjən
hawser	HAW zer	ˈhɔzər
hawthorn, -e, H-	HAW thawrn	ˈhɔθɔrn
Haya de la Torre	IGH yah day lah TAW ray	ˈaɪjɑ de lɑ ˈtɔre
Hayden	HAY duhn	ˈhedən
Haydn	HIGH duhn	ˈhaɪdən
Hayes	hayz	hez
hazardous	HA zer duhs	ˈhæzərdəs

sing [ŋ] ; *oh* [o] ; *oil* [ɔɪ] ; *foot* [ʊ] ; *foo* :d [u] ; *how* [aʊ] ; *pie* [p] ; *ray* [r] ; *so* [s] ; *shall* [ʃ] ; *to* [t] ; *thin* [θ] ; *th* :en [ð] ; *above* (*uh BUHV*) [ə, ˈʌ] ; *vine* [v] ; *wine* [w] ; *whine* [hw] ; *you* [j] ; *zoo* [z] ; *rouge* (*roo* :*zh*) [ʒ].

Hazlitt	HAZ lit	ˈhæzlɪt
headcheese	HED cheez	ˈhɛdtʃiz
Hearn, Lafcadio	hern, laf KA di oh	hɜrn, læfˈkædɪo
Hearst	herst	hɜrst
hearth	hahrth	hɑrθ
heath, H-	heeth	hiθ
heather	HE th : er	ˈhɛðər
heaume	hohm	hom
Hebbel	HE buhl	ˈhɛbəl
hebdomadal	heb DAH muh duhl	hɛbˈdɑmədəl
Hebe	HEE bi	ˈhibɪ
Hebraic	hi BRAY ik	hɪˈbreɪk
Hebrew	HEE broo :	ˈhibru
Hebrides	HE bruh deez	ˈhɛbrədiz
Hebron	HEE bruhn	ˈhibrən
Hecate	HE kuh ti	ˈhɛkətɪ
Hecate (Shakespeare)	HE kit	ˈhɛkɪt
hecatomb	HE kuh tohm	ˈhɛkətom
Hecht	hekt	hɛkt
hector, H-	HEK ter	ˈhɛktər
Hecuba	HE kyoo buh	ˈhɛkjʊbə
Hedmark	HED mahrk	ˈhɛdmɑrk
hedonism	HEE duh ni zuhm	ˈhidənɪzəm
hegari	huh GAI ri	həˈgɛrɪ
Hegel	HAY guhl	ˈhegəl
Hegelian	hay GAY li uhn	heˈgelɪən
hegemony	hi JE muh ni	hɪˈdʒɛmənɪ
hegira, H-	hi JIGH ruh	hɪˈdʒaɪrə
Heidelberg	HIGH duhl berg	ˈhaɪdəlbərg
heifer	HE fer	ˈhɛfər
Heifetz, Jascha	HIGH fets, YAH shah	ˈhaɪfɛts, ˈjɑʃɑ
heigh	high	haɪ
heigh-ho	high hoh	haɪ ho
height	hight	haɪt
Heijo	hay joh	he dʒo
heil	highl	haɪl
Heilbronn	HIGHL brawn	ˈhaɪlbrɔn
Heimdall	HAYM dahl	ˈhemdɑl
Heimweh	HIGHM vay	ˈhaɪmve
Heine	HIGH nuh	ˈhaɪnə
Heinlein	HIGHN lighn	ˈhaɪnlaɪn
heinous	HAY nuhs	ˈhenəs
Heinz	highnz	haɪnz
heir	air	ɛr
Hejaz	he JAHZ	hɛˈdʒɑz
heldentenor	HEL duhn te ner	ˈhɛldəntɛnər
Helena	HE li nuh	ˈhɛlɪnə
Helgoland	HEL goh land	ˈhɛlgolænd
helianthus	hee li AN thuhs	hilɪˈænθəs
Helicon, h-	HE li kahn	ˈhɛlɪkɑn
helicopter	HE li kahp ter	ˈhɛlɪkɑptər
Heligoland	HE li goh land	ˈhɛlɪgolænd

at [æ]; ah [ɑ]; air [ɛ]; awful [ɔ]; say [e]; back [b]; chair [tʃ]; do [d]; elm [ɛ]; eel [i];
server [ˈɜ, ər]; fit [f]; go [g]; hurt [h]; is [ɪ]; high [aɪ]; jet [dʒ]; kiss [k]; lamb [l]; my [m];
nice [n];

heliocentric	hee li oh SEN trik	hilɪoˈsɛntrɪk
Heliogabalus	hee li uh GA buh luhs	hilɪəˈgæbələs
heliographic	hee li uh GRA fik	hilɪəˈgræfɪk
heliometer	hee li AH muh ter	hilɪˈɑmətər
heliotherapy	hee li oh THE ruh pi	hilɪoˈθɛrəpɪ
heliotrope	HEE li uh trohp	ˈhilɪətrop
heliport	HE li pawrt	ˈhɛlɪpɔrt
helium	HEE li uhm	ˈhilɪəm
helix	HEE liks	ˈhilɪks
hellebore	HE luh bawr	ˈhɛləbɔr
Hellenic	he LE nik	hɛˈlɛnɪk
helleri	HE luh ri	ˈhɛlərɪ
Hellespont	HE luh spahnt	ˈhɛləspɑnt
helm	helm	hɛlm
Helmholtz	HELM hohlts	ˈhɛlmholts
helot, H-	HE luht	ˈhɛlət
helotry	HE luh tri	ˈhɛlətrɪ
helpmate	HELP mayt	ˈhɛlpmet
Helsingfors	HEL sing fawrz	ˈhɛlsɪŋfɔrz
Helsinki	HEL sing ki	ˈhɛlsɪŋkɪ
Helvetia	hel VEE shuh	hɛlˈviʃə
Hemans	HE muhnz	ˈhɛmənz
hematin	HE muh tin	ˈhɛmətɪn
hematite	HE muh tight	ˈhɛmətaɪt
hematology	he muh TAH luh ji	hɛməˈtɑlədʒɪ
Hemingway	HE ming way	ˈhɛmɪŋwe
hemiplegia	he mi PLEE ji uh	hɛmɪˈplidʒɪə
hemipterous	hi MIP tuh ruhs	hɪˈmɪptərəs
hemistich	HE mi stik	ˈhɛmɪstɪk
hemoglobin	hee muh GLOH bin	himəˈglobɪn
hemophilia	hee muh FI li uh	himəˈfɪlɪə
henceforth	hens FAWRTH	hɛnsˈfɔrθ
hendiadys	hen DIGH uh dis	hɛnˈdaɪədɪs
henequen	HE nuh kin	ˈhɛnəkɪn
Hengist	HENG gist	ˈhɛŋgɪst
Henie	HE ni	ˈhɛnɪ
Henley	HEN li	ˈhɛnlɪ
henna	HE nuh	ˈhɛnə
Henslowe	HENZ loh	ˈhɛnzlo
heparin	HE puh rin	ˈhɛpərɪn
hepatic	hi PA tik	hɪˈpætɪk
hepatica	hi PA ti kuh	hɪˈpætɪkə
hepatitis	he puh TIGH tis	hɛpəˈtaɪtɪs
Hephaestus	hi FE stuhs	hɪˈfɛstəs
Hephzibah	HEF zi buh	ˈhɛfzɪbə
Hepplewhite	HE puhl hwight	ˈhɛpəlhwaɪt
Heptateuch	HEP tuh too:k	ˈhɛptətuk
Hera	HI ruh	ˈhɪrə
Heracles	he ruh KLEEZ	hɛrəˈkliz
Heraclitus	he ruh KLIGH tuhs	hɛrəˈklaɪtəs
heraldic	he RAL dik	hɛˈrældɪk
heraldry	HE ruhl dri	ˈhɛrəldrɪ

sing [ŋ]; oh [o]; oil [ɔɪ]; foot [ʊ]; foo:d [u]; how [aʊ]; pie [p]; ray [r]; so [s]; shall [ʃ];
to [t]; thin [θ]; th:en [ð]; above (uh BUHV) [ə, ˈʌ]; vine [v]; wine [w]; whine [hw];
you [j]; zoo [z]; rouge (roo:zh) [ʒ].

herb	erb	ɝb
herbaceous	her BAY shuhs	hərˈbeʃəs
herbage	ER bij	ˈɝbɪdʒ
herbarium	her BAI ri uhm	hərˈbɛrɪəm
herbivorous	her BI vuh ruhs	hərˈbɪvərəs
Herculaneum	her kyoo LAY ni uhm	hərkjuˈlenɪəm
Herculean, h-	her KYOO : li uhn	hərˈkjulɪən
Hercules, h-	HER kyoo leez	ˈhɝkjʊliz
hereditary	huh RE duh tai ri	həˈrɛdətɛrɪ
herein	hir IN	hɪrˈɪn
heresy	HE ruh si	ˈhɛrəsɪ
heretic	HE ruh tik	ˈhɛrətɪk
heretical	huh RE ti kuhl	həˈrɛtɪkəl
Hergesheimer	HER guhs high mer	ˈhɝgəshaɪmər
heritage	HE ruh tij	ˈhɛrətɪdʒ
hermaphrodite	her MA fruh dight	hərˈmæfrədaɪt
hermeneutics	her mi NYOO : tiks	hərmɪˈnjutɪks
Hermes	HER meez	ˈhɝmiz
Hermione	her MIGH uh ni	hərˈmaɪənɪ
Hermon	HER muhn	ˈhɝmən
Hernandez	air NAHN dez	ɛrˈnɑndɛz
hernia	HER ni uh	ˈhɝnɪə
hero, H-	HI roh	ˈhɪro
Herod	HE ruhd	ˈhɛrəd
Herodiade	ay roh di AD	erodɪˈæd
Herodias	hi ROH di uhs	hɪˈrodɪəs
Herodotus	hi RAH duh tuhs	hɪˈrɑdətəs
heroic	hi ROH ik	hɪˈroɪk
heroin	HE roh in	ˈhɛroɪn
heroine	HE roh in	ˈhɛroɪn
heroism	HE roh i zuhm	ˈhɛroɪzəm
herpes	HER peez	ˈhɝpiz
herpetology	her pi TAH luh ji	hərpɪˈtɑlədʒɪ
Herr	hair	hɛr
Herrenvolk	HAI ruhn fawlk	ˈhɛrənfɔlk
Herrera	e RAI rah	ɛˈrɛrɑ
Herrick	HE rik	ˈhɛrɪk
herring	HE ring	ˈhɛrɪŋ
Herriot	e ri OH	ɛrɪˈo
Herschel	HER shuhl	ˈhɝʃəl
Hersey	HER see	ˈhɝsi
Herter	HER ter	ˈhɝtər
Hertford (England)	HAHR ferd	ˈhɑrfərd
Hertford (U.S.)	HERT ferd	ˈhɝtfərd
Hertz	herts	hɝts
Hertzog	HERT zawg	ˈhɝtzɔg
Herzegovina	hert si goh VEE nuh	hɝtsɪgoˈvinə
Herzl	HERT suhl	ˈhɝtsəl
Heshvan	HESH van	ˈhɛʃvæn
Hesiod	HEE si uhd	ˈhisɪəd
hesitant	HE zuh tuhnt	ˈhɛzətənt
hesitate	HE zuh tayt	ˈhɛzətet

at [æ] ; *ah* [ɑ] ; *air* [ɛ] ; *awful* [ɔ] ; *say* [e] ; *back* [b] ; *chair* [tʃ] ; *do* [d] ; *elm* [ɛ] ; *eel* [i] ; *server* [ˈɝ, ər] ; *fit* [f] ; *go* [g] ; *hurt* [h] ; *is* [ɪ] ; *high* [aɪ] ; *jet* [dʒ] ; *kiss* [k] ; *lamb* [l] ; *my* [m] ; *nice* [n] ;

Hesperia	he SPI ri uh	hɛˈspɪrɪə
Hesperides	he SPE ruh deez	hɛˈspɛrədiz
hesperidin	he SPE ruh din	hɛˈspɛrədɪn
Hesperus	HE spuh ruhs	ˈhɛspərəs
Hess	hes	hɛs
Hesse	hes	hɛs
Hessian	HE shuhn	ˈhɛʃən
hetaera	hi TI ruh	hɪˈtɪrə
heterodox	HE tuh ruh dahks	ˈhɛtərədɑks
heterodoxy	HE tuh ruh dahk si	ˈhɛtərədɑksɪ
heterogamy	he tuh RAH guh mi	hɛtəˈragəmɪ
heterogeneity	he tuh roh juh NEE uh ti	hɛtərodʒəˈniətɪ
heterogeneous	he tuh ruh JEE ni uhs	hɛtərəˈdʒiniəs
Heteroousian	he tuh roh OO : si uhn	hɛtəroˈusiən
heterosexual	he tuh roh SEK shoo uhl	hɛtəroˈsɛkʃuəl
heuristic	hyoo RI stik	hjuˈrɪstɪk
hexachloride	hek suh KLAW righd	hɛksəˈklɔraɪd
hexagonal	hek SA guh nuhl	hɛkˈsægənəl
hexameter	hek SA muh ter	hɛkˈsæmətər
hey	hay	he
heyday	HAY day	ˈhede
Heyerdahl, Thor	HIGH er dahl, thawr	ˈhaɪərdɑl, θɔr
Heyse	HIGH zuh	ˈhaɪzə
Heywood	HAY wood	ˈhewʊd
Hezekiah	he zuh KIGH uh	hɛzəˈkaɪə
Hialeah	hih uh LEE uh	haɪəˈliə
hiatus	high AY tuhs	haɪˈetəs
Hiawatha	high uh WAH thuh	haɪəˈwɑθə
hibernate	HIGH ber nayt	ˈhaɪbərnet
Hibernia	high BER ni uh	haɪˈbɚnɪə
hiccup, hiccough	HI kuhp	ˈhɪkəp
hidalgo, H-	hi DAL goh	hɪˈdælgo
hideous	HI di uhs	ˈhɪdɪəs
hierarchy	HIGH uh rahr ki	ˈhaɪərɑrkɪ
hieroglyph	HIGH uh ruh glif	ˈhaɪərəglɪf
hieroglyphic	high uh ruh GLI fik	haɪərəˈglɪfɪk
Hieronymus	high uh RAH nuh muhs	haɪəˈranəməs
hi-fi	high figh	haɪ faɪ
Highet	HIGH uht	ˈhaɪət
highfalutin, -g	high fuh LOO : tuhn	haɪfəˈlutən
highland, H-	HIGH luhnd	ˈhaɪlənd
highwayman	HIGH way muhn	ˈhaɪwemən
Hiiumaa	HEE oo mah	ˈhiʊmɑ
hilarious	hi LAI ri uhs	hɪˈlɛrɪəs
hilarity	hi LA ruh ti	hɪˈlærətɪ
Hildebrand	HIL duh brand	ˈhɪldəbrænd
Hillyer	HIL yer	ˈhɪljər
Hilo	HEE loh	ˈhilo
Himachal Pradesh	hi MAH chuhl PRAH desh	hɪˈmɑtʃəl ˈpradɛʃ
Himalaya	hi MAHL yuh	hɪˈmɑlyə
Himalayan, Himilayan	hi muh LAY uhn	hɪməˈleən
Himmler	HIM ler	ˈhɪmlər

sing [ŋ] ; oh [o] ; oil [ɔɪ] ; foot [ʊ] ; foo:d [u] ; how [aʊ] ; pie [p] ; ray [r] ; so [s] ; shall [ʃ] ;
to [t] ; thin [θ] ; th:en [ð] ; above (uh BUHV) [ə, ˈʌ] ; vine [v] ; wine [w] ; whine [hw] ;
you [j] ; zoo [z] ; rouge (roo:zh) [ʒ].

Hindemith	HIN duh muhth	ˈhɪndəməθ
Hindenburg	HIN duhn berg	ˈhɪndənbərg
Hindi	HIN di	ˈhɪndɪ
hindrance	HIN druhns	ˈhɪndrəns
Hindu, Hindoo	HIN doo:	ˈhɪndu
Hindustan	hin doo STAN	hɪnduˈstæn
Hindustani	hin doo STA ni	hɪnduˈstænɪ
hinterland	HIN ter land	ˈhɪntərlænd
Hipparchus	hi PAHR kuhs	hɪˈpɑrkəs
Hippocrates	hi PAH kruh teez	hɪˈpɑkrətiz
Hippocratic	hi puh KRA tik	hɪpəˈkrætɪk
Hippocrene	HI puh kreen	ˈhɪpəkrin
hippodrome	HI puh drohm	ˈhɪpədrom
hippogriff, hippogryph	HI puh grif	ˈhɪpəgrɪf
Hippolytus	hi PAH li tuhs	hɪˈpɑlɪtəs
Hippomenes	hi PAH muh neez	hɪˈpɑməniz
hippophagous	hi PAH fuh guhs	hɪˈpɑfəgəs
hippopotamus	hi puh PAH tuh muhs	hɪpəˈpɑtəməs
Hiram	HIGH ruhm	ˈhaɪrəm
Hirohito	hi roh HEE toh	hɪroˈhito
Hiroshige	hi roh SHEE guh	hɪroˈʃigə
Hiroshima	hi roh SHEE mah	hɪroˈʃimɑ
hirsute	HER soo:t	ˈhɜsut
Hispaniola	hi spuhn YOH luh	hɪspənˈjolə
histamine	HI stuh meen	ˈhɪstəmin
histology	hi STAH luh ji	hɪˈstɑlədʒɪ
historian	hi STAW ri uhn	hɪˈstɔrɪən
historical	hi STAW ri kuhl	hɪˈstɔrɪkəl
historiographer	hi staw ri AH gruh fer	hɪstɔrɪˈɑgrəfər
history	HI stuh ri	ˈhɪstərɪ
histrionic	hi stri AH nik	hɪstrɪˈɑnɪk
Hitler	HIT ler	ˈhɪtlər
Hitlerism	HIT luh ri zuhm	ˈhɪtlərɪzəm
Hittite	HI tight	ˈhɪtaɪt
hives	highvz	haɪvz
Hjalmar	YAHL mahr	ˈjɑlmɑr
ho, H-	hoh	ho
Hoagy	HOH gi	ˈhogɪ
Hobart (Tasmania)	HOH bert	ˈhobərt
Hobbes	hahbz	hɑbz
hobby, H-	HAH bi	ˈhɑbɪ
hobo	HOH boh	ˈhobo
Hoboken	HOH boh kuhn	ˈhobokən
Hoch	hohk	hok
Ho Chi Minh	hoh chi min	ho tʃɪ mɪn
Hódmezóvásárhely	HAWD me zer VAH shahr hay	ˈhɔdmɛzərˈvɑʃɑrhe
Hodur, Hoder	HOH der	ˈhodər
Hoenir	HUH ner	ˈhʌnər
Hoffa	HAH fuh	ˈhɑfə
Hoffmann	HAWF mahn	ˈhɔfmɑn
Hofstra	HAHF struh	ˈhɑfstrə

at [æ] ; ah [ɑ] ; air [ɛ] ; awful [ɔ] ; say [e] ; back [b] ; chair [tʃ] ; do [d] ; elm [ɛ] ; eel [i] ; server [ˈɜ, ər] ; fit [f] ; go [g] ; hurt [h] ; is [ɪ] ; high [aɪ] ; jet [dʒ] ; kiss [k] ; lamb [l] ; my [m] ; nice [n] ;

hogan	HOH gawn	ˈhogɔn
Hogarth	HOH gahrth	ˈhogɑrθ
Hohenzollern	HOH uhn zah lern	ˈhoənzɑlərn
hoist	hoist	hɔɪst
hoity-toity	HOI ti TOI ti	ˈhɔɪtɪ ˈtɔɪtɪ
Hokkaido	hoh KIGH doh	hoˈkaɪdo
Holbein	HOHL bighn	ˈholbaɪn
Holinshed	HAH linz hed	ˈhɑlɪnzhɛd
holla	HAH luh	ˈhɑlə
Holland	HAH luhnd	ˈhɑlənd
hollandaise	HAH luhn dayz	ˈhɑləndez
holloa	huh LOH	həˈlo
hollyhock	HAH li hahk	ˈhɑlɪhɑk
Hollywood	HAH li wood	ˈhɑlɪwʊd
Holman	HOHL muhn	ˈholmən
Holmes	hohmz	homz
holocaust	HAH luh kawst	ˈhɑləkɔst
Holofernes	hah luh FER neez	hɑləˈfɚniz
Holstein	HOHL stighn	ˈholstaɪn
Holyhead	HAH li hed	ˈhɑlɪhɛd
Holyoke (Massachusetts)	HOHL yohk	ˈholyok
Holyrood (Scotland)	HAH li roo : d	ˈhɑlɪrud
homage	HAH mij	ˈhɑmɪdʒ
Homburg	HAHM berg	ˈhɑmbɚg
homely	HOHM li	ˈhomlɪ
homeopath	HOH mi uh path	ˈhomɪəpæθ
homeopathy	hoh mi AH puh thi	homɪˈɑpəθɪ
homer, H-	HOH mer	ˈhomər
Homeric	hoh ME rik	hoˈmɛrɪk
homicide	HAH muh sighd	ˈhɑməsaɪd
homiletic	hah muh LE tik	hɑməˈlɛtɪk
homily	HAH muh li	ˈhɑməlɪ
hominy	HAH muh ni	ˈhɑmənɪ
homo, H-	HOH moh	ˈhomo
homogeneity	hoh muh juh NEE uh ti	homədʒəˈniətɪ
homogeneous	hoh muh JEE ni uhs	homəˈdʒinɪəs
Homolka	HOH mawl kah	ˈhomɔlkɑ
homologous	hoh MAH luh guhs	hoˈmɑləgəs
homonym	HAH muh nim	ˈhɑmənɪm
homophone	HAH muh fohn	ˈhɑməfon
homo sapiens, H-	HOH moh SAY pi enz	ˈhomo ˈsepɪɛnz
Honan	hoh nahn	ho nɑn
Honduras	hahn DOO ruhs	hɑnˈdʊrəs
Honegger	HOH ne ger	ˈhonɛgər
honest	AH nist	ˈɑnɪst
Hong Kong	hahng kahng	hɑŋ kɑŋ
Honolulu	hah nuh LOO : loo :	hɑnəˈlulu
honorable	AH nuh ruh buhl	ˈɑnərəbəl
honorarium	ah nuh RAI ri uhm	ɑnəˈrɛrɪəm
Honshu	hahn shoo :	hɑn ʃu
Hooch	hohk	hok
hoodlum	HOO : D luhm	ˈhudləm

---

sing [ŋ] ; *oh* [o] ; *oil* [ɔɪ] ; *foot* [ʊ] ; *foo* :d [u] ; *how* [aʊ] ; *pie* [p] ; *ray* [r] ; *so* [s] ; *shall* [ʃ] ; *to* [t] ; *thin* [θ] ; *th* :en [ð] ; *above* (*uh* BUHV) [ə, ˈʌ] ; *vine* [v] ; *wine* [w] ; *whine* [hw] ; *you* [j] ; *zoo* [z] ; *rouge* (roo:*zh*) [ʒ].

hoodoo	HOO : doo :	ˈhudu
hoof	hoof	huf
hooligan	HOO : li guhn	ˈhulɪgən
hoop	hoo : p	hup
hoosegow, hoosgow	HOO : S gow	ˈhusgaʊ
Hoosier	HOO : zher	ˈhuʒər
Hopei, Hopeh	hoh pay	ho pe
Hopi	HOH pi	ˈhopɪ
Horace	HAW ris	ˈhɔrɪs
Horatio	huh RAY shoh	həˈreʃo
Horatius	huh RAY shuhs	həˈreʃəs
Horeb	HOH reb	ˈhorɛb
Hore-Belisha	HOHR buh LEE shuh	ˈhor bəˈliʃə
horizon	huh RIGH zuhn	həˈraɪzən
horizontal	haw ruh ZAHN tuhl	hɔrəˈzɑntəl
hormone	HAWR mohn	ˈhɔrmon
Hormuz	HAWR muhz	ˈhɔrməz
hornblende	HAWRN blend	ˈhɔrnblɛnd
horologist	haw RAH luh just	hɔˈrɑlədʒɪst
horoscope	HAW ruh skohp	ˈhɔrəskop
Horowitz	HAH roh wits	ˈhɑrowɪts
horrendous	haw REN duhs	hɔˈrɛndəs
horrible	HAW ruh buhl	ˈhɔrəbəl
horrid	HAW rid	ˈhɔrɪd
horror	HAW rer	ˈhɔrər
Horsa	HAWR suh	ˈhɔrsə
hors de combat	awr duh kohn BA	ɔr də konˈbæ
hors d'oeuvre	awr DERV	ɔr ˈdɜv
Horst Wessel	HAWRST VE suhl	ˈhɔrst ˈvɛsəl
Horten	HAWR tuhn	ˈhɔrtən
Horthy von Nagybánya	HAWR ti fawn NAH di bah nyah	ˈhɔrtɪ fɔn ˈnɑdɪbɑnjɑ
hosanna	hoh ZA nuh	hoˈzænə
Hosea	hoh SEE uh	hoˈsiə
hosier	HOH zher	ˈhoʒər
hosiery	HOH zhuh ri	ˈhoʒərɪ
hospice	HAH spis	ˈhɑspɪs
hospitable	HAH spi tuh buhl	ˈhɑspɪtəbəl
hospital	HAH spi tuhl	ˈhɑspɪtəl
hostage	HAH stij	ˈhɑstɪdʒ
hostel	HAH stuhl	ˈhɑstəl
hosteler	HAH stuh ler	ˈhɑstələr
hostelry	HAH stuhl ri	ˈhɑstəlrɪ
hostile	HAH stuhl	ˈhɑstəl
hostler	HAH sler	ˈhɑslər
Hotchner	HAHCH ner	ˈhɑtʃnər
hotel	hoh TEL	hoˈtɛl
hôtel de ville	oh TEL duh VEEL	oˈtɛl də ˈvil
Houdini	hoo : DEE ni	huˈdinɪ
Houdon	HOO : dahn	ˈhudɑn
Houdry	HOO : dri	ˈhudrɪ
Hough	huhf	hʌf

at [æ] ; *ah* [ɑ] ; *air* [ɛ] ; *aw*ful [ɔ] ; *say* [e] ; *b*ack [b] ; *ch*air [tʃ] ; *do* [d] ; *elm* [ɛ] ; *eel* [i] ; *server* [ˈɜ, ər] ; *f*it [f] ; *go* [g] ; *h*urt [h] ; *is* [ɪ] ; *high* [aɪ] ; *j*et [dʒ] ; *k*iss [k] ; *l*amb [l] ; *my* [m] ; *n*ice [n] ;

Houghton	HOH tuhn	ˈhotən
Hounslow	HOWNZ loh	ˈhaʊnzlo
houri	HOO ri	ˈhʊrɪ
Housatonic	hoo : suh TAH nik	husəˈtɑnɪk
housel	HOW zuhl	ˈhaʊzəl
housewife	HOWS wighf	ˈhaʊswaɪf
housewife (small bag)	HUH zif	ˈhʌzɪf
Housman	HOWS muhn	ˈhaʊsmən
Houston (English botanist and Scotland)	HOO : stuhn	ˈhustən
Houston (New York street and Georgia county)	HOW stuhn	ˈhaʊstən
Houston (Texas soldier and city)	HYOO : stuhn	ˈhjustən
Houyhnhnm	HWI nuhm	ˈhwɪnəm
hovel	HUH vuhl	ˈhʌvəl
hover	HUH ver	ˈhʌvər
Hovey	HUH vi	ˈhʌvɪ
howdah	HOW duh	ˈhaʊdə
howdy	HOW di	ˈhaʊdɪ
Howe	how	haʊ
Howells	HOW uhlz	ˈhaʊəlz
howitzer	HOW it ser	ˈhaʊɪtsər
hoyden	HOI duhn	ˈhɔɪdən
Hoyle	hoil	hɔɪl
Hrdlička	HERD lich ka	ˈhɝdlɪtʃkæ
Hsinking	shin king	ʃɪn kɪŋ
Hsiung	shyoong	ʃjʊŋ
huarache	huh RAH chi	həˈratʃɪ
Huascarán	wah skah RAHN	wɑskɑˈrɑn
Hubbard	HUH berd	ˈhʌbərd
hubbub	HUH buhb	ˈhʌbəb
hubris	HYOO : bris	ˈhjubrɪs
huckster	HUHK ster	ˈhʌkstər
Hudibras	HYOO : di bras	ˈhjudɪbræs
Huelva	WEL vah	ˈwɛlvɑ
Huesca	WE skah	ˈwɛskɑ
Huguenot	HYOO : guh naht	ˈhjugənɑt
Ḥuila	WEE lah	ˈwilɑ
Huk	hoo : k	huk
Hukbalahap	HOO : K bah lah HAHP	ˈhukbɑlɑˈhɑp
hula-hula	HOO : luh HOO : luh	ˈhulə ˈhulə
Hull, h-	huhl	hʌl
hullabaloo	HUH luh buh LOO :	ˈhʌləbəˈlu
hullo	huh LOH	həˈlo
Hulme (British)	hyoo : m	hjum
Hulme (U.S.)	huhlm	hʌlm
human	HYOO : muhn	ˈhjumən
humane	hyoo MAYN	hjuˈmen
humanism, H-	HYOO : muh ni zuhm	ˈhjumənɪzəm
humanitarian	hyoo ma nuh TAI ri uhn	hjʊmænəˈtɛrɪən

---

sing [ŋ] ; *oh* [o] ; *oi*l [ɔɪ] ; *foo*t [ʊ] ; *foo :*d [u] ; *how* [aʊ] ; *pie* [p] ; *ray* [r] ; *so* [s] ; *shall* [ʃ] ;
to [t] ; *thin* [θ] ; *th :*en [ð] ; *above* (*uh* B*UH*V) [ə, ˈʌ] ; *vine* [v] ; *wine* [w] ; *whine* [hw] ;
*y*ou [j] ; *zoo* [z] ; *rouge* (roo :*zh*) [ʒ].

humanization	HYOO : muh ni ZAY shuhn	ˈhjumənɪˈzeʃən
Humber	HUHM ber	ˈhʌmbər
humble	HUHM buhl	ˈhʌmbəl
Humboldt	HUHM bohlt	ˈhʌmbolt
humdrum	HUHM druhm	ˈhʌmdrʌm
Hume	hyoo : m	hjum
humid	HYOO : mid	ˈhjumɪd
humidity	hyoo MI duh ti	hjʊˈmɪdətɪ
humiliate	hyoo MI li ayt	hjʊˈmɪlɪet
humiliation	hyoo mi li AY shuhn	hjumɪlɪˈeʃən
humility	hyoo MI luh ti	hjʊˈmɪlətɪ
humor	HYOO : mer	ˈhjumər
humorist	HYOO : muh rist	ˈhjumərɪst
humorous	HYOO : muh ruhs	ˈhjumərəs
Humperdinck	HUHM per dingk	ˈhʌmpərdɪŋk
humus	HYOO : muhs	ˈhjuməs
Hunan	hoo : nahn	hu nɑn
hundred	HUHN druhd	ˈhʌndrəd
hundredth	HUHN druhdth	ˈhʌndrədθ
Huneker	HUH nuh ker	ˈhʌnəkər
Hungarian	huhng GAI ri uhn	həŋˈgɛrɪən
Hungary	HUHNG guh ri	ˈhʌŋgərɪ
hunger	HUHNG ger	ˈhʌŋgər
hungry	HUHNG gri	ˈhʌŋgrɪ
Hurok	HYOO : rahk	ˈhjurɑk
hurrah	hoo RAH	hʊˈrɑ
hurray	hoo RAY	hʊˈre
hurricane	HER i kayn	ˈhɝɪken
hurry	HER i	ˈhɝɪ
Hurst	herst	hɝst
Husky, h-	HUH ski	ˈhʌskɪ
Huss	huhs	hʌs
hussar	hoo ZAHR	hʊˈzɑr
Hussein	hoo SAYN	hʊˈsen
hussy	HUH zi	ˈhʌzɪ
hustings	HUH stingz	ˈhʌstɪŋz
hustle	HUH suhl	ˈhʌsəl
huswife	HUH zif	ˈhʌzɪf
Huxley	HUHK sli	ˈhʌkslɪ
Huygens	HIGH guhnz	ˈhaɪgənz
Huysmans	HOIS mahns	ˈhɔɪsmɑns
huzza	huh ZAH	həˈzɑ
Hwang Hai	hwahng high	hwɑŋ haɪ
Hwang Ho	hwahng hoh	hwɑŋ ho
hyacinth	HIGH uh sinth	ˈhaɪəsɪnθ
Hyacinthus	high uh SIN thuhs	haɪəˈsɪnθəs
Hyades	HIGH uh deez	ˈhaɪədiz
Hyannis	high A nis	haɪˈænɪs
hybrid	HIGH brid	ˈhaɪbrɪd
hybridization	high bri duh ZAY shuhn	haɪbrɪdəˈzeʃən
Hyderabad	high duh ruh BAD	haɪdərəˈbæd
Hydra, h-	HIGH druh	ˈhaɪdrə

at [æ]; *ah* [ɑ]; *air* [ɛ]; *awful* [ɔ]; *say* [e]; *back* [b]; *chair* [tʃ]; *do* [d]; *elm* [ɛ]; *eel* [i]; *server* [ˈɝ, ər]; *fit* [f]; *go* [g]; *hurt* [h]; *is* [ɪ]; *high* [aɪ]; *jet* [dʒ]; *kiss* [k]; *lamb* [l]; *my* [m]; *nice* [n];

hydrangea	high DRAYN juh	haɪˈdrendʒə
hydraulic	high DRAW lik	haɪˈdrɔlɪk
hydrocephalous	high druh SE fuh luhs	haɪdrəˈsɛfələs
hydrogen	HIGH druh juhn	ˈhaɪdrədʒən
hydrography	high DRAH gruh fi	haɪˈdrɑgrəfɪ
hydrology	high DRAH luh ji	haɪˈdrɑlədʒɪ
hydrometer	high DRAH muh ter	haɪˈdrɑmətər
hydropathy	high DRAH puh thi	haɪˈdrɑpəθɪ
hydrophobia	high druh FOH bi uh	haɪdrəˈfobɪə
hydroplane	HIGH druh playn	ˈhaɪdrəplen
hydroponic	high druh PAH nik	haɪdrəˈpɑnɪk
Hydrus	HIGH druhs	ˈhaɪdrəs
Hygeia	high JEE uh	haɪˈdʒiə
hygiene	HIGH jeen	ˈhaɪdʒin
hygienic	high ji E nik	haɪdʒɪˈɛnɪk
hygienist	HIGH ji uh nist	ˈhaɪdʒɪənɪst
Hyksos	HIK sohs	ˈhɪksos
hyla	HIGH luh	ˈhaɪlə
Hymen, h-	HIGH muhn	ˈhaɪmən
hymeneal	high muh NEE uhl	haɪməˈniəl
Hymettus	high ME tuhs	haɪˈmɛtəs
hymn	him	hɪm
hymnal	HIM nuhl	ˈhɪmnəl
hyperbola	high PER buh luh	haɪˈpɝbələ
hyperbole	high PER buh li	haɪˈpɝbəlɪ
hyperbolic	high per BAH lik	haɪpərˈbɑlɪk
hyperborean, H-	high per BAW ri uhn	haɪpərˈbɔrɪən
hypercritical	high per KRI ti kuhl	haɪpərˈkrɪtɪkəl
hyperesthesia	high per es THEE zhuh	haɪpərɛsˈθiʒə
hypergolic	high per GAH lik	haɪpərˈgɑlɪk
Hyperion	high PI ri uhn	haɪˈpɪrɪən
hypertension	high per TEN shuhn	haɪpərˈtɛnʃən
hypertrophy	high PER truh fi	haɪˈpɝtrəfɪ
Hypnos	HIP nahs	ˈhɪpnɑs
hypnosis	hip NOH sis	hɪpˈnosɪs
hypnotic	hip NAH tik	hɪpˈnɑtɪk
hypnotism	HIP nuh ti zuhm	ˈhɪpnətɪzəm
hypnotist	HIP nuh tist	ˈhɪpnətɪst
hypochondria	high puh KAHN dri uh	haɪpəˈkɑndrɪə
hypochondriac	high puh KAHN dri ak	haɪpəˈkɑndrɪæk
hypochondriacal	high puh kuhn DRIGH uh kuhl	haɪpəkənˈdraɪəkəl
hypocrisy	hi PAH kruh si	hɪˈpɑkrəsɪ
hypocrite	HI puh krit	ˈhɪpəkrɪt
hypodermic	high puh DER mik	haɪpəˈdɝmɪk
hypognathous	high PAHG nuh thuhs	haɪˈpɑgnəθəs
hypostasis	high PAH stuh sis	haɪˈpɑstəsɪs
hypotenuse	high PAH tuh noo : s	haɪˈpɑtənus
hypothecate	high PAH thuh kayt	haɪˈpɑθəket
hypothecation	high pah thuh KAY shuhn	haɪpɑθəˈkeʃən
hypothermia	high puh THER mi uh	haɪpəˈθɝmɪə
hypotheses	high PAH thuh seez	haɪˈpɑθəsiz

sing [ŋ] ; *oh* [o] ; *oil* [ɔɪ] ; *foot* [ʊ] ; *foo :*d [u] ; *how* [aʊ] ; *pie* [p] ; *ray* [r] ; *so* [s] ; *shall* [ʃ] ;
to [t] ; *thin* [θ] ; *th :*en [ð] ; *above* (*uh BUHV*) [ə, ˈʌ] ; *vine* [v] ; *wine* [w] ; *whine* [hw] ;
you [j] ; *zoo* [z] ; *rouge* (*roo :zh*) [ʒ].

hypothesis	high PAH thuh sis	haɪˈpɑθəsɪs
hypothetical	high puh THE ti kuhl	haɪpəˈθɛtɪkəl
hypoxia	high PAHK si uh	haɪˈpɑksɪə
hyrax	HIGH raks	ˈhaɪræks
Hyrcania	her KAY ni uh	hərˈkenɪə
hyson	HIGH suhn	ˈhaɪsən
hyssop	HI suhp	ˈhɪsəp
hysterectomy	hi stuh REK tuh mi	hɪstəˈrɛktəmɪ
hysteria	hi STI ri uh	hɪˈstɪrɪə
hysteric	hi STE rik	hɪˈstɛrɪk
hysterotomy	hi stuh RAH tuh mi	hɪstəˈrɑtəmɪ

I

Iago	i AH goh	ɪˈɑgo
iamb	IGH amb	ˈaɪæmb
iambic	igh AM bik	aɪˈæmbɪk
Iapetus	igh A puh tuhs	aɪˈæpətəs
Ibadan	ee BAH dahn	iˈbadɑn
Ibáñez	ee BAH nyeth	iˈbɑnjeθ
Iberia	igh BI ri uh	aɪˈbɪrɪə
Iberian	igh BI ri uhn	aɪˈbɪrɪən
ibidem	i BIGH dem	ɪˈbaɪdɛm
ibis	IGH bis	ˈaɪbɪs
Ibn Saud, i-	I buhn sah OO : D	ˈɪbən sɑˈud
Ibo	EE boh	ˈibo
Ibsen	IB suhn	ˈɪbsən
Icarian	i KE ri uhn	ɪˈkɛrɪən
Icarus	I kuh ruhs	ˈɪkərəs
Iceland	IGHS luhnd	ˈaɪslənd
Iceni	igh SEE nigh	aɪˈsinaɪ
ich	ik	ɪk
Ichabod	I kuh bahd	ˈɪkəbad
ich dien	ik DEEN	ɪk ˈdin
ichneumon	ik NYOO : muhn	ɪkˈnjumən
ichor	IGH kawr	ˈaɪkɔr
ichthyology	ik thi AH luh ji	ɪkθɪˈɑlədʒɪ
ichthyosaurus	ik thi uh SAW ruhs	ɪkθɪəˈsɔrəs
ichthyosis	ik thi OH sis	ɪkθɪˈosɪs
Ickes	I kis	ˈɪkɪs
icon	IGH kahn	ˈaɪkɑn
iconoclasm	igh KAH nuh kla zuhm	aɪˈkɑnəklæzəm
iconoclast	igh KAH nuh klast	aɪˈkɑnəklæst
iconolatry	igh kuh NAH luh tri	aɪkəˈnɑlətrɪ
iconoscope	igh KAH nuh skohp	aɪˈkɑnəskop
icosahedron	igh koh suh HEE druhn	aɪkosəˈhidrən
ictus	IK tuhs	ˈɪktəs
Ida	IGH duh	ˈaɪdə

at [æ]; *ah* [ɑ]; *air* [ɛ]; *awful* [ɔ]; *say* [e]; *back* [b]; *chair* [tʃ]; *do* [d]; *elm* [ɛ]; *eel* [i]; *server* [ˈɝ, ər]; *fit* [f]; *go* [g]; *hurt* [h]; *is* [ɪ]; *high* [aɪ]; *jet* [dʒ]; *kiss* [k]; *lamb* [l]; *my* [m]; *nice* [n];

Idaho	IGH duh hoh	ˈaɪdəho
idea	igh DEE uh	aɪˈdiə
ideal	igh DEE uhl	aɪˈdiəl
idealism	igh DEE uh li zuhm	aɪˈdiəlɪzəm
ideality	igh di A luh ti	aɪdɪˈælətɪ
idée fixe	ee day FEEKS	ide ˈfiks
idem	IGH dem	ˈaɪdɛm
identically	igh DEN ti kuh li	aɪˈdɛntɪkəlɪ
identity	igh DEN tuh ti	aɪˈdɛntətɪ
ideogram	I di uh gram	ˈɪdɪəgræm
ideograph	I di uh graf	ˈɪdɪəgræf
ideology	igh di AH luh ji	aɪdɪˈɑlədʒɪ
ides, I-	ighdz	aɪdz
id est	id est	ɪd ɛst
idiocy	I di uh si	ˈɪdɪəsɪ
idiom	I di uhm	ˈɪdɪəm
idiomatic	i di uh MA tik	ɪdɪəˈmætɪk
idiosyncrasy	i di uh SING kruh si	ɪdɪəˈsɪŋkrəsɪ
idiosyncratic	i di oh sin KRA tik	ɪdɪosɪnˈkrætɪk
idiot	I di uht	ˈɪdɪət
idle	IGH duhl	ˈaɪdəl
Ido	EE doh	ˈido
idol	IGH duhl	ˈaɪdəl
idolater	igh DAH luh ter	aɪˈdɑlətər
Idomeneus	igh DAH muh nyoo : s	aɪˈdɑmənjus
idyl, idyll	IGH duhl	ˈaɪdəl
idyllic	igh DI lik	aɪˈdɪlɪk
Igdrasil	IG druh sil	ˈɪgdrəsɪl
Ignatius	ig NAY shuhs	ɪgˈneʃəs
ignis fatuus	IG nis FA choo uhs	ˈɪgnɪs ˈfætʃuəs
ignition	ig NI shuhn	ɪgˈnɪʃən
ignoble	ig NOH buhl	ɪgˈnobəl
ignominious	ig nuh MI ni uhs	ɪgnəˈmɪnɪəs
ignominy	IG nuh mi ni	ˈɪgnəmɪnɪ
ignoramus	ig nuh RAY muhs	ɪgnəˈreməs
Igorot	i guh ROHT	ɪgəˈrot
Igraine	i GRAYN	ɪˈgren
iguana	i GWAH nuh	ɪˈgwɑnə
Iguassú	ee gwah SOO :	igwɑˈsu
ihram	i RAHM	ɪˈrɑm
Ijssel	IGH suhl	ˈaɪsəl
Ijsselmeer	IGH suhl mair	ˈaɪsəlmɛr
il, I- (Italian)	eel	il
île, Î-	eel	il
Ileana	ee lay AH nah	ileˈɑna
ileitis	i li IGH tis	ɪlɪˈaɪtɪs
ileum	I li uhm	ˈɪlɪəm
ilex	IGH leks	ˈaɪlɛks
Iliad	I li uhd	ˈɪlɪəd
Ilium, i-	I li uhm	ˈɪlɪəm
Illampu	ee YAHM poo :	iˈjɑmpu
illative	I luh tiv	ˈɪlətɪv

sing [ŋ] ; *oh* [o] ; *oil* [ɔɪ] ; *foot* [ʊ] ; *foo:d* [u] ; *how* [aʊ] ; *pie* [p] ; *ray* [r] ; *so* [s] ; *shall* [ʃ] ;
to [t] ; *thin* [θ] ; *th:en* [ð] ; *above* (*uh BUH*V) [ə, ˈʌ] ; *vine* [v] ; *wine* [w] ; *whine* [hw] ;
you [j] ; *zoo* [z] ; *rouge* (roo:*zh*) [ʒ].

illegal	i LEE guhl	ɪˈligəl
illegible	i LE juh buhl	ɪˈlɛdʒəbəl
illegitimate	i li JI tuh mit	ɪlɪˈdʒɪtəmɪt
illicit	i LI sit	ɪˈlɪsɪt
Illimani	ee yee MAH nee	ijiˈmɑni
Illinois	i luh NOI	ɪləˈnɔɪ
illiterate	i LI tuh rit	ɪˈlɪtərɪt
illuminate	i LOO : muh nayt	ɪˈlumənet
illumination	i loo : muh NAY shuhn	ɪluməˈneʃən
illusion	i LOO : zhuhn	ɪˈluʒən
illusive	i LOO : siv	ɪˈlusɪv
illusory	i LOO : suh ri	ɪˈlusərɪ
illustrate	I luh strayt	ˈɪləstret
illustrative	i LUH struh tiv	ɪˈlʌstrətɪv
illustrator	I luh stray ter	ˈɪləstretər
illustrious	i LUH stri uhs	ɪˈlʌstrɪəs
Illyria	i LI ri uh	ɪˈlɪrɪə
image	I mij	ˈɪmɪdʒ
imagery	I mij ri	ˈɪmɪdʒrɪ
imago	i MAY goh	ɪˈmego
imam	i MAHM	ɪˈmɑm
imbecile	IM buh suhl	ˈɪmbəsəl
imbecility	im buh SI luh ti	ɪmbəˈsɪlətɪ
imbroglio	im BROHL yoh	ɪmˈbroljo
immaculate	i MA kyoo lit	ɪˈmækjʊlɪt
immanent	I muh nuhnt	ˈɪmənənt
Immanuel	i MAY nyoo uhl	ɪˈmænjʊəl
immature	i muh TYOOR	ɪməˈtjur
immeasurable	i ME zhuh ruh buhl	ɪˈmeʒərəbəl
immediate	i MEE di it	ɪˈmidɪt
immediately	i MEE di it li	ɪˈmidɪtlɪ
Immelmann	I muhl mahn	ˈɪməlmɑn
immerse	i MERS	ɪˈmɜˑs
immersion	i MER zhuhn	ɪˈmɜˑʒən
immigrant	I muh gruhnt	ˈɪməgrənt
immigrate	I muh grayt	ˈɪməgret
imminent	I muh nuhnt	ˈɪmənənt
immitigable	i MI ti guh buhl	ɪˈmɪtɪgəbəl
immobile	i MOH buhl	ɪˈmobəl
immolate	I muh layt	ˈɪmələt
immoral	i MAW ruhl	ɪˈmɔrəl
immortality	i mawr TA luh ti	ɪmɔrˈtælətɪ
immune	i MYOO : N	ɪˈmjun
immunization	i myoo ni ZAY shuhn	ɪmjʊnɪˈzeʃən
immunize	I myoo nighz	ˈɪmjʊnaɪz
immure	i MYOOR	ɪˈmjʊr
immutable	i MYOO : tuh buhl	ɪˈmjutəbəl
Imogen	I muh juhn	ˈɪmədʒən
Imogene	I muh jeen	ˈɪmədʒin
impartial	im PAHR shuhl	ɪmˈpɑrʃəl
impartiality	im pahr shi A luh ti	ɪmpɑrʃɪˈælətɪ
impasse	IM pas	ˈɪmpæs

at [æ] ; ah [ɑ] ; air [ɛ] ; awful [ɔ] ; say [e] ; back [b] ; chair [tʃ] ; do [d] ; elm [ɛ] ; eel [i] ; server [ˈɝ, ər] ; fit [f] ; go [g] ; hurt [h] ; is [ɪ] ; high [aɪ] ; jet [dʒ] ; kiss [k] ; lamb [l] ; my [m] ; nice [n] ;

impeccable	im PE kuh buhl	ɪmˈpɛkəbəl
impecunious	im pi KYOO : ni uhs	ɪmpɪˈkjunɪəs
impediment	im PE duh muhnt	ɪmˈpɛdəmənt
impedimenta	im pe duh MEN tuh	ɪmpɛdəˈmɛntə
impenetrable	im PE ni truh buhl	ɪmˈpɛnɪtrəbəl
impenitent	im PE ni tuhnt	ɪmˈpɛnɪtənt
imperial	im PI ri uhl	ɪmˈpɪrɪəl
imperialism	im PI ri uh li zuhm	ɪmˈpɪrɪəlɪzəm
imperialistic	im pi ri uh LI stik	ɪmpɪrɪəˈlɪstɪk
impertinent	im PER tuh nuhnt	ɪmˈpɜˈtənənt
imperturbable	im per TER buh buhl	ɪmpərˈtɜˈbəbəl
impervious	im PER vi uhs	ɪmˈpɜˈvɪəs
impetigo	im pi TIGH goh	ɪmpɪˈtaɪgo
impetuous	im PE choo uhs	ɪmˈpɛtʃʊəs
impetus	IM puh tuhs	ˈɪmpətəs
impiety	im PIGH uh ti	ɪmˈpaɪətɪ
impious	IM pi uhs	ˈɪmpɪəs
impiousness	IM pi uhs nis	ˈɪmpɪəsnɪs
implacable	im PLAY kuh buhl	ɪmˈplekəbəl
implement (n)	IM pluh muhnt	ˈɪmpləmənt
implement (v)	IM pluh ment	ˈɪmpləmɛnt
implemental	im pluh MEN tuhl	ɪmpləˈmɛntəl
implicate	IM pli kayt	ˈɪmplɪket
implicit	im PLI sit	ɪmˈplɪsɪt
import (n)	IM pawrt	ˈɪmpɔrt
import (v)	im PAWRT	ɪmˈpɔrt
important	im PAWR tuhnt	ɪmˈpɔrtənt
importunate	im PAWR chuh nit	ɪmˈpɔrtʃənɪt
importune	im pawr TOO : N	ɪmpɔrˈtun
impostor	im PAH ster	ɪmˈpɑstər
impotence	IM puh tuhns	ˈɪmpətəns
impotency	IM puh tuhn si	ˈɪmpətənsɪ
impotent	IM puh tuhnt	ˈɪmpətənt
imprecatory	IM pri kuh taw ri	ˈɪmprɪkətɔrɪ
impregnate	im PREG nayt	ɪmˈprɛgnet
impresario	im pri SAH ri oh	ɪmprɪˈsɑrɪo
impress (n)	IM pres	ˈɪmprɛs
impress (v)	im PRES	ɪmˈprɛs
imprimatur	im pri MAY ter	ɪmprɪˈmetər
imprimis	im PRIGH mis	ɪmˈpraɪmɪs
improvisation	im prah vuh ZAY shuhn	ɪmprɑvəˈzeʃən
improvvisatore	eem praw vee zah TAW re	ɪmprɔvizɑˈtɔrɛ
imprudent	im PROO : duhnt	ɪmˈprudənt
impudence	IM pyoo duhns	ˈɪmpjʊdəns
impudent	IM pyoo duhnt	ˈɪmpjʊdənt
impugn	im PYOO : N	ɪmˈpjun
impuissance	im PYOO : i suhns	ɪmˈpjuɪsəns
impunity	im PYOO : nuh ti	ɪmˈpjunətɪ
impute	im PYOO : T	ɪmˈpjut
in absentia	in ab SEN shi uh	ɪn æbˈsɛnʃɪə
inadvertent	i nuhd VER tuhnt	ɪnədˈvertənt
inalienable	in AY lyuh nuh buhl	ɪnˈeljənəbəl

sing [ŋ] ; *oh* [o] ; *oil* [ɔɪ] ; *foot* [ʊ] ; *foo:*d [u] ; *how* [aʊ] ; *pie* [p] ; *ray* [r] ; *so* [s] ; *shall* [ʃ] ;
to [t] ; *thin* [θ] ; *th:*en [ð] ; above (*uh* B*UH*V) [ə, ˈʌ] ; *vine* [v] ; *wine* [w] ; *whine* [hw] ;
you [j] ; *zoo* [z] ; rouge (roo:*zh*) [ʒ].

inane	in AYN	ɪnˈen
inanition	i nuh NI shuhn	ɪnəˈnɪʃən
inanity	in A nuh ti	ɪnˈænətɪ
inapplicable	in A pli kuh buhl	ɪnˈæplɪkəbəl
inarticulate	i nahr TI kyoo lit	ɪnɑrˈtɪkjʊlɪt
inaugural	in AW gyoo ruhl	ɪnˈɔgjʊrəl
inaugurate	in AW gyoo rayt	ɪnˈɔgjʊret
Inca	ING kuh	ˈɪŋkə
incandescence	in kuhn DE suhns	ɪnkənˈdɛsəns
incandescent	in kuhn DE suhnt	ɪnkənˈdɛsənt
incarnate (a)	in KAHR nit	ɪnˈkɑrnɪt
incarnate (v)	in KAHR nayt	ɪnˈkɑrnet
incendiary	in SEN di ai ri	ɪnˈsɛndɪɛrɪ
incense (n)	IN sens	ˈɪnsɛns
incense (" anger ")	in SENS	ɪnˈsɛns
incestuous	in SES choo uhs	ɪnˈsɛstʃʊəs
inchoate	in KOH it	ɪnˈkoɪt
inchoative	in KOH uh tiv	ɪnˈkoətɪv
incinerate	in SI nuh rayt	ɪnˈsɪnəret
incipient	in SI pi uhnt	ɪnˈsɪpɪənt
incipit	IN si pit	ˈɪnsɪpɪt
incision	in SI zhuhn	ɪnˈsɪʒən
incisive	in SIGH siv	ɪnˈsaɪsɪv
incisor	in SIGH zer	ɪnˈsaɪzər
inclement	in KLE muhnt	ɪnˈklɛmənt
incline (n)	IN klighn	ˈɪnklaɪn
incline (v)	in KLIGHN	ɪnˈklaɪn
inclose	in KLOHZ	ɪnˈkloz
inclosure	in KLOH zher	ɪnˈkloʒər
include	in KLOO : D	ɪnˈklud
inclusion	in KLOO : zhuhn	ɪnˈkluʒən
inclusive	in KLOO : siv	ɪnˈklusɪv
incogitant	in KAH juh tuhnt	ɪnˈkɑdʒətənt
incognito	in KAHG ni toh	ɪnˈkɑgnɪto
incoherent	in koh HI ruhnt	ɪnkoˈhɪrənt
income	IN kuhm	ˈɪnkəm
incommensurate	in kuh MEN shoo rit	ɪnkəˈmɛnʃʊrɪt
incommodious	in kuh MOH di uhs	ɪnkəˈmodɪəs
incommunicado	in kuh myoo : ni KAH doh	ɪnkəmjunɪˈkado
incomparable	in KAHM puh ruh buhl	ɪnˈkɑmpərəbəl
incompatibility	in kuhm pa tuh BI luh ti	ɪnkəmpætəˈbɪlətɪ
incompatible	in kuhm PA tuh buhl	ɪnkəmˈpætəbəl
incompetence	in KAHM puh tuhns	ɪnˈkɑmpətəns
incompetent	in KAHM puh tuhnt	ɪnˈkɑmpətənt
incongruent	in KAHNG groo uhnt	ɪnˈkɑŋgruənt
incongruity	in kuhn GROO : uh ti	ɪnkənˈgruətɪ
incongruous	in KAHNG groo uhs	ɪnˈkɑŋgruəs
inconsequential	in kahn si KWEN shuhl	ɪnkɑnsɪˈkwɛnʃəl
inconsolable	in kuhn SOH luh buhl	ɪnkənˈsoləbəl
incontinent	in KAHN tuh nuhnt	ɪnˈkɑntənənt
incontrovertible	in kahn truh VER tuh buhl	ɪnkɑntrəˈvɝtəbəl
incorporate (a)	in KAWR puh rit	ɪnˈkɔrpərɪt

at [æ] ; ah [ɑ] ; air [ɛ] ; awful [ɔ] ; say [e] ; back [b] ; chair [tʃ] ; do [d] ; elm [ɛ] ; eel [i] ; server [ˈɝ, ər] ; fit [f] ; go [g] ; hurt [h] ; is [ɪ] ; high [aɪ] ; jet [dʒ] ; kiss [k] ; lamb [l] ; my [m] ; nice [n] ;

incorporate (v)	in KAWR puh rayt	ɪnˈkɔrpəret
incorporeal	in kawr PAW ri uhl	ɪnkɔrˈpɔrɪəl
incorrigible	in KAW ri juh buhl	ɪnˈkɔrɪdʒəbəl
increase(n)	IN krees	ˈɪnkris
increase (v)	in KREES	ɪnˈkris
incredible	in KRE duh buhl	ɪnˈkrɛdəbəl
incredulity	in kruh DOO : luh ti	ɪnkrəˈdulətɪ
incredulous	in KRE joo luhs	ɪnˈkrɛdʒʊləs
increment	IN kruh muhnt	ˈɪnkrəmənt
incubate	IN kyoo bayt	ˈɪnkjʊbet
incubator	IN kyoo bay ter	ˈɪnkjʊbetər
incubus	IN kyoo buhs	ˈɪnkjʊbəs
inculcate	in KUHL kayt	ɪnˈkʌlket
inculpable	in KUHL puh buhl	ɪnˈkʌlpəbəl
inculpate	in KUHL payt	ɪnˈkʌlpet
incumbent	in KUHM buhnt	ɪnˈkʌmbənt
incunabula	in kyoo NA byoo luh	ɪnkjʊˈnæbjʊlə
incursion	in KER zhuhn	ɪnˈkɝʒən
incus	ING kuhs	ˈɪŋkəs
indecorous	in DE kuh ruhs	ɪnˈdɛkərəs
indefatigable	in di FA ti guh buhl	ɪndɪˈfætɪgəbəl
indenture	in DEN cher	ɪnˈdɛntʃər
indescribable	in di SKRIGH buh buhl	ɪndɪˈskraɪbəbəl
Index Expurgatorius	IN deks ek sper guh TOH ri uhs	ˈɪndɛks ɛkspɜrgəˈtorɪəs
Index Librorum Prohibitorum	IN deks ligh BRAW ruhm proh hi bi TAW ruhm	ˈɪndɛks laɪˈbrɔrəm prohɪbɪˈtɔrəm
India	IN di uh	ˈɪndɪə
Indian	IN di uhn	ˈɪndɪən
Indiana	in di A nuh	ɪndɪˈænə
Indianapolis	in di uh NA puh lis	ɪndɪəˈnæpəlɪs
Indianian	in di A ni uhn	ɪndɪˈænɪən
Indic	IN dik	ˈɪndɪk
indicative	in DI kuh tiv	ɪnˈdɪkətɪv
indices	IN duh seez	ˈɪndəsiz
indict	in DIGHT	ɪnˈdaɪt
indictable	in DIGH tuh buhl	ɪnˈdaɪtəbəl
indictment	in DIGHT muhnt	ɪnˈdaɪtmənt
indigenous	in DI juh nuhs	ɪnˈdɪdʒənəs
indigent	IN di juhnt	ˈɪndɪdʒənt
indignant	in DIG nuhnt	ɪnˈdɪgnənt
indigo	IN di goh	ˈɪndɪgo
indiscreet	in di SKREET	ɪndɪˈskrit
indiscrete	in di SKREET	ɪndɪˈskrit
indiscretion	in di SKRE shuhn	ɪndɪˈskrɛʃən
indiscriminate	in di SKRI muh nit	ɪndɪˈskrɪmənɪt
indisputable	in di SPYOO : tuh buhl	ɪndɪˈspjutəbəl
indissoluble	in di SAH lyoo buhl	ɪndɪˈsɑljubəl
individual	in duh VI joo uhl	ɪndəˈvɪdʒual
indivisible	in duh VI zuh buhl	ɪndəˈvɪzəbel
Indo-	IN doh	ˈɪndo
Indo-China, Indochina	IN doh CHIGH nuh	ˈɪndo ˈtʃaɪnə

sing [ŋ]; *oh* [o]; *oil* [ɔɪ]; *foot* [ʊ]; *foo:d* [u]; *how* [aʊ]; *pie* [p]; *ray* [r]; *so* [s]; *shall* [ʃ]; *to* [t]; *thin* [θ]; *th:en* [ð]; *above* (*uh BUH*V) [ə, ˈʌ]; *vine* [v]; *wine* [w]; *whine* [hw]; *you* [j]; *zoo* [z]; *rouge* (roo:zh) [ʒ].

H.P.—N

indolence	IN duh luhns	ˈɪndələns
indomitable	in DAH mi tuh buhl	ɪnˈdɑmɪtəbəl
Indonesia	in doh NEE zhuh	ɪndoˈniʒə
Indore	in DAWR	ɪnˈdɔr
Indra	IN druh	ˈɪndrə
indubitable	in DOO : bi tuh buhl	ɪnˈdubɪtəbəl
induce	in DOOS	ɪnˈdus
Indus	IN duhs	ˈɪndəs
industrial	in DUH stri uhl	ɪnˈdʌstrɪəl
industry	IN duh stri	ˈɪndəstrɪ
Indy, d'	dan DEE	dænˈdi
inebriate (a, n)	in EE bri it	ɪnˈibrɪɪt
inebriate (v)	in EE bri ayt	ɪnˈibrɪet
inebriation	i nee bri AY shuhn	ɪnibrɪˈeʃən
inedible	in E duh buhl	ɪnˈɛdəbəl
ineffable	in E fuh buhl	ɪnˈɛfəbəl
inefficacy	in E fi kuh si	ɪnˈɛfɪkəsɪ
inefficient	i nuh FI shuhnt	ɪnəˈfɪʃənt
ineluctable	i ni LUHK tuh buhl	ɪnɪˈlʌktəbəl
inept	in EPT	ɪnˈɛpt
ineptitude	in EP tuh too : d	ɪnˈɛptətud
inequity	in E kwi ti	ɪnˈɛkwɪtɪ
ineradicable	i ni RA di kuh buhl	ɪnɪˈrædɪkəbəl
inert	in ERT	ɪnˈɝt
inertia	in ER shuh	ɪnˈɝʃə
in esse	in E si	ɪn ˈɛsɪ
inestimable	in E sti muh buhl	ɪnˈɛstɪməbəl
inevitable	in E vi tuh buhl	ɪnˈɛvɪtəbəl
inexorable	in EK suh ruh buhl	ɪnˈɛksərəbəl
inexplicable	in EK spli kuh buhl	ɪnˈɛksplɪkəbəl
in extenso	in ik STEN soh	ɪn ɪkˈstɛnso
inextricable	in EK stri kuh buhl	ɪnˈɛkstrɪkəbəl
infallible	in FA luh buhl	ɪnˈfæləbəl
infamous	IN fuh muhs	ˈɪnfəməs
infamy	IN fuh mi	ˈɪnfəmɪ
infancy	IN fuhn si	ˈɪnfənsɪ
infanta	in FAN tuh	ɪnˈfæntə
infante	in FAN tay	ɪnˈfænte
infantile	IN fuhn tighl	ˈɪnfəntaɪl
inference	IN fuh ruhns	ˈɪnfərəns
inferiority	in fi ri AW ruh ti	ɪnfɪrɪˈɔrətɪ
infernal	in FER nuhl	ɪnˈfɝnəl
inferno	in FER noh	ɪnˈfɝno
infest	in FEST	ɪnˈfɛst
infidel	IN fuh duhl	ˈɪnfədəl
infiltrate	in FIL trayt	ɪnˈfɪltret
infiltration	in fil TRAY shuhn	ɪnfɪlˈtreʃən
infinite	IN fuh nit	ˈɪnfənɪt
infinitesimal	in fi nuh TE suh muhl	ɪnfɪnəˈtɛsəməl
infinity	in FI nuh ti	ɪnˈfɪnətɪ
infix (n)	IN fiks	ˈɪnfɪks
infix (v)	in FIKS	ɪnˈfɪks

at [æ] ; ah [ɑ] ; air [ɛ] ; awful [ɔ] ; say [e] ; back [b] ; chair [tʃ] ; do [d] ; elm [ɛ] ; eel [i] ;
server [ˈɝ, ər] ; fit [f] ; go [g] ; hurt [h] ; is [ɪ] ; high [aɪ] ; jet [dʒ] ; kiss [k] ; lamb [l] ; my [m] ;
nice [n] ;

inflammable	in FLA muh buhl	ɪnˈflæməbəl
inflammation	in fluh MAY shuhn	ɪnfləˈmeʃən
inflate	in FLAYT	ɪnˈflet
inflexible	in FLEK suh buhl	ɪnˈflɛksəbəl
inflorescence	in flaw RE suhns	ɪnfloˈrɛsəns
influence	IN floo uhns	ˈɪnfluəns
influential	in floo EN shuhl	ɪnfluˈɛnʃəl
influenza	in floo EN zuh	ɪnfluˈɛnzə
informative	in FAWR muh tiv	ɪnˈfɔrmətɪv
infra dignitatem	IN fruh dig ni TAY tuhm	ˈɪnfrə dɪgnɪˈtetəm
infrangible	in FRAN juh buhl	ɪnˈfrændʒəbəl
infrequent	in FREE kwuhnt	ɪnˈfrikwənt
infusoria, I-	in fyoo SAW ri uh	ɪnfjuˈsɔrɪə
Inge	ing	ɪŋ
Ingelow	IN juh loh	ˈɪndʒəlo
Ingeman, -n	ING guh muhn	ˈɪŋgəmən
ingenious	in JEE nyuhs	ɪnˈdʒinjəs
ingénue	an zhi NOO:	ænʒɪˈnu
ingenuity	in juh NOO: uh ti	ɪndʒəˈnuətɪ
ingenuous	in JE nyoo uhs	ɪnˈdʒɛnjuəs
Ingersol, -l	ING ger suhl	ˈɪŋgərsəl
Ingham	ING uhm	ˈɪŋəm
inglenook	ING guhl nook	ˈɪŋgəlnʊk
Ingold	IN gohld	ˈɪngold
Ingoldsby	ING guhlz bi	ˈɪŋgəlzbɪ
ingot	ING guht	ˈɪŋgət
Ingram	ING gruhm	ˈɪŋgrəm
ingrate	IN grayt	ˈɪngret
ingratiate	in GRAY shi ayt	ɪnˈgreʃɪet
ingredient	in GREE di uhnt	ɪnˈgridɪənt
Ingres	AN gruh	ˈæŋgrə
ingress	IN gres	ˈɪŋgrɛs
Ingwinian	ing GWI ni uhn	ɪŋˈgwɪnɪən
inhere	in HIR	ɪnˈhɪr
inherent	in HI ruhnt	ɪnˈhɪrənt
inheritance	in HE ri tuhns	ɪnˈhɛrɪtəns
inhibition	in hi BI shuhn	ɪnhɪˈbɪʃən
inhospitable	in HAH spi tuh buhl	ɪnˈhɑspɪtəbəl
inimical	in I mi kuhl	ɪnˈɪmɪkəl
inimitable	in I mi tuh buhl	ɪnˈɪmɪtəbəl
iniquitous	i NI kwuh tuhs	ɪˈnɪkwətəs
iniquity	i NI kwuh ti	ɪˈnɪkwətɪ
initiate (a, n)	i NI shi it	ɪˈnɪʃɪt
initiate (v)	i NI shi ayt	ɪˈnɪʃɪet
initiation	i ni shi AY shuhn	ɪnɪʃɪˈeʃən
initiative	i NI shi uh tiv	ɪˈnɪʃɪətɪv
injudicious	in joo DI shuhs	ɪndʒuˈdɪʃəs
injunction	in JUHNGK shuhn	ɪnˈdʒʌŋkʃən
inlay (n)	IN lay	ˈɪnle
inlay (v)	in LAY	ɪnˈle
in loco parentis	in LOH koh puh REN tis	ɪn ˈloko pəˈrɛntɪs
inmate	IN mayt	ˈɪnmet

si*ng* [ŋ] ; *oh* [o] ; *oil* [ɔɪ] ; *foot* [ʊ] ; *foo*:d [u] ; *how* [aʊ] ; *p*ie [p] ; *ray* [r] ; *so* [s] ; *sh*all [ʃ] ;
to [t] ; *thin* [θ] ; *th*:en [ð] ; *above* (*uh* B*U*H*V*) [ə, ˈʌ] ; *vine* [v] ; *wine* [w] ; *wh*ine [hw] ;
*y*ou [j] ; *zoo* [z] ; *rouge* (roo:*zh*) [ʒ].

in medias res	in MEE di uhs REEZ	ɪn ˈmidɪəs ˈriz
in memoriam	in muh MAW ri uhm	ɪn məˈmɔrɪəm
Inness	I nis	ˈɪnɪs
innocent, I-	I nuh suhnt	ˈɪnəsənt
innocuous	i NAH kyoo uhs	ɪˈnɑkjuəs
innovate	I nuh vayt	ˈɪnəvet
Innsbruck	INZ brook	ˈɪnzbrʊk
innuendo	in yoo EN doh	ɪnjuˈɛndo
Inönü	EE noh noo	ˈinonʊ
inordinate	in AWR duh nit	ɪnˈɔrdənɪt
in perpetuum	in per PE too uhm	ɪn pərˈpɛtuəm
inquest	IN kwest	ˈɪnkwɛst
inquire	in KWIGHR	ɪnˈkwaɪr
inquiry	in KWIGH ri	ɪnˈkwaɪrɪ
inquisition, I-	in kwuh ZI shuhn	ɪnkwəˈzɪʃən
inquisitive	in KWI zuh tiv	ɪnˈkwɪzətɪv
inquisitor	in KWI zuh ter	ɪnˈkwɪzətər
insalubrious	in suh LOO : bri uhs	ɪnsəˈlubrɪəs
insane	in SAYN	ɪnˈsen
insatiable	in SAY shuh buhl	ɪnˈseʃəbəl
insatiate	in SAY shi it	ɪnˈseʃɪɪt
inscrutable	in SKROO : tuh buhl	ɪnˈskrutəbəl
insecticide	in SEK tuh sighd	ɪnˈsɛktəsaɪd
insectivora, I-	in sek TI vuh ruh	ɪnsɛkˈtɪvərə
insensate	in SEN sit	ɪnˈsɛnsɪt
insentient	in SEN shuhnt	ɪnˈsɛnʃənt
insert (n)	IN sert	ˈɪnsərt
insert (v)	in SERT	ɪnˈsɝt
insidious	in SI di uhs	ɪnˈsɪdɪəs
insignia	in SIG ni uh	ɪnˈsɪgnɪə
insinuation	in si nyoo AY shuhn	ɪnsɪnjuˈeʃən
insipid	in SI pid	ɪnˈsɪpɪd
insolent	IN suh luhnt	ˈɪnsələnt
insomnia	in SAHM ni uh	ɪnˈsɑmnɪə
insomniac	in SAHM ni ak	ɪnˈsɑmnɪæk
insouciance	in SOO : si uhns	ɪnˈsusɪəns
insouciant	in SOO : si uhnt	ɪnˈsusɪənt
inspiration	in spuh RAY shuhn	ɪnspəˈreʃən
in statu quo	in STAY too KWOH	ɪn ˈstetʊ ˈkwo
instinct (a)	in STINGKT	ɪnˈstɪŋkt
instinct (n)	IN stingkt	ˈɪnstɪŋkt
institut	an stee TOO :	ænstiˈtu
institute	IN stuh too : t	ˈɪnstətut
insubordinate	in suh BAWR duh nit	ɪnsəˈbɔrdənɪt
insufferable	in SUH fuh ruh buhl	ɪnˈsʌfərəbəl
insular	IN suh ler	ˈɪnsələr
insularity	in suh LA ruh ti	ɪnsəˈlærətɪ
insulate	IN suh layt	ˈɪnsəlet
insulation	in suh LAY shuhn	ɪnsəˈleʃən
insulator	IN suh lay ter	ˈɪnsəletər
insulin	IN suh lin	ˈɪnsəlɪn
insult (n)	IN suhlt	ˈɪnsəlt

at [æ] ; ah [ɑ] ; air [ɛ] ; awful [ɔ] ; say [e] ; back [b] ; chair [tʃ] ; do [d] ; elm [ɛ] ; eel [i] ;
server [ˈɝ, ər] ; fit [f] ; go [g] ; hurt [h] ; is [ɪ] ; high [aɪ] ; jet [dʒ] ; kiss [k] ; lamb [l] ; my [m] ;
nice [n] ;

insult (v)	in SUHLT	ɪnˈsʌlt
insuperable	in SOO : puh ruh buhl	ɪnˈsupərəbəl
insurable	in SHOO ruh buhl	ɪnˈʃurəbəl
insurance	in SHOO ruhns	ɪnˈʃurəns
insure	in SHOOR	ɪnˈʃur
insurgent	in SER juhnt	ɪnˈsɝdʒənt
insurrectionary	in suh REK shuh nai ri	ɪnsəˈrɛkʃənɛrɪ
intact	in TAKT	ɪnˈtækt
intaglio	in TA lyoh	ɪnˈtæljo
integer	IN tuh jer	ˈɪntədʒər
integral	IN tuh gruhl	ˈɪntəgrəl
integrate	IN tuh grayt	ˈɪntəgret
integration	in tuh GRAY shuhn	ɪntəˈgreʃən
integrity	in TEG ruh ti	ɪnˈtɛgrətɪ
integument	in TEG yoo muhnt	ɪnˈtɛgjumənt
intellectual	in tuh LEK choo uhl	ɪntəˈlɛktʃuəl
intelligent	in TE luh juhnt	ɪnˈtɛlədʒənt
intelligentsia	in te luh JENT si uh	ɪntɛləˈdʒɛntsɪə
intelligible	in TE li juh buhl	ɪnˈtɛlɪdʒəbəl
intemperate	in TEM puh rit	ɪnˈtɛmpərɪt
inter	in TER	ɪnˈtɝ
inter alia	IN ter AY li uh	ˈɪntər ˈelɪə
inter alios	IN ter AY li ohs	ˈɪntər ˈelɪos
intercalate	in TER kuh layt	ɪnˈtɝkəlet
intercept (n)	IN ter sept	ˈɪntərsept
intercept (v)	in ter SEPT	ɪntərˈsept
intercom	IN ter kahm	ˈɪntərkɑm
interdict (n)	IN ter dikt	ˈɪntərdɪkt
interdict (v)	in ter DIKT	ɪntərˈdɪkt
interest	IN trist	ˈɪntrɪst
interested	IN tri stid	ˈɪntrɪstɪd
interesting	IN tri sting	ˈɪntrɪstɪŋ
interfere	in ter FIR	ɪntərˈfɪr
interference	in ter FI ruhns	ɪntərˈfɪrəns
interim	IN tuh rim	ˈɪntərɪm
Interlaken	IN ter lah kuhn	ˈɪntərlɑkən
interlocutor	in ter LAH kyoo ter	ɪntərˈlɑkjutər
interloper	IN ter loh per	ˈɪntərlopər
interlude	IN ter loo : d	ˈɪntərlud
intermediary	in ter MEE di ai ri	ɪntərˈmidɪɛrɪ
intermediate	in ter MEE di it	ɪntərˈmidɪɪt
interment	in TER muhnt	ɪnˈtɝmənt
intermezzo	in ter MET soh	ɪntərˈmɛtso
interminable	in TER mi nuh buhl	ɪnˈtɝmɪnəbəl
intern, -e (n)	IN tern	ˈɪntərn
intern (v)	in TERN	ɪnˈtɝn
internecine	in ter NEE sin	ɪntərˈnisɪn
internist	in TER nist	ɪnˈtɝnɪst
inter nos	IN ter NOHS	ˈɪntər ˈnos
interpolate	in TER puh layt	ɪnˈtɝpəlet
interpolation	in ter puh LAY shuhn	ɪntɝpəˈleʃən
interpretative	in TER pri tay tiv	ɪnˈtɝprɪtetɪv

sing [ŋ] ; *oh* [o] ; *oil* [ɔɪ] ; *foot* [ʊ] ; *foo:d* [u] ; *how* [aʊ] ; *pie* [p] ; *ray* [r] ; *so* [s] ; *shall* [ʃ] ;
to [t] ; *thin* [θ] ; *th:en* [ð] ; *above* (*uh BUHV*) [ə, ˈʌ] ; *vine* [v] ; *wine* [w] ; *whine* [hw] ;
you [j] ; *zoo* [z] ; *rouge* (*roo:zh*) [ʒ].

interpreter	in TER pri ter	ɪnˈtɜːprɪtər
interrogate	in TE ruh gayt	ɪnˈtɛrəget
interrogator	in TE ruh gay ter	ɪnˈtɛrəgetər
interrogatory	in tuh RAH guh taw ri	ɪntəˈrɑgətɔrɪ
interstice	in TER stis	ɪnˈtɜːstɪs
interstitial	in ter STI shuhl	ɪntərˈstɪʃəl
intestate	in TE stayt	ɪnˈtɛstet
intestinal	in TE sti nuhl	ɪnˈtɛstɪnəl
intestine	in TE stin	ɪnˈtɛstɪn
intimacy	IN tuh muh si	ˈɪntəməsɪ
intimate (a)	IN tuh mit	ˈɪntəmɪt
intimate (v)	IN tuh mayt	ˈɪntəmet
intimation	in tuh MAY shuhn	ɪntəˈmeʃən
intimidate	in TI muh dayt	ɪnˈtɪmədet
intolerable	in TAH luh ruh buhl	ɪnˈtɑlərəbəl
intonation	in tuh NAY shuhn	ɪntəˈneʃən
in toto	in TOH toh	ɪn ˈtoto
intoxicant	in TAHK suh kuhnt	ɪnˈtɑksəkənt
intransigence	in TRAN si juhns	ɪnˈtrænsɪdʒəns
intravenous	in truh VEE nuhs	ɪntrəˈvinəs
intrepid	in TRE pid	ɪnˈtrɛpɪd
intrepidity	in truh PI duh ti	ɪntrəˈpɪdətɪ
intricacy	IN tri kuh si	ˈɪntrɪkəsɪ
intricate	IN tri kit	ˈɪntrɪkɪt
intrigue	in TREEG	ɪnˈtrig
intrinsic	in TRIN sik	ɪnˈtrɪnsɪk
introduce	in truh DOO : S	ɪntrəˈdus
introit	in TROH it	ɪnˈtroɪt
introversion	in truh VER zhuhn	ɪntrəˈvɜːʒən
introvert (a, n)	IN truh vert	ˈɪntrəvərt
introvert (v)	in truh VERT	ɪntrəˈvɜːt
intrude	in TROO : D	ɪnˈtrud
intrusion	in TROO : zhuhn	ɪnˈtruʒən
intuition	in too I shuhn	ɪntʊˈɪʃən
intuitive	in TOO : i tiv	ɪnˈtuɪtɪv
intumescence	in too ME suhns	ɪntʊˈmɛsəns
inundate	I nuhn dayt	ˈɪnəndet
inure	in YOOR	ɪnˈjʊr
invalid (" ill "; a, n, v)	IN vuh lid	ˈɪnvəlɪd
invalid (" void ")	in VA lid	ɪnˈvælɪd
Invalides	an vah LEED	ænvɑˈlid
inveigh	in VAY	ɪnˈve
inveigle	in VEE guhl	ɪnˈvigəl
inventory	IN vuhn taw ri	ˈɪnvəntɔrɪ
Inverness, i-	in ver NES	ɪnvərˈnɛs
inversion	in VER zhuhn	ɪnˈvɜːʒən
invert (a, n)	IN vert	ˈɪnvərt
invert (v)	in VERT	ɪnˈvɜːt
invertebrate	in VER tuh brit	ɪnˈvɜːtəbrɪt
inveterate	in VE tuh rit	ɪnˈvɛtərɪt
invidious	in VI di uhs	ɪnˈvɪdɪəs
invigorate	in VI guh rayt	ɪnˈvɪgəret

at [æ] ; ah [ɑ] ; air [ɛ] ; awful [ɔ] ; say [e] ; back [b] ; chair [tʃ] ; do [d] ; elm [ɛ] ; eel [i] ; server [ˈɜ, ər] ; fit [f] ; go [g] ; hurt [h] ; is [ɪ] ; high [aɪ] ; jet [dʒ] ; kiss [k] ; lamb [l] ; my [m] ; nice [n] ;

inviolable	in VIGH uh luh buhl	ɪnˈvaɪələbəl
inviolate	in VIGH uh lit	ɪnˈvaɪəlɪt
invoice	IN vois	ˈɪnvɔɪs
involute	IN vuh loo꞉t	ˈɪnvəlut
Io	IGH oh	ˈaɪo
iodic	igh AH dik	aɪˈɑdɪk
iodine	IGH uh dighn	ˈaɪədaɪn
iodoform	igh OH duh fawrm	aɪˈodəfɔrm
Iola	igh OH luh	aɪˈolə
Iolanthe	igh uh LAN thi	aɪəˈlænθɪ
ion	IGH uhn	ˈaɪən
Ionesco	ee uh NE skoh	iəˈnɛsko
Ionia	igh OH ni uh	aɪˈonɪə
Ionic	igh AH nik	aɪˈɑnɪk
ionize	IGH uh nighz	ˈaɪənaɪz
ionosphere	igh AH nuh sfir	aɪˈɑnəsfɪr
Iowa	IGH uh wuh	ˈaɪəwə
Iowan	IGH uh wuhn	ˈaɪəwən
ipecac	I pi kak	ˈɪpɪkæk
Iphigenia	i fuh ji NIGH uh	ɪfədʒɪˈnaɪə
Ippolitov-Ivanov	i paw LEE tawf i VAH nawf	ɪpɔˈlitəf ɪˈvɑnɔf
ipse dixit	IP si DIK sit	ˈɪpsɪ ˈdɪksɪt
ipso facto	IP soh FAK toh	ˈɪpso ˈfækto
Ipswich	IP swich	ˈɪpswɪtʃ
Irak	i RAHK	ɪˈrɑk
Iran	i RAHN	ɪˈrɑn
Iranian	i RAY ni uhn	ɪˈrenɪən
Iraq	i RAHK	ɪˈrɑk
Iraqi	i RAH ki	ɪˈrɑkɪ
irascible	i RA suh buhl	ɪˈræsəbəl
irate	IGH rayt	ˈaɪret
Irazú	ee rah ZOO꞉	irɑˈzu
ire	ighr	aɪr
Ireland	IGHR luhnd	ˈaɪrlənd
Irene (not myth)	igh REEN	aɪˈrin
Irene (myth)	igh REE nee	aɪˈrini
Irgun	IR goon	ˈɪrgʊn
iridescence	i ruh DE suhns	ɪrəˈdɛsəns
iridium	i RI di uhm	ɪˈrɪdɪəm
iris, I-	IGH ris	ˈaɪrɪs
Irish	IGH rish	ˈaɪrɪʃ
iritis	igh RIGH tis	aɪˈraɪtɪs
Irkutsk	ir KOOTSK	ɪrˈkʊtsk
iron	IGH ern	ˈaɪərn
ironic	igh RAH nik	aɪˈrɑnɪk
irony	IGH ruh ni	ˈaɪrənɪ
Iroquois	I ruh kwoi	ˈɪrəkwɔɪ
irradiate	i RAY di ayt	ɪˈredɪet
Irrawaddi	i ruh WAH di	ɪrəˈwɑdɪ
irreconcilable	i re kuhn SIGH luh buhl	ɪrɛkənˈsaɪləbəl
Irredentist	i ri DEN tist	ɪrɪˈdɛntɪst

sing [ŋ]; oh [o]; oil [ɔɪ]; foot [ʊ]; foo꞉d [u]; how [aʊ]; pie [p]; ray [r]; so [s]; shall [ʃ];
to [t]; thin [θ]; th꞉en [ð]; above (uh BUHV) [ə, ˈʌ]; vine [v]; wine [w]; whine [hw];
you [j]; zoo [z]; rouge (roo꞉zh) [ʒ].

irrefragable	i RE fruh guh buhl	ɪˈrɛfrəgəbəl
irrefutable	i RE fyoo tuh buhl	ɪˈrɛfjʊtəbəl
irrelevant	i RE luh vuhnt	ɪˈrɛləvənt
irremediable	i ri MEE di uh buhl	ɪrɪˈmidɪəbəl
irreparable	i RE puh ruh buhl	ɪˈrɛpərəbəl
irresolute	i RE zuh loo : t	ɪˈrɛzəlut
irreverent	i RE vuh ruhnt	ɪˈrɛvərənt
irrevocable	i RE vuh kuh buhl	ɪˈrɛvəkəbəl
irritability	i ruh tuh BI luh ti	ɪrətəˈbɪlətɪ
irritable	I ruh tuh buhl	ˈɪrətəbəl
irritant	I ruh tuhnt	ˈɪrətənt
irruption	i RUHP shuhn	ɪˈrʌpʃən
Irtish	ir TISH	ɪrˈtɪʃ
Irving	ER ving	ˈɜvɪŋ
Isador, -e	I suh dawr	ˈɪsədɔr
Isaiah	igh ZAY uh	aɪˈzeə
Isaias	igh ZAY uhs	aɪˈzeəs
Isar	EE zahr	ˈizɑr
Iscariot	i SKA ri uht	ɪˈskærɪət
Iseult	i SOO : LT	ɪˈsult
Isfahan	is fa HAHN	ɪsfæˈhɑn
Ishbosheth	ish BOH shith	ɪʃˈboʃɪθ
Isherwood	I sher wood	ˈɪʃərwʊd
Ishikawa	ee shee KAH wah	iʃiˈkɑwɑ
Ishmael	ISH mi uhl	ˈɪʃmɪəl
Ishtar	ISH tahr	ˈɪʃtɑr
Isidor, -e	I zuh dawr	ˈɪzədɔr
isinglass	IGH zing glas	ˈaɪzɪŋglæs
Isis	IGH sis	ˈaɪsɪs
Islam	I sluhm	ˈɪsləm
Islamic	i SLA mik	ɪˈslæmɪk
island	IGH luhnd	ˈaɪlənd
isle	ighl	aɪl
islet	IGH lit	ˈaɪlɪt
Islington	IZ ling tuhn	ˈɪzlɪŋtən
Islip	IGH slip	ˈaɪslɪp
isobar	IGH suh bahr	ˈaɪsəbɑr
Isocrates	igh SAH kruh teez	aɪˈsɑkrətiz
isolate	IGH suh layt	ˈaɪsəlet
isolation	igh suh LAY shuhn	aɪsəˈleʃən
Isolde	i SOHLD	ɪˈsold
isomer	IGH suh mer	ˈaɪsəmər
isotherm	IGH suh therm	ˈaɪsəθərm
isotope	IGH suh tohp	ˈaɪsətop
Israel	IZ ri uhl	ˈɪzrɪəl
Israeli	iz RAY li	ɪzˈrelɪ
Israelite	Iz ri uh light	ˈɪzrɪəlaɪt
issei	ees say	is se
issue	I shoo	ˈɪʃʊ
Istanbul	i stan BOO : L	ɪstænˈbul
isthmus	IS muhs	ˈɪsməs
Istria	I stri uh	ˈɪstrɪə

at [æ] ; ah [ɑ] ; air [ɛ] ; awful [ɔ] ; say [e] ; back [b] ; chair [tʃ] ; do [d] ; elm [ɛ] ; eel [i] ;
server [ˈɜ, ər] ; fit [f] ; go [g] ; hurt [h] ; is [ɪ] ; high [aɪ] ; jet [dʒ] ; kiss [k] ; lamb [l] ; my [m] ;
nice [n] ;

Italian	i TA lyuhn	ɪˈtæljən
italic, I-	i TA lik	ɪˈtælɪk
italicize	i TA luh sighz	ɪˈtæləsaɪz
italienne	ee tah li EN	itɑlɪˈɛn
Italy	I tuh li	ˈɪtəli
Itasca	igh TA skuh	aɪˈtæskə
item	IGH tuhm	ˈaɪtəm
iterate	I tuh rayt	ˈɪtəret
iterative	I tuh ray tiv	ˈɪtəretɪv
Ithaca	I thuh kuh	ˈɪθəkə
Ithuriel	i THYOO ri uhl	ɪˈθjʊrɪəl
itinerant	igh TI nuh ruhnt	aɪˈtɪnərənt
itinerary	igh TI nuh rai ri	aɪˈtɪnərɛrɪ
Iturbi	ee TOOR bee	iˈtʊrbi
Ivan	IGH vuhn	ˈaɪvən
Ivan (Russian)	i VAHN	ɪˈvɑn
Ivanhoe	IGH vuhn hoh	ˈaɪvənho
Ivanovo	i VAH naw vaw	ɪˈvɑnɔvɔ
Ives	ighvz	aɪvz
ivory, I-	IGHV ri	ˈaɪvrɪ
iwis	i WIS	ɪˈwɪs
Iwo Jima	EE woh JEE mah	ˈiwo ˈdʒimɑ
ixia, I-	IK si uh	ˈɪksɪə
Ixion	ik SIGH uhn	ɪkˈsaɪən
Izvestia	iz VE sti ah	ɪzˈvɛstɪɑ

J

Jabesh	JAY besh	ˈdʒebɛʃ
Jabloneč	YAH blaw nets	ˈjɑblɔnɛts
jabot	zha BOH	ʒæˈbo
jacinth	JAY sinth	ˈdʒesɪnθ
jackal	JA kawl	ˈdʒækɔl
jackanapes	JA kuh nayps	ˈdʒækəneps
Jacobean	ja kuh BEE uhn	dʒækəˈbiən
Jacobin	JA kuh bin	ˈdʒækəbɪn
Jacoby	juh KOH bi	dʒɜˈkobɪ
Jacquard	juh KAHRD	dʒɜˈkɑrd
Jacqueline	JA kwuh lin	ˈdʒækwəlɪn
Jacqueminot	JAK mi noh	ˈdʒækmɪno
Jacquerie, j-	zha KREE	ʒæˈkri
Jacques (French)	ZHAHK	ʒɑk
Jacques (in Shakespeare)	JAY kweez	ˈdʒekwiz
Jacquinot	zhah kee NOH	ʒɑkiˈno
jaeger	YAY ger	ˈjegər
Jael	JAY uhl	ˈdʒeəl
Jaffa	JA fuh	ˈdʒæfə
jaguar	JA gwahr	ˈdʒægwɑr
Jahve, -h	YAH ve	ˈjɑvɛ

sing [ŋ]; _oh_ [o]; _oil_ [ɔɪ]; _foot_ [ʊ]; _foo:d_ [u]; _how_ [aʊ]; _pie_ [p]; _ray_ [r]; _so_ [s]; _shall_ [ʃ];
_to_ [t]; _thin_ [θ]; _th:en_ [ð]; _above_ (_uh BUHV_) [ə, ˈʌ]; _vine_ [v]; _wine_ [w]; _whine_ [hw];
you [j]; _zoo_ [z]; _rouge_ (roo:_zh_) [ʒ].

jai-alai	high uh LIGH	haɪ əˈlaɪ
Jain	jighn	dʒaɪn
Jaipur	JIGH poor	ˈdʒaɪpʊr
Jairus	jay IGH ruhs	dʒeˈaɪrəs
Jakarta	jah KAHR tah	dʒɑˈkɑrtɑ
Jalisco	hah LEE skoh	hɑˈlisko
jalopy, jallopy	juh LAH pi	dʒəˈlɑpɪ
jalousie	JA loo see	ˈdʒælʊsi
Jamaica	juh MAY kuh	dʒɑˈmekə
Jamali	jah MAH li	dʒɑˈmɑlɪ
jamb, -e	jam	dʒæm
jamboree	jam buh REE	dʒæmbəˈri
Jamestown	JAYMZ town	ˈdʒemztaʊn
Jammu	JUH moo :	ˈdʒʌmu
Jan (European)	yahn	jɑn
Jan (U.S.)	jan	dʒæn
Janáček	YA nah chek	ˈjænɑtʃɛk
jangle	JANG guhl	ˈdʒæŋgəl
janiculum	juh NI kyuh luhm	dʒəˈnɪkjələm
Janigro, Antonio	YAH nee groh, ahn TOH nee oh	ˈjɑnigro ɑnˈtonio
Janis	JA nis	ˈdʒænɪs
janissary, J-	JA nuh sai ri	ˈdʒænəsɛrɪ
janizary, J-	JA nuh zai ri	ˈdʒænəzɛrɪ
Jansen	JAN suhn	ˈdʒænsən
January	JA nyoo ai ri	ˈdʒænjʊɛrɪ
Janus	JAY nuhs	ˈdʒenəs
japan, J-	juh PAN	dʒəˈpæn
Japanese	ja puh NEEZ	dʒæpəˈniz
jape	jayp	dʒep
Japheth	JAY fith	ˈdʒefɪθ
japonica	juh PAH ni kuh	dʒəˈpɑnɪkə
Jaques (Shakespeare)	JAY kweez	ˈdʒekwiz
jardiniere	jahr duh NIR	dʒɑrdəˈnɪr
jardinière	zhahr dee ni AIR	ʒɑrdinɪˈɛr
jargon	JAHR guhn	ˈdʒɑrgən
Jaroslaw	yah RAW slahf	jɑˈrɔslɑf
Jarrow	JA roh	ˈdʒæro
jasmin, -e	JAS min	ˈdʒæsmɪn
Jason	JAY suhn	ˈdʒesən
jasper, J-	JA sper	ˈdʒæspər
jaundice	JAWN dis	ˈdʒɔndɪs
jaunt	jawnt	dʒɔnt
Java	JAH vuh	ˈdʒɑvə
Javanese	ja vuh NEEZ	dʒævəˈniz
Javel, -le	zhuh VEL	ʒəˈvɛl
javelin	JAV lin	ˈdʒævlɪn
Javits	JA vits	ˈdʒævɪts
jaw	jaw	dʒɔ
ja wohl	yah VOHL	jɑ ˈvol
Jean (French)	zhah	ʒɑ
Jeanne (French)	zhahn	ʒɑn

at [æ]; *ah* [ɑ]; *air* [ɛ]; *aw*ful [ɔ]; s*ay* [e]; *b*ack [b]; *ch*air [tʃ]; *d*o [d]; *e*lm [ɛ]; *ee*l [i]; *server* [ˈɝ, ər]; *f*it [f]; *g*o [g]; *h*urt [h]; *i*s [ɪ]; h*igh* [aɪ]; *j*et [dʒ]; *k*iss [k]; *l*amb [l]; *m*y [m]; *n*ice [n];

Jebel Musa	JE buhl MOO : sah	ˈdʒɛbəl ˈmusɑ
jehad	ji HAHD	dʒɪˈhɑd
Jehoiakim	ji HOI uh kim	dʒɪˈhɔɪəkɪm
Jehol	juh HOHL	dʒəˈhol
Jehoram	ji HAW ruhm	dʒɪˈhɔrəm
Jehoshaphat	ji HAH shuh fat	dʒɪˈhɑʃəfæt
Jehovah	ji HOH vuh	dʒɪˈhovə
Jehu	JEE hoo :	ˈdʒihu
jejune	ji JOO : N	dʒɪˈdʒun
Jekyll	JEE kuhl	ˈdʒikəl
Jellicoe	JE li koh	ˈdʒɛlɪko
jellied	JE lid	ˈdʒɛlɪd
Jemima	juh MIGH muh	dʒəˈmaɪmə
Jena	YAY nah	ˈjenɑ
Jenner	JE ner	ˈdʒɛnər
jennet	JE nit	ˈdʒɛnɪt
Jennifer	JE ni fer	ˈdʒɛnɪfər
jenny, J-	JE ni	ˈdʒɛnɪ
Jensen	JEN suhn	ˈdʒɛnsən
jeopardize	JE per dighz	ˈdʒɛpərdaɪz
jeopardy	JE per di	ˈdʒɛpərdɪ
Jephthah	JEF thuh	ˈdʒɛfθə
jerboa	jer BOH uh	dʒɜrˈboə
jeremiad	je ruh MIGH uhd	dʒɛrəˈmaɪəd
Jeremiah	je ruh MIGH uh	dʒɛrəˈmaɪə
Jerez	he RETH	hɛˈrɛθ
Jericho	JE ruh koh	ˈdʒɛrəko
Jericó (Colombia)	he ri KOH	hɛrɪˈko
Jeritza	YE rit suh	ˈjɛrɪtsə
jerkin	JER kin	ˈdʒɝkɪn
Jeroboam, j-	je ruh BOH uhm	dʒɛrəˈboəm
Jerome	juh ROHM	dʒəˈrom
Jersey, j-	JER zi	ˈdʒɝzɪ
Jerusalem	juh ROO suh luhm	dʒəˈrusələm
Jervis (British)	JAHR vis	ˈdʒɑrvɪs
Jervis (U.S.)	JER vis	ˈdʒɝvɪs
Jespersen	YE sper suhn	ˈjɛspərsən
jessamine, J-	JE suh min	ˈdʒɛsəmɪn
Jesse, Jessie	JE si	ˈdʒɛsɪ
Jessica	JE si kuh	ˈdʒɛsɪkə
Jesu	JEE zoo :	ˈdʒizu
Jesuit	JE zhoo it	ˈdʒɛʒʊɪt
jet	jet	dʒɛt
Jethro	JE throh	ˈdʒɛθro
jetsam	JET suhm	ˈdʒɛtsəm
jettison	JE tuh suhn	ˈdʒɛtəsən
jeu de mots	zher duh MOH	ʒər də ˈmo
jeu d'esprit	zher de SPREE	ʒər dɛ ˈspri
jeune fille	zhern FEE yuh	ʒɜrn ˈfijə
Jevons	JE vuhnz	ˈdʒɛvənz
Jew	joo :	dʒu
jewel	JOO : uhl	ˈdʒuəl

jewelry	JOO : uhl ri	ˈdʒuəlrɪ
Jewett	JOO : it	ˈdʒuɪt
Jewry	JOO : ri	ˈdʒurɪ
Jezebel	JE zuh buhl	ˈdʒɛzəbəl
Jezreel	JEZ ri uhl	ˈdʒɛzrɪəl
Jhelum	JAY luhm	ˈdʒeləm
jibe	jighb	dʒaɪb
Jibuti	jee BOO : ti	dʒiˈbutɪ
Jicamarca	hee kah MAHR kuh	hikaˈmɑrkə
jihad	ji HAHD	dʒɪˈhɑd
Jiménez	hee MAY neth	hiˈmɛnɛθ
jimson, J-	JIM suhn	ˈdʒɪmsən
jingle	JING guhl	ˈdʒɪŋgəl
jingly	JING gli	ˈdʒɪŋglɪ
jingo	JING goh	ˈdʒɪŋgo
jingoism	JING goh i zuhm	ˈdʒɪŋgoɪzəm
jinn	jin	dʒɪn
Jinnah	JI nuh	ˈdʒɪnə
jinni	ji NEE	dʒɪˈni
jinriksha, jinrikisha	jin RIK shuh	dʒɪnˈrɪkʃə
jipijapa	hee pi HAH pah	hipɪˈhɑpɑ
jitney	JIT ni	ˈdʒɪtnɪ
jive	jighv	dʒaɪv
Joab	JOH ab	ˈdʒoæb
Joachim (Bible)	JOH uh kim	ˈdʒoəkɪm
Joachim (violinist)	YOH uh kim	ˈjoəkɪm
Joan	john	dʒon
Joanna	joh A nuh	dʒoˈænə
Joanne	joh AN	dʒoˈæn
Joaquin	wah KEEN	wɑˈkin
job	jahb	dʒɑb
Job	johb	dʒob
Jocasta	joh KA stuh	dʒoˈkæstə
Jochum, Eugen	YOH kuhm, OH zhin	ˈjokəm, ˈoʒɪn
jocose	joh KOHS	dʒoˈkos
jocular	JAH kyoo ler	ˈdʒɑkjʊlər
jocund	JAH kuhnd	ˈdʒɑkənd
Jodhpur	johd POOR	dʒodˈpʊr
jodhpurs	JAHD perz	ˈdʒɑdpərz
Joel	JOH uhl	ˈdʒoəl
Joffre	ZHAW fruh	ˈʒɔfrə
Johann (German)	YOH hahn	ˈjohɑn
Johannes (German)	yoh HAH nes	joˈhɑnɛs
Johannesburg	joh HA nis berg	dʒoˈhænɪsbərg
John, j-	jahn	dʒɑn
Johore	juh HAWR	dʒəˈhɔr
joie de vivre	zhwah duh VEE vruh	ʒwɑ də ˈvivrə
Joinville	zhwan VEEL	ʒwænˈvil
Jókai	YOH koi	ˈjokɔi
Jokjakarta	jahk yah KAHR tah	dʒɑkyaˈkɑrtɑ
Joliet	JOH li et	ˈdʒolɪɛt
Joliot-Curie	zhaw LYOH koo REE	ʒɔˈljo kuˈri

at [æ] ; ah [ɑ] ; air [ɛ] ; awful [ɔ] ; say [e] ; back [b] ; chair [tʃ] ; do [d] ; elm [ɛ] ; eel [i] ; server [ˈɝ, ər] ; fit [f] ; go [g] ; hurt [h] ; is [ɪ] ; high [aɪ] ; jet [dʒ] ; kiss [k] ; lamb [l] ; my [m] ; nice [n] ;

Jolo	haw LAW	hɔˈlo
Jonah	JOH nuh	ˈdʒonə
Jonathan	JAH nuh thuhn	ˈdʒɑnəθən
jongleur	JAHNG gler	ˈdʒɑŋglər
jonquil	JAHNG kwil	ˈdʒɑŋkwɪl
Joplin	JAH plin	ˈdʒɑplɪn
Jordaens	YAWR dans	ˈjɔrdæns
Jordan	JAWR duhn	ˈdʒɔrdən
Jordanian	jawr DAY ni uhn	dʒɔrˈdenɪən
jorum	JOH ruhm	ˈdʒorəm
Josephus	joh SEE fuhs	dʒoˈsifəs
Joshua	JAH shoo uh	ˈdʒɑʃʊə
Josiah	joh SIGH uh	dʒoˈsaɪə
joss	jahs	dʒɑs
jostle	JAH suhl	ˈdʒɑsəl
jota	HOH tuh	ˈhotə
Jouhaud	zhoo : OH	ʒuˈo
Joule, j-	jowl	dʒaul
Jourdain, Louis	zhawr DAN, loo : EE	ʒɔrˈdæn, luˈi
joust	juhst	dʒʌst
Jove	johv	dʒov
Jowett	JOW it	ˈdʒauɪt
jowl	jowl	dʒaul
Joyce	jois	ˈdʒɔɪs
Juan (English)	JOO : uhn	ˈdʒuən
Juan (Spanish)	hwahn	hwɑn
Juan de Fuca (strait)	JOO : uhn duh FYOO : kuh	ˈdʒuən də ˈfjukə
Juanita	waw NEE tuh	wɑˈnitə
Juarez	HWAH res	ˈhwɑrɛs
Juba	JOO : bah	ˈdʒubɑ
Jubal	JOO : buhl	ˈdʒubəl
Jubbulpore	juh buhl PAWR	dʒəbəlˈpɔr
Jubilate	joo : buh LAY tee	dʒubəˈleti
jubilate	JOO : buh layt	ˈdʒubəlet
jubilee	JOO : buh lee	ˈdʒubəli
Judaea	joo : DEE uh	dʒuˈdiə
Judah	JOO : duh	ˈdʒudə
Judaic	joo : DAY ik	dʒuˈdeɪk
Judaism	JOO : di i zuhm	ˈdʒudɪɪzəm
Judas	JOO : duhs	ˈdʒudəs
Judea	joo : DEE uh	dʒuˈdiə
judicable	JOO : di kuh buhl	ˈdʒudɪkəbəl
judicatory	JOO : di kuh taw ri	ˈdʒudɪkətɔrɪ
judicature	JOO : di kuh cher	ˈdʒudɪkətʃər
judicial	joo : DI shuhl	dʒuˈdɪʃəl
judiciary	joo : DI shi ai ri	dʒuˈdɪʃɪɛrɪ
judicious	joo : DI shuhs	dʒuˈdɪʃəs
judo	JOO : doh	ˈdʒudo
Juggernaut, j-	JUH ger nawt	ˈdʒʌgərnɔt
Jugoslavia	yoo : guh SLAH vi uh	jugəˈslɑvɪə
jugular	JUH gyoo ler	ˈdʒʌgjʊlər
Juilliard	JOO : lee ahrd	ˈdʒuliɑrd

sing [ŋ] ; *oh* [o] ; *oil* [ɔɪ] ; *foot* [ʊ] ; *foo*:d [u] ; *how* [aʊ] ; *p*ie [p] ; *ray* [r] ; *so* [s] ; *sh*all [ʃ] ;
to [t] ; *th*in [θ] ; *th*:en [ð] ; above (*uh* BUH*V*) [ə, ˈʌ] ; *v*ine [v] ; *w*ine [w] ; *wh*ine [hw] ;
*y*ou [j] ; *z*oo [z] ; rouge (roo:*zh*) [ʒ].

jujitsu	joo : JIT soo :	dʒuˈdʒɪtsu
juju	JOO : joo :	ˈdʒudʒu
jujube	JOO : joo : b	ˈdʒudʒub
juke	joo : k	dʒuk
Jukes	joo : ks	dʒuks
julep	JOO : lip	ˈdʒulɪp
julienne	joo : li EN	dʒulɪˈɛn
juncaceous	juhng KAY shuhs	dʒəŋˈkeʃəs
junco	JUHNG koh	ˈdʒʌŋko
juncture	JUHNGK cher	ˈdʒʌŋtʃər
Juneau	JOO : noh	ˈdʒuno
Jung	yoong	juŋ
Jungfrau	YOONG frow	ˈjuŋfrau
Juniata	joo : nee AH tuh	dʒuniˈatə
juniper	JOO : nuh per	ˈdʒunəpər
Junker, j-	YOONG ker	ˈjuŋkər
junket	JUHNG kit	ˈdʒʌŋkɪt
Juno	JOO : noh	ˈdʒuno
Junoesque	joo : noh ESK	dʒunoˈɛsk
junta	JUHN tuh	ˈdʒʌntə
junto	JUHN toh	ˈdʒʌnto
Jupiter	JOO : puh ter	ˈdʒupətər
Jura	JOO ruh	ˈdʒurə
Jurassic	joo RA sik	dʒuˈræsɪk
jurat	JOO rat	ˈdʒuræt
Jurgens	JER guhnz	ˈdʒɝgənz
juridical	joo RI di kuhl	dʒuˈrɪdɪkəl
Jurinac, Sena	yoo : ri NAHK, SAY nah	jurɪˈnɑk, ˈsenɑ
jurisdiction	joo ris DIK shuhn	dʒurɪsˈdɪkʃən
jurisprudence	joo ris PROO : duhns	dʒurɪsˈprudəns
jurist	JOO rist	ˈdʒurɪst
juror	JOO rer	ˈdʒurər
Juruá	zhoo : roo : AH	ʒuruˈɑ
jury	JOO ri	ˈdʒurɪ
jus, au	oh ZHOO	o ˈʒu
Jusserand	zhoos RAHN	ʒusˈrɑn
jussive	JUH siv	ˈdʒʌsɪv
just	juhst	dʒʌst
justificatory	juh STI fuh kuh taw ri	dʒəˈstɪfəkətɔrɪ
Justin	JUH stin	ˈdʒʌstɪn
Justinian	juh STI ni uhn	dʒəˈstɪnɪən
justle	JUH suhl	ˈdʒʌsəl
Jute, j-	joo : t	ˈdʒut
Jutish	JOO : tish	ˈdʒutɪʃ
Jutland	JUHT luhnd	ˈdʒʌtlənd
jutty	JUH ti	ˈdʒʌtɪ
Juvenal	JOO : vuh nuhl	ˈdʒuvənəl
juvenescence	joo : vuh NE suhns	dʒuvəˈnɛsəns
juvenile	JOO : vuh nuhl	ˈdʒuvənəl
juvenilia	joo : vuh NI li uh	dʒuvəˈnɪlɪə
juxtapose	JUHK stuh pohz	ˈdʒʌkstəpoz
juxtaposition	juhk stuh puh ZI shuhn	dʒʌkstəpəˈzɪʃən

_at_ [æ] ; _ah_ [ɑ] ; _air_ [ɛ] ; _aw_ful [ɔ] ; _say_ [e] ; _b_ack [b] ; _ch_air [tʃ] ; _do_ [d] ; _e_lm [ɛ] ; _ee_l [i] ;
server [ɝ, ər] ; _f_it [f] ; _go_ [g] ; _h_urt [h] ; _is_ [ɪ] ; _high_ [aɪ] ; _j_et [dʒ] ; _k_iss [k] ; _l_amb [l] ; _m_y [m] ;
_n_ice [n] ;

K

ka	kah	kɑ
Kaaba	KAH buh	ˈkɑbə
Kabalevsky	kah bah LYEF ski	kɑbɑˈljɛfskɪ
kabobs	kuh BAHBZ	kəˈbɑbz
kabuki	kah BOO : kee	kɑˈbuki
Kabul	KAH bool	ˈkɑbʊl
Kabyle	kuh BIGHL	kəˈbaɪl
Kadar, Janos	KAH dahr, YAH nohsh	ˈkɑdɑr, ˈjɑnoʃ
kaddish	KAH dish	ˈkɑdɪʃ
Kadesh	KAY desh	ˈkedɛʃ
Kaffir, k-	KA fer	ˈkæfər
Kaffraria	kuh FRAI ri uh	kəˈfrɛrɪə
Kafka	KAHF kah	ˈkɑfkɑ
Kagawa	KAH gah WAH	ˈkɑgɑˈwɑ
Kagoshima	kah gaw SHEE mah	kɑgɔˈʃimɑ
Kaifeng	kigh fuhng	kaɪ fʌŋ
kailyard	KAYL yahrd	ˈkeljɑrd
kaiser, K-	KIGH zer	ˈkaɪzər
Kakatiya	kah KAH tee yah	kɑˈkɑtijɑ
Kalahari	kah lah HAH ri	kɑlɑˈhɑrɪ
Kalamazoo	ka luh muh ZOO :	kæləməˈzu
Kalat	kuh LAHT	kəˈlɑt
kale	kayl	kel
kaleidoscope	kuh LIGH duh skohp	kəˈlaɪdəskop
kaleidoscopic	kuh ligh duh SKAH pik	kəlaɪdəˈskɑpɪk
Kalevala	kah li VAH lah	kɑlɪˈvɑlɑ
Kalgan	kal GAHN	kælˈgɑn
Kalinin	kah LEE nin	kɑˈlinɪn
Kalisz	KAH lish	ˈkɑlɪʃ
Kalmuck	KAL muhk	ˈkælmək
Kamchatka	kam CHAT kuh	kæmˈtʃætkə
Kamerad	kah muh RAHT	kɑməˈrat
kamikaze	kah mi KAH zi	kɑmɪˈkɑzɪ
Kaminsky	kah MIN ski	kɑˈmɪnskɪ
Kanaka	kuh NA kuh	kəˈnækə
Kanara	kuh NAH ruh	kəˈnɑrə
Kanarese	kah nuh REEZ	kɑnəˈriz
Kanazawa	kah na ZAH wah	kɑnæˈzɑwɑ
Kanchenjunga	kahn chuhn JOONG guh	kɑntʃənˈdʒʊŋgə
Kandinsky	kan DIN skee	kænˈdɪnski
Kandy	KAN di	ˈkændɪ
Kanelopoulos	kah ne LAW poo : laws	kɑnɛˈlɔpulɔs
kangaroo	kang guh ROO :	kæŋgəˈru
Kanin	KAY nin	ˈkenɪn
Kansas	KAN zuhs	ˈkænzəs
Kant	kant	kænt

sing [ŋ]; *oh* [o]; *oil* [ɔɪ]; *foot* [ʊ]; *foo:*d [u]; *how* [aʊ]; *pie* [p]; *ray* [r]; *so* [s]; *sh*all [ʃ];
to [t]; *thin* [θ]; *th:*en [ð]; *above* (*uh* B*UH*V) [ə, ˈʌ]; *vine* [v]; *wine* [w]; *whine* [hw];
you [j]; *zoo* [z]; *rouge* (roo:*zh*) [ʒ].

Kantian	KAN ti uhn	ˈkæntɪən
Kantor	KAN ter	ˈkæntər
kaoliang	kah oh li ANG	kɑolɪˈæŋ
kaolin, -e	KAY uh lin	ˈkeəlɪn
Kapellmeister	kah PEL migh ster	kɑˈpɛlmaɪstər
Kaplan	KA pluhn	ˈkæplən
kapok	KAY pahk	ˈkepɑk
Kaposvár	KAH pawsh vahr	ˈkɑpoʃvɑr
kaput	kuh POO : T	kəˈput
Kara	KAH rah	ˈkɑrɑ
Karachi	kuh RAH chi	kəˈrɑtʃɪ
Karajan	KA ruh yahn	ˈkærəjɑn
Kara-Kalpak	kah RAH kahl PAHK	kɑˈrɑ kɑlˈpɑk
Karakoram	kah rah KAW ruhm	kɑrɑˈkorəm
karakul	KA ruh kuhl	ˈkærəkəl
Kara Kum	kah RAH KOO : M	kɑˈrɑ ˈkum
Kardelj	kahr DEL yuh	kɑrˈdɛljə
Karelian	kuh REE li uhn	kəˈrilɪən
Karenina, Anna	kah RE nyi nuh, AH nah	kɑˈrɛnjɪnə, ˈɑnɑ
Karlovac	KAHR law vahts	ˈkɑrlovɑts
Karlsbad	KAHRLZ bad	ˈkɑrlzbæd
Karlsruhe	KAHRLZ roo : uh	ˈkɑrlzruə
karma	KAHR muh	ˈkɑrmə
Karnak	KAHR nak	ˈkɑrnæk
Karolyi	KAH raw lyi	ˈkɑrɔljɪ
karoo, karoo	kuh ROO :	kəˈru
kasba, -h, K-	KAHZ bah	ˈkɑzbɑ
Kashmir	kash MIR	kæʃˈmɪr
Kassim	kah SEEM	kɑˈsim
Katahdin	kuh TAH din	kəˈtɑdɪn
Katanga	ka TAHNG gah	kæˈtɑŋgɑ
Katmai	KAT migh	ˈkætmaɪ
Katmandu	kaht mahn DOO :	kɑtmɑnˈdu
Katowice	kah taw VEET se	kɑtɔˈvitsɛ
Katrine	KA trin	ˈkætrɪn
Kattegat	KA ti gat	ˈkætɪgæt
Kauai	kah oo : AH ee	kɑuˈɑi
Kauffmann	KOWF mahn	ˈkaʊfmɑn
Kaufman	KAWF muhn	ˈkɔfmən
Kaunas	KOW nahs	ˈkaʊnɑs
Kavir	kuh VIR	kəˈvɪr
Kawasaki	kah wa SAH ki	kɑwæˈsɑkɪ
kayak	KIGH ak	ˈkaɪæk
Kaye	kay	ke
Kazak, Kazakh	ka ZAHK	kæˈzɑk
Kazan	kuh ZAHN	kəˈzɑn
Kazan (U.S.S.R.)	kah ZAHN	kɑˈzɑn
Kazbek	kaz BEK	kæzˈbɛk
Kazin	KAY zin	ˈkezɪn
kazoo	kuh ZOO :	kəˈzu
kea	KAY ah	ˈkeɑ
Kearny	KAHR ni	ˈkɑrnɪ

at [æ]; ah [ɑ]; air [ɛ]; awful [ɔ]; say [e]; back [b]; chair [tʃ]; do [d]; elm [ɛ]; eel [i];
server [ˈɜ, ər]; fit [f]; go [g]; hurt [h]; is [ɪ]; high [aɪ]; jet [dʒ]; kiss [k]; lamb [l]; my [m];
nice [n];

Keats	keets	kits
Keble	KEE buhl	ˈkibəl
Kecskemét	KECH ke mayt	ˈkɛtʃkɛmet
Kedah	KAY dah	ˈkedɑ
Kedar	KEE der	ˈkidər
kedgeree	KE juh ree	ˈkɛdʒərɪ
Kedron	KEE druhn	ˈkidrən
Keewatin	kee WAH tin	kiˈwɑtɪn
Kefauver	KEE faw ver	ˈkifɔvər
keg	keg	kɛg
Keijo	kay joh	ke dʒo
Keith	keeth	kiθ
Keller	KE ler	ˈkɛlər
Kellogg	KE luhg	ˈkɛləg
Kelmscot	KEM skuht	ˈkɛmskət
keloid	KEE loid	ˈkilɔɪd
kelpie, kelpy	KEL pi	ˈkɛlpɪ
Kelvin	KEL vin	ˈkɛlvɪn
Kemal Ataturk	ke MAHL ah tah TERK	kɛˈmɑl ɑtɑˈtɝk
Kemi	KE mee	ˈkɛmi
Kempe	KEM puh	ˈkɛmpə
Kempff	kempf	ˈkɛmpf
Kenilworth	KE nuhl werth	ˈkɛnəlwərθ
Kennebec	KE nuh bek	ˈkɛnəbɛk
Kennedy	KE nuh di	ˈkɛnədɪ
Kennelly	KE nuh li	ˈkɛnəlɪ
Kennesaw	KE nuh saw	ˈkɛnəsɔ
kenning	KE ning	ˈkɛnɪŋ
keno	KEE noh	ˈkino
kenosis	ki NOH sis	kɪˈnosɪs
kenotron	KE nuh trahn	ˈkɛnətrɑn
Kensington	KEN zing tuhn	ˈkɛnzɪŋtən
Kentucky	kuhn TUH ki	kənˈtʌkɪ
Kenya	KEN yuh	ˈkɛnjə
Kenyon	KEN yuhn	ˈkɛnjən
Keokuk	KEE uh kuhk	ˈkiəkək
Keos	KE aws	ˈkɛɔs
kepi	KE pi	ˈkɛpɪ
Kepler	KE pler	ˈkɛplər
keratogenous	ke ruh TAH juh nuhs	kɛrəˈtɑdʒənəs
Kerch	kairch	kɛrtʃ
kerchief	KER chif	ˈkɝtʃɪf
Kerensky, Kerenski	kuh REN ski	kəˈrɛnskɪ
Kermanshah	ker mahn SHAH	kərmɑnˈʃa
kermis, kermess	KER mis	ˈkɝmɪs
Kern	kern	kɝn
Kerouac	KER oh ak	ˈkɛroæk
Kerr (British)	kahr	kɑr
Kerr (U.S.)	ker	kɝ
Keszthely	KEST hay	ˈkɛsthe
ketchup	KE chuhp	ˈkɛtʃəp
ketogenic	kee tuh JE nik	kitəˈdʒɛnɪk

sing [ŋ]; oh [o]; oil [ɔɪ]; foot [ʊ]; foo:d [u]; how [aʊ]; pie [p]; ray [r]; so [s]; shall [ʃ];
to [t]; thin [θ]; th:en [ð]; above (uh BUHV) [ə, ˈʌ]; vine [v]; wine [w]; whine [hw];
you [j]; zoo [z]; rouge (roo:zh) [ʒ].

ketone	KEE tohn	ˈkiton
ketosis	ki TOH sis	kɪˈtosɪs
Keturah	ki TJOO ruh	kɪˈtyurə
Kevin	KE vin	ˈkɛvɪn
Kew	kyoo :	kju
Keynes	kaynz	kenz
Keynesian	KAYN zi uhn	ˈkenzɪən
Keyserling	KIGH zer ling	ˈkaɪzərlɪŋ
Khabarovsk	kah BAH rawfsk	kɑˈbɑrɔfsk
Khachaturian	ka chuh TOO : ree uhn	kætʃəˈturiən
Khaibar, Khaiber	KIGH ber	ˈkaɪbər
khaki	KA ki	ˈkækɪ
khan, K-	kahn	kɑn
Khanaqin	KA nuh kin	ˈkænəkin
Kharkov	KAHR kawf	ˈkɑrkɔf
Khartoum, Khartum	kahr TOO : M	kɑrˈtum
Khayyám	kigh AHM	kaɪˈɑm
khedive	kuh DEEV	kəˈdiv
Khrushchev	kroo : s CHAWF	krusˈtʃɔf
Khyber	KIGH ber	ˈkaɪbər
Kiam	kigh AHM	kaɪˈɑm
Kiangsi	kyang see	kjæŋ si
Kiangsu	kyang soo :	kjæŋ su
kibbutz	ki BOO : TS	kɪˈbuts
kibei	kee bay	ki be
kibitz	KI bits	ˈkɪbɪts
kibitzer	KI bit ser	ˈkɪbɪtsər
kibosh	KIGH bahsh	ˈkaɪbɑʃ
Kickapoo	KI kuh poo :	ˈkɪkəpu
kickshaw	KIK shaw	ˈkɪkʃɔ
kidney	KID ni	ˈkɪdnɪ
Kiel	keel	kil
Kieran	KI ruhn	ˈkɪrən
Kierkegaard	KIR kuh gawr	ˈkɪrkəgɔr
Kieta	kee E tah	kiˈɛtɑ
Kiev	kee EV	kiˈɛv
Kilauea	kee low AY uh	kilauˈeə
Kildare	kil DAIR	kɪlˈdɛr
Kilgallen	kil GA luhn	kɪlˈgælən
Kilimanjaro	ki li mahn JAH roh	kɪlɪmɑnˈdʒɑro
Kilkenny	kil KE ni	kɪlˈkɛnɪ
Killarney	ki LAHR ni	kɪˈlɑrnɪ
Killiecrankie	ki li KRANG ki	kɪlɪˈkræŋkɪ
Kilmarnock	kil MAHR nuhk	kɪlˈmɑrnək
Kilmer	KIL mer	ˈkɪlmər
kiln	kil	kɪl
kilo	KEE loh	ˈkilo
kilogram, -me	KI luh gram	ˈkɪləgræm
kilometer, kilometre	KI luh mee ter	ˈkɪləmitər
kilowatt	KI luh waht	ˈkɪləwɑt
Kimberley	KIM ber li	ˈkɪmbərlɪ
Kimbrough	KIM broh	ˈkɪmbro

at [æ] ; *ah* [ɑ] ; *air* [ɛ] ; *awful* [ɔ] ; *say* [e] ; *back* [b] ; *chair* [tʃ] ; *do* [d] ; *elm* [ɛ] ; *eel* [i] ; *server* [ˈɝ, ər] ; *f*it [f] ; *go* [g] ; *h*urt [h] ; *is* [ɪ] ; *high* [aɪ] ; *jet* [dʒ] ; *kiss* [k] ; *lamb* [l] ; *my* [m] ; *n*ice [n] ;

kimono	kuh MOH nuh	kəˈmonə
kindergarten	KIN der gahr tuhn	ˈkɪndərgɑrtən
kinescope, K-	KI nuh skohp	ˈkɪnəskop
kinesics	ki NEE siks	kɪˈnisɪks
kinesthesia	ki nis THEE zhuh	kɪnɪsˈθiʒə
kinesthesis	ki nis THEE sis	kɪnɪsˈθisɪs
kinesthetic	ki nis THE tik	kɪnɪsˈθɛtɪk
kinetic	ki NE tik	kɪˈnɛtɪk
Kingsley	KINGZ li	ˈkɪŋzlɪ
Kingston	KINGZ tuhn	ˈkɪŋztən
kinkajou	KING kuh joo :	ˈkɪŋkədʒu
Kinsey	KIN zi	ˈkɪnzɪ
kiosk	ki AHSK	kɪˈɑsk
Kiplinger	KIP ling er	ˈkɪplɪŋər
Kirghiz	kir GEEZ	kɪrˈgiz
kirk	kerk	kɝk
Kirkcudbright	ker KOO : bri	kərˈkubrɪ
Kirov	KEE rawf	ˈkirɔf
kirschwasser	KIRSH vah ser	ˈkɪrʃvɑsər
Kirsten	KIR sten	ˈkɪrstɛn
kirtle	KER tuhl	ˈkɝtəl
Kishinev	KI shi nef	ˈkɪʃɪnɛf
Kiska	KI skuh	ˈkɪskə
Kittredge	KI trij	ˈkɪtrɪdʒ
Kiushu	kyoo : shoo :	kju ʃu
Kiwanis	kuh WAH nis	kəˈwɑnɪs
kiwi	KEE wi	ˈkiwɪ
Klagenfurt	KLAH guhn foort	ˈklɑgənfʊrt
Klamath	KLA muth	ˈklæməθ
Kléber	klay BAIR	kleˈbɛr
Kleberg	KLAY berg	ˈklebɝg
Klee	klay	kle
kleig	kleeg	klig
Klemperer	KLEM puh ruhr	ˈklɛmpərər
kleptomania	klep tuh MAY ni uh	klɛptəˈmenɪə
kleptomaniac	klep tuh MAY ni ak	klɛptəˈmenɪæk
klieg	kleeg	klig
Klingsor	KLING zawr	ˈklɪŋzɔr
Klondike	KLAHN dighk	ˈklɑndaɪk
klystron	KLI struhn	ˈklɪstrən
knavish	NAY vish	ˈnevɪʃ
Kneller	NE ler	ˈnɛlər
Knesset	kuh NE set	kəˈnɛsset
knew	noo :	nu
Knickerbocker	NI ker bah ker	ˈnɪkərbɑkər
knob	nahb	nɑb
knoll	nohl	nol
Knopf	knahpf	knɑpf
Knossos	NAH suhs	ˈnɑsəs
knout	nowt	naʊt
Knowland	NOH luhnd	ˈnolənd
knowledge	NAH lij	ˈnɑlɪdʒ

sing [ŋ] ; oh [o] ; oil [ɔi] ; foot [ʊ] ; foo:d [u] ; how [aʊ] ; pie [p] ; ray [r] ; so [s] ; shall [ʃ] ; to [t] ; thin [θ] ; th:en [ð] ; above (uh BUHV) [ə, ˈʌ] ; vine [v] ; wine [w] ; whine [hw] ; you [j] ; zoo [z] ; rouge (roo:zh) [ʒ].

Knowles	nohlz	nolz
Knox	nahks	nɑks
Knudsen	NOO : D suhn	ˈnudsən
Knut	kuh NOO : T	kəˈnut
koala	koh AH luh	koˈɑlə
Kobe	KOH bi	ˈkobɪ
Koblenz	KOH blents	ˈkoblɛnts
kodak, K-	KOH dak	ˈkodæk
Kodály	koh DAH lyi	koˈdɑljɪ
Kodiak, k-	KOH di ak	ˈkodɪæk
Koestler	KEST ler	ˈkɛstlər
Kohinoor, Kohinur	KOH i noor	ˈkoɪnur
kohlrabi	KOHL rah bi	ˈkolrɑbɪ
koine, K-	KOI ni	ˈkɔɪnɪ
koksagyz	KOHK sa geez	ˈkoksægiz
kolinsky	kuh LIN ski	kəˈlɪnskɪ
kolkhoz	kawl KAWZ	kɔlˈkɔz
Kol Nidre	kohl NI druh	kol ˈnɪdrə
Komarno	kaw MAHR naw	kɔˈmɑrnɔ
Kondrashin	kahn DRAH shin	kɑnˈdrɑʃɪn
Konev	KAW nef	ˈkɔnɛf
Königsberg	KAY nigz berg	ˈkenɪgzbərg
Konitsa	KAW neet sah	ˈkɔnitsɑ
Konoye	KAW naw ye	ˈkɔnɔjɛ
Kootenay, Kootenai	KOO : tuh nay	ˈkutəne
kop	kahp	kɑp
kopeck, kopek	KOH pek	ˈkopɛk
kopje	KAH pi	ˈkɑpɪ
Koran	kaw RAHN	kəˈrɑn
Korea	kaw REE uh	kəˈriə
Korzybski	kawr ZIB ski	kɔrˈzɪbskɪ
Kosciusko	kah si UH skoh	kɑsɪˈʌsko
kosher	KOH sher	ˈkoʃər
Košice	KAW shit se	ˈkɔʃɪtsɛ
Kossuth	KAH soo : th	ˈkɑsuθ
Kostelanetz	kah stuh LAH nets	kɑstəˈlɑnɛts
Koster	KAH ster	ˈkɑstər
Kotka	KAWT kah	ˈkɔtkɑ
koumis, -s, koumyss	KOO : mis	ˈkumɪs
Koussevitzky	koo : suh VIT ski	kusəˈvɪtskɪ
Kovno	KAWV naw	ˈkɔvnɔ
kowtow	kow tow	kau tau
kraal	krahl	krɑl
Krafft-Ebing	KRAHFT AY bing	ˈkrɑft ˈebɪŋ
Kragerö, Krageroe	KRAH yai rer	ˈkrɑjɛrər
Krakatoa	krah kah TOW	krɑkɑˈtau
Kraków	KRAY koh	ˈkreko
Krasnodar	KRAHS naw dahr	ˈkrɑsnɔdɑr
Kreisler	KRIGH sler	ˈkraɪslər
kremlin, K-	KREM lin	ˈkrɛmlɪn
Křenek, Ernst	KRE nik	ˈkrɛnɪk
Kreutzer, k-	KROIT ser	ˈkrɔɪtsər

at [æ] ; ah [ɑ] ; air [ɛ] ; awful [ɔ] ; say [e] ; back [b] ; chair [tʃ] ; do [d] ; elm [ɛ] ; eel [i] ;
server [ˈɝ, ər] ; fit [f] ; go [g] ; hurt [h] ; is [ɪ] ; high [aɪ] ; jet [dʒ] ; kiss [k] ; jamb [l] ; my [m] ;
nice [n] ;

Kreymborg	KRAYM bawrg	ˈkrembɔrg
krieg, K-	kreeg	krig
Kriemhild	KREEM hild	ˈkrimhɪld
kris	krees	kris
Krishna	KRISH nuh	ˈkrɪʃnə
Kriss Kringle	kris KRING guhl	krɪs ˈkrɪŋgəl
Kristiansand	kris tyahn SAHN	krɪstjɑnˈsɑn
Kristiansund	kris tyahn SOON	krɪstjɑnˈsʊn
Krk	kerk	kɝk
Krnov	KER nawf	ˈkɝnɔf
Krokodil	kroh koh DEEL	krokoˈdil
krona	KROH nuh	ˈkronə
krone	KROH nuh	ˈkronə
Kronstadt	KRAWN staht	ˈkrɔnstɑt
Kropotkin	kruh PAHT kin	krəˈpɑtkɪn
Kruger	KROO : ger	ˈkrugər
kruller	KRUH ler	ˈkrʌlər
Krupa	KROO : puh	ˈkrupə
Krupp	kruhp	krʌp
Kruševac	KROO : she vahts	ˈkruʃɛvɑts
Krutch	kroo : ch	krutʃ
Krylov	kri LAWF	krɪˈlɔf
krypton	KRIP tahn	ˈkrɪptɑn
Krzemieniec	kerzh MYAY nyets	kɜrʒˈmjenjɛts
Kuala Lumpur	KWAH lah LOO : M pawr	ˈkwɑlɑ ˈlumpɔr
Kubango	koo BAHN goh	kʊˈbɑngo
Kubelik	KOO buh lik	ˈkʊbəlɪk
Kubla Khan	KOO : bluh KAHN	ˈkublə ˈkɑn
Kublai Khan	KOO : bligh KAHN	ˈkublaɪ ˈkɑn
kudos	KYOO : dahs	ˈkjudɑs
Kufic	KYOO : fik	ˈkjufɪk
Kuibyshev	KWEE bi shef	ˈkwibɪʃɛf
Ku Klux Klan	kyoo : kluhks klan	kju klʌks klæn
kula	KOO : luh	ˈkulə
kulak	koo : LAHK	kuˈlɑk
Kuldiga	KOOL di gah	ˈkʊldɪgɑ
Kultur	kool TOO : R	kʊlˈtur
kumiss	KOO : mis	ˈkumɪs
kümmel	KI muhl	ˈkɪməl
kumquat	KUHM kwaht	ˈkʌmkwɑt
Kun, Béla	KOON, BAY lah	ˈkʊn, ˈbelɑ
Kundry	KOON dri	ˈkʊndrɪ
Kuner	KYOO : ner	ˈkjunər
Kung Fu-tse	koong foo : d zuh	kʊŋ fud zʌ
Kunz, Erich	koonz, AIR ish	kʊnz, ˈɛrɪʃ
Kuomintang	KWOH min TAHNG	ˈkwomɪnˈtɑŋ
Kura	koo : RAH	kuˈrɑ
Kurdish	KER dish	ˈkɝdɪʃ
Kurdistan	KER di stan	ˈkɝdɪstæn
Kure	KOO : re	ˈkurɛ
Kuril, -e	KOO : ril	ˈkurɪl
Kursk	koo : rsk	kursk

si*ng* [ŋ] ; *oh* [o] ; *oil* [ɔɪ] ; *foot* [ʊ] ; *foo* :d [u] ; *how* [aʊ] ; *p*ie [p] ; *r*ay [r] ; *s*o [s] ; *sh*all [ʃ] ; *t*o [t] ; *th*in [θ] ; *th* :en [ð] ; *above* (*uh* B*UH*V) [ə, ˈʌ] ; *v*ine [v] ; *w*ine [w] ; *wh*ine [hw] ; *y*ou [j] ; *z*oo [z] ; *rouge* (roo:*zh*) [ʒ].

Kush (India)	koo : sh	kuʃ
kuvasz	KOO : vahs	ˈkuvɑs
Kuwait	koo : WIGHT	kuˈwaɪt
Kuznetsk	koo : z NETSK	kuzˈnɛtsk
Kwangchowan	kwahng choh wahn	kwɑŋ tʃo wɑn
Kwangsi	kwang see	kwæŋ si
Kwangtung	kwang toong	kwæŋ tʊŋ
Kwantung	kwan toong	kwæn tʊŋ
Kweichow	kway chow	kwe tʃaʊ
Kweihwacheng	kway hwah chuhng	kwe hwɑ tʃʌŋ
Kweilin	kway lin	kwe lɪn
Kweiyang	kway yahng	kwe jɑŋ
kyack	KIGH ak	ˈkaɪæk
Kyd	kid	kɪd
kymograph	KIGH muh graf	ˈkaɪməgræf
Kymry, Kymri, -e	KIM ri	ˈkɪmrɪ
Kyoto, Kioto	KYAW taw	ˈkjɔto
Kyrie eleison	KI ri ay ay LAY i suhn	ˈkɪrɪe eˈleɪsən
Kyushu	kyoo : shoo :	kju ʃu

L

Laban	LAY buhn	ˈlebən
labial	LAY bi uhl	ˈlebɪəl
laboratory	LA bruh taw ri	ˈlæbrətɔrɪ
Labrador	LA bruh dawr	ˈlæbrədɔr
Labuan	lah boo : AHN	lɑbuˈɑn
laburnum	luh BER nuhm	ləˈbɚnəm
labyrinth, L-	LA buh rinth	ˈlæbərɪnθ
labyrinthine	la buh RIN thin	læbəˈrɪnθɪn
Laccadive	LA kuh dighv	ˈlækədaɪv
Lacedaemon	la suh DEE muhn	læsəˈdimən
Lacedaemonian	la suh di MOH ni uhn	læsədɪˈmonɪən
Lachaise, La Chaise	la SHEZ	læˈʃez
Lachesis	LA kuh sis	ˈlækəsɪs
lachrymal	LA kruh muhl	ˈlækrəməl
lachrymose	LA kruh mohs	ˈlækrəmos
lackadaisical	la kuh DAY zi kuhl	lækəˈdezɪkəl
Lackawanna	la kuh WAH nuh	lækəˈwɑnə
Laconia	luh KOH ni uh	ləˈkonɪə
laconic	luh KAH nik	ləˈkɑnɪk
lacquer	LA ker	ˈlækər
lacrosse	luh KRAWS	ləˈkrɔs
lactation	lak TAY shuhn	lækˈteʃən
lactose	LAK tohs	ˈlæktos
lacuna	luh KYOO : nuh	ləˈkjunə
Ladakh	lah DAHK	lɑˈdɑk
Ladino	lah DEE noh	lɑˈdino

at [æ] ; *ah* [ɑ] ; *air* [ɛ] ; *aw*ful [ɔ] ; s*ay* [e] ; *b*ack [b] ; *ch*air [tʃ] ; *d*o [d] ; *e*lm [ɛ] ; *ee*l [i] ; ser*ver* [ˈɝ, ər] ; *f*it [f] ; *g*o [g] ; *h*urt [h] ; *i*s [ɪ] ; *high* [aɪ] ; *j*et [dʒ] ; *k*iss [k] ; *l*amb [l] ; *m*y [m] ; *n*ice [n] ;

lado, L-	LAH doh	ˈlɑdo
Ladoga (U.S.)	luh DOH guh	ləˈdogə
Ladoga (U.S.S.R)	LAH daw gah	ˈlɑdɔgɑ
Ladrone, l-	luh DROHN	ləˈdron
Lae	LAH e	ˈlɑɛ
Laertes	lay ER teez	leˈɜtiz
La Farge	luh FAHRZH	ləˈfɑrʒ
Lafayette (French general)	lah fi ET	lɑfɪˈɛt
Lafayette (U.S.)	LA fi yet	ˈlæfɪjɛt
Lafcadio	laf KA di oh	læfˈkædɪo
La Follette	luh FAH lit	ləˈfɑlɪt
La Fontaine	luh fahn TAYN	lə fɑnˈten
Lagerkvist, Pär	LAH guhr kvist, pair	ˈlɑgərkvɪst, pɛər
Lagerlöf	LAH ger lerf	ˈlɑgərlərf
lagniappe, lagnappe	lan YAP	lænˈjæp
lagoon	luh GOO : N	ləˈgun
Lagos (Nigeria)	LAH gohs	ˈlɑgos
Lagting, Lagthing	LAHG ting	ˈlɑg tɪŋ
La Guardia	luh GWAHR di uh	lə ˈgwɑrdɪə
Lahore	luh HAWR	ləˈhɔr
laic	LAY ik	ˈleɪk
lair	lair	lɛr
laird	laird	lɛrd
laissez-faire	le say FAIR	lɛseˈfɛr
laity	LAY uh ti	ˈleətɪ
Laius	LAY yuhs	ˈlejəs
Lakmé	lak MAY	lækˈme
Lalo	la LOH	læˈlo
lama, L-	LAH muh	ˈlɑmə
Lamarck	luh MAHRK	ləˈmɑrk
Lamartine	la mahr TEEN	læmɑrˈtin
lamb, L-	lam	læm
lambaste	lam BAYST	læmˈbest
lambda	LAM duh	ˈlæmdə
Lambeth	LAM buhth	ˈlæmbəθ
lamé	la MAY	læˈme
Lamech	LAY muhk	ˈlemək
lament	luh MENT	ləˈmɛnt
lamentable	LA muhn tuh buhl	ˈlæməntəbəl
lamia, L-	LAY mi uh	ˈlemɪə
Lamia (Greece)	lah MEE ah	lɑˈmiɑ
laminate (a)	LA muh nit	ˈlæmənɪt
laminate (v)	LA muh nayt	ˈlæmənet
Lammas	LA muhs	ˈlæməs
Lamont	luh MAHNT	ləˈmɑnt
Lampedusa	lahm pe DOO : zah	lɑmpɛˈduzɑ
lampoon	lam POO : N	læmˈpun
lamprey	LAM pri	ˈlæmprɪ
Lamy	LAY mi	ˈlemɪ
lanai, L-	lah NAH ee	lɑˈnɑi
Lanark	LA nerk	ˈlænərk

sing [ŋ]; *oh* [o]; *oil* [ɔɪ]; *foot* [ʊ]; *foo*:d [u]; ho*w* [aʊ]; *p*ie [p]; *r*ay [r]; *s*o [s]; *sh*all [ʃ];
*t*o [t]; *th*in [θ]; *th*:en [ð]; above (*uh* BUHV) [ə, ˈʌ]; *v*ine [v]; *w*ine [w]; *wh*ine [hw];
*y*ou [j]; *z*oo [z]; rouge (roo:*zh*) [ʒ].

Lancashire	LANG kuh shir	ˈlæŋkəʃɪr
Lancaster	LANG kuh ster	ˈlæŋkəstər
Lancastrian	lang KA stri uhn	læŋˈkæstrɪən
lance	lans	læns
Lancelot	LAN suh luht	ˈlænsələt
lancet	LAN sit	ˈlænsɪt
Lanchester, Elsa	LAN che ster, EL suh	ˈlæntʃestər, ˈɛlsə
Lanchow	lahn choh	lɑn tʃo
landau	LAN daw	ˈlændɔ
länderrat	LEN de raht	ˈlɛndɛrɑt
Ländler	LENT ler	ˈlɛntlər
Landowska, Wanda	lahn DAWF skah, WAHN dah	lɑnˈdɔfskɑ, ˈwɑndɑ
Landsteiner	LAND stigh ner	ˈlændstaɪnər
Landsturm	LAHNT shtoorm	ˈlɑntʃturm
Landwehr	LAHNT vair	ˈlɑntvɛr
Lang	lang	læŋ
Lange (North European)	LAHNG uh	ˈlɑŋə
Langer	LANG er	ˈlæŋər
Langland	LANG luhnd	ˈlæŋlənd
Langley	LANG li	ˈlæŋlɪ
Langmuir	LANG myoor	ˈlæŋmjʊr
Langtry	LANG tri	ˈlæŋtrɪ
language	LANG gwij	ˈlæŋgwɪdʒ
langue d'oc, Languedoc	lahng DAWK	lɑnˈdɔk
langue d'oïl	lahng daw EEL	lɑndɔˈil
languid	LANG gwid	ˈlæŋgwɪd
languish	LANG gwish	ˈlæŋgwɪʃ
languor	LANG ger	ˈlæŋgər
Lanier	luh NIR	ləˈnɪr
Lao	LAH oh	ˈlɑo
Laoag	lah WAHG	lɑˈwɑg
Laocoön	lay AH koh ahn	leˈɑkoɑn
Laodamia	lay oh duh MIGH uh	leodəˈmaɪə
Laodicea	lay uh duh SEE uh	leədəˈsiə
Laodicean	lay uh duh SEE uhn	leədəˈsiən
Laomedon	lay AH muh dahn	leˈɑmədɑn
Laos	LAH ohs	ˈlaos
Laotse	lowd zuh	laud zʌ
La Paz	lah PAHS	lɑ ˈpɑs
lapel	luh PEL	ləˈpɛl
lapis lazuli	LA pis LAZ yoo ligh	ˈlæpɪs ˈlæzjʊlaɪ
Lapland	LAP land	ˈlæplænd
La Plata	lah PLAH tah	lɑ ˈplɑtɑ
Lapp	lap	læp
lapsus linguae	LAP suhs LING gwee	ˈlæpsəs ˈlɪŋgwi
lapsus memoriae	LAP suhs me MOH ri ee	ˈlæpsəs mɛˈmorɪi
Laputa	luh PYOO: tuh	ləˈpjutə
Laramie	LA ruh mi	ˈlærəmɪ
larboard	LAHR berd	ˈlɑrbərd
larcenous	LAHR suh nuhs	ˈlɑrsənəs

at [æ] ; *ah* [ɑ] ; *air* [ɛ] ; *aw*ful [ɔ] ; *say* [e] ; *b*ack [b] ; *ch*air [tʃ] ; *d*o [d] ; *e*lm [ɛ] ; *ee*l [i] ; *server* [ˈɝ, ər] ; *f*it [f] ; *g*o [g] ; *h*urt [h] ; *is* [ɪ] ; *high* [aɪ] ; *j*et [dʒ] ; *k*iss [k] ; *l*amb [l] ; *my* [m] ; *n*ice [n] ;

larceny	LAHR suh ni	ˈlɑrsənɪ
lard	lahrd	lɑrd
Lardner	LAHRD ner	ˈlɑrdnər
lardon	LAHR duhn	ˈlɑrdən
Laredo	luh RAY doh	ləˈredo
Lares	LAI reez	ˈlɛriz
largando	lahr GAHN daw	lɑrˈgɑndɔ
largess, -e	LAHR jis	ˈlɑrdʒɪs
larghetto	lahr GE taw	lɑrˈgɛtɔ
largo	LAHR goh	ˈlɑrgo
lariat	LA ri uht	ˈlærɪət
Larousse	la ROO : S	læˈrus
Larvik	LAHR veek	ˈlɑrvik
laryngal	luh RING guhl	ləˈrɪŋgəl
laryngeal	luh RIN ji uhl	ləˈrɪndʒɪəl
laryngitis	la rin JIGH tis	lærɪnˈdʒaɪtɪs
laryngology	la ring GAH luh ji	lærɪŋˈgɑlədʒɪ
laryngotomy	la ring GAH tuh mi	lærɪŋˈgɑtəmɪ
larynx	LA ringks	ˈlærɪŋks
lasagna	lah ZAH nyuh	lɑˈzɑnjə
La Salle	luh SAL	lə ˈsæl
La Scala	lah SKAH lah	lɑ ˈskɑlɑ
lascivious	luh SI vi uhs	ləˈsɪvɪəs
Lashio	LAHSH yoh	ˈlɑʃjo
Laski	LA ski	ˈlæskɪ
La Spezia	lah SPET syah	lɑ ˈspɛtsjɑ
lass	las	læs
Lassen	LA suhn	ˈlæsən
lassie	LA si	ˈlæsɪ
lasso	LA soh	ˈlæso
last	last	læst
lastex, L-	LA steks	ˈlæstɛks
Las Vegas	lahs VAY guhs	lɑs ˈvegəs
Latakia	lah tah KEE ah	lɑtɑˈkiɑ
lateen	la TEEN	læˈtin
latent	LAY tuhnt	ˈletənt
Lateran	LA tuh ruhn	ˈlætərən
latex	LAY teks	ˈletɛks
lath	lath	læθ
lathe	layth :	leð
lather	LA th : er	ˈlæðər
Latimer	LA tuh mer	ˈlætəmər
Latium	LAY shi uhm	ˈleʃɪəm
Latona	luh TOH nuh	ləˈtonə
Latourette	la too RET	lætuˈrɛt
Latvia	LAT vi uh	ˈlætvɪə
laud, L-	lawd	lɔd
laudanum	LAW duh nuhm	ˈlɔdənəm
Lauder	LAW der	ˈlɔdər
laugh	laf	læf
laughter	LAF ter	ˈlæftər
Laughton	LAW tuhn	ˈlɔtən

sing [ŋ] ; *oh* [o] ; *oil* [ɔɪ] ; *foot* [ʊ] ; *foo :* d [u] ; *how* [aʊ] ; *pie* [p] ; *ray* [r] ; *so* [s] ; *sh*all [ʃ] ;
to [t] ; *thin* [θ] ; *th :* en [ð] ; above (*uh* B*UH*V) [ə, ˈʌ] ; *v*ine [v] ; *w*ine [w] ; *wh*ine [hw] ;
*y*ou [j] ; *z*oo [z] ; rouge (roo :*zh*) [ʒ].

launch	lawnch	lɔntʃ
launder	LAWN der	ˈlɔndər
laundry	LAWN dri	ˈlɔndrɪ
laurel	LAW ruhl	ˈlɔrəl
Laurel, José	low REL, haw SAY	lauˈrɛl, hɔˈse
Laurencin	loh rahn SAN	lorɑnˈsæn
Laurentian	law REN shi uhn	lɔˈrɛnʃɪən
Laurents	LAW rents	ˈlɔrɛnts
Laurie	LAW ri	ˈlɔrɪ
Lausanne	loh ZAN	loˈzæn
lava	LAH vuh	ˈlɑvə
Laval	luh VAL	ləˈvæl
lavalier, -e	la vuh LIR	lævəˈlɪr
lavatory	LA vuh taw ri	ˈlævətɔrɪ
Lavoisier	la vwa ZYAY	lævwæˈzje
law	law	lɔ
lawyer	LAW yer	ˈlɔjər
Layamon	LAY uh muhn	ˈleəmən
layette	lay ET	leˈɛt
lazar	LAY zer	ˈlezər
Lazarus	LA zuh ruhs	ˈlæzərəs
Lazear	luh ZIR	ləˈzɪr
lazzarone	la zuh ROH nay	læzəˈrone
Le, Kong	lee, kawng	li, kɔŋ
lea, L-	lee	li
Leacock	LEE kahk	ˈlikɑk
league	leeg	lig
Leah	LEE uh	ˈliə
Leahy	LAY hi	ˈlehɪ
Leander	li AN der	lɪˈændər
Lear	lir	lɪr
learned (a)	LER nid	ˈlɜnɪd
leash	leesh	liʃ
Leavenworth	LE vuhn werth	ˈlɛvənwərθ
Leavis	LEV is	ˈlɛvɪs
Lebanese	LE buh neez	ˈlɛbəniz
Lebanon	LE buh nuhn	ˈlɛbənən
Lebensraum	LAY buhns rowm	ˈlebənsraum
Lebrija	le BREE hah	lɛˈbrihɑ
Lebrun	luh BRERN	ləˈbrɜn
lecher	LE cher	ˈlɛtʃər
Leconte	luh KOHNT	ləˈkont
Le Corbusier	luh kawr boo ZYAY	lə kɔrbuˈzje
lectern	LEK tern	ˈlɛktərn
lecture	LEK cher	ˈlɛktʃər
Leczyca	lan CHIT sah	lænˈtʃɪtsɑ
Leda	LEE duh	ˈlidə
Lederle	LAY der lee	ˈledərli
leek	leek	lik
Leeuwenhoek	LAY vuhn hoo:k	ˈlevənhuk
leeward, L-	LEE werd	ˈliwərd
leeward (nautical)	LOO: erd	ˈluərd

at [æ]; ah [ɑ]; air [ɛ]; awful [ɔ]; say [e]; back [b]; chair [tʃ]; do [d]; elm [ɛ]; eel [i]; server [ˈɜ, ər]; fit [f]; go [g]; hurt [h]; is [ɪ]; high [aɪ]; jet [dʒ]; kiss [k]; lamb [l]; my [m]; nice [n];

Lefevre (French)	luh FEV ruh	lə'fɛvrə
Lefevre, Le Fevre (U.S.)	luh FEE ver	lə 'fi vər
legacy	LE guh si	'lɛgəsɪ
Le Gallienne	luh GAL yuhn	lə 'gæljən
legate	LE git	'lɛgɪt
legatee	LE guh tee	'lɛgəti
legend	LE juhnd	'lɛdʒənd
legendary	LE juhn dai ri	'lɛdʒəndɛrɪ
Léger	lay ZHAY	le'ʒe
legerdemain	le jer di MAYN	lɛdʒərdɪ'men
leghorn, L-	LE gern	'lɛgərn
Leghorn (Italy)	LEG hawrn	'lɛghɔrn
legible	LE juh buhl	'lɛdʒəbəl
legionnaire	lee juhn AIR	lidʒən'ɛr
legislature	LE ji slay cher	'lɛdʒɪsletʃər
Legree	li GREE	lɪ'gri
legume	LEG yoo : m	'lɛgjum
Lehár	LAY hahr	'lehɑr
Le Havre	luh HAH ver	lə 'hɑvər
Lehman, Herbert	LEE muhn	'limən
Lehman, -n	LAY muhn	'lemən
lehua	lay HOO : ah	le'huɑ
lei	LAY i	'leɪ
Leibnitz	LIGHB nits	'laɪbnɪts
Leibowitz	LEE buh wits	'libəwɪts
Leica	LIGH kuh	'laɪkə
Leicester	LE ster	'lɛstər
Leiden	LIGH duhn	'laɪdən
Leif	leef	lif
Leigh	lee	li
Leinsdorf	LIGHNZ dawrf	'laɪnzdɔrf
Leinster	LEN ster	'lɛnstər
Leipzig	LIGHP sig	'laɪpsɪg
leisure	LEE zher	'liʒər
Leith	leeth	liθ
leitmotif, leitmotiv	LIGHT moh teef	'laɪtmotif
Lely	LEE li	'lilɪ
leman	LE muhn	'lɛmən
Leman	LEE muhn	'limən
lemming	LE ming	'lɛmɪŋ
Lemnitzer	LEM nit ser	'lɛmnɪtsər
Lemnos	LEM nahs	'lɛmnɑs
Lemoyne	luh MOIN	lə'mɔɪn
Lemuel	LEM yoo uhl	'lɛmjʊəl
lemur	LEE mer	'limər
Lemuria	li MYOO ri uh	lɪ'mjʊrɪə
Lena (river)	LYE nah	'ljɛnɑ
L'Enfant	LAHN fahnt	'lɑnfɑnt
length	length	lɛŋθ
leniency	LEE ni uhn si	'linɪənsɪ
lenient	LEE ni uhnt	'linɪənt

sing [ŋ] ; *oh* [o] ; *oil* [ɔɪ] ; *foot* [ʊ] ; *foo:d* [u] ; *how* [aʊ] ; *pie* [p] ; *ray* [r] ; *so* [s] ; *shall* [ʃ] ;
to [t] ; *thin* [θ] ; *th:en* [ð] ; *above (uh BUHV)* [ə, 'ʌ] ; *vine* [v] ; *wine* [w] ; *whine* [hw] ;
you [j] ; *zoo* [z] ; *rouge (roo:zh)* [ʒ].

Lenin	LE nin	ˈlɛnɪn
Leningrad	LE nin grad	ˈlɛnɪngræd
lenis	LEE nis	ˈlinɪs
lenity	LE nuh ti	ˈlɛnətɪ
lens	lenz	lɛnz
lento	LEN toh	ˈlɛnto
Lenya, Lotte	LAY nyuh, LAH tuh	ˈlɛnjə, ˈlɑtə
Leo	LEE oh	ˈlio
Leonard	LE nerd	ˈlɛnərd
Leonardo	lay oh NAHR doh	leoˈnardo
Leoncavallo	lay awn kah VAH loh	leɔnkaˈvɑlo
Leonid	LEE uh nid	ˈliənɪd
Leonidas	lee AH nuh duhs	liˈɑnədəs
Leopardi	lay aw PAHR di	leɔˈpɑrdɪ
Léopoldville	LEE uh pohld vil	ˈliəpoldvɪl
leotard	LEE uh tahrd	ˈliətɑrd
Lepanto	li PAN toh	lɪˈpænto
Lepidus	LE pi duhs	ˈlɛpɪdəs
Lepontine	li PAHN tin	lɪˈpɑntɪn
leprechaun	LE pruh kawn	ˈlɛprəkɔn
leprosarium	le pruh SAI ri uhm	lɛprəˈsɛrɪəm
leprosy	LE pruh si	ˈlɛprəsɪ
Lepus	LEE puhs	ˈlipəs
Lequerica, José Félix de	lay kay REE kah, ho ZAY FAY leeks day	lekeˈrika, hoˈze ˈfeliks de
Lermontov	LYAIR mahn tawf	ˈljɛrmɑntɔf
Leschetizky	le she TIT ski	lɛʃɛˈtɪtskɪ
lese majesty	LEEZ MA ji sti	ˈliz ˈmædʒɪstɪ
lesion	LEE zhen	ˈliʒən
Leslie (American)	LES li	ˈlɛslɪ
Leslie (British)	LEZ li	ˈlɛzlɪ
Lesseps	LE suhps	ˈlɛsəps
Le Sueur	luh SOOR	lə ˈsur
lethal	LEE thuhl	ˈliθəl
lethargic	li THAHR jik	lɪˈθɑrdʒɪk
lethargy	LE ther ji	ˈlɛθərdʒɪ
Lethe	LEE thi	ˈliθɪ
leucocyte	LOO: kuh sight	ˈlukəsaɪt
leukemia, leukaemia	loo: KEE mi uh	luˈkimɪə
Levant	luh VANT	ləˈvænt
Levantine	luh VAN tin	ləˈvæntɪn
levee	LE vi	ˈlɛvɪ
lever	LE ver	ˈlɛvər
leverage	LE vuh rij	ˈlɛvərɪdʒ
Levi	LEE vigh	ˈlivaɪ
leviathan, L-	luh VIGH uh thuhn	ləˈvaɪəθən
Levice	LE vit se	ˈlɛvɪtsɛ
Levin, Meyer	LEV in, MIGH uhr	ˈlɛvɪn, ˈmaɪər
Levine	luh VEEN	ləˈvin
Levit, -t	LE vit	ˈlɛvɪt
Leviticus	luh VI ti kuhs	ləˈvɪtɪkəs
levy	LE vi	ˈlɛvɪ

---

at [æ]; *ah* [ɑ]; *air* [ɛ]; *awful* [ɔ]; *say* [e]; *back* [b]; *chair* [tʃ]; *do* [d]; *elm* [ɛ]; *eel* [i];
server [ˈɚ, ər]; *f*it [f]; *go* [g]; *hurt* [h]; *is* [ɪ]; *high* [aɪ]; *jet* [dʒ]; *kiss* [k]; *lamb* [l]; *my* [m];
nice [n];

Levy	LEE vi	ˈliːvɪ
Lewisohn	LOO : i zuhn	ˈluːɪzən
lexicography	lek suh KAH gruh fi	lɛksəˈkɑgrəfɪ
lexicon	LEK si kuhn	ˈlɛksɪkən
Ley, Willy	lay, WI lee	le, ˈwɪli
Leyden	LIGH duhn	ˈlaɪdən
Leyte	LAY te	ˈleteɛ
Lhasa	LAH suh	ˈlɑsə
Lhevinne	lay VEEN	leˈvin
liability	ligh uh BI luh ti	laɪəˈbɪlətɪ
liable	LIGH uh buhl	ˈlaɪəbəl
liaison	LEE uh zahn	ˈliəzɑn
Liao	lyow	ljaʊ
libation	ligh BAY shuhn	laɪˈbeʃən
Libby	LI bi	ˈlɪbɪ
libelous, libellous	LIGH buh luhs	ˈlaɪbələs
Liberia	ligh BI ri uh	laɪˈbɪrɪə
libertine	LI ber teen	ˈlɪbərtin
libidinous	li BI duh nuhs	lɪˈbɪdənəs
libra, L-	LIGH bruh	ˈlaɪbrə
librarian	ligh BRAI ri uhn	laɪˈbrɛrɪən
library	LIGH bre ri	ˈlaɪbrɛrɪ
libration	ligh BRAY shuhn	laɪˈbreʃən
librettist	li BRE tist	lɪˈbrɛtɪst
libretto	li BRE toh	lɪˈbrɛto
Libya	LI bi uh	ˈlɪbɪə
Libyan	LI bi uhn	ˈlɪbɪən
licentiate	ligh SEN shi it	laɪˈsɛnʃɪɪt
licentious	ligh SEN shuhs	laɪˈsɛnʃəs
licet	LIGH set	ˈlaɪsɛt
lichee	LEE chee	ˈlitʃi
lichen	LIGH kuhn	ˈlaɪkən
licorice	LI kuh ris	ˈlɪkərɪs
Lidice	LI duh si	ˈlɪdəsɪ
Lido	LEE doh	ˈlido
Lie, Trygve	LEE, TRIG vuh	ˈli, ˈtrɪgvə
Liebknecht	LEEP nekt	ˈlipnɛkt
Liechtenstein	LIK tuhn stighn	ˈlɪktənstaɪn
lied (" song ")	leed	lid
lieder (pl. of *lied*)	LEE der	ˈlidər
lief, L-	leef	lif
liege	leej	lidʒ
Liège	li AYZH	liˈeʒ
lien	leen	lin
lieu	loo :	lu
lieutenant	loo : TE nuhnt	luˈtɛnənt
lieutenant (British army)	lef TE nuhnt	lɛfˈtɛnənt
ligament	LI guh muhnt	ˈlɪgəmənt
ligature	LI guh cher	ˈlɪgətʃər
lightning	LIGHT ning	ˈlaɪtnɪŋ
ligneous	LIG ni uhs	ˈlɪgnɪəs

sing [ŋ] ; *oh* [o] ; *oil* [ɔɪ] ; *foot* [ʊ] ; *foo*:d [u] ; *how* [aʊ] ; *pie* [p] ; *ray* [r] ; *so* [s] ; *shall* [ʃ] ; *to* [t] ; *thin* [θ] ; *th:*en [ð] ; *above* (*uh* B*UH*V) [ə, ˈʌ] ; *vine* [v] ; *wine* [w] ; *whine* [hw] ; *you* [j] ; *zoo* [z] ; *rouge* (roo:*zh*) [ʒ].

lignite	LIG night	ˈlɪgnaɪt
Ligurian	li GYOO ri uhn	lɪˈgjʊrɪən
lilac	LIGH luhk	ˈlaɪlək
Lilienthal	LI lyuhn thahl	ˈlɪljənθɑl
Lilith	LI lith	ˈlɪlɪθ
Liliuokalani	li LEE oo : oh kah LAH ni	lɪˈliuokɑˈlɑnɪ
Lille	leel	lil
Lilliput	LI luh puht	ˈlɪləpət
Lilliputian	li luh PYOO : shuhn	lɪləˈpjuʃən
Lima (Ohio)	LIGH muh	ˈlaɪmə
Lima (Peru)	LEE muh	ˈlimə
limbo	LIM boh	ˈlɪmbo
Limbourg, Limburg	LIM berg	ˈlɪmbərg
limen	LIGH men	ˈlaɪmɛn
limn	lim	lɪm
Limoges	li MOHZH	lɪˈmoʒ
Limon, José	lee MOHN, hoh ZAY	liˈmon, hoˈze
limousine	LI muh zeen	ˈlɪməzin
Limpopo	lim POH poh	lɪmˈpopo
linage	LIGH nij	ˈlaɪnɪdʒ
Lincoln	LING kuhn	ˈlɪŋkən
Lindbergh	LIND berg	ˈlɪndbərg
lineage (" family ")	LI ni ij	ˈlɪnɪɪdʒ
lineament	LI ni uh muhnt	ˈlɪnɪəmənt
linear	LI ni er	ˈlɪnɪər
Lingayen	ling gah YEN	lɪŋgɑˈjɛn
lingerie	LAHN zhuh ree	ˈlɑnʒəri
lingua	LING gwuh	ˈlɪŋgwə
Linguaphone	LING gwuh fohn	ˈlɪŋgwəfon
linguistic	ling GWI stik	lɪŋˈgwɪstɪk
Linley	LIN lee	ˈlɪnli
Linlithgow	lin LITH goh	lɪnˈlɪθgo
Linnaean, Linnean	li NEE uhn	lɪˈnɪən
Linnaeus	li NEE uhs	lɪˈnɪəs
linotype	LIGH nuh tighp	ˈlaɪnətaɪp
lintel	LIN tuhl	ˈlɪntəl
Linton	LIN tuhn	ˈlɪntən
Lin Yutang	LIN yoo : TANG	ˈlɪn juˈtæŋ
Linz	lints	lɪnts
Lipari	LI puh ri	ˈlɪpərɪ
Lipatti, Dinu	li PAH tee, DEE noo :	lɪˈpɑti, ˈdinu
Li Po	lee poh	li po
Lippe	LI puh	ˈlɪpə
Lippi	LI pi	ˈlɪpɪ
Lippmann	LIP muhn	ˈlɪpmən
liqueur	li KER	lɪˈkɝ
liquidity	li KWI duh ti	lɪˈkwɪdətɪ
liquor	LI ker	ˈlɪkər
lira	LI ruh	ˈlɪrə
lire	LI ray	ˈlɪre
Lisbon	LIZ buhn	ˈlɪzbən
Lisle, l-	lighl	laɪl

at [æ] ; ah [ɑ] ; air [ɛ] ; awful [ɔ] ; say [e] ; back [b] ; chair [tʃ] ; do [d] ; elm [ɛ] ; eel [i] ; server [ˈɝ, ər] ; fit [f] ; go [g] ; hurt [h] ; is [ɪ] ; high [aɪ] ; jet [dʒ] ; kiss [k] ; lamb [l] ; my [m] ; nice [n] ;

lissom, -e	LI suhm	ˈlɪsəm
Liszt	list	lɪst
litany, L-	LI tuh ni	ˈlɪtənɪ
litchi	LEE chee	ˈlitʃi
literary	LI tuh rai ri	ˈlɪtərɛrɪ
literate	LI tuh rit	ˈlɪtərɪt
literati	li tuh RAY tigh	lɪtəˈretaɪ
literature	LI tuh ruh cher	ˈlɪtərətʃər
lithe	lighth :	laɪð
lithograph	LI thuh graf	ˈlɪθəgræf
lithography	li THAH gruh fi	lɪˈθagrəfɪ
lithotomy	li THAH tuh mi	lɪˈθatəmɪ
Lithuania	li thoo WAY ni uh	lɪθuˈwenɪə
litigant	LI tuh guhnt	ˈlɪtəgənt
litigious	li TI juhs	lɪˈtɪdʒəs
litotes	LIGH tuh teez	ˈlaɪtətiz
littérateur	li tuh ruh TER	lɪtərəˈtɝ
littoral	LI tuh ruhl	ˈlɪtərəl
liturgical	li TER ji kuhl	lɪˈtɝdʒɪkəl
liturgy	LI ter ji	ˈlɪtərdʒɪ
Litvinov	lit VEE nawf	lɪtˈvinɔf
livelong	LIV lawng	ˈlɪvlɔŋ
liver	LI ver	ˈlɪvər
Liverpudlian	li ver PUHD li uhn	lɪvərˈpʌdlɪən
liverwort	LI ver wert	ˈlɪvərwɝt
liverwurst	LI ver werst	ˈlɪvərwɝst
livery	LI vuh ri	ˈlɪvərɪ
livid	LI vid	ˈlɪvɪd
Livonia	li VOH ni uh	lɪˈvonɪə
Livorno	li VAWR naw	lɪˈvɔrnɔ
Livy	LI vi	ˈlɪvɪ
lixiviate	lik SI vi ayt	lɪkˈsɪvɪet
Ljubljana	lyoo : BLYAH nah	ljuˈbljana
llama	LAH muh	ˈlamə
Llanelly	lan E li	lænˈɛlɪ
Llanera	lyah NAY rah	ljaˈnera
Llewellyn	loo E lin	luˈɛlɪn
loach	lohch	lotʃ
Loanda	law AHN duh	lɔˈandə
loath	lohth	loθ
loathe	lohth :	loð
lobar	LOH ber	ˈlobər
lobe	lohb	lob
lobectomy	loh BEK tuh mi	loˈbɛktəmɪ
lobelia	loh BEE li uh	loˈbilɪə
loblolly	LAHB lah li	ˈlablalɪ
lobo	LOH boh	ˈlobo
lobotomy	loh BAH tuh mi	loˈbatəmɪ
Locarno	loh KAHR noh	loˈkarno
locative	LAH kuh tiv	ˈlakətɪv
loch, L-	lahk	lak
Lochinvar	lah kin VAHR	lakɪnˈvar

sing [ŋ] ; oh [o] ; oil [ɔɪ] ; foot [ʊ] ; foo :d [u] ; how [aʊ] ; pie [p] ; ray [r] ; so [s] ; shall [ʃ] ; to [t] ; thin [θ] ; th :en [ð] ; above (uh BUHV) [ə, ˈʌ] ; vine [v] ; wine [w] ; whine [hw] ; you [j] ; zoo [z] ; rouge (roo :zh) [ʒ].

Locke	lahk	lɑk
loco	LOH koh	ˈloko
locofoco	LOH koh FOH koh	ˈlokoˈfoko
locus	LOH kuhs	ˈlokəs
locution	loh KYOO : shuhn	loˈkjuʃən
Lodge, l-	lahj	lɑdʒ
Lodi	LAW dee	ˈlɔdi
Lodz	lahdz	lɑdz
Loeffler	LE fler	ˈlɛflər
Loesser	LE ser	ˈlɛsər
Loewe	loh	lo
Loewy	Loh i	ˈloɪ
Lofoten	LOH foo tuhn	ˈlofʊtən
Logan	LOH guhn	ˈlogən
logarithm	LAW guh ri th : uhm	ˈlɔgərɪðəm
loge	lohzh	loʒ
loggia	LOH juh	ˈlodʒə
logia	LAH gi uh	ˈlɑgɪə
logic	LAH jik	ˈlɑdʒɪk
logistic	luh JI stik	ləˈdʒɪstɪk
logomachy	loh GAH muh ki	loˈgɑməkɪ
logomania	lah guh MAY ni uh	lɑgəˈmenɪə
logos, L-	LAH gahs	ˈlɑgɑs
logy	LOH gi	ˈlogɪ
Lohengrin	LOH uhn grin	ˈloəngrɪn
Loire	lwahr	lwɑr
Loki	LOH ki	ˈlokɪ
Lola	LOH luh	ˈlolə
loll	lahl	lɑl
Lollard	LAH lerd	ˈlɑlərd
Lollobrigida, Gina	law law BREE zhee dah, ZHEE nah	lɔlɔˈbriʒidɑ, ʒinɑ
Lombard	LAHM berd	ˈlɑmbərd
Lombardy	LAHM ber di	ˈlɑmbərdɪ
Lombrosian	lahm BROH zi uhn	lɑmˈbrozɪən
Lomé	loh MAY	loˈme
Lomond	LOH muhnd	ˈlomənd
London	LUHN duhn	ˈlʌndən
longevity	lahn JE vuh ti	lɑnˈdʒɛvətɪ
Longines-Wittnauer	LAWNG jeen WIT now er	ˈlɔŋdʒin ˈwɪtnaʊər
Longinus	lahn JIGH nuhs	lɑnˈdʒaɪnəs
longitude	LAHN juh too : d	ˈlɑndʒətud
long-lived	lawng lighvd	lɔŋ laɪvd
Longobardi	lahng guh BAHR di	lɑŋɡəˈbɑrdɪ
López	LOH pez	ˈlopɛz
loquacious	loh KWAY shuhs	loˈkweʃəs
loquacity	loh KWA suh ti	loˈkwæsətɪ
Lorain	luh RAYN	ləˈren
loran, L-	LOH ran	ˈloræn
Lorca	LAWR kah	ˈlɔrka
lordosis	lawr DOH sis	lɔrˈdosɪs
Lorelei	LAW ruh ligh	ˈlɔrəlaɪ

at [æ] ; ah [ɑ] ; air [ɛ] ; awful [ɔ] ; say [e] ; back [b] ; chair [tʃ] ; do [d] ; elm [ɛ] ; eel [i] ; server [ˈɝ, ər] ; fit [f] ; go [g] ; hurt [h] ; is [ɪ] ; high [aɪ] ; jet [dʒ] ; kiss [k] ; lamb [l] ; my [m] ; nice [n] ;

lorgnette	lawr NYET	lɔrˈnjɛt
lorica	loh RIGH kuh	loˈraɪkə
Lorica	law REE kuh	lɔˈrikə
Lorre	LAW ree	ˈlɔri
lorry	LAW ri	ˈlɔrɪ
Los Alamos	laws A luh mohs	lɔs ˈæləmos
Los Angeles	lahs AN juh luhs	lɑs ˈændʒələs
L'Osservatore Romano	loh ser vah TAW re roh MAH noh	losərvaˈtɔre roˈmano
Lothario	loh THAI ri oh	loˈθerɪo
Lothian	LOH th:i uhn	ˈloðɪən
Loti	law TEE	lɔˈti
lough	lahk	lɑk
Louis (English)	LOO: is	ˈluɪs
Louis (French)	lwee	lwi
Louisiana	loo i zi A nuh	luɪzɪˈænə
lour	lowr	laʊr
Lourdes	loord	lʊrd
Lourenço Marques	loh REN soh MAHR kes	loˈrɛnso ˈmarkɛs
Louvain	loo: VAYN	luˈven
louver	LOO: ver	ˈluvər
Louvre	LOO: vruh	ˈluvrə
Lowell	LOH uhl	ˈloəl
lower (" scowl ")	LOW er	ˈlaʊər
Lowestoft	LOHS tahft	ˈlostɑft
lox	lahks	lɑks
loxodromic	lahk suh DRAH mik	lɑksəˈdrɑmɪk
lozenge	LAH zinj	ˈlɑzɪndʒ
Luanda	loo: AHN duh	luˈɑndə
Luang Prabang	loo: AHNG prah BAHNG	luˈaŋ prɑˈbaŋ
Lubang	loo: BAHNG	luˈbaŋ
lube	loo:b	lub
Lübeck	LOO: bek	ˈlubɛk
Lublin	LOO: blin	ˈlublɪn
lubricity	loo: BRI suh ti	luˈbrɪsətɪ
Lucan	LOO: kuhn	ˈlukən
Lucania	loo: KAY ni uh	luˈkenɪə
Lucas	LOO: kuhs	ˈlukəs
luce, L-	loo:s	lus
Lucena	loo: THE nah	luˈθenɑ
Lucenec	LOO: che nets	ˈlutʃenɛts
Lucerne, l-	loo: SERN	luˈsɜn
Lucia (Italian)	loo: CHEE uh	luˈtʃiə
Lucian	LOO: shuhn	ˈluʃən
lucid	LOO: sid	ˈlusɪd
lucida	LOO: si duh	ˈlusɪdə
Lucifer, l-	LOO: suh fer	ˈlusəfər
lucite, L-	LOO: sight	ˈlusaɪt
Lucius	LOO: shuhs	ˈluʃəs
Lucknow	LUHK now	ˈlʌknaʊ
lucrative	LOO: kruh tiv	ˈlukrətɪv
lucre	LOO: ker	ˈlukər

sing [ŋ] ; *oh* [o] ; *oil* [ɔI] ; *foot* [ʊ] ; *foo:*d [u] ; *how* [aʊ] ; *p*ie [p] ; *r*ay [r] ; *s*o [s] ; *sh*all [ʃ] ; *t*o [t] ; *th*in [θ] ; *th:*en [ð] ; above (*uh* B*UH*V) [ə, ˈʌ] ; *v*ine [v] ; *w*ine [w] ; *wh*ine [hw] ; *y*ou [j] ; *z*oo [z] ; rouge (roo:*zh*) [ʒ].

H.P.—P

Lucrece	loo : KREES	luˈkris
Lucretius	loo : KREE shuhs	luˈkriʃəs
Lucrezia	loo : KRAYT si uh	luˈkretsɪə
Lucullan	loo : KUH luhn	luˈkʌlən
Lucullus	loo : KUH luhs	luˈkʌləs
Luddite	LUH dight	ˈlʌdaɪt
Ludendorff	LOO : duhn dawrf	ˈludəndɔrf
ludicrous	loo : di kruhs	ˈludɪkrəs
Ludwig	LUHD wig	ˈlʌdwɪg
lues	LOO : eez	ˈluiz
Luftwaffe	LOOFT vah fuh	ˈlʊftvɑfə
lugubrious	loo GOO : bri uhs	lʊˈgubrɪəs
Lukow	LOO koof	ˈlʊkʊf
Lully	loo LEE	lʊˈli
lumbago	luhm BAY goh	ləmˈbego
lumbar	LUHM ber	ˈlʌmbər
luminal, L-	LOO : muh nuhl	ˈlumənəl
luminescence	loo : muh NE suhns	luməˈnɛsəns
luminous	LOO : muh nuhs	ˈlumənəs
lummox	LUH muhks	ˈlʌməks
Lumumba, Patrice	loo MOOM buh, pa TREES	lʊˈmʊmbə, pæˈtris
Luna, l-	LOO : nuh	ˈlunə
lunar	LOO : ner	ˈlunər
lunarian	loo : NAI ri uhn	luˈnɛrɪən
lunation	loo : NAY shuhn	luˈneʃən
lunet, -te	loo : NET	luˈnɛt
lunik, L-	LOO : nik	ˈlunɪk
Lupercalia	loo : per KAY li uh	lupərˈkelɪə
Lupescu	loo : PE skoo	luˈpɛskʊ
lupine (plant)	LOO : pin	ˈlupɪn
lupine (" wolfish ")	LOO : pighn	ˈlupaɪn
lupus, L-	LOO : puhs	ˈlupəs
lure	loor	lʊr
lurid	LOO rid	ˈlʊrɪd
Lusitania	loo : si TAY ni uh	lusɪˈtenɪə
lustrous	LUH struhs	ˈlʌstrəs
lusus naturae	LOO : suhs nuh TYOO ree	ˈlusəs nəˈtjʊri
lutanist, lutenist	LOO : tuh nist	ˈlutənɪst
lute	loo : t	lut
Lutsk	loo : tsk	lutsk
lux, L-	luhks	lʌks
luxe	looks	lʊks
Luxembourg, Luxemburg	LUHK suhm berg	ˈlʌksəmbərg
Luxor	LUHK sawr	ˈlʌksɔr
luxuriance	luhg ZHOO ri uhns	ləgˈʒʊrɪəns
luxurious	luhg ZHOO ri uhs	ləgˈʒʊrɪəs
luxury	LUHK shuh ri	ˈlʌkʃərɪ
Luzon	loo : ZAHN	luˈzɑn
Lwów	luh VOO : F	ləˈvuf
lycanthropy	ligh KAN thruh pi	laɪˈkænθrəpɪ
Lycaon	ligh KAY uhn	laɪˈkeən
Lycaonia	li ki OH ni uh	lɪkɪˈonɪə

at [æ] ; ah [ɑ] ; air [ɛ] ; awful [ɔ] ; say [e] ; back [b] ; chair [tʃ] ; do [d] ; elm [ɛ] ; eel [i] ; server [ˈɝ, ər] ; fit [f] ; go [g] ; hurt [h] ; is [ɪ] ; high [aɪ] ; jet [dʒ] ; kiss [k] ; lamb [l] ; my [m] ; nice [n] ;

lycée	lee SAY	liˈse
lyceum	ligh SEE uhm	laɪˈsiəm
lych	lich	lɪtʃ
Lycian	LI shi uhn	ˈlɪʃɪən
Lycidas	LI suh duhs	ˈlɪsədəs
Lycurgus	ligh KER guhs	laɪˈkɝgəs
lyddite	LI dight	ˈlɪdaɪt
Lydgate	LID gayt	ˈlɪdget
Lyly	LI li	ˈlɪlɪ
lymph	limf	lɪmf
lymphocyte	LIM fuh sight	ˈlɪmfəsaɪt
lynx	lingks	lɪŋks
lyonnaise	ligh uh NAYZ	laɪəˈnez
Lyonnesse	ligh uh NES	laɪəˈnɛs
Lyra	LIGH ruh	ˈlaɪrə
lyre	lighr	laɪr
lyric	LI rik	ˈlɪrɪk
Lysander	ligh SAN der	laɪˈsændər
Lysenko	li SEN koh	lɪˈsɛnko
Lysistrata	ligh SI struh tuh	laɪˈsɪstrətə
lysol, L-	LIGH sahl	ˈlaɪsɑl
lyssophobia	li suh FOH bi uh	lɪsəˈfobɪə
Lystra	LI struh	ˈlɪstrə
Lytton	LI tuhn	ˈlɪtən

M

ma'am	mam	mæm
Maas	mahs	mɑs
Mabbott	MA buht	ˈmæbət
Mabinogion	ma buh NOH gi uhn	mæbəˈnogɪən
macabre, macaber	muh KAH ber	məˈkɑbər
macadam	muh KA duhm	məˈkædəm
McAdoo	MA kuh doo:	ˈmækədu
McAleer	MA kuh lir	ˈmækəlɪr
Macao	muh KOW	məˈkau
macaronic	ma kuh RAH nik	mækəˈrɑnɪk
MacArthur	muhk AHR ther	məkˈɑrθər
Macassar	muh KA ser	məˈkæsər
Macaulay	muh KAW li	məˈkɔlɪ
McAuliffe	muh KAW lif	məˈkɔlɪf
macaw	muh KAW	məˈkɔ
McBride	muhk BRIGHD	məkˈbraɪd
Maccabaeus, Maccabeus	ma kuh BEE uhs	mækəˈbiəs
Maccabees	MA kuh beez	ˈmækəbiz
McCarthy	muh KAHR thi	məˈkɑrθɪ
McCreery	muh KRAI ri	məˈkrɛrɪ
McCulloch	muh KUH luhk	məˈkʌlək

---

sing [ŋ] ; *oh* [o] ; *oil* [ɔɪ] ; *foot* [ʊ] ; *foo:*d [u] ; *how* [aʊ] ; *p*ie [p] ; *ray* [r] ; *so* [s] ; *sh*all [ʃ] ;
to [t] ; *th*in [θ] ; *th:*en [ð] ; *above* (*uh* B*U*H*V*) [ə, ˈʌ] ; *v*ine [v] ; *w*ine [w] ; *wh*ine [hw] ;
*y*ou [j] ; *z*oo [z] ; *rouge* (roo:*zh*) [ʒ].

MacCurdy	muh KER di	məˈkɚdɪ
McDougal, -l	muhk DOO : guhl	məkˈdugəl
MacDowell	muhk DOW uhl	məkˈdauəl
macédoine	ma say DWAHN	mæseˈdwɑn
Macedonia	ma suh DOH ni uh	mæsəˈdonɪə
maceration	ma suh RAY shuhn	mæsəˈreʃən
Macgillicuddy, MacG-	muh GI luh kuh di	məˈgɪləkʌdɪ
McGlinchee	muh GLIN chi	məˈglɪntʃɪ
McGuffey	muh GUH fi	məˈgʌfɪ
Mach, m-	mahk	mɑk
Machado	mah CHAH doh	mɑˈtʃɑdo
Machen, Arthur	MA kuhn	ˈmækən
ma chère	mah SHAIR	mɑ ˈʃɛr
ma chérie	mah shai REE	mɑ ʃɛˈri
machete	mah CHAY tay	mɑˈtʃete
Machiavelli	ma ki uh VE li	mækɪəˈvɛlɪ
machination	ma kuh NAY shuhn	mækəˈneʃən
machree	muh KREE	məˈkri
Maciejowice	mah che yaw VEET se	mɑtʃɛjɔˈvitsɛ
Mackinac	MA kuh naw	ˈmækənɔ
Mackinaw	MA kuh naw	ˈmækənɔ
MacLean, McLean	muh KLAYN	məˈklen
MacLeish	muhk LEESH	məkˈliʃ
Macleod, McLeod	muhk LOWD	məkˈlaud
McMahon Line	mik MAN lighn	mɪkˈmæn laɪn
MacMillan, Macmillan	muhk MI luhn	məkˈmɪlən
MacMonnies	muhk MAH niz	məkˈmɑnɪz
McNamara	mak nuh MA ruh	mæknəˈmærə
McNaughton	muhk NAW tuhn	məkˈnɔtən
Macon	MAY kuhn	ˈmekən
MacPherson	muhk FER suhn	məkˈfɚsən
macramé	MA kruh may	ˈmækrəme
Macris	MA kris	ˈmækrɪs
Macrobius	muh KROH bi uhs	məˈkrobɪəs
macrocosm	MA kruh kah zuhm	ˈmækrəkɑzəm
macron	MAY kruhn	ˈmekrən
macula	MA kyuh luh	ˈmækjələ
Macy	MAY see	ˈmesi
Madagascar	ma duh GA sker	mædəˈgæskər
madam	MA duhm	ˈmædəm
madame (French)	ma DAHM	mæˈdɑm
Madariaga	mah th : ah RYAH gah	mɑðɑˈrjɑgɑ
Madeira	muh DI ruh	məˈdɪrə
Madeleine	mad LEN	mædˈlɛn
mademoiselle	ma duh muh ZEL	mædəməˈzɛl
Madhya Bharat	MUHD hyuh BUH ruht	ˈmʌdhjə ˈbʌrət
Madhya Pradesh	MUHD hyuh PRAH desh	ˈmʌdhjə ˈprɑdɛʃ
madonna, M-	muh DAH nuh	məˈdɑnə
madras	MA druhs	ˈmædrəs
Madras	muh DRAS	məˈdræs
Madrid (Spain)	muh DRID	məˈdrɪd
madrigal	MA dri guhl	ˈmædrɪgəl

at [æ] ; ah [ɑ] ; air [ɛ] ; awful [ɔ] ; say [e] ; back [b] ; chair [tʃ] ; do [d] ; elm [ɛ] ; eel [i] ; server [ˈɚ, ər] ; fit [f] ; go [g] ; hurt [h] ; is [ɪ] ; high [aɪ] ; jet [dʒ] ; kiss [k] ; lamb [l] ; my [m] ; nice [n] ;

Madura (India)	MA joo ruh	'mædʒʊrə
Madura (Indonesia)	mah DOO : rah	mɑ'durɑ
Maecenas	mi SEE nuhs	mɪ'sinəs
maelstrom	MAYL struhm	'melstrəm
maenad	MEE nad	'minæd
maestoso	mah es TAW saw	mɑes'tɔsɔ
maestro	MIGH stroh	'maɪstro
Maeterlinck	MAY ter lingk	'metərlɪŋk
Mafeking	MAH fuh king	'mɑfəkɪŋ
maffia, mafia, M-	MAH fi ah	'mɑfɪɑ
Magallanes	mah gah YAH nes	mɑgɑ'jɑnɛs
magazine	MA guh zeen	'mægəzin
Magdalen (Oxford)	MAWD lin	'mɔdlɪn
Magdalena	mahg dah LE nah	mɑgdɑ'lɛnɑ
Magdalene, m-	MAG duh leen	'mægdəlin
Magdalene (Cambridge)	MAWD lin	'mɔdlɪn
mage	mayj	medʒ
Magellan	muh JE luhn	mə'dʒɛlən
Magellanic	ma juh LA nik	mædʒə'lænɪk
magenta	muh JEN tuh	mə'dʒɛntə
Maggiore	muh JAW ri	mə'dʒɔri
Magi	MAY jigh	'medʒaɪ
Magindanao	mah geen dah NAH oh	mɑgindɑ'nɑo
Maginot	MA zhuh noh	'mæʒəno
magistracy	MA ji struh si	'mædʒɪstrəsɪ
Magloire	mah GLWAHR	mɑ'glwɑr
magma	MAG muh	'mægmə
Magna Charta, -Carta	MAG nuh KAHR tuh	'mægnə 'kɑrtə
Magnani	mahn YAH nee	mɑn'jɑni
magnanimity	mag nuh NI muh ti	mægnə'nɪmətɪ
magnanimous	mag NA nuh muhs	mæg'nænəməs
magnate	MAG nit	'mægnɪt
Magnavox	MAG nuh vahks	'mægnəvɑks
magnesium	mag NEE shi uhm	mæg'niʃɪəm
magnet	MAG nit	'mægnɪt
magneto	mag NEE toh	mæg'nito
magnetometer	mag nuh TAH muh ter	mægnə'tɑmətər
magnetron	MAG nuh trahn	'mægnətrɑn
Magnificat, m-	mag NI fi kat	mæg'nɪfɪkæt
magnifico	mag NI fuh koh	mæg'nɪfəko
magniloquent	mag NI luh kwuhnt	mæg'nɪləkwənt
Magnin, I.	MAG nin	'mægnɪn
magnitude	MAG nuh too : d	'mægnətud
magnum	MAG nuhm	'mægnəm
magnum opus	MAG nuhm OH puhs	'mægnəm 'opəs
Magnus	MAG nuhs	'mægnəs
Magog	MAY gahg	'megɑg
Magus, m-	MAY guhs	'megəs
Magyar	MAG yahr	'mægjɑr
Magyarorszag	MAWD yahr awr sahg	'mɔdjɑrɔrsɑg
Mahabharata	muh HAH BAH ruh tuh	mə'hɑ'bɑrətə

sing [ŋ] ; oh [o] ; oil [ɔɪ] ; foot [ʊ] ; foo:d [u] ; how [aʊ] ; pie [p] ; ray [r] ; so [s] ; shall [ʃ] ; to [t] ; thin [θ] ; th:en [ð] ; above (uh BUHV) [ə, 'ʌ] ; vine [v] ; wine [w] ; whine [hw] ; you [j] ; zoo [z] ; rouge (roo:zh) [ʒ].

Mahan	muh HAN	mə¹hæn
maharaja, -h	mah huh RAH juh	mɑhə¹rɑdʒə
maharanee, maharani	mah huh RAH nee	mɑhə¹rɑni
mahatma, M-	muh HAT muh	mə¹hætmə
Mahdi	MAH di	¹mɑdɪ
mah jong, -g	mah jawng	mɑ dʒɔŋ
Mahler	MAH ler	¹mɑlər
mahout	muh HOWT	mə¹haʊt
Mahratti, Mahrati	muh RA ti	mə¹rætɪ
Maia	MAY yuh	¹mejə
Maidanek	MIGH duh nek	¹maɪdənɛk
maigre	MAY ger	¹megər
Maillol	ma YAWL	mæ¹jɔl
maillot	migh YOH	maɪ¹jo
maim	maym	mem
Maimonides	migh MAH nuh deez	maɪ¹mɑnədiz
Mainbocher	man boh SHAY	mænbo¹ʃe
mainsail (nautical)	MAYN suhl	¹mensəl
maintain	mayn TAYN	men¹ten
maintenance	MAYN tuh nuhns	¹mentənəns
Mainz	mighnts	maɪnts
maître d'hôtel	ME truh daw TEL	¹mɛtrə dɔ¹tɛl
majolica	muh JAH li kuh	mə¹dʒɑlɪkə
Majorca	muh JAWR kuh	mə¹dʒɔrkə
major-domo	MAY jer DOH moh	¹medʒər ¹domo
majuscule	muh JUH skyoo : l	mə¹dʒʌskjul
Makarios	mah KAH ri aws	mɑ¹kɑrɪos
Makhach Kala	mah HAHCH kah LAH	mɑ¹hɑtʃ kɑ¹lɑ
Malabar	MA luh bahr	¹mæləbɑr
Malacca	muh LA kuh	mə¹lækə
Malachi	MA luh kigh	¹mæləkaɪ
maladroit	MA luh droit	¹mælədrɔɪt
Málaga	MA luh guh	¹mæləgə
Malagasy	ma luh GA si	mælə¹gæsɪ
malagueña	ma luh GAY nyuh	mælə¹genjə
malaise	ma LAYZ	mə¹lez
malamute, malemute	MAH luh myoo : t	¹mɑləmjut
malapert	MA luh pert	¹mæləpərt
Malaprop	MA luh prahp	¹mæləprɑp
malapropism	MA luh prah pi zuhm	¹mæləprɑpɪzəm
malaria	muh LAI ri uh	mə¹lɛrɪə
malarkey, malarky	muh LAHR ki	mə¹lɑrkɪ
Malawi	mah LAH wee	mɑ¹lɑwi
Malay	MAY lay	¹mele
Malaya	muh LAY uh	mə¹leə
Malayalam	ma luh YAH luhm	mælə¹jɑləm
mal de mer	mal duh MAIR	mæl də ¹mɛr
Malden	MAWL duhn	¹mɔldən
Maldive	MAL dighv	¹mældaɪv
malediction	ma luh DIK shuhn	mælə¹dɪkʃən
malefactor	MA luh fak ter	¹mæləfæktər
Malenkov	MA len kawf	¹mælɛnkɔf

at [æ]; ah [ɑ]; air [ɛ]; awful [ɔ]; say [e]; back [b]; chair [tʃ]; do [d]; elm [ɛ]; eel [i]; server [¹ɝ, ər]; fit [f]; go [g]; hurt [h]; is [ɪ]; high [aɪ]; jet [dʒ]; kiss [k]; lamb [l]; my [m]; nice [n];

malevolent	muh LE vuh luhnt	mə'lɛvələnt
malfeasance	mal FEE zuhns	mæl'fizəns
Malherbe	ma LAIRB	mæ'lɛrb
Mali	MAH li	'malɪ
malign	muh LIGHN	mə'laɪn
malignant	muh LIG nuhnt	mə'lɪgnənt
Malik, Charles	MA lik	'mælɪk
Malik, Yakov	MAH lik, YAH kawf	'malɪk, 'jakɔf
maline, -s	muh LEEN	mə'lin
malinger	muh LING ger	mə'lɪŋgər
Malinovsky	mah li NAWF ski	malɪ'nɔfskɪ
Malinowski	mah li NAWF ski	malɪ'nɔfskɪ
malkin	MAW kin	'mɔkɪn
mall	mawl	mɔl
mallard	MA lerd	'mælərd
Mallarmé	ma lahr MAY	mælar'me
malleable	MA li uh buhl	'mælɪəbəl
Mallorca	mah LYAWR kah	ma'ljɔrka
Malmédy	mal me DEE	mælmɛ'di
Malmesbury	MAHMZ buh ri	'mamzbərɪ
Malmö	MAL moh	'mælmo
malmsey	MAHM zi	'mamzɪ
Malory	MA luh ri	'mælərɪ
Malraux	mal ROH	mæl'ro
Malta	MAWL tuh	'mɔltə
Malthus	MAL thuhs	'mælθəs
Malthusian	mal THOO : zhuhn	mæl'θu : ʒən
maltreat	mal TREET	mæl'trit
Malvern	MAL vern	'mælvərn
mamba	MAHM buh	'mambə
mambo	MAHM boh	'mambo
Mameluke, m-	MA muh loo : k	'mæməluk
mammary	MA muh ri	'mæmərɪ
Mammon, m-	MA muhn	'mæmən
Managua	mah NAH gwah	ma'nagwa
mañana	mah NYAH nah	ma'njana
Manassas	muh NA suhs	mə'næsəs
Manasseh	muh NA suh	mə'næsə
manatee	ma nuh TEE	mænə'ti
manavelins, manavilins	muh NA vuh linz	mə'nævəlɪnz
Manchukuo, Manchoukuo	man choo : KWOH	mæntʃu'kwo
Manchuria	man CHOO ri uh	mæn'tʃʊrɪə
Mancunian	man KYOO : ni uhn	mæn'kjunɪən
Mandalay	MAN duh lay	'mændəle
mandamus	man DAY muhs	mæn'deməs
mandarin, M-	MAN duh rin	'mændərɪn
mandate	MAN dayt	'mændet
mandatory	MAN duh taw ri	'mændətɔrɪ
Mandeville	MAN duh vil	'mændəvɪl
Mandingo	man DING goh	mæn'dɪŋgo
mandolin	MAN duh lin	'mændəlɪn

sing [ŋ] ; oh [o] ; oil [ɔi] ; foot [ʊ] ; foo:d [u] ; how [aʊ] ; pie [p] ; ray [r] ; so [s] ; shall [ʃ] ; to [t] ; thin [θ] ; th:en [ð] ; above (uh BUHV) [ə, 'ʌ] ; vine [v] ; wine [w] ; whine [hw] ; you [j] ; zoo [z] ; rouge (roo:zh) [ʒ].

manège	ma NEZH	mæˈnɛʒ
manes, M-	MAY neez	ˈmeniz
Manet	muh NAY	məˈne
maneuver	muh NOO : ver	məˈnuvər
manganese	MANG guh neez	ˈmæŋgəniz
mango	MANG goh	ˈmæŋgo
mania	MAY ni uh	ˈmenɪə
maniacal	muh NIGH uh kuhl	məˈnaɪəkəl
manifesto	ma nuh FE stoh	mænəˈfɛsto
manifold	MA nuh fohld	ˈmænəfold
Manila	muh NI luh	məˈnɪlə
Manipur	muh ni POOR	mənɪˈpʊr
Manitoba	ma nu TOH buh	mænəˈtobə
Mankiewicz	MEN kuh wits	ˈmɛnkəwɪts
mankind	MAN kighnd	ˈmænkaɪnd
Mann (Heinrich, Thomas)	mahn	mɑn
Mann (Horace)	man	mæn
mannequin	MA nuh kin	ˈmænəkɪn
Mannerheim	MA ner highm	ˈmænərhaɪm
Mannheim	MAN highm	ˈmænhaɪm
Manoah	muh NOH uh	məˈnoə
manoeuvre	muh NOO : ver	məˈnuvər
Manolete	mah noh LAY tay	mɑnoˈlete
Manon Lescaut	ma NAWN le SKOH	mæˈnɔn lɛˈsko
mansard	MAN sahrd	ˈmænsɑrd
mansuetude	MAN swi too : d	ˈmænswɪtud
manta	MAN tuh	ˈmæntə
manteau	MAN toh	ˈmænto
Mantegna	mahn TE nyah	mɑnˈtɛnjɑ
mantel, mantle, M-	MAN tuhl	ˈmæntəl
mantilla	mahn TEE yuh	mɑnˈtijə
Mantoux (test)	MAN too :	ˈmæntu
Mantua, m-	MAN choo uh	ˈmæntʃʊə
manumission	ma nyoo MI shuhn	mænjuˈmɪʃən
Manutius	muh NYOO : shi uhs	məˈnjuʃɪəs
Manx, m-	mangks	mæŋks
Manzanillo	mahn sah NEE yaw	mɑnsɑˈnijɔ
Manzoni	mahnd ZAW nee	mɑndˈzɔni
Maori	MAH oh ri	ˈmɑorɪ
Mao Tse-tung	MAH oh dzuh DOONG	ˈmao dzəˈdʊŋ
Mapai	mah PIGH	mɑˈpaɪ
maquillage	ma kee YAHZH	mækiˈjɑʒ
Maquis, m-	mah KEE	mɑˈki
marabou	MA ruh boo :	ˈmærəbu
maraca	muh RAH kuh	məˈrɑkə
Maracaibo	ma ruh KIGH boh	mærəˈkaɪbo
maraschino	ma ruh SKEE noh	mærəˈskino
Marasesti	muh ruh SHESHT	mərəˈʃɛʃt
Maratha	muh RAH tuh	məˈrɑtə
Marathi	muh RAH ti	məˈrɑtɪ
Marathon, m-	MA ruh thahn	ˈmærəθɑn

maraud	muh RAWD	məˈrɔd
Marceline	mahr suh LEEN	ˌmɑrsəˈlin
marchesa	mahr KE zah	mɑrˈkɛzɑ
marchese	mahr KE ze	mɑrˈkɛzɛ
marchioness	MAHR shuh nis	ˈmɑrʃənɪs
marchpane	MAHRCH payn	ˈmɑrtʃpen
Marcia	MAHR shuh	ˈmɑrʃə
Marckwardt, Marckwart	MAHR kwahrt	ˈmɑrkwɑrt
Marconi	mahr KOH ni	mɑrˈkonɪ
Mardi gras	MAHR di GRAH	ˈmɑrdɪ ˈgrɑ
mare (" sea ; moon area ")	MAI ri	ˈmɛrɪ
Marengo	muh RENG goh	məˈrɛŋgo
margarin, -e	MAHR juh rin	ˈmɑrdʒərɪn
Margesson	MAHR juh suhn	ˈmɑrdʒəsən
maria (" seas ")	MAI ri uh	ˈmɛrɪə
Marianas (islands)	mah ree AH nahs	mɑriˈɑnɑs
marigold	MA ri gohld	ˈmærɪgold
marijuana, marihuana	mai ri WAH nuh	ˌmɛrɪˈwɑnə
marimba	muh RIM buh	məˈrɪmbə
marina	muh REE nuh	məˈrinə
marinate	MA ruh nayt	ˈmærənet
marine, M-	muh REEN	məˈrin
mariner	MA ruh ner	ˈmærənər
Maritain	ma ree TAN	ˌmæriˈtæn
marital	MA ruh tuhl	ˈmærətəl
maritime, M-	MA ruh tighm	ˈmærətaɪm
Mariveles	mah ree VE les	mɑriˈvɛles
marjoram	MAHR juh ruhm	ˈmɑrdʒərəm
market	MAHR kit	ˈmɑrkɪt
Markevitch	mahr KAY vich	mɑrˈkevɪtʃ
Markham	MAHR kuhm	ˈmɑrkəm
Marlborough (British)	MAWL bruh	ˈmɔlbrə
Marlborough (U.S.)	MAHRL buh ruh	ˈmɑrlbərə
Marmara, Marmora	MAHR muh ruh	ˈmɑrmərə
marmoset	MAHR muh zet	ˈmɑrməzet
marmot	MAHR muht	ˈmɑrmət
maroon	muh ROO : N	məˈrun
Marquand	mahr KWAHND	mɑrˈkwɑnd
Marquardt, Marquart	MAHR kwahrt	ˈmɑrkwɑrt
marquee	mahr KEE	mɑrˈki
Marquesas (islands)	mahr KAY suhs	mɑrˈkesəs
marquess	MAHR kwis	ˈmɑrkwɪs
marquetry, marqueterie	MAHR kuh tri	ˈmɑrkətrɪ
Marquette	mahr KET	mɑrˈkɛt
marquis, M-	MAHR kwis	ˈmɑrkwɪs
marquis (French)	mahr KEE	mɑrˈki
marquise	mahr KEEZ	mɑrˈkiz
Marrakech, Marrakesh	mah RAH kesh	mɑˈrɑkeʃ
marron	MA ruhn	ˈmærən
marrow	MA roh	ˈmæro
marry	MA ri	ˈmærɪ

sing [ŋ] ; oh [o] ; oil [ɔɪ] ; foot [ʊ] ; foo:d [u] ; how [aʊ] ; pie [p] ; ray [r] ; so [s] ; shall [ʃ] ; to [t] ; thin [θ] ; th:en [ð] ; above (uh BUHV) [ə, ˈʌ] ; vine [v] ; wine [w] ; whine [hw] ; you [j] ; zoo [z] ; rouge (roo:zh) [ʒ].

Marryat	MA ri uht	ˈmærɪət
Marsala	mahr SAH lah	mɑrˈsɑlɑ
Marschner	MAHRSH ner	ˈmɑrʃnər
Marseillaise	mahr se YEZ	mɑrsɛˈjɛz
Marseille, -s (France)	mahr SAY	mɑrˈse
Marseilles (U.S.), m-	mahr SAYLZ	mɑrˈselz
marshal, -l, M-	MAHR shuhl	ˈmɑrʃəl
marsupial	mahr SOO : pi uhl	mɑrˈsupɪəl
Martaban	mahr tuh BAHN	mɑrtəˈbɑn
Martel	mahr TEL	mɑrˈtɛl
martial, M-	MAHR shuhl	ˈmɑrʃəl
Martian	MAHR shuhn	ˈmɑrʃən
Martineau	MAHR ti noh	ˈmɑrtɪno
Martinelli	mahr tuh NE li	mɑrtəˈnɛlɪ
martinet	mahr tuh NET	mɑrtəˈnɛt
Martínez	mahr TEE nes	mɑrˈtinɛs
martini, M-	mahr TEE ni	mɑrˈtinɪ
Martinique	mahr tuh NEEK	mɑrtəˈnik
martyr	MAHR ter	ˈmɑrtər
Marx	mahrks	mɑrks
marzipan	MAHR zi pan	ˈmɑrzɪpæn
Masaryk	MA sa rik	ˈmæsærɪk
Masbate	mahs BAH te	mɑsˈbɑtɛ
Mascagni	mah SKAH nyee	mɑˈskɑnji
mascara	ma SKA ruh	mæˈskærə
Masharbrum, Masherbrum	MUH sher broom	ˈmʌʃərbrʊm
masochism	MA zuh ki zuhm	ˈmæzəkɪzəm
masochist	MA zuh kist	ˈmæzəkɪst
Masonic, m-	muh SAH nik	məˈsɑnɪk
masonite, M-	MAY suh night	ˈmesənaɪt
Masora, -h	muh SOH ruh	məˈsorə
masque	mask	mæsk
mass, M-	mas	mæs
Massachusetts	ma suh CHOO : sits	mæsəˈtʃusɪts
massacre	MA suh ker	ˈmæsəkər
massage	muh SAHZH	məˈsɑʒ
Massenet	ma suh NAY	mæsəˈne
masseur	ma SER	mæˈsɝ
masseuse	ma SOOZ	mæˈsʊz
massif	MA sif	ˈmæsɪf
Massine	ma SEEN	mæˈsin
mastaba, -b	MA stuh buh	ˈmæstəbə
mastectomy	ma STEK tuh mi	mæˈstɛktəmɪ
mastodon	MA stuh dahn	ˈmæstədɑn
mastoid	MA stoid	ˈmæstɔɪd
matador	MA tuh dawr	ˈmætədɔr
Matamoros	ma tuh MAW ruhs	mætəˈmɔrəs
Matanuska	ma tuh NOO : skuh	mætəˈnuskə
matelote	MA tuh loht	ˈmætəlot
Mateos	mah TE aws	mɑˈtɛɔs
mater	MAY ter	ˈmetər

at [æ] ; ah [ɑ] ; air [ɛ] ; awful [ɔ] ; say [e] ; back [b] ; chair [tʃ] ; do [d] ; elm [ɛ] ; eel [i] ;
server [ˈɝ, ər] ; fit [f] ; go [g] ; hurt [h] ; is [ɪ] ; high [aɪ] ; jet [dʒ] ; kiss [k] ; lamb [l] ; my [m] ;
nice [n] ;

material	muh TI ri uhl	məˈtɪrɪəl
materia medica	muh TI ri uh ME di kuh	məˈtɪrɪə ˈmɛdɪkə
materiel	muh ti ri EL	mətɪrɪˈɛl
Mather	MA th:er	ˈmæðər
Mathias	muh THIGH uhs	məˈθaɪəs
matin, M-	MA tin	ˈmætɪn
matinee	ma tuh NAY	mætəˈne
Matisse	ma TEES	mæˈtis
Mato Grosso	MAH too GRAW soo	ˈmɑtʊ ˈgrɔsʊ
matriarch	MAY tri ahrk	ˈmetrɪɑrk
matricide	MAY truh sighd	ˈmetrəsaɪd
matrix	MAY triks	ˈmetrɪks
matronly	MAY truhn li	ˈmetrənlɪ
Matsuoka	MAHT soo OH kah	ˈmɑtsʊˈokɑ
Matterhorn	MA ter hawrn	ˈmætərhɔrn
mature, M-	muh TYOOR	məˈtjʊr
matzoth	MAHT sohth	ˈmɑtsoθ
maudlin	MAWD lin	ˈmɔdlɪn
Maugham	mawm	mɔm
Maui	MOW ee	ˈmaʊi
Mau Mau	mow mow	maʊ maʊ
Mauna Kea	MOW nah KAY ah	ˈmaʊnɑ ˈkeɑ
Mauna Loa	MOW nah LOH ah	ˈmaʊnɑ ˈloɑ
maunder	MAWN der	ˈmɔndər
Maundy	MAWN di	ˈmɔndɪ
Maupassant	MOH puh sahnt	ˈmopəsɑnt
Mauriac	maw ri AK	mɔrɪˈæk
Mauritania, Mauretania	maw ruh TAY ni uh	mɔrəˈtenɪə
Mauritius	maw RI shi uhs	mɔˈrɪʃɪəs
Maurois	mawr WAH	mɔrˈwɑ
Mauser, m-	MOW zer	ˈmaʊzər
mausoleum, M-	maw suh LEE uhm	mɔsəˈliəm
mauve	mohv	mov
maverick, M-	MA vuh rik	ˈmævərɪk
mavis, M-	MAY vis	ˈmevɪs
mavourneen, mavournin	muh VOOR neen	məˈvʊrnin
maxim, M-	MAK sim	ˈmæksɪm
Maximilian	mak suh MIL yuhn	mæksəˈmɪljən
Maya	MAH yuh	ˈmɑjə
Mayaguez	mah yah GWES	mɑjɑˈgwɛs
Mayan	MAH yuhn	ˈmɑjən
Mayo	MAY oh	ˈmeo
Mayon	mah YAWN	mɑˈjɔn
mayonnaise	MAY uh nayz	ˈmeənez
mayoralty	MAY uh ruhl ti	ˈmeərəltɪ
Mazarin	MA zuh rin	ˈmæzərɪn
Mazda, m-	MAZ duh	ˈmæzdə
mazurka, mazourka	muh ZER kuh	məˈzɝkə
mazzeltov	MAH zuhl tohv	ˈmɑzəltov
Mazzini	mad ZEE ni	mædˈzini
mea culpa	MEE uh KUHL puh	ˈmiə ˈkʌlpə

sing [ŋ] ; oh [o] ; oil [ɔɪ] ; foot [ʊ] ; foo:d [u] ; how [aʊ] ; pie [p] ; ray [r] ; so [s] ; shall [ʃ] ; to [t] ; thin [θ] ; th:en [ð] ; above (uh BUHV) [ə, ˈʌ] ; vine [v] ; wine [w] ; whine [hw] ; you [j] ; zoo [z] ; rouge (roo:zh) [ʒ].

mead, M-	meed	mid
meadow	ME doh	'mɛdo
meager, meagre	MEE ger	'migər
meander, M-	mi AN der	mɪ'ændər
Meany	MEE ni	'minɪ
measles	MEE zuhlz	'mizəlz
measure	ME zher	'mɛʒər
meatus	mi AY tuhs	mɪ'etəs
Mecca, m-	ME kuh	'mɛkə
mechanize	ME kuh nighz	'mɛkənaɪz
Mechlin	ME klin	'mɛklɪn
Mecklenburg, Mecklenberg	ME kluhn berg	'mɛklənbərg
Medaglia d'Oro	may DAH lyah DOH roh	me'dɑlja 'doro
medallion	muh DAL yuhn	mə'dæljən
Medea	mi DEE uh	mə'diə
Medellín	me de YEEN	mɛdɛ'ljin
media, M-	MEE di uh	'midɪə
mediaeval	mee di EE vuhl	midɪ'ivəl
mediant	MEE di uhnt	'midɪənt
mediastinum	mee di a STIGH nuhm	midɪæ'staɪnəm
mediate (a)	MEE di it	'midɪɪt
mediate (v)	MEE di ayt	'midɪet
medic, M-	ME dik	'mɛdɪk
Medici	ME duh chee	'mɛdətʃi
medicinal	muh DI suh nuhl	mə'dɪsənəl
medicine	ME duh suhn	'mɛdəsən
medico	ME di koh	'mɛdɪko
medieval	mee di EE vuhl	midɪ'ivəl
mediocre	MEE di oh ker	'midɪokər
mediocrity	mee di AH kruh ti	midɪ'ɑkrətɪ
Mediterranean	me duh tuh RAY ni uhn	mɛdətə'renɪən
medley	MED li	'mɛdlɪ
medulla	mi DUH luh	mɪ'dʌlə
medullary	ME duh lai ri	'mɛdəlɛrɪ
Medusa, m-	muh DOO: suh	mə'dusə
Meehan	MEE uhn	'miən
Meer	mair	mɛr
meerschaum	MIR shuhm	'mɪrʃəm
megacycle	ME guh sigh kuhl	'mɛgəsaɪkəl
megalomania	me guh luh MAY ni uh	mɛgələ'menɪə
megalopolis	me guh LAH puh luhs	mɛgə'lɑpələs
Meganthropus	me guhn THROH puhs	mɛgən'θropəs
megaton	ME guh tuhn	'mɛgətʌn
Megiddo	muh GI doh	mə'gɪdo
megrim	MEE grim	'migrɪm
Meiji	may jee	me dʒi
Mein Kampf	mighn KAHMPF	maɪn 'kɑmpf
meiosis	migh OH sis	maɪ'osɪs
Meir, Golda	ME eer, GOHL dah	'mɛir, 'goldɑ
Meissen	MIGH suhn	'maɪsən
Meistersinger	MIGH ster sing er	'maɪstərsɪŋər

at [æ] ; ah [ɑ] ; air [ɛ] ; awful [ɔ] ; say [e] ; back [b] ; chair [tʃ] ; do [d] ; elm [ɛ] ; eel [i] ;
server ['ɝ, ər] ; fit [f] ; go [g] ; hurt [h] ; is [ɪ] ; high [aɪ] ; jet [dʒ] ; kiss [k] ; lamb [l] ; my [m] ;
nice [n] ;

mejicano	may hi KAH naw	mehɪˈkɑnɔ
Méjico	MAY hi kaw	ˈmehɪkɔ
Meklong	ma KLAWNG	mæˈklɔŋ
Mekong	MAY kahng	ˈmekɑŋ
melancholia	me luhn KOH li uh	mɛlənˈkolɪə
melancholy	ME luhn kah li	ˈmɛlənkɑlɪ
Melanchthon,	muh LANGK thuhn	məˈlæŋkθən
Melancthon		
Melanesia	me luh NEE zhuh	mɛləˈniʒə
mélange	may LAHNZH	meˈlɑnʒ
Melba	MEL buh	ˈmɛlbə
Melbourne	MEL bern	ˈmɛlbərn
Melchior, Lauritz	MEL kyawr, LOW rits	ˈmɛlkjɔr, ˈlaurɪts
Melchizedek,	mel KI zuh dek	mɛlˈkɪzədɛk
Melchisedec		
Meleager	me li AY jer	mɛlɪˈedʒər
melee, mêlée	may LAY	meˈle
meliorate	MEE lyuh rayt	ˈmiljəret
mellifluous	muh LI floo uhs	məˈlɪfluəs
Mellon	ME luhn	ˈmɛlən
Melnik (Czechoslovakia)	MYEL neek	ˈmjɛlnik
melodeon	muh LOH di uhn	məˈlodɪən
melodrama	ME luh drah muh	ˈmɛlədrɑmə
Melos	MEE lahs	ˈmiiɑs
Melpomene	mel PAH muh nee	mɛlˈpɑməni
Melville	MEL vil	ˈmɛlvɪl
membrane	MEM brayn	ˈmɛmbren
membranous	MEM bruh nuhs	ˈmɛmbrənəs
Memel	ME muhl	ˈmɛməl
memento	mi MEN toh	mɪˈmɛnto
memento mori	mi MEN toh MOH righ	mɪˈmɛnto ˈmoraɪ
Memnon	MEM nahn	ˈmɛmnɑn
memoir	MEM wahr	ˈmɛmwɑr
memorable	ME muh ruh buhl	ˈmɛmərəbəl
memory	ME muh ri	ˈmɛmərɪ
Memphis	MEM fis	ˈmɛmfɪs
memsahib	MEM sah ib	ˈmɛmsɑɪb
menage, ménage	may NAHZH	meˈnɑʒ
menagerie	muh NA juh ri	məˈnædʒərɪ
Menam	me NAHM	meˈnɑm
Menander	mi NAN der	mɪˈnændər
Mencius	MEN shi uhs	ˈmɛnʃɪəs
Mencken	MENG kuhn	ˈmɛŋkən
mendacious	men DAY shuhs	mɛnˈdeʃəs
mendacity	men DA suh ti	mɛnˈdæsətɪ
Mendeleev	men duh LAY ef	mɛndəˈleef
mendelevium	men duh LEE vi uhm	mɛndəˈlivɪəm
Mendelian	men DEE li uhn	mɛnˈdilɪən
Mendelssohn	MEN duhl suhn	ˈmɛndəlsən
Menderes	men de RES	mɛndɛˈrɛs
mendicant	MEN di kuhnt	ˈmɛndɪkənt
Menelaus	me nuh LAY uhs	mɛnəˈleəs

sing [ŋ]; oh [o]; oil [ɔɪ]; foot [ʊ]; foo:d [u]; how [aʊ]; pie [p]; ray [r]; so [s]; shall [ʃ];
to [t]; thin [θ]; th:en [ð]; above (uh BUHV) [ə, ˈʌ]; vine [v]; wine [w]; whine [hw];
you [j]; zoo [z]; rouge (roo:zh) [ʒ].

Menelik	ME nuh lik	ˈmɛnəlɪk
menhaden	men HAY duhn	mɛnˈhedən
menial	MEE ni uhl	ˈminiəl
meninges	muh NIN jeez	məˈnɪndʒiz
meningitis	me nin JIGH tis	mɛnɪnˈdʒaɪtɪs
Menjou	mahn ZHOO:	manˈʒu
Menninger	ME nin jer	ˈmɛnɪndʒər
Mennonite	ME nuh night	ˈmɛnənaɪt
Menon, Krishna	ME nuhn, KRISH nuh	ˈmɛnən, ˈkrɪʃnə
Menotti, Gian-Carlo	me NAW ti, JAHN KAHR loh	mɛˈnɔtɪ, ˈdʒan ˈkarlo
menshevik, M-	MEN shuh vik	ˈmɛnʃəvɪk
menthol	MEN thahl	ˈmɛnθɑl
menu	ME nyoo:	ˈmɛnju
Menuhin, Yehudi	MEN yoo in, yuh HOO: di	ˈmɛnjuɪn, yəˈhudɪ
Mephisto	mi FI stoh	mɪˈfɪsto
Mephistopheles	me fuh STAH fuh leez	mɛfəˈstafəliz
mephitis	me FIGH tis	mɛˈfaɪtɪs
mercantile	MER kuhn til	ˈmɝkəntɪl
mercaptan	mer KAP tan	mərˈkæptæn
Mercator	mer KAY ter	mərˈketər
mercenary	MER suh nai ri	ˈmɝsənɛrɪ
merci	mair SEE	mɛrˈsi
Mercian	MER shuhn	ˈmɝʃən
mercurial	mer KYOO ri uhl	mərˈkjʊriəl
mercury, M-	MER kuh ri	ˈmɝkərɪ
Mercutio	mer KYOO: shi oh	mərˈkjuʃɪo
merengue	muh RENG gay	məˈrɛŋge
meretricious	me ruh TRI shuhs	mɛrəˈtrɪʃəs
Mérida	ME ree dah	ˈmɛridɑ
meridian	muh RI di uhn	məˈrɪdɪən
Mérimée	may ree MAY	meriˈme
meringue	muh RANG	məˈræŋ
merino	muh REE noh	məˈrino
Merkel	MER kuhl	ˈmɝkəl
merl, -e, M-	merl	mɝl
mermaid	MER mayd	ˈmɝmed
Merovingian	me ruh VIN ji uhn	mɛrəˈvɪndʒɪən
Merrimac, -k	ME ruh mak	ˈmɛrəmæk
merry	ME ri ·	ˈmɛrɪ
Mersey	MER zi	ˈmɝzɪ
merthiolate	mer THIGH uh layt	mərˈθaɪəlet
mesa	MAY suh	ˈmesə
mescal	me SKAL	mɛˈskæl
mesdames	may DAHM	meˈdam
mesenteric	me suhn TE rik	mɛsənˈtɛrɪk
Meshach	MEE shak	ˈmiʃæk
Meshed	muh SHED	məˈʃɛd
mesial	MEE zi uhl	ˈmizɪəl
mesmerize	MES muh righz	ˈmɛsməraɪz
mesne	meen	min
meson	ME suhn	ˈmɛsən

Mesopotamia	me suh puh TAY mi uh	mɛsəpə'temɪə
mesothelium	me suh THEE li uhm	mɛsə'θiliəm
mesotron	ME suh trahn	'mɛsətrɑn
Mesozoic	me suh ZOH ik	mɛsə'zoɪk
mesquit, -e	me SKEET	mɛ'skit
Messalina	me suh LIGH nuh	mɛsə'laɪnə
messaline	me suh LEEN	mɛsə'lin
Messiah, m-	muh SIGH uh	mə'saɪə
messieurs	ME serz	'mɛsərz
Messina	muh SEE nuh	mə'sinə
Messrs.	ME serz	'mɛsərz
mestizo	me STEE zoh	mɛ'stizo
Mestrovic	MESH traw vich	'mɛʃtrɔvɪtʃ
metabolism	muh TA buh li zuhm	mə'tæbəlɪzəm
metallic	muh TA lik	mə'tælɪk
metallurgy	ME tuh ler ji	'mɛtələrdʒɪ
metamorphoses	me tuh MAWR fuh seez	mɛtə'mɔrfəsiz
metamorphosis	me tuh MAWR fuh sis	mɛtə'mɔrfəsɪs
metaphor	ME tuh fer	'mɛtəfər
metaphorical	me tuh FAW ri kuhl	mɛtə'fɔrɪkəl
metaphysical	me tuh FI zi kuhl	mɛtə'fɪzɪkəl
metaphysics	me tuh FI ziks	mɛtə'fɪzɪks
metathesis	muh TA thuh sis	mə'tæθəsɪs
Metaxas	mi TAK suhs	mɪ'tæksəs
Metchnikoff	mech nee KAWF	mɛtʃni'kɔf
metempsychosis	me tuhm sigh KOH sis	mɛtəmsaɪ'kosɪs
meteor	MEE ti er	'mitɪər
meteorite	MEE ti uh right	'mitɪəraɪt
meteorology	mee ti uh RAH luh ji	mitɪə'rɑlədʒɪ
methane	ME thayn	'mɛθen
Methuselah	muh THOO : zuh luh	mə'θuzələ
methyl	ME thuhl	'mɛθəl
métier	may TYAY	me'tje
metonymy	muh TAH nuh mi	mə'tɑnəmɪ
metronome	ME truh nohm	'mɛtrənom
metropolis	muh TRAH puh lis	mə'trɑpəlɪs
metropolitan	me truh PAH luh tuhn	mɛtrə'pɑlətən
Metternich	ME ter nik	'mɛtərnɪk
Metz	mets	mɛts
Meuse	myoo : z	mjuz
Mexico	MEK si koh	'mɛksɪko
Meyerbeer	MIGH er bir	'maɪərbɪr
Meynell	ME nuhl	'mɛnəl
Mezokovesd	ME zuh KUH vezd	'mɛzə'kʌvɛzd
Mezuza, -h	muh ZOO zuh	mə'zuzə
mezzanine	ME zuh neen	'mɛzənin
mezzo	MET soh	'mɛtso
mezzotint	MET suh tint	'mɛtsətɪnt
Miami	migh A mi	maɪ'æmɪ
miasma	migh AZ muh	maɪ'æzmə
mica	MIGH kuh	'maɪkə
Micah	MIGH kuh	'maɪkə

sing [ŋ]; *oh* [o]; *oil* [ɔɪ]; *foot* [ʊ]; *foo*:d [u]; *how* [aʊ]; *pie* [p]; *ray* [r]; *so* [s]; *shall* [ʃ]; *to* [t]; *thin* [θ]; *th*:en [ð]; above (*uh BUH*V) [ə, 'ʌ]; *vine* [v]; *wine* [w]; *whine* [hw]; *you* [j]; *zoo* [z]; *rouge* (roo:*zh*) [ʒ].

Micaiah	migh KAY uh	maɪˈkeə
Micawber	mi KAW ber	mɪˈkɔbər
Michelangelo	migh kuhl AN juh loh	maɪkəlˈændʒəlo
Michigan	MI shuh guhn	ˈmɪʃəgən
Michiko	MI chi koh	ˈmɪtʃiko
microbe	MIGH krohb	ˈmaɪkrob
micrococcus	migh kruh KAH kuhs	maɪkrəˈkɑkəs
microcosm	MIGH kruh kah zuhm	ˈmaɪkrəkɑzəm
micrometer	migh KRAH muh ter	maɪˈkrɑmətər
Micronesia	migh kruh NEE zhuh	maɪkrəˈniʒə
microphone	MIGH kruh fohn	ˈmaɪkrəfon
microscope	MIGH kruh skohp	ˈmaɪkrəskop
microwaves	MIGH kroh wayvz	ˈmaɪkrowevz
Midas	MIGH duhs	ˈmaɪdəs
Midgard	MID gahrd	ˈmɪdgɑrd
Midi	mee DEE	miˈdi
Midian	MI di uhn	ˈmɪdɪən
Midlothian	mid LOH th:i uhn	mɪdˈloðɪən
midwifery	MID wigh fri	ˈmɪdwaɪfrɪ
mien	meen	min
Mies van der Rohe,	MEES fahn der ROH uh,	ˈmis fɑn dər ˈroə,
Ludwig	LOO:D wik	ˈludwɪk
mignon, M-	MIN yahn	ˈmɪnjɑn
mignonette	min yuh NET	mɪnjəˈnɛt
migraine	MIGH grayn	ˈmaɪgren
migrant	MIGH gruhnt	ˈmaɪgrənt
migratory	MIGH gruh taw ri	ˈmaɪgrətɔrɪ
Miguel	mee GEL	miˈgɛl
Mihailovitch,	mi HIGH law vich, DRAH	mɪˈhaɪlovɪtʃ, ˈdrɑʒɑ
Mikhailovic, Draja,	zhah	
Draza		
mikado, M-	mi KAH doh	mɪˈkɑdo
Mikolajczyk	mi kaw LIGH chik	mɪkəˈlaɪtʃɪk
Mikoyan, Mikoian	mi kaw YAHN	mɪkəˈjɑn
Milan	mi LAN	mɪˈlæn
milanaise	mee lah NEZ	milɑˈnɛz
Milanese	mi luh NEEZ	mɪləˈniz
Milano	mee LAH naw	miˈlɑnɔ
Milanov, Zinka	MEE lah nuf, ZING kuh	ˈmilɑnəf, ˈzɪŋkə
milch	milch	mɪltʃ
Milesian	muh LEE zhuhn	məˈliʒən
Milhaud, Darius	mee LOH, da RYOO:Z	miˈlo dæˈrjuz
milieu	meel YOO	milˈju
militaire	mee lee TAIR	miliˈtɛr
militant	MI li tuhnt	ˈmɪlɪtənt
militia	muh LI shuh	məˈlɪʃə
Millais	mi LAY	mɪˈle
Millay	mi LAY	mɪˈle
millennium	mi LE ni uhm	mɪˈlɛnɪəm
millet	MI lit	ˈmɪlɪt
Millet, Jean François	mi LAY	mɪˈle
milliampere	mi li AM pir	mɪlɪˈæmpɪr

at [æ]; ah [ɑ]; air [ɛ]; awful [ɔ]; say [e]; back [b]; chair [tʃ]; do [d]; elm [ɛ]; eel [i]; server [ˈɝ, ər]; fit [f]; go [g]; hurt [h]; is [ɪ]; high [aɪ]; jet [dʒ]; kiss [k]; lamb [l]; my [m]; nice [n];

Millikan	MI luh kuhn	ˈmɪləkən
millimeter, millimetre	mi luh MEE ter	mɪləˈmitər
millimicron	mi luh MIGH krahn	mɪləˈmaɪkrɑn
millinery	MI luh nai ri	ˈmilənɛrɪ
Milne	miln	mɪln
milo, M-	MIGH loh	ˈmaɪlo
Milo (Melos)	MEE loh	ˈmilo
milquetoast, M-	MILK tohst	ˈmɪlktost
Milstein	MIL stighn	ˈmɪlstaɪn
Miltiades	mil TIGH uh deez	mɪlˈtaɪədiz
Miltonic	mil TAH nik	mɪlˈtɑnɪk
Milwaukee	mil WAW ki	mɪlˈwɔkɪ
Mimas	MIGH muhs	ˈmaɪməs
mime	mighm	maɪm
mimeograph, M-	MI mi uh graf	ˈmɪmɪəgræf
mimesis	mi MEE sis	mɪˈmisɪs
mimetic	mi ME tik	mɪˈmɛtɪk
mimic	MI mik	ˈmɪmɪk
mimicry	MI mi kri	ˈmɪmɪkrɪ
Mimir	MEE mir	ˈmimɪr
mimosa	mi MOH suh	mɪˈmosə
minaret	mi nuh RET	mɪnəˈrɛt
minatory	MI nuh taw ri	ˈmɪnətɔrɪ
Mindanao	min dah NOW	mɪndɑˈnaʊ
Mindoro	min DOH roh	mɪnˈdoro
Mindszenty	mind ZEN ti	mɪndˈzɛntɪ
mineralogy	mi nu RA luh ji	mɪnəˈrælədʒɪ
Minerva	mi NER vuh	mɪˈnɝvə
minestrone	mi nuh STROH ni	mɪnəˈstronɪ
Ming	ming	mɪŋ
miniature	MI ni uh cher	ˈmɪnɪətʃər
minicam, M-	MI ni kam	ˈmɪnɪkæm
Minion	MIN yuhn	ˈmɪnjən
Minneapolis	mi ni A puh lis	mɪnɪˈæpəlɪs
minnesinger	MI ni sing er	ˈmɪnɪsɪŋər
Minnesota	mi ni SOH tuh	mɪnɪˈsotə
Minoan	mi NOH uhn	mɪˈnoən
Minorca	mi NAWR kuh	mɪˈnɔrkə
Minos	MIGH nuhs	ˈmaɪnəs
Minotaur	MI nuh tawr	ˈmɪnətor
Minsk	minsk	mɪnsk
minuend	MIN yoo end	ˈmɪnjʊɛnd
minuet	min yoo ET	mɪnjʊˈɛt
Minuit	MIN yoo it	ˈmɪnjʊɪt
minuscule	mi NUH skyool	mɪˈnʌskjʊl
minute (a)	migh NOO꞉T	maɪˈnut
minute (n, v)	MI nit	ˈmɪnɪt
minutia	mi NOO꞉ shi uh	mɪˈnuʃɪə
minutiae	mi NOO꞉ shi ee	mɪˈnuʃri
Miocene	MIGH uh seen	ˈmaɪəsin
miotic	migh AH tik	maɪˈɑtɪk
Miquelon	mi kuh LAHN	mɪkəˈlɑn

---

sing [ŋ] ; oh [o] ; oil [ɔɪ] ; foot [ʊ] ; foo꞉d [u] ; how [aʊ] ; pie [p] ; ray [r] ; so [s] ; shall [ʃ] ; to [t] ; thin [θ] ; th꞉en [ð] ; above (uh BUHV) [ə, ˈʌ] ; vine [v] ; wine [w] ; whine [hw] ; you [j] ; zoo [z] ; rouge (roo꞉zh) [ʒ].

H.P.—Q

Mirabeau	MI ruh boh	ˈmɪrəbo
mirabile dictu	mi RA bi li DIK too:	mɪˈræbɪlɪ ˈdɪktu
Miraflores	mee rah FLAW res	mirɑˈflorɛs
mirage	mi RAHZH	mɪˈrɑʒ
Miranda	mi RAN duh	mɪˈrændə
Miriam	MI ri uhm	ˈmɪrɪəm
Miró	mi RAW	mɪˈrɔ
miry	MIGH ri	ˈmaɪrɪ
mirza, M-	MIR zah	ˈmɪrzɑ
misalliance	mi suh LIGH uhns	mɪsəˈlaɪəns
misanthrope	MI suhn throhp	ˈmɪsənθrop
miscegenation	mi si juh NAY shuhn	mɪsɪdʒəˈneʃən
miscellaneous	mi suh LAY ni uhs	mɪsəˈlenɪəs
miscellany	MI suh lay ni	ˈmɪsəlenɪ
mischief	MIS chif	ˈmɪstʃɪf
mischievous	MIS chi vuhs	ˈmɪstʃɪvəs
miscreant	MI skri uhnt	ˈmɪskrɪənt
misdemeanor	mis di MEE ner	mɪsdɪˈminər
mise en scène	mee zahn SEN	mi zɑn ˈsɛn
miser	MIGH zer	ˈmaɪzər
Miserere, m-	mi zuh RAI ri	mizəˈrɛrɪ
misericord, -e	mi zuh ri KAWRD	mɪzɛrɪˈkɔrd
mishap	MIS hap	ˈmɪshæp
misnomer	mis NOH mer	mɪsˈnomər
misogamy	mi SAH guh mi	mɪˈsɑgəmɪ
misogynist	mi SAH juh nist	mɪˈsɑdʒənɪst
misology	mi SAH luh ji	mɪˈsɑlədʒɪ
missal	MI suhl	ˈmɪsəl
missile	MI suhl	ˈmɪsəl
missilery, missilry	MI suhl ri	ˈmɪsəlrɪ
Missouri	mi ZOO ri	mɪˈzʊrɪ
mistletoe	MI suhl toh	ˈmɪsəlto
miter, mitre	MIGH ter	ˈmaɪtər
Mithridates	mi thruh DAY teez	mɪθrəˈdetiz
mitigate	MI tuh gayt	ˈmɪtəget
mitosis	mi TOH sis	mɪˈtosɪs
Mitropoulos	mi TRAH puh luhs	mɪˈtrɑpələs
Mitrovica	MEE traw vit sah	ˈmitrɔvɪtsɑ
mittimus	MI ti muhs	ˈmɪtɪməs
mitzvah, mitsvah	MITS vah	ˈmɪtsvɑ
Mizpah, Mizpeh	MIZ puh	ˈmɪzpə
Mlada Boleslav	muh LAH dah BAW le slahf	məˈlɑdɑ ˈbɔlɛslɑf
Mlava, Mlawa	muh LAH vah	məˈlɑvɑ
mnemonic	ni MAH nik	nɪˈmɑnɪk
Mnemosyne	ni MAH suh nee	nɪˈmɑsəni
moa	MOH uh	ˈmoə
Moab	MOH ab	ˈmoæb
mobile (a)	MOH buhl	ˈmobəl
mobile (sculpture)	MOH beel	ˈmobil
Mobile	moh BEEL	moˈbil
mobilize	MOH buh lighz	ˈmobəlaɪz

at [æ] ; ah [ɑ] ; air [ɛ] ; awful [ɔ] ; say [e] ; back [b] ; chair [tʃ] ; do [d] ; elm [ɛ] ; eel [i] ; server [ˈɝ, ər] ; fit [f] ; go [g] ; hurt [h] ; is [ɪ] ; high [aɪ] ; jet [dʒ] ; kiss [k] ; lamb [l] ; my [m] ; nice [n] ;

mobocracy	mahb AH kruh si	mɑb'ɑkrəsɪ
Mocha, m-	MOH kuh	'mokə
modal	MOH duhl	'modəl
mode	mohd	mod
moderato	mah duh RAH toh	mɑdə'rɑto
modern	MAH dern	'mɑdərn
Modigliani	maw deel YAH nee	mɔdil'yɑni
modiste	moh DEEST	mo'dist
Modjeska	muh JE skuh	mə'dʒɛskə
Modred	MOH drid	'modrɪd
modulate	MAH juh layt	'mɑdʒəlet
modulation	mah juh LAY shuhn	mɑdʒə'leʃən
module	MAH joo : l	'mɑdʒul
modus operandi	MOH duhs ah puh RAN digh	'modəs ɑpə'rændaɪ
modus vivendi	MOH duhs vi VEN digh	'modəs vɪ'vɛndaɪ
Mogadishu	moh gah DEE shoo :	mogɑ'diʃu
Mogul, m-	MOH guhl	'mogəl
Mohammed	moh HA mid	mo'hæmɪd
Mohave	moh HAH vi	mo'hɑvɪ
Mohican	moh HEE kuhn	mo'hikən
Mohs (scale)	mohz	moz
moiety	MOI uh ti	'mɔɪətɪ
Moira	MOI ruh	'mɔɪrə
moire	mwahr	mwɑr
moiré	mwah RAY	mwɑ're
Moisewitch	moi SE vich	mɔɪ'sɛvɪtʃ
Mojave	moh HAH vi	mo'hɑvɪ
Moji	maw jee	mɔ dʒi
molar	MOH ler	'molər
molasses	muh LA siz	mə'læsɪz
Moldau	MAWL dow	'mɔldau
Moldavia	mahl DAY vi uh	mɑl'devɪə
Molech	MOH lek	'molɛk
molecular	muh LEK yuh ler	mə'lɛkjelər
molecule	MAH luh kyoo : l	'mɑləkjul
molest	muh LEST	mə'lɛst
molestation	moh le STAY shuhn	molɛ'steʃən
Molière	MOH li air	'molɪɛr
Molina	maw LEE nah	mo'linɑ
Molinari-Pradelli	moh lee NAH ree-prah DE lee	moli'nɑri prɑ'dɛli
mollify	MAH luh figh	'mɑləfaɪ
mollusk, mollusc	MAH luhsk	'mɑləsk
Molnar, Ferenc	MAWL nahr, FE rents	'mɔlnɑr, 'fɛrɛnts
Moloch	MOH lahk	'molɑk
Molokai	moh loh KIGH	molo'kaɪ
Molotov	MAW law tawf	'mɔlɔtɔf
Molucca	moh LUH kuh	mo'lʌkə
moly	MOH li	'molɪ
Mombasa	mahm BA suh	mɑm'bæsə
momentous	moh MEN tuhs	mo'mɛntəs

si*ng* [ŋ] ; *oh* [o] ; *oi*l [ɔɪ] ; *foot* [ʊ] ; *foo*:d [u] ; *how* [aʊ] ; *p*ie [p] ; *r*ay [r] ; *s*o [s] ; *sh*all [ʃ] ; *t*o [t] ; *th*in [θ] ; *th*:en [ð] ; above (*uh* BUHV) [ə, 'ʌ] ; *v*ine [v] ; *w*ine [w] ; *wh*ine [hw] ; *y*ou [j] ; *z*oo [z] ; rouge (roo:*zh*) [ʒ].

momentum	moh MEN tuhm	moˈmɛntəm
Mommsen	MAHM suhn	ˈmɑmsən
Momus	MOH muhs	ˈmoməs
Monaco	MAH nuh koh	ˈmɑnəko
monadnock, M-	muh NAD nahk	məˈnædnɑk
Monaghan	MAH nuh guhn	ˈmɑnəgən
Mona Lisa	MOH nuh LEE zuh	ˈmonə ˈlizə
mon ami	maw na MEE	mɔ næˈmi
monandrous	muh NAN druhs	məˈnændrəs
monarchial	muh NAHR ki uhl	məˈnɑrkɪəl
monaural	mahn AW ruhl	mɑnˈɔrəl
mon cher	mawn SHAIR	mɔn ˈʃɛr
Monel, -l, m-	moh NEL	moˈnɛl
Monet	moh NAY	moˈne
monger	MUHNG ger	ˈmʌnger
Mongol	MAHNG guhl	ˈmɑngəl
Mongolia	mahng GOH li uh	mɑŋˈgolɪə
mongoloid, M-	MAHNG guh loid	ˈmɑngəlɔɪd
mongoos, -e	MAHNG goo:s	ˈmɑngus
mongrel	MUHNG gruhl	ˈmʌngrəl
Monique	moh NEEK	moˈnik
monitor	MAH nuh ter	ˈmɑnətər
Monmouth	MAHN muhth	ˈmɑnməθ
monocle	MAH nuh kuhl	ˈmɑnəkəl
monocracy	muh NAH kruh si	məˈnɑkrəsɪ
monody	MAH nuh di	ˈmɑnədɪ
monogamy	muh NAH guh mi	məˈnɑgəmɪ
monogram	MAH nuh gram	ˈmɑnəgræm
monograph	MAH nuh graf	ˈmɑnəgræf
monogyny	muh NAH juh ni	məˈnɑdʒənɪ
monolatry	muh NAH luh tri	məˈnɑlətrɪ
monolith	MAH nuh lith	ˈmɑnəlɪθ
monolog, -ue	MAH nuh lawg	ˈmɑnəlɔg
monologist, monologuist	MAH nuh law gist	ˈmɑnəlɔgɪst
monomania	mah nuh MAY ni uh	mɑnəˈmenɪə
Monongahela	muh nahng guh HEE luh	mənɑŋgəˈhilə
mononucleosis	mah nuh noo:kli OH sis	mɑnənuklɪˈosɪs
monophonic	mah nuh FAH nik	mɑnəˈfɑnɪk
monophthong	MAH nuhf thawng	ˈmɑnəfθɔŋ
Monophysite	muh NAH fuh sight	məˈnɑfəsaɪt
monoplane	MAH nuh playn	ˈmɑnəplen
monoplegia	mah nuh PLEE ji uh	mɑnəˈplidʒɪə
monopoly	muh NAH puh li	məˈnɑpəlɪ
monopsony	muh NAHP suh ni	məˈnɑpsənɪ
monostich	MAH nuh stik	ˈmɑnəstɪk
monosyllabic	mah nuh si LA bik	mɑnəsɪˈlæbɪk
monotheism	mah nuh THEE i zuhm	mɑnəˈθiɪzəm
monotony	muh NAH tuh ni	məˈnɑtənɪ
monotype	MAH nuh tighp	ˈmɑnətaɪp
monovalent	mah nuh VAY luhnt	mɑnəˈvelənt
Monrovia	mahn ROH vi uh	mɑnˈrovɪə
Monsarrat	MAHN suh raht	ˈmɑnsərɑt

at [æ] ; *ah* [ɑ] ; *air* [ɛ] ; *awful* [ɔ] ; *say* [e] ; *back* [b] ; *ch*air [tʃ] ; *do* [d] ; *elm* [ɛ] ; *eel* [i] ; *server* [ˈɝ, ər] ; *f*it [f] ; *go* [g] ; *h*urt [h] ; *is* [ɪ] ; *high* [aɪ] ; *jet* [dʒ] ; *kiss* [k] ; *l*amb [l] ; *my* [m] ; *n*ice [n] ;

Monseigneur, m-	mahn sen YER	mɑnsɛnˈjɝ
Monsieur, m-	muh SYER	məˈsjɝ
Monsignor, m-	mahn SEEN yer	mɑnˈsinjər
Monson	MUHN suhn	ˈmʌnsən
monsoon	mahn SOON:N	mɑnˈsun
montage	mahn TAHZH	mɑnˈtɑʒ
Montagu, -e	MAHN tuh gyoo:	ˈmɑntəgju
Montaigne	mahn TAYN	mɑnˈten
Montana	mahn TA nuh	mɑnˈtænə
Montauk	MAHN tawk	ˈmɑntɔk
Monte Cassino	MAWN te kah SEE noh	ˈmɔntɛ kɑˈsino
Montenegro	mahn tuh NEE groh	mɑntəˈnigro
Monterey, Monterrey	mahn tuh RAY	mɑntəˈre
Montespan	MAHN tuh span	ˈmɑntəspæn
Montesquieu	mahn tuh SKYOO:	mɑntəˈskju
Montessori	mahn tuh SAW ri	mɑntəˈsɔrɪ
Monteux	mawn TER	mɔnˈtɝ
Monteverdi	mawn te VAIR dee	mɔntɛˈvɛrdi
Montevideo	mahn tuh vi DAY oh	mɑntəvɪˈdeo
Montezuma	mahn tuh ZOO: muh	mɑntəˈzumə
Montgomery	muhn GUHM ri	mənˈgʌmrɪ
Monticello	mahn tuh SE loh	mɑntəˈsɛlo
Montmartre	mohn MA er truh	monˈmæərtrə
Montpellier (France)	mawn pe LYAY	mɔnpɛˈlje
Montpellier (Vermont)	mahnt PEE lyer	mɑntˈpiljər
Montreal	mahn tri AWL	ˈmɑntrɪˈɔl
Montserrat	mahnt suh RAT	mɑntsəˈræt
moraine	muh RAYN	məˈren
moral	MAW ruhl	ˈmɔrəl
morale	muh RAL	məˈræl
Morales	maw RAH les	mɔˈrɑlɛs
morass	muh RAS	məˈræs
Morava	MAW rah vah	ˈmɔrɑvɑ
Moravia	maw RAY vi uh	mɔˈrevɪə
moray	MAW ray	ˈmɔre
morceau	mawr SOH	mɔrˈso
mordant	MAWR duhnt	ˈmɔrdənt
Mordecai	MAWR di kigh	ˈmɔrdɪkaɪ
mordent	MAWR duhnt	ˈmɔrdənt
Mordovian	mawr DOH vi uhn	mɔrˈdovɪən
Mordred	MAWR drid	ˈmɔrdrɪd
Morea	maw REE uh	mɔˈriə
Moreau	maw ROH	mɔˈro
moreen	muh REEN	məˈrin
morel	muh REL	məˈrɛl
mores	MOH reez	ˈmoriz
Moresby	MAWRZ bi	ˈmɔrzbɪ
morganatic	mawr guh NA tik	mɔrgəˈnætɪk
morgen	MAWR guhn	ˈmɔrgən
Morgenstierne	mawr guhn sti YAIR nuh	mɔrgənstɪˈjɛrnə
Morgenthau	MAWR guhn thaw	ˈmɔrgənθɔ
Moriah	muh RIGH uh	məˈraɪə

sing [ŋ]; oh [o]; oil [ɔɪ]; foot [ʊ]; foo:d [u]; how [aʊ]; pie [p]; ray [r]; so [s]; shall [ʃ];
to [t]; thin [θ]; th:en [ð]; above (uh BUHV) [ə, ˈʌ]; vine [v]; wine [w]; whine [hw];
you [j]; zoo [z]; rouge (roo:zh) [ʒ].

Moriarty	maw ri AHR ti	mɔrɪˈɑrtɪ
moribund	MAW ruh buhnd	ˈmɔrəbənd
Morini	maw REE ni	mɔˈrinɪ
Morinigo	maw REE nee gaw	mɔˈrinigɔ
Mornay	mawr NAY	mɔrˈne
Morocco	muh RAH koh	məˈrako
moron	MAW rahn	ˈmɔran
Morón	maw RAWN	mɔˈrɔn
morose	muh ROHS	məˈros
morpheme	MAWR feem	ˈmɔrfim
morphemic	mawr FEE mik	mɔrˈfimɪk
Morpheus	MAWR fi uhs	ˈmɔrfɪəs
morphine	MAWR feen	ˈmɔrfin
morphology	mawr FAH luh ji	mɔrˈfɑlədʒɪ
morphophonemic	mawr fuh fuh NEE mik	mɔrfəfəˈnimɪk
morphosis	mawr FOH sis	mɔrˈfosɪs
mortgage	MAWR gij	ˈmɔrgɪdʒ
mortician	mawr TI shuhn	mɔrˈtɪʃən
mortise	MAWR tis	ˈmɔrtɪs
mortmain	MAWRT mayn	ˈmɔrtmen
mortuary	MAWR choo ai ri	ˈmɔrtʃuɛrɪ
mosaic, M-	moh ZAY ik	moˈzeɪk
Moscow	MAH skow	ˈmɑskaʊ
Moselle	moh ZEL	moˈzɛl
Moslem	MAHZ luhm	ˈmɑzləm
Moson	MAW shawn	ˈmɔʃɔn
mosque	mahsk	mɑsk
Moss (Norway)	maws	mɔs
Mostel, Zero	mahs TEL, ZEE roh	mɑsˈtɛl, ˈziro
Mosul	moh SOO:L	moˈsul
motel	moh TEL	moˈtɛl
motet	moh TET	moˈtɛt
motif	moh TEEF	moˈtif
motile	MOH tuhl	ˈmotəl
motive	MOH tiv	ˈmotɪv
motley, M-	MAHT li	ˈmɑtlɪ
motorcycle	MOH ter sigh kuhl	ˈmotərsaɪkəl
mouchoir	moo : SHWAHR	muˈʃwar
moue	moo :	mu
moulage	moo : LAHZH	muˈlaʒ
mould	mohld	mold
moulin, M-, -s	moo : LAN	muˈlæn
Moulmein	mool MAYN	mʊlˈmen
moult	mohlt	molt
Mountbatten	mownt BA tuhn	maʊntˈbætən
mountebank	MOWN tuh bangk	ˈmaʊntəbæŋk
mouser	MOW zer	ˈmaʊzər
mousquetaire, M-	moo : skuh TAIR	muskəˈtɛr
Moussa	MOO : sah	ˈmusɑ
mousse	moo : s	mus
mousseline	moo : SLEEN	muˈslin
Moussorgsky	moo SAWRG ski	mʊˈsɔrgskɪ

at [æ] ; ah [ɑ] ; air [ɛ] ; awful [ɔ] ; say [e] ; back [b] ; chair [tʃ] ; do [d] ; elm [ɛ] ; eel [i] ;
server [ˈɝ, ər] ; fit [f] ; go [g] ; hurt [h] ; is [ɪ] ; high [aɪ] ; jet [dʒ] ; kiss [k] ; lamb [l] ; my [m] ;
nice [n] ;

Mousterian, Moustierian	moo : STI ri uhn	mu'stɪrɪən
mouton	MOO : tahn	'mutɑn
movement	MOO : V muhnt	'muvmənt
mow (" cut ")	moh	mo
mow (" grimace "; " stack ")	mow	mau
Mowbray	MOH bri	'mobrɪ
Mowgli	MOW gli	'mauglɪ
Mozambique	moh zuhm BEEK	mozəm'bik
Mozart	MOHT sahrt	'motsɑrt
Mrs.	MI siz	'mɪsɪz
mucin	MYOO : sin	'mjusɪn
mucous, mucus	MYOO : kuhs	'mjukəs
muezzin	myoo : E zin	mju'ɛzɪn
mufti, M-	MUHF ti	'mʌftɪ
mug	muhg	mʌg
mugwump	MUHG wuhmp	'mʌgwəmp
Muir	myoor	mjʊr
Mukacevo	MOO : kah CHE vaw	'mukɑ'tʃɛvɔ
Mukden	mook den	mʊk dɛn
mukluk	MUHK luhk	'mʌklək
mulatto	muh LA toh	mə'læto
mulct	muhlkt	mʌlkt
mulla, -h	MUH luh	'mʌlə
mullein, mullen	MUH lin	'mʌlɪn
mulligan, M-	MUH li guhn	'mʌlɪgən
mulligatawny	muh li guh TAW ni	mʌlɪgə'tɔnɪ
mullion	MUH lyuhn	'mʌljən
multifarious	muhl tuh FAI ri uhs	mʌltə'fɛrɪəs
multum in parvo	MUHL tuhm in PAHR voh	'mʌltəm in 'pɑrvo
Munch	moonch	'mʊntʃ
Munchausen	MUHN chow zuhn	'mʌntʃauzən
mundane	MUHN dayn	'mʌnden
Mundt	muhnt	mʌnt
Munich	MYOO : nik	'mjunɪk
municipal	myoo : NI suh puhl	mju'nɪsəpəl
municipality	myoo : ni suh PA luh ti	mjunɪsə'pælətɪ
munificent	myoo : NI fuh suhnt	mju'nɪfəsənt
muniment	MYOO : ni muhnt	'mjunɪmənt
munition	myoo : NI shuhn	mju'nɪʃən
Munkacsy	MOON kah chi	'mʊnkɑtʃɪ
Muñoz	moo : NYAWS	mu'njɔs
Munro	muhn ROH	mən'ro
Munsel, Patrice	muhn SEL, puh TREES	mʌn'sɛl, pətris
Munsingwear	MUHN zing wair	'mʌnzɪŋwɛr
Münster (Germany)	MIN ster	'mɪnstər
Munster (Ireland)	MUHN ster	'mʌnstər
muntjac, muntjak	MUHNT jak	'mʌntdʒæk
mural	MYOO ruhl	'mjʊrəl
Murasaki	MOO : rah SAH ki	'murɑ'sɑkɪ
Murat	myoo : RAT	mju'ræt

Murillo	myoo RI loh	mjʊˈrɪlo
Murman	moor MAHN	mʊrˈmɑn
Murmansk	moor MAHNSK	mʊrˈmɑnsk
murmur	MER mer	ˈmɝmər
Murrow	MER oh	ˈmɝo
Musa	MOO : sah	ˈmusɑ
Musca	MUH skuh	ˈmʌskə
muscadine	MUH skuh din	ˈmʌskədɪn
muscat	MUH skuht	ˈmʌskət
Muscat	MUH skat	ˈmʌskæt
muscatel	muh skuh TEL	məskəˈtɛl
muscle	MUH suhl	ˈmʌsəl
Muscovite, m-	MUH skuh vight	ˈmʌskəvaɪt
Muscovy	MUH skuh vi	ˈmʌskəvɪ
muse, M-	myoo : z	mjuz
musette	myoo : ZET	mjuˈzɛt
museum	myoo : ZEE uhm	mjuˈziəm
mushroom	MUHSH roo : m	ˈmʌʃrum
musicale	myoo : zi KAL	mjuzɪˈkæl
Musici, I	MOO : zee chee, ee	ˈmuzitʃi, i
muskellunge, muskallunge	MUH skuh luhnj	ˈmʌskələndʒ
muskrat	MUHSK rat	ˈmʌskræt
Muslem, Muslim	MUHZ luhm	ˈmʌzləm
muslin	MUHZ lin	ˈmʌzlɪn
mussel	MUH suhl	ˈmʌsəl
Musset	muh SAY	məˈse
Mussolini, Benito	moo suh LEE ni, be NEE taw	musəˈlini, bɛˈnito
Mussulman	MUH suhl muhn	ˈmʌsəlmən
mustache	MUH stash	ˈmʌstæʃ
mustang	MUH stang	ˈmʌstæŋ
mutant	MYOO : tuhnt	ˈmjutənt
mutation	myoo : TAY shuhn	mjuˈteʃən
Mutsuhito	MOOT soo HEE taw	ˈmutsuˈhito
mutual	MYOO : choo uhl	ˈmjutʃuəl
muzhik, muzjik	moo : ZHEEK	muˈʒik
Mweru	MWAY roo :	ˈmweru
Mycenae	migh SEE nee	maɪˈsini
mycosis	migh KOH sis	maɪˈkosɪs
myelitis	migh uh LIGH tis	maɪəˈlaɪtɪs
myna, -h	MIGH nuh	ˈmaɪnə
Mynheer, m-	mighn HAIR	maɪnˈhɛr
myopia	migh OH pi uh	maɪˈopɪə
Myra	MIGH ruh	ˈmaɪrə
Myrdal, Gunnar	MIR dahl, GUH ner	ˈmɪrdɑl, ˈgʌnər
myriad	MI ri uhd	ˈmɪrɪəd
Myrmidon, m-	MER mi dahn	ˈmɝmɪdɑn
myrrh	mer	mɝ
Mysore	migh SAWR	maɪˈsɔr
mystery	MI stuh ri	ˈmɪstərɪ
mysticism	MI stuh si zuhm	ˈmɪstəsɪzəm

at [æ] ; *ah* [ɑ] ; *air* [ɛ] ; *awful* [ɔ] ; *say* [e] ; *back* [b] ; *ch*air [tʃ] ; *do* [d] ; *elm* [ɛ] ; *eel* [i] ; *server* [ˈɝ, ər] ; *f*it [f] ; *go* [g] ; *h*urt [h] ; *is* [ɪ] ; *high* [aɪ] ; *jet* [dʒ] ; *k*iss [k] ; *l*amb [l] ; *my* [m] ; *n*ice [n] ;

mystique	mi STEEK	mɪˈstik
mythical	MI thi kuhl	ˈmɪθɪkəl
Mytilene, Mytileni	mi tuh LEE ni	mɪtəˈlinɪ

N

Naaman	NAY uh muhn	ˈneəmən
nabob	NAY bahb	ˈnebɑb
Naboth	NAY bahth	ˈnebɑθ
nacelle	nuh SEL	nəˈsɛl
nacre	NAY ker	ˈnekər
nacreous	NAY kri uhs	ˈnekrɪəs
nadir	NAY der	ˈnedər
Naga	NAH gah	ˈnɑgɑ
Nagasaki	NAH gah SAH kee	ˈnɑgɑˈsɑki
Nagoya	nah GAW yah	nɑˈgɔjɑ
Nagy (Hungarian)	nawj	nɔdʒ
Nagykoros	NAWJ KUH ruhsh	ˈnɔdʒˈkʌrəʃ
Nahant	nuh HANT	nəˈhænt
Nahua	NAH wah	ˈnɑwɑ
Nahum	NAY uhm	ˈneəm
naiad	NAY ad	ˈneæd
naïf	nah EEF	nɑˈif
Nairobi	nigh ROH bi	naɪˈrobɪ
naive	nah EEV	nɑˈiv
naiveté	nah EEV tay	nɑˈivte
naked	NAY kid	ˈnekɪd
Nakhichevan	nah kee che VAHN	nɑkitʃɛˈvɑn
Nama	NAH mah	ˈnɑmɑ
Namaqua	nah MAHK wuh	nɑˈmɑkwə
Nanda Devi	NUHN dah DAY vee	ˈnʌndɑ ˈdevi
Nanga Parbat	NUHNG gah PER buht	ˈnʌŋgɑ ˈpɝbət
nankeen, nankin	nan KEEN	nænˈkin
Nanking	nan king	næn kɪŋ
Nansen	NAN suhn	ˈnænsən
Nantes	nants	nænts
Nantucket	nan TUH kit	nænˈtʌkɪt
napalm	NAY pahm	ˈnepɑm
nape	nayp	nep
napery	NAY puh ri	ˈnepərɪ
Naphtali	NAF tuh ligh	ˈnæftəlaɪ
naphtha	NAF thuh	ˈnæfθə
Naples	NAY puhlz	ˈnepəlz
napoleon, N-	nuh POH li uhn	nəˈpolɪən
naprapathy	nuh PRA puh thi	nəˈpræpəθɪ
Narbonne	nahr BAWN	nɑrˈbɔn
narcissism	nahr SI si zuhm	nɑrˈsɪsɪzəm
narcolepsy	NAHR kuh lep si	ˈnɑrkəlɛpsɪ

sing [ŋ]; *oh* [o]; *oil* [ɔɪ]; *foot* [ʊ]; *foo:*d [u]; *how* [aʊ]; *pie* [p]; *ray* [r]; *so* [s]; *shall* [ʃ];
to [t]; *thin* [θ]; *th:*en [ð]; *above* (*uh* B*UH*V) [ə, ˈʌ]; *vine* [v]; *wine* [w]; *whine* [hw];
you [j]; *zoo* [z]; *rouge* (roo:*zh*) [ʒ].

narcosis	nahr KOH sis	nɑr'kosɪs
narcotic	nahr KAH tik	nɑr'kɑtɪk
narghile, nargile	NAHR guh li	'nɑrgəlɪ
Narragansett	na ruh GAN sit	nærə'gænsɪt
narrate	na RAYT	næ'ret
Narva	NAHR vah	'nɑrvɑ
Narvik	NAHR vik	'nɑrvɪk
narwal, narwhal	NAHR wuhl	'nɑrwəl
nascent	NAY suhnt	'nesənt
Nashua	NA shoo uh	'næʃʊə
Nassau	NA saw	'næsɔ
Nasser, Gamal Abdel	NAH ser, gah MAHL AHB duhl	'nɑsər, gɑ'mɑl 'ɑbdəl
nasturtium	nuh STER shuhm	nə'stɝʃəm
natal	NAY tuhl	'netəl
Natal	nuh TAL	nə'tæl
natatorium	NAY tuh taw ri uhm	'netətɔrɪəm
Natchez	NA chiz	'nætʃɪz
Nathan	NAY thuhn	'neθən
national	NA shuh nuhl	'næʃənəl
nationale (French)	na syaw NAL	næsjɔ'næl
nativity, N-	nuh TI vuh ti	nə'tɪvətɪ
naturalization	na chuh ruh li ZAY shuhn	nætʃərəlɪ'zeʃən
naturally	NA chuh ruh li	'nætʃərəlɪ
nature	NAY cher	'netʃər
naught	nawt	nɔt
nausea	NAW zhuh	'nɔʒə
nauseate	NAW zhi ayt	'nɔʒɪet
nauseous	NAW zhuhs	'nɔʒəs
Nausicaä	naw SI kay uh	nɔ'sɪkeə
nautch	nawch	nɔtʃ
nautical	NAW ti kuhl	'nɔtɪkəl
nautilus	NAW tuh luhs	'nɔtələs
Navaho, Navajo	NA vuh hoh	'nævəho
naval	NAY vuhl	'nevəl
navar	NA vahr	'nævɑr
Navarra	nah VAH rah	nɑ'vɑrɑ
Navarre	nuh VAHR	nə'vɑr
navel	NAY vuhl	'nevəl
navicert	NA vi sert	'nævɪsərt
navvy	NA vi	'nævɪ
nawab, N-	nuh WAWB	nə'wɔb
Naxos	NAK sahs	'næksɑs
Nazi	NAHT si	'nɑtsɪ
Nazimova, Alla	nuh ZI muh vuh, AH luh	nə'zɪməvə, 'ɑlə
Neanderthal	ni AN der thawl	nɪ'ændərθɔl
Neapolitan	nee uh PAH luh tuhn	niə'pɑlətən
Nebiim	ne bi EEM	nɛbɪ'im
Nebo	NEE boh	'nibo
Nebraska	nuh BRA skuh	nə'bræskə
Nebuchadnessar	neb yoo kuhd NE zer	nɛbjʊkəd'nɛzər
nebular	NE byuh ler	'nɛbjələr

at [æ]; ah [ɑ]; air [ɛ]; awful [ɔ]; say [e]; back [b]; chair [tʃ]; do [d]; elm [ɛ]; eel [i]; server ['ɝ, ər]; fit [f]; go [g]; hurt [h]; is [ɪ]; high [aɪ]; jet [dʒ]; kiss [k]; lamb [l]; my [m]; nice [n];

nebulous	NE byuh luhs	ˈnɛbjələs
necessarily	NE suh sai ruh li	ˈnɛsəsɛrəlɪ
necessary	NE suh sai ri	ˈnɛsəsɛrɪ
necklace	NE klis	ˈnɛklɪs
necrology	ne KRAH luh ji	nɛˈkrɑlədʒɪ
necromancer	NE kruh man ser	ˈnɛkrəmænsər
necropolis	ne KRAH puh lis	nɛˈkrɑpəlɪs
necrosis	ne KROH sis	nɛˈkrosɪs
nectar	NEK ter	ˈnɛktər
nectarine	NEK tuh reen	ˈnɛktərin
nee, née	nay	ne
ne'er-do-well	NAIR doo wel	ˈnɛrdʊwɛl
nefarious	ni FAI ri uhs	nɪˈfɛrɪəs
negate	ni GAYT	nɪˈget
negatron	NE guh trahn	ˈnɛgətrɑn
Negev	NE gev	ˈnɛgɛv
negligee	NE gli zhay	ˈnɛglɪʒe
negligence	NE gli juhns	ˈnɛglɪdʒəns
negotiable	ni GOH shuh buhl	nɪˈgoʃəbəl
negotiate	ni GOH shi ayt	nɪˈgoʃiet
negotiation	ni goh shi AY shuhn	nɪgoʃɪˈeʃən
Negrillo	ni GRI loh	nɪˈgrɪlo
Negri Sembilan	NAY gree sem bee LAHN	ˈnegri sɛmbiˈlɑn
Negrito	ni GREE toh	nɪˈgrito
Negro	NEE groh	ˈnigro
Negro, Río	NAY groh, REE oh	ˈnegro, ˈrio
Negros (island)	NAY grohs	ˈnegros
negus, N-	NEE guhs	ˈnigəs
Nehemiah	nee uh MIGH uh	niəˈmaɪə
Nehru, Jawaharlal	NAY roo :, juh WAH her lahl	ˈneru, dʒəˈwɑhərlɑl
Neiman-Marcus	NEE muhn MAHR kuhs	ˈnimən ˈmɑrkəs
neither	NEE th : er	ˈniðər
Nejd	nezhd	nɛʒd
nekton	NEK tahn	ˈnɛktɑn
Nembutal	NEM byuh tahl	ˈnɛmbjətɑl
Nemea	NEE mi uh	ˈnimɪə
nemesis, N-	NE muh sis	ˈnɛməsɪs
Neocene	NEE uh seen	ˈniəsin
neolithic	NEE uh li thik	ˈniəlɪθɪk
neologism	nee AH luh ji zuhm	niˈɑlədʒɪzəm
neomycin	nee uh MIGH sin	niəˈmaɪsɪn
neon	NEE ahn	ˈniɑn
neophyte	NEE uh fight	ˈniəfaɪt
neoprene	NEE uh preen	ˈniəprin
Nepal	ni PAWL	nɪˈpɔl
Nepalese	ne puh LEEZ	nɛpəˈliz
nepenthe	ni PEN thi	nɪˈpɛnθɪ
nephew	NE fyoo :	ˈnɛfju
nephritis	ne FRIGH tis	nɛˈfraɪtɪs
ne plus ultra	nee pluhs UHL truh	ni plʌs ˈʌltrə
nepotism	NE puh ti zuhm	ˈnɛpətɪzəm

---

sing [ŋ] ; *oh* [o] ; *oil* [ɔɪ] ; *foot* [ʊ] ; *foo:d* [u] ; *how* [aʊ] ; *pie* [p] ; *ray* [r] ; *so* [s] ; *shall* [ʃ] ; *to* [t] ; *thin* [θ] ; *th:en* [ð] ; above (*uh BUH*V) [ə, ˈʌ] ; *vine* [v] ; *wine* [w] ; *whine* [hw] ; *you* [j] ; *zoo* [z] ; *rouge* (roo:*zh*) [ʒ].

Neptune	NEP too : n	ˈnɛptun
Nereid	NI ri id	ˈnɪrɪɪd
Nereus	NI roo : s	ˈnɪrus
Nero	NI roh	ˈnɪro
Nesselrode, n-	NE suhl rohd	ˈnɛsəlrod
Nessus	NE suhs	ˈnɛsəs
n'est-ce pas	nes PAH	nɛs ˈpɑ
nestle	NE suhl	ˈnɛsəl
Nestor	NE ster	ˈnɛstər
Nestorianism	ne STAW ri uh ni zuhm	nɛˈstɔrɪənɪzəm
nether	NE th : er	ˈnɛðər
Netherlands	NE th : er luhndz	ˈnɛðərləndz
Neuchâtel	ner sha TEL	nərʃæˈtɛl
Neufchâtel (cheese)	noo : shuh TEL	nuʃəˈtɛl
Neufchâtel (France)	ner sha TEL	nərʃæˈtɛl
Neuilly	ner YEE	nərˈji
neum, -e	noo : m	num
neuralgia	noo RAL juh	nʊˈrældʒə
neurasthenia	noo ruhs THEE ni uh	nʊrəsˈθinɪə
neuritis	noo RIGH tis	nʊˈraɪtɪs
neuroses (pl.)	noo ROH seez	nʊˈrosiz
neurosis	noo ROH sis	nʊˈrosɪs
neurotic	noo RAH tik	nʊˈrɑtɪk
neutral	NOO : truhl	ˈnutrəl
neutrino	noo : TREE noh	nuˈtrino
neutron	NOO : trahn	ˈnutrɑn
Neva	NEE vuh	ˈnivə
Nevada (state)	nuh VA duh	nəˈvædə
névé	nay VAY	neˈve
Neversink	NE ver singk	ˈnɛvərsɪŋk
nevus	NEE vuhs	ˈnivəs
new	noo :	nu
Newark	NOO : erk	ˈnuərk
Newberg, Newburg, -h	NOO : berg	ˈnubərg
Newcastle	NOO : ka suhl	ˈnukæsəl
Newfoundland	NOO : fuhnd luhnd	ˈnufəndlənd
New Orleans	noo : AWR li uhnz	nu ˈɔrlɪənz
news	noo : z	nuz
Ngaio	NIGH oh	ˈnaɪo
niacin	NIGH uh suhn	ˈnaɪəsən
Niagara	nigh A gruh	naɪˈægrə
Niarchos, Stavros	NYAHR hohs, STAHV rohs	ˈnjɑrhos, ˈstɑvros
Nibelung	NEE buh loong	ˈnibəlʊŋ
Nibelungenlied	NEE buh loong uhn leed	ˈnibəlʊŋənlid
Nicaea	nigh SEE uh	naɪˈsiə
Nicaragua	ni kuh RAH gwuh	nɪkəˈrɑgwə
Nice (France)	nees	nis
nicety	NIGH suh ti	ˈnaɪsətɪ
niche	nich	nɪtʃ
nickelodeon	ni kuh LOH di uhn	nɪkəˈlodɪən
Nicobar	ni kuh BAHR	nɪkəˈbɑr
Nicolette	ni kuh LET	nɪkəˈlɛt

at [æ] ; ah [ɑ] ; air [ɛ] ; awful [ɔ] ; say [e] ; back [b] ; chair [tʃ] ; do [d] ; elm [ɛ] ; eel [i] ;
server [ˈɝ, ər] ; fit [f] ; go [g] ; hurt [h] ; is [ɪ] ; high [aɪ] ; jet [dʒ] ; kiss [k] ; lamb [l] ; my [m] ;
nice [n] ;

Nicosia	nee kaw ZEE uh	nikɔˈziə
nicotine	NI kuh teen	ˈnɪkətin
nidus	NIGH duhs	ˈnaɪdəs
Niebuhr	NEE boor	ˈnibʊr
Niemoeller	NEE mi ler	ˈnimɪlər
Nietzsche	NEE chuh	ˈnitʃə
Niger	NIGH jer	ˈnaɪdʒər
Nigeria	nigh JI ri uh	naɪˈdʒɪrɪə
niggard	NI gerd	ˈnɪgərd
nightingale, N-	NIGH tuhn gayl	ˈnaɪtəngel
nigrescence	nigh GRE suhns	naɪˈgresəns
nigrify	NI gruh figh	ˈnɪgrəfaɪ
nihil	NIGH hil	ˈnaɪhɪl
nihilism	NIGH uh li zuhm	ˈnaɪəlɪzəm
nihilist	NIGH uh list	ˈnaɪəlɪst
Nihon	nee hahn	ni hɑn
Niihau	NEE ee HAH oo:	ˈniiˈhɑu
Nijinsky	nuh JIN ski	nəˈdʒɪnskɪ
Nijmegen	NIGH may guhn	ˈnaɪmegən
Nike	NIGH kee	ˈnaɪki
Niksic	NEE shich	ˈniʃɪtʃ
nil	nil	nɪl
Nile	nighl	naɪl
Nilotic	nigh LAH tik	naɪˈlɑtɪk
nimbus	NIM buhs	ˈnɪmbəs
Nîmes	neem	nim
Nimitz	NI mits	ˈnɪmɪts
Nineveh	NI nuh vuh	ˈnɪnəvə
Niobe	NIGH uh bi	ˈnaɪəbɪ
niobium	nigh OH bi uhm	naɪˈobɪəm
Nippon	NI pahn	ˈnɪpɑn
Nipponese	ni puh NEEZ	nɪpəˈniz
nirvana	ner VA nuh	nərˈvænə
nisei	nee say	ni se
nisi	NIGH sigh	ˈnaɪsaɪ
Nissen	NI suhn	ˈnɪsən
nisus	NIGH suhs	ˈnaɪsəs
niter	NIGH ter	ˈnaɪtər
nitric	NIGH trik	ˈnaɪtrɪk
nitrogen	NIGH truh juhn	ˈnaɪtrədʒən
nitrogenous	nigh TRAH juh nuhs	naɪˈtrɑdʒənəs
nitroglycerin, -e	nigh truh GLI suh rin	naɪtrəˈglɪsərɪn
nitrous	NIGH truhs	ˈnaɪtrəs
Nixon	NIK suhn	ˈnɪksən
nizam, N-	ni ZAHM	nɪˈzam
Noah	NOH uh	ˈnoə
Nobel	noh BEL	noˈbɛl
nobelium	noh BE li uhm	noˈbɛlɪəm
noblesse oblige	noh BLES oh BLEEZH	noˈblɛs oˈbliʒ
nocturn, -e	NAHK tern	ˈnɑktərn
nocturnal	nahk TER nuhl	nɑkˈtɜnəl
nocuous	NAH kyoo uhs	ˈnɑkjuəs

---

sing [ŋ] ; *oh* [o] ; *oil* [ɔɪ] ; *foot* [ʊ] ; *foo:d* [u] ; *how* [aʊ] ; *pie* [p] ; *ray* [r] ; *so* [s] ; *shall* [ʃ] ; *to* [t] ; *thin* [θ] ; *th:en* [ð] ; above (*uh BUH*V) [ə, ˈʌ] ; *vine* [v] ; *wine* [w] ; *whine* [hw] ; *you* [j] ; *zoo* [z] ; *rouge* (roo:*zh*) [ʒ].

nodal	NOH duhl	ˈnodəl
node	nohd	nod
nodule	NAH jool	ˈnadʒʊl
Noel (personal name)	NOH uhl	ˈnoəl
Noel, n- (Christmas)	noh EL	noˈɛl
noesis	noh EE sis	noˈisɪs
Noguchi	noh GOO : chi	noˈgutʃɪ
nolens, volens	NOH lenz VOH lenz	ˈnolɛnz ˈvolɛnz
noli me tangere	NOH ligh mee TAN juh ri	ˈnolaɪ mi ˈtændʒərɪ
nolle prosequi	NAH li PRAH si kwigh	ˈnalɪ ˈprasɪkwaɪ
nolo contendere	NOH loh kuhn TEN duh ri	ˈnolo kənˈtɛndərɪ
nol-pros	nahl PRAHS	nalˈpras
noma	NOH muh	ˈnomə
nomad	NOH mad	ˈnomæd
nomadic	noh MA dik	noˈmædɪk
nom de guerre	nahm duh GAIR	nɑm də ˈgɛr
nom de plume	nahm duh PLOO : M	nɑm də ˈplum
Nome	nohm	nom
nomenclature	NOH muhn klay cher	ˈnomənkletʃər
nominal	NAH muh nuhl	ˈnamənəl
Nomura	NAW moo : rah	ˈnɔmurɑ
nonchalance	NAHN shuh luhns	ˈnɑnʃələns
nonchalant	NAHN shuh luhnt	ˈnɑnʃələnt
noncombatant	nahn KAHM buh tuhnt	nɑnˈkɑmbətənt
non compos mentis	nahn KAHM puhs MEN tis	nɑn ˈkɑmpəs ˈmɛntɪs
nonconformist	nahn kuhn FAWR mist	nɑnkənˈfɔrmɪst
nondescript	NAHN di skript	ˈnɑndɪskrɪpt
nonentity	nahn EN tuh ti	nɑnˈɛntətɪ
non obstante	nahn ahb STAN ti	nɑn ɑbˈstæntɪ
nonpareil	nahn puh REL	nɑnpəˈrɛl
nonplus	nahn PLUHS	nɑnˈplʌs
non prosequitur	nahn proh SE kwi ter	nɑn proˈsɛkwɪtər
non sequitur	nahn SE kwi ter	nɑn ˈsɛkwɪtər
nook	nook	nʊk
Norfolk	NAWR fuhk	ˈnɔrfək
normalcy	NAWR muhl si	ˈnɔrməlsɪ
Norse	nawrs	nɔrs
Norstad, Lauris	NAWR stad, LAW ris	ˈnɔrstæd, ˈlɔrɪs
Northumberland	nawr THUHM ber luhnd	nɔrˈθʌmbərlənd
Norwalk	NAWR wawk	ˈnɔrwɔk
Norway	NAWR way	ˈnɔrwe
Norwegian	nawr WEE juhn	nɔrˈwidʒən
Norwich (Connecticut)	NAWR wich	ˈnɔrwɪtʃ
Norwich (England)	NAW rij	ˈnɔrɪdʒ
nosology	noh SAH luh ji	noˈsalədʒɪ
nostalgia	nah STAL juh	nɑˈstældʒə
Nostradamus	nah struh DAY muhs	nɑstrəˈdeməs
Nostrand	NOH struhnd	ˈnostrənd
nostril	NAH struhl	ˈnastrəl
nostrum	NAH struhm	ˈnastrəm
not	naht	nɑt
nota bene	NOH tuh BEE ni	ˈnotə ˈbini

at [æ] ; ah [ɑ] ; air [ɛ] ; awful [ɔ] ; say [e] ; back [b] ; chair [tʃ] ; do [d] ; elm [ɛ] ; eel [i] ;
server [ˈɝ, ər] ; fit [f] ; go [g] ; hurt [h] ; is [ɪ] ; high [aɪ] ; jet [dʒ] ; kiss [k] ; lamb [l] ; my [m] ;
nice [n] ;

noteworthy	NOHT wer th:i	ˈnotwərði
nothing	NUH thing	ˈnʌθɪŋ
notoriety	noh tuh RIGH uh ti	notəˈraɪətɪ
Notre Dame (Paris)	NOH truh DAHM	ˈnotrə ˈdam
Notre Dame (U.S.)	NOH ter DAYM	ˈnotər ˈdem
Nottingham	NAH ting uhm	ˈnɑtɪŋəm
nougat	NOO: guht	ˈnugət
nought	nawt	nɔt
Nouméa	noo: may AH	numeˈɑ
noumenon	NOO: mi nahn	ˈnumɪnɑn
nourish	NER ish	ˈnɝɪʃ
nous (French)	noo:	nu
nouveau riche	noo: voh REESH	nuvo ˈriʃ
nova, N-	NOH vuh	ˈnovə
Novaes, Guiomar	noh VIGH ays, GEE oh mahr	noˈvaɪes, ˈgiomɑr
Nova Scotia	NOH vuh SKOH shuh	ˈnovə ˈskoʃə
Novaya Zemlya	NAW vah yah ZEM lyah	ˈnɔvɑjə ˈzɛmljɑ
novel	NAH vuhl	ˈnɑvəl
novella	naw VE luh	nɔˈvɛlə
novelle (pl.)	naw VE le	nɔˈvɛlɛ
November	noh VEM ber	noˈvɛmbər
novena	noh VEE nuh	noˈvinə
Novgorod	NAHV guh rahd	ˈnɑvgərɑd
novice	NAH vis	ˈnɑvɪs
Novikov	NAW vi kawf	ˈnɔvɪkɔf
Novi Sad	NAW vi SAHD	ˈnɔvɪ ˈsad
novitiate, noviciate	noh VI shi it	noˈvɪʃɪɪt
novocain, -e, N-	NOH vuh kayn	ˈnovəken
Novorossiisk	naw vaw raw SEESK	novɔrɔˈsisk
Novosibirsk	naw vaw si BIRSK	novɔsɪˈbɪrsk
Novotna	nuh VAHT nuh	nəˈvɑtnə
novus ordo seclorum	NOH vuhs AWR doh suh KLOH ruhm	ˈnovəs ˈɔrdo səˈklorəm
Nowy Sacz	NAW vi SAWNCH	ˈnɔvɪ ˈsɔntʃ
Nox	nahks	nɑks
noxious	NAHK shuhs	ˈnɑkʃəs
Noyes	noiz	nɔɪz
Nu, see U Nu		
nuance	noo: AHNS	nuˈɑns
Nuba	NOO: bah	ˈnubɑ
Nubian	NOO: bi uhn	ˈnubɪən
nubile	NOO: buhl	ˈnubəl
nuclear	NOO: kli er	ˈnuklɪər
nuclei (pl.)	NOO: kli igh	ˈnuklɪaɪ
nucleon	NOO: kli ahn	ˈnuklɪɑn
nucleonics	noo: kli AH niks	nuklɪˈɑnɪks
nucleus	NOO: kli uhs	ˈnuklɪəs
nude	noo:d	nud
Nuevo Leon	NWE vaw le AWN	ˈnwɛvɔ lɛˈon
nugatory	NOO: guh taw ri	ˈnugətɔrɪ
nugget	NUH git	ˈnʌgɪt

sing [ŋ]; oh [o]; oil [ɔɪ]; foot [ʊ]; foo:d [u]; how [aʊ]; pie [p]; ray [r]; so [s]; shall [ʃ]; to [t]; thin [θ]; th:en [ð]; above (uh BUHV) [ə, ˈʌ]; vine [v]; wine [w]; whine [hw]; you [j]; zoo [z]; rouge (roo:zh) [ʒ].

nuisance	NOO : suhns	ˈnusəns
null	nuhl	nʌl
nullity	NUH luh ti	ˈnʌlətɪ
numeral	NOO : muh ruhl	ˈnumərəl
numismatic	noo : miz MA tik	numɪzˈmætɪk
numismatist	noo : MIZ muh tist	nuˈmɪzmətɪst
nunc dimittis	nuhngk di MI tis	nʌŋk dɪˈmɪtɪs
nuncio	NUHN shi oh	ˈnʌnʃɪo
Nuñez	NOO : nyes	ˈnunjɛs
nuptial	NUHP shuhl	ˈnʌpʃəl
Nuremberg	NOO ruhm berg	ˈnurəmbərg
Nürnberg	NIRN bairk	ˈnɪrnbɛrk
nurture	NER cher	ˈnɝtʃər
nutation	noo : TAY shuhn	nuˈteʃən
nutmeg	NUHT meg	ˈnʌtmɛg
nutrient	NOO : tri uhnt	ˈnutrɪənt
nutriment	NOO : truh muhnt	ˈnutrəmənt
nutrition	noo : TRI shuhn	nuˈtrɪʃən
nux vomica	NUHKS VAH mi kuh	ˈnʌks ˈvɑmɪkə
Nyasa	nigh A suh	naɪˈæsə
Nyasaland	nigh A suh land	naɪˈæsəlænd
nyctophobia	nik tuh FOH bi uh	nɪktəˈfobɪə
Nygaarsdvold	NI gawrs vawl	ˈnɪgɔrsvɔl
Nyiregyhaza	NYI rej HAH zaw	ˈnjɪrɛdʒˈhɑzɔ
nylon	NIGH lahn	ˈnaɪlɑn
nymph	nimf	nɪmf
nymphomania	nim fuh MAY ni uh	nɪmfəˈmenɪə
Nyx	niks	nɪks

O

Oahu	oh AH hoo :	oˈɑhu
oases	oh AY seez	oˈesiz
oasis	oh AY sis	oˈesɪs
oath	ohth	oθ
Oaxaca	wah HAH kah	wɑˈhɑkɑ
Ob	ohb	ob
Obadiah	oh buh DIGH uh	obəˈdaɪə
obbligato	ah bli GAH toh	ɑblɪˈgɑto
obdurate	AHB doo rit	ˈɑbdʊrɪt
obeah	OH bi uh	ˈobɪə
Obed	OH bid	ˈobɪd
obeisance	oh BAY suhns	oˈbesəns
obelisk	AH buh lisk	ˈɑbəlɪsk
obelus	AH buh luhs	ˈɑbələs
Oberammergau	oh ber A mer gow	obərˈæmərgaʊ
Oberon	OH buh rahn	ˈobərɑn
obese	oh BEES	oˈbis

---

at [æ]; ah [ɑ]; air [ɛ]; awful [ɔ]; say [e]; back [b]; chair [tʃ]; do [d]; elm [ɛ]; eel [i]; server [ˈɝ, ər]; fit [f]; go [g]; hurt [h]; is [ɪ]; high [aɪ]; jet [dʒ]; kiss [k]; lamb [l]; my [m]; nice [n];

obesity	oh BEE suh ti	oˈbisətɪ
obfuscate	AHB fuh skayt	ˈɑbfəsket
obi	OH bi	ˈobɪ
obiit	AH bi it	ˈɑbɪɪt
obit	OH bit	ˈobɪt
obiter dictum	AH bi ter DIK tuhm	ˈɑbɪtər ˈdɪktəm
obituary	uh BI choo ai ri	əˈbɪtʃʊɛrɪ
object (n)	AHB jikt	ˈɑbdʒɪkt
object (v)	uhb JEKT	əbˈdʒɛkt
objet d'art	awb zhe DAR	ɔbʒɛ ˈdær
objurgate	AHB jer gayt	ˈɑbdʒərget
oblation	uh BLAY shuhn	əˈbleʃən
obligato	ah bli GAH toh	ɑblɪˈgɑto
obligatory	uh BLI guh taw ri	əˈblɪgətɔrɪ
oblige	uh BLIGHJ	əˈblaɪdʒ
oblique	uh BLEEK	əˈblik
oblique (military)	uh BLIGHK	əˈblaɪk
obliquity	uh BLI kwuh ti	əˈblɪkwətɪ
obliterate	uh BLI tuh rayt	əˈblɪtəret
oblivion	uh BLI vi uhn	əˈblɪvɪən
oblivious	uh BLI vi uhs	əˈblɪvɪəs
oblong	AHB lawng	ˈɑblɔŋ
obloquy	AH bluh kwi	ˈɑbləkwɪ
oboe	OH boh	ˈobo
Oboler	OH buh ler	ˈobələr
Oborin, Lev	ah BAW rin, lef	ɑˈbɔrɪn, lɛf
Obregón	aw bre GAWN	ɔbrɛˈgɔn
obscenity	uhb SE nuh ti	əbˈsɛnətɪ
obscurantism	uhb SKYOO ruhn ti zuhm	əbˈskjʊrəntɪzəm
obsequious	uhb SEE kwi uhs	əbˈsikwɪəs
obsequy	AHB si kwi	ˈɑbsɪkwɪ
obsolete	AHB suh leet	ˈɑbsəlit
obstacle	AHB stuh kuhl	ˈɑbstəkəl
obstetric	ahb STE trik	ɑbˈstɛtrɪk
obstetrician	ahb ste TRI shuhn	ɑbstɛˈtrɪʃən
obstinate	AHB stuh nit	ˈɑbstənɪt
obstreperous	uhb STRE puh ruhs	əbˈstrɛpərəs
obtrusive	uhb TROO : siv	əbˈtrusɪv
obtuse	uhb TOO : S	əbˈtus
obverse	AHB vers	ˈɑbvərs
O'Casey, Sean	oh KAY si, SHAWN	oˈkesɪ, ˈʃɔn
Occam	AH kuhm	ˈɑkəm
occasion	uh KAY zhuhn	əˈkeʒən
occident, O-	AHK suh duhnt	ˈɑksədənt
occipital	ahk SI puh tuhl	ɑkˈsɪpətəl
occult	uh KUHLT	əˈkʌlt
occultation	ah kuhl TAY shuhn	ɑkəlˈteʃən
Oceania	oh shi A ni uh	oʃɪˈænɪə
oceanographer	oh shi uh NAH gruh fer	oʃɪəˈnɑgrəfər
Oceanus	oh SEE uh nuhs	oˈsiənəs
ocher, ochre	OH ker	ˈokər
ochlocracy	ahk LAH kruh si	ɑkˈlɑkrəsɪ

sing [ŋ]; *oh* [o]; *oil* [ɔɪ]; *foot* [ʊ]; *foo*:d [u]; *how* [aʊ]; *pie* [p]; *ray* [r]; *so* [s]; *shall* [ʃ]; *to* [t]; *thin* [θ]; *th*:en [ð]; *above* (*uh* B*UH*V) [ə, ˈʌ]; *vine* [v]; *wine* [w]; *whine* [hw]; *you* [j]; *zoo* [z]; rouge (roo:*zh*) [ʒ].

H.P.—R

Ochs	ahks	ɑks
Ockham	AH kuhm	ˈɑkəm
octagon	AHK tuh guhn	ˈɑktəgən
octagonal	ahk TA guh nuhl	ɑkˈtægənəl
octahedron	ahk tuh HEE druhn	ɑktəˈhidrən
octameter	ahk TA muh ter	ɑkˈtæmətər
octane	AHK tayn	ˈɑkten
Octans	AHK tanz	ˈɑktænz
octant	AHK tuhnt	ˈɑktənt
octave	AHK tayv	ˈɑktev
octave (music)	AHK tiv	ˈɑktɪv
octavo	ahk TAY voh	ɑkˈtevo
octogenarian	ahk tuh ji NAI ri uhn	ɑktədʒɪˈnɛrɪən
octopus	AHK tuh puhs	ˈɑktəpəs
octoroon	ahk tuh ROO:N	ɑktəˈrun
ocular	AHK yuh ler	ˈɑkjələr
oculist	AHK yuh list	ˈɑkjəlɪst
odalisque, odalisk	OH duh lisk	ˈodəlɪsk
Odegard	OH duh gahrd	ˈodəgɑrd
Oder	OH der	ˈodər
Odessa	oh DE suh	oˈdɛsə
odeum	oh DEE uhm	oˈdiəm
Odin	OH din	ˈodɪn
odious	OH di uhs	ˈodɪəs
odium	OH di uhm	ˈodɪəm
Odoacer	oh doh AY ser	odoˈesər
odoriferous	oh duh RI fuh ruhs	odəˈrɪfərəs
odorous	OH duh ruhs	ˈodərəs
Odysseus	oh DI si uhs	oˈdɪsɪəs
Odyssey	AH duh si	ˈɑdəsɪ
oecumenical	e kyoo ME ni kuhl	ɛkjuˈmɛnɪkəl
Oedipal	E duh puhl	ˈɛdəpəl
Oedipus	E duh puhs	ˈɛdəpəs
Oenone	ee NOH ni	iˈnonɪ
oeuvre	ER vruh	ˈɝvrə
Offenbach	AW fuhn bahk	ˈɔfənbɑk
officer	AW fuh ser	ˈɔfəsər
official	uh FI shuhl	əˈfɪʃəl
officious	uh FI shuhs	əˈfɪʃəs
O'Flaherty	oh FLA her ti	oˈflæhərtɪ
often	AW fuhn	ˈɔfən
ogee	oh JEE	oˈdʒi
Ogilvie	OH guhl vi	ˈogəlvɪ
ogive	OH jighv	ˈodʒaɪv
ogle	OH guhl	ˈogəl
Oglethorpe	OH guhl thawrp	ˈogəlθɔrp
Ogpu	AHG poo:	ˈɑgpu
ogre	OH ger	ˈogər
O'Hara	oh HA ruh	oˈhærə
ohm, O-	ohm	om
oil	oil	ɔɪl
Oireachtas	AI ruhk tuhs	ˈɛrəktəs

at [æ]; *ah* [ɑ]; *air* [ɛ]; *awful* [ɔ]; *say* [e]; *back* [b]; *chair* [tʃ]; *do* [d]; *elm* [ɛ]; *eel* [i]; *server* [ˈɝ, ər]; *fit* [f]; *go* [g]; *hurt* [h]; *is* [ɪ]; *high* [aɪ]; *jet* [dʒ]; *kiss* [k]; *lamb* [l]; *my* [m]; *nice* [n];

Oise	wahz	wɑz
Oistrakh	OI strahk	ˈɔɪstrɑk
Ojibwa, -y	oh JIB way	oˈdʒɪbwe
okapi	oh KAH pi	oˈkɑpɪ
Okeechobee	oh ki CHOH bi	okɪˈtʃobɪ
Okhotsk	oh KAHTSK	oˈkatsk
Okie	OH ki	ˈokɪ
Okinawa	oh ki NAH wah	okɪˈnɑwɑ
Oklahoma	oh kluh HOH muh	oklǝˈhomǝ
okra	OH kruh	ˈokrǝ
Olav	OH lahf	ˈolɑf
Oldham	OHL duhm	ˈoldǝm
oleander	oh li AN der	olɪˈændǝr
oleomargarin, -e	oh li oh MAHR juh rin	olɪoˈmɑrdʒǝrɪn
olfactory	ahl FAK tuh ri	alˈfæktǝrɪ
oligarchy	ah li GAHR ki	alɪˈgɑrkɪ
Oligocene	AH li guh seen	ˈalɪgǝsin
oligopoly	ah li GAH puh li	alɪˈgɑpǝlɪ
oligopsony	ah li GAHP suh ni	alɪˈgɑpsǝnɪ
olio	OH li oh	ˈolɪo
Olivier	oh LI vee ay	oˈlɪvie
olla	OH luh	ˈolǝ
olla-podrida	OH luh puh DREE duh	ˈolǝ pǝˈdridǝ
Olympia	oh LIM pi uh	oˈlɪmpɪǝ
Omaha	OH muh haw	ˈomǝhɔ
O'Mahoney	oh MA huh ni	oˈmæhǝnɪ
Oman	oh MAHN	oˈmɑn
Omar Khayyám	OH mahr kigh YAHM	ˈomɑr kaɪˈjɑm
omber, ombre	AHM ber	ˈambǝr
omelet, -te	AHM lit	ˈamlɪt
omen	OH muhn	ˈomǝn
ominous	AH muh nuhs	ˈamǝnǝs
omnia vincit amor	AHM ni uh VIN sit AY mawr	ˈamnɪǝ ˈvɪnsɪt ˈemɔr
omnibus	AHM nuh buhs	ˈamnǝbǝs
omnifarious	ahm ni FAI ri uhs	amnɪˈfɛrɪǝs
omnipotent	ahm NI puh tuhnt	amˈnɪpǝtǝnt
omnipresent	ahm ni PRE zuhnt	amnɪˈprɛzǝnt
omniscience	ahm NI shuhns	amˈnɪʃǝns
omniscient	ahm NI shuhnt	amˈnɪʃǝnt
omnivorous	ahm NI vuh ruhs	amˈnɪvǝrǝs
Omphale	AHM fuh lee	ˈamfǝli
Omsk	awmsk	ɔmsk
Onan	OH nuhn	ˈonǝn
onanism	OH nuh ni zuhm	ˈonǝnɪzǝm
Onassis	oh NAH sis	oˈnɑsɪs
once	wuhns	wʌns
Ondine	awn DEEN	ɔnˈdin
Onega	oh NEE guh	oˈnigǝ
Onegin, Eugene	ah NE gin, yoo JEEN	aˈnɛgɪn, juˈdʒin
Oneida	oh NIGH duh	oˈnaɪdǝ
onerous	AH nuh ruhs	ˈanǝrǝs

si*ng* [ŋ] ; *oh* [o] ; *oil* [ɔɪ] ; *foot* [ʊ] ; *foo:d* [u] ; *how* [aʊ] ; *pie* [p] ; *ray* [r] ; *so* [s] ; *sh*all [ʃ] ;
to [t] ; *thin* [θ] ; *th:*en [ð] ; *above* (*uh* B*U*H*V*) [ǝ, ˈʌ] ; *vine* [v] ; *wine* [w] ; *wh*ine [hw] ;
you [j] ; *zoo* [z] ; *rouge* (roo:*zh*) [ʒ].

onion	UHN yuhn	ˈʌnjən
onomatopoeia	ah nuh ma tuh PEE uh	ɑnəmætəˈpiə
Onondaga	ah nuhn DAW guh	ɑnənˈdɔgə
Ontario	ahn TAI ri oh	ɑnˈtɛrio
ontological	ahn tuh LAH ji kuhl	ɑntəˈlɑdʒɪkəl
ontogeny	ahn TAH juh ni	ɑnˈtɑdʒəni
ontology	ahn TAH luh ji	ɑnˈtɑlədʒɪ
onus	OH nuhs	ˈonəs
onyx	AH niks	ˈɑnɪks
oolong	OO : lawng	ˈulɔŋ
opal	OH puhl	ˈopəl
opaque	oh PAYK	oˈpek
Opéra	oh pay RAH	opeˈrɑ
opera bouffe	AH puh ruh BOO : F	ˈɑpərə ˈbuf
opera buffa	OH per ah BOO : fah	ˈopɑrɑ ˈbufɑ
operative (a)	AH puh ruh tiv	ˈɑpərətɪv
operative (n)	AH puh ray tiv	ˈɑpəretɪv
operetta	ah puh RE tuh	ɑpəˈrɛtə
ophiolatry	ah fi AH luh tri	ɑfɪˈɑlətrɪ
Ophir	OH fer	ˈofər
Ophiuchus	ah fi YOO : kuhs	ɑfɪˈjukəs
ophthalmia	ahf THAL mi uh	ɑfˈθælmɪə
ophthalmologist	ahf thuhl MAH luh jist	ɑfθəlˈmɑlədʒɪst
opiate (a, n)	OH pi it	ˈopɪt
opinion	uh PIN yuhn	əˈpɪnjən
opinionaire	uh pin yuh NAIR	əpɪnjəˈnɛr
opisthognathous	ah pis THAHG nuh thuhs	ɑpɪsˈθɑgnəθəs
opium	OH pi uhm	ˈopɪəm
Oporto	oh PAWR toh	oˈpɔrto
opossum	uh PAH suhm	əˈpɑsəm
Oppenheim	AH puhn highm	ˈɑpənhaɪm
oppidan	AH pi duhn	ˈɑpɪdən
opponent	uh POH nuhnt	əˈponənt
opportune	ah per TOO : N	ɑpərˈtun
opportunism	ah per TOO : ni zuhm	ɑpərˈtunɪzəm
opportunity	ah per TOO : nuh ti	ɑpərˈtunətɪ
oppose	uh POHZ	əˈpoz
opposite	AH puh zit	ˈɑpəzɪt
oppressor	uh PRE ser	əˈprɛsər
opprobrious	uh PROH bri uhs	əˈprobrɪəs
opprobrium	uh PROH bri uhm	əˈprobrɪəm
oppugnant	uh PUHG nuhnt	əˈpʌgnənt
optative	AHP tuh tiv	ˈɑptətɪv
optic	AHP tik	ˈɑptɪk
optician	ahp TI shuhn	ɑpˈtɪʃən
optimism	AHP tuh mi zuhm	ˈɑptəmɪzəm
optimum	AHP tuh muhm	ˈɑptəməm
option	AHP shuhn	ˈɑpʃən
optometrist	ahp TAH muh trist	ɑpˈtɑmətrɪst
optometry	ahp TAH muh tri	ɑpˈtɑmətrɪ
opulent	AH pyuh luhnt	ˈɑpjələnt
opus	OH puhs	ˈopəs

---

at [æ]; *ah* [ɑ]; *air* [ɛ]; *awful* [ɔ]; *say* [e]; *back* [b]; *chair* [tʃ]; *do* [d]; *elm* [ɛ]; *eel* [i]; *server* [ˈɝ, ər]; *f*it [f]; *go* [g]; *h*urt [h]; *is* [ɪ]; *high* [aɪ]; *jet* [dʒ]; *kiss* [k]; *lamb* [l]; *my* [m]; *nice* [n];

oracular	aw RAK yuh ler	ɔˈrækjələr
Oradea	aw RAH di ah	ɔˈrɑdɪɑ
orangoutang	oh RANG oo tang	oˈræŋʊtæŋ
orangutan	oh RANG oo tan	oˈræŋʊtæn
ora pro nobis	OH ruh proh NOH bis	ˈorə pro ˈnobɪs
orator	AW ruh ter	ˈɔrətər
oratorio	aw ruh TAW ri oh	ɔrəˈtɔrɪo
oratory	AW ruh taw ri	ˈɔrətɔrɪ
orbit	AWR bit	ˈɔrbɪt
orbital	AWR bi tuhl	ˈɔrbɪtəl
orchard	AWR cherd	ˈɔrtʃərd
orchestra	AWR ki struh	ˈɔrkɪstrə
orchestral	awr KE struhl	ɔrˈkɛstrəl
orchid	AWR kid	ˈɔrkɪd
orchidaceous	awr ki DAY shuhs	ɔrkɪˈdeʃəs
ordeal	awr DEEL	ɔrˈdil
ordinal	AWR duh nuhl	ˈɔrdənəl
ordinance	AWR duh nuhns	ˈɔrdənəns
ordinarily	AWR duh nai ruh li	ˈɔrdənɛrəlɪ
ordinary	AWR duh nai ri	ˈɔrdənɛrɪ
ordinate	AWR duh nit	ˈɔrdənɪt
ordnance	AWRD nuhns	ˈɔrdnəns
Ordovician	awr duh VI shuhn	ɔrdəˈvɪʃən
ordure	AWR jer	ˈɔrdʒər
Ordzhonikidze	awr jaw ni KEED ze	ɔrdʒɔnɪˈkidzɛ
oread	AW ri ad	ˈɔrɪæd
oregano	oh RE guh noh	oˈrɛgəno
Oregon	AW ri gahn	ˈɔrɪgɑn
Oregonian	aw ri GOH ni uhn	ɔrɪˈgonɪən
Orel	oh REL	oˈrɛl
Orestes	aw RE steez	ɔˈrɛstiz
organ	AWR guhn	ˈɔrgən
organdy, organdie	AWR guhn di	ˈɔrgəndɪ
organization	awr guh ni ZAY shuhn	ɔrgənɪˈzeʃən
orgiastic	awr ji A stik	ɔrdʒɪˈæstɪk
orgy	AWR ji	ˈɔrdʒɪ
oriel	AW ri uhl	ˈɔrɪəl
orient, O- (a, n)	AW ri uhnt	ˈɔrɪənt
orient (v)	AW ri ent	ˈɔrɪɛnt
oriental, O-	aw ri EN tuhl	ɔrɪˈɛntəl
orientation	aw ri en TAY shuhn	ɔrɪɛnˈteʃən
Oriente	aw ri EN te	ɔrɪˈɛntɛ
orifice	AW ruh fis	ˈɔrəfɪs
oriflamme	AW ruh flam	ˈɔrəflæm
origan	AW ri guhn	ˈɔrɪgən
Origen	AW ri juhn	ˈɔrɪdʒən
origin	AW ruh jin	ˈɔrədʒɪn
Orinoco	aw ruh NOH koh	ɔrəˈnoko
oriole	AW ri ohl	ˈɔrɪol
Orion	oh RIGH uhn	oˈraɪən
Oriskany	oh RI skuh ni	oˈrɪskənɪ
orison	AW ri zuhn	ˈɔrɪzən

sing [ŋ] ; *oh* [o] ; *oil* [ɔɪ] ; *foot* [ʊ] ; *foo:*d [u] ; *how* [aʊ] ; *pie* [p] ; *ray* [r] ; *so* [s] ; *shall* [ʃ] ;
to [t] ; *thin* [θ] ; *th:en* [ð] ; *above* (*uh* B*U*HV) [ə, ˈʌ] ; *vine* [v] ; *wine* [w] ; *whine* [hw] ;
you [j] ; *zoo* [z] ; *rouge* (roo:*zh*) [ʒ].

Orissa	oh RI suh	oˈrɪsə
Orizaba	aw ree SAH bah	ɔriˈsabɑ
Orkney	AWRK ni	ˈɔrknɪ
Orlando	awr LAN doh	ɔrˈlændo
Orleans	AWR li uhnz	ˈɔrlɪənz
orlon	AWR lahn	ˈɔrlɑn
Ormandy	AWR muhn dee	ˈɔrməndi
Ormazd	AWR muhzd	ˈɔrməzd
ormolu	AWR muh loo:	ˈɔrməlu
ornithology	awr ni THAH luh ji	ɔrnɪˈθalədʒɪ
ornithorhynchus	awr ni thoh RING kuhs	ɔrnɪθoˈrɪŋkəs
ornithosis	awr ni THOH sis	ɔrnɪˈθosɪs
orography	aw RAH gruh fi	ɔˈragrəfɪ
orology	aw RAH luh ji	ɔˈralədʒɪ
orometer	aw RAH muh ter	ɔˈramətər
Orosius	aw ROH zhi uhs	ɔˈroʒɪəs
orotund	AW ruh tuhnd	ˈɔrətənd
Orozco	aw RAW skaw	ɔˈrɔskɔ
Orpen	AWR puhn	ˈɔrpən
orphan	AWR fuhn	ˈɔrfən
Orpheus	AWR fi uhs	ˈɔrfɪəs
orris, orrice	AW ris	ˈɔrɪs
Ortega y Gasset, José	awr TE gah ee gah SET, haw SE	ɔrˈtega i gaˈsɛt, hɔˈsɛ
orthicon, O-	AWR thi kahn	ˈɔrθɪkɑn
orthocephalic	awr thoh suh FA lik	ɔrθosəˈfælɪk
orthodontia	awr thuh DAHN shuh	ɔrθəˈdɑnʃə
orthodox	AWR thuh dahks	ˈɔrθədɑks
orthodoxy	AWR thuh dahk si	ˈɔrθədɑksɪ
orthoepist	awr THOH i pist	ɔrˈθoɪpɪst
orthoepy	awr THOH i pi	ɔrˈθoɪpɪ
orthognathous	awr THAHG nuh thuhs	ɔrˈθagnəθəs
orthographic	awr thuh GRA fik	ɔrθəˈgræfɪk
orthography	awr THAH gruh fi	ɔrˈθagrəfɪ
orthopedic, orthopaedic	awr thuh PEE dik	ɔrθəˈpidɪk
orthophonic	awr thuh FAH nik	ɔrθəˈfanɪk
Osage	OH sayj	ˈosedʒ
Osaka	oh SAH kuh	oˈsakə
Osborn, -e	AHZ bern	ˈazbərn
Oscan	AH skuhn	ˈaskən
Osceola	ah si OH luh	asɪˈolə
oscillate	AH suh layt	ˈasəlet
oscilloscope	uh SI luh skohp	əˈsɪləskop
Osco-Umbrian	AH skoh UHM bri uhn	ˈasko ˈʌmbrɪən
osculate	AH skyuh layt	ˈaskjəlet
Oshkosh	AHSH kahsh	ˈaʃkaʃ
osier	OH zher	ˈoʒər
Osijek	AW si yek	ˈɔsijɛk
Osiris	oh SIGH ris	oˈsaɪrɪs
Osler	OH sler	ˈoslər
Oslo	AH sloh	ˈaslo
osmosis	ahz MOH sis	azˈmosɪs

---

at [æ]; *ah* [ɑ]; *air* [ɛ]; *aw*ful [ɔ]; *say* [e]; *back* [b]; *chair* [tʃ]; *do* [d]; *elm* [ɛ]; *eel* [i]; *server* [ˈɝ, ər]; *f*it [f]; *go* [g]; *hurt* [h]; *is* [ɪ]; *high* [aɪ]; *jet* [dʒ]; *kiss* [k]; *lamb* [l]; *my* [m]; *nice* [n];

Osnaburg	AHZ nuh berg	ˈɑznəbɜrg
Ospina	aw SPEE nah	ɔˈspinɑ
osprey	AH spri	ˈɑsprɪ
Ossa	AH suh	ˈɑsə
Ossetia	ah SEE shuh	ɑˈsiʃə
Ossian	AH shuhn	ˈɑʃən
Ossietzky	ah si ET ski	ɑsɪˈɛtskɪ
ossify	AH suh figh	ˈɑsəfaɪ
Ossining	AH suh ning	ˈɑsənɪŋ
osteitis	ah sti IGH tis	ɑstɪˈaɪtɪs
Ostend	ah STEND	ɑˈstɛnd
ostensible	ah STEN suh buhl	ɑˈstɛnsəbəl
ostentatious	ah stuhn TAY shuhs	ɑstənˈteʃəs
osteopath	AH sti uh path	ˈɑstɪəpæθ
osteopathy	ah sti AH puh thi	ɑstɪˈɑpəθɪ
Ostia	AH sti uh	ˈɑstɪə
ostler	AH sler	ˈɑslər
Ostmark	AWST mahrk	ˈɔstmɑrk
ostracize	AH struh sighz	ˈɑstrəsaɪz
ostrich	AW strich	ˈɔstrɪtʃ
Ostrogoth	AH struh gahth	ˈɑstrəgɑθ
Ostrowiec	aw STRAW vyets	ɔˈstrɔvjɛts
Ostwald	OHST vahlt	ˈostvɑlt
Ostyak, Ostiak	AH sti ak	ˈɑstɪæk
Oswego	ah SWEE goh	ɑˈswigo
Oswiecim	awsh VYANT sim	ɔʃˈvjæntsɪm
otalgia	oh TAL ji uh	oˈtældʒɪə
Othello	uh THE loh	əˈθɛlo
otiose	OH shi ohs	ˈoʃɪos
otitis	oh TIGH tis	oˈtaɪtɪs
otology	oh TAH luh ji	oˈtɑlədʒɪ
Otranto	oh TRAHN toh	oˈtrɑnto
ottava rima	uh TAH vuh REE muh	əˈtɑvə ˈrimə
Ottawa	AH tuh wuh	ˈɑtəwə
Ottoman	AH tuh muhn	ˈɑtəmən
Ouachita	WAH shi taw	ˈwɑʃɪtɔ
Ouagadougou	wah gah DOO : goo :	wɑgɑˈdugu
oubliette	oo : bli ET	ublɪˈɛt
Ouida	WEE duh	ˈwidə
ouija	WEE juh	ˈwidʒə
Oulu	OH loo	ˈolu
Oursler	OWZ ler	ˈaʊzlər
outnumber	owt NUHM ber	aʊtˈnʌmbər
outrance	oo : TRAHNS	uˈtrɑns
outré	oo : TRAY	uˈtre
outremer	oo : truh MAIR	utrəˈmɛr
outward	OWT werd	ˈaʊtwərd
ouzel, ousel	OO : zuhl	ˈuzəl
ovary	OH vuh ri	ˈovərɪ
overalls	OH ver awlz	ˈovərɔlz
overdraft, overdraught	OH ver draft	ˈovərdræft
overt	OH vert	ˈovərt

sing [ŋ] ; *oh* [o] ; *oil* [ɔɪ] ; *foot* [ʊ] ; *foo*:d [u] ; *how* [aʊ] ; *p*ie [p] ; *r*ay [r] ; *s*o [s] ; *sh*all [ʃ] ;
*t*o [t] ; *thin* [θ] ; *th:*en [ð] ; *above (uh BUHV)* [ə, ˈʌ] ; *v*ine [v] ; *w*ine [w] ; *wh*ine [hw] ;
*y*ou [j] ; *z*oo [z] ; *rouge (roo:zh)* [ʒ].

overture	OH ver cher	ˈovərtʃər
Ovid	AH vid	ˈɑvɪd
Oviedo	aw VYE th : aw	ɔˈvjeðɔ
oviparous	oh VI puh ruhs	oˈvɪpərəs
ovoid	OH void	ˈovɔɪd
ovum	OH vuhm	ˈovəm
owe	oh	o
oxalic	ahk SA lik	ɑkˈsælɪk
oxalis	AHK suh lis	ˈɑksəlɪs
Oxford	AHKS ferd	ˈɑksfərd
oxidation	ahk suh DAY shuhn	ɑksəˈdeʃən
oxide	AHK sighd	ˈɑksaɪd
oxidize	AHK suh dighz	ˈɑksədaɪz
Oxonian	ahk SOH ni uhn	ɑkˈsonɪən
oxyacetylene	ahk si uh SE tuh leen	ɑksɪəˈsɛtəlin
oxycephalic	ahk si suh FA lik	ɑksɪsəˈfælɪk
oxygen	AHK si juhn	ˈɑksɪdʒən
oxymoron	ahk si MAW rahn	ɑksɪˈmɔrɑn
oyster	OI ster	ˈɔɪstər
Ozark	OH zahrk	ˈozɑrk
ozone	OH zohn	ˈozon

P

Paasikivi, Juho	PAH see kee vee, YOO : haw	ˈpɑsikivi, ˈjuhɔ
pabulum	PA byuh luhm	ˈpæbjələm
Pacelli	pah CHE lee	pɑˈtʃeli
pachisi	puh CHEE zi	pəˈtʃizɪ
pachyderm	PA kuh derm	ˈpækədərm
pacific, P-	puh SI fik	pəˈsɪfɪk
pacifism	PA suh fi zuhm	ˈpæsəfɪzəm
pacify	PA suh figh	ˈpæsəfaɪ
Packard	PA kerd	ˈpækərd
Padang	pah DAHNG	pɑˈdɑŋ
paddock	PA duhk	ˈpædək
paddy, P-	PA di	ˈpædɪ
Paderewski, Ignace Jan	pa duh REF ski, EE nyas YAHN	pædəˈrɛfskɪ, ˈinjæs ˈjɑn
Padilla	pah DEE yah	pɑˈdija
padishah	PAH di shah	ˈpɑdɪʃɑ
padre	PAH dri	ˈpɑdrɪ
padrone	puh DROH ni	pəˈdronɪ
Padua	PA joo uh	ˈpædʒuə
Paducah	puh DOO : kuh	pəˈdukə
paean	PEE uhn	ˈpiən
pagan	PAY guhn	ˈpegən
Paganini	pa guh NEE ni	pægəˈ ninɪ
pageant	PA juhnt	ˈpædʒənt

at [æ] ; ah [ɑ] ; air [ɛ] ; awful [ɔ] ; say [e] ; back [b] ; chair [tʃ] ; do [d] ; elm [ɛ] ; eel [i] ;
server [ˈɝ, ər] ; fit [f] ; go [g] ; hurt [h] ; is [ɪ] ; high [aɪ] ; jet [dʒ] ; kiss [k] ; lamb [l] ; my [m] ;
nice [n] ;

Paget	PA jit	ˈpædʒɪt
paginate	PA juh nayt	ˈpædʒənet
pagoda	puh GOH duh	pəˈgodə
Pago Pago	PAHNG oh PAHNG oh	ˈpɑŋo ˈpɑŋo
Pahang	pah HAHNG	pɑˈhɑŋ
Pahlavi, p-	PAH luh vee	ˈpɑləvi
paillaise, pallaise	pal YAS	pælˈjæs
paillette	pal YET	pælˈjɛt
pain	payn	pen
paisley, P-	PAYZ li	ˈpezlɪ
Paiute	pigh YOO:T	paɪˈjut
pajamas	puh JA muhz	pəˈdʒæməz
Pakistan	PA ki stan	ˈpækɪstæn
Pakistani	pa ki STA ni	pækɪˈstænɪ
paladin	PA luh din	ˈpælədɪn
palaestra	puh LE struh	pəˈlɛstrə
Palais-Royal	PA lay roi YAL	ˈpæle rɔɪˈjæl
Palamon	PA luh muhn	ˈpæləmən
palanquin, palankeen	pa luhn KEEN	pælənˈkin
palatable	PA luh tuh buhl	ˈpælətəbəl
palatal	PA luh tuhl	ˈpælətəl
palate	PA lit	ˈpælɪt
palatial	puh LAY shuhl	pəˈleʃəl
palatinate, P-	puh LA tuh nit	pəˈlætənɪt
palatine, P-	PA luh tighn	ˈpælətaɪn
Palau	pah LOW	pɑˈlaʊ
palaver	puh LA ver	pəˈlævər
Palawan	pah LAH wahn	pɑˈlawɑn
palazzo	pah LAHT soh	pɑˈlatso
Palembang	PAH lem bahng	ˈpɑlɛmbɑŋ
Palenque	pah LENG kay	pɑˈlɛŋke
Paleocene	PAY li uh seen	ˈpelɪəsin
paleography	pay li AH gruh fi	pelɪˈɑgrəfɪ
paleolithic	pay li uh LI thik	pelɪəˈlɪθɪk
paleontology	pay li uhn TAH luh ji	pelɪənˈtɑlədʒɪ
Paleozoic	pay li uh ZOH ik	pelɪəˈzoɪk
Palermo	puh LER moh	pəˈlɝmo
Palestine	PA luh stighn	ˈpæləstaɪn
palestra	puh LE struh	pəˈlɛstrə
Palestrina	pa luh STREE nuh	pæləˈstrinə
palette	PA lit	ˈpælɪt
palfrey	PAWL fri	ˈpɔlfrɪ
Palgrave	PAWL grayv	ˈpɔlgrev
Pali	PAH lee	ˈpɑli
palimpsest	PA limp sest	ˈpælɪmpsɛst
palindrome	PA lin drohm	ˈpælɪndrom
palisade, P-	PA luh sayd	ˈpæləsed
pall	pawl	pɔl
Palladian	puh LAY di uhn	pəˈledɪən
Palladio	pah LAH dyaw	pɑˈladjɔ
palladium, P-	puh LAY di uhm	pəˈledɪəm
Pallas	PA luhs	ˈpæləs

---

sing [ŋ] ; oh [o] ; oil [ɔɪ] ; foot [ʊ] ; foo:d [u] ; how [aʊ] ; pie [p] ; ray [r] ; so [s] ; shall [ʃ] ; to [t] ; thin [θ] ; th:en [ð] ; above (uh BUHV) [ə, ˈʌ] ; vine [v] ; wine [w] ; whine [hw] ; you [j] ; zoo [z] ; rouge (roo:zh) [ʒ].

pallet	PA lit	ˈpælɪt
palliative	PA li ay tiv	ˈpælɪetɪv
pallid	PA lid	ˈpælɪd
pall-mall, Pall Mall	pel mel	pɛl mɛl
palm	pahm	pɑm
Palma	PAHL mah	ˈpɑlmɑ
Palmas	PAHL mahs	ˈpɑlmɑs
palmer	PAH mer	ˈpɑmər
palmetto	pal ME toh	pælˈmɛto
palmistry	PAH mi stri	ˈpɑmɪstrɪ
Palmyra, p-	pal MIGH ruh	pælˈmaɪrə
Palo Alto	PA loh AL toh	ˈpælo ˈælto
Palomar	PA luh mahr	ˈpæləmɑr
palomino	pa luh MEE nuh	pæləˈmino
palooka	puh LOO : kuh	pəˈlukə
Palos	PAH laws	ˈpɑlɔs
palpable	PAL puh buhl	ˈpælpəbəl
palpitation	pal puh TAY shuhn	pælpəˈteʃən
palsgrave	PAWLZ grayv	ˈpɔlzgrev
palsy	PAWL zi	ˈpɔlzɪ
palter	PAWL ter	ˈpɔltər
paltry	PAWL tri	ˈpɔltrɪ
Pamela	PA muh luh	ˈpæmələ
Pamir	pah MIR	pɑˈmɪr
Pamlico	PAM li koh	ˈpæmlɪko
pampa, P-	PAM puh	ˈpæmpə
pampero	pahm PE roh	pɑmˈpɛro
pamphlet	PAM flit	ˈpæmflɪt
panacea	pa nuh SEE uh	pænəˈsiə
panache	puh NASH	pəˈnæʃ
Panama	PA nuh mah	ˈpænəmɑ
Panamanian	pa nuh MAY ni uhn	pænəˈmenɪən
Pan-Americanism	pan uh MAI ruh kuh ni zuhm	pæn əˈmɛrəkənɪzəm
Panay	puh NIGH	pəˈnaɪ
panchromatic	pan kroh MA tik	pænkroˈmætɪk
pancreas	PAN kri uhs	ˈpænkrɪəs
pancreatic	pan kri A tik	pænkrɪˈætɪk
panda	PAN duh	ˈpændə
Pandarus	PAN duh ruhs	ˈpændərəs
pandect, P-	PAN dekt	ˈpændɛkt
pandemic	pan DE mik	pænˈdɛmɪk
pandemonium, P-	pan di MOH ni uhm	pændɪˈmonɪəm
pandit, P-	PUHN dit	ˈpʌndɪt
Pandora	pan DAW ruh	pænˈdɔrə
pandowdy	pan DOW di	pænˈdaʊdɪ
panegyric	pa nuh JI rik	pænəˈdʒɪrɪk
panegyrist	pa nuh JI rist	pænəˈdʒɪrɪst
panegyrize	PA nuh ji righz	ˈpænədʒɪraɪz
panel	PA nuhl	ˈpænəl
panelist	PA nuh list	ˈpænəlɪst
panetela, panetella	pa nuh TE luh	pænəˈtɛlə

at [æ] ; *ah* [ɑ] ; *air* [ɛ] ; *aw*ful [ɔ] ; s*ay* [e] ; *b*ack [b] ; *ch*air [tʃ] ; *d*o [d] ; *e*lm [ɛ] ; *ee*l [i] ; s*er*ver [ˈɝ, ər] ; *f*it [f] ; *g*o [g] ; *h*urt [h] ; *i*s [ɪ] ; *high* [aɪ] ; *j*et [dʒ] ; *k*iss [k] ; *l*amb [l] ; *m*y [m] ; *n*ice [n] ;

pangolin	pang GOH lin	pæŋˈgolɪn
Pango Pango	PAHNG oh PAHNG oh	ˈpɑŋo ˈpɑŋo
Panhellenic	pan huh LE nik	pænhəˈlɛnɪk
Panjabi	puhn JAH bi	pʌnˈdʒɑbɪ
panjandrum	pan JAN druhm	pænˈdʒændrəm
pannier	PA nyer	ˈpænjər
panocha	puh NOH chuh	pəˈnotʃə
panoply	PA nuh pli	ˈpænəplɪ
panorama	pa nuh RA muh	pænəˈræmə
pansophy	PAN suh fi	ˈpænsəfɪ
Pantagruel	pan TA groo el	pænˈtægruɛl
pantechnicon	pan TEK ni kahn	pænˈtɛknɪkɑn
Pantelleria	pahn te le REE ah	pɑntɛlɛˈriɑ
pantheism	PAN thee i zuhm	ˈpænθiɪzəm
pantheon, P-	PAN thee ahn	ˈpænθiɑn
Panthéon	pahn tay OHN	pɑnteˈon
pantomime	PAN tuh mighm	ˈpæntəmaɪm
pantomimic	pan tuh MI mik	pæntəˈmɪmɪk
pantothenic	pan tuh THE nik	pæntəˈθɛnɪk
Panurge	pa NERJ	pæˈnɝdʒ
panzer, P-	PAN zer	ˈpænzər
papacy	PAY puh si	ˈpepəsɪ
papal	PAY puhl	ˈpepəl
Papanicalaou	pah puh NEE kuh low	pɑpəˈnikəlau
papaw	PAW paw	ˈpɔpɔ
papaya	puh PAH yuh	pəˈpajə
Papeete	pah pi AY tay	pɑpɪˈete
papeterie	PA puh tri	ˈpæpətrɪ
papier-mâché	PAY per muh SHAY	ˈpepər məˈʃe
papilla	puh PI luh	pəˈpɪlə
papillary	PA puh lai ri	ˈpæpəlɛrɪ
papillon	PA puh lahn	ˈpæpəlɑn
papilloma	pa puh LOH muh	pæpəˈlomə
papist	PAY pist	ˈpepɪst
papoose	pa POO:S	pæˈpus
paprika, paprica	puh PREE kuh	pəˈprikə
Papua	PA pyoo uh	ˈpæpjuə
papyrus	puh PIGH ruhs	pəˈpaɪrəs
par, P-	pahr	pɑr
Pará	pah RAH	pɑˈrɑ
para-aminobenzoic	PA ruh uh MEE noh ben ZOH ik	ˈpærə əˈminobɛnˈzoɪk
parable	PA ruh buhl	ˈpærəbəl
parabola	puh RA buh luh	pəˈræbələ
parabolic	pa ruh BAH lik	pærəˈbɑlɪk
Paracelsus	pa ruh SEL suhs	pærəˈsɛlsəs
parachute	PA ruh shoo:t	ˈpærəʃut
paraclete	PA ruh kleet	ˈpærəklit
parade	puh RAYD	pəˈred
paradichlorobenzene	PA ruh digh KLAW ruh BEN zeen	ˈpærədaɪˈklɔrəˈbɛnzin
paradigm	PA ruh dim	ˈpærədɪm

sing [ŋ]; *oh* [o]; *oil* [ɔɪ]; *foot* [ʊ]; *foo:*d [u]; *how* [aʊ]; *pie* [p]; *ray* [r]; *so* [s]; *shall* [ʃ];
to [t]; *thin* [θ]; *th:*en [ð]; *above* (*uh BUHV*) [ə, ˈʌ]; *vine* [v]; *wine* [w]; *whine* [hw];
you [j]; *zoo* [z]; *rouge* (roo:*zh*) [ʒ].

paradigmatic	pa ruh dig MA tik	pærədɪɡˈmætɪk
paradise, P-	PA ruh dighs	ˈpærədaɪs
paradisiac	pa ruh DI si ak	pærəˈdɪsɪæk
paradox	PA ruh dahks	ˈpærədɑks
paradoxical	pa ruh DAHK si kuhl	pærəˈdɑksɪkəl
paraffin	PA ruh fin	ˈpærəfɪn
paragon	PA ruh gahn	ˈpærəgɑn
Paraguay	PA ruh gway	ˈpærəgwe
parakeet	PA ruh keet	ˈpærəkit
paraleipsis	pa ruh LIGHP sis	pærəˈlaɪpsɪs
parallax	PA ruh laks	ˈpærəlæks
parallel	PA ruh lel	ˈpærəlɛl
parallelogram	pa ruh LE luh gram	pærəˈlɛləgræm
paralysis	puh RA luh sis	pəˈræləsɪs
paralytic	pa ruh LI tik	pærəˈlɪtɪk
Paramaribo	pa ruh MA ri boh	pærəˈmærɪbo
paramecium	pa ruh MEE shi uhm	pærəˈmiʃɪəm
paramount	PA ruh mownt	ˈpærəmaʊnt
paramour	PA ruh moor	ˈpærəmʊr
Paraná	pa ruh NAH	pærəˈnɑ
paralogia	pa ruh LOH ji uh	pærəˈlodʒɪə
paranoia	pa ruh NOI uh	pærəˈnɔɪə
paranoiac	pa ruh NOI ak	pærəˈnɔɪæk
Paranthropus	pa ran THROH puhs	pærænˈθropəs
parapet	PA ruh pit	ˈpærəpɪt
paraphernalia	pa ruh fer NAY li uh	pærəfərˈnelɪə
paraphrase	PA ruh frayz	ˈpærəfrez
paraphrastic	pa ruh FRA stik	pærəˈfræstɪk
paraplegia	pa ruh PLEE ji uh	pærəˈplidʒɪə
paraplegic	pa ruh PLE jik	pærəˈplɛdʒɪk
parapsychology	pa ruh sigh KAH luh ji	pærəsaɪˈkɑlədʒɪ
parasite	PA ruh sight	ˈpærəsaɪt
parasitic	pa ruh SI tik	pærəˈsɪtɪk
parasol	PA ruh sawl	ˈpærəsɔl
paratactic	pa ruh TAK tik	pærəˈtæktɪk
parataxis	pa ruh TAK sis	pærəˈtæksɪs
parathyroid	pa ruh THIGH roid	pærəˈθaɪrɔɪd
Paray	pah RAY	pɑˈre
parboil	PAHR boil	ˈpɑrbɔɪl
Parcae	PAHR see	ˈpɑrsi
parcheesi, parchesi, parchisi	pahr CHEE zi	pɑrˈtʃizi
pardie, pardi	pahr DEE	pɑrˈdi
paregoric	pa ruh GAW rik	pærəˈgɔrɪk
parent	PAI ruhnt	ˈpɛrənt
paresis	puh REE sis	pəˈrisɪs
par excellence	pahr EK suh lahns	pɑr ˈɛksəlɑns
parfait	pahr FAY	pɑrˈfe
parhelion	pahr HEE li uhn	pɑrˈhilɪən
pariah	puh RIGH uh	pəˈraɪə
Paricutín	pah ree koo : TEEN	pɑrikuˈtin
pari-mutuel	PA ri MYOO : choo uhl	ˈpærɪ ˈmjutʃʊəl

---

at [æ]; *ah* [ɑ]; *air* [ɛ]; *aw*ful [ɔ]; *say* [e]; *b*ack [b]; *ch*air [tʃ]; *d*o [d]; *e*lm [ɛ]; *ee*l [i];
*ser*ver [ɜ, ər]; *f*it [f]; *g*o [g]; *h*urt [h]; *i*s [ɪ]; *high* [aɪ]; *j*et [dʒ]; *k*iss [k]; *l*amb [l]; *m*y [m];
*n*ice [n];

pari passu	PA ri PA soo:	ˈpærɪ ˈpæsu
Paris	PA ris	ˈpærɪs
parish	PA rish	ˈpærɪʃ
parishioner	puh RI shuh ner	pəˈrɪʃənər
Parisian	puh RI zhunh	pəˈrɪʒən
parisien, -ne, P-	pa ree zi EN	pæriziˈɛn
parka	PAHR kuh	ˈpɑrkə
parlance	PAHR luhns	ˈpɑrləns
parlando	pahr LAHN daw	pɑrˈlɑndɔ
parlay, parley	PAHR li	ˈpɑrlɪ
parliament	PAHR luh muhnt	ˈpɑrləmənt
parliamentarian	pahr luh men TAI ri uhn	pɑrləmɛnˈtɛrɪən
parliamentary	pahr luh MEN tuh ri	pɑrləˈmɛntɛrɪ
Parma	PAHR mah	ˈpɑrmɑ
Parmesan	PAHR mi zan	ˈpɑrmɪzæn
Parnassian	pahr NA si uhn	pɑrˈnæsɪən
Parnassus	pahr NA suhs	pɑrˈnæsəs
Parnu	PAR noo:	ˈpærnu
parochial	puh ROH ki uhl	pəˈrokɪəl
parody	PA ruh di	ˈpærədɪ
parole	puh ROHL	pəˈrol
paronomasia	pa ruh noh MAY zhuh	pærənoˈmeʒə
parotitis	pa ruh TIGH tis	pærəˈtaɪtɪs
paroxysm	PA ruhk si zuhm	ˈpærəksɪzəm
parquet	pahr KAY	pɑrˈke
parquetry	PAHR ki tri	ˈpɑrkɪtrɪ
Parran	PA ruhn	ˈpærən
parricide	PA ruh sighd	ˈpærəsaɪd
Parrington	PA ring tuhn	ˈpærɪŋtən
Parrish	PA rish	ˈpærɪʃ
parrot	PA ruht	ˈpærət
parry, P-	PA ri	ˈpærɪ
parse	pahrs	pɑrs
parsec	PAHR sek	ˈpɑrsɛk
Parsee, Parsi	PAHR see	ˈpɑrsi
Parsifal	PAHR si fahl	ˈpɑrsɪfɑl
parsimonious	pahr suh MOH ni uhs	pɑrsəˈmonɪəs
parsimony	PAHR suh moh ni	ˈpɑrsəmonɪ
parsley	PAHR sli	ˈpɑrslɪ
parsnip	PAHR snip	ˈpɑrsnɪp
parterre	pahr TAIR	pɑrˈtɛr
parthenogenesis	pahr thuh noh JE nuh sis	pɑrθənoˈdʒɛnəsɪs
Parthenon	PAHR thuh nahn	ˈpɑrθənɑn
Parthenope	pahr THE nuh pee	pɑrˈθɛnəpi
Parthenos	PAHR thuh nahs	ˈpɑrθənɑs
Parthian	PAHR thi uhn	ˈpɑrθɪən
participial	pahr tuh SI pi uhl	pɑrtəˈsɪpɪəl
participle	PAHR tuh si puhl	ˈpɑrtəsɪpəl
particular	per TI kyuh ler	pərˈtɪkjələr
partisan	PAHR tuh zuhn	ˈpɑrtəzən
partite	PAHR tight	ˈpɑrtaɪt
partitive	PAHR tuh tiv	ˈpɑrtətɪv

---

sing [ŋ]; oh [o]; oil [ɔɪ]; foot [ʊ]; foo:d [u]; how [aʊ]; pie [p]; ray [r]; so [s]; shall [ʃ];
to [t]; thin [θ]; th:en [ð]; above (uh BUHV) [ə, ˈʌ]; vine [v]; wine [w]; whine [hw];
you [j]; zoo [z]; rouge (roo:zh) [ʒ].

partner	PAHRT ner	ˈpɑrtnər
partridge	PAHR trij	ˈpɑrtrɪdʒ
parturient	pahr TYOO ri uhnt	pɑrˈtjʊrɪənt
parturition	pahr choo RI shuhn	pɑrtʃuˈrɪʃən
parure	puh ROOR	pəˈrʊr
parvenu	PAHR vuh noo:	ˈpɑrvənu
pas (French)	pah	pɑ
Pasadena	pa suh DEE nuh	pæsəˈdinə
Pascal, Blaise	pah SKAHL, BLEZ	pɑˈskɑl, ˈblɛz
paschal	PA skuhl	ˈpæskəl
pasha	PAH shuh	ˈpɑʃɑ
Pasiphaë	puh SI fuh ee	pəˈsɪfəi
Pasquale	pah SKWAH lay	pɑˈskwɑle
Pasquini	pahs KWEE nee	pɑsˈkwini
passacaglia	pa suh KAHL yuh	pæsəˈkɑljə
passade	puh SAYD	pəˈsed
passado	puh SAH doh	pəˈsɑdo
Passaic	puh SAY ik	pəˈseɪk
Passamaquoddy	pa suh muh KWAH di	pæsəməˈkwɑdɪ
passé	pa SAY	pæˈse
passementerie	pas MEN tri	pæsˈmɛntrɪ
passe partout	pas pahr TOO:	pæs pɑrˈtu
passerine	PA suh rin	ˈpæsərɪn
passim	PA sim	ˈpæsɪm
passivism	PA si vi zuhm	ˈpæsɪvɪzəm
Passover	PAS oh ver	ˈpæsover
passus	PA suhs	ˈpæsəs
Passy	pa SEE	pæˈsi
pasta	PAH stuh	ˈpɑstə
pastel	pa STEL	pæˈstɛl
Pasternak	PA ster nak	ˈpæstərnæk
Pasteur	pa STER	pæˈstɝ
pasticcio	pah STEE chaw	pɑˈstitʃɔ
pastiche	pa STEESH	pæˈstiʃ
pastille	pa STEEL	pæˈstil
pastime	PAS tighm	ˈpæstaɪm
Pasto	PAH staw	ˈpɑstɔ
pastor	PA ster	ˈpæstər
pastoral	PA stuh ruhl	ˈpæstərəl
pastorate	PA stuh rit	ˈpæstərɪt
pastrami	puh STRAH mi	pəˈstrɑmɪ
Patagonia	pa tuh GOH ni uh	pætəˈgonɪə
patchouli, patchouly	PA choo li	ˈpætʃʊlɪ
pâte	paht	pɑt
pâté	pah TAY	pɑˈte
pâté de foie gras	pah TAY duh fwah GRAH	pɑˈte də fwɑ ˈgrɑ
patent (" obvious ")	PAY tuhnt	ˈpetənt
patent (except " obvious ")	PA tuhnt	ˈpætənt
patently	PAY tuhnt li	ˈpetəntlɪ
Pater, p-	PAY ter	ˈpetər
paterfamilias	PAY ter fuh MI li uhs	ˈpetərfəˈmɪlɪəs

---

at [æ]; *ah* [ɑ]; *air* [ɛ]; *aw*ful [ɔ]; *say* [e]; *b*ack [b]; *ch*air [tʃ]; *d*o [d]; *e*lm [ɛ]; *ee*l [i];
*ser*ver [ˈɝ, ər]; *f*it [f]; *g*o [g]; *h*urt [h]; *is* [ɪ]; *high* [aɪ]; *j*et [dʒ]; *k*iss [k]; *l*amb [l]; *m*y [m];
*n*ice [n];

paternoster, Pater Noster	PAY ter NAH ster	ˈpetərˈnɑstər
Paterson	PA ter suhn	ˈpætərsən
path	path	pæθ
Pathanistan	pah THAH nis tahn	pɑˈθɑnɪstɑn
pathetic	puh THE tik	pəˈθɛtɪk
Pathet Lao	PAH thuht LAH oh	ˈpɑθətˈlɑo
pathogen	PA thuh jen	ˈpæθədʒɛn
pathogenesis	pa thuh JE nuh sis	pæθəˈdʒɛnəsɪs
pathological	pa thuh LAH ji kuhl	pæθəˈlɑdʒɪkəl
pathology	puh THAH luh ji	pəˈθɑlədʒɪ
pathos	PAY thahs	ˈpeθɑs
Patiala	puh ti AH luh	pətɪˈɑlə
patina	PA tuh nuh	ˈpætənə
Patiño	pah TEE nyaw	pɑˈtinjɔ
patio	PA ti oh	ˈpætɪo
Patmos	PAT muhs	ˈpætməs
Patna	PUHT nuh	ˈpʌtnə
patois	PA twah	ˈpætwɑ
Paton	PAY tuhn	ˈpetən
Patras	pah TRAHS	pɑˈtrɑs
patriarch	PAY tri ahrk	ˈpetrɪɑrk
patriarchal	pay tri AHR kuhl	petrɪˈɑrkəl
patrician	puh TRI shuhn	pəˈtrɪʃən
patricidal	pa truh SIGH duhl	pætrəˈsaɪdəl
patricide	PA truh sighd	ˈpætrəsaɪd
patrimony	PA truh moh ni	ˈpætrəmonɪ
patriot	PAY tri uht	ˈpetrɪət
patriotic	pa tri AH tik	petrɪˈɑtɪk
patriotism	PAY tri uh ti zuhm	ˈpetrɪətɪzəm
patristic	puh TRI stik	pəˈtrɪstɪk
Patroclus	puh TROH kluhs	pəˈtrokləs
patrol	puh TROHL	pəˈtrol
patron	PAY truhn	ˈpetrən
patronage	PAY truh nij	ˈpetrənɪdʒ
patroness	PAY truh nis	ˈpetrənɪs
patronize	PAY truh nighz	ˈpetrənaɪz
patronymic	pa truh NI mik	pætrəˈnɪmɪk
Patti	PA ti	ˈpætɪ
Patton	PA tuhn	ˈpætən
paucity	PAW suh ti	ˈpɔsətɪ
Pauling, Linus	PAW ling, LIGH nuhs	ˈpɔlɪŋ, ˈlaɪnəs
Paumoto	pah oo MOH too:	pɑuˈmotu
paunch	pawnch	pɔntʃ
pauper	PAW per	ˈpɔpər
Pausanias	paw SAY ni uhs	pɔˈsenɪəs
pavan, -e	PA vuhn	ˈpævən
pavé	pa VAY	pæˈve
Pavia	pah VEE ah	pɑˈviɑ
pavilion	puh VI lyuhn	pəˈvɪljən
pavior, paviour	PAY vyer	ˈpevjər
Pavlov	PAHV lawf	ˈpɑvlɔf

Pavlova	PAHV law vah	ˈpɑvlɔvɑ
Pavo	PAY voh	ˈpevo
Pawnee	paw NEE	pɔˈni
Pawtucket	paw TUH kit	pɔˈtʌkɪt
pax, P-	paks	pæks
pax in bello	PAKS in BE loh	ˈpæks in ˈbɛlo
Paxinou, Katina	pahk see NOO :, kah TEE nuh	pɑksiˈnu, kɑˈtinə
Pax Romana	PAKS roh MAY nuh	ˈpæks roˈmenə
pax vobiscum	PAKS voh BI skuhm	ˈpæks voˈbɪskəm
Pearsall	PIR suhl	ˈpɪrsəl
Pearson	PIR suhn	ˈpɪrsən
Peary	PI ri	ˈpɪrɪ
pease	peez	piz
pecan	pi KAN	pɪˈkæn
peccadillo	pe kuh DI loh	pɛkəˈdɪlo
peccant	PE kuhnt	ˈpɛkənt
peccary	PE kuh ri	ˈpɛkərɪ
peccavi	pe KAY vigh	pɛˈkevaɪ
Pecksniffian	pek SNI fi uhn	pɛkˈsnɪfɪən
Pecos	PAY kohs	ˈpekos
Pecs	paych	petʃ
pectoral	PEK tuh ruhl	ˈpɛktərəl
peculation	pe kyuh LAY shuhn	pɛkjəˈleʃən
peculiar	pi KYOO : lyer	pɪˈkjuljər
peculiarity	pi kyoo : li A ruh ti	pɪkjulɪˈærətɪ
pecuniary	pi KYOO : ni ai ri	pɪˈkjunɪɛrɪ
pedagog, -ue	PE duh gahg	ˈpɛdəgɑg
pedagogy	PE duh goh ji	ˈpɛdəgodʒɪ
pedant	PE duhnt	ˈpɛdənt
pedantic	pi DAN tik	pɪˈdæntɪk
pedantry	PE duhn tri	ˈpɛdəntrɪ
pederast	PE duh rast	ˈpɛdəræst
pediatric	pee di A trik	pidɪˈætrɪk
pediatrician	pee di uh TRI shuhn	pidɪəˈtrɪʃən
pediatrist	pee di A trist	pidɪˈætrɪst
pedicure	PE di kyoor	ˈpɛdɪkjʊr
pedograph	PE duh graf	ˈpɛdəgræf
pedology	pi DAH luh ji	pɪˈdɑlədʒɪ
pedometer	pi DAH muh ter	pɪˈdɑmətər
peduncle	pi DUHNG kuhl	pɪˈdʌŋkəl
peer	pir	pɪr
peerage	PI rij	ˈpɪrɪdʒ
Pegasus	PE guh suhs	ˈpɛgəsəs
pegmatite	PEG muh tight	ˈpɛgmətaɪt
peignoir	payn WAHR	penˈwɑr
Peiping	PAY ping	ˈpepɪŋ
Peixoto, Amaral	pay SHAW too, ah muh RAHL	peˈʃɔtu, ɑməˈrɑl
pejoration	pee juh RAY shuhn	pidʒəˈreʃən
pejorative	PEE juh ray tiv	ˈpidʒəretɪv
Pekin, p-	PEE kin	ˈpikɪn
Peking	PEE king	ˈpikɪŋ

at [æ] ; ah [ɑ] ; air [ɛ] ; awful [ɔ] ; say [e] ; back [b] ; chair [tʃ] ; do [d] ; elm [ɛ] ; eel [i] ;
server [ˈɜ, ər] ; fit [f] ; go [g] ; hurt [h] ; is [ɪ] ; high [aɪ] ; jet [dʒ] ; kiss [k] ; lamb [l] ; my [m] ;
nice [n] ;

Pekingese	PEE ki neez	ˈpikɪniz
pekoe	PEE koh	ˈpiko
pelage	PE lij	ˈpɛlɪdʒ
pelagic	puh LA jik	pəˈlædʒɪk
pelargonium	pe lahr GOH ni uhm	pɛlɑrˈgonɪəm
Pelée	puh LAY	pəˈle
Peleliu	PE le lyoo:	ˈpɛlɛlju
Peleus	PEE lyoos	ˈpiljʊs
Pelew	pee LOO:	piˈlu
Pelham	PE luhm	ˈpɛləm
Pelias	PEE li uhs	ˈpilɪəs
pelican	PE li kuhn	ˈpɛlɪkən
Pelion	PEE li uhn	ˈpilɪən
pelisse	puh LEES	pəˈlis
pellagra	puh LAY gruh	pəˈlegrə
pell mell	pel mel	pɛl mɛl
pellucid	puh LOO: sid	pəˈlusɪd
Peloponnesian	pe luh puh NEE shuhn	pɛləpəˈniʃən
Peloponnesus	pe luh puh NEE suhs	pɛləpəˈnisəs
Pelops	PEE lahps	ˈpilɑps
pelota	pe LOH tuh	pɛˈlotə
pelvis	PEL vis	ˈpɛlvɪs
pemmican, pemican	PE mi kuhn	ˈpɛmɪkən
Peña	PE nyah	ˈpɛnjɑ
penal	PEE nuhl	ˈpinəl
penalize	PEE nuh lighz	ˈpinəlaɪz
penalty	PE nuhl ti	ˈpɛnəltɪ
penance	PE nuhns	ˈpɛnəns
Penang	pi NANG	pɪˈnæŋ
Peñaranda	pe nyah RAHN dah	pɛnjɑˈrɑndɑ
penates	pi NAY teez	pɪˈnetiz
penchant	PEN chuhnt	ˈpɛntʃənt
pendant, pendent	PEN duhnt	ˈpɛndənt
pendulous	PEN juh luhs	ˈpɛndʒələs
pendulum	PEN juh luhm	ˈpɛndʒələm
Penelope	puh NE luh pi	pəˈnɛləpɪ
peneplain, peneplane	PEE nuh playn	ˈpinəplen
penetralia	pe nuh TRAY li uh	pɛnəˈtrelɪə
Peneus	pi NEE uhs	pɪˈniəs
penguin	PENG gwin	ˈpɛŋgwɪn
penicillin	pe nuh SI lin	pɛnəˈsɪlɪn
peninsula	puh NIN suh luh	pəˈnɪnsələ
penitence	PE nuh tuhns	ˈpɛnətəns
penitentiary	pe nuh TEN shuh ri	pɛnəˈtɛnʃərɪ
pennant	PE nuhnt	ˈpɛnənt
Pennario	pe NAH ree oh	pɛˈnɑrio
Pennine	PE nighn	ˈpɛnaɪn
pennon	PE nuhn	ˈpɛnən
Pennsylvania	pen suhl VAY nyuh	pɛnsəlˈvenjə
Penobscot	pi NAHB skaht	pɪˈnɑbskɑt
penology	pee NAH luh ji	piˈnɑlədʒɪ
Pensacola	pen suh KOH luh	pɛnsəˈkolə

H.P.—S

pensée	pawn SAY	pɔnˈse
Penseroso	pen suh ROH soh	pɛnsəˈroso
pension (" boarding place ")	PAHN si ahn	ˈpɑnsɪɑn
pentadactyl	pen tuh DAK til	pɛntəˈdæktɪl
pentagon, P-	PEN tuh gahn	ˈpɛntəgɑn
pentameter	pen TA muh ter	pɛnˈtæmətər
Pentateuch	PEN tuh too : k	ˈpɛntətuk
Pentecost	PEN ti kawst	ˈpɛntɪkɔst
Penthesilea	pen the suh LEE uh	pɛnθɛsəˈliə
pentobarbital	pen tuh BAHR bi tawl	pɛntəˈbɑrbɪtɔl
pentothal	PEN tuh thal	ˈpɛntəθæl
pentstemon	pent STEE muhn	pɛntˈstimən
penuche, penuchi	puh NOO : chi	pəˈnutʃɪ
penult	PEE nuhlt	ˈpinʌlt
penultimate	pi NUHL tuh mit	pɪˈnʌltəmɪt
penumbra	pi NUHM bruh	pɪˈnʌmbrə
penurious	puh NYOO ri uhs	pəˈnjʊrɪəs
penury	PE nyuh ri	ˈpɛnjərɪ
peon	PEE uhn	ˈpiən
peonage	PEE uh nij	ˈpiənɪdʒ
peony	PEE uh ni	ˈpiənɪ
Pepin	PE pin	ˈpɛpɪn
peplos, peplus	PE pluhs	ˈpɛpləs
peplum	PE pluhm	ˈpɛpləm
peppercorn	PE per kawrn	ˈpɛpərkɔrn
pepperidge	PE puh rij	ˈpɛpərɪdʒ
peptic	PEP tik	ˈpɛptɪk
Pepys	peeps	pips
Pequot	PEE kwaht	ˈpikwɑt
Perak	PAY rak	ˈperæk
per annum	per A nuhm	pər ˈænəm
per aspera ad astra	per A spuh ruh ad A struh	pər ˈæspərə æd ˈæstrə
percale	per KAYL	pərˈkel
per capita	per KA puh tuh	pər ˈkæpətə
per cent, percent	per SENT	pərˈsɛnt
Perceval	PER suh vuhl	ˈpɜˑsəvəl
Percheron	PER chuh rahn	ˈpɜˑtʃərɑn
percipient	per SI pi uhnt	pərˈsɪpɪənt
Percival, -e	PER suh vuhl	ˈpɜˑsəvəl
percolate	PER kuh layt	ˈpɜˑkəlet
percolator	PER kuh lay ter	ˈpɜˑkəletər
percussion	per KUH shuhn	pərˈkʌʃən
per diem	per DIGH uhm	pər ˈdaɪəm
perdition	per DI shuhn	pərˈdɪʃən
père, P-	pair	pɛr
peregrinate	PE ruh gri nayt	ˈpɛrəgrɪnet
peregrination	pe ruh gri NAY shuhn	pɛrəgrɪˈneʃən
peregrine	PE ruh grin	ˈpɛrəgrɪn
pereira, P-	puh RAY ruh	pəˈrerə
Pereira (Spanish, Portuguese)	pe RAY rah	pɛˈrerɑ

at [æ]; ah [ɑ]; air [ɛ]; awful [ɔ]; say [e]; back [b]; chair [tʃ]; do [d]; elm [ɛ]; eel [i]; server [ˈɜˑ, ər]; fit [f]; go [g]; hurt [h]; is [ɪ]; high [aɪ]; jet [dʒ]; kiss [k]; lamb [l]; my [m]; nice [n];

peremptory	puh REMP tuh ri	pəˈrɛmptərɪ
perennial	puh RE ni uhl	pəˈrɛnɪəl
Perez	puh REZ	pəˈrɛz
perfect (a)	PER fikt	ˈpɝfɪkt
perfect (v)	per FEKT	pərˈfɛkt
perfecto	per FEK toh	pərˈfɛkto
perfervid	per FER vid	pərˈfɝvɪd
perfidious	per FI di uhs	pərˈfɪdɪəs
perfidy	PER fi di	ˈpɝfɪdɪ
perforate	PER fuh rayt	ˈpɝfəret
perforce	per FAWRS	pərˈfɔrs
perfume (n)	PER fyoo:m	ˈpɝfjum
perfume (v)	per FYOO:M	pərˈfjum
perfunctory	per FUHNGK tuh ri	pərˈfʌŋktərɪ
pergola	PER guh luh	ˈpɝgələ
Pergolesi	pair gaw LE si	pɛrgɔˈlɛsɪ
perhaps	per HAPS	pərˈhæps
peri	PI ri	ˈpɪrɪ
pericardium	pe ruh KAHR di uhm	pɛrəˈkɑrdɪəm
perichondrium	pe ruh KAHN dri uhm	pɛrəˈkɑndrɪəm
Periclean	pe ruh KLEE uhn	pɛrəˈkliən
Pericles	PE ruh kleez	ˈpɛrəkliz
pericranium	pe ruh KRAY ni uhm	pɛrəˈkrenɪəm
perigee	PE ruh jee	ˈpɛrədʒi
perihelion	pe ruh HEE li uhn	pɛrəˈhilɪən
peril	PE ruhl	ˈpɛrəl
perimeter	puh RI muh ter	pəˈrɪmətər
perimetry	puh RI muh tri	pəˈrɪmətrɪ
perinephrium	pe ruh NE fri uhm	pɛrəˈnɛfrɪəm
perineum	pe ruh NEE uhm	pɛrəˈniəm
perineuritis	pe ri nyoo RIGH tis	pɛrɪnjuˈraɪtɪs
perineurium	pe ruh NYOO ri uhm	pɛrəˈnjʊrɪəm
periodic	pi ri AH dik	pɪrɪˈɑdɪk
periodical	pi ri AH di kuhl	pɪrɪˈɑdɪkəl
periosteum	pe ri AH sti uhm	pɛrɪˈɑstɪəm
periostitis	pe ri ah STIGH tis	pɛrɪɑˈstaɪtɪs
peripatetic	pe ri puh TE tik	pɛrɪpəˈtɛtɪk
periphery	puh RI fuh ri	pəˈrɪfərɪ
periphrasis	puh RI fruh sis	pəˈrɪfrəsɪs
periphrastic	pe ruh FRA stik	pɛrəˈfræstɪk
periscope	PE ruh skohp	ˈpɛrəskop
perish	PE rish	ˈpɛrɪʃ
peristalsis	pe ruh STAL sis	pɛrəˈstælsɪs
peristyle	PE ruh stighl	ˈpɛrəstaɪl
peritoneum, peritonaeum	pe ri tuh NEE uhm	pɛrɪtəˈniəm
peritonitis	pe ri tuh NIGH tis	pɛrɪtəˈnaɪtɪs
perjure	PER jer	ˈpɝdʒər
perjury	PER juh ri	ˈpɝdʒərɪ
Perm (U.S.S.R.)	pairm	pɛrm
permeability	per mi uh BI luh ti	pɝmɪəˈbɪlətɪ
permeable	PER mi uh buhl	ˈpɝmɪəbəl
permeate	PER mi ayt	ˈpɝmiet

---

si*ng* [ŋ] ; *oh* [o] ; *oil* [ɔɪ] ; *foot* [ʊ] ; *foo:*d [u] ; *how* [aʊ] ; *pie* [p] ; *ray* [r] ; *so* [s] ; *shall* [ʃ] ;
to [t] ; *thin* [θ] ; *th:*en [ð] ; *above* (*uh* B*UH*V) [ə, ˈʌ] ; *vine* [v] ; *wine* [w] ; *whine* [hw] ;
*y*ou [j] ; *zoo* [z] ; *rouge* (roo:*zh*) [ʒ].

Permian	PER mi uhn	ˈpɝmiən
permit (n)	PER mit	ˈpɝmɪt
permit (v)	per MIT	pərˈmɪt
permutation	per myuh TAY shuhn	pərmjəˈteʃən
Pernambuco	per nuhm BOO : koh	pərnəmˈbuko
pernicious	per NI shuhs	pərˈnɪʃəs
Perón	pe RAWN	pɛˈrɔn
peroration	pe ruh RAY shuhn	pɛrəˈreʃən
perpetual	per PE choo uhl	pərˈpɛtʃuəl
perpetuity	per puh TOO : uh ti	pərpəˈtuətɪ
perquisite	PER kwuh zit	ˈpɝkwəzɪt
Perrault	pe ROH	pɛˈro
per se	per SEE	pər ˈsi
Perseid	PER si id	ˈpɝsɪɪd
Persephone	per SE fuh ni	pərˈsɛfənɪ
Perseus	PER syoo : s	ˈpɝsjus
perseverance	per suh VI ruhns	pərsəˈvɪrəns
persevere	per suh VIR	pərsəˈvɪr
Pershing	PER shing	ˈpɝʃɪŋ
Persia	PER zhuh	ˈpɝʒə
Persian	PER zhuhn	ˈpɝʒən
persiflage	PER si flahzh	ˈpɝsɪflɑʒ
persimmon	per SI muhn	pərˈsɪmən
persist	per SIST	pərˈsɪst
persona	per SOH nuh	pərˈsonə
personae	per SOH nee	pərˈsoni
personal	PER suh nuhl	ˈpɝsənəl
persona non grata	per SOH nuh nahn GRAH tuh	pərˈsonə nɑn ˈgrɑtə
personification	per sah nuh fi KAY shuhn	pərsɑnəfɪˈkeʃən
personify	per SAH nuh figh	pərˈsɑnəfaɪ
personnel	per suh NEL	pərsəˈnɛl
perspective	per SPEK tiv	pərˈspɛktɪv
perspicacious	per spi KAY shuhs	pərspɪˈkeʃəs
perspicacity	per spi KA suh ti	pərspɪˈkæsətɪ
perspicuity	per spi KYOO : uh ti	pərspɪˈkjuətɪ
perspicuous	per SPI kyoo uhs	pərˈspɪkjuəs
perspiration	per spuh RAY shuhn	pərspəˈreʃən
perspire	per SPIGHR	pərˈspaɪr
persuade	per SWAYD	pərˈswed
persuasion	per SWAY zhuhn	pərˈsweʒən
persuasive	per SWAY siv	pərˈswesɪv
Perth	perth	pɝθ
pertinacious	per tuh NAY shuhs	pərtəˈneʃəs
pertinacity	per tuh NA suh ti	pərtəˈnæsətɪ
pertinent	PER tuh nuhnt	ˈpɝtənənt
perturbation	per ter BAY shuhn	pərtərˈbeʃən
pertussal	per TUH suhl	pərˈtʌsəl
pertussis	per TUH sis	pərˈtʌsɪs
Peru	puh ROO :	pəˈru
Perugia	pe ROO : jah	pɛˈrudʒɑ
Perugino	pe roo : JEE naw	pɛruˈdʒino

at [æ] ; *ah* [ɑ] ; *air* [ɛ] ; *awful* [ɔ] ; *say* [e] ; *back* [b] ; *chair* [tʃ] ; *do* [d] ; *elm* [ɛ] ; *eel* [i] ; *server* [ˈɝ, ər] ; *f*it [f] ; *go* [g] ; *h*urt [h] ; *is* [ɪ] ; *high* [aɪ] ; *jet* [dʒ] ; *kiss* [k] ; *l*amb [l] ; *my* [m] ; *nice* [n] ;

peruke	puh ROO : K	pəˈruk
perusal	puh ROO : zuhl	pəˈruzəl
peruse	puh ROO : Z	pəˈruz
Peruvian	puh ROO : vi uhn	pəˈruvɪən
pervasive	per VAY siv	pərˈvesɪv
perverse	per VERS	pərˈvɝs
perversion	per VER zhuhn	pərˈvɝʒən
pervert (n)	PER vert	ˈpɝvərt
pervert (v)	per VERT	pərˈvɝt
pervious	PER vi uhs	ˈpɝvɪəs
Pesach	PAY sahk	ˈpesɑk
pesade	puh SAYD	pəˈsed
Pescadores	pe skah DAW res	peskɑˈdɔres
peseta	puh SAY tuh	pəˈsetə
Peshawar	pe SHAH wer	pɛˈʃɑwər
peso	PAY soh	ˈpeso
pessimal	PE suh muhl	ˈpɛsəməl
pessimum	PE suh muhm	ˈpɛsəməm
Pestalozzi	pe stah LAWT si	pɛstɑˈlɔtsɪ
pestiferous	pe STI fuh ruhs	pɛˈstɪfərəs
pestilence	PE stuh luhns	ˈpɛstələns
pestilential	pe stuh LEN shuhl	pɛstəˈlɛnʃəl
pestle	PE suhl	ˈpɛsəl
Pesto	PE staw	ˈpɛstɔ
Pétain	pay TAN	peˈtæn
petard	pi TAHRD	pɪˈtɑrd
petit	PE ti	ˈpɛtɪ
Petit, Roland	puh TEE, roh LAHN	pəˈti, roˈlɑn
petite	puh TEET	pəˈtit
petit four	PE ti FAWR	ˈpɛtɪ ˈfɔr
petition	puh TI shuhn	pəˈtɪʃən
petit point	PE ti POINT	ˈpɛtɪ ˈpɔɪnt
petits pois	puh TEE PWAH	pəˈti ˈpwɑ
Petöfi	PE ter fi	ˈpɛtərfɪ
Petrarch	PEE trahrk	ˈpitrɑrk
Petrarchan	pee TRAHR kuhn	pɪˈtrɑrkən
petrel	PE truhl	ˈpɛtrəl
Petrie	PEE tri	ˈpitrɪ
petrify	PE truh figh	ˈpɛtrəfaɪ
Petrillo	puh TRI loh	pəˈtrɪlo
petroglyph	PE truh glif	ˈpɛtrəglɪf
Petrograd	PE truh grad	ˈpɛtrəgræd
petrography	pi TRAH gruh fi	pɪˈtrɑgrəfɪ
petrol	PE truhl	ˈpɛtrəl
petrolatum	pe truh LAY tuhm	pɛtrəˈletəm
petroleum	puh TROH li uhm	pəˈtrolɪəm
petrology	pi TRAH luh ji	pɪˈtrɑlədʒɪ
Petronius	pi TROH ni uhs	pɪˈtronɪəs
Petropavlovsk	pe traw PAHV lawfsk	petroˈpavlɔfsk
Petrosani	pe traw SHAHN	petrɔˈʃɑn
Petruchio	puh TROO : ki oh	pəˈtrukɪo
Petsamo	PET sah maw	ˈpɛtsɑmɔ

pettifoggery	pe ti FAH guh ri	pɛtɪˈfɑgərɪ
petulance	PE chuh luhns	ˈpɛtʃələns
petulant	PE chuh luhnt	ˈpɛtʃələnt
petunia	puh TOO: nyuh	pəˈtunjə
pew	pyoo:	pju
pewter	PYOO: ter	ˈpjutər
peyote	pay OH ti	peˈotɪ
Pfeiffer	FIGH fer	ˈfaɪfər
pfennig	FE nig	ˈfɛnɪg
Pfizer	FIGH zer	ˈfaɪzer
Phaedra	FEE druh	ˈfidrə
Phaethon	FAY uh thuhn	ˈfeəθən
phaeton	FAY uh tuhn	ˈfeətən
phagocyte	FA guh sight	ˈfægəsaɪt
phalanstery	FA luhn stai ri	ˈfælənstɛrɪ
phalanx	FAY langks	ˈfelæŋks
phalarope	FA luh rohp	ˈfælərop
phallic	FA lik	ˈfælɪk
phallus	FA luhs	ˈfæləs
phanatron	FA nuh trahn	ˈfænətrɑn
phantasm	FAN ta zuhm	ˈfæntæzəm
phantasmagoria	fan taz muh GAW ri uh	fæntæzməˈgɔrɪə
phantasmal	fan TAZ muhl	fænˈtæzməl
phantom	FAN tuhm	ˈfæntəm
Pharaoh	FAI roh	ˈfɛro
Pharaonic	fai ray AH nik	fɛreˈɑnɪk
pharisaic, P-	fa ruh SAY ik	færəˈseɪk
Pharisee, p-	FA ruh see	ˈfærəsi
pharmaceutical	fahr muh SOO: ti kuhl	fɑrməˈsutɪkəl
pharmacopoeia	fahr muh kuh PEE uh	fɑrməkəˈpiə
Pharos, p-	FAI rahs	ˈfɛrɑs
Pharpar	FAHR pahr	ˈfɑrpɑr
Pharsalus	fahr SAY luhs	fɑrˈseləs
pharyngeal	fuh RIN ji uhl	fəˈrɪndʒɪəl
pharyngitis	fa rin JIGH tis	færɪnˈdʒaɪtɪs
pharynx	FA ringks	ˈfærɪŋks
Phebe	FEE bi	ˈfibɪ
phenacaine	FEE nuh kayn	ˈfinəken
phenacetin, -e	fi NA suh tin	fɪˈnæsətɪn
phenobarbital	fee nuh BAHR bi tal	finəˈbɑrbɪtæl
phenol	FEE nawl	ˈfinɔl
phenology	fi NAH luh ji	fɪˈnɑlədʒɪ
phenomenal	fi NAH muh nuhl	fɪˈnɑmənəl
phenomenon	fi NAH muh nahn	fɪˈnɑmənɑn
phial	FIGH uhl	ˈfaɪəl
Phidias	FI di uhs	ˈfɪdɪəs
philanderer	fi LAN duh rer	fɪˈlændərər
philanthropic	fi luhn THRAH pik	fɪlənˈθrɑpɪk
philanthropist	fi LAN thruh pist	fɪˈlænθrəpɪst
philanthropy	fi LAN thruh pi	fɪˈlænθrəpɪ
philatelic	fi luh TE lik	fɪləˈtɛlɪk
philatelist	fi LA tuh list	fɪˈlætəlɪst

at [æ]; *ah* [ɑ]; *air* [ɛ]; *awful* [ɔ]; *say* [e]; *back* [b]; *chair* [tʃ]; *do* [d]; *elm* [ɛ]; *eel* [i]; *server* [ˈɝ, ər]; *f*it [f]; *go* [g]; *h*urt [h]; *is* [ɪ]; *high* [aɪ]; *jet* [dʒ]; *kiss* [k]; *l*amb [l]; *my* [m]; *n*ice [n];

philately	fi LA tuh li	fɪˈlætəlɪ
Philemon	fi LEE muhn	fɪˈlimən
philharmonic	fil hahr MAH nik	fɪlhɑrˈmɑnɪk
Philippi	fi LI pigh	fɪˈlɪpaɪ
Philippian	fi LI pi uhn	fɪˈlɪpɪən
Philippic, p-	fi LI pik	fɪˈlɪpɪk
Philippine	FI luh peen	ˈfɪləpin
Philistine	fuh LI stin	fəˈlɪstɪn
philodendron	fi luh DEN druhn	fɪləˈdɛndrən
philogyny	fi LAH juh ni	fɪˈlɑdʒənɪ
philologian	fi luh LOH juhn	fɪləˈlodʒən
philologist	fi LAH luh jist	fɪˈlɑlədʒɪst
philology	fi LAH luh ji	fɪˈlɑlədʒɪ
philomel	FI luh mel	ˈfɪləmɛl
Philomela	fi luh MEE luh	fɪləˈmilə
philoprogenitive	fi luh proh JE nuh tiv	fɪləproˈdʒɛnətɪv
philosophical	fi luh SAH fi kuhl	fɪləˈsɑfɪkəl
philosophism	fi LAH suh fi zuhm	fɪˈlɑsəfɪzəm
philosophy	fi LAH suh fi	fɪˈlɑsəfɪ
Phineas	FI ni uhs	ˈfɪnɪəs
phlebitis	fli BIGH tis	flɪˈbaɪtɪs
phlebosclerosis	fle boh skli ROH sis	flɛbosklɪˈrosɪs
phlebotomy	fli BAH tuh mi	flɪˈbɑtəmɪ
Phlegethon	FLE guh thahn	ˈflɛgəθɑn
phlegm	flem	flɛm
phlegmatic	fleg MA tik	flɛgˈmætɪk
phlogiston	floh JI stuhn	floˈdʒɪstən
phlox	flahks	flɑks
phlyctena	flik TEE nuh	flɪkˈtinə
phobia	FOH bi uh	ˈfobɪə
Phoebe, p-	FEE bi	ˈfibɪ
Phoebus	FEE buhs	ˈfibəs
Phoenicia	fuh NI shuh	fəˈnɪʃə
Phoenix, p-	FEE niks	ˈfinɪks
phonasthenia	foh nas THEE ni uh	fonæsˈθinɪə
phonation	foh NAY shuhn	foˈneʃən
phoneme	FOH neem	ˈfonim
phonemic	foh NEE mik	foˈnimɪk
phonetic	fuh NE tik	fəˈnɛtɪk
phonetician	foh nuh TI shuhn	fonəˈtɪʃən
phoneticist	fuh NE tuh sist	fəˈnɛtəsɪst
phonic	FAH nik	ˈfɑnɪk
phonotypy	FOH nuh tigh pi	ˈfonətaɪpɪ
phosgene	FAHS jeen	ˈfɑsdʒin
phosphate	FAHS fayt	ˈfɑsfet
phosphorescence	fahs fuh RE suhns	fɑsfəˈrɛsəns
phosphoric	fahs FAW rik	fɑsˈfɔrɪk
phosphorous, phosphorus	FAHS fuh ruhs	ˈfɑsfərəs
photic	FOH tik	ˈfotɪk
photochromy	FOH tuh kroh mi	ˈfotəkromɪ
photogene	FOH tuh jeen	ˈfotədʒin
photogenic	foh tuh JE nik	fotəˈdʒɛnɪk

sing [ŋ] ; *oh* [o] ; *oil* [ɔi] ; *foot* [ʊ] ; *foo:*d [u] ; *how* [aʊ] ; *p*ie [p] ; *r*ay [r] ; *s*o [s] ; *sh*all [ʃ] ;
*t*o [t] ; *th*in [θ] ; *th:*en [ð] ; *above* (*uh* B*U*HV) [ə, ˈʌ] ; *v*ine [v] ; *w*ine [w] ; *wh*ine [hw] ;
*y*ou [j] ; *z*oo [z] ; *rouge* (roo:*zh*) [ʒ].

photography	fuh TAH gruh fi	fə'tɑgrəfɪ
photogravure	foh tuh gruh VYOOR	fotəgrə'vjʊr
photolytic	foh tuh LI tik	fotə'lɪtɪk
photometer	foh TAH muh ter	fo'tɑmətər
photometry	foh TAH muh tri	fo'tɑmətrɪ
photon	FOH tahn	'fotɑn
photostat	FOH tuh stat	'fotəstæt
phototypy	FOH tuh tigh pi	'fotətaɪpɪ
phraseology	fray zi AH luh ji	frezɪ'ɑlədʒɪ
phrenetic	fri NE tik	frɪ'nɛtɪk
phrenic	FRE nik	'frɛnɪk
phrenology	fre NAH luh ji	frɛ'nɑlədʒɪ
Phrygia	FRI ji uh	'frɪdʒɪə
phthalic	THA lik	'θælɪk
phthisic	TI zik	'tɪzɪk
phthisis	THIGH sis	'θaɪsɪs
Phyfe	fighf	faɪf
phylactery	fi LAK tuh ri	fɪ'læktərɪ
phylaxis	fi LAK sis	fɪ'læksɪs
phylogeny	figh LAH juh ni	faɪ'lɑdʒənɪ
phylum	FIGH luhm	'faɪləm
physician	fuh ZI shuhn	fə'zɪʃən
physicist	FI zuh sist	'fɪzəsɪst
physiocrat	FI zi uh krat	'fɪzɪəkræt
physiognomy	fi zi AHG nuh mi	fɪzɪ'ɑgnəmɪ
physiography	fi zi AH gruh fi	fɪzɪ'ɑgrəfɪ
physiological	fi zi uh LAH ji kuhl	fɪzɪə'lɑdʒɪkəl
physiology	fi zi AH luh ji	fɪzɪ'ɑlədʒɪ
physiotherapy	fi zi oh THE ruh pi	fɪzɪo'θɛrəpɪ
physique	fi ZEEK	fɪ'zik
phytogenesis	figh toh JE nuh sis	faɪto'dʒɛnəsɪs
pi	pigh	paɪ
Piacenza	pyah CHENT sah	pjɑ'tʃɛntsɑ
Piaf, Edith	pee AHF, ay DEET	pi'ɑf, e'dit
pia mater	PIGH uh MAY ter	'paɪə 'metər
pianissimo	pee uh NI suh moh	piə'nɪsəmo
pianist	pi A nist	pɪ'ænɪst
piano (a, adv.)	pi AH noh	pɪ'ɑno
piano (n)	pi A noh	pɪ'æno
pianoforte	pi A nuh fawrt	pɪ'ænəfɔrt
piaster, piastre	pi A ster	pɪ'æstər
Piatigorsky	pyah ti GAWR ski	pjɑtɪ'gɔrskɪ
piazza	pi A zuh	pɪ'æzə
pibroch	PEE brahk	'pibrɑk
pica	PIGH kuh	'paɪkə
picador	PI kuh dawr	'pɪkədɔr
Picardy	PI ker di	'pɪkərdɪ
picaresque	pi kuh RESK	pɪkə'rɛsk
Picasso	pi KAH soh	pɪ'kɑso
picayune	pi ki YOO : N	pɪkɪ'jun
Piccadilly	pi kuh DI li	pɪkə'dɪlɪ
piccalilli	PI kuh li li	'pɪkəlɪlɪ

at [æ]; ah [ɑ]; air [ɛ]; awful [ɔ]; say [e]; back [b]; chair [tʃ]; do [d]; elm [ɛ]; eel [i];
server ['ɝ, ər]; fit [f]; go [g]; hurt [h]; is [ɪ]; high [aɪ]; jet [dʒ]; kiss [k]; lamb [l]; my [m];
nice [n];

Piccard	pi KAHRD	pɪˈkɑrd
piccolo	PI kuh loh	ˈpɪkəlo
Pickwickian	pik WI ki uhn	pɪkˈwɪkɪən
picot	PEE koh	ˈpiko
Pict	pikt	pɪkt
Pictor	PIK ter	ˈpɪktər
pictorial	pik TAW ri uhl	pɪkˈtɔrɪəl
picture	PIK cher	ˈpɪktʃər
picturesque	pik chuh RESK	pɪktʃəˈrɛsk
picul	PI kuhl	ˈpɪkəl
pidgin	PI jin	ˈpɪdʒɪn
piebald	PIGH bawld	ˈpaɪbɔld
pièce de résistance	pyes duh ray zee STAHNS	pjɛs də reziˈstɑns
Pieck	peek	pik
pied	pighd	paɪd
pied à terre	pye da TAIR	pjɛ dæ ˈtɛr
Piedmont, p-	PEED mahnt	ˈpidmɑnt
Pierian	pigh I ri uhn	paɪˈɪrɪən
Pierre	pyair	pjɛr
Pierre (South Dakota)	pir	pɪr
Pierrot	PEE uh roh	ˈpiəro
Piestany	PYESH tyah ni	ˈpjɛʃtjɑnɪ
Pietà	pyay TAH	pjeˈtɑ
Pietermaritzburg	PEE ter MAI rits berg	ˈpitərˈmɛrɪtsbərg
pietism	PIGH uh ti zuhm	ˈpaɪətɪzəm
pietistic	pigh uh TI stik	paɪəˈtɪstɪk
piety	PIGH uh ti	ˈpaɪətɪ
piezoelectric	pigh ee zoh i LEK trik	paɪizoɪˈlɛktrɪk
pigeon	PI juhn	ˈpɪdʒən
Pigmy, p-	PIG mi	ˈpɪgmɪ
pilaf, -f	pi LAHF	pɪˈlɑf
pilaster	pi LA ster	pɪˈlæstər
Pilate, Pontius	PIGH luht, PAHN chuhs	ˈpaɪlət, ˈpɑntʃəs
pilau, pilaw	pi LAW	pɪˈlɔ
Pilcomayo	peel kaw MAH yaw	pilkɔˈmɑjɔ
pileus	PIGH li uhs	ˈpaɪlɪəs
pilgarlic	pil GAHR lik	pɪlˈgɑrlɪk
pilgrim, P-	PIL grim	ˈpɪlgrɪm
pilgrimage	PIL gruh mij	ˈpɪlgrəmɪdʒ
pili	pee LEE	piˈli
pillion	PI lyuhn	ˈpɪljən
pillory	PI luh ri	ˈpɪlərɪ
pillow	PI loh	ˈpɪlo
pilose	PIGH lohs	ˈpaɪlos
pilot	PIGH luht	ˈpaɪlət
Pilsen	PIL zuhn	ˈpɪlzən
Pilsudski	pil SUHD ski	pɪlˈsʌdskɪ
Piltdown	PILT down	ˈpɪltdaʊn
Pima	PEE muh	ˈpimə
pimento	pi MEN toh	pɪˈmɛnto
pimiento	pi MYEN toh	pɪˈmjɛnto
pimpernel, P-	PIM per nel	ˈpɪmpərnɛl

sing [ŋ] ; *oh* [o] ; *oil* [ɔɪ] ; *foot* [ʊ] ; *foo:d* [u] ; *how* [aʊ] ; *pie* [p] ; *ray* [r] ; *so* [s] ; *shall* [ʃ] ; *to* [t] ; *thin* [θ] ; *th:en* [ð] ; *above* (*uh* B*UH*V) [ə, ˈʌ] ; *vine* [v] ; *wine* [w] ; *whine* [hw] ; *you* [j] ; *zoo* [z] ; *rouge* (roo:*zh*) [ʒ].

pinaceous	pigh NAY shuhs	paɪˈneʃəs
pinafore	PI nuh fawr	ˈpɪnəfɔr
pince-nez	PANS nay	ˈpænsne
pincers	PIN serz	ˈpɪnsərz
Pindar	PIN der	ˈpɪndər
Pindaric	pin DA rik	pɪnˈdærɪk
pineal	PI ni uhl	ˈpɪnɪəl
Pinero	pi NAI roh	pɪˈnɛro
Piñero	pee NYE roh	piˈnjɛro
pinion	PI nyuhn	ˈpɪnjən
pinnace	PI nis	ˈpɪnɪs
pinnacle	PI nuh kuhl	ˈpɪnəkəl
pinochle, pinocle	PEE nuh kuhl	ˈpinəkəl
pinole	pi NOH lay	pɪˈnole
Pinza, Ezio	PEENT sah, AYT si oh	ˈpintsɑ, ˈetsɪo
pioneer	pigh uh NIR	paɪəˈnɪr
pious	PIGH uhs	ˈpaɪəs
pipage	PIGH pij	ˈpaɪpɪdʒ
pipet, -te	pigh PET	paɪˈpɛt
pipit	PI pit	ˈpɪpɪt
piquancy	PEE kwuhn si	ˈpikwənsɪ
piquant	PEE kwuhnt	ˈpikwənt
piquante	pee KAHNT	piˈkɑnt
pique	peek	pik
piqué	pi KAY	pɪˈke
piquet	pi KET	pɪˈkɛt
piracy	PIGH ruh si	ˈpaɪrəsɪ
Piraeus	pigh REE uhs	paɪˈriəs
piragua	pi RAH gwuh	pɪˈrɑgwə
Pirandello	pi ruhn DE loh	pɪrənˈdɛlo
piranha	pi RAHN yuh	pɪˈrɑnjə
piratical	pigh RA ti kuhl	paɪˈrætɪkəl
Pirithous	pigh RI thoh uhs	paɪˈrɪθoəs
pirn	pern	pɜn
Pirnie	PER ni	ˈpɜnɪ
pirogue	pi ROHG	pɪˈrog
pirouette	pi roo : ET	pɪruˈet
Pisa	PEE zuh	ˈpizə
pis aller	pee za LAY	pizæˈle
Pisano	pi SAH noh	pɪˈsɑno
piscatorial	pi skuh TAW ri uhl	pɪskəˈtɔrɪəl
Pisces	PI seez	ˈpɪsiz
pisciculture	PI si kuhl cher	ˈpɪsɪkʌltʃər
Pisgah	PIZ guh	ˈpɪzgə
Pisistratus	pi SI struh tuhs	pɪˈsɪstrətəs
pismire	PIS mighr	ˈpɪsmaɪr
Pissarro	pee sa ROH	pisæˈro
pistachio	pi STAH shi oh	pɪˈstaʃɪo
piston	PI stuhn	ˈpɪstən
Pitcairn	PIT kairn	ˈpɪtkɛrn
pitchblende	PICH blend	ˈpɪtʃblɛnd
pitcher	PI cher	ˈpɪtʃər

at [æ]; ah [ɑ]; air [ɛ]; awful [ɔ]; say [e]; back [b]; chair [tʃ]; do [d]; elm [ɛ]; eel [i];
server [ˈɜ, ər]; fit [f]; go [g]; hurt [h]; is [ɪ]; high [aɪ]; jet [dʒ]; kiss [k]; lamb [l]; my [m];
nice [n];

piteous	PI ti uhs	ˈpɪtɪəs
Pithecanthropus	pi thuh kan THROH puhs	pɪθəkænˈθropəs
pithy	PI thi	ˈpɪθɪ
pitiable	PI ti uh buhl	ˈpɪtɪəbəl
Pitot	pee TOH	piˈto
pittance	PI tuhns	ˈpɪtəns
pituitary	pi TOO : uh tai ri	pɪˈtuətɛrɪ
pituitous	pi TOO uh tuhs	pɪˈtuətəs
pityriasis	pi tuh RIGH uh sis	pɪtəˈraɪəsɪs
più	pyoo :	pju
Pius	PIGH uhs	ˈpaɪəs
pivot	PI vuht	ˈpɪvət
pivotal	PI vuh tuhl	ˈpɪvətəl
pixilated	PIK suh lay tid	ˈpɪksəletɪd
pixy	PIK si	ˈpɪksɪ
Pizarro	pi ZAH roh	pɪˈzɑro
pizza	PEET suh	ˈpitsə
pizzeria	peet suh REE uh	pitsəˈriə
pizzicato	pit suh KAH toh	pɪtsəˈkɑto
placable	PLAY kuh buhl	ˈplekəbəl
placard (n)	PLA kahrd	ˈplækɑrd
placard (v)	pluh KAHRD	pləˈkɑrd
placate	PLAY kayt	ˈpleket
placebo	pluh SEE boh	pləˈsibo
Place de la Concorde	plas duh lah kohn KAWRD	plæs də lɑ konˈkɔrd
placenta	pluh SEN tuh	pləˈsɛntə
placet	PLAY sit	ˈplesɪt
placid	PLA sid	ˈplæsɪd
placket	PLA kit	ˈplækɪt
plagal	PLAY guhl	ˈplegəl
plagiarism	PLAY juh ri zuhm	ˈpledʒərɪzəm
plagiarize	PLAY juh righz	ˈpledʒəraɪz
plague	playg	pleg
plaguy	PLAY gi	ˈplegɪ
plaice	plays	ples
plaid	plad	plæd
plaint	playnt	plent
plaintiff	PLAYN tif	ˈplentɪf
plait	playt	plet
planchette	plan SHET	plænˈʃɛt
Planck, Max	plahngk, mahks	plɑŋk, mɑks
planetarium	pla nuh TAI ri uhm	plænəˈtɛrɪəm
planetary	PLA nuh tai ri	ˈplænətɛrɪ
planetesimal	pla nuh TE si muhl	plænəˈtɛsɪməl
planetoid	PLA nuh toid	ˈplænətɔɪd
plangent	PLAN juhnt	ˈplændʒənt
planimeter	pluh NI muh ter	pləˈnɪmətər
planish	PLA nish	ˈplænɪʃ
plankton	PLANGK tuhn	ˈplæŋktən
planometer	pluh NAH muh ter	pləˈnɑmətər
Plantagenet	plan TA juh nit	plænˈtædʒənɪt
plantain	PLAN tin	ˈplæntɪn

si*ng* [ŋ] ; *oh* [o] ; *oil* [ɔɪ] ; *foot* [ʊ] ; *foo*:*d* [u] ; *how* [aʊ] ; *pie* [p] ; *ray* [r] ; *so* [s] ; *shall* [ʃ] ; *to* [t] ; *thin* [θ] ; *th*:*en* [ð] ; *above* (*uh BUHV*) [ə, ˈʌ] ; *vine* [v] ; *wine* [w] ; *whine* [hw] ; *you* [j] ; *zoo* [z] ; *rouge* (roo:*zh*) [ʒ].

plaque	plak	plæk
plasma	PLAZ muh	ˈplæzmə
plasmochin, P-	PLAZ muh kin	ˈplæzməkɪn
plasmodium	plaz MOH di uhm	plæzˈmodɪəm
Plassey	PLAH si	ˈplɑsɪ
plaster	PLA ster	ˈplæstər
plastic	PLA stik	ˈplæstɪk
plastron	PLA struhn	ˈplæstrən
plat	plat	plæt
Plata	PLAH tah	ˈplɑtɑ
plateau	pla TOH	plæˈto
platen	PLA tuhn	ˈplætən
platinum	PLA tuh nuhm	ˈplætənəm
platitude	PLA tuh too:d	ˈplætətud
platitudinous	pla tuh TOO: duh nuhs	plætəˈtudənəs
Plato	PLAY toh	ˈpleto
Platonic, p-	pluh TAH nik	pləˈtɑnɪk
Platonism	PLAY tuh ni zuhm	ˈpletənɪzəm
platoon	pluh TOO:N	pləˈtun
Plattdeutsch	PLAHT doich	ˈplɑtdɔɪtʃ
Platte	plat	plæt
platy	PLA ti	ˈplætɪ
platypus	PLA tuh puhs	ˈplætəpəs
platyrrhinian	pla tuh RI ni uhn	plætəˈrɪnɪən
plaudit	PLAW dit	ˈplɔdɪt
plausible	PLAW zuh buhl	ˈplɔzəbəl
Plautus	PLAW tuhs	ˈplɔtəs
playa	PLAH yuh	ˈplɑjə
plaza	PLA zuh	ˈplæzə
Plaza (Latin America)	PLAH sah	ˈplɑsɑ
pleasance	PLE zuhns	ˈplɛzəns
pleasant	PLE zuhnt	ˈplɛzənt
pleasure	PLE zher	ˈplɛʒər
pleat	pleet	plit
pleb	pleb	plɛb
plebe	pleeb	plib
plebeian	pli BEE uhn	plɪˈbiən
plebiscite	PLE buh sight	ˈplɛbəsaɪt
plebs	plebz	plɛbz
plectrum	PLEK truhm	ˈplɛktrəm
Pleiades	PLEE uh deez	ˈpliədiz
plein-air	playn AIR	plenˈɛr
Pleiocene	PLIGH uh seen	ˈplaɪəsin
Pleistocene	PLIGH stuh seen	ˈplaɪstəsin
plenary	PLEE nuh ri	ˈpli nuh rɪ
plenipotentiary	ple ni puh TEN shi ai ri	plɛnɪpəˈtɛnʃɪɛrɪ
plenteous	PLEN ti uhs	ˈplɛntɪəs
plenum	PLEE nuhm	ˈplinəm
pleonasm	PLEE uh na zuhm	ˈpliənæzəm
pleonastic	plee uh NA stik	pliəˈnæstɪk
Plesianthropus	plee si an THROH puhs	plisɪænˈθropəs
plesiosaur	PLEE si uh sawr	ˈplisɪəsɔr

at [æ]; *ah* [ɑ]; *air* [ɛ]; *aw*ful [ɔ]; *say* [e]; *b*ack [b]; *ch*air [tʃ]; *d*o [d]; *e*lm [ɛ]; *ee*l [i]; *ser*ver [ˈɝ, ər]; *f*it [f]; *g*o [g]; *h*urt [h]; *is* [ɪ]; *h*igh [aɪ]; *j*et [dʒ]; *k*iss [k]; *l*amb [l]; *m*y [m]; *n*ice [n];

plethora	PLE thuh ruh	ˈplɛθərə
plethoric	ple THAW rik	plɛˈθɔrɪk
pleurisy	PLOO ruh si	ˈplʊrəsɪ
pleuston	PLOO : stuhn	ˈplustən
plexiglass, P-	PLEK si glas	ˈplɛksɪglæs
plexus	PLEK suhs	ˈplɛksəs
pliable	PLIGH uh buhl	ˈplaɪəbəl
pliant	PLIGH uhnt	ˈplaɪənt
plication	pligh KAY shuhn	plaɪˈkeʃən
plinth	plinth	plɪnθ
Pliny	PLI ni	ˈplɪnɪ
Pliocene	PLIGH uh seen	ˈplaɪəsin
pliofilm	PLIGH uh film	ˈplaɪəfɪlm
plioflex	PLIGH uh fleks	ˈplaɪəflɛks
Ploesti	plaw YESHT	plɔˈjɛʃt
Plotinus	ploh TIGH nuhs	ploˈtaɪnəs
Plovdiv	PLAWV dif	ˈplɔvdɪf
plover	PLUH ver	ˈplʌvər
plow, plough	plow	plaʊ
plumb	pluhm	plʌm
plumbago	pluhm BAY goh	plʌmˈbego
plumbeous	PLUHM bi uhs	ˈplʌmbɪəs
plumber	PLUH mer	ˈplʌmər
plumbery	PLUH muh ri	ˈplʌmərɪ
plumbic	PLUM bik	ˈplʌmbɪk
plumbing	PLUH ming	ˈplʌmɪŋ
plumbism	PLUHM bi zuhm	ˈplʌmbɪzəm
plummet	PLUH mit	ˈplʌmɪt
plumose	PLOO : mohs	ˈplumos
plumule	PLOO : myoo : l	ˈplumjul
plural	PLOO ruhl	ˈplʊrəl
plurality	ploo RA luh ti	pluˈrælətɪ
plus	pluhs	plʌs
plush	pluhsh	plʌʃ
Plutarch	PLOO : tahrk	ˈplutɑrk
Pluto	PLOO : toh	ˈpluto
plutocracy	ploo : TAH kruh si	pluˈtɑkrəsɪ
plutocrat	PLOO : tuh krat	ˈplutəkræt
Plutonic, p-	ploo : TAH nik	pluˈtɑnɪk
plutonium	ploo : TOH ni uhm	pluˈtonɪəm
Plutus	PLOO : tuhs	ˈplutəs
pluvial	PLOO : vi uhl	ˈpluvɪəl
pluviometry	ploo : vi AH muh tri	pluvɪˈɑmətrɪ
pluvious	PLOO : vi uhs	ˈpluvɪəs
ply	pligh	plaɪ
Plymouth	PLI muhth	ˈplɪməθ
pneumatic	noo : MA tik	nuˈmætɪk
pneumectomy	noo : MEK tuh mi	nuˈmɛktəmɪ
pneumococcus	noo : muh KAH kuhs	numəˈkɑkəs
pneumoconiosis	noo : muh kah ni OH sis	numəkɑnɪˈosɪs
pneumonia	noo : MOH nyuh	nuˈmonjə
Pnom-Penh	nahm pen	nɑm pɛn

sing [ŋ] ; oh [o] ; oil [ɔɪ] ; foot [ʊ] ; foo:d [u] ; how [aʊ] ; pie [p] ; ray [r] ; so [s] ; shall [ʃ] ;
to [t] ; thin [θ] ; th:en [ð] ; above (uh BUHV) [ə, ˈʌ] ; vine [v] ; wine [w] ; whine [hw] ;
you [j] ; zoo [z] ; rouge (roo:zh) [ʒ].

Po	poh	po
Pocahontas	poh kuh HAHN tuhs	pokəˈhɑntəs
poco	POH koh	ˈpoko
pococurante	poh koh koo RAN ti	pokokʊˈrænti
podagra	puh DA gruh	pəˈdægrə
podesta	poh DE stuh	poˈdɛstə
podiatrist	poh DIGH uh trist	poˈdaɪətrɪst
podium	POH di uhm	ˈpodɪəm
podophyllin	pah duh FI lin	padəˈfɪlɪn
Podunk	POH duhngk	ˈpodʌŋk
poem	POH im	ˈpoɪm
poesy	POH i si	ˈpoɪsɪ
poet	POH it	ˈpoɪt
poetaster	POH i ta ster	ˈpoɪtæstər
poetess	POH i tis	ˈpoɪtɪs
poetic	poh E tik	poˈɛtɪk
poetry	POH i tri	ˈpoɪtrɪ
pogo	POH goh	ˈpogo
pogonip	PAH guh nip	ˈpagənɪp
pogrom	POH gruhm	ˈpogrəm
pogy	POH gi	ˈpogɪ
Pohai	poh high	po haɪ
poi	poi	pɔɪ
poignancy	POI nuhn si	ˈpɔɪnənsɪ
poignant	POI nuhnt	ˈpɔɪnənt
poilu	PWAH loo:	ˈpwɑlu
Poincaré	pwan ka RAY	pwænkæˈre
poinciana	poin si A nuh	pɔɪnsɪˈænə
poinsettia	poin SE ti uh	pɔɪnˈsɛtɪə
pointillism	PWAN tuh li zuhm	ˈpwæntəlɪzəm
Poitiers	poi TIRZ	pɔɪˈtɪrz
Poitou	pwa TOO:	pwæˈtu
polacca	poh LAH kah	poˈlɑkɑ
Poland	POH luhnd	ˈpolənd
polar	POH ler	ˈpolər
Polaris	poh LAI ris	poˈlɛrɪs
polariscope	poh LA ruh skohp	poˈlærəskop
polarity	poh LA ruh ti	poˈlærətɪ
polaroid, P-	POH luh roid	ˈpolərɔɪd
polemic	poh LE mik	poˈlɛmɪk
police	puh LEES	pəˈlis
policeman	puh LEES muhn	pəˈlismən
polio	POH li oh	ˈpolɪo
poliomyelitis	pah li oh MIGH uh LIGH tis	palioˈmaɪəˈlaɪtɪs
Politburo	puh LIT byoo roh	pəˈlɪtbjʊro
polite	puh LIGHT	pəˈlaɪt
politesse	pah luh TES	paləˈtɛs
politic	PAH luh tik	ˈpalətɪk
politico	puh LI ti koh	pəˈlɪtiko
polity	PAH luh ti	ˈpalətɪ
Polk	pohk	pok

at [æ]; ah [ɑ]; air [ɛ]; awful [ɔ]; say [e]; back [b]; chair [tʃ]; do [d]; elm [ɛ]; eel [i]; server [ˈɜ, ər]; fit [f]; go [g]; hurt [h]; is [ɪ]; high [aɪ]; jet [dʒ]; kiss [k]; lamb [l]; my [m]; nice [n];

polka (dance)	POHL kuh	ˈpolkə
polka (dot)	POH kuh	ˈpokə
poll	pohl	pol
pollen	PAH luhn	ˈpɑlən
pollex	PAH leks	ˈpɑlɛks
Pollock	PAH luhk	ˈpɑlək
pollute	puh LOO : T	pəˈlut
Pollux	PAH luhks	ˈpɑləks
polo, P-	POH loh	ˈpolo
polonaise	pah luh NAYZ	pɑləˈnez
polonium	puh LOH ni uhm	pəˈloniəm
Polonius	puh LOH ni uhs	pəˈloniəs
Poltava	pawl TAH vah	pɔlˈtɑvɑ
poltergeist	POHL ter gighst	ˈpoltərgaɪst
poltroon	pahl TROO : N	pɑlˈtrun
polyandrist	pah li AN drist	pɑlɪˈændrɪst
Polybius	puh LI bi uhs	pəˈlɪbiəs
Polycarp	PAH li kahrp	ˈpɑlɪkɑrp
polychrome	PAH li krohm	ˈpɑlɪkrom
polyclinic	pah li KLI nik	pɑlɪˈklɪnɪk
Polyclitus, Polycleitus	pah li KLIGH tuhs	pɑlɪˈklaɪtəs
Polycrates	puh LI kruh teez	pəˈlɪkrətiz
polydactyl, -e	pah li DAK til	pɑlɪˈdæktɪl
Polydorus	pah li DAW ruhs	pɑlɪˈdɔrəs
polyester	PAH li e ster	ˈpɑlɪestər
polygamy	puh LI guh mi	pəˈlɪgəmɪ
polyglot	PAH li glaht	ˈpɑlɪglɑt
Polygnotus	pah lig NOH tuhs	pɑlɪgˈnotəs
polygon	PAH li gahn	ˈpɑlɪgɑn
polygonal	puh LI guh nuhl	pəˈlɪgənəl
polygraph	PAH li graf	ˈpɑlɪgræf
polygyny	puh LI juh ni	pəˈlɪdʒənɪ
Polyhymnia	pah li HIM ni uh	pɑlɪˈhɪmnɪə
polymer	PAH li mer	ˈpɑlɪmər
polymerization	pah li muh ri ZAY shuhn	pɑlɪmərɪˈzeʃən
Polymnia	puh LIM ni uh	pəˈlɪmnɪə
Polynesia	pah luh NEE zhuh	pɑləˈniʒə
Polynices	pah li NIGH seez	pɑlɪˈnaɪsiz
polynomial	pah li NOH mi uhl	pɑlɪˈnomɪəl
polyp	PAH lip	ˈpɑlɪp
polyphagia	pah li FAY ji uh	pɑlɪˈfedʒɪə
Polyphemus	pah li FEE muhs	pɑlɪˈfiməs
polyphonic	pah li FAH nik	pɑlɪˈfɑnɪk
polyphony	puh LI fuh ni	pəˈlɪfənɪ
polyptych	PAH lip tik	ˈpɑlɪptɪk
polysyllabic	pah li si LA bik	pɑlɪsɪˈlæbɪk
polysyllable	PAH li si luh buhl	ˈpɑlɪsɪləbəl
polytechnic	pah li TEK nik	pɑlɪˈtɛknɪk
polytheism	PAH li thee i zuhm	ˈpɑlɪθiɪzəm
Polyxena	puh LIK suh nuh	pəˈlɪksənə
pomade	poh MAYD	poˈmed
pomander	puh MAN der	pəˈmændər

sing [ŋ] ; *oh* [o] ; *oil* [ɔɪ] ; *foot* [ʊ] ; *foo:d* [u] ; *how* [aʊ] ; *pie* [p] ; *ray* [r] ; *so* [s] ; *sh*all [ʃ] ;
to [t] ; *thin* [θ] ; *th:*en [ð] ; *above* (*uh BUH*V) [ə, ˈʌ] ; *vine* [v] ; *wine* [w] ; *whine* [hw] ;
you [j] ; *zoo* [z] ; *rouge* (*roo:zh*) [ʒ].

pomegranate	PAHM gra nit	ˈpɑmgrænɪt
pomelo	PAH muh loh	ˈpɑməlo
Pomerania	pah muh RAY ni uh	pɑməˈrenɪə
pommel	PUH muhl	ˈpʌməl
Pomona	puh MOH nuh	pəˈmonə
pomp	pahmp	pɑmp
pompadour, P-	PAHM puh dawr	ˈpɑmpədɔr
Pompeii	pahm PAY ee	pɑmˈpei
Pompeius	pahm PEE uhs	pɑmˈpiəs
Pompey	PAHM pi	ˈpɑmpɪ
pom-pom	PAHM pahm	ˈpɑmpɑm
pompon	PAHM pahn	ˈpɑmpɑn
pomposity	pahm PAH suh ti	pɑmˈpɑsətɪ
pompous	PAHM puhs	ˈpɑmpəs
Ponca	PAHNG kuh	ˈpɑŋkə
Ponce	PAWN se	ˈpɔnsɛ
Ponce de León	PAWN se de le AWN	ˈpɔnsɛ dɛ lɛˈɔn
Ponchielli	pahn KYE li	pɑnˈkjɛlɪ
poncho	PAHN choh	ˈpɑntʃo
ponderous	PAHN duh ruhs	ˈpɑndərəs
Pondicherry	pahn di CHE ri	pɑndɪˈtʃɛrɪ
pongee	pahn JEE	pɑnˈdʒi
poniard	PAHN yerd	ˈpɑnjərd
pons, P-	pahnz	pɑnz
Ponta Delgada	PAHN tuh del GAH duh	ˈpɑntə dɛlˈgɑdə
Pontchartrain	PAHN cher trayn	ˈpɑntʃərtren
Pontiac	PAHN ti ak	ˈpɑntɪæk
pontifex	PAHN tuh feks	ˈpɑntəfɛks
pontifical	pahn TI fi kuhl	pɑnˈtɪfɪkəl
Pontius	PAHN chuhs	ˈpɑntʃəs
pontlevis	pahnt LE vis	pɑntˈlevɪs
ponton	PAHN tuhn	ˈpɑntən
pontoon	pahn TOO:N	pɑnˈtun
Pontoppidan	pahn TAH pi dahn	pɑnˈtɑpɪdɑn
Pontus	PAHN tuhs	ˈpɑntəs
pood	poo:d	pud
Poona	POO:nuh	ˈpunə
poor	poor	pʊr
Poperinghe	PAH puh ring	ˈpɑpərɪŋ
poplin	PAH plin	ˈpɑplɪn
Popocatepetl	poh puh KA tuh pe tuhl	popəˈkætəpetəl
Popovic	PAW paw vich	ˈpɔpovɪtʃ
populace	PAH pyuh lis	ˈpɑpjəlɪs
popular	PAH pyuh ler	ˈpɑpjələr
popularity	pah pyuh LA ruh ti	pɑpjəˈlærətɪ
populous	PAH pyuh luhs	ˈpɑpjələs
porcelain	PAWR suh lin	ˈpɔrsəlɪn
porcine	PAWR sighn	ˈpɔrsaɪn
porcupine	PAWR kyuh pighn	ˈpɔrkjəpaɪn
porgy, P-	PAWR gi	ˈpɔrgɪ
Pori	PAW ree	ˈpɔri
pornographic	pawr nuh GRA fik	pɔrnəˈgræfɪk

at [æ]; ah [ɑ]; air [ɛ]; awful [ɔ]; say [e]; back [b]; chair [tʃ]; do [d]; elm [ɛ]; eel [i];
server [ˈɝ, ər]; fit [f]; go [g]; hurt [h]; is [ɪ]; high [aɪ]; jet [dʒ]; kiss [k]; lamb [l]; my [m];
nice [n];

pornography	pawr NAH gruh fi	pɔrˈnɑgrəfɪ
porosity	paw RAH suh ti	poˈrɑsətɪ
porous	PAW ruhs	ˈpɔrəs
porphyry	PAWR fuh ri	ˈpɔrfərɪ
porpoise	PAWR puhs	ˈpɔrpəs
porridge	PAW rij	ˈpɔrɪdʒ
porringer	PAW rin jer	ˈpɔrɪndʒər
Porsena	PAWR si nuh	ˈpɔrsɪnə
portamento	pawr tuh MEN toh	pɔrtəˈmɛnto
Port-au-Prince	pawrt oh PRINS	pɔrt o ˈprɪns
portcullis	pawrt KUH lis	pɔrtˈkʌlɪs
porte-cochere	pawrt koh SHAIR	pɔrtkoˈʃɛr
portend	pawr TEND	pɔrˈtɛnd
Porteño	pawr TAY nyoh	pɔrˈtenjo
portent	PAWR tent	ˈpɔrtɛnt
portentous	pawr TEN tuhs	pɔrˈtɛntəs
Porte St. Denis	pawrt san doo NEE	pɔrt sæn duˈni
Porte St. Martin	pawrt san mahr TAN	pɔrt sæn mɑrˈtæn
portfolio	pawrt FOH li oh	pɔrtˈfolɪo
Portia	PAWR shuh	ˈpɔrʃə
portico	PAWR ti koh	ˈpɔrtɪko
portiere	pawr TYAIR	pɔrˈtjɛr
Portland	PAWRT luhnd	ˈpɔrtlənd
portmanteau	pawrt MAN toh	pɔrtˈmænto
Porto (Portugal)	PAWR too	ˈpɔrtu
Porto Alegre	PAWR too ah LE gri	ˈpɔrtu ɑˈlɛgrɪ
Porto Rico	PAWR tuh REE kuh	ˈpɔrtə ˈrikə
portrait	PAWR trit	ˈpɔrtrɪt
portraiture	PAWR tri cher	ˈpɔrtrɪtʃər
Port Said	PAWRT sah EED	ˈpɔrt sɑˈid
Portsmouth	PAWRTS muhth	ˈpɔrtsməθ
Portugal	PAWR chuh guhl	ˈpɔrtʃəgəl
Portuguese	PAWR chuh geez	ˈpɔrtʃəgiz
portulaca	pawr chuh LA kuh	pɔrtʃəˈlækə
Poseidon	poh SIGH duhn	poˈsaɪdən
Posen	POH zuhn	ˈpozən
poseur	poh ZER	poˈzɝ
posit	PAH zit	ˈpɑzɪt
positive	PAH zuh tiv	ˈpɑzətɪv
positively	PAH zuh tiv li	ˈpɑzətɪvlɪ
positron	PAH zuh trahn	ˈpɑzətrɑn
posse	PAH si	ˈpɑsɪ
possess	puh ZES	pəˈzɛs
possession	puh ZE shuhn	pəˈzɛʃən
posset	PAH sit	ˈpɑsɪt
possible	PAH suh buhl	ˈpɑsəbəl
possum	PAH suhm	ˈpɑsəm
post bellum	pohst BE luhm	post ˈbɛləm
post-chaise	POHST shayz	ˈpost ʃez
postdiluvian	pohst di LOO : vi uhn	postdɪˈluvɪən
posterity	pah STE ruh ti	pɑˈstɛrətɪ
postern	POH stern	ˈpostərn

---

sing [ŋ] ; *oh* [o] ; *oil* [ɔi] ; foot [ʊ] ; foo:d [u] ; *how* [aʊ] ; *pie* [p] ; ray [r] ; *so* [s] ; *shall* [ʃ] ;
to [t] ; *thin* [θ] ; *th*:en [ð] ; above (*uh* B*UH*V) [ə, ˈʌ] ; *vine* [v] ; *wine* [w] ; *whine* [hw] ;
you [j] ; *zoo* [z] ; *rouge* (roo:*zh*) [ʒ].

H.P.—T

posthumous	PAHS choo muhs	ˈpɑstʃuməs
postiche	paw STEESH	pɔˈstiʃ
postilion, postillion	poh STI lyuhn	poˈstɪljən
postman	POHST muhn	ˈpostmən
postmeridian	pohst muh RI diuhn	postməˈrɪdiən
post meridiem	pohst muh RI di em	post məˈrɪdiɛm
post mortem	pohst MAWR tuhm	post ˈmɔrtəm
postprandial	pohst PRAN di uhl	postˈprændɪəl
postulant	PAHS chuh luhnt	ˈpɑstʃələnt
postulate (n)	PAHS chuh lit	ˈpɑstʃəlɪt
postulate (v)	PAHS chuh layt	ˈpɑstʃəlet
posture	PAHS cher	ˈpɑstʃər
posy	POH zi	ˈpozɪ
potable	POH tuh buhl	ˈpotəbəl
potage	paw TAHZH	pɔˈtɑʒ
potash	PAHT ash	ˈpɑtæʃ
potassic	puh TA sik	pəˈtæsɪk
potassium	puh TA si uhm	pəˈtæsɪəm
potation	poh TAY shuhn	poˈteʃən
potato	puh TAY toh	pəˈteto
pot-au-feu	paw toh FER	potoˈfɝ
poteen	poh TEEN	poˈtin
Potemkin	poh TEM kin	poˈtɛmkɪn
potency	POH tuhn si	ˈpotənsɪ
potent	POH tuhnt	ˈpotənt
potentate	POH tuhn tayt	ˈpotəntet
potential	puh TEN shuhl	pəˈtɛnʃəl
potentiality	puh ten shi A luh ti	pətɛnʃɪˈælətɪ
potentially	puh TEN shuh li	pəˈtɛnʃəlɪ
potentiometer	puh ten shi AH muh ter	pətɛnʃɪˈɑmətər
potheen	poh THEEN	poˈθin
pother	PAH th : er	ˈpɑðər
potiche	paw TEESH	pɔˈtiʃ
potion	POH shuhn	ˈpoʃən
Potiphar	PAH tuh fer	ˈpɑtəfər
Potomac	puh TOH muhk	pəˈtomək
Potosí	paw taw SEE	pɔtɔˈsi
potpie	PAHT pigh	ˈpɑtpaɪ
potpourri	poh poo REE	popuˈri
Potsdam	PAHTS dam	ˈpɑtsdæm
potsherd	PAHT sherd	ˈpɑtʃɝd
pottage	PAH tij	ˈpɑtɪdʒ
pouf	poo : f	puf
Poughkeepsie	puh KIP si	pəˈkɪpsɪ
Poulenc	poo : LAHNGK	puˈlɑŋk
poult	pohlt	polt
poultice	POHL tis	ˈpoltɪs
pour	pawr	pɔr
pourboire	poor BWAHR	pʊrˈbwar
pourparler	poor pahr LAY	pʊrparˈle
pousse-café	poo : s ka FAY	puskæˈfe
Poussin	poo : SAN	puˈsæn

at [æ]; ah [ɑ]; air [ɛ]; awful [ɔ]; say [e]; back [b]; chair [tʃ]; do [d]; elm [ɛ]; eel [i];
server [ˈɝ, ər]; fit [f]; go [g]; hurt [h]; is [ɪ]; high [aɪ]; jet [dʒ]; kiss [k]; lamb [l]; my [m];
nice [n];

Powhatan	pow uh TAN	paʊəˈtæn
Powys	POH is	ˈpoɪs
Pozarevac	PAW zhah re vahts	ˈpɔʒɑrɛvɑts
Pozega	PAW zhe gah	ˈpɔʒɛgɑ
Poznań	PAWZ nah nyuh	ˈpɔznɑnjə
practitioner	prak TI shuh ner	prækˈtɪʃənər
praenomen	pree NOH men	priˈnomɛn
praetor	PREE ter	ˈpritər
praetorian, P-	pri TAW ri uhn	prɪˈtɔrɪən
pragmatic	prag MA tik	prægˈmætɪk
pragmatism	PRAG muh ti zuhm	ˈprægmətɪzəm
Prague	prahg	prɑg
Praha	PRAH hah	ˈprɑhɑ
prairie	PRAI ri	ˈprɛrɪ
Prajadhipok	pruh CHAH ti pahk	prəˈtʃɑtɪpɑk
Prakrit	PRAH krit	ˈprɑkrɪt
praline	PRAH leen	ˈprɑlin
prance	prans	præns
prandial	PRAN di uhl	ˈprændɪəl
Prasad, Rajendra	pruh SAHD, rah JAYN druh	prəˈsɑd, rɑˈdʒɛndrə
pratfall	PRAT fawl	ˈprætfɔl
pratique	pra TEEK	præˈtik
Pravda	PRAHV dah	ˈprɑvdɑ
prawn	prawn	prɔn
praxis	PRAK sis	ˈpræksɪs
Praxiteles	prak SI tuh leez	prækˈsɪtəliz
prayer (" act of praying ")	prair	prɛr
prayer (" one who prays ")	PRAY er	ˈprɛər
preadamite	pree A duh might	priˈædəmaɪt
prebendary	PRE buhn dai ri	ˈprɛbəndɛrɪ
Pre-Cambrian	pree KAM bri uhn	priˈkæmbrɪən
precarious	pri KAI ri uhs	prɪˈkɛrɪəs
precatory	PRE kuh taw ri	ˈprɛkətɔrɪ
precedence	pri SEE duhns	prɪˈsidəns
precedent (a)	pri SEE duhnt	prɪˈsidənt
precedent (n)	PRE suh duhnt	ˈprɛsədənt
precedent (v)	PRE suh dent	ˈprɛsədɛnt
precept	PREE sept	ˈprisɛpt
preceptive	pri SEP tiv	prɪˈsɛptɪv
preceptory	pri SEP tuh ri	prɪˈsɛptərɪ
precession	pri SE shuhn	prɪˈsɛʃən
precinct	PREE singkt	ˈprisɪŋkt
preciosity	pre shi AH suh ti	prɛʃɪˈɑsətɪ
precipice	PRE suh pis	ˈprɛsəpɪs
precipitant	pri SI puh tuhnt	prɪˈsɪpətənt
precipitous	pri SI puh tuhs	prɪˈsɪpətəs
précis	pray SEE	preˈsi
precise	pri SIGHS	prɪˈsaɪs
precisely	pri SIGHS li	prɪˈsaɪslɪ

sing [ŋ] ; *oh* [o] ; *oil* [ɔɪ] ; *foot* [ʊ] ; *foo*:d [u] ; *how* [aʊ] ; *p*ie [p] ; *ray* [r] ; *so* [s] ; *sh*all [ʃ] ;
to [t] ; *thin* [θ] ; *th*:en [ð] ; *above* (*uh* B*U*H*V*) [ə, ˈʌ] ; *v*ine [v] ; *w*ine [w] ; *wh*ine [hw] ;
*y*ou [j] ; *zoo* [z] ; *rouge* (roo:*zh*) [ʒ].

precisian	pri SI zhuhn	prɪˈsɪʒən
precision	pri SI zhuhn	prɪˈsɪʒən
preclude	pri KLOO : D	prɪˈklud
precocious	pri KOH shuhs	prɪˈkoʃəs
precocity	pri KAH suh ti	prɪˈkɑsətɪ
precursor	pri KER ser	prɪˈkɝsər
predator	PRE duh ter	ˈprɛdətər
predatory	PRE duh taw ri	ˈprɛdətɔrɪ
predecessor	PRE duh se ser	ˈprɛdəsɛsər
predestination	pri de stuh NAY shuhn	prɪdɛstəˈneʃən
predicament	pri DI kuh muhnt	prɪˈdɪkəmənt
predicate (a, n)	PRE di kit	ˈprɛdɪkɪt
predicate (v)	PRE di kayt	ˈprɛdɪket
predilection	pree duh LEK shuhn	prɪdəˈlɛkʃən
pre-eminence, preëminence	pree E muh nuhns	priˈɛmənəns
pre-empt, preëmpt	pree EMPT	priˈɛmpt
preface	PRE fis	ˈprɛfɪs
prefatory	PRE fuh taw ri	ˈprɛfətɔrɪ
prefect	PREE fekt	ˈprifɛkt
prefecture	PREE fek cher	ˈprifɛktʃər
preferable	PRE fuh ruh buhl	ˈprɛfərəbəl
preferably	PRE fuh ruh bli	ˈprɛfərəblɪ
preference	PRE fuh ruhns	ˈprɛfərəns
preferential	pre fuh REN shuhl	prɛfəˈrɛnʃəl
preferment	pri FER muhnt	prɪˈfɝmənt
prefix (n)	PREE fiks	ˈprifɪks
prefix (v)	pree FIKS	priˈfɪks
pregnancy	PREG nuhn si	ˈprɛgnənsɪ
prehensile	pri HEN sil	prɪˈhɛnsɪl
prehistory	pree HI stuh ri	priˈhɪstərɪ
prejudge	pree JUHJ	priˈdʒʌdʒ
prejudice	PRE juh dis	ˈprɛdʒədɪs
prejudicial	pre juh DI shuhl	prɛdʒəˈdɪʃəl
prelacy	PRE luh si	ˈprɛləsɪ
prelate	PRE lit	ˈprɛlɪt
preliminary	pri LI muh nai ri	prɪˈlɪmənɛrɪ
Prelle	prel	prɛl
prelude	PRE loo : d	ˈprɛlud
premature	pree muh TYOOR	priməˈtjʊr
premier (a)	PREE mi er	ˈprimɪər
premier (n)	pri MIR	prɪˈmɪr
première	pri MIR	prɪˈmɪr
premillennial	pree muh LE ni uhl	priməˈlɛnɪəl
premise (n)	PRE mis	ˈprɛmɪs
premise (v)	pri MIGHZ	prɪˈmaɪz
premium	PREE mi uhm	ˈprimɪəm
premonition	pree muh NI shuhn	priməˈnɪʃən
prenatal	pree NAY tuhl	priˈnetəl
preparative	pri PA ruh tiv	prɪˈpærətɪv
preparatory	pri PA ruh taw ri	prɪˈpærətɔrɪ
preponderance	pri PAHN duh ruhns	prɪˈpɑndərəns

at [æ] ; *ah* [ɑ] ; *air* [ɛ] ; *awful* [ɔ] ; *say* [e] ; *back* [b] ; *chair* [tʃ] ; *do* [d] ; *elm* [ɛ] ; *eel* [i] ; *server* [ˈɝ, ər] ; *f*it [f] ; *go* [g] ; *hurt* [h] ; *is* [ɪ] ; *high* [aɪ] ; *jet* [dʒ] ; *kiss* [k] ; *lamb* [l] ; *my* [m] ; *nice* [n] ;

preposition	pre puh ZI shuhn	prɛpəˈzɪʃən
prepossession	pree puh ZE shuhn	pripəˈzɛʃən
preposterous	pri PAH stuh ruhs	prɪˈpɑstərəs
Pre-Raphaelite	pree RA fi uh light	priˈræfɪəlaɪt
prerequisite	pree RE kwuh zit	priˈrɛkwəzɪt
prerogative	pri RAH guh tiv	prɪˈrɑgətɪv
presage (n)	PRE sij	ˈprɛsɪdʒ
presage (v)	pri SAYJ	prɪˈsɛdʒ
presbyter	PREZ bi ter	ˈprɛzbɪtər
Presbyterian	prez buh TI ri uhn	prɛzbəˈtɪrɪən
presbytery	PREZ bi tai ri	ˈprɛzbɪtɛrɪ
prescience	PREE shi uhns	ˈpriʃɪəns
prescient	PREE shi uhnt	ˈpriʃɪənt
present (a, n)	PRE zuhnt	ˈprɛzənt
present (v)	pri ZENT	prɪˈzɛnt
presentation	pre zuhn TAY shuhn	prɛzənˈteʃən
presentiment	pri ZEN tuh muhnt	prɪˈzɛntəmənt
preside	pri ZIGHD	prɪˈzaɪd
presidency	PRE zuh duhn si	ˈprɛzədənsɪ
president	PRE zuh duhnt	ˈprɛzədənt
presidential	pre zuh DEN shuhl	prɛzəˈdɛnʃəl
presidio	pri SI di oh	prɪˈsɪdɪo
presidium	pri SI di uhm	prɪˈsɪdɪəm
pressure	PRE sher	ˈprɛʃər
prester, P-	PRE ster	ˈprɛstər
prestidigitation	pre stuh di ji TAY shuhn	prɛstədɪdʒɪˈteʃən
prestidigitator	pre stuh DI ji tay ter	prɛstəˈdɪdʒɪtetər
prestige	pre STEEZH	prɛˈstiʒ
prestissimo	pre STI suh moh	prɛˈstɪsəmo
presto	PRE stoh	ˈprɛsto
presume	pri ZOO : M	prɪˈzum
presumptive	pri ZUHMP tiv	prɪˈzʌmptɪv
presumptuous	pri ZUHMP choo uhs	prɪˈzʌmptʃuəs
presupposition	pree suh puh ZI shuhn	prisəpəˈzɪʃən
pretense, pretence	pri TENS	prɪˈtɛns
pretentious	pri TEN shuhs	prɪˈtɛnʃəs
preterit, -e	PRE tuh rit	ˈprɛtərɪt
preternatural	pree ter NA chuh ruhl	pritərˈnætʃərəl
pretext	PREE tekst	ˈpritɛkst
Pretoria	pri TAW ri uh	prɪˈtɔrɪə
pretty	PRI ti	ˈprɪtɪ
pretzel	PRET suhl	ˈprɛtsəl
prevalence	PRE vuh luhns	ˈprɛvələns
prevalent	PRE vuh luhnt	ˈprɛvələnt
prevaricator	pri VA ruh kay ter	prɪˈværəketər
preventive	pri VEN tiv	prɪˈvɛntɪv
Prévost	pray VOH	preˈvo
Priam	PRIGH uhm	ˈpraɪəm
Priamus	pree AH muhs	priˈɑməs
priapism	PRIGH uh pi zuhm	ˈpraɪəpɪzəm
Priapus, p-	prigh AY puhs	praɪˈepəs
Pribilof	PRI buh lawf	ˈprɪbəlɔf

sing [ŋ]; *oh* [o]; *oil* [ɔɪ]; *foot* [ʊ]; *foo*:d [u]; *how* [aʊ]; *pie* [p]; *ray* [r]; *so* [s]; *shall* [ʃ]; *to* [t]; *thin* [θ]; *th*:en [ð]; *above* (*uh* B*U*HV) [ə, ˈʌ]; *vine* [v]; *wine* [w]; *whine* [hw]; *you* [j]; *zoo* [z]; *rouge* (roo:zh) [ʒ].

prie-dieu	pree DYER	pri'djɚ
primacy	PRI muh si	'prɪməsɪ
prima donna	PREE muh DAH nuh	'primə 'dɑnə
prima facie	PRIGH muh FAY shi ee	'praɪmə 'feʃiɪ
primarily	PRIGH mai ruh li	'praɪmɛrəlɪ
primary	PRIGH mai ri	'praɪmɛrɪ
primate	PRIGH mit	'praɪmɪt
primer (book)	PRI mer	'prɪmər
primer (not " book ")	PRIGH mer	'praɪmər
primeval	prigh MEE vuhl	praɪ'mivəl
primogenitor	prigh muh JE nuh ter	praɪmə'dʒɛnətər
primogeniture	prigh muh JE nuh cher	praɪmə'dʒɛnətʃər
primordial	prigh MAWR di uhl	praɪ'mɔrdɪəl
primula	PRI myoo luh	'prɪmjʊlə
primum mobile	PRIGH muhm MAH buh lee	'praɪməm 'mɑbəli
primus, P-	PRIGH muhs	'praɪməs
prince	prins	prɪns
princes	PRIN siz	'prɪnsɪz
princess	PRIN sis	'prɪnsɪs
princesse	prin SES	prɪn'sɛs
princesses	PRIN si siz	'prɪnsɪsɪz
Princeton	PRIN stuhn	'prɪnstən
principal	PRIN suh puhl	'prɪnsəpəl
principality	prin suh PA luh ti	prɪnsə'pælətɪ
principium	prin SI pi uhm	prɪn'sɪpɪəm
principle	PRIN suh puhl	'prɪnsəpəl
prior, P-	PRIGH er	'praɪər
priorate	PRIGH uh rit	'praɪərɪt
prioress	PRIGH uh ris	'praɪərɪs
priority	prigh AW ruh ti	praɪ'ɔrətɪ
priory	PRIGH uh ri	'praɪərɪ
Pripet	PREE pet	'prɪpɛt
Priscian	PRI shuhn	'prɪʃən
prism	prizm	prɪzm
prismatic	priz MA tik	prɪz'mætɪk
pristine	PRI steen	'prɪstin
prithee	PRI th : i	'prɪðɪ
privacy	PRIGH vuh si	'praɪvəsɪ
Privatdocent, Privatdozent, p-	pree VAHT dawt SENT	pri'vɑt dɔt'sɛnt
privateer	prigh vuh TIR	praɪvə'tɪr
privet	PRI vit	'prɪvɪt
privilege	PRI vuh lij	'prɪvəlɪdʒ
privily	PRI vuh li	'prɪvəlɪ
privy	PRI vi	'prɪvɪ
prix fixe	pree feeks	pri fiks
pro	proh	pro
proa	PROH uh	'proə
probably	PRAH buh bli	'prɑbəblɪ
probate	PROH bayt	'probet
probationary	proh BAY shuh nai ri	pro'beʃənɛrɪ
probity	PROH buh ti	'probətɪ

---

at [æ] ; *ah* [ɑ] ; *air* [ɛ] ; *aw*ful [ɔ] ; *say* [e] ; *back* [b] ; *ch*air [tʃ] ; *do* [d] ; *elm* [ɛ] ; *eel* [i] ; *server* ['ɝ, ər] ; *f*it [f] ; *go* [g] ; *hurt* [h] ; *is* [ɪ] ; *high* [aɪ] ; *jet* [dʒ] ; *kiss* [k] ; *lamb* [l] ; *my* [m] ; *nice* [n] ;

problematical	prah bluh MA ti kuhl	prɑblə'mætɪkəl
pro bono publico	proh BOH noh PUH bli koh	pro 'bono 'pʌblɪko
proboscis	proh BAH sis	pro'bɑsɪs
procaine	proh KAYN	pro'ken
procedural	pruh SEE juh ruhl	prə'sidʒərəl
procedure	pruh SEE jer	prə'sidʒər
proceeds (" result ")	PROH seedz	'prosidz
process	PRAH ses	'prɑsɛs
proclitic	proh KLI tik	pro'klɪtɪk
proclivity	proh KLI vuh ti	pro'klɪvətɪ
Procne	PRAHK ni	'prɑknɪ
Procopius	proh KOH pi uhs	pro'kopɪəs
procrastinate	proh KRA stuh nayt	pro'kræstənet
procreant	PROH kri uhnt	'prokrɪənt
Procrustean	proh KRUH sti uhn	pro'krʌstɪən
Procrustes	proh KRUH steez	pro'krʌstiz
proctology	prahk TAH luh ji	prɑk'tɑlədʒɪ
proctor	PRAHK ter	'prɑktər
procurance	proh KYOO ruhns	pro'kjʊrəns
procuration	prah kyuh RAY shuhn	prɑkjə'reʃən
procurator	PRAH kyuh ray ter	'prɑkjəretər
procure	proh KYOOR	pro'kjʊr
procurer	proh KYOO rer	pro'kjʊrər
procuress	proh KYOO ris	pro'kjʊrɪs
Procyon	PROH si ahn	'prosɪɑn
prodigal	PRAH di guhl	'prɑdɪgəl
prodigality	prah di GA luh ti	prɑdɪ'gælətɪ
prodigious	pruh DI juhs	prə'dɪdʒəs
prodigy	PRAH duh ji	'prɑdədʒɪ
prodrome	PROH drohm	'prodrom
produce (n)	PRAH doo : s	'prɑdus
produce (v)	pruh DOO : S	prə'dus
proem	PROH em	'proɛm
profanation	prah fuh NAY shuhn	prɑfə'neʃən
profane	pruh FAYN	prə'fen
profanity	pruh FA nuh ti	prə'fænətɪ
profess	pruh FES	prə'fɛs
profession	pruh FE shuhn	prə'fɛʃən
professor	pruh FE ser	prə'fɛsər
professorial	proh fuh SAW ri uhl	profɔ'sorɪəl
proffer	PRAH fer	'prɑfər
proficiency	pruh FI shuhn si	prə'fɪʃənsɪ
proficient	pruh FI shuhnt	prə'fɪʃənt
profile	PROH fighl	'profaɪl
profiteer	prah fuh TIR	prɑfə'tɪr
profligacy	PRAH fluh guh si	'prɑfləgəsɪ
profligate	PRAH fluh git	'prɑfləgɪt
pro forma	proh FAWR muh	pro 'fɔrmə
profound	pruh FOWND	prə'faund
profundity	pruh FUHN duh ti	prə'fʌndətɪ
profuse	pruh FYOO : S	prə'fjus
profusion	pruh FYOO : zhuhn	prə'fjuʒən

sing [ŋ] ; *oh* [o] ; *oil* [ɔɪ] ; *foot* [ʊ] ; *foo*:d [u] ; *how* [au] ; *pie* [p] ; *ray* [r] ; *so* [s] ; *shall* [ʃ] ; *to* [t] ; *thin* [θ] ; *th*:en [ð] ; *above* (*uh* B*UH*V) [ə, 'ʌ] ; *vine* [v] ; *wine* [w] ; *whine* [hw]; *you* [j] ; *zoo* [z] ; *rouge* (roo:*zh*) [ʒ].

progenitor	proh JE nuh ter	pro'dʒɛnətər
progeny	PRAH juh ni	'prɑdʒənɪ
progesterone	proh JE stuh rohn	pro'dʒɛstəron
prognathous	PRAHG nuh thuhs	'prɑgnəθəs
prognosis	prahg NOH sis	prɑg'nosɪs
prognostic	prahg NAH stik	prɑg'nɑstɪk
prognosticate	prahg NAH stuh kayt	prɑg'nɑstəket
program, -me	PROH gruhm	'progrəm
programmatic	proh gruh MA tik	progrə'mætɪk
progress (n)	PRAH gres	'prɑgrɛs
progress (v)	pruh GRES	prə'grɛs
progression	pruh GRE shuhn	prə'grɛʃən
progressive	pruh GRE siv	prə'grɛsɪv
Prohaska, Felix	proh HAHS kah, FE liks	pro'hɑskɑ, 'fɛlɪks
prohibition	proh uh BI shuhn	proə'bɪʃən
prohibitive	proh HI buh tiv	pro'hɪbətɪv
project (n)	PRAH jekt	'prɑdʒɛkt
project (v)	pruh JEKT	prə'dʒɛkt
projectile	pruh JEK tuhl	prə'dʒɛktəl
Prokofieff, Prokofiev	praw KAW fyef	pro'kɔfjɛf
Prokopievsk	praw kaw PYEFSK	prɔko'pjɛfsk
prolactin	proh LAK tin	pro'læktɪn
prolan	PROH lan	'prolæn
prolapse	proh LAPS	pro'læps
prolegomenon	proh li GAH muh nahn	prolɪ'gɑmənɑn
prolepsis	proh LEP sis	pro'lɛpsɪs
proletarian	proh luh TAI ri uhn	prolə'tɛrɪən
proletariat	proh luh TAI ri uht	prolə'tɛrɪət
proliferate	proh LI fuh rayt	pro'lifəret
proliferous	proh LI fu ruhs	pro'lɪfərəs
prolific	pruh LI fik	prə'lɪfɪk
prolix	proh LIKS	pro'lɪks
prolixity	proh LIK suh ti	pro'lɪksətɪ
prolocutor	proh LAH kyuh ter	pro'lɑkjətər
prolog, -ue	PROH lawg	'prolɔg
prolongation	proh lawng GAY shuhn	prolɔŋ'geʃən
prom	prahm	prɑm
promenade	prah muh NAYD	prɑmə'ned
Promethean	pruh MEE thi uhn	prə'miθɪən
Prometheus	pruh MEE thyuhs	prə'miθjəs
promethium	proh MEE thi uhm	pro'miθɪəm
prominence	PRAH muh nuhns	'prɑmənəns
prominent	PRAH muh nuhnt	'prɑmənənt
promiscuity	prah mi SKYOO : uh ti	prɑmɪ'skjuətɪ
promiscuous	pruh MI skyoo uhs	prə'mɪskjʊəs
promissory	PRAH muh saw ri	'prɑməsɔrɪ
promontory	PRAH muhn taw ri	'prɑməntɔrɪ
promulgate	pruh MUHL gayt	prə'mʌlget
promulgation	proh muhl GAY shuhn	promʌl'geʃən
promulgator	pruh MUHL gay ter	prə'mʌlgetər
pronoun	PROH nown	'pronaun
pronounce	pruh NOWNS	prə'nauns

at [æ] ; *ah* [ɑ] ; *air* [ɛ] ; *awful* [ɔ] ; *say* [e] ; *back* [b] ; *chair* [tʃ] ; *do* [d] ; *elm* [ɛ] ; *eel* [i] ; *server* ['ɜ, ər] ; *f* it [f] ; *go* [g] ; *hurt* [h] ; *is* [ɪ] ; *high* [aɪ] ; *jet* [dʒ] ; *kiss* [k] ; *lamb* [l] ; *my* [m] ; *nice* [n] ;

pronto	PRAHN toh	ˈprɑnto
pronunciamento	pruh nuhn si uh MEN toh	prənʌnsɪəˈmɛnto
pronunciation	pruh nuhn si AY shuhn	prənʌnsɪˈeʃən
propaganda	prah puh GAN duh	prɑpəˈgændə
propagate	PRAH puh gayt	ˈprɑpəget
propane	PROH payn	ˈpropen
pro patria	proh PAY tri uh	pro ˈpetrɪə
propel	pruh PEL	prəˈpɛl
propellant, propellent	pruh PE luhnt	prəˈpɛlənt
propensity	pruh PEN suh ti	prəˈpɛnsətɪ
Propertius	proh PER shuhs	proˈpɝʃəs
prophecy	PRAH fuh si	ˈprɑfəsɪ
prophesy	PRAH fuh sigh	ˈprɑfəsaɪ
prophet	PRAH fit	ˈprɑfɪt
prophetic	pruh FE tik	prəˈfɛtɪk
prophylactic	proh fuh LAK tik	profəˈlæktɪk
prophylaxis	proh fuh LAK sis	profəˈlæksɪs
propinquity	proh PING kwuh ti	proˈpɪŋkwətɪ
propitiate	pruh PI shi ayt	prəˈpɪʃɪet
propitious	pruh PI shuhs	prəˈpɪʃəs
proponent	pruh POH nuhnt	prəˈponənt
proportion	pruh PAWR shuhn	prəˈpɔrʃən
proportionate (a)	pruh PAWR shuh nit	prəˈpɔrʃənɪt
proportionate (v)	pruh PAWR shuh nayt	prəˈpɔrʃənet
proposal	pruh POH zuhl	prəˈpozəl
proprietary	pruh PRIGH uh tai ri	prəˈpraɪətɛrɪ
proprietor	pruh PRIGH uh ter	prəˈpraɪətər
propriety	pruh PRIGH uh ti	prəˈpraɪətɪ
pro rata	proh RAY tuh	pro ˈretə
prorogue	proh ROHG	proˈrog
prosaic	proh ZAY ik	proˈzeɪk
proscenium	proh SEE ni uhm	proˈsinɪəm
proselyte	PRAH suh light	ˈprɑsəlaɪt
proselytize	PRAH suh li tighz	ˈprɑsəlɪtaɪz
Proserpina	proh SER pi nuh	proˈsɝpɪnə
Proserpine	proh SER pi nee	proˈsɝpɪni
prosit	PROH sit	ˈprosɪt
prosodic	pruh SAH dik	prəˈsɑdɪk
prosodist	PRAH suh dist	ˈprɑsədɪst
prosody	PRAH suh di	ˈprɑsədɪ
prosopopoeia	pruh soh poh PEE uh	prəsopoˈpiə
prospectus	pruh SPEK tuhs	prəˈspɛktəs
Prospero	PRAH spuh roh	ˈprɑspəro
prostate	PRAH stayt	ˈprɑstet
prosthesis	PRAHS thuh sis	ˈprɑsθəsɪs
prosthetic	prahs THE tik	prɑsˈθɛtɪk
prosthodontia	prahs thuh DAHN shuh	prɑsθəˈdɑnʃə
Prostigmin, p-	praw STIG min	proˈstɪgmɪn
prostitute	PRAH stuh too:t	ˈprɑstətut
prostrate	PRAH strayt	ˈprɑstret
prostyle	PROH stighl	ˈprostaɪl
prosy	PROH zi	ˈprozɪ

protactinium	proh tak TI ni uhm	proˌtækˈtɪniəm
protagonist	proh TA guh nist	proˈtægənɪst
Protagoras	proh TA guh ruhs	proˈtægərəs
protamine	PROH tuh meen	ˈprotəmin
protean, P-	PROH ti uhn	ˈprotɪən
protectorate	pruh TEK tuh rit	prəˈtɛktərɪt
protégé, -e	PROH tuh zhay	ˈprotəʒe
proteide	PROH ti ighd	ˈprotɪaɪd
protein	PROH teen	ˈprotin
pro tempore	proh TEM puh ree	pro ˈtɛmpəri
Proterozoic	prah tuh ruh ZOH ik	pratərəˈzoɪk
protest (n)	PROH test	ˈprotɛst
protest (v)	pruh TEST	prəˈtɛst
Protestant, p-	PRAH ti stuhnt	ˈpratɪstənt
protestation	prah tuh STAY shuhn	pratəˈsteʃən
Proteus	PROH ti uhs	ˈprotɪəs
prothalamion	proh thuh LAY mi ahn	proθəˈlemɪɑn
prothesis	PRAH thuh sis	ˈpraθəsɪs
protium	PROH ti uhm	ˈprotɪəm
protocol	PROH tuh kahl	ˈprotəkɑl
proton	PROH tahn	ˈprotɑn
protoplasm	PROH tuh pla zuhm	ˈprotəplæzəm
prototype	PROH tuh tighp	ˈprotətaɪp
Protozoa	proh tuh ZOH uh	protəˈzoə
protozoic	proh tuh ZOH ik	protəˈzoɪk
protract	proh TRAKT	proˈtrækt
protrude	proh TROO : D	proˈtrud
protrusion	proh TROO : zhuhn	proˈtruʒən
protrusive	proh TROO : siv	proˈtrusɪv
protuberance	proh TOO : buh ruhns	proˈtubərəns
protyle	PROH tighl	ˈprotaɪl
Proust	proo : st	prust
provenance	PRAH vuh nuhns	ˈpravənəns
Provençal	proh vuhn SAHL	provənˈsal
Provence	proh VAHNS	proˈvans
provender	PRAH vuhn der	ˈpravəndər
provenience	proh VEE ni uhns	proˈvinɪəns
proverb	PRAH verb	ˈpravərb
proverbial	pruh VER bi uhl	prəˈvɝbɪəl
providence, P-	PRAH vuh duhns	ˈpravədəns
provident	PRAH vuh duhnt	ˈpravədənt
province	PRAH vins	ˈpravɪns
provincial	pruh VIN shuhl	prəˈvɪnʃəl
provision	pruh VI zhuhn	prəˈvɪʒən
proviso	pruh VIGH zoh	prəˈvaɪzo
provocation	prah vuh KAY shuhn	pravəˈkeʃən
provocative	pruh VAH kuh tiv	prəˈvakətɪv
provoke	pruh VOHK	prəˈvok
provost	PRAH vuhst	ˈpravəst
provost (military)	PROH voh	ˈprovo
prow	prow	praʊ
prowess	PROW is	ˈpraʊɪs

at [æ] ; *ah* [ɑ] ; *air* [ɛ] ; *awful* [ɔ] ; *say* [e] ; *back* [b] ; *chair* [tʃ] ; *do* [d] ; *elm* [ɛ] ; *eel* [i] ;
server [ˈɝ, ər] ; *f* it [f] ; *go* [g] ; *hurt* [h] ; *is* [ɪ] ; *high* [aɪ] ; *jet* [dʒ] ; *kiss* [k] ; *lamb* [l] ; *my* [m] ;
nice [n] ;

proximal	PRAHK suh muhl	ˈprɑksəməl
proximity	prahk SI muh ti	prɑkˈsɪmətɪ
proximo	PRAHK suh moh	ˈprɑksəmo
proxy	PRAHK si	ˈprɑksɪ
prudery	PROO : duh ri	ˈprudərɪ
prunella	proo : NE luh	pruˈnɛlə
prurient	PROO ri uhnt	ˈprʊrɪənt
prurigo	proo RIGH goh	prʊˈraɪgo
Prussia	PRUH shuh	ˈprʌʃə
Prussian	PRUH shuhn	ˈprʌʃən
prussic	PRUH sik	ˈprʌsɪk
Pruszkow	PROOSH koof	ˈpruʃkʊf
Prut, -h	proo : t	prut
pruta, -h	proo : TAH	pruˈtɑ
Prynne	prin	prɪn
prythee	PRI th : i	ˈprɪðɪ
psalm	sahm	sɑm
psalmodist	SAH muh dist	ˈsɑmədɪst
psalmody	SAH muh di	ˈsɑmədɪ
psalter, P-	SAWL ter	ˈsɔltər
psaltery, P-	SAWL tuh ri	ˈsɔltərɪ
psammite	SA might	ˈsæmaɪt
psephite	SEE fight	ˈsifaɪt
pseudepigrapha	soo : duh PI gruh fuh	sudəˈpɪgrəfə
pseudo	SOO : doh	ˈsudo
pseudonym	SOO : duh nim	ˈsudənɪm
pseudonymous	soo : DAH nuh muhs	suˈdɑnəməs
pseudopod	SOO : duh pahd	ˈsudəpɑd
pseudopodium	soo : duh POH di uhm	sudəˈpodɪəm
psi	sigh	saɪ
psilanthropy	sigh LAN thruh pi	saɪˈlænθrəpɪ
psilosis	sigh LOH sis	saɪˈlosɪs
psittacosis	si tuh KOH sis	sɪtəˈkosɪs
psoriasis	soh RIGH uh sis	soˈraɪəsɪs
psychasthenia	sigh kas THEE ni uh	saɪkæsˈθinɪə
psyche, P-	SIGH ki	ˈsaɪkɪ
psychiatric	sigh ki A trik	saɪkɪˈætrɪk
psychiatrist	sigh KIGH uh trist	saɪˈkaɪətrɪst
psychiatry	sigh KIGH uh tri	saɪˈkaɪətrɪ
psychic	SIGH kik	ˈsaɪkɪk
psychoanalysis	SIGH koh uh NA luh sis	saɪkoəˈnæləsɪs
psychoanalyst	SIGH koh A nuh list	saɪkoˈænəlɪst
psychogenic	sigh kuh JE nik	saɪkəˈdʒɛnɪk
psychological	sigh kuh LAH ji kuhl	saɪkəˈlɑdʒɪkəl
psychologist	sigh KAH luh jist	saɪˈkɑlədʒɪst
psychology	sigh KAH luh ji	saɪˈkɑlədʒɪ
psychometry	sigh KAH muh tri	saɪˈkɑmətrɪ
psychoneuroses	SIGH koh nyoo ROH seez	ˌsaɪkonjʊˈrosiz
psychoneurosis	SIGH koh nyoo ROH sis	ˌsaɪkonjʊˈrosɪs
psychopath	SIGH kuh path	ˈsaɪkəpæθ
psychopathic	sigh kuh PA thik	saɪkəˈpæθɪk
psychopathology	SIGH koh puh THAH luh ji	ˈsaɪkopəˈθɑlədʒɪ

psychoses	sigh KOH seez	saɪˈkosiz
psychosis	sigh KOH sis	saɪˈkosɪs
psychosomatic	SIGH koh soh MA tik	ˈsaɪkosoˈmætɪk
psychotherapeutics	SIGH koh the ruh PYOO: tiks	ˈsaɪkoθɛrəˈpjutɪks
psychotherapy	SIGH koh THE ruh pi	ˈsaɪkoˈθɛrəpɪ
psychotic	sigh KAH tik	saɪˈkatɪk
psychrometer	sigh KRAH muh ter	saɪˈkramətər
Ptah	puh TAH	pəˈta
ptarmigan	TAHR muh guhn	ˈtarməgən
pterodactyl	te ruh DAK tuhl	tɛrəˈdæktəl
pteropod	TE ruh pahd	ˈtɛrəpad
Ptolemaic	tah luh MAY ik	taləˈmeɪk
Ptolemy	TAH luh mi	ˈtaləmɪ
ptomain, -e	TOH mayn	ˈtomen
ptosis	TOH sis	ˈtosɪs
puberty	PYOO: ber ti	ˈpjubərtɪ
pubescent	pyoo: BE suhnt	pjuˈbɛsənt
pubic	PYOO: bik	ˈpjubɪk
publican	PUH bli kuhn	ˈpʌblɪkən
Puccini	poo: CHEE ni	puˈtʃini
puce	pyoo: s	pjus
pucka	PUH kuh	ˈpʌkə
pudendum	pyoo: DEN duhm	pjuˈdɛndəm
Puebla	PWE blah	ˈpwɛbla
pueblo, P-	PWE bloh	ˈpwɛblo
puerile	PYOO: uh ril	ˈpjuərɪl
puerperal	pyoo: ER puh ruhl	pjuˈɜpərəl
Puerto Rican	PWAIR tuh REE kuhn	ˈpwɛrtə ˈrikən
Puerto Rico	PWAIR tuh REE koh	ˈpwɛrtə ˈriko
puffin	PUH fin	ˈpʌfɪn
pug	puhg	pʌg
Puget	PYOO: jit	ˈpjudʒɪt
puggree, puggry	PUH gri	ˈpʌgrɪ
pugilist	PYOO: juh list	ˈpjudʒəlɪst
pugnacious	puhg NAY shuhs	pʌgˈneʃəs
puisne	PYOO: ni	ˈpjunɪ
puissance	PYOO: i suhns	ˈpjuɪsəns
puissant	PYOO: i suhnt	ˈpjuɪsənt
pukka	PUH kuh	ˈpʌkə
Pulaski	poo LA ski	puˈlæskɪ
pulchritude	PUHL kruh too: d	ˈpʌlkrətud
pulchritudinous	puhl kruh TOO: duh nuhs	pʌlkrəˈtudənəs
pule	pyoo: l	pjul
puli	POO: li	ˈpulɪ
Pulitzer	PYOO: lit ser	ˈpjulɪtsər
pullet	POO lit	ˈpʊlɪt
Pullman	POOL muhn	ˈpʊlmən
pullulate	PUH lyuh layt	ˈpʌljəlet
pulmonary	PUHL muh nai ri	ˈpʌlmənɛrɪ
pulmotor	PUHL moh ter	ˈpʌlmotər
pulpit	POOL pit	ˈpʊlpɪt

at [æ]; *ah* [a]; *air* [ɛ]; *awful* [ɔ]; *say* [e]; *back* [b]; *chair* [tʃ]; *do* [d]; *elm* [ɛ]; *eel* [i]; *server* [ˈɜ, ər]; *f*it [f]; *go* [g]; *hurt* [h]; *is* [ɪ]; *high* [aɪ]; *jet* [dʒ]; *kiss* [k]; *lamb* [l]; *my* [m]; *nice* [n];

pulque	POOL kay	ˈpʊlke
pulsate	PUHL sayt	ˈpʌlset
pulse	puhls	pʌls
Pultusk	POOL toosk	ˈpʊltʊsk
pulverize	PUHL vuh righz	ˈpʌlvəraɪz
puma	PYOO : muh	ˈpjumə
pumice	PUH mis	ˈpʌmɪs
pummel	PUH muhl	ˈpʌməl
pumpernickel	PUHM per ni kuhl	ˈpʌmpərnɪkəl
pumpkin	PUHMP kin	ˈpʌmpkɪn
puna	POO : nah	ˈpunɑ
puncheon	PUHN chuhn	ˈpʌntʃən
punchinello, P-	puhn chuh NE loh	pʌntʃəˈnɛlo
punctation	puhngk TAY shuhn	pʌŋkˈteʃən
punctilio	puhngk TI li oh	pʌŋkˈtɪlɪo
punctilious	puhngk TI li uhs	pʌŋkˈtɪlɪəs
punctual	PUHNKG choo uhl	ˈpʌŋktʃʊəl
punctuality	puhngk choo A luh ti	pʌŋktʃuˈælətɪ
punctuate	PUNGK choo ayt	ˈpʌŋktʃuet
punctuation	puhngk choo AY shuhn	pʌŋtʃuˈeʃən
puncture	PUHNGK cher	ˈpʌŋktʃər
pundit	PUHN dit	ˈpʌndɪt
pungent	PUHN juhnt	ˈpʌndʒənt
Punic	PYOO : nik	ˈpjunɪk
punitive	PYOO : nuh tiv	ˈpjunətɪv
Punjab	puhn JAHB	pʌnˈdʒɑb
Punjabi	puhn JAH bi	pʌnˈdʒɑbɪ
punka, -h	PUHNG kuh	ˈpʌŋkə
Punta Arenas	POO : N tah ah RE nahs	ˈpuntɑ ɑˈrɛnɑs
puny	PYOO : ni	ˈpjunɪ
pupa	PYOO : puh	ˈpjupə
Pupin	pyoo PEEN	pjuˈpin
puppet	PUH pit	ˈpʌpɪt
Puppis	PUH pis	ˈpʌpɪs
purblind	PER blighnd	ˈpɝˈblaɪnd
Purcell (composer)	PER suhl	ˈpɝsəl
purdah	PER duh	ˈpɝdə
purée	pyoo RAY	pjuˈre
purgative	PER guh tiv	ˈpɝgətɪv
purgatory	PER guh taw ri	ˈpɝgətɔrɪ
Purim	PYOO rim	ˈpjʊrɪm
puritanical, P-	pyoo ruh TA ni kuhl	pjʊrəˈtænɪkəl
Puritanism, p-	PYOO ruh tuh ni zuhm	ˈpjʊrətənɪzəm
purl	perl	pɝl
purlieu	PER loo :	ˈpɝlu
purloin	per LOIN	pərˈlɔɪn
purport (n)	PER pawrt	ˈpɝpɔrt
purport (v)	per PAWRT	pərˈpɔrt
purposive	PER puh siv	ˈpɝpəsɪv
purpura	PER pyuh ruh	ˈpɝpjərə
purslane	PER slin	ˈpɝslɪn
pursuance	per SOO : uhns	pərˈsuəns

---

sing [ŋ] ; *oh* [o] ; *oil* [ɔɪ] ; *foot* [ʊ] ; *foo*:d [u] ; *how* [aʊ] ; *pie* [p] ; *ray* [r] ; *so* [s] ; *sh*all [ʃ] ;
to [t] ; *th*in [θ] ; *th:*en [ð] ; *above* (*uh* B*UH*V) [ə, ˈʌ] ; *v*ine [v] ; *w*ine [w] ; *wh*ine [hw] ;
*y*ou [j] ; *z*oo [z] ; *rouge* (roo:*zh*) [ʒ].

pursuant	per SOO : uhnt	pərˈsuənt
pursue	per SOO :	pərˈsu
pursuit	per SOO : T	pərˈsut
pursuivant	PER swi vuhnt	ˈpɝswɪvənt
pursy	PER si	ˈpɝsɪ
purulence	PYOO ruh luhns	ˈpjʊrələns
purulent	PYOO ruh luhnt	ˈpjʊrələnt
purveyor	per VAY er	pərˈveər
purview	PER vyoo :	ˈpɝvju
Pusan	poo : sahn	pusɑn
Pusey	PYOO : see	ˈpjusi
Puseyism	PYOO : zi i zuhm	ˈpjuzɪɪzəm
Pushkin	POOSH kin	ˈpʊʃkɪn
Pushtu	POOSH too :	ˈpʊʃtu
pusillanimity	pyoo : suh luh NI muh ti	pjusələˈnɪmətɪ
pusillanimous	pyoo : suh LA nuh muhs	pjusəˈlænəməs
pustule	PUHS chool	ˈpʌstʃʊl
put	poot	pʊt
putamen	pyoo : TAY muhn	pjuˈtemən
putative	PYOO : tuh tiv	ˈpjutətɪv
Putnam	PUHT nuhm	ˈpʌtnəm
putrefaction	pyoo : truh FAK shuhn	pjutrəˈfækʃən
putrescent	pyoo : TRE suhnt	pjuˈtresənt
putrid	PYOO : trid	ˈpjutrɪd
Putsch, p-	pooch	pʊtʃ
putt	puht	pʌt
puttee	puh TEE	pʌˈti
putty	PUH ti	ˈpʌtɪ
Putumayo	poo : too : MAH yaw	putuˈmɑjɔ
Pu-yi	poo : yee	puji
pycnometer	pik NAH muh ter	pɪkˈnɑmətər
Pydna	PID nuh	ˈpɪdnə
pyelitis	pigh uh LIGH tis	paɪəˈlaɪtɪs
pyemia	pigh EE mi uh	paɪˈimɪə
Pygmalion	pig MAY lyuhn	pɪgˈmeljən
Pygmy, p-	PIG mi	ˈpɪgmɪ
pyjamas	puh JA muhz	pəˈdʒæməz
pyknic	PIK nik	ˈpɪknɪk
Pyle	pighl	paɪl
pylon	PIGH lahn	ˈpaɪlɑn
pylorus	pigh LAW ruhs	paɪˈlɔrəs
Pym	pim	pɪm
pyogenic	pigh uh JE nik	paɪəˈdʒenɪk
Pyongyang	pyerng yahng	pjɝˈnjɑŋ
pyorrhea, pyorrhoea	pigh uh REE uh	paɪəˈriə
pyosis	pigh OH sis	paɪˈosɪs
pyramid	PI ruh mid	ˈpɪrəmɪd
pyramidal	pi RA muh duhl	pɪˈræmədəl
pyramidic	pi ruh MI dik	pɪrəˈmɪdɪk
Pyramus	PI ruh muhs	ˈpɪrəməs
pyre	pighr	paɪr
pyrene	PIGH reen	ˈpaɪrin

at [æ] ; *ah* [ɑ] ; *air* [ɛ] ; *awful* [ɔ] ; *say* [e] ; *back* [b] ; *chair* [tʃ] ; *do* [d] ; *elm* [ɛ] ; *eel* [i] ; *server* [ˈɝ, ər] ; *f*it [f] ; *go* [g] ; *hurt* [h] ; *is* [ɪ] ; *high* [aɪ] ; *jet* [dʒ] ; *kiss* [k] ; *lamb* [l] ; *my* [m] ; *nice* [n] ;

Pyrenean	pi ruh NEE uhn	pɪrəˈniən
Pyrenees	PI ruh neez	ˈpɪrəniz
pyretic	pigh RE tik	paɪˈrɛtɪk
pyretology	pi ruh TAH luh ji	pɪrəˈtɑlədʒɪ
pyrex, P-	PIGH reks	ˈpaɪrɛks
pyrexia	pigh REK si uh	paɪˈrɛksɪə
pyridine	PI ruh deen	ˈpɪrədin
pyridoxine	pi ruh DAHK seen	pɪrəˈdɑksin
pyriform	PI ruh fawrm	ˈpɪrəfɔrm
pyrite	PIGH right	ˈpaɪraɪt
pyrogenic	pigh ruh JE nik	paɪrəˈdʒɛnɪk
pyrography	pigh RAH gruh fi	paɪˈrɑgrəfɪ
pyrolysis	pigh RAH luh sis	paɪˈrɑləsɪs
pyrolyze	PIGH ruh lighz	ˈpaɪrəlaɪz
pyromania	pigh ruh MAY ni uh	paɪrəˈmenɪə
pyrope	PIGH rohp	ˈpaɪrop
pyrophobia	pigh ruh FOH bi uh	paɪrəˈfobɪə
pyrosis	pigh ROH sis	paɪˈrosɪs
pyrotechnic	pigh ruh TEK nik	paɪrəˈtɛknɪk
Pyrrh	PI ruh	ˈpɪrə
pyrrhic, P-	PI rik	ˈpɪrɪk
Pyrrhonism	PI ruh ni zuhm	ˈpɪrənɪzəm
Pyrrhus	PI ruhs	ˈpɪrəs
Pythagoras	pi THA guh ruhs	pɪˈθægərəs
Pythagorean	pi tha guh REE uhn	pɪθægəˈriən
Pythia	PI thi uh	ˈpɪθɪə
Pythian	PI thi uhn	ˈpɪθɪən
Pythias	PI thi uhs	ˈpɪθɪəs
python, P-	PIGH thahn	ˈpaɪθɑn
pythoness	PIGH thuh nis	ˈpaɪθənɪs
pyuria	pigh OO ri uh	paɪˈurɪə
pyx	piks	pɪks
Pyxis, p-	PIK sis	ˈpɪksɪs

Q

Qara Qum	kah RAH KOOM	kɑˈrɑ ˈkum
Qattara	kah TAH rah	kɑˈtɑrɑ
Qirghiz	kir GEEZ	kɪrˈgiz
Qizhm	KI shuhm	ˈkɪʃəm
Qizil Qum	KI zil KOOM	ˈkɪzɪl ˈkum
qua	kway	kwe
quack	kwak	kwæk
quacksalver	KWAK sal ver	ˈkwæksælvər
quad	kwahd	kwɑd
quadragenarian	kwah druh ji NAI ri uhn	kwɑdrədʒɪˈnɛrɪən
Quadragesima	kwah druh JE si muh	kwɑdrəˈdʒɛsɪmə
quadrant	KWAH druhnt	ˈkwɑdrənt

sing [ŋ]; *oh* [o]; *oil* [ɔɪ]; *foot* [ʊ]; *foo:d* [u]; *how* [aʊ]; *pie* [p]; *ray* [r]; *so* [s]; *shall* [ʃ];
to [t]; *thin* [θ]; *th:en* [ð]; above (*uh BUH*V) [ə, ˈʌ]; *vine* [v]; *wine* [w]; *whine* [hw];
you [j]; *zoo* [z]; *rouge* (roo:*zh*) [ʒ].

quadrate (a, n)	KWAH drit	ˈkwɑdrɪt
quadrate (v)	KWAH drayt	ˈkwɑdret
quadratic	kwah DRA tik	kwɑˈdrætɪk
quadrature	KWAH druh cher	ˈkwɑdretʃər
quadrennial	kwah DRE ni uhl	kwɑˈdrɛnɪəl
quadricentennial	kwah dri sen TE ni uhl	kwɑdrɪsɛnˈtɛnɪəl
quadrille	kwuh DRIL	kwəˈdrɪl
quadriplegia	kwah druh PLEE ji uh	kwɑdrəˈplidʒɪə
quadrivium	kwah DRI vi uhm	kwɑˈdrɪvɪəm
quadroon	kwah DROO : N	kwɑˈdrun
quadruped	KWAH druh ped	ˈkwɑdrəpɛd
quadruple	KWAH droo puhl	ˈkwɑdrʊpəl
quadruplet	KWAH droo plit	ˈkwɑdrʊplɪt
quadruplicate (a, n)	kwah DROO : pli kit	kwɑˈdruplɪkɪt
quadruplicate (v)	kwah DROO : pli kayt	kwɑˈdruplɪket
quaere	KWEE ri	ˈkwirɪ
quaestor	KWE ster	ˈkwɛstər
quaff	kwahf	kwɑf
quagmire	KWAG mighr	ˈkwægmaɪr
quahog, quahaug	KWAW hawg	ˈkwɔhɔg
Quai de la Concorde	kay duh lah kohn KAWRD	ke də lɑ konˈkɔrd
Quai d'Orsay	KAY dawr SAY	ˈke dɔrˈse
quaint	kwaynt	kwent
qualm	kwahm	kwɑm
quandary	KWAHN dri	ˈkwɑndrɪ
quandong, quandang	KWAHN dahng	ˈkwɑndɑŋ
quant	kwant	kwænt
quanta	KWAHN tuh	ˈkwɑntə
quantic	KWAHN tik	ˈkwɑntɪk
quantity	KWAHN tuh ti	ˈkwɑntətɪ
quantum	KWAHN tuhm	ˈkwɑntəm
quarantine	KWAW ruhn teen	ˈkwɔrəntin
Quarles	kwawrlz	kwɔrlz
Quarnero	kwahr NE raw	kwɑrˈnɛrɔ
quarrel	KWAW ruhl	ˈkwɔrəl
quarry	KWAW ri	ˈkwɔrɪ
quart (measure)	kwawrt	kwɔrt
quartan	KWAWR tuhn	ˈkwɔrtən
quartern	KWAWR tern	ˈkwɔrtərn
quartile	KWAWR tighl	ˈkwɔrtaɪl
quartz	kwawrts	kwɔrts
quash	kwahsh	kwɑʃ
quasi	KWAY sigh	ˈkwesaɪ
quassia	KWAH shi uh	ˈkwɑʃɪə
Quathlamba	KWAHT lahm bah	ˈkwɑtlɑmbɑ
quatrefoil	KA ter foil	ˈkætərfɔɪl
quattrocento	KWAH traw CHEN taw	ˈkwɑtrɔ ˈtʃɛntɔ
quay	kee	ki
quean	kween	kwin
queasy	KWEE zi	ˈkwizɪ
Quebec	kwi BEK	kwɪˈbɛk
quebracho	kay BRAH choh	keˈbratʃo

at [æ] ; ah [ɑ] ; air [ɛ] ; awful [ɔ] ; say [e] ; back [b] ; chair [tʃ] ; do [d] ; elm [ɛ] ; eel [i] ;
server [ˈɜ, ər] ; fit [f] ; go [g] ; hurt [h] ; is [ɪ] ; high [aɪ] ; jet [dʒ] ; kiss [k] ; lamb [l] ; my [m] ;
nice [n] ;

Quechua	KECH wah	ˈkɛtʃwɑ
Queensland	KWEENZ land	ˈkwinzlænd
Quelpart	KWEL pahrt	ˈkwɛlpɑrt
quelque chose	kel kuh SHOHZ	kɛlkə ˈʃoz
Quemoy	kee MOI	kiˈmɔɪ
quenelle	kuh NEL	kəˈnɛl
Querétaro	ke RE tah raw	kɛˈrɛtɑrɔ
quern	kwern	kwɜn
querulous	KWE ruh luhs	ˈkwɛrələs
query	KWI ri	ˈkwɪrɪ
Quesada (Elwood)	kuh SAH duh	kəˈsɑdə
question	KWES chuhn	ˈkwɛstʃən
questionnaire	kwes chuh NAIR	kwɛstʃəˈnɛr
Quetta	KWE tah	ˈkwɛtɑ
quetzal	ket SAHL	kɛtˈsɑl
queue	kyoo:	kju
Quezon	KAY zahn	ˈkezɑn
quiddity	KWI duh ti	ˈkwɪdətɪ
quidnunc	KWID nuhngk	ˈkwɪdnʌŋk
quid pro quo	KWID proh KWOH	ˈkwɪd pro ˈkwo
quién sabe	kyen SAH be	kjɛn ˈsɑbe
quiescence	kwigh E suhns	kwaɪˈɛsəns
quiescent	kwigh E suhnt	kwaɪˈɛsənt
quietism	KWIGH uh ti zuhm	ˈkwaɪətɪzəm
quietude	KWIGH uh too: d	ˈkwaɪətud
quietus	kwigh EE tuhs	kwaɪˈitəs
Quiller-Couch	KWI ler KOO: CH	ˈkwɪlər ˈkutʃ
quinacrine	KWI nuh kreen	ˈkwɪnəkrin
quincunx	KWIN kuhngks	ˈkwɪnkʌŋks
Quincy (Illinois)	KWIN si	ˈkwɪnsɪ
Quincy (Massachusetts)	KWIN zi	ˈkwɪnzɪ
quindecagon	kwin DE kuh gahn	kwɪnˈdɛkəgɑn
quindecennial	kwin di SE ni uhl	kwɪndɪˈsɛnɪəl
quinidine	KWI nuh deen	ˈkwɪnədin
quinine	KWIGH nighn	ˈkwaɪnaɪn
quinnat	KWI nat	ˈkwɪnæt
quinquagenarian	kwing kwuh ji NAI ri uhn	kwɪŋkwədʒɪˈnɛrɪən
Quinquagesima	kwing kwuh JE suh muh	kwɪŋkwəˈdʒɛsəmə
quinquennial	kwing KWE ni uhl	kwɪŋˈkwɛnɪəl
quinquennium	kwing KWE ni uhm	kwɪŋˈkwɛnɪəm
quinquereme	KWING kwuh reem	ˈkwɪŋkwərim
quinsy	KWIN zi	ˈkwɪnzɪ
quintal	KWIN tuhl	ˈkwɪntəl
quintan	KWIN tuhn	ˈkwɪntən
Quintero	keen TE raw	kinˈtɛrɔ
quintessence	kwin TE suhrs	kwɪnˈtɛsəns
quintessential	kwin tuh SEN shuhl	kwɪntəˈsɛnʃəl
Quintilian	kwin TI lyuhn	kwɪnˈtɪljən
quintillion	kwin TI lyuhn	kwɪnˈtɪljən
quintuple	KWIN too puhl	ˈkwɪntʊpəl
quintuplet	KWIN too plit	ˈkwɪntʊplɪt
quipu	KEE poo:	ˈkipu

sing [ŋ] ; oh [o] ; oil [ɔɪ] ; foot [ʊ] ; foo:d [u] ; how [aʊ] ; pie [p] ; ray [r] ; so [s] ; shall [ʃ] ;
to [t] ; thin [θ] ; th:en [ð] ; above (uh BUHV) [ə, ˈʌ] ; vine [v] ; wine [w] ; whine [hw] ;
you [j] ; zoo [z] ; rouge (roo:zh) [ʒ].

quire	kwighr	kwaɪr
Quirinal	KWI ri nuhl	ˈkwɪrɪnəl
Quirinus	kwi RIGH nuhs	kwɪˈraɪnəs
Quirites	kwi RIGH teez	kwɪˈraɪtiz
quirk	kwerk	kwɜˑk
quirt	kwert	kwɜˑt
quisle	KWI zuhl	ˈkwɪzəl
quisling	KWIZ ling	ˈkwɪzlɪŋ
Quito	KEE taw	ˈkitɔ
qui vive	kee VEEV	ki ˈviv
quixotic	kwik SAH tik	kwɪkˈsɑtɪk
Qumran	koom RAN	kʊmˈræn
quoit	kwoit	kwɔɪt
quondam	KWAHN duhm	ˈkwɑndəm
Quonset	KWAHN sit	ˈkwɑnsɪt
quorum	KWAW ruhm	ˈkwɔrəm
quota	KWOH tuh	ˈkwotə
quotation	kwoh TAY shuhn	kwoˈteʃən
quoth	kwohth	kwoθ
quotidian	kwoh TI di uhn	kwoˈtɪdɪən
Quo Vadis	KWOH VAY dis	ˈkwo ˈvedɪs

R

Ra	rah	rɑ
Rabat	rah BAHT	rɑˈbɑt
Rabaul	rah BOWL	rɑˈbaʊl
Rabbath	RA buhth	ˈræbəθ
rabbi	RA bigh	ˈræbaɪ
Rabbinic, r-	ruh BI nik	rəˈbɪnɪk
rabbinist	RA bi nist	ˈræbɪnɪst
Rabelais	ra buh LAY	ræbəˈle
Rabelaisian	ra buh LAY zhuhn	ræbəˈleʒən
rabid	RA bid	ˈræbɪd
rabies	RAY beez	ˈrebiz
Rabinowitz	ruh BI nuh wits	rəˈbɪnəwɪts
raccoon	ra KOO:N	ræˈkun
raceme	ray SEEM	reˈsim
Rachel	RAY chuhl	ˈretʃəl
Rachel (French actress)	ra SHEL	ræˈʃɛl
rachis	RAY kis	ˈrekɪs
rachitic	ruh KI tik	rəˈkɪtɪk
rachitis	ruh KIGH tis	rəˈkaɪtɪs
Rachmaninoff, Rachmaninov	rak MAH ni nawf	rækˈmɑnɪnɔf
racial	RAY shuhl	ˈreʃəl
Racine	rah SEEN	rɑˈsin
racket	RA kit	ˈrækɪt

---

at [æ]; *ah* [ɑ]; *air* [ɛ]; *aw*ful [ɔ]; *say* [e]; *back* [b]; *chair* [tʃ]; *do* [d]; *elm* [ɛ]; *eel* [i]; *server* [ˈɜ, ər]; *f*it [f]; *go* [g]; *h*urt [h]; *is* [ɪ]; *high* [aɪ]; *jet* [dʒ]; *kiss* [k]; *lamb* [l]; *my* [m]; *n*ice [n];

Rackham	RA kuhm	ˈrækəm
racon	RAY kahn	ˈrekɑn
raconteur	ra kahn TER	rækɑnˈtɜ
racquet	RA kit	ˈrækɪt
radar	RAY dahr	ˈredɑr
Radauti	ruh duh OOTS	rədəˈuts
Radek	RAH dek	ˈrɑdɛk
radial	RAY di uhl	ˈredɪəl
radiant	RAY di uhnt	ˈredɪənt
radiate	RAY di ayt	ˈredɪet
radiation	ray di AY shuhn	redɪˈeʃən
radiator	RAY di ay ter	ˈredɪetər
radical	RA di kuhl	ˈrædɪkəl
radii (pl.)	RAY di igh	ˈredɪaɪ
radio	RAY di oh	ˈredɪo
radioactive, radio-active	RAY di oh AK tiv	ˈredɪoˈæktɪv
radiogenic	RAY di oh JE nik	ˈredɪoˈdʒɛnɪk
radiogram	RAY di oh gram	ˈredɪogræm
radiography	ray di AH gruh fi	redɪˈɑgrəfɪ
radiology	ray di AH luh ji	redɪˈɑlədʒɪ
radiometer	ray di AH muh ter	redɪˈɑmətər
radionics	ray di AH niks	redɪˈɑnɪks
radioscopy	ray di AH skuh pi	redɪˈɑskəpɪ
radiosonde	RAY di oh sahnd	ˈredɪosɑnd
radish	RA dish	ˈrædɪʃ
radium	RAY di uhm	ˈredɪəm
radius	RAY di uhs	ˈredɪəs
radix	RAY diks	ˈredɪks
radome	RAY dohm	ˈredom
radon	RAY dahn	ˈredɑn
Radziwillow	rah ji VEE loof	rɑdʒɪˈviluf
raffia	RA fi uh	ˈræfɪə
raffinate	RA fi nayt	ˈræfɪnet
raffinose	RA fuh nohs	ˈræfənos
raffish	RA fish	ˈræfɪʃ
raft	raft	ræft
ragamuffin	RA guh muh fin	ˈrægəmʌfɪn
raglan	RAG luhn	ˈræglən
Ragnarok	RAHG nuh rahk	ˈrɑgnərɑk
ragout	ra GOO:	ræˈgu
Ragusa	rah GOO: zah	rɑˈguzɑ
raia	RAH yuh	ˈrɑjə
raillery	RAY luh ri	ˈrelərɪ
raiment	RAY muhnt	ˈremənt
Rainier (Mount)	ray NEER	reˈnir
Rainier (Prince)	ray nyay	renje
raison d'être	RAY zawn DET	ˈrezɔn ˈdɛt
raj	rahj	rɑdʒ
raja, -h	RAH juh	ˈrɑdʒə
Rajagopalachari	rah juh gaw pah luh CHAH ree	rɑdʒəgɔpɑləˈtʃɑri

---

sing [ŋ] ; *oh* [o] ; *oil* [ɔɪ] ; *foot* [ʊ] ; *foo:d* [u] ; *how* [aʊ] ; *pie* [p] ; *ray* [r] ; *so* [s] ; *shall* [ʃ] ;
to [t] ; *thin* [θ] ; *th:en* [ð] ; *above* (*uh BUHV*) [ə, ˈʌ] ; *vine* [v] ; *wine* [w] ; *whine* [hw] ;
you [j] ; *zoo* [z] ; *rouge* (*roo:zh*) [ʒ].

Rajasthan	RAH juh stahn	ˈrɑdʒəstɑn
Rajput	RAHJ poo : t	ˈrɑdʒput
Rajputana	rahj poo TAH nuh	rɑjpuˈtɑnə
raki	ruh KEE	rəˈki
rakish	RAY kish	ˈrekɪʃ
rale (disease)	rahl	rɑl
Raleigh, Ralegh	RAW li	ˈrɔlɪ
rallentando	rah len TAHN doh	rɑlɛnˈtɑndo
Ralph	ralf	rælf
Ralph (British)	rayf	ref
Rama	RAH muh	ˈrɑmə
Ramachandra	rah muh CHUHN druh	rɑməˈtʃʌndrə
Ramadan	ra muh DAHN	ræməˈdɑn
Ramapo	RA muh poh	ˈræməpo
Ramayana	rah MAH yuh nuh	rɑˈmɑjənə
Rambouillet	RAM boo lay	ˈræmbʊle
rambunctious	ram BUHNGK shuhs	ræmˈbʌŋkʃəs
Rameau	ra MOH	ræˈmo
ramekin, ramequin	RA muh kin	ˈræməkɪn
Rameses	RA muh seez	ˈræməsiz
ramification	ra muh fi KAY shuhn	ræməfɪˈkeʃən
ramjet	RAM jet	ˈræmdʒɛt
ramose	RAY mohs	ˈremos
rampage (n)	RAM payj	ˈræmpedʒ
rampage (v)	ram PAYJ	ræmˈpedʒ
rampant	RAM puhnt	ˈræmpənt
Ramsay	RAM zi	ˈræmzɪ
Ramses	RAM seez	ˈræmsiz
ramshackle	RAM sha kuhl	ˈræmʃækəl
ranchero	ran CHAY roh	rænˈtʃero
rancho	RAN choh	ˈræntʃo
rancid	RAN sid	ˈrænsɪd
rancor	RANG ker	ˈræŋkər
Rand, Ayn	rand, AY in	rænd, ˈem
randkluft	RAHNT klooft	ˈrɑntklʊft
ranee	RAH ni	ˈrɑnɪ
Rangoon	rang GOO : N	ræŋˈgun
rani	RAH ni	ˈrɑnɪ
Ranjit Singh	RUHN jit SIN huh	ˈrʌndʒɪt ˈsɪnhə
ransack	RAN sak	ˈrænsæk
ranunculus	ruh NUHNG kyuh luhs	rəˈnʌŋkjələs
rapacious	ruh PAY shuhs	rəˈpeʃəs
rapacity	ruh PA suh ti	rəˈpæsətɪ
Rapallo	rah PAH law	rɑˈpɑlɔ
Raphael	RA fi uhl	ˈræfɪəl
Rapidan	ra puh DAN	ræpəˈdæn
rapidity	ruh PI duh ti	rəˈpɪdətɪ
rapier	RAY pi er	ˈrepɪər
rapine	RA pin	ˈræpɪn
Rappahannock	ra puh HA nuhk	ræpəˈhænək
rappel	ruh PEL	rəˈpɛl
rapport	ra PAWRT	ræˈpɔrt

at [æ] ; ah [ɑ] ; air [ɛ] ; awful [ɔ] ; say [e] ; back [b] ; chair [tʃ] ; do [d] ; elm [ɛ] ; eel [i] ; server [ˈɜ, ər] ; fit [f] ; go [g] ; hurt [h] ; is [ɪ] ; high [aɪ] ; jet [dʒ] ; kiss [k] ; lamb [l] ; my [m] ; nice [n] ;

rapprochement	ra prawsh MAHN	ræprɔʃˈmɑn
rapscallion	rap SKA lyuhn	ræpˈskæljən
rapt	rapt	ræpt
raptorial	rap TAW ri uhl	ræpˈtɔrɪəl
rapture	RAP cher	ˈræptʃər
rapturous	RAP chuh ruhs	ˈræptʃərəs
rara avis	RAY ruh AY vis	ˈrerə ˈevɪs
rarebit	RAIR bit	ˈrɛrbɪt
rarefaction	rai ruh FAK shuhn	rɛrəˈfækʃən
rarefy	RAI ruh figh	ˈrɛrəfaɪ
rarity	RAI ruh ti	ˈrɛrətɪ
Rarotonga	rah raw TAWNG guh	rɑrɔˈtɔŋgə
rascality	ra SKA luh ti	ræˈskælətɪ
rash	rash	ræʃ
rasher	RA sher	ˈræʃər
rasorial	ruh SAW ri uhl	rəˈsɔrɪəl
raspberry	RAZ be ri	ˈræzbɛrɪ
Rasputin	ra SPYOO : tin	ræˈspjutɪn
raster	RA ster	ˈræstər
ratafia	ra tuh FEE uh	rætəˈfiə
ratan	ra TAN	ræˈtæn
rataplan	ra tuh PLAN	rætəˈplæn
ratchet	RA chit	ˈrætʃɪt
rathe	rayth :	reð
rather	RA th : er	ˈræðər
rathskeller	RAHT ske ler	ˈrɑtskɛlər
ratiné	ra tuh NAY	rætəˈne
ratio	RAY shoh	ˈreʃo
ratiocinate	ra shi AH suh nayt	ræʃɪˈɑsənet
ratiocination	ra shi ah suh NAY shuhn	ræʃɪɑsəˈneʃən
ratiocinative	ra shi AH suh nay tiv	ræʃɪˈɑsənetɪv
ration	RA shuhn	ˈræʃən
rational	RA shuh nuhl	ˈræʃənəl
rationale	ra shuh NAL	ræʃəˈnæl
rationalism	RA shuh nuh li zuhm	ˈræʃənəlɪzəm
rationality	ra shuh NA luh ti	ræʃəˈnælətɪ
rationalization	ra shuh nuh li ZAY shuhn	ræʃənəlɪˈzeʃən
ratsbane	RATS bayn	ˈrætsben
rattan	ra TAN	ræˈtæn
ratteen	ra TEEN	ræˈtin
Rau	row	rau
raucous	RAW kuhs	ˈrɔkəs
ravage	RA vij	ˈrævɪdʒ
ravel	RA vuhl	ˈrævəl
Ravel	ra VEL	ræˈvɛl
raven	RAY vuhn	ˈrevən
Ravenna	ruh VE nuh	rəˈvɛnə
ravenous	RA vuh nuhs	ˈrævənəs
ravigote	ra vee GAWT	ræviˈgɔt
ravin	RA vuhn	ˈrævən
ravine	ruh VEEN	rəˈvin
ravioli	ra vi OH li	rævɪˈolɪ

---

sing [ŋ] ; *oh* [o] ; *oil* [ɔɪ] ; *foot* [ʊ] ; *foo:*d [u] ; *how* [aʊ] ; *pie* [p] ; *ray* [r] ; *so* [s] ; *shall* [ʃ] ;
to [t] ; *thin* [θ] ; *th:*en [ð] ; *above* (*uh* B*UH*V) [ə, ˈʌ] ; *vine* [v] ; *wine* [w] ; *whine* [hw] ;
you [j] ; *zoo* [z] ; *rouge* (roo:*zh*) [ʒ].

ravish	RA vish	ˈrævɪʃ
Rawalpindi	rah wuhl PIN di	rɑwəlˈpɪndɪ
rayah	RAH yuh	ˈrɑjə
Rayburn	RAY bern	ˈrebərn
Rayleigh	RAY li	ˈrelɪ
rayon	RAY ahn	ˈreɑn
razon	RAY zahn	ˈrezɑn
Re, re	ray	re
reaction	ri AK shuhn	rɪˈækʃən
reactionary	ri AK shuh nai ri	rɪˈækʃənɛrɪ
reactor	ri AK ter	rɪˈæktər
Reading (Pennsylvania, England)	RE ding	ˈredɪŋ
Reagan	REE guhn	ˈrigən
reagent	ree AY juhnt	riˈedʒənt
real	REE uhl	ˈriəl
reality	ri A luh ti	rɪˈælətɪ
realization	ree uh li ZAY shuhn	riəlɪˈzeʃən
really	REE uh li	ˈriəlɪ
realm	relm	rɛlm
Realpolitik, r-	ray AHL paw li TEEK	reˈɑlpɔlɪˈtik
realtor	REE uhl ter	ˈriəltər
realty	REE uhl ti	ˈriəltɪ
Réaumur	RAY uh myoor	ˈreəmjʊr
rebec, -k	REE bek	ˈribɛk
Rebecca, Rebekah	ri BE kuh	rɪˈbɛkə
rebel (n)	RE buhl	ˈrɛbəl
rebel (v)	ri BEL	rɪˈbɛl
rebellion	ri BE lyuhn	rɪˈbɛljən
rebellious	ri BE lyuhs	rɪˈbɛljəs
rebop	REE bahp	ˈribɑp
rebuke	ri BYOO : K	rɪˈbjuk
rebus	REE buhs	ˈribəs
rebut	ri BUHT	rɪˈbʌt
rebuttal	ri BUH tuhl	rɪˈbʌtəl
recalcitrance	ri KAL si truhns	rɪˈkælsɪtrəns
recalcitrant	ri KAL si truhnt	rɪˈkælsɪtrənt
recall (n)	REE kawl	ˈrikɔl
recall (v)	ri KAWL	rɪˈkɔl
Récamier	ray ka MYAY	rekæˈmje
recant	ri KANT	rɪˈkænt
recapitulate	ree kuh PI chuh layt	rikəˈpɪtʃəlet
recco	RE koh	ˈrɛko
reccy	RE ki	ˈrɛkɪ
receipt	ri SEET	rɪˈsit
recency	REE suhn si	ˈrisənsɪ
recension	ri SEN shuhn	rɪˈsɛnʃən
recept	REE sept	ˈrisɛpt
receptacle	ri SEP tuh kuhl	rɪˈsɛptəkəl
recess (n)	REE ses	ˈrisɛs
recess (v)	ri SES	rɪˈsɛs
recessional	ri SE shuh nuhl	rɪˈsɛʃənəl

at [æ] ; *ah* [ɑ] ; *air* [ɛ] ; *awful* [ɔ] ; *say* [e] ; *back* [b] ; *chair* [tʃ] ; *do* [d] ; *elm* [ɛ] ; *eel* [i] ; *server* [ˈɚ, ər] ; *fit* [f] ; *go* [g] ; *hurt* [h] ; *is* [ɪ] ; *high* [aɪ] ; *jet* [dʒ] ; *kiss* [k] ; *lamb* [l] ; *my* [m] ; *nice* [n] ;

réchauffé	ray shoh FAY	reʃoˈfe
recherché	ruh SHAIR shay	rəˈʃɛrʃe
recidivism	ri SI duh vi zuhm	rɪˈsɪdəvɪzəm
recidivist	ri SI duh vist	rɪˈsɪdəvɪst
Recife	re SEE fuh	rɛˈsifə
recipe	RE suh pi	ˈrɛsəpɪ
recipient	ri SI pi uhnt	rɪˈsɪpɪənt
reciprocal	ri SI pruh kuhl	rɪˈsɪprəkəl
reciprocate	ri SI pruh kayt	rɪˈsɪprəket
reciprocity	re suh PRAH suh ti	rɛsəˈprɑsətɪ
recital	ri SIGH tuhl	rɪˈsaɪtəl
recitation	re suh TAY shuhn	rɛsəˈteʃən
recitative (music)	re suh tuh TEEV	rɛsətəˈtiv
recitativo	re chee tah TEE voh	rɛtʃitaˈtivo
reclamation	re kluh MAY shuhn	rɛkləˈmeʃən
recluse (a)	ri KLOO : S	rɪˈklus
recluse (n)	RE kloo : s	ˈrɛklus
recognition	re kuhg NI shuhn	rɛkəgˈnɪʃən
recognizable	RE kuhg nigh zuh buhl	ˈrɛkəgnaɪzəbəl
recognizance	ri KAHG ni zuhns	rɪˈkɑgnɪzəns
recognize	RE kuhg nighz	ˈrɛkəgnaɪz
recoil	ri KOIL	rɪˈkɔɪl
recollect (" recall ")	re kuh LEKT	rɛkəˈlɛkt
recollect (" collect again ")	ree kuh LEKT	rikəˈlɛkt
recollection	re kuh LEK shuhn	rɛkəˈlɛkʃən
recompense	RE kuhm pens	ˈrɛkəmpɛns
recon	REE kahn	ˈrikɑn
reconcilable	RE kuhn sigh luh buhl	ˈrɛkənsaɪləbəl
reconciliation	re kuhn si li AY shuhn	rɛkənsɪlɪˈeʃən
reconciliatory	re kuhn SI li uh taw ri	rɛkənˈsɪlɪətɔrɪ
recondite	RE kuhn dight	ˈrɛkəndaɪt
reconnaissance, reconnoissance	ri KAH nuh suhns	rɪˈkɑnəsəns
reconnoiter, reconnoitre	re kuh NOI ter	rɛkəˈnɔɪtər
record (a, n)	RE kerd	ˈrɛkərd
record (v)	ri KAWRD	rɪˈkɔrd
recorder	ri KAWR der	rɪˈkɔrdər
recoup	ri KOO : P	rɪˈkup
recourse	REE kawrs	ˈrikɔrs
recreant	RE kri uhnt	ˈrɛkrɪənt
recreate (" relax ")	RE kri ayt	ˈrɛkriet
re-create (" create again ")	ree kri AYT	rikrɪˈet
recreation (" relaxation ")	re kri AY shuhn	rɛkrɪˈeʃən
re-creation (" creation anew ")	ree kri AY shuhn	rikrɪˈeʃən
recrement	RE kruh muhnt	ˈrɛkrəmənt
recrimination	ri kri muh NAY shuhn	rɪkrɪməˈneʃən
recriminatory	ri KRI muh nuh taw ri	rɪˈkrɪmənətɔrɪ
recrudescence	ree kroo : DE suhns	rikruˈdɛsəns

sing [ŋ] ; oh [o] ; oil [ɔɪ] ; foot [ʊ] ; foo:d [u] ; how [aʊ] ; pie [p] ; ray [r] ; so [s] ; shall [ʃ] ;
to [t] ; thin [θ] ; th:en [ð] ; above (uh BUHV) [ə, ˈʌ] ; vine [v] ; wine [w] ; whine [hw] ;
you [j] ; zoo [z] ; rouge (roo:zh) [ʒ].

recruit	ri KROO : T	rɪˈkrut
rectangle	REK tang guhl	ˈrɛktæŋgəl
rectangular	rek TANG gyuh ler	rɛkˈtæŋgjələr
rectify	REK tuh figh	ˈrɛktəfaɪ
rectilinear	rek tuh LI ni er	rɛktəˈlɪnɪər
rectitude	REK tuh too : d	ˈrɛktətud
recto	REK toh	ˈrɛkto
rector	REK ter	ˈrɛktər
rectory	REK tuh ri	ˈrɛktərɪ
rectum	REK tuhm	ˈrɛktəm
recumbent	ri KUHM buhnt	rɪˈkʌmbənt
recuperate	ri KOO : puh rayt	rɪˈkupəret
recuperative	ri KOO : puh ray tiv	rɪˈkupəretɪv
recur	ri KER	rɪˈkɝ
recurrence	ri KER uhns	rɪˈkɝəns
recusant	RE kyoo zuhnt	ˈrɛkjuzənt
redact	ri DAKT	rɪˈdækt
redaction	ri DAK shuhn	rɪˈdækʃən
redan	ri DAN	rɪˈdæn
redeploy	ree di PLOI	ridɪˈplɔɪ
redingote	RE ding goht	ˈrɛdɪŋgot
redolent	RE duh luhnt	ˈrɛdələnt
Redon, Odilon	ruh DOHN, oh dee LOHN	rəˈdon, odiˈlon
redoubt	ri DOWT	rɪˈdaʊt
redoubtable	ri DOW tuh buhl	rɪˈdaʊtəbəl
redound	ri DOWND	rɪˈdaʊnd
redowa	RE duh wuh	ˈrɛdəwə
redress (n)	REE dres	ˈridrɛs
redress (v)	ri DRES	rɪˈdrɛs
reduce	ri DOO : S	rɪˈdus
reductio ad absurdum	ri DUHK shi oh ad ab SER duhm	rɪˈdʌkʃɪo æd æbˈsɝdəm
redundancy	ri DUHN duhn si	rɪˈdʌndənsɪ
redundant	ri DUHN duhnt	rɪˈdʌndənt
reduplicate (a, n)	ri DOO : pluh kit	rɪˈdupləkɪt
reduplicate (v)	ri DOO : pluh kayt	rɪˈdupləket
reefer	REE fer	ˈrifər
refection	ri FEK shuhn	rɪˈfɛkʃən
refectory	ri FEK tuh ri	rɪˈfɛktərɪ
referable	RE fuh ruh buhl	ˈrɛfərəbəl
referee (n)	RE fuh ree	ˈrɛfəri
referee (v)	re fuh REE	rɛfəˈri
reference	RE fuh ruhns	ˈrɛfərəns
referendum	re fuh REN duhm	rɛfəˈrɛndəm
referent	RE fuh ruhnt	ˈrɛfərənt
referential	re fuh REN shuhl	rɛfəˈrɛnʃəl
referral	ri FER uhl	rɪˈfɝəl
reflection	ri FLEK shuhn	rɪˈflɛkʃən
reflector	ri FLEK ter	rɪˈflɛktər
reflet	ruh FLE	rəˈflɛ
reflex (a, n)	REE fleks	ˈriflɛks
reflex (v)	ri FLEKS	rɪˈflɛks

at [æ]; ah [ɑ]; air [ɛ]; awful [ə]; say [e]; back [b]; chair [tʃ]; do [d]; elm [ɛ]; eel [i]; server [ˈɝ, ər]; fit [f]; go [g]; hurt [h]; is [ɪ]; high [aɪ]; jet [dʒ]; kiss [k]; lamb [l]; my [m]; nice [n];

reflexive	ri FLEK siv	rɪˈflɛksɪv
refluent	RE floo uhnt	ˈrɛfluənt
reflux	REE fluhks	ˈriflʌks
reforestation	ree faw ri STAY shuhn	rifɔrɪˈsteʃən
reformation	re fer MAY shuhn	rɛfərˈmeʃən
reformatory	ri FAWR muh taw ri	rɪˈfɔrmətɔrɪ
refraction	ri FRAK shuhn	rɪˈfrækʃən
refractory	ri FRAK tuh ri	rɪˈfræktərɪ
refrain	ri FRAYN	rɪˈfren
refrangible	ri FRAN juh buhl	rɪˈfrændʒəbəl
refuge	RE fyoo : j	ˈrɛfjudʒ
refugee	RE fyoo jee	ˈrɛfjʊdʒi
refulgent	ri FUHL juhnt	rɪˈfʌldʒənt
refund (n)	REE fuhnd	ˈrifʌnd
refund (v)	ri FUHND	rɪˈfʌnd
refurbish	ree FER bish	riˈfɝbɪʃ
refusal	ri FYOO : zuhl	rɪˈfjuzəl
refuse (a, n)	RE fyoo : s	ˈrɛfjus
refuse (v)	ri FYOO : Z	rɪˈfjuz
refutable	RE fyoo tuh buhl	ˈrɛfjʊtəbəl
refutation	re fyoo TAY shuhn	rɛfjʊˈteʃən
refute	ri FYOO : T	rɪˈfjut
regal	REE guhl	ˈrigəl
regalia	ri GAY li uh	rɪˈgelɪə
Regan	REE guhn	ˈrigən
regatta	ri GA tuh	rɪˈgætə
regency	REE juhn si	ˈridʒənsɪ
regenerate (a)	ri JE nuh rit	rɪˈdʒɛnərɪt
regenerate (v)	ri JE nuh rayt	rɪˈdʒɛnəret
Regensburg	RAY guhnz berg	ˈregənzbɔrg
regent	REE juhnt	ˈridʒənt
Reggan	ray GAHN	reˈgɑn
Reggio di Calabria	RE jaw dee kah LAH bree ah	ˈrɛdʒɔ di kɑˈlabriɑ
regicide	RE juh sighd	ˈrɛdʒəsaɪd
regime, régime	ri ZHEEM	rɪˈʒim
regimen	RE juh men	ˈrɛdʒəmɛn
regiment	RE juh muhnt	ˈrɛdʒəmənt
Regina	ri JIGH nuh	rɪˈdʒaɪnə
reginal	ri JIGH nuhl	rɪˈdʒaɪnəl
region	REE juhn	ˈridʒən
registrant	RE ji struhnt	ˈrɛdʒɪstrənt
registrar	RE ji strahr	ˈrɛdʒɪstrɑr
registry	RE ji stri	ˈrɛdʒɪstrɪ
regius	REE ji uhs	ˈridʒɪəs
regress (n)	REE gres	ˈrigrɛs
regress (v)	ri GRES	rɪˈgrɛs
regression	ri GRE shuhn	rɪˈgrɛʃən
regular	RE gyuh ler	ˈrɛgjələr
regularity	re gyuh LA ruh ti	regjəˈlærətɪ
regularly	RE gyuh ler li	ˈrɛgjələrlɪ
regulatory	RE gyuh luh taw ri	ˈrɛgjələtɔrɪ

sing [ŋ] ; *oh* [o] ; *oil* [ɔɪ] ; *foot* [ʊ] ; *foo:d* [u] ; *how* [aʊ] ; *pie* [p] ; *ray* [r] ; *so* [s] ; *shall* [ʃ] ; *to* [t] ; *th*in [θ] ; *th:*en [ð] ; *above* (*uh* BUHV) [ə, ˈʌ] ; *vine* [v] ; *wine* [w] ; *whine* [hw] ; *you* [j] ; *zoo* [z] ; *rouge* (roo:*zh*) [ʒ].

Regulus, r-	RE gyuh luhs	ˈrɛgjələs
regurgitate	ree GER juh tayt	riˈgɝdʒətet
rehabilitate	ree huh BI luh tayt	rihəˈbɪlətet
rehabilitation	ree huh bi luh TAY shuhn	rihəbɪləˈteʃən
rehabilitative	ree huh BI luh tay tiv	rihəˈbɪlətetɪv
Rehan	REE uhn	ˈriən
rehash (n)	REE hash	ˈrihæʃ
rehash (v)	ree HASH	riˈhæʃ
Rehoboam	ree uh BOH uhm	riəˈboəm
Rehoboth (Africa)	RAY uh bohth	ˈreəboθ
Rehoboth (U.S.)	ri HOH buhth	rɪˈhobəθ
Reich	righk	raɪk
Reichstag	RIGHKS tahg	ˈraɪkstɑg
Reichswehr	RIGHKS vair	ˈraɪksvɛr
reify	REE uh figh	ˈriəfaɪ
Reik	righk	raɪk
Reikjavik	RAY kyuh veek	ˈrekjɔvik
Reims	reemz	rimz
reindeer	RAYN dir	ˈrendɪr
reine	ren	rɛn
Reiner	RIGH ner	ˈraɪnər
Reinhardt	RIGHN hahrt	ˈraɪnhɑrt
reis, R-	rays	res
reiterate	ree I tuh rayt	riˈɪtəret
reiteration	ree i tuh RAY shuhn	riɪtəˈreʃən
rejectamenta	ri jek tuh MEN tuh	rɪdʒɛktəˈmɛntə
rejoinder	ri JOIN der	rɪˈdʒɔɪndər
rejuvenate	ri JOO : vuh nayt	rɪˈdʒuvənet
rejuvenescence	ri joo : vuh NE suhns	rɪdʒuvəˈnɛsəns
relative	RE luh tiv	ˈrɛlətɪv
relativism	RE luh ti vi zuhm	ˈrɛlətɪvɪzəm
relativity	re luh TI vuh ti	rɛləˈtɪvətɪ
relaxation	ree lak SAY shuhn	rilækˈseʃən
relay (a, n)	REE lay	ˈrile
relay (v)	ri LAY	rɪˈle
relegate	RE luh gayt	ˈrɛləget
relegation	re luh GAY shuhn	rɛləˈgeʃən
relent	ri LENT	rɪˈlɛnt
relevance	RE luh vuhns	ˈrɛləvəns
relevant	RE luh vuhnt	ˈrɛləvənt
reliable	ri LIGH uh buhl	rɪˈlaɪəbəl
relic	RE lik	ˈrɛlɪk
relict (a)	ri LIKT	rɪˈlɪkt
relict (n)	RE likt	ˈrɛlɪkt
relief	ri LEEF	rɪˈlif
relieve	ri LEEV	rɪˈliv
relievo	ri LEE voh	rɪˈlivo
religieuse	ruh lee ZHYERZ	rəliˈʒjɝz
religieux	ruh lee ZHYER	rəliˈʒjɝ
religiosity	ri li ji AH suh ti	rɪlɪdʒɪˈɑsətɪ
relinquish	ri LING kwish	rɪˈlɪŋkwɪʃ
reliquary	RE luh kwai ri	ˈrɛləkwɛrɪ

at [æ] ; ah [ɑ] ; air [ɛ] ; awful [ɔ] ; say [e] ; back [b] ; chair [tʃ] ; do [d] ; elm [ɛ] ; eel [i] ; server [ˈɝ, ər] ; fit [f] ; go [g] ; hurt [h] ; is [ɪ] ; high [aɪ] ; jet [dʒ] ; kiss [k] ; lamb [l] ; my [m] ; nice [n] ;

relique	RE lik	ˈrɛlɪk
reliquiae	ri LI kwi ee	rɪˈlɪkwɪi
rely	ri LIGH	rɪˈlaɪ
remanent	RE muh nuhnt	ˈrɛmənənt
remarque	ri MAHRK	rɪˈmɑrk
Remarque	ruh MAHRK	rəˈmɑrk
Rembrandt	REM brant	ˈrɛmbrænt
remedial	ri MEE di uhl	rɪˈmidɪəl
remedy	RE muh di	ˈrɛmədɪ
remembrance	ri MEM bruhns	rɪˈmɛmbrəns
reminisce	re muh NIS	rɛməˈnɪs
reminiscence	re muh NI suhns	rɛməˈnɪsəns
remiss	ri MIS	rɪˈmɪs
remission	ri MI shuhn	rɪˈmɪʃən
remittance	ri MI tuhns	rɪˈmɪtəns
remnant	REM nuhnt	ˈrɛmnənt
remolade	ray muh LAHD	reməˈlɑd
remonstrance	ri MAHN struhns	rɪˈmɑnstrəns
remonstrate	ri MAHN strayt	rɪˈmɑnstret
remonstrative	ri MAHN struh tiv	rɪˈmɑnstrətɪv
remora	RE muh ruh	ˈrɛmərə
remorse	ri MAWRS	rɪˈmɔrs
rémoulade	ray muh LAHD	reməˈlɑd
remuneration	ri myoo: nuh RAY shuhn	rɪmjunəˈreʃən
remunerative	ri MYOO: nuh ray tiv	rɪˈmjunəretɪv
Remus	REE muhs	ˈriməs
Renaissance (of or like the revival in the 14-16 centuries)	re nuh SAHNS	rɛnəˈsɑns
renaissance (" rebirth " or " revival " but not pertaining to that of 14-16 centuries)	ri NAY suhns	rɪˈnesəns
renal	REE nuhl	ˈrinəl
Renan	ri NAN	rɪˈnæn
Renard	RE nerd	ˈrɛnərd
renascence, R-	ri NAY suhns	rɪˈnesəns
Renault	ruh NOH	rəˈno
rencontre	ren KAHN ter	rɛnˈkɑntər
rencounter	ren KOWN ter	rɛnˈkaʊntər
render	REN der	ˈrɛndər
rendezvous	RAHN duh voo:	ˈrɑndəvu
renegade	RE nuh gayd	ˈrɛnəged
renege	ri NIG	rɪˈnɪg
Reni	RE nee	ˈreni
renin	REE nin	ˈrinɪn
Rennes	ren	rɛn
rennet	RE nit	ˈrɛnɪt
rennin	RE nin	ˈrɛnɪn
Renoir	ruh NWAHR	rəˈnwɑr
renovate	RE nuh vayt	ˈrɛnəvet
renown	ri NOWN	rɪˈnaʊn

sing [ŋ]; oh [o]; oil [ɔɪ]; foot [ʊ]; foo:d [u]; how [aʊ]; pie [p]; ray [r]; so [s]; shall [ʃ]; to [t]; thin [θ]; th:en [ð]; above (uh BUHV) [ə, ˈʌ]; vine [v]; wine [w]; whine [hw]; you [j]; zoo [z]; rouge (roo:zh) [ʒ].

renowned	ri NOWND	rɪˈnaʊnd
Rensselaer	REN suh ler	ˈrɛnsələr
rentier	rahn TYAY	rɑnˈtje
renunciation	ri nuhn si AY shuhn	rɪnʌnsɪˈeʃən
repairable	ri PAI ruh buhl	rɪˈpɛrəbəl
reparable	RE puh ruh buhl	ˈrɛpərəbəl
reparation	re puh RAY shuhn	rɛpəˈreʃən
repartee	re per TEE	rɛpərˈti
repast	ri PAST	rɪˈpæst
repatriate	ree PAY tri ayt	riˈpetrɪet
repay	ri PAY	rɪˈpe
repellent	ri PE luhnt	rɪˈpɛlənt
repercussion	ree per KUH shuhn	ripərˈkʌʃən
repertoire	RE per twahr	ˈrɛpərtwɑr
repertory	RE per taw ri	ˈrɛpərtɔrɪ
repetitive	ri PE tuh tiv	rɪˈpɛtətɪv
replete	ri PLEET	rɪˈplit
repletion	ri PLEE shuhn	rɪˈpliʃən
replevin	ri PLE vin	rɪˈplɛvɪn
replica	RE pli kuh	ˈrɛplɪkə
replicate (a, n)	RE pli kit	ˈrɛplɪkɪt
replicate (v)	RE pli kayt	ˈrɛplɪket
répondez s'il vous plaît	ray pohn DAY seel voo : PLE	reponˈde sil vu ˈplɛ
reportorial	re per TAW ri uhl	rɛpərˈtɔrɪəl
reposit	ri PAH zit	rɪˈpɑzɪt
reposition	re puh ZI shuhn	rɛpəˈzɪʃən
repository	ri PAH zuh taw ri	rɪˈpɑzətɔrɪ
repoussé	ruh poo : SAY	rəpuˈse
Repplier	RE plir	ˈrɛplɪr
reprehend	re pri HEND	rɛprɪˈhɛnd
reprehensible	re pri HEN suh buhl	rɛprɪˈhɛnsəbəl
reprehension	re pri HEN shuhn	rɛprɪˈhɛnʃən
representation	re pri zen TAY shuhn	rɛprɪzɛnˈteʃən
representative	re pri ZEN tuh tiv	rɛprɪˈzɛntətɪv
reprieve	ri PREEV	rɪˈpriv
reprimand (n)	RE pruh mand	ˈrɛprəmænd
reprimand (v)	re pruh MAND	rɛprəˈmænd
reprint (n)	REE print	ˈriprɪnt
reprint (v)	ree PRINT	riˈprɪnt
reprisal	ri PRIGH zuhl	rɪˈpraɪzəl
reprise (law)	ri PRIGHZ	rɪˈpraɪz
reprise (music)	ruh PREEZ	rəˈpriz
reprobate	RE pruh bayt	ˈrɛprəbet
reprobation	re pruh BAY shuhn	rɛprəˈbeʃən
reproof	ri PROO : F	rɪˈpruf
reprove	ri PROO : V	rɪˈpruv
reptile	REP til	ˈrɛptɪl
reptilian	rep TI li uhn	rɛpˈtɪlɪən
repudiate	ri PYOO : di ayt	rɪˈpjudɪet
repugnance	ri PUHG nuhns	rɪˈpʌgnəns
repugnant	ri PUHG nuhnt	rɪˈpʌgnənt

at [æ] ; ah [ɑ] ; air [ɛ] ; awful [ɔ] ; say [e] ; back [b] ; chair [tʃ] ; do [d] ; elm [ɛ] ; eel [i] ; server [ˈɝ, ər] ; fit [f] ; go [g] ; hurt [h] ; is [ɪ] ; high [aɪ] ; jet [dʒ] ; kiss [k] ; lamb [l] ; my [m] ; nice [n] ;

repulse	ri PUHLS	rɪˈpʌls
repulsion	ri PUHL shuhn	rɪˈpʌlʃən
repulsive	ri PUHL siv	rɪˈpʌlsɪv
reputable	RE pyuh tuh buhl	ˈrɛpjətəbəl
reputation	re pyuh TAH shuhn	rɛpjəˈteʃən
repute	ri PYOO:T	rɪˈpjut
requiem, R-	REE kwi uhm	ˈrikwɪəm
requiescat in pace	re kwi E skat in PAY si	rɛkwɪˈɛskæt ɪn ˈpesɪ
requisite	RE kwuh zit	ˈrɛkwəzɪt
requisition	re kwuh ZI shuhn	rɛkwəˈzɪʃən
requital	ri KWIGH tuhl	rɪˈkwaɪtəl
requite	ri KWIGHT	rɪˈkwaɪt
reredos	RIR dahs	ˈrɪrdɑs
rescind	ri SIND	rɪˈsɪnd
rescript	REE skript	ˈriskrɪpt
research (n)	REE serch	ˈrisɚtʃ
research (v)	ri SERCH	rɪˈsɚtʃ
reseau, réseau	ray ZOH	reˈzo
resemblance	ri ZEM bluhns	rɪˈzɛmbləns
resent	ri ZENT	rɪˈzɛnt
reserpine	ri SER peen	rɪˈsɚpin
reservist	ri ZER vist	rɪˈzɚvɪst
reservoir	RE zer vawr	ˈrɛzərvɔr
res gestae	REEZ JE stee	ˈriz ˈdʒɛsti
residence	RE zuh duhns	ˈrɛzədəns
residential	re zuh DEN shuhl	rɛzəˈdɛnʃəl
residual	ri ZI joo uhl	rɪˈzɪdʒuəl
residue	RE zuh doo:	ˈrɛzədu
resignation	re zig NAY shuhn	rɛzɪgˈneʃən
resilient	ri ZI li uhnt	rɪˈzɪlɪənt
resin	RE zuhn	ˈrɛzən
resistor	ri ZI ster	rɪˈzɪstər
resnatron	REZ nuh trahn	ˈrɛznətrɑn
Resnik	REZ nik	ˈrɛznɪk
resojet	RE zuh jet	ˈrɛzədʒɛt
resolute	RE zuh loo:t	ˈrɛzəlut
resolution	re zuh LOO: shuhn	rɛzəˈluʃən
resolve	ri ZAHLV	rɪˈzɑlv
resolvent	ri ZAHL vuhnt	rɪˈzɑlvənt
resonance	RE zuh nuhns	ˈrɛzənəns
resonant	RE zuh nuhnt	ˈrɛzənənt
resonator	RE zuh nay ter	ˈrɛzənetər
resort	ri ZAWRT	rɪˈzɔrt
resound	ri ZOWND	rɪˈzaʊnd
resource	REE sawrs	ˈrisɔrs
resourceful	ri SAWRS fuhl	rɪˈsɔrsfəl
Respighi	re SPEE gee	reˈspigi
respirable	ri SPIGH ruh buhl	rɪˈspaɪrəbəl
respiration	re spuh RAY shuhn	rɛspəˈreʃən
respirator	RE spuh ray ter	ˈrɛspəretər
respiratory	ri SPIGH ruh taw ri	rɪˈspaɪrətɔrɪ
respite	RE spit	ˈrɛspɪt

sing [ŋ]; oh [o]; oil [ɔɪ]; foot [ʊ]; foo:d [u]; how [aʊ]; pie [p]; ray [r]; so [s]; shall [ʃ]; to [t]; thin [θ]; th:en [ð]; above (uh BUHV) [ə, ˈʌ]; vine [v]; wine [w]; whine [hw]; you [j]; zoo [z]; rouge (roo:zh) [ʒ].

resplendent	ri SPLEN duhnt	rɪˈsplɛndənt
respondent	ri SPAHN duhnt	rɪˈspɑndənt
responsory	ri SPAHN suh ri	rɪˈspɑnsərɪ
res publica	REEZ PUH bli kuh	ˈriz ˈpʌblɪkə
restaurant	RE stuh ruhnt	ˈrɛstərənt
restaurateur	re stuh ruh TER	rɛstərəˈtɝ
restitution	re stuh TOO : shuhn	rɛstəˈtuʃən
restoration	re stuh RAY shuhn	rɛstəˈreʃən
restorative	ri STAW ruh tiv	rɪˈstɔrətɪv
resume	ri ZOO : M	rɪˈzum
résumé	ray zoo MAY	rezʊˈme
resumption	ri ZUHMP shuhn	rɪˈzʌmpʃən
resurgence	ri SER juhns	rɪˈsɝdʒəns
resurrect	re zuh REKT	rɛzəˈrɛkt
resuscitate	ri SUH suh tayt	rɪˈsʌsətet
resuscitation	ri suh suh TAY shuhn	rɪsʌsəˈteʃən
Reszke	RESH ke	ˈrɛʃkɛ
retail	REE tayl	ˈritel
retailer	REE tay ler	ˈritelər
retake (n)	REE tayk	ˈritek
retake (v)	ree TAYK	riˈtek
retaliate	ri TA li ayt	rɪˈtælɪet
retaliatory	ri TA li uh taw ri	rɪˈtælɪətɔrɪ
retard	ri TAHRD	rɪˈtɑrd
retardation	ree tahr DAY shuhn	ritɑrˈdeʃən
rete	REE tee	ˈriti
retepore	REE ti pawr	ˈritɪpor
retiarius	ree shi AI ri uhs	riʃɪˈɛrɪəs
reticence	RE tuh suhns	ˈrɛtəsəns
reticent	RE tuh suhnt	ˈrɛtəsənt
reticle	RE ti kuhl	ˈrɛtɪkəl
reticular	ri TI kyuh ler	rɪˈtɪkjələr
reticule	RE ti kyoo : l	ˈrɛtɪkjul
reticulum, R-	ri TI kyuh luhm	rɪˈtɪkjələm
retina	RE tuh nuh	ˈrɛtənə
retinene	RE tuh neen	ˈrɛtənin
retinue	RE tuh noo :	ˈrɛtənu
retort	ri TAWRT	rɪˈtɔrt
retral	REE truhl	ˈritrəl
retribution	re truh BYOO : shuhn	rɛtrəˈbjuʃən
retrieve	ri TREEV	rɪˈtriv
retro	RE troh	ˈrɛtro
retroactive	re troh AK tiv	rɛtroˈæktɪv
retrocede	re troh SEED	rɛtroˈsid
retroflex	RE truh fleks	ˈrɛtrəflɛks
retrograde	RE truh grayd	ˈrɛtrəgred
retrogress	RE truh gres	ˈrɛtrəgrɛs
retropack	RE truh pak	ˈrɛtrəpæk
retrospect	RE truh spekt	ˈrɛtrəspɛkt
retroussé	re troo : SAY	rɛtruˈse
retroversion	re truh VER zhuhn	rɛtrəˈvɝʒən
Reuben	ROO : bin	ˈrubɪn

at [æ] ; ah [ɑ] ; air [ɛ] ; awful [ɔ] ; say [e] ; back [b] ; chair [tʃ] ; do [d] ; elm [ɛ] ; eel [i] ;
server [ˈɝ, ər] ; fit [f] ; go [g] ; hurt [h] ; is [ɪ] ; high [aɪ] ; jet [dʒ] ; kiss [k] ; lamb [l] ; my [m] ;
nice [n] ;

Reuters	ROI terz	ˈrɔɪtərz
Reuther	ROO : ther	ˈruθər
reveille	RE vuh li	ˈrɛvəlɪ
revel, R-	RE vuhl	ˈrɛvəl
revenant	RE vuh nuhnt	ˈrɛvənənt
revenue	RE vuh noo :	ˈrɛvənu
reverberatory	ri VER buh ruh taw ri	rɪˈvɝbərətɔrɪ
revere, R-	ri VIR	rɪˈvɪr
reverence	RE vuh ruhns	ˈrɛvərəns
reverend	RE vuh ruhnd	ˈrɛvərənd
reverent	RE vuh ruhnt	ˈrɛvərənt
reverential	re vuh REN shuhl	rɛvəˈrɛnʃəl
reverie	RE vuh ri	ˈrɛvərɪ
revers	ruh VIR	rəˈvɪr
reversion	ri VER zhuhn	rɪˈvɝʒən
revery	RE vuh ri	ˈrɛvərɪ
revetment	ri VET muhnt	rɪˈvɛtmənt
revisal	ri VIGH zuhl	rɪˈvaɪzəl
revision	ri VI zhuhn	rɪˈvɪʒən
revivify	ri VI vuh figh	rɪˈvɪvəfaɪ
reviviscence	re vuh VI suhns	rɛvəˈvɪsəns
revocable	RE vuh kuh buhl	ˈrɛvəkəbəl
revocation	re vuh KAY shuhn	rɛvəˈkeʃən
revolt	ri VOHLT	rɪˈvolt
revue	ri VYOO :	rɪˈvju
revulsion	ri VUHL shuhn	rɪˈvʌlʃən
rex, R-	reks	rɛks
Rexist	REK sist	ˈrɛksɪst
Rexroth	REKS rawth	ˈrɛksrɔθ
Reykjavik	RAY kyuh veek	ˈrekjəvik
Reymont	RAY mawnt	ˈremɔnt
Reynard	RE nerd	ˈrɛnərd
Reynaud	ray NOH	reˈno
Reynolds	RE nuhldz	ˈrɛnəldz
Rezekne	RAY zek ne	ˈrezɛknɛ
rhabdomancy	RAB duh man si	ˈræbdəmænsɪ
Rhadamanthine	ra duh MAN thin	rædəˈmænθɪn
Rhadamanthus	ra duh MAN thuhs	rædəˈmænθəs
Rhaetian	REE shuhn	ˈriʃən
Rhaetic	REE tik	ˈritɪk
Rhaeto-Romanic	REE toh roh MA nik	ˈrito roˈmænɪk
rhapsodic	rap SAH dik	ræpˈsɑdɪk
rhapsody	RAP suh di	ˈræpsədɪ
rhatany	RA tuh ni	ˈrætənɪ
Rhea	REE uh	ˈriə
Rhee	ree	ˈri
Rheims	reemz	rimz
Rhein	righn	raɪn
Rheingold	RIGHN gohld	ˈraɪngold
rhematic	ri MA tik	rɪˈmætɪk
Rhenish	RE nish	ˈrɛnɪʃ
rhenium	REE ni uhm	ˈrinɪəm

sing [ŋ] ; *oh* [o] ; *oil* [ɔɪ] ; *foot* [ʊ] ; *foo*:d [u] ; *how* [aʊ] ; *pie* [p] ; *ray* [r] ; *so* [s] ; *sh*all [ʃ] ;
to [t] ; *th*in [θ] ; *th*:en [ð] ; *above* (*uh BUH*V) [ə, ˈʌ] ; *v*ine [v] ; *w*ine [w] ; *wh*ine [hw] ;
*y*ou [j] ; *z*oo [z] ; rouge (roo:*zh*) [ʒ].

rheostat	REE uh stat	ˈriəstæt
rhesus, R-	REE suhs	ˈrisəs
rhetoric	RE tuh rik	ˈrɛtərɪk
rhetorical	ri TAW ri kuhl	rɪˈtɔrɪkəl
rhetorician	re tuh RI shuhn	rɛtəˈrɪʃən
rheum	roo : m	rum
rheumatic	roo : MA tik	ruˈmætɪk
rheumatism	ROO : muh ti zuhm	ˈrumətɪzəm
rheumy	ROO : mi	ˈrumɪ
rhigolene	RI guh leen	ˈrɪgəlin
rhinal	RIGH nuhl	ˈraɪnəl
Rhine	righn	raɪn
rhinencephalon	righ nen SE fuh lahn	raɪnɛnˈsɛfəlɑn
rhinestone	RIGHN stohn	ˈraɪnston
rhinitis	righ NIGH tis	raɪˈnaɪtɪs
rhinoceros	righ NAH suh ruhs	raɪˈnɑsərəs
rhinology	righ NAH luh ji	raɪˈnɑlədʒɪ
rhinoplasty	RIGH nuh pla sti	ˈraɪnəplæstɪ
rhizobium	righ ZOH bi uhm	raɪˈzobɪəm
rhizome	RIGH zohm	ˈraɪzom
rhizotomy	righ ZAH tuh mi	raɪˈzɑtəmɪ
rho	roh	ro
Rhoda	ROH duh	ˈrodə
Rhodes	rohdz	rodz
Rhodesia	roh DEE zhuh	roˈdiʒə
rhododendron	roh duh DEN druhn	rodəˈdɛndrən
rhodolite	ROH duh light	ˈrodəlaɪt
rhodonite	ROH duh night	ˈrodənaɪt
Rhodope, Rhodopi	RAH duh pi	ˈrɑdəpɪ
rhodopsin	roh DAHP sin	roˈdɑpsɪn
rhombencephalon	rahm ben SE fuh lahn	rɑmbɛnˈsɛfəlɑn
rhombic	RAHM bik	ˈrɑmbɪk
rhombus	RAHM buhs	ˈrɑmbəs
rhonchus	RAHNG kuhs	ˈrɑŋkəs
Rhone	rohn	ron
rhubarb	ROO : bahrb	ˈrubɑrb
rhumb	ruhm	rʌm
rhumba	RUHM buh	ˈrʌmbə
rhumbatron	RUHM buh trahn	ˈrʌmbətrɑn
rhyme	righm	raɪm
rhyolite	RIGH uh light	ˈraɪəlaɪt
Rhys	rees	ris
rhythm	RI th : uhm	ˈrɪðəm
rial	RIGH uhl	ˈraɪəl
Rialto	ri AL toh	rɪˈælto
riant	RIGH uhnt	ˈraɪənt
riata	ri AH tuh	rɪˈɑtə
ribald	RI buhld	ˈrɪbəld
ribaldry	RI buhl dri	ˈrɪbəldrɪ
Ribbentrop	RI buhn trawp	ˈrɪbəntrɔp
Ribera	ree BE rah	riˈbɛrɑ
Ribicoff	RI buh kawf	ˈrɪbəkɔf

at [æ]; ah [ɑ]; air [ɛ]; awful [ɔ]; say [e]; back [b]; chair [tʃ]; do [d]; elm [ɛ]; eel [i];
server [ˈɜ, ər]; fit [f]; go [g]; hurt [h]; is [ɪ]; high [aɪ]; jet [dʒ]; kiss [k]; lamb [l]; my [m];
nice [n];

riboflavin	righ buh FLAY vin	ˈraɪbəˈflevɪn
Ricardo	ri KAHR doh	rɪˈkɑrdo
Ricci, Nina	REE chee, NEE nah	ˈritʃi, ˈninɑ
riccia	RIK si uh	ˈrɪksɪə
Riccio	RI chi oh	ˈrɪtʃɪo
Richelieu	ri shuh LOO:	rɪʃəˈlu
Richter	RIK ter	ˈrɪktər
ricin	RIGH sin	ˈraɪsɪn
Rickenbacker	RI kuhn ba ker	ˈrɪkənbækər
rickets	RI kits	ˈrɪkɪts
rickettsia	ri KET si uh	rɪˈkɛtsɪə
rickettsial	ri KET si uhl	rɪˈkɛtsɪəl
rickety	RI ki ti	ˈrɪkɪtɪ
rickey	RI ki	ˈrɪkɪ
ricksha, -w	RIK shaw	ˈrɪkʃɔ
ricochet	ri kuh SHAY	rɪkəˈʃe
riddance	RI duhns	ˈrɪdəns
Riegger	REE ger	ˈrigər
Rienzi	ri EN zi	rɪˈɛnz
Rif, -f, r-	rif	rɪf
Riga	REE guh	ˈrigə
rigadoon	ri guh DOO:N	rɪgəˈdun
Rigel	RIGH guhl	ˈraɪgəl
righteous	RIGH chuhs	ˈraɪtʃəs
Rigi	REE gee	ˈrigi
rigmarole	RIG muh rohl	ˈrɪgmərol
Rigoletto	ri guh LE toh	rɪgəˈlɛto
rigor	RI ger	ˈrɪgər
rigorous	RI guh ruhs	ˈrɪgərəs
Rig-Veda	rig VAY duh	rɪgˈvedə
Riis	rees	ris
rilievo	ree LYE vaw	riˈljɛvo
Rilke	RIL kuh	ˈrɪlkə
rill, -e	ril	rɪl
Rimbaud	ran BOH	rænˈbo
Rimini	RI muh ni	ˈrɪmənɪ
Rimmon	RI muhn	ˈrɪmən
Rimski-Korsakov	RIM ski KAWR suh kawf	ˈrɪmskɪ ˈkɔrsəkɔf
Rinaldo	ri NAL doh	rɪˈnældo
rind	righnd	raɪnd
rinderpest	RIN der pest	ˈrɪndərpɛst
rinse	rins	rɪns
Rio, Río, r-	REE oh	ˈrio
Rio Bravo	REE aw BRAH vaw	ˈriɔ ˈbrɑvɔ
Rio de Janeiro	REE oh duh zhuh NAY roh	ˈrio də ʒəˈnero
Rio de Oro	REE aw de AW raw	ˈriɔ dɛ ˈɔrɔ
Rio Grande (Brazil)	REE oo GRAHN di	ˈriu ˈgrɑndɪ
Rio Grande (U.S.)	REE oh GRAND	ˈrio ˈgrænd
Rio Muni	REE aw MOO:nee	ˈriɔ ˈmuni
riotous	RIGH uh tuhs	ˈraɪətəs
riparian	ri PAI ri uhn	rɪˈpɛrɪən
Ripon	RI puhn	ˈrɪpən

sing [ŋ]; *oh* [o]; *oil* [ɔɪ]; *foot* [ʊ]; *foo:*d [u]; *how* [aʊ]; *pie* [p]; *ray* [r]; *so* [s]; *shall* [ʃ];
to [t]; *thin* [θ]; *th:*en [ð]; above (*uh* BUHV) [ə, ˈʌ]; *vine* [v]; *wine* [w]; *whine* [hw];
you [j]; *zoo* [z]; *rouge* (roo:*zh*) [ʒ].

ripost, -e	ri POHST	rɪˈpost
rise	righz	raɪz
risibility	ri zuh BI luh ti	rɪzəˈbɪlətɪ
risible	RI zuh buhl	ˈrɪzəbəl
Risorgimento	ree sawr jee MEN taw	risɔrdʒiˈmɛntɔ
risotto	ree SAW taw	riˈsɔtɔ
risqué	ri SKAY	rɪˈske
rissole	RI sohl	ˈrɪsol
ritardando	ree tahr DAHN doh	ritɑrˈdɑndo
ritual	RI choo uhl	ˈrɪtʃʊəl
ritzy	RIT si	ˈrɪtsɪ
Rivas	REE vahs	ˈrivɑs
rive	righv	raɪv
riven	RI vuhn	ˈrɪvən
Rivera	ree VE rah	riˈvɛrɑ
rivet	RI vit	ˈrɪvɪt
Riviera	ri vi AI ruh	rɪviˈɛrə
rivière	ree VYAIR	riˈvjɛr
rivulet	RI vyuh lit	ˈrɪvjəlɪt
Riyadh	ree YAHD	riˈjɑd
Rizal	ree SAHL	riˈsɑl
Rizzio	RIT si oh	ˈrɪtsio
Roa	ROO : ah	ˈruɑ
Roanoke	ROH uh nohk	ˈroənok
rob	rahb	rɑb
Robbia	RAW byah	ˈrɔbjɑ
Robeson	ROHB suhn	ˈrobsən
Robespierre	ROHBZ pyair	ˈrobzpjɛr
robomb	ROH bahm	ˈrobɑm
roborant	RAH buh ruhnt	ˈrɑbərənt
robot	ROH buht	ˈrobət
roburite	ROH buh right	ˈrobəraɪt
robust	roh BUHST	roˈbʌst
robustious	roh BUHS chuhs	roˈbʌstʃəs
roc	rahk	rɑk
rocambole	RAH kuhm bohl	ˈrɑkəmbol
Rocha	RAW chah	ˈrɔtʃɑ
Rochambeau	raw shahn BOH	rɔʃɑnˈbo
Rochdale	RAHCH dayl	ˈrɑtʃdel
Rochefoucauld, La	rawsh foo KOH, la	rɔʃfuˈko, læ
Rochelle	roh SHEL	roˈʃɛl
Rockefeller	RAH kuh fe ler	ˈrɑkəfɛlər
Rockne, Knute	RAHK ni, NOO : T	ˈrɑknɪ, ˈnut
rococo	ruh KOH koh	rəˈkoko
rodent	ROH duhnt	ˈrodənt
rodeo	ROH di oh	ˈrodɪo
rodeo (southwestern U.S.)	roh DAY oh	roˈdeo
Rodin	roh DAN	roˈdæn
rodomontade	rah duh mahn TAYD	rɑdəmɑnˈted
Rodzinski, Artur	roh DZIN skee, AHR too : r	roˈdzɪnski, ˈɑrtur
roentgen, R-	RENT guhn	ˈrɛntgən

at [æ] ; ah [ɑ] ; air [ɛ] ; awful [ɔ] ; say [e] ; back [b] ; chair [tʃ] ; do [d] ; elm [ɛ] ; eel [i] ; server [ˈɝ, ər] ; fit [f] ; go [g] ; hurt [h] ; is [ɪ] ; high [aɪ] ; jet [dʒ] ; kiss [k] ; lamb [l] ; my [m] ; nice [n] ;

Roethke (Theodore)	RET kee	ˈrɛtki
rogation	roh GAY shuhn	roˈgeʃən
rogatory	RAH guh taw ri	ˈrɑgətɔrɪ
rogue	rohg	rog
roguery	ROH guh ri	ˈrogərɪ
roguish	ROH gish	ˈrogɪʃ
roil	roil	rɔɪl
roily	ROI li	ˈrɔɪlɪ
roister	ROI ster	ˈrɔɪstər
Rojas	ROH hahs	ˈrohɑs
Rok	rahk	rɑk
role, rôle	rohl	rol
roll	rohl	rol
Rolland, Romain	raw LAHN, raw MAN	rɔˈlɑn, rɔˈmæn
Rollo	RAH loh	ˈrɑlo
Rolvaag	ROHL vahg	ˈrolvɑg
roly-poly	ROH li POH li	ˈrolɪ ˈpolɪ
Romaic	roh MAY ik	roˈmeɪk
romaine	roh MAYN	roˈmen
Romains	raw MAN	rɔˈmæn
roman	raw MAHN	rɔˈmɑn
roman à clef	raw MAHN a KLAY	rɔˈmɑn æ ˈkle
romance, R-	roh MANS	roˈmæns
Romanesque	roh muh NESK	roməˈnɛsk
roman-fleuve	raw MAHN FLERV	rɔˈmɑn ˈflɝv
Romania	roh MAY ni uh	roˈmenɪə
Romanic	roh MA nik	roˈmænɪk
Romanism	ROH muh ni zuhm	ˈromənɪzəm
Romanov, Romanoff	ROH muh nawf	ˈromənɔf
Romansh, Romansch	roh MANSH	roˈmænʃ
romantic	roh MAN tik	roˈmæntɪk
Romany	RAH muh ni	ˈrɑmənɪ
Rome	rohm	rom
Romeo	ROH mi oh	ˈromɪo
Rommany	RAH muh ni	ˈrɑmənɪ
Rommel	RAW muhl	ˈrɔməl
Romney	RUHM ni	ˈrʌmnɪ
Romola	RAH muh luh	ˈrɑmələ
Romulo	RAW moo loh	ˈrɔmulo
Romulus	RAH myuh luhs	ˈrɑmjələs
Roncesvalles	RAHN suh valz	ˈrɑnsəvælz
rondeau	RAHN doh	ˈrɑndo
rondel	RAHN duhl	ˈrɑndəl
Rondelet	RAHN duh let	ˈrɑndəlɛt
rondo	RAHN doh	ˈrɑndo
Ronsard	rohn SAHR	ronˈsɑr
Röntgen, r-	RENT guhn	ˈrɛntgən
rood, R-	roo : d	rud
rook	rook	rʊk
rookery	ROO kuh ri	ˈrʊkərɪ
rookie	ROO ki	ˈrʊkɪ
roorback, roorbach	ROOR bak	ˈrʊrbæk

sing [ŋ] ; *oh* [o] ; *oil* [ɔɪ] ; *foot* [ʊ] ; *foo:d* [u] ; *how* [aʊ] ; *pie* [p] ; *ray* [r] ; *so* [s] ; *shall* [ʃ] ;
to [t] ; *thin* [θ] ; *th:en* [ð] ; *above* (*uh* BUHV) [ə, ˈʌ] ; *vine* [v] ; *wine* [w] ; *whine* [hw] ;
you [j] ; *zoo* [z] ; *rouge* (roo:*zh*) [ʒ].

Roosevelt	ROH zuh velt	ˈrozəvɛlt
roost	roo : st	rust
roque	rohk	rok
Roquefort	ROHK fert	ˈrokfərt
roquet	roh KAY	roˈke
rorqual	RAWR kwuhl	ˈrɔrkwəl
Rorschach	RAWR shahk	ˈrɔrʃak
rosaceous	roh ZAY shuhs	roˈzeʃəs
rosary	ROH zuh ri	ˈrozərɪ
roseate	ROH zi it	ˈrozɪɪt
roseola	roh ZEE uh luh	roˈziələ
Rosetta	roh ZE tuh	roˈzɛtə
rosette	roh ZET	roˈzɛt
Rosh Hashana	ROHSH hah SHAH nuh	ˈroʃ haˈʃanə
Rosicrucian	roh zuh KROO : shuhn	rozəˈkruʃən
rosin	RAH zuhn	ˈrazən
Rosinante	rah zuh NAN ti	razəˈnæntɪ
rosolio	roh ZAW lyoh	roˈzɔljo
Rossellini, Roberto	roh se LEE ni, roh BAIR toh	roseˈlini, roˈbeərto
Rossetti	roh SE ti	roˈsetɪ
Rossi-Lemeni	ROH see lay MAY nee	ˈrosi leˈmeni
Rossini	roh SEE ni	roˈsinɪ
Rostand	RAH stand	ˈrastænd
roster	RAH ster	ˈrastər
Rostock	RAH stahk	ˈrastak
Rostov	RAH stahv	ˈrastav
rostrum	RAH struhm	ˈrastrəm
rota, R-	ROH tuh	ˈrotə
Rotarian	roh TAI ri uhn	roˈtɛrɪən
rotary, R-	ROH tuh ri	ˈrotərɪ
rotative	ROH tuh tiv	ˈrotətɪv
rotatory	ROH tuh taw ri	ˈrotətɔrɪ
rotch, -e	rahch	ratʃ
rote	roht	rot
rotenone	ROH tuh nohn	ˈrotənon
Rothschild	RAWTH chighld	ˈrɔθtʃaɪld
rotifer	ROH ti fer	ˈrotɪfər
rotiform	ROH tuh fawrm	ˈrotəfɔrm
rotisserie	roh TI suh ri	roˈtɪsərɪ
rotl	RAH tuhl	ˈratəl
rotogravure	ROH tuh gruh VYOOR	ˈrotəgrəˈvjur
rotor	ROH ter	ˈrotər
Rotterdam	RAH ter dam	ˈratərdæm
rotund	roh TUHND	roˈtʌnd
rotunda	roh TUHN duh	roˈtʌndə
Rouault	roo : OH	ruˈo
Roubaix	roo : BE	ruˈbɛ
rouche	roo : sh	ruʃ
roué	roo : AY	ruˈe
Rouen	roo : AHN	ruˈan
rouge	roo : zh	ruʒ
Rougemont	ROO : ZH mahnt	ˈruʒmant

at [æ]; *ah* [ɑ]; *air* [ɛ]; *awful* [ɔ]; *say* [e]; *back* [b]; *chair* [tʃ]; *do* [d]; *elm* [ɛ]; *eel* [i];
server [ˈ�, ər]; *f*it [f]; *go* [g]; *hurt* [h]; *is* [ɪ]; *high* [aɪ]; *jet* [dʒ]; *kiss* [k]; *lamb* [l]; *my* [m];
nice [n];

Rouget de Lisle	roo : ZHAY duh LEEL	ruˈʒe də ˈlil
roulade	roo : LAHD	ruˈlɑd
rouleau	roo : LOH	ruˈlo
roulette	roo : LET	ruˈlɛt
Roumania	roo : MAY ni uh	ruˈmenɪə
roundel	ROWN duhl	ˈraʊndəl
roundelay	ROWN duh lay	ˈraʊndəle
roup	roo : p	rup
Rousseau	roo : SOH	ruˈso
route	roo : t	rut
route (military)	rowt	raʊt
routine	roo : TEEN	ruˈtin
roux	roo :	ru
Rovigno	raw VEE nyaw	rɔˈvinjɔ
Rovno	RAWV naw	ˈrɔvnɔ
rowdy	ROW di	ˈraʊdɪ
rowel	ROW uhl	ˈraʊəl
rowen	ROW uhn	ˈraʊən
Rowena	roh EE nuh	roˈinə
Rowne	ROOV ne	ˈruvnɛ
Roxana	rahk SA nuh	rɑkˈsænə
Roxas	RAW hahs	ˈrɔhɑs
Ruanda-Urundi	roo : AHN dah oo ROON di	ruˈɑndɑ ʊˈrʊndɪ
Rubaiyat	ROO : bigh yaht	ˈrubaɪjɑt
Rub' al Khali	ROOB ahl KAH lee	ˈrʊb ɑl ˈkɑli
rubato	roo : BAH toh	ruˈbɑto
rubble	RUH buhl	ˈrʌbəl
rubefacient	roo : buh FAY shuhnt	rubəˈfeʃənt
rubella	roo BE luh	rʊˈbɛlə
Rubens	ROO : buhnz	ˈrubənz
rubeola	roo BEE uh luh	rʊˈbiələ
rubescent	roo BE suhnt	rʊˈbɛsənt
Rubicon	ROO : bi kahn	ˈrubɪkɑn
rubicund	ROO : bi kuhnd	ˈrubɪkənd
rubidium	roo BI di uhm	rʊˈbɪdɪəm
rubiginous	roo BI juh nuhs	rʊˈbɪdʒənəs
Rubinstein	ROO : bin stighn	ˈrubɪnstaɪn
Rubirosa, Porfirio	roo : buh ROH suh, pawr FEE ree oh	rubəˈrosə, pɔrˈfirio
ruble	ROO : buhl	ˈrubəl
rubric	ROO : brik	ˈrubrɪk
ruche	roo : sh	ruʃ
rucksack	RUHK sak	ˈrʌksæk
ruction	RUHK shuhn	ˈrʌkʃən
rudiment	ROO : duh muhnt	ˈrudəmənt
rudimentary	roo : duh MEN tuh ri	rudəˈmɛntərɪ
rue	roo :	ru
rueful	ROO : fuhl	ˈrufəl
ruffian	RUH fi uhn	ˈrʌfɪən
rufous	ROO : fuhs	ˈrufəs
Rugby	RUHG bi	ˈrʌgbɪ
Ruhr	roor	rʊr

si*ng* [ŋ] ; *oh* [o] ; *oi*l [ɔɪ] ; *foo*t [ʊ] ; *foo*:d [u] ; h*ow* [aʊ] ; *p*ie [p] ; *r*ay [r] ; *s*o [s] ; *sh*all [ʃ] ;
*t*o [t] ; *th*in [θ] ; *th*:en [ð] ; *a*bove (*uh* B*U*HV) [ə, ˈʌ] ; *v*ine [v] ; *w*ine [w] ; *wh*ine [hw] ;
*y*ou [j] ; *z*oo [z] ; *r*ouge (roo:*zh*) [ʒ].

ruin	ROO : in	ˈruɪn
ruinate	ROO : uh nayt	ˈruənet
ruinous	ROO : i nuhs	ˈruɪnəs
Ruis	roo EES	ruˈis
Ruisdael	ROIS dahl	ˈrɔɪsdɑl
Rukeyser	ROO kigh zer	ˈrʊkaɪzər
Rumania	roo : MAY ni uh	ruˈmenɪə
rumba	RUHM buh	ˈrʌmbə
ruminate	ROO : muh nayt	ˈrumənet
Ruml	RUH muhl	ˈrʌməl
rummage	RUH mij	ˈrʌmɪdʒ
rummy	RUH mi	ˈrʌmɪ
Rumpelstiltskin	ruhm puhl STILT skin	rʌmpəlˈstɪltskɪn
runcible	RUHN suh buhl	ˈrʌnsəbəl
runcinate	RUHN si nit	ˈrʌnsɪnɪt
rundle	RUHN duhl	ˈrʌndəl
rune	roo : n	run
runic	ROO : nik	ˈrunɪk
runnel	RUH nuhl	ˈrʌnəl
Runnymede	RUH ni meed	ˈrʌnɪmid
rupee	roo : PEE	ruˈpi
rupiah	roo : PEE uh	ruˈpiə
rupture	RUHP cher	ˈrʌptʃər
rural	ROO ruhl	ˈrʊrəl
rurban	RER buhn	ˈrɝbən
Rurik	ROO rik	ˈrʊrɪk
ruse	roo : z	ruz
rus in urbe	RUHS in ER bi	ˈrʌs ɪn ˈɝbɪ
rusk, R-	ruhsk	rʌsk
Ruskin	RUH skin	ˈrʌskɪn
russe	roos	rʊs
russet	RUH sit	ˈrʌsɪt
Russia	RUH shuh	ˈrʌʃə
Russian	RUH shuhn	ˈrʌʃən
Russophile	RUH soh fighl	ˈrʌsofaɪl
Russophobe	RUH soh fohb	ˈrʌsofob
rustic	RUH stik	ˈrʌstɪk
rusticity	ruh STI suh ti	rʌˈstɪsətɪ
rustle	RUH suhl	ˈrʌsəl
rut	ruht	rʌt
rutabaga	roo : tuh BAY guh	rutəˈbegə
rutaceous	roo : TAY shuhs	ruˈteʃəs
ruth, R-	roo : th	ruθ
Ruthenia	roo : THEE ni uh	ruˈθinɪə
ruthenium	roo : THEE ni uhm	ruˈθinɪəm
Rutherford, Rutherfurd	RUH th : er ferd	ˈrʌðərfərd
ruthless	ROO : TH lis	ˈruθlɪs
Rutland	RUHT luhnd	ˈrʌtlənd
Rutledge	RUHT lij	ˈrʌtlɪdʒ
Ruwenzori	roo : wen ZOH ri	ruwɛnˈzorɪ
Ruysdael	ROIS dahl	ˈrɔɪsdɑl
Ruyter	ROI ter	ˈrɔɪtər

at [æ] ; *ah* [ɑ] ; *air* [ɛ] ; *aw*ful [ɔ] ; *say* [e] ; *b*ack [b] ; *ch*air [tʃ] ; *do* [d] ; *e*lm [ɛ] ; *ee*l [i] ; *ser*ver [ˈɝ, ər] ; *f*it [f] ; *g*o [g] ; *h*urt [h] ; *is* [ɪ] ; *high* [aɪ] ; *j*et [dʒ] ; *k*iss [k] ; *l*amb [l] ; *m*y [m] ; *n*ice [n] ;

Rwanda	roo : AHN duh	ru'ɑndə
ryania	righ AY ni uh	raɪ'enɪə
Ryazan	ryah ZAHN	rjɑ'zɑn
Ryder	RIGH der	'raɪdər
ryot	RIGH uht	'raɪət
Ryswick	RIZ wik	'rɪzwɪk
Ryti, Risto	RI tee, RI staw	'rɪti, 'rɪstɔ
Ryukyu	ryoo : kyoo :	rjukju
Rzeszow	ZHE shoof	'ʒɛʃuf

S

Saar	sahr	sɑr
Saarbrucken	SAHR broo kuhn	'sɑrbrʊkən
Saarinen	SAH ree nen	'sɑrinɛn
Saba	SAY buh	'sebə
Sabac	SHAH bahts	'ʃɑbɑts
Sabaean	suh BEE uhn	sə'biən
Sabaism, s-	SAY bi i zuhm	'sebɪɪzəm
Sabaoth	SA bi ahth	'sæbɪɑθ
Sabatini	sa buh TEE ni	sæbə'tini
Sabbatical, s-	suh BA ti kuhl	sə'bætɪkəl
Sabean	suh BEE uhn	sə'biən
Sabena	suh BEE nuh	sə'binə
saber	SAY ber	'sebər
Sabin	SAY bin	'sebɪn
Sabine (Italy)	SAY bighn	'sebaɪn
Sabine (Texas)	suh BEEN	sə'bin
sabot	SA boh	'sæbo
sabotage	SA buh tahzh	'sæbətɑʒ
saboteur	sa buh TER	sæbə'tɚ
sabra, S-	SAH bruh	'sɑbrə
sabre	SAY ber	'sebər
sabretache	SAY ber tash	'sebərtæʃ
sabulous	SA byuh luhs	'sæbjələs
sac, S-	sak	sæk
saccharic	suh KA rik	sə'kærɪk
saccharin, -e	SA kuh rin	'sækərɪn
Sacco	SA koh	'sæko
sacerdotal	sa ser DOH tuhl	sæsər'dotəl
sachem	SAY chuhm	'setʃəm
sachet	sa SHAY	sæ'ʃe
Sacheverell	suh SHE vuh ruhl	sə'ʃevərəl
Sachs (German)	zahks	zɑks
Sachs (U.S.)	saks	sæks
sacral	SAY kruhl	'sekrəl
sacrament	SA kruh muhnt	'sækrəmənt
sacramental	sa kruh MEN tuhl	sækrə'mɛntəl

sing [ŋ] ; oh [o] ; oil [ɔɪ] ; foot [ʊ] ; foo:d [u] ; how [aʊ] ; pie [p] ; ray [r] ; so [s] ; shall [ʃ] ;
to [t] ; thin [θ] ; th:en [ð] ; above (uh BUHV) [ə, 'ʌ] ; vine [v] ; wine [w] ; whine [hw] ;
you [j] ; zoo [z] ; rouge (roo:zh) [ʒ].

Sacramento	sa kruh MEN toh	sækrə'mɛnto
sacrarium	suh KRAI ri uhm	sə'krɛrɪəm
sacrifice	SA kruh fighs	'sækrəfaɪs
sacrificial	sa kruh FI shuhl	sækrə'fɪʃəl
sacrilege	SA kruh lij	'sækrəlɪdʒ
sacrilegious	sa kri LEE juhs	sækrɪ'lidʒəs
sacristan	SA kri stuhn	'sækrɪstən
sacristy	SA kri sti	'sækrɪstɪ
sacroiliac	say kroh I li ak	sekro'ɪlɪæk
sacrosanct	SA kroh sangkt	'sækrosæŋkt
sacrum	SAY kruhm	'sekrəm
Sadducean	sa juh SEE uhn	sædʒə'siən
Sadducee	SA juh see	'sædʒəsi
sadism	SAY di zuhm	'sedɪzəm
sadist	SAY dist	'sedɪst
sadistic	suh DI stik	sə'dɪstɪk
Sadowa	SAH daw vah	'sadɔvɑ
safari	suh FAH ri	sə'fɑrɪ
saffron	SA fruhn	'sæfrən
Safid Rud	sa FEED ROOD	sæ'fid 'rud
saga	SAH guh	'sɑgə
sagacious	suh GAY shuhs	sə'geʃəs
sagacity	suh GA suh ti	sə'gæsətɪ
sagamore	SA guh mawr	'sægəmɔr
Sagan, Françoise	sa GAHN, frahn SWAHZ	sæ'gɑn, frɑn'swɑz
Saghalien	SAH gah lyen	'sɑgɑljɛn
Saginaw	SA guh naw	'sægənɔ
Sagitta	suh JI tuh	sə'dʒɪtə
sagittal	SA ji tuhl	'sædʒɪtəl
Sagittarius	sa ji TAI ri uhs	sædʒɪ'tɛrɪəs
sago, S-	SAY goh	'sego
sagrada	suh GRAY duh	sə'gredə
Saguenay	sa guh NAY	sægə'ne
Sahara	suh HAI ruh	sə'hɛrə
sahib, S-	SAH ib	'sɑɪb
said	sed	sɛd
Saida	SAH ee dah	'saɪdɑ
Saigon	sigh GAHN	saɪ'gɑn
St. Albans	saynt AWL buhnz	sent 'ɔlbənz
Saint Bernard	SAYNT ber NAHRD	'sent bər'nɑrd
St. Bernard (pass)	saynt ber NAHRD	sent bər'nɑrd
St.-Cloud (France)	san KLOO:	sæn 'klu
St. Croix	saynt KROI	sent 'krɔɪ
St. Denis	san duh NEE	san də'ni
Ste. Anne de Beaupré	saynt AN duh boh PRAY	sent 'æn də bo'pre
Sainte-Beuve	sant BERV	sænt 'bɜ·v
St.-Étienne	san tay TYEN	sænte'tjɛn
Saint-Exupéry	san teg zoo pay REE	sæntɛgzupe'ri
Saint-Gaudens	saynt GAW duhnz	sent'gɔdənz
St.-Germain	san zher MAN	sænʒɔr'mæn
St. Gotthard	saynt GAH terd	sent 'gɑtərd
St. Helena	saynt he LEE nuh	sent he'linə

at [æ] ; ah [ɑ] ; air [ɛ] ; awful [ɔ] ; say [e] ; back [b] ; chair [tʃ] ; do [d] ; elm [ɛ] ; eel [i] ; server ['ɜ·, ər] ; fit [f] ; go [g] ; hurt [h] ; is [ɪ] ; high [aɪ] ; jet [dʒ] ; kiss [k] ; lamb [l] ; my [m] ; nice [n] ;

St. Helier	saynt HE lyer	sent ˈhɛljər
St. Laurent	san loh RAHN	sænloˈrɑn
St.-Lô	san LOH	sænˈlo
St. Louis	saynt LOO : is	sent ˈluɪs
St.-Malo	san mah LOH	sæn mɑˈlo
St.-Mihiel	san mee YEL	sæn miˈjɛl
St.-Moritz	saynt MOH rits	sent ˈmorɪts
St.-Nazaire	san nah ZAIR	sæn nɑˈzɛr
St.-Ouen	san TWAHN	sænˈtwɑn
St.-Pierre	san PYAIR	sænˈpjɛr
Saint-Saëns	san SAHN	sænˈsɑn
St. Tropez	sahn troh PAY	ˈsɑn troˈpe
Saintsbury	SAYNTS buh ri	ˈsentsbərɪ
Saint-Simon	san see MOHN	sænsiˈmon
Saipan	sigh PAHN	saɪˈpɑn
saith	seth	sɛθ
sake (" drink ")	SAH ki	ˈsɑkɪ
Sakhalin	SA kuh leen	ˈsækəlin
Saki	SAH ki	ˈsɑkɪ
salaam	suh LAHM	səˈlɑm
salacious	suh LAY shuhs	səˈleʃəs
salacity	suh LA suh ti	səˈlæsətɪ
Saladin	SA luh din	ˈsælədɪn
Salado	sah LAH doh	sɑˈlado
Salamanca	sah luh MAHNG kuh	sɑləˈmɑŋkə
salamander	SA luh man der	ˈsæləmændər
Salambria	suh LAM bri uh	səˈlæmbrɪə
salami	suh LAH mi	səˈlɑmɪ
Salamis	SA luh mis	ˈsæləmɪs
salary	SA luh ri	ˈsælərɪ
Salazar	sah lah ZAHR	sɑlɑˈzɑr
Salem	SAY luhm	ˈseləm
saleratus	sa luh RAY tuhs	sæləˈretəs
Salerno	suh LER noh	səˈlɝno
Salic	SA lik	ˈsælɪk
salicylate	SA luh si layt	ˈsæləsɪlet
salience	SAY li uhns	ˈselɪəns
salient	SAY li uhnt	ˈselɪənt
Salina, s-	suh LIGH nuh	səˈlaɪnə
saline	SAY lighn	ˈselaɪn
Salisbury	SAWLZ be ri	ˈsɔlzbɛrɪ
Salishan	SAY li shuhn	ˈselɪʃən
saliva	suh LIGH vuh	səˈlaɪvə
salivary	SA luh ve ri	ˈsæləvɛrɪ
salivate	SA luh vayt	ˈsæləvet
Salk	sawlk	sɔlk
salle à manger	sal a mahn ZHAY	sæl æ mɑnˈʒe
Sallust	SA luhst	ˈsæləst
Sally Lunn	SA li LUHN	ˈsælɪ ˈlʌn
salmagundi	sal muh GUHN di	sælməˈgʌndɪ
salmi, -s	SAL mi	ˈsælmɪ
salmon, S-	SA muhn	ˈsæmən

sing [ŋ] ; oh [o] ; oil [ɔɪ] ; foot [ʊ] ; foo:d [u] ; how [aʊ] ; pie [p] ; ray [r] ; so [s] ; shall [ʃ] ;
to [t] ; thin [θ] ; th:en [ð] ; above (uh BUHV) [ə, ˈʌ] ; vine [v] ; wine [w] ; whine [hw] ;
you [j] ; zoo [z] ; rouge (roo:zh) [ʒ].

salol	SA lohl	ˈsælol
Salome	suh LOH mi	səˈlomɪ
Salomé	sa law MAY	sælɔˈme
salon	suh LAHN	səˈlɑn
Salonika	sa luh NEE kuh	sæləˈnikə
salsify	SAL suh figh	ˈsælsəfaɪ
saltarello	sal tuh RE loh	sæltəˈrɛlo
Saltillo	sahl TEE yaw	sɑlˈtijɔ
Salton	SAWL tuhn	ˈsɔltən
salubrious	suh LOO : bri uhs	səˈlubrɪəs
salubrity	suh LOO : bruh ti	səˈlubrətɪ
Saluki	suh LOO : ki	səˈlukɪ
Salus	SAY luhs	ˈseləs
salutary	SA lyuh tai ri	ˈsæljətɛrɪ
salutation	sa lyuh TAY shuhn	sæljəˈteʃən
salutatorian	suh loo : tuh TAW ri uhn	səlutəˈtɔrɪən
salute	suh LOO : T	səˈlut
Salvador, El	SAL vuh dawr, el	ˈsælvədɔr, ɛl
Salvadori	sahl vah DAW ree	sɑlvɑˈdɔri
salvage	SAL vij	ˈsælvɪdʒ
salve (" hail ")	SAL vi	ˈsælvɪ
salve (" ointment ")	sav	sæv
salve (" salvage ")	salv	sælv
salver	SAL ver	ˈsælvər
salvia	SAL vi uh	ˈsælvɪə
salvo	SAL voh	ˈsælvo
Salween	SAL ween	ˈsælwin
Salzburg	SAWLZ berg	ˈsɔlzbərg
Samar	SAH mahr	ˈsɑmɑr
Samaria	suh MAI ri uh	səˈmɛrɪə
Samaritan	suh MA ruh tuhn	səˈmærətən
samarium	suh MAI ri uhm	səˈmɛrɪəm
Samarkand	sa mer KAND	sæmərˈkænd
samarskite	suh MAHR skight	səˈmɑrskaɪt
samba	SAM buh	ˈsæmbə
samiel	SAM yel	ˈsæmjɛl
samisen	SA mi sen	ˈsæmɪsɛn
samite	SA might	ˈsæmaɪt
Samoa	suh MOH uh	səˈmoə
Samos	SAY mahs	ˈsemɑs
Samothrace	SA muh thrays	ˈsæməθres
samovar	SA muh vahr	ˈsæməvɑr
Samoyed, -e	sa muh YED	sæməˈjɛd
sampan	SAM pan	ˈsæmpæn
Sampang	SAHM pahng	ˈsɑmpɑŋ
samphire	SAM fighr	ˈsæmfaɪr
sample	SAM puhl	ˈsæmpəl
Samsun	sahm SOON	sɑmˈsun
samurai	SA moo righ	ˈsæmʊraɪ
Sanaa, San'a	sah NAH	sɑˈnɑ
San Agustín	sahn ah goo STEEN	sɑn ɑguˈstin
San Andrés	sahn ahn DRES	sɑn ɑnˈdres

at [æ] ; ah [ɑ] ; air [ɛ] ; awful [ɔ] ; say [e] ; back [b] ; chair [tʃ] ; do [d] ; elm [ɛ] ; eel [i] ; server [ˈɝ, ər] ; fit [f] ; go [g] ; hurt [h] ; is [ɪ] ; high [aɪ] ; jet [dʒ] ; kiss [k] ; lamb [l] ; my [m] ; nice [n] ;

San Angelo	san AN juh loh	sæn ˈændʒəlo
San Antonio	san uhn TOH ni oh	sæn ənˈtonɪo
sanatorium	sa nuh TAW ri uhm	sænəˈtɔrɪəm
sanatory	SA nuh taw ri	ˈsænətɔrɪ
sanbenito	san buh NEE toh	sænbəˈnito
San Benito	san buh NEE toh	sæn bəˈnito
San Bernardino	san ber ner DEE noh	sæn bərnərˈdino
Sancho Panza	SAHN choh PAHN zuh	ˈsɑntʃo ˈpɑnzə
San Cristóbal	san kri STOH buhl	sæn krɪˈstobəl
sanctify	SANGK tuh figh	ˈsæŋktəfaɪ
sanctimonious	sangk tuh MOH ni uhs	sæŋktəˈmonɪəs
sanctimony	SANGK tuh moh ni	ˈsæŋktəmonɪ
sanctuary	SANGK choo ai ri	ˈsæŋktʃuɛrɪ
sanctum	SANGK tuhm	ˈsæŋktəm
sanctum sanctorum	SANGK tuhm sangk TAW ruhm	ˈsæŋktəm sæŋkˈtɔrəm
Sanctus	SANGK tuhs	ˈsæŋktəs
Sandakan	san DAH kuhn	sænˈdɑkən
sandarac	SAN duh rak	ˈsændəræk
Sandburg	SAND berg	ˈsændbərg
Sandefjord	SAH nuh fyohr	ˈsɑnəfjor
sandhi	SAN di	ˈsændɪ
Sandhurst	SAND herst	ˈsændhərst
San Diego	san di AY goh	sæn dɪˈego
Sandoz	SAN dohz	ˈsændoz
Sandusky	san DUH ski	sænˈdʌskɪ
sandwich, S-	SAND wich	ˈsændwɪtʃ
San Fernando	san fer NAN doh	sæn fərˈnændo
Sanforize, s-	SAN fuh righz	ˈsænfəraɪz
San Francisco	san fruhn SI skoh	sæn frɔnˈsɪsko
sangaree	sang guh REE	sæŋgəˈri
Sanger	SANG ger	ˈsæŋgər
sang-froid	sahn FRWAH	sɑnˈfrwɑ
Sangre de Cristo	SAHNG gre de KREE staw	ˈsɑŋgrɛ dɛ ˈkristɔ
sanguinary	SANG gwi nai ri	ˈsæŋgwɪnɛrɪ
sanguine	SANG gwin	ˈsæŋgwɪn
sanguineous	sang GWI ni uhs	sæŋˈgwɪnɪəs
Sanhedrim	SAN hi drim	ˈsænhɪdrɪm
Sanhedrin	SAN hi drin	ˈsænhɪdrɪn
sanitarium	sa nuh TAI ri uhm	sænəˈtɛrɪəm
sanitary	SA nuh tai ri	ˈsænətɛrɪ
sanitation	sa nuh TAY shuhn	sænəˈteʃən
sanity	SA nuh ti	ˈsænətɪ
San Jacinto	san juh SIN toh	sæn dʒəˈsɪnto
San Joaquín	san waw KEEN	sæn wɔˈkin
San Jorge	sahn HAWR he	sɑn ˈhɔrhɛ
San Jose (California)	san hoh ZAY	sæn hoˈze
San José (Spanish)	sahn haw SE	sɑn hɔˈsɛ
San Juan	san HWAHN	sæn ˈhwɑn
Sankhya	SAHNG kyuh	ˈsɑŋkjə
San Luis Potosí	sahn loo: EES paw taw SEE	sɑn luˈis pɔtɔˈsi
San Marino	san muh REE noh	sæn məˈrino

---

sing [ŋ]; oh [o]; oil [ɔɪ]; foot [ʊ]; foo:d [u]; how [aʊ]; pie [p]; ray [r]; so [s]; shall [ʃ]; to [t]; thin [θ]; th:en [ð]; above (uh BUHV) [ə, ˈʌ]; vine [v]; wine [w]; whine [hw]; you [j]; zoo [z]; rouge (roo:zh) [ʒ].

San Martín	sahn mahr TEEN	sɑn mɑr'tin
San Remo	san REE moh	sæn 'rimo
sans	sanz	sænz
San Salvador	san SAL vuh dawr	sæn 'sælvədɔr
Sanscrit	SAN skrit	'sænskrɪt
sans-culotte	sanz koo LAHT	sænz ku'lɑt
sans-culottism	sanz koo LAH ti zuhm	sænz ku'lɑtɪzəm
San Sebastian	san si BAS chuhn	sæn sɪ'bæstʃən
sansei	SAN say	'sænse
sans gêne	sahn ZHEN	sɑn 'ʒɛn
Sanskrit	SAN skrit	'sænskrɪt
sans-serif	san SAI rif	sæn'sɛrɪf
sans souci	sahn soo : SEE	sɑn su'si
Santa (in English names)	SAN tuh	'sæntə
Santa (in Spanish and Italian names)	SAHN tah	'sɑntɑ
Santa Barbara	SAN tuh BAHR buh ruh	'sæntə 'bɑrbərə
Santa Catalina	SAN tuh ka tuh LEE nuh	'sæntə kætə'linə
Santa Claus, Santa Klaus	SAN tuh KLAWZ	'sæntə 'klɔz
Santa Cruz	SAN tuh KROO : Z	'sæntə 'kruz
Santa Fe	SAN tuh FAY	'sæntə 'fe
Santa María	SAHN tah mah REE ah	'sɑntɑ mɑ'riɑ
Santa Monica	SAN tuh MAH ni kuh	'sæntə 'mɑnɪkə
Santander	sahn tahn DAIR	sɑntɑn'der
Santayana	san ti A nuh	sæntɪ'ænə
Santiago	san ti AY goh	sæntɪ'ego
Santiago de Cuba	sahn tee AH gaw de KOO : bah	sɑnti'ɑgɔ dɛ 'kubɑ
Santo Domingo	SAN toh duh MING goh	'sænto də'mɪŋgo
Santos	SAHN toos	'sɑntus
São Francisco	sown frahn SEE skoo	saun frɑn'siskʊ
são Luiz	sown LWEES	saun 'lwis
São Miguel	sown mee GEL	saun mi'gɛl
Saône	sohn	son
São Paulo	sown POW loo	saun 'paulʊ
Saorstat Eireann	SAIR stawt AI ruhn	'sɛrstɔt 'ɛrən
São Salvador	sown sahl vuh DAWR	saun sɑlvə'dɔr
sapajou	sa puh JOO :	sæpə'dʒu
saphena	suh FEE nuh	sə'finə
sapience	SAY pi uhns	'sepɪəns
sapient	SAY pi uhnt	'sepɪənt
sapodilla	sa puh DI luh	sæpə'dɪlə
saponaceous	sa puh NAY shuhs	sæpə'neʃəs
saponify	suh PAH nuh figh	sə'pɑnəfaɪ
sapor	SAY per	'sepər
sapota	suh POH tuh	sə'potə
sapper	SA per	'sæpər
Sapphic	SA fik	'sæfɪk
Sapphira	suh FIGH ruh	sə'faɪrə
sapphire	SA fighr	'sæfaɪr

at [æ]; ah [ɑ]; air [ɛ]; awful [ɔ]; say [e]; back [b]; chair [tʃ]; do [d]; elm [ɛ]; eel [i]; server ['ɝ, ər]; fit [f]; go [g]; hurt [h]; is [ɪ]; high [aɪ]; jet [dʒ]; kiss [k]; lamb [l̩]; my [m]; nice [n];

sapphism	SA fi zuhm	ˈsæfɪzəm
Sappho	SA foh	ˈsæfo
Sapporo	SAH paw raw	ˈsɑpɔrɔ
sapremia, sapraemia	suh PREE mi uh	səˈprimɪə
saprogenic	sa pruh JE nik	sæprəˈdʒɛnɪk
saprolite	SA pruh light	ˈsæprəlaɪt
saprophyte	SA pruh fight	ˈsæprəfaɪt
sapsago	SAP suh goh	ˈsæpsəgo
saraband	SA ruh band	ˈsærəbænd
Saracen	SA ruh suhn	ˈsærəsən
Saracoglu	sah RAH jaw gloo	sɑˈrɑdʒɔglʊ
Saragossa	sa ruh GAH suh	særəˈgɑsə
Sarajevo	sah ruh YE voh	sɑrəˈjɛvo
saran, S-	suh RAN	səˈræn
Saranac	SA ruh nak	ˈsærənæk
Sarasota	sa ruh SOH tuh	særəˈsotə
Saratoga	sa ruh TOH guh	særəˈtogə
Saratov	sah RAH tawf	sɑˈrɑtɔf
Sarawak	suh RAH wahk	səˈrɑwɑk
sarcasm	SAHR ka zuhm	ˈsɑrkæzəm
sarcastic	sahr KA stik	sɑrˈkæstɪk
sarcenet	SAHR snet	ˈsɑrsnɛt
sarcocarp	SAHR kuh kahrp	ˈsɑrkəkɑrp
sarcology	sahr KAH luh ji	sɑrˈkɑlədʒɪ
sarcoma	sahr KOH muh	sɑrˈkomə
sarcomatosis	sahr koh muh TOH sis	sɑrkoməˈtosɪs
sarcomatous	sahr KOH muh tuhs	sɑrˈkomətəs
sarcophagi	sahr KAH fuh jigh	sɑrˈkɑfədʒaɪ
sarcophagus	sahr KAH fuh guhs	sɑrˈkɑfəgəs
sarcous	SAHR kuhs	ˈsɑrkəs
sard	sahrd	sɑrd
Sardinia	sahr DI ni uh	sɑrˈdɪnɪə
sardius	SAHR di uhs	ˈsɑrdɪəs
sardonic	sahr DAH nik	sɑrˈdɑnɪk
sardonyx	SAHR duh niks	ˈsɑrdənɪks
Sardou	sahr DOO :	sɑrˈdu
Sarg	sahrg	sɑrg
sargasso, S-	sahr GA soh	sɑrˈgæso
sargassum	sahr GA suhm	sɑrˈgæsəm
Sargent	SAHR juhnt	ˈsɑrdʒənt
sari	SAH ree	ˈsɑri
sarong	suh RAWNG	səˈrɔŋ
Saroyan	suh ROI uhn	səˈrɔɪən
Sarpedon	sahr PEE duhn	sɑrˈpidən
sarsaparilla	sahr spuh RI luh	sɑrspəˈrilə
Sarto	SAHR taw	ˈsɑrtɔ
sartor	SAHR ter	ˈsɑrtər
sartorial	sahr TAW ri uhl	sɑrˈtɔrɪəl
sartorius	sahr TAW ri uhs	sɑrˈtɔrɪəs
Sartre	SAHR truh	ˈsɑrtrə
sashay	sa SHAY	sæˈʃe
Saskatchewan	sa SKA chuh wahn	sæˈskætʃəwɑn

---

sing [ŋ] ; *oh* [o] ; *oil* [ɔɪ] ; *foot* [ʊ] ; *foo*:d [u] ; *how* [aʊ] ; *p*ie [p] ; *r*ay [r] ; *s*o [s] ; *sh*all [ʃ] ;
*t*o [t] ; *th*in [θ] ; *th*:en [ð] ; above (*uh* B*U*HV) [ə, ˈʌ] ; *v*ine [v] ; *w*ine [w] ; *wh*ine [hw] ;
*y*ou [j] ; *z*oo [z] ; rouge (roo:*zh*) [ʒ].

Saskatoon, s-	sa skuh TOO : N	sæskəˈtun
sassaby	SA suh bi	ˈsæsəbɪ
sassafras	SA suh fras	ˈsæsəfræs
Sassenach	SA suh nak	ˈsæsənæk
Sassoon	suh SOO : N	səˈsun
satanic, S-	suh TA nik	səˈtænɪk
Satanism	SAY tuh ni zuhm	ˈsetənɪzəm
sateen	sa TEEN	sæˈtin
satellite	SA tuh light	ˈsætəlaɪt
satiate	SAY shi ayt	ˈseʃɪet
satiety	suh TIGH uh ti	səˈtaɪətɪ
satin	SA tuhn	ˈsætən
satinet, -te	sa tuh NET	sætəˈnɛt
satire	SA tighr	ˈsætaɪr
satirical	suh TI ri kuhl	səˈtɪrɪkəl
satirize	SA tuh righz	ˈsætəraɪz
satrap	SAY trap	ˈsetræp
satrapy	SAY truh pi	ˈsetrəpɪ
Satsuma	sat SOO : muh	sætˈsumə
saturant	SA chuh ruhnt	ˈsætʃərənt
saturate	SA chuh rayt	ˈsætʃəret
Saturday	SA ter di	ˈsætərdɪ
Saturn	SA tern	ˈsætərn
Saturnalia, s-	sa ter NAY li uh	sætərˈnelɪə
Saturnian, s-	suh TER ni uhn	səˈtɜnɪən
saturnine	SA ter nighn	ˈsætərnaɪn
Satyagraha	SUHT yuh gruh huh	ˈsʌtjəgrʌhə
satyr	SA ter	ˈsætər
satyriasis	sa tuh RIGH uh sis	sætəˈraɪəsɪs
satyric	suh TI rik	səˈtɪrɪk
sauce	saws	sɔs
saucer	SAW ser	ˈsɔsər
Saud, Ibn	sah OOD, I buhn	sɑˈud, ˈɪbən
Saudi Arabia	sah OO : di uh RAY bi uh	sɑˈudɪ əˈrebɪə
sauerbraten	SOW er brah tuhn	ˈsauərbrɑtən
sauerkraut	SOWR krowt	ˈsaurkraut
Sauk	sawk	sɔk
Sault Sainte Marie	SOO : saynt muh REE	ˈsu sent məˈri
sauna	SOW nuh	ˈsaunə
saunter	SAWN ter	ˈsɔntər
Saurashtra	SOW ruhsh truh	ˈsaurʌʃtrə
saurian	SAW ri uhn	ˈsɔrɪən
sauropod	SAW ruh pahd	ˈsɔrəpad
sausage	SAW sij	ˈsɔsɪdʒ
sauté	soh TAY	soˈte
sauterne	soh TERN	soˈtɜn
sauve-qui-peut	sohv kee PER	sov ki ˈpɜ
Sava	SAH vah	ˈsɑvɑ
savage	SA vij	ˈsævɪdʒ
savanna, -h, S-	suh VA nuh	səˈvænə
savant	SA vuhnt	ˈsævənt
saveloy	SA vuh loi	ˈsævəlɔɪ

at [æ] ; ah [ɑ] ; air [ɛ] ; awful [ɔ] ; say [e] ; back [b] ; chair [tʃ] ; do [d] ; elm [ɛ] ; eel [i] ;
server [ˈɜ, ər] ; fit [f] ; go [g] ; hurt [h] ; is [ɪ] ; high [aɪ] ; jet [dʒ] ; kiss [k] ; lamb [l] ; my [m] ;
nice [n] ;

savior, saviour, S-	SAY vyer	ˈsevjər
savoir-faire	sa vwahr FAIR	sævwɑrˈfɛr
Savonarola	sa vuh nuh ROH luh	sævənəˈrolə
savor	SAY ver	ˈsevər
savory	SAY vuh ri	ˈsevərɪ
Savoy, s-	suh VOI	səˈvɔɪ
Savoyard	suh VOI erd	səˈvɔɪərd
savvy	SA vi	ˈsævɪ
Sawatch	suh WAHCH	səˈwɑtʃ
Saxe-Coburg-Gotha	SAKS KOH berg GOH thuh	ˈsæks ˈkobərg ˈgoθə
saxifrage	SAK si frij	ˈsæksɪfrɪdʒ
Saxon	SAK suhn	ˈsæksən
Saxony	SAK suh ni	ˈsæksənɪ
saxophone	SAK suh fohn	ˈsæksəfon
Sayan	sah YAHN	sɑˈjɑn
Sayão, Bidú	sigh YAH oh, bee DOO:	saɪˈjɑo, biˈdu
sayid, sayyid	SAH yid	ˈsɑjɪd
Sayre	sair	sɛr
says	sez	sɛz
scabies	SKAY bi eez	ˈskebɪiz
scabiosa	skay bi OH suh	skebɪˈosə
scabious	SKAY bi uhs	ˈskebɪəs
scabrous	SKAY bruhs	ˈskebrəs
Scafell	SKAW fel	ˈskɔfɛl
scaffold	SKA fuhld	ˈskæfəld
scagliola	skal YOH luh	skælˈjolə
scalar	SKAY ler	ˈskelər
scalawag	SKA luh wag	ˈskæləwæg
scald	skawld	skɔld
scallion	SKA lyuhn	ˈskæljən
scallop	SKAH luhp	ˈskɑləp
scalpel	SKAL puhl	ˈskælpəl
Scanderbeg	SKAN der beg	ˈskændərbɛg
Scandian	SKAN di uhn	ˈskændɪən
Scandinavia	skan duh NAY vi uh	skændəˈnevɪə
scandium	SKAN di uhm	ˈskændɪəm
scansion	SKAN shuhn	ˈskænʃən
Scapa Flow	SKA puh FLOH	ˈskæpə ˈflo
scapegoat	SKAYP goht	ˈskepgot
scapula	SKA pyuh luh	ˈskæpjələ
scapular	SKA pyuh ler	ˈskæpjələr
scarab	SKA ruhb	ˈskærəb
Scaramouch, s-	SKA ruh mowch	ˈskærəmaʊtʃ
scarce	skairs	skɛrs
scarify	SKA ruh figh	ˈskærəfaɪ
Scarlatti	skahr LAH ti	skɑrˈlɑtɪ
scathe	skayth:	skeð
scatheless	SKAYTH: lis	ˈskeðlɪs
scatological	ska tuh LAH ji kuhl	skætəˈlɑdʒɪkəl
scatology	skuh TAH luh ji	skəˈtɑlədʒɪ
scavenge	SKA vinj	ˈskævɪndʒ
scavenger	SKA vin jər	ˈskævɪndʒər

sing [ŋ]; oh [o]; oil [ɔɪ]; foot [ʊ]; foo:d [u]; how [aʊ]; þie [p]; ray [r]; so [s]; shall [ʃ]; to [t]; thin [θ]; th:en [ð]; above (uh BUHV) [ə, ˈʌ]; vine [v]; wine [w]; whine [hw]; you [j]; zoo [z]; rouge (roo:zh) [ʒ].

Scelba	SHEL bah	ˈʃɛlbɑ
scenario	si NAI ri oh	sɪˈnɛrɪo
scenic	SEE nik	ˈsinɪk
scenography	see NAH gruh fi	siˈnɑgrəfɪ
scepter, sceptre	SEP ter	ˈsɛptər
sceptic	SKEP tik	ˈskɛptɪk
Schacht	shahkt	ʃɑkt
Scharnhorst	SHAHRN hawrst	ˈʃɑrnhɔrst
schatchen	SHAHT kuhn	ˈʃɑtkən
Schaumburg-Lippe	SHOWM boork LI puh	ˈʃaʊmbʊrk ˈlɪpə
schedule	SKE jool	ˈskɛdʒʊl
scheelite	SHEE light	ˈʃilaɪt
schefferite	SHE fuh right	ˈʃɛfəraɪt
Scheherazade	shuh hai ruh ZAH duh	ʃəhɛrəˈzɑdə
Scheldt	skelt	skɛlt
Schelling	SHE ling	ˈʃɛlɪŋ
schema	SKEE muh	ˈskimə
schematic	skee MA tik	skiˈmætɪk
schematize	SKEE muh tighz	ˈskimətaɪz
scheme	skeem	skim
Schenectady	skuh NEK tuh di	skəˈnɛktədɪ
Schenk	shengk	ˈʃɛŋk
Scherchen	SHAIR shin	ˈʃɛərʃɪn
scherzando	skairt SAHN doh	skɛrtˈsɑndo
scherzo	SKAIRT soh	ˈskɛrtso
Schiaparelli	skyah pah RE lee	skjɑpɑˈrɛli
Schick	shik	ʃɪk
Schiller, s-	SHI ler	ˈʃɪlər
schilling	SHI ling	ˈʃɪlɪŋ
Schipa	SKEE pah	ˈskipɑ
schipperke	SKI per ki	ˈskɪpərkɪ
Schippers	SHI perz	ˈʃɪpərz
Schirra	shi RAH	ʃɪˈrɑ
schism	SI zuhm	ˈsɪzəm
schismatic	siz MA tik	sɪzˈmætɪk
schist	shist	ʃɪst
schistosome	SHI stuh sohm	ˈʃɪstəsom
schistosomiasis	shi stuh soh MIGH uh sis	ʃɪstəsoˈmaɪəsɪs
schizogenesis	ski zuh JE nuh sis	skɪzəˈdʒɛnəsɪs
schizoid	SKI zoid	ˈskɪzɔɪd
schizomycete	ski zoh migh SET	skɪzomaɪˈsɛt
schizomycosis	ski zoh migh KOH sis	skɪzomaɪˈkosɪs
schizophrene	SKI zuh freen	ˈskɪzəfrin
schizophrenia	ski zuh FREE ni uh	skɪzəˈfrinɪə
schizophrenic	ski zuh FRE nik	skɪzəˈfrɛnɪk
schizopod	SKI zuh pahd	ˈskɪzəpɑd
schizothymia	ski zuh THIGH mi uh	skɪzəˈθaɪmɪə
Schlegel	SHLAY guhl	ˈʃlegəl
Schleiermacher	SHLIGH uh mah ker	ˈʃlaɪəmɑkər
schlemiel, schlemihl	shluh MEEL	ʃləˈmil
Schlesinger (Arthur M., Jr.)	SHLAY zing er	ˈʃlezɪŋər

at [æ]; ah [ɑ]; air [ɛ]; awful [ɔ]; say [e]; back [b]; chair [tʃ]; do [d]; elm [ɛ]; eel [i];
server [ˈɜ, ər]; fit [f]; go [g]; hurt [h]; is [ɪ]; high [aɪ]; jet [dʒ]; kiss [k]; lamb [l]; my [m];
nice [n];

Schleswig	SHLES wig	ˈʃlɛswɪg
Schley	sligh	slaɪ
Schliemann	SHLEE mahn	ˈʃlimɑn
schlieren	SHLI ruhn	ˈʃlɪrən
schmaltz	shmahlts	ʃmɑlts
Schnabel	SHNAH buhl	ˈʃnɑbəl
schnapps, schnaps	shnaps	ʃnæps
schnauzer	SHNOW zer	ˈʃnaʊzər
schnitzel	SHNIT suhl	ˈʃnɪtsəl
Schnitzler	SHNIT sler	ˈʃnɪtslər
schnorchel, schnorkel	SHNAWR kuhl	ˈʃnɔrkəl
schnorrer	SHNAW rer	ˈʃnɔrər
schnozzle	SHNAH zuhl	ˈʃnɑzəl
Schoenberg	SHOHN berg	ˈʃonbərg
Schoendienst	SHAYN deenst	ˈʃendinst
scholastic	skuh LA stik	skəˈlæstɪk
scholasticism	skuh LA stuh si zuhm	skəˈlæstəsɪzəm
scholiast	SKOH li ast	ˈskolɪæst
scholium	SKOH li uhm	ˈskolɪəm
Schönberg	SHOHN berg	ˈʃonbərg
schoolhouse	SKOO : L hows	ˈskulhaʊs
schooner	SKOO : ner	ˈskunər
Schoonover	SKOO : noh ver	ˈskunovər
Schopenhauer	SHOH puhn how er	ˈʃopənhaʊər
Schorer	SHAW rer	ˈʃɔrər
schorl	shawrl	ʃɔrl
schottische, schottish	SHAH tish	ˈʃatɪʃ
Schottky	SHAHT ki	ˈʃatkɪ
Schrödinger	SHRAY ding er	ˈʃredɪŋər
Schubert	SHOO : bert	ˈʃubərt
Schueler	SHOO : ler	ˈʃulər
Schumann	SHOO : mahn	ˈʃumɑn
Schumann-Heink	SHOO : muhn HIGHNGK	ˈʃumən ˈhaɪŋk
Schurz	shoorts	ʃʊrts
schuss	shoos	ʃʊs
Schuster	SHOO : ster	ˈʃustər
Schutzstaffel	SHOOTS shtah fuhl	ˈʃʊtsʃtɑfəl
Schuyler	SKIGH ler	ˈskaɪlər
Schuylkil	SKOO : L kil	ˈskulkɪl
schwa	shwah	ʃwɑ
Schwab	shwahb	ʃwɑb
Schwarzkopf	SHVARTS kuhpf	ˈʃvɑrtskəpf
Schweitzer	SHWIGHT ser	ˈʃwaɪtsər
Schwerin	SHVE rin	ˈʃvɛrɪn
sciamachy	sigh A muh ki	saɪˈæməkɪ
sciatica	sigh A ti kuh	saɪˈætɪkə
sciential	sigh EN shuhl	saɪˈɛnʃəl
scilicet	SI li set	ˈsɪlɪset
Scilla	SI luh	ˈsɪlə
Scilly	SI li	ˈsɪlɪ
scimitar, scimiter	SI muh ter	ˈsɪmətər
scintilla	sin TI luh	sɪnˈtɪlə

sing [ŋ]; oh [o]; oil [ɔɪ]; foot [ʊ]; foo:d [u]; how [aʊ]; pie [p]; ray [r]; so [s]; shall [ʃ]; to [t]; thin [θ]; th:en [ð]; above (uh BUHV) [ə, ˈʌ]; vine [v]; wine [w]; whine [hw]; you [j]; zoo [z]; rouge (roo:zh) [ʒ].

H.P.—Y

scintillate	SIN tuh layt	ˈsɪntəlet
sciolism	SIGH uh li zuhm	ˈsaɪəlɪzəm
scion	SIGH uhn	ˈsaɪən
Scipio	SI pi oh	ˈsɪpɪo
scire facias	SIGH ree FAY shi as	ˈsaɪri ˈfeʃɪæs
scirrhus	SKI ruhs	ˈskɪrəs
scleriasis	skli RIGH uh sis	sklɪˈraɪəsɪs
scleritis	skli RIGH tis	sklɪˈraɪtɪs
scleroma	skli ROH muh	sklɪˈromə
sclerosis	skli ROH sis	sklɪˈrosɪs
scoliosis	skoh li OH sis	skolɪˈosɪs
sconce	skahns	skɑns
scone	skohn	skon
Scone	skoo : n	skun
scop	skahp	skɑp
scopolamine	skoh PAH luh meen	skoˈpɑləmin
scoptophilia	skahp tuh FI li uh	skɑptəˈfɪlɪə
scoria	SKAW ri uh	ˈskɔrɪə
Scorpio	SKAWR pi oh	ˈskɔrpɪo
scorpion	SKAWR pi uhn	ˈskɔrpɪən
Scorpius	SKAWR pi uhs	ˈskɔrpɪəs
scotia, S-	SKOH shuh	ˈskoʃə
Scotism	SKOH ti zuhm	ˈskotɪzəm
Scotland	SKAHT luhnd	ˈskɑtlənd
scotoma	skuh TOH muh	skəˈtomə
Scourby	SKAWR bi	ˈskɔrbɪ
scourge	skerj	skɝdʒ
scow	skow	skaʊ
scrabble	SKRA buhl	ˈskræbəl
scrag	skrag	skræg
scrapple	SKRA puhl	ˈskræpəl
Scriabin	skri AH bin	skrɪˈɑbɪn
scribal	SKRIGH buhl	ˈskraɪbəl
scrimshaw	SKRIM shaw	ˈskrɪmʃɔ
scripsit	SKRIP sit	ˈskrɪpsɪt
scriptorium	skrip TAW ri uhm	skrɪpˈtɔrɪəm
scrivener	SKRIV ner	ˈskrɪvnər
scrofula	SKRAH fyuh luh	ˈskrɑfjələ
scrofulous	SKRAH fyuh luhs	ˈskrɑfjələs
Scrooge	skroo : j	skrudʒ
scrotum	SKROH tuhm	ˈskrotəm
scrouge	skroo : j	skrudʒ
scrounge	skrownj	skraʊndʒ
scruff	skruhf	skrʌf
scrumptious	SKRUHMP shuhs	ˈskrʌmpʃəs
scrunch	skruhnch	skrʌntʃ
scull	skuhl	skʌl
scullery	SKUH luh ri	ˈskʌlərɪ
scullion	SKUH lyuhn	ˈskʌljən
sculptor	SKUHLP ter	ˈskʌlptər
sculpture	SKUHLP cher	ˈskʌlptʃər
sculpturesque	skuhlp chuh RESK	skʌlpʃəˈrɛsk

at [æ] ; ah [ɑ] ; air [ɛ] ; awful [ɔ] ; say [e] ; back [b] ; chair [tʃ] ; do [d] ; elm [ɛ] ; eel [i] ;
server [ˈɝ, ər] ; fit [f] ; go [g] ; hurt [h] ; is [ɪ] ; high [aɪ] ; jet [dʒ] ; kiss [k] ; lamb [l] ; my [m] ;
nice [n] ;

scuppernong	SKUH per nahng	ˈskʌpərnɑŋ
scurrility	skuh RI luh ti	skəˈrɪlətɪ
scurrilous	SKER uh luhs	ˈskɝələs
scurry	SKER i	ˈskɝɪ
scurvy	SKER vi	ˈskɝvɪ
Scutari	SKOO : tah ri	ˈskutɑrɪ
scutcheon	SKUH chuhn	ˈskʌtʃən
scuttlebutt	SKUH tuhl buht	ˈskʌtəlbʌt
scutum, S-	SKYOO : tuhm	ˈskjutəm
Scylla	SI luh	ˈsɪlə
scyphus	SIGH fuhs	ˈsaɪfəs
scythe	sighth :	saɪð
Scythian	SI thi uhn	ˈsɪθɪən
sealette	see LET	siˈlɛt
Sealyham	SEE li uhm	ˈsilɪəm
seamstress	SEEM stris	ˈsimstrɪs
Seanad Eireann	SA nahd AI ruhn	ˈsænɑd ˈɛrən
séance	SAY ahns	ˈseɑns
Seattle	see A tuhl	siˈætəl
sebaceous	si BAY shuhs	sɪˈbeʃəs
Sebastopol	si BA stuh pohl	sɪˈbæstəpol
seborrhea, seborrhoea	se buh REE uh	sɛbəˈriə
sebum	SEE buhm	ˈsibəm
secant	SEE kuhnt	ˈsikənt
secco	SE kaw	ˈsɛkɔ
secession	si SE shuhn	sɪˈsɛʃən
Sechuana	se CHWAH nah	sɛˈtʃwɑnɑ
Seckel	SE kuhl	ˈsɛkəl
seclude	si KLOO : D	sɪˈklud
second	SE kuhnd	ˈsɛkənd
secondary	SE kuhn dai ri	ˈsɛkəndɛrɪ
secondhand	SE kuhnd HAND	ˈsɛkəndˈhænd
secondo	se KAWN daw	sɛˈkɔndɔ
secretaire	se kruh TAIR	sɛkrəˈtɛr
secretarial	se kruh TAI ri uhl	sɛkrəˈtɛrɪəl
secretariat, -e	se kruh TAI ri it	sɛkrəˈtɛrɪɪt
secretary	SE kruh tai ri	ˈsɛkrətɛrɪ
secrete	si KREET	sɪˈkrit
secretion	si KREE shuhn	sɪˈkriʃən
secretive	si KREE tiv	sɪˈkritɪv
secretiveness	si KREE tiv nis	sɪˈkritɪvnɪs
secretory	si KREE tuh ri	sɪˈkritərɪ
sectarian	sek TAI ri uhn	sɛkˈtɛrɪən
sector	SEK ter	ˈsɛktər
sects	sekts	sɛkts
secular	SE kyuh ler	ˈsɛkjələr
secunderabad	see KUHN duh rah BAHD	siˈkʌndərɑˈbɑd
secundum	si KUHN duhm	sɪˈkʌndəm
Sedalia	si DAY li uh	sɪˈdelɪə
sedan, S-	si DAN	sɪˈdæn
sedate	si DAYT	sɪˈdet
sedation	si DAY shuhn	sɪˈdeʃən

---

sing [ŋ] ; *oh* [o] ; *oil* [ɔɪ] ; *foot* [ʊ] ; *foo*:d [u] ; *how* [aʊ] ; *pie* [p] ; *ray* [r] ; *so* [s] ; *shall* [ʃ] ;
to [t] ; *thin* [θ] ; *th*:en [ð] ; above (*uh* BUHV) [ə, ˈʌ] ; *vine* [v] ; *wine* [w] ; *whine* [hw] ;
you [j] ; *zoo* [z] ; rouge (roo:*zh*) [ʒ].

sedative	SE duh tiv	ˈsɛdətɪv
sedentary	SE duhn tai ri	ˈsɛdəntɛrɪ
Seder	SAY der	ˈsedər
sediment	SE duh muhnt	ˈsɛdəmənt
sedition	si DI shuhn	sɪˈdɪʃən
seduce	si DOO : S	sɪˈdus
seductive	si DUHK tiv	sɪˈdʌktɪv
sedulity	si DYOO : luh ti	sɪˈdjulətɪ
sedulous	SE juh luhs	ˈsɛdʒələs
sedum	SEE duhm	ˈsidəm
Seefried, Irmgard	ZAY freet, EERM gahrt	ˈzefrit, ˈirmgɑrt
segno	SE nyaw	ˈsɛnjɔ
sego	SEE goh	ˈsigo
Segovia	se GAW vyah	sɛˈgɔvjɑ
segregate (n)	SE gri git	ˈsɛgrɪgɪt
segregate (v)	SE gri gayt	ˈsɛgrɪget
segregation	se gri GAY shuhn	sɛgrɪˈgeʃən
segregationist	se gri GAY shuh nist	sɛgrɪˈgeʃənɪst
segregative	SE gri gay tiv	ˈsɛgrɪgetɪv
segreto	se GRE taw	sɛˈgrɛtɔ
segue	SAY gway	ˈsegwe
seguidilla	se gee DEE lyah	sɛgiˈdiljɑ
Segura	se GOO rah	sɛˈgurɑ
seicento	se CHEN taw	sɛˈtʃɛntɔ
seiche	saysh	seʃ
seidel, S-	SIGH duhl	ˈsaɪdəl
Seidlitz	SED lits	ˈsɛdlɪts
seigneur	SAY nyer	ˈsenjər
seignior	SEE nyer	ˈsinjər
seigniorage	SEE nyuh rij	ˈsinjərɪdʒ
seigniory	SEE nyuh ri	ˈsinjərɪ
Seine, s-	sayn	sen
seismic	SIGHZ mik	ˈsaɪzmɪk
seismograph	SIGHZ muh graf	ˈsaɪzməgræf
seismology	sighz MAH luh ji	saɪzˈmɑlədʒɪ
sejant, sejeant	SEE juhnt	ˈsidʒənt
sejm	saym	sem
selah	SEE luh	ˈsilə
selamlik	se LAHM lik	sɛˈlɑmlɪk
Selangor	se LAHNG gawr	sɛˈlɑŋgɔr
Selene	si LEE nee	sɪˈlini
selenic	si LEE nik	sɪˈlinɪk
selenite	SE luh night	ˈsɛlənait
selenium	si LEE ni uhm	sɪˈlinɪəm
selenology	se li NAH luh ji	sɛlɪˈnɑlədʒɪ
selenosis	see luh NOH sis	sɛləˈnosis
Seleucus	si LOO : kuhs	sɪˈlukəs
Seljuk	sel JOO : K	sɛlˈdʒuk
Seltzer, s-	SELT ser	ˈsɛltsər
selvage, selvedge	SEL vij	ˈsɛlvɪdʒ
semantic	suh MAN tik	səˈmæntɪk
semaphore	SE muh fawr	ˈsɛməfor

at [æ] ; *ah* [ɑ] ; *air* [ɛ] ; *awful* [ɔ] ; *say* [e] ; *back* [b] ; *chair* [tʃ] ; *do* [d] ; *elm* [ɛ] ; *eel* [i] ; *server* [ˈɝ, ər] ; *fit* [f] ; *go* [g] ; *hurt* [h] ; *is* [ɪ] ; *high* [aɪ] ; *jet* [dʒ] ; *kiss* [k] ; *lamb* [l] ; *my* [m] ; *nice* [n] ;

Semarang	suh MAH rahng	səˈmɑrɑŋ
semasiology	suh may si AH luh ji	səmesɪˈɑlədʒɪ
Sembrich	SEM brik	ˈsɛmbrɪk
semé	suh MAY	səˈme
Semele	SE muh lee	ˈsɛməli
semen	SEE muhn	ˈsimən
semester	suh ME ster	səˈmɛstər
seminal	SE muh nuhl	ˈsɛmənəl
seminar	SE muh nahr	ˈsɛmənɑr
seminary	SE muh nai ri	ˈsɛmənɛrɪ
Seminole	SE muh nohl	ˈsɛmənol
semiology	se mi AH luh ji	sɛmɪˈɑlədʒɪ
semiotic	se mi AH tik	sɛmɪˈɑtɪk
Semiramis	si MI ruh mis	sɪˈmɪrəmɪs
Semite	SE might	ˈsɛmaɪt
Semitic	suh MI tik	səˈmɪtɪk
Semitism	SE muh ti zuhm	ˈsɛmətɪzəm
semolina	se muh LEE nuh	sɛməˈlinə
semper fidelis	SEM per fi DEE lis	ˈsɛmpər fɪˈdilɪs
semper paratus	SEM per puh RAY tuhs	ˈsɛmpər pəˈretəs
sempiternal	sem pi TER nuhl	sɛmpɪˈtɝnəl
sen	sen	sɛn
senate	SE nit	ˈsɛnɪt
senator	SE nuh ter	ˈsɛnətər
Sendai	sen digh	sɛndaɪ
sendal	SEN duhl	ˈsɛndəl
Seneca	SE ni kuh	ˈsɛnɪkə
Senegal	se ni GAWL	sɛnɪˈgɔl
Senegalese	se ni gaw LEEZ	sɛnɪgɔˈliz
Senegambia	se nuh GAM bi uh	sɛnəˈgæmbɪə
senescent	suh NE suhnt	səˈnɛsənt
seneshal	SE nuh shuhl	ˈsɛnəʃəl
senhor (Portuguese)	se NYAWR	sɛˈnjɔr
senhora (Portuguese)	se NYAW rah	sɛˈnjɔrɑ
senhorita (Portuguese)	se nyaw REE tah	sɛnjɔˈritɑ
senile	SEE nighl	ˈsinaɪl
senility	suh NI luh ti	səˈnɪlətɪ
Senlac	SEN lak	ˈsɛnlæk
senna	SE nuh	ˈsɛnə
Sennacherib	suh NA kuh rib	səˈnækərɪb
sennet	SE nit	ˈsɛnɪt
sennit	SE nit	ˈsɛnɪt
señor (Spanish)	se NYAWR	sɛˈnjɔr
señora (Spanish)	se NYAW rah	sɛˈnjɔrɑ
señorita (Spanish)	se nyaw REE tah	sɛnjɔˈritɑ
sensorium	sen SAW ri uhm	sɛnˈsɔrɪəm
sensory	SEN suh ri	ˈsɛnsərɪ
sensual	SEN shoo uhl	ˈsɛnʃʊəl
sensuality	sen shoo A luh ti	sɛnʃʊˈælətɪ
sensuous	SEN shoo uhs	ˈsɛnʃʊəs
Senta	SEN tah	ˈsɛntɑ
sentential	sen TEN shuhl	sɛnˈtɛnʃəl

---

sing [ŋ] ; oh [o] ; oil [ɔɪ] ; foot [ʊ] ; foo:d [u] ; how [aʊ] ; pie [p] ; ray [r] ; so [s] ; shall [ʃ] ; to [t] ; thin [θ] ; th:en [ð] ; above (uh BUHV) [ə, ˈʌ] ; vine [v] ; wine [w] ; whine [hw] ; you [j] ; zoo [z] ; rouge (roo:zh) [ʒ].

sententious	sen TEN shuhs	sɛnˈtɛnʃəs
sentience	SEN shuhns	ˈsɛnʃəns
sentient	SEN shuhnt	ˈsɛnʃənt
sentimental	sen tuh MEN tuhl	sɛntəˈmɛntəl
sentinel	SEN tuh nuhl	ˈsɛntənəl
sentry	SEN tri	ˈsɛntrɪ
Senusi, Senussi	se NOO : si	sɛˈnusɪ
Seoul	sohl	sol
sepal	SEE puhl	ˈsipəl
separate (a, n)	SE puh rit	ˈsɛpərɪt
separate (v)	SE puh rayt	ˈsɛpəret
Sephardic	si FAHR dik	sɪˈfɑrdɪk
Sephardim	si FAHR dim	sɪˈfɑrdɪm
sepia	SEE pi uh	ˈsipɪə
sepiolite	SEE pi uh light	ˈsipɪəlaɪt
sepoy	SEE poi	ˈsipɔɪ
seppuku	se POO : koo	sɛˈpukʊ
sepsis	SEP sis	ˈsɛpsɪs
September	sep TEM ber	sɛpˈtɛmbər
septenary	SEP tuh nai ri	ˈsɛptənɛrɪ
septennial	sep TE ni uhl	sɛpˈtɛnɪəl
septentrional	sep TEN tri uh nuhl	sɛpˈtɛntrɪənəl
septet, -te	sep TET	sɛpˈtɛt
septic	SEP tik	ˈsɛptɪk
septicemia, septicaemia	sep tuh SEE mi uh	sɛptəˈsimɪə
septuagenarian	SEP choo uh ji NAI ri uhn	ˈsɛptʃʊədʒɪˈnɛrɪən
Septuagesima	SEP choo uh JE si muh	ˈsɛptʃʊəˈdʒɛsɪmə
Septuagint	SEP too uh jint	ˈsɛptʊədʒɪnt
septum	SEP tuhm	ˈsɛptəm
septuple	SEP too puhl	ˈsɛptʊpəl
sepulcher, sepulchre	SE puhl ker	ˈsɛpəlkər
sepulchral	suh PUHL kruhl	səˈpʌlkrəl
sepulture	SE puhl cher	ˈsɛpəltʃər
sequacious	si KWAY shuhs	sɪˈkweʃəs
sequel	SEE kwuhl	ˈsikwəl
sequela	si KWEE luh	sɪˈkwilə
sequence	SEE kwuhns	ˈsikwəns
sequential	si KWEN shuhl	sɪˈkwɛnʃəl
sequester	si KWE ster	sɪˈkwɛstər
sequestration	see kwe STRAY shuhn	sikwɛˈstreʃən
sequin	SEE kwin	ˈsikwɪn
sequitur	SE kwi ter	ˈsɛkwɪtər
sequoia	si KWOI uh	sɪˈkwɔɪə
Serafin, Tullio	say rah FEEN, TOO : lee oh	sɛrɑˈfin, ˈtulio
seraglio	si RA lyoh	sɪˈræljo
serai	suh RAH i	səˈrɑɪ
seral	SI ruhl	ˈsɪrəl
Serang	se RAHNG	sɛˈrɑŋ
serape	se RAH pi	sɛˈrɑpɪ
seraph	SE ruhf	ˈsɛrəf
seraphic	suh RA fik	səˈræfɪk
seraphim	SE ruh fim	ˈsɛrəfɪm

at [æ] ; *ah* [ɑ] ; *air* [ɛ] ; *awful* [ɔ] ; *say* [e] ; *back* [b] ; *chair* [tʃ] ; *do* [d] ; *elm* [ɛ] ; *eel* [i] ; *server* [ˈɝ, ər] ; *f*it [f] ; *go* [g] ; *h*urt [h] ; *is* [ɪ] ; *high* [aɪ] ; *jet* [dʒ] ; *k*iss [k] ; *l*amb [l] ; *my* [m] ; *n*ice [n] ;

Serapis	suh RAY pis	sə'repɪs
Serb	serb	sɝb
Serbia	SER bi uh	'sɝbɪə
Serbo-	SER boh	'sɝbo
sere	sir	sɪr
serenata	se ruh NAH tuh	sɛrə'nɑtə
serendipity	se ruhn DI puh ti	sɛrən'dɪpətɪ
serene	suh REEN	sə'rin
serenity	suh RE nuh ti	sə'rɛnətɪ
serf	serf	sɝf
sergeant	SAHR juhnt	'sɑrdʒənt
seriatim	si ri AY tim	sɪrɪ'etɪm
sericeous	si RI shuhs	sɪ'rɪʃəs
sericulture	SE ri kuhl cher	'sɛrɪkʌltʃər
serif	SE rif	'sɛrɪf
serigraph	SE ri graf	'sɛrɪgræf
serigraphy	suh RI gruh fi	sə'rɪgrəfɪ
Serkin	SER kin	'sɝkɪn
serology	si RAH luh ji	sɪ'rɑlədʒɪ
serous	SI ruhs	'sɪrəs
Serpens	SER penz	'sɝpɛnz
serpentine	SER puhn teen	'sɝpəntin
serpiginous	ser PI juh nuhs	sər'pɪdʒənəs
serpigo	ser PIGH goh	sər'paɪgo
serried	SE rid	'sɛrɪd
serum	SI ruhm	'sɪrəm
serval	SER vuhl	'sɝvəl
serviette	ser vi ET	sɝvɪ'et
servile	SER vuhl	'sɝvəl
servility	ser VI luh ti	sər'vɪlətɪ
sesame	SE suh mee	'sɛsəmi
sesquicentennial	SE skwi sen TE ni uhl	'sɛskwɪsɛn'tɛnɪəl
sesquipedalian	SE skwi puh DAY li uhn	'sɛskwɪpə'delɪən
sestet	se STET	sɛ'stɛt
sestina	se STEE nuh	sɛ'stinə
setaceous	si TAY shuhs	sɪ'teʃəs
seton, S-	SEE tuhn	'sitən
settecento	se te CHEN taw	sɛtɛ'tʃɛnto
settee	se TEE	sɛ'ti
Seurat	ser RAH	sər'rɑ
Sevareid	SE vuh righd	'sɛvəraɪd
Sevastopol	si VA stuh pohl	sɪ'væstəpol
sever	SE ver	'sɛvər
several	SE vuh ruhl	'sɛvərəl
severance	SE vuh ruhns	'sɛvərəns
severe	suh VIR	sə'vɪr
severity	suh VE ruh ti	sə'vɛrətɪ
Severn	SE vern	'sɛvərn
Sévigné	say vee NYAY	sevi'nje
Sevilla	se VEE lyah	sɛ'vilja
Seville	suh VIL	sə'vɪl
Sèvres	SE vruh	'sɛvrə

sing [ŋ] ; oh [o] ; oil [ɔɪ] ; foot [ʊ] ; foo:d [u] ; how [aʊ] ; pie [p] ; ray [r] ; so [s] ; shall [ʃ] ;
to [t] ; thin [θ] ; th:en [ð] ; above (uh BUHV) [ə, 'ʌ] ; vine [v] ; wine [w] ; whine [hw] ;
you [j] ; zoo [z] ; rouge (roo:zh) [ʒ].

sewage	soo : ij	ˈsuɪdʒ
Sewall	SOO : uhl	ˈsuəl
Seward	SOO : erd	ˈsuərd
sewerage	SOO : uh rij	ˈsuərɪdʒ
sexagenarian	SEK suh ji NAI ri uhn	ˌsɛksədʒɪˈnɛrɪən
Sexagesima	sek suh JE si muh	sɛksəˈdʒɛsɪmə
sexennial	sek SE ni uhl	sɛkˈsɛnɪəl
sexology	sek SAH luh ji	sɛkˈsalədʒɪ
sextain	SEK stayn	ˈsɛksten
Sextans	SEK stuhnz	ˈsɛkstənz
sextant	SEK stuhnt	ˈsɛkstənt
sextet, -te	sek STET	sɛkˈstɛt
sextuple	SEK stoo puhl	ˈsɛkstʊpəl
sextuplet	SEK stoo plit	ˈsɛkstʊplɪt
sexuality	sek shoo A luh ti	sɛkʃuˈælətɪ
Seychelles	say SHELZ	seˈʃɛlz
Sfantul-Gheorghe	SFUHN tool GYAWR ge	ˈsfʌntul ˈgjɔrgɛ
Sfax	sfahks	sfɑks
sferics	SFE riks	ˈsfɛrɪks
Sforza	SFAWRT sah	ˈsfɔrtsɑ
sforzando	sfawrt SAHN daw	sfɔrtˈsandɔ
sforzato	sfawrt SAH taw	sfɔrtˈsatɔ
's-Gravenhage	skrah vuhn HAH kuh	skrɑvənˈhɑkə
Shabuoth	shah VOO : ohth	ʃɑˈvuoθ
shaddock	SHA duhk	ˈʃædək
Shadrach	SHAY drak	ˈʃedræk
shagreen	shuh GREEN	ʃəˈgrin
shah, S-	shah	ʃɑ
Shah Jahan, Shah Jehan	SHAH juh HAHN	ˈʃɑ dʒəˈhɑn
Shahjahanpur	SHAH juh hahn POOR	ˈʃɑdʒəhɑnˈpʊr
shaitan, S-	shigh TAHN	ʃaɪˈtɑn
Shakespeare, Shakespere, etc.	SHAYK spir	ˈʃekspɪr
Shakespearean, Shakespearian, etc.	shayk SPI ri uhn	ʃekˈspɪrɪən
shako	SHA koh	ˈʃæko
Shakti, s-	SHUHK ti	ˈʃʌktɪ
shalloon	sha LOO : N	ʃæˈlun
shallop	SHA luhp	ˈʃæləp
shallot	shuh LAHT	ʃəˈlɑt
shaman	SHAH muhn	ˈʃɑmən
Shamash	SHAH mahsh	ˈʃɑmɑʃ
Shan	shahn	ʃɑn
shandrydan	SHAN dri dan	ˈʃændrɪdæn
shandygaff	SHAN di gaf	ˈʃændɪgæf
Shanghai	shang high	ʃæŋ haɪ
Shangri-La	shang gri LAH	ʃæŋgrɪˈlɑ
Shansi	shan see	ʃænsi
shan't	shant	ʃænt
Shantung, s-	shan tuhng	ʃæn tʌŋ
Shaohsing	show shing	ʃaʊ ʃɪŋ

at [æ]; *ah* [ɑ]; *air* [ɛ]; *awful* [ɔ]; *say* [e]; *back* [b]; *chair* [tʃ]; *do* [d]; *elm* [ɛ]; *eel* [i]; *server* [ˈɝ, ər]; *f*it [f]; *go* [g]; *h*urt [h]; *is* [ɪ]; *high* [aɪ]; *jet* [dʒ]; *kiss* [k]; *lamb* [l]; *my* [m]; *nice* [n];

Shapley	SHA pli	ˈʃæplɪ
Shara	SHAH ruh	ˈʃɑrə
Shari	SHAH ri	ˈʃɑrɪ
Sharon	SHAI ruhn	ˈʃɛrən
Sharra	SHAH ruh	ˈʃɑrə
Shasta	SHA stuh	ˈʃæstə
Shatt-al-Arab	sha tuhl AH rahb	ʃætəlˈɑrab
Shavian	SHAY vi uhn	ˈʃevɪən
Shaw, s-	shaw	ʃɔ
Shawinigan	shuh WI nuh guhn	ʃəˈwɪnəgən
Shcherbakov	cher bah KAWF	tʃərbɑˈkɔf
shea	shee	ʃi
sheath	sheeth	ʃiθ
sheathe	sheeth :	ʃið
shebeen	shi BEEN	ʃɪˈbin
Shebeli	shay BE li	ʃeˈbɛlɪ
sheik, -h	sheek	ʃik
shekel	SHE kuhl	ˈʃɛkəl
Shekinah	shi KIGH nuh	ʃɪˈkaɪnə
shellac, -k	shuh LAK	ʃəˈlæk
Shenandoah	she nuhn DOH uh	ʃɛnənˈdoə
shenanigan	shi NA ni guhn	ʃɪˈnænɪgən
Sheol, s-	SHEE ohl	ˈʃiol
shepherd	SHE perd	ˈʃɛpərd
Sheraton	SHE ruh tuhn	ˈʃɛrətən
sherbet	SHER bit	ˈʃɚbɪt
sherif	shuh REEF	ʃəˈrif
sheriff	SHE rif	ˈʃɛrɪf
's Hertogenbosch	SAIR toh kuhn BAWS	ˈsɛrtokənˈbɔs
Shetland	SHET luhnd	ˈʃɛtlənd
Shevuoth	shuh VOO : ohth	ʃəˈvuoθ
shew	shoh	ʃo
shewbread	SHOH bred	ˈʃobrɛd
shibboleth	SHI buh luhth	ˈʃɪbələθ
shield	sheeld	ʃild
Shiite	SHEE ight	ˈʃiaɪt
shikari, shikaree	shi KAH ree	ʃɪˈkɑri
Shikoku	SHEE kaw koo :	ˈʃikɔku
shillelagh, shillalah	shi LAY luh	ʃɪˈlelə
Shillong	shi LAWNG	ʃɪˈlɔŋ
Shiloh	SHIGH loh	ˈʃaɪlo
Shimonoseki	SHEE maw naw SAY ki	ˈʃimɔnɔˈsekɪ
Shinar	SHIGH nahr	ˈʃaɪnɑr
Shinnecock	SHI nuh kahk	ˈʃɪnəkɑk
Shinto	SHIN toh	ˈʃɪnto
Shipka	SHIP kah	ˈʃɪpkɑ
Shiraz	shee RAHZ	ʃiˈrɑz
Shiré	SHEE re	ˈʃirɛ
Shirer	SHIGH rer	ˈʃaɪrər
shirr	sher	ʃɚ
shish kebab	SHISH kuh BAHB	ˈʃɪʃ kəˈbab
shittah	SHI tuh	ˈʃɪtə

sing [ŋ] ; *oh* [o] ; *oil* [ɔɪ] ; *foot* [ʊ] ; *foo*:d [u] ; *how* [aʊ] ; *pie* [p] ; *ray* [r] ; *so* [s] ; *sh*all [ʃ] ; *to* [t] ; *thin* [θ] ; *th*:en [ð] ; *above* (*uh* B*U*HV) [ə, ˈʌ] ; *vine* [v] ; *wine* [w] ; *wh*ine [hw] ; *you* [j] ; *zoo* [z] ; *rouge* (roo:*zh*) [ʒ].

shittim	SHI tim	ˈʃɪtɪm
Shiva	SHEE vuh	ˈʃivə
shivaree	shi vuh REE	ʃɪvəˈri
Shizuoka	SHEE zoo : AW kah	ˈʃizuˈɔkɑ
shoal	shohl	ʃol
shoat	shoht	ʃot
shofar	SHOH fahr	ˈʃofɑr
shogun	SHOH goo : n	ˈʃogun
shogunate	SHOH goo : nayt	ˈʃogunet
Sholapur	SHOH luh poor	ˈʃoləpur
Sholokhov	SHAH lah kawf	ˈʃɑlakɔf
shone	shohn	ʃon
shoon	shoo : n	ʃun
shophar	SHOH fahr	ˈʃofɑr
shoran	SHAW ran	ˈʃɔræn
short-lived	shawrt lighvd	ʃɔrt laɪvd
Shoshone, Shoshoni	shoh SHOH ni	ʃoˈʃoni
Shostakovich	shah stuh KOH vich	ʃɑstəˈkovɪtʃ
shrapnel	SHRAP nuhl	ˈʃræpnəl
Shreveport	SHREEV pawrt	ˈʃrivpɔrt
Shrewsbury	SHROO : Z be ri	ˈʃruzbɛrɪ
shrive	shrighv	ʃraɪv
shriven	SHRI vuhn	ˈʃrɪvən
shroud	shrowd	ʃraʊd
Shulamite	SHOO : luh might	ˈʃuləmaɪt
Shuster	SHOO : ster	ˈʃustər
Shvernik	SHVAIR nik	ˈʃvɛrnɪk
si, S-, sí	see	si
Sialkot	si AHL koht	sɪˈɑlkot
Siam	sigh AM	saɪˈæm
siamang	SEE uh mang	ˈsiəmæŋ
Sibelius	suh BAY lyuhs	səˈbeljəs
Siberia	sigh BI ri uh	saɪˈbɪrɪə
sibilant	SI buh luhnt	ˈsɪbələnt
sibling	SIB ling	ˈsɪblɪŋ
Sibyl, s-	SI buhl	ˈsɪbəl
sibylline, S-	SI buh leen	ˈsɪbəlin
sic	sik	sɪk
siccative	SI kuh tiv	ˈsɪkətɪv
Sicilian	si SI li uhn	sɪˈsɪlɪən
Sicily	SI suh li	ˈsɪsəlɪ
sickle	SI kuhl	ˈsɪkəl
sicklemia	si KLEE mi uh	sɪˈklimɪə
sic passim	sik PA sim	sɪk ˈpæsɪm
sic semper tyrannis	sik SEM per ti RA nis	sɪk ˈsɛmpər tɪˈrænɪs
sic transit gloria mundi	sik TRAN sit GLOH ri uh MUHN di	sɪk ˈtrænsɪt ˈglorɪə ˈmʌndɪ
Siddhartha	si DAHR tuh	sɪˈdɑrtə
Siddons	SI duhnz	ˈsɪdənz
siddur	SI door	ˈsɪdur
sidereal	sigh DI ri uhl	saɪˈdɪrɪəl
siderite	SI duh right	ˈsɪdəraɪt

at [æ] ; *ah* [ɑ] ; *air* [ɛ] ; *awful* [ɔ] ; *say* [e] ; *back* [b] ; *chair* [tʃ] ; *do* [d] ; *elm* [ɛ] ; *eel* [i] ; *server* [ˈɝ, ər] ; *fit* [f] ; *go* [g] ; *hurt* [h] ; *is* [ɪ] ; *high* [aɪ] ; *jet* [dʒ] ; *kiss* [k] ; *lamb* [l] ; *my* [m] ; *nice* [n] ;

siderosis	si duh ROH sis	sɪdəˈrosɪs
siderostat	SI duh roh stat	ˈsɪdərostæt
Sidi Barrani	SEE dee bah RAH nee	ˈsidi bɑˈrɑni
sidle	SIGH duhl	ˈsaɪdəl
Sidon	SIGH duhn	ˈsaɪdən
Sidonian	sigh DOH ni uhn	saɪˈdonɪən
siècle	SYE kluh	ˈsjɛklə
Siegbahn	SEEG bahn	ˈsigbɑn
Siegel	SEE guhl	ˈsigəl
Siegfried	SEEG freed	ˈsigfrid
Sieg heil	zeek highl	zik haɪl
Siemens	SEE muhnz	ˈsimənz
Siena	si E nuh	sɪˈɛnə
Sienkiewicz	shen KYE vich	ʃɛnˈkjɛvɪtʃ
sienna	si E nuh	sɪˈɛnə
Siepi	see E pee	siˈɛpi
Sierpc	shairpts	ʃɛrpts
sierra, S-	si AI ruh	sɪˈɛrə
Sierra Leone	si AI ruh lee OH ni	sɪˈɛrə liˈonɪ
Sierra Madre	si AI ruh MAH dray	sɪˈɛrə ˈmɑdre
Sierra Nevada	si AI ruh nuh VA duh	sɪˈɛrə nəˈvædə
siesta	si E stuh	sɪˈɛstə
sieve	siv	sɪv
Sighisoara	see gee SHWAH rah	sigiˈʃwɑrɑ
sigil	SI juhl	ˈsɪdʒəl
Sigismund	SI jis muhnd	ˈsɪdʒɪsmənd
sigma	SIG muh	ˈsɪgmə
Sigmund	SIG muhnd	ˈsɪgmənd
signal	SIG nuhl	ˈsɪgnəl
signatory	SIG nuh taw ri	ˈsɪgnətɔrɪ
signet	SIG nit	ˈsɪgnɪt
signor (Italian)	see NYAWR	siˈnjɔr
signora (Italian)	see NYAW rah	siˈnjɔrɑ
signore (Italian)	see NYAW re	siˈnjɔrɛ
signorina (Italian)	see nyaw REE nah	sinjɔˈrinɑ
signorino (Italian)	see nyaw REE naw	sinjɔˈrinɔ
Sigurd	SI gerd	ˈsɪgərd
Sikandarabad	see KUHN duh rah BAHD	siˈkʌndərɑˈbɑd
Sikh	seek	sik
Sikkim	SI kim	ˈsɪkɪm
Sikorsky	si KAWR ski	sɪˈkɔrskɪ
silage	SIGH lij	ˈsaɪlɪdʒ
silenus, S-	sigh LEE nuhs	saɪˈlinəs
Silesia, s-	sigh LEE shi uh	saɪˈliʃɪə
silex, S-	SIGH leks	ˈsaɪlɛks
silhouette	si loo ET	sɪluˈɛt
silica	SI li kuh	ˈsɪlɪkə
siliceous	suh LI shuhs	səˈlɪʃəs
silicic	suh LI sik	səˈlɪsɪk
silicon	SI li kuhn	ˈsɪlɪkən
silicone	SI luh kohn	ˈsɪləkon
silicosis	si luh KOH sis	sɪləˈkosɪs

sing [ŋ] ; *oh* [o] ; *oil* [ɔɪ] ; *foot* [ʊ] ; *foo:d* [u] ; *how* [aʊ] ; *pie* [p] ; *ray* [r] ; *so* [s] ; *shall* [ʃ] ; *to* [t] ; *thin* [θ] ; *th:en* [ð] ; *above* (*uh* BUHV) [ə, ˈʌ] ; *vine* [v] ; *wine* [w] ; *whine* [hw] ; *you* [j] ; *zoo* [z] ; *rouge* (roo:zh) [ʒ].

silkaline, silkalene	sil kuh LEEN	ˈsɪlkəˈlin
sillabub	SI luh buhb	ˈsɪləbʌb
Sillanpaa	SI lan pa	ˈsɪlænpæ
Sillitoe	SI li toh	ˈsɪlɪto
silo	SIGH loh	ˈsaɪlo
Siloam	sigh LOH uhm	saɪˈloəm
Silone	see LAW ne	siˈlɔnɛ
Silurian	suh LOO ri uhn	səˈlʊrɪən
silva	SIL vuh	ˈsɪlvə
Silvia	SIL vi uh	ˈsɪlvɪə
silviculture	SIL vi kuhl cher	ˈsɪlvɪkʌltʃər
s'il vous plaît	seel voo: PLE	sil vu ˈplɛ
simar	si MAHR	sɪˈmɑr
Simchath Torah	sim KAHTH toh RAH	sɪmˈkɑθ toˈrɑ
Simferopol	sim fe RAW pawl	sɪmfɛˈrɔpɔl
simian	SI mi uhn	ˈsɪmɪən
similar	SI muh ler	ˈsɪmələr
similarity	si muh LA ruh ti	sɪməˈlærətɪ
simile	SI muh lee	ˈsɪməli
similitude	suh MI luh too: d	səˈmɪlətud
Simionato, Giuletta	si mee uh NAH toh, joo: lee E tuh	sɪmɪəˈnɑto, dʒuliˈɛtə
Simla	SIM luh	ˈsɪmlə
Simoneau, Leopold	see moh NOH, lee oh POHL	simoˈno, lioˈpol
simoniac	si MOH ni ak	sɪˈmonɪæk
Simonides	sigh MAH nuh deez	saɪˈmɑnədiz
Simonize	SIGH muh nighz	ˈsaɪmənaɪz
Simon Legree	SIGH muhn luh GREE	ˈsaɪmən ləˈgri
simony	SIGH muh ni	ˈsaɪmənɪ
simoom	si MOO: M	sɪˈmum
simoon	si MOO: N	sɪˈmun
Simplon	SIM plahn	ˈsɪmplɑn
simulacrum	sim yoo LAY kruhm	sɪmjuˈlekrəm
simulcast	SIGH muhl kast	ˈsaɪməlkæst
simultaneity	sigh muhl tuh NEE uh ti	saɪməltəˈniətɪ
simultaneous	sigh muhl TAY ni uhs	saɪməlˈtenɪəs
Sinai	SIGH nigh	ˈsaɪnaɪ
Sinaloa	see nah LAW ah	sinɑˈlɔɑ
sinarchism, sinarquism	si NAHR ki zuhm	sɪˈnɑrkɪzəm
sinarquista	si nahr KI stuh	snɑrˈkɪstə
Sinbad	SIN bad	ˈsɪnbæd
sincerity	sin SAI ruh ti	sɪnˈsɛrətɪ
sine (mathematics)	sighn	saɪn
sine ("without")	SIGH ni	ˈsaɪnɪ
sinecure	SIGH ni kyoor	ˈsaɪnɪkjʊr
sine die	SIGH ni DIGH ee	ˈsaɪnɪ ˈdaɪi
sine prole	SIGH ni PROH li	ˈsaɪnɪ ˈprolɪ
sine qua non	SIGH ni kway NAHN	ˈsaɪnɪ kwe ˈnɑn
sinew	SI nyoo:	ˈsɪnju
sinewy	SI nyuh wi	ˈsɪnjəwɪ
sinfonia	sin fuh NEE uh	sɪnfəˈniə
sinfonietta	sin fuh NYE tuh	sɪnfəˈnjɛtə

at [æ]; *ah* [ɑ]; *air* [ɛ]; *aw*ful [ɔ]; *say* [e]; *back* [b]; *chair* [tʃ]; *do* [d]; *elm* [ɛ]; *eel* [i]; *server* [ˈɜ, ər]; *f*it [f]; *go* [g]; *hurt* [h]; *is* [ɪ]; *high* [aɪ]; *jet* [dʒ]; *kiss* [k]; *lamb* [l]; *my* [m]; *nice* [n];

Singapore	SING guh pawr	ˈsɪŋgəpɔr
Singaraja, Singaradja	sing gah RAH jah	sɪŋgɑˈrɑdʒɑ
singer	SING er	ˈsɪŋər
Singhalese	sing guh LEEZ	sɪŋgəˈliz
singularity	sing gyuh LA ruh ti	sɪŋgjəˈlærətɪ
Sinhalese	sin huh LEEZ	sɪnhəˈliz
Sinicism	SI nuh si zuhm	ˈsɪnəsɪzəm
sinister	SI ni ster	ˈsɪnɪstər
sinistral	SI ni struhl	ˈsɪnɪstrəl
Sinitic	si NI tik	sɪˈnɪtɪk
sink	singk	sɪŋk
Sinkiang	sin kyang	sɪn kjæŋ
Sinn Fein	shin fayn	ʃɪn fen
Sino-	SIGH noh	ˈsaɪno
Sinology	sigh NAH luh ji	saɪˈnɑlədʒɪ
Sinon	SIGH nuhn	ˈsaɪnən
sinuosity	si nyoo AH suh ti	sɪnjʊˈɑsətɪ
sinuous	SI nyoo uhs	ˈsɪnjʊəs
sinus	SIGH nuhs	ˈsaɪnəs
sinusitis	sigh nuh SIGH tis	saɪnəˈsaɪtɪs
Sion	SIGH uhn	ˈsaɪən
Siouan	SOO : uhn	ˈsuən
Sioux	soo :	su
siphon	SIGH fuhn	ˈsaɪfən
Siqueiros	see KAY raws	siˈkerɔs
sirdar	ser DAHR	sərˈdɑr
siren	SIGH ruhn	ˈsaɪrən
sirenian	sigh REE ni uhn	saɪˈrinɪən
Siret	si RET	sɪˈrɛt
Sirius	SI ri uhs	ˈsɪrɪəs
sirloin	SER loin	ˈsɚlɔɪn
sirocco	suh RAH koh	səˈrɑko
sirrah	SI ruh	ˈsɪrə
sirup	SI ruhp	ˈsɪrəp
sisal	SIGH suhl	ˈsaɪsəl
Sismondi	sis MAHN di	sɪsˈmɑndɪ
Sistine	SI steen	ˈsɪstin
sistrum	SI struhm	ˈsɪstrəm
Sisyphean	si suh FEE uhn	sɪsəˈfiən
Sisyphus	SI suh fuhs	ˈsɪsəfəs
Sitka	SIT kuh	ˈsɪtkə
sitology	sigh TAH luh ji	saɪˈtɑlədʒɪ
sitomania	sigh tuh MAY ni uh	saɪtəˈmenɪə
sitophobia	sigh tuh FOH bi uh	saɪtəˈfobɪə
sitosterol	sigh TAH stuh rohl	saɪˈtɑstərol
Sittang	si tang	sɪtæŋ
situate (a)	SI choo it	ˈsɪtʃʊɪt
situate (v)	SI choo ayt	ˈsɪtʃʊet
situs	SIGH tuhs	ˈsaɪtəs
Sitwell	SIT wuhl	ˈsɪtwəl
sitz	sits	sɪts
Siva	SEE vuh	ˈsivə

sing [ŋ]; *oh* [o]; *oil* [ɔɪ]; *foot* [ʊ]; *foo*:d [u]; *how* [aʊ]; *pie* [p]; *ray* [r]; *so* [s]; *sh*all [ʃ];
to [t]; *th*in [θ]; *th*:en [ð]; *above* (*uh* B*U*H*V*) [ə, ˈʌ]; *vine* [v]; *wine* [w]; *wh*ine [hw];
you [j]; *zoo* [z]; *rouge* (roo:*zh*) [ʒ].

Sivas	see VAHZ	si'vɑz
Siwa	SEE wah	'siwɑ
Sixtine	SIK stin	'sɪkstɪn
Sixtus	SIK stuhs	'sɪkstəs
sizar, sizer	SIGH zer	'saɪzər
Skagen	SKAH guhn	'skɑgən
Skagerrak, Skagerak, Skager Rack, etc.	SKA guh rak	'skægeræk
skald	skawld	skɔld
skaldic	SKAWL dik	'skɔldɪk
Skaneateles	ska ni AT luhs	skænɪ'ætləs
skein	skayn	sken
skeletal	SKE luh tuhl	'skɛlətəl
skep	skep	skɛp
skew	skyoo :	skju
skewer	SKYOO : er	'skjuər
ski	skee	ski
skiagraph	SKIGH uh graf	'skaɪəgræf
skijoring	SKEE jaw ring	'skidʒɔrɪŋ
skiogram	SKIGH uh gram	'skaɪəgræm
skirl	skerl	skɜl
skirmish	SKER mish	'skɜmɪʃ
skiver	SKIGH ver	'skaɪvər
skivvy	SKI vi	'skɪvɪ
skoal	skohl	skol
Skoplje	SKAWP lye	'skɔpljɛ
Skouras	SKOO rahs	'skurɑs
skulduggery	skuhl DUH guh ri	skʌl'dʌgərɪ
skulk	skuhlk	skʌlk
Skye	skigh	skaɪ
skyey	SKIGH i	'skaɪɪ
Skyros	SKEE raws	'skirɔs
slalom	SLAH lawm	'slɑlɔm
slather	SLA th : er	'slæðər
slattern	SLA tern	'slætərn
slavey	SLAY vi	'slevɪ
Slavic	SLAH vik	'slɑvɪk
slavish	SLAY vish	'slevɪʃ
slavocracy	slay VAH kruh si	sle'vɑkrəsɪ
Slavonia	sluh VOH ni uh	slə'vonɪə
Slavonic	sluh VAH nik	slə'vɑnɪk
Slavophile	SLAH vuh fighl	'slɑvəfaɪl
Slavophobe	SLAH vuh fohb	'slɑvəfob
Slavophobia	slah vuh FOH bi uh	slɑvə'fobɪə
sleazy	SLEE zi	'slizɪ
sleek	sleek	slik
sleigh	slay	sle
sleight	slight	slaɪt
slept	slept	slɛpt
sleuth	sloo : th	sluθ
Sligo	SLIGH goh	'slaɪgo
slither	SLI th : er	'slɪðər

at [æ] ; ah [ɑ] ; air [ɛ] ; awful [ɔ] ; say [e] ; back [b] ; chair [tʃ] ; do [d] ; elm [ɛ] ; eel [i] ; server ['ɜ, ər] ; fit [f] ; go [g] ; hurt [h] ; is [ɪ] ; high [aɪ] ; jet [dʒ] ; kiss [k] ; lamb [l] ; my [m] ; nice [n] ;

slithery	SLI th:uh ri	ˈslɪðərɪ
sliver	SLI ver	ˈslɪvər
slivovitz	SLI vuh vits	ˈslɪvəvɪts
sloe	sloh	slo
Sloka	SLAW kah	ˈslɔkɑ
sloth	slohth	sloθ
slough ("cast off")	sluhf	slʌf
slough ("marsh")	sloo:	slu
slough ("mudhole")	slow	slaʊ
Slovak	SLOH vak	ˈslovæk
Slovakia	sloh VAH ki uh	sloˈvɑkɪə
sloven	SLUH vuhn	ˈslʌvən
Slovene	SLOH veen	ˈslovin
Slovenia	sloh VEE ni uh	sloˈvinɪə
slovenly	SLUH vuhn li	ˈslʌvənlɪ
sluggard	SLUH gerd	ˈslʌgərd
sluice	SLOO:S	slus
slur	sler	slɝ
slype	slighp	slaɪp
small	smawl	smɔl
smallage	SMAW lij	ˈsmɔlɪdʒ
smalto	ZMAHL taw	ˈzmɑltɔ
smaragd	SMA ragd	ˈsmærægd
smaragdine	smuh RAG din	sməˈrægdɪn
smaragdite	smuh RAG dight	sməˈrægdaɪt
smaze	smayz	smez
Smetana	SME tuh nuh	ˈsmɛtənə
Smethwick	SME th:ik	ˈsmɛðɪk
smidgen	SMI jin	ˈsmɪdʒɪn
smilax	SMIGH laks	ˈsmaɪlæks
smirch	smerch	smɝtʃ
smirk	smerk	smɝk
smithy	SMI thi	ˈsmɪθɪ
smolder	SMOHL der	ˈsmoldər
Smolensk	smah LENSK	smɑˈlɛnsk
Smollett	SMAH lit	ˈsmɑlɪt
smolt	smohlt	smolt
smooch	smoo:ch	smutʃ
smooth	smoo:th:	smuð
smorgasbord	SMAWR guhs bawrd	ˈsmɔrgəsbɔrd
smorzando	smawrt SAHN daw	smɔrtˈsɑndɔ
smother	SMUH th:er	ˈsmʌðər
Smuts	smuhts	smʌts
Smyrna	SMER nuh	ˈsmɝnə
snafu (a, n)	SNA foo:	ˈsnæfu
snafu (v)	sna FOO:	snæˈfu
snivel	SNI vuhl	ˈsnɪvəl
snood	snoo:d	snud
Snoqualmie	snoh KWAHL mi	snoˈkwɑlmɪ
snorkel	SNAWR kuhl	ˈsnɔrkəl
Sobolev	SAW bah lef	ˈsɔbɑlɛf
sobriety	soh BRIGH uh ti	soˈbraɪətɪ

---

sing [ŋ]; *oh* [o]; *oil* [ɔɪ]; *foot* [ʊ]; *foo:d* [u]; *how* [aʊ]; *pie* [p]; *ray* [r]; *so* [s]; *shall* [ʃ]; *to* [t]; *thin* [θ]; *th:en* [ð]; *above* (*uh BUH*V) [ə, ˈʌ]; *vine* [v]; *wine* [w]; *whine* [hw]; *you* [j]; *zoo* [z]; *rouge* (*roo:zh*) [ʒ].

sobriquet	SOH bri kay	ˈsobrɪke
soccer	SAH ker	ˈsɑkər
Sochi	SAW chi	ˈsɔtʃɪ
social	SOH shuhl	ˈsoʃəl
sociality	soh shi A luh ti	soʃɪˈælətɪ
socialize	SOH shuh lighz	ˈsoʃəlaɪz
societal	suh SIGH uh tuhl	səˈsaɪətəl
society	suh SIGH uh ti	səˈsaɪətɪ
Socinian	soh SI ni uhn	soˈsɪnɪən
Socinus	soh SIGH nuhs	soˈsaɪnəs
sociological	soh si uh LAH ji kuhl	sosɪəˈlɑdʒɪkəl
sociology	soh si AH luh ji	sosɪˈɑlədʒɪ
sociometry	soh si AH muh tri	sosɪˈɑmətrɪ
socket	SAH kit	ˈsɑkɪt
sockeye	SAH kigh	ˈsɑkaɪ
Socony	suh KOH ni	səˈkonɪ
Socorro	suh KAW raw	səˈkɔrɔ
Socotra	soh KOH truh	soˈkotrə
Socrates	SAH kruh teez	ˈsɑkrətiz
Socratic	soh KRA tik	soˈkrætɪk
sodality	soh DA luh ti	soˈdælətɪ
Söderström	SER der strerm	ˈSɝdərstrɔrm
sodium	SOH di uhm	ˈsodɪəm
Sodom	SAH duhm	ˈsadəm
Sodomite, s-	SAH duh might	ˈsadəmaɪt
sodomy	SAH duh mi	ˈsadəmɪ
Soekarno	soo : KAHR noh	suˈkɑrno
Soemba	SOO : M bah	ˈsumbɑ
Soembawa	soo : m BAH wah	sumˈbɑwɑ
Soenda	SOO : N dah	ˈsundɑ
Soerabaja	soo : rah BAH yah	surɑˈbɑjɑ
Soerakarta	soo : rah KAHR tah	surɑˈkɑrtɑ
sofa	SOH fuh	ˈsofə
sofar	SOH fahr	ˈsofɑr
Sofia	SOH fi uh	ˈsofɪə
soft	sawft	sɔft
soften	SAW fuhn	ˈsɔfən
Sogdian	SAHG di uhn	ˈsɑgdɪən
Sogdiana	sahg di AY nuh	sɑgdɪˈenə
soggy	SAH gi	ˈsagɪ
Soho	soh HOH	soˈho
soi-disant	swah dee ZAHN	swa diˈzɑn
soigné, -e	swah NYAY	swaˈnje
soilure	SOI lyoor	ˈsɔɪljur
soiree, soirée	swah RAY	swaˈre
Soissons	swah SOHN	swaˈson
sojourn (n)	SOH jern	ˈsodʒərn
sojourn (v)	soh JERN	soˈdʒɝn
Sokoto	SOH koh toh	ˈsokoto
solace	SAH lis	ˈsalɪs
solanum	soh LAY nuhm	soˈlenəm
solar	SOH ler	ˈsolər

at [æ] ; ah [ɑ] ; air [ɛ] ; awful [ɔ] ; say [e] ; back [b] ; chair [tʃ] ; do [d] ; elm [ɛ] ; eel [i] ;
server [ˈɝ, ər] ; fit [f] ; go [g] ; hurt [h] ; is [ɪ] ; high [aɪ] ; jet [dʒ] ; kiss [k] ; lamb [l] ; my [m] ;
nice [n] ;

solarium	soh LAI ri uhm	soˈlɛrɪəm
solarize	SOH luh righz	ˈsoləraɪz
solder	SAH der	ˈsɑdər
solecism	SAH luh si zuhm	ˈsɑləsɪzəm
solemn	SAH luhm	ˈsɑləm
solemnify	suh LEM nuh figh	səˈlɛmnəfaɪ
solemnity	suh LEM nuh ti	səˈlɛmnətɪ
solemnize	SAH luhm nighz	ˈsɑləmnaɪz
solenoid	SOH luh noid	ˈsolənɔɪd
Solent	SOH luhnt	ˈsolənt
solfa	sohl FAH	solˈfɑ
solfatara	sawl fah TAH rah	sɔlfaˈtɑrɑ
solfeggio	sahl FE joh	salˈfɛdʒo
solicitor	suh LI suh ter	səˈlɪsətər
solicitous	suh LI suh tuhs	səˈlɪsətəs
solidarity	sah luh DA ruh ti	sɑləˈdærətɪ
solidify	suh LI duh figh	səˈlɪdəfaɪ
solidity	suh LI duh ti	səˈlɪdətɪ
solidus	SAH li duhs	ˈsɑlɪdəs
solifidian	sah luh FI di uhn	sɑləˈfɪdɪən
soliloquist	suh LI luh kwist	səˈlɪləkwɪst
soliloquize	suh LI luh kwighz	səˈlɪləkwaɪz
soliloquy	suh LI luh kwi	səˈlɪləkwɪ
solipsism	SAH lip si zuhm	ˈsɑlɪpsɪzəm
solipsist	SAH lip sist	ˈsɑlɪpsɪst
Solisti di Zagreb, I	soh LEES tee di DZAH greb, ee	soˈlisti dɪ ˈdzɑgrɛb, i
solitaire	sah luh TAIR	sɑləˈtɛr
solitary	SAH luh tai ri	ˈsɑlətɛrɪ
solo, S-	SOH loh	ˈsolo
Solomon	SAH luh muhn	ˈsɑləmən
Solon, s-	SOH luhn	ˈsolən
solstice	SAHL stis	ˈsɑlstɪs
Solti	SOHL tee	ˈsol ti
soluble	SAH lyuh buhl	ˈsɑljəbəl
solus	SOH luhs	ˈsoləs
solute	SAH lyoo : t	ˈsɑljut
solution	suh LOO : shuhn	səˈluʃən
Solvay	SAHL vay	ˈsɑlve
solve	sahlv	sɑlv
solvent	SAHL vuhnt	ˈsɑlvənt
Solway Firth	SAHL way FERTH	ˈsɑlwe ˈfɜθ
soma	SOH muh	ˈsomə
Somali	suh MAH li	səˈmɑlɪ
Somalia	suh MAH li uh	səˈmɑlɪə
Somaliland	suh MAH li land	səˈmɑlɪlænd
somatic	soh MA tik	soˈmætɪk
somatology	soh muh TAH luh ji	soməˈtɑlədʒɪ
somatoplasm	SOH muh tuh pla zuhm	ˈsomətəplæzəm
somatotonic	soh muh tuh TAH nik	somətəˈtɑnɪk
somber, sombre	SAHM ber	ˈsɑmbər
sombrero	sahm BRAI roh	sɑmˈbrero

sing [ŋ] ; *oh* [o] ; *oil* [ɔɪ] ; *foot* [ʊ] ; *foo:*d [u] ; *how* [aʊ] ; *pie* [p] ; *ray* [r] ; *so* [s] ; *sh*all [ʃ] ;
to [t] ; *th*in [θ] ; *th:*en [ð] ; *above* (*uh* BUHV) [ə, ˈʌ] ; *vine* [v] ; *wine* [w] ; *wh*ine [hw] ;
you [j] ; *zoo* [z] ; *rouge* (roo:*zh*) [ʒ].

H.P.—Z

somersault	SUH mer sawlt	ˈsʌmərsɔlt
Somerset, s-	SUH mer set	ˈsʌmərsɛt
somewhat	SUHM hwaht	ˈsʌmhwɑt
Somme	suhm	sʌm
somnambulate	sahm NAM byuh layt	sɑmˈnæmbjəlet
somnambulation	sahm nam byuh LAY shuhn	sɑmnæmbjəˈleʃən
somniferous	sahm NI fuh ruhs	sɑmˈnɪfərəs
somniloquy	sahm NI luh kwi	sɑmˈnɪləkwɪ
somnolence	SAHM nuh luhns	ˈsɑmnələns
Somnus	SAHM nuhs	ˈsɑmnəs
Somoza	saw MAW sah	sɔˈmɔsɑ
sonant	SOH nuhnt	ˈsonənt
sonar	SOH nahr	ˈsonɑr
sonata	suh NAH tuh	səˈnɑtə
sonatina	sah nuh TEE nuh	sɑnəˈtinə
song	sawng	sɔŋ
sonic	SAH nik	ˈsɑnɪk
Sonnambula, La	soh NAHM byoo : lah, lah	soˈnɑmbjulɑ, lɑ
sonnet	SAH nit	ˈsɑnɪt
Sonora	saw NAW rah	sɔˈnɔrɑ
sonorant	soh NAW ruhnt	soˈnɔrənt
sonority	suh NAW ruh ti	səˈnɔrətɪ
sonorous	suh NAW ruhs	səˈnɔrəs
Sonotone	SAH nuh tohn	ˈsɑnəton
Soochow	soo : chow	su tʃau
Soong	soong	suŋ
soot	soot	sʊt
sooth	soo : th	suθ
soothe	soo : th :	suð
Sophia	soh FIGH uh	soˈfaɪə
sophism	SAH fi zuhm	ˈsɑfɪzəm
sophister	SAH fi ster	ˈsɑfɪstər
sophisticate (n)	suh FI stuh kit	səˈfɪstəkɪt
sophisticate (v)	suh FI stuh kayt	səˈfɪstəket
sophistry	SAH fi stri	ˈsɑfɪstrɪ
Sophocles	SAH fuh kleez	ˈsɑfəkliz
sophomore	SAH fuh mawr	ˈsɑfəmɔr
sophomoric	sah fuh MAW rik	sɑfəˈmɔrɪk
sopor	SOH per	ˈsopər
soporific	sah puh RI fik	sɑpəˈrɪfɪk
soprano	suh PRA noh	səˈpræno
Sopron	SHAW prawn	ˈʃɔprɔn
Sorbian	SAWR bi uhn	ˈsɔrbɪən
Sorbonne	sawr BAHN	sɔrˈbɑn
sorcerer	SAWR suh rer	ˈsɔrsərər
sordid	SAWR did	ˈsɔrdɪd
sordino	sawr DEE naw	sɔrˈdino
Sorenson	SAWR uhn suhn	ˈsɔrənsən
sorghum	SAWR guhm	ˈsɔrgəm
sorites	soh RIGH teez	soˈraɪtiz
Soroptimist	suh RAHP tuh mist	səˈrɑptəmɪst
sororicide	suh RAW ruh sighd	səˈrɔrəsaɪd

at [æ] ; ah [ɑ] ; air [ɛ] ; awful [ɔ] ; say [e] ; back [b] ; chair [tʃ] ; do [d] ; elm [ɛ] ; eel [i] ; server [ˈɝ, ər] ; fit [f] ; go [g] ; hurt [h] ; is [ɪ] ; high [aɪ] ; jet [dʒ] ; kiss [k] ; lamb [l] ; my [m] ; nice [n] ;

sorority	suh RAW ruh ti	sǝˈrɔrǝtɪ
sorosis	suh ROH sis	sǝˈrosɪs
sorrel	SAW ruhl	ˈsɔrǝl
Sorrento	suh REN toh	sǝˈrɛnto
sorrow	SAH roh	ˈsɑro
sorry	SAW ri	ˈsɔrɪ
sortie	SAWR ti	ˈsɔrtɪ
sortilege	SAWR ti lij	ˈsɔrtɪlɪdʒ
Sosnowiec	saws NAW vyets	sɔsˈnɔvjɛts
sostenuto	sah stuh NOO : toh	sɑstǝˈnuto
Sotheby's	SUHTH : beez	ˈsʌðbiz
Sothern	SUH th : ern	ˈsʌðǝrn
sotto voce	SAH toh VOH chi	ˈsɑto ˈvotʃɪ
sou	soo :	su
Soubise, s-	soo : BEEZ	suˈbiz
soubrette	soo : BRET	suˈbrɛt
soubriquet	SOO : bri kay	ˈsubrɪke
souchong	soo : shawng	suʃɔŋ
souffle	SOO : fuhl	ˈsufǝl
soufflé	soo : FLAY	suˈfle
sough	suhf	sʌf
sought	sawt	sɔt
soupçon	soo : p SOHN	supˈson
sourdine	soor DEEN	sʊrˈdin
sourdough	SOWR doh	ˈsaʊrdo
Sousa	SOO : zuh	ˈsuzǝ
sousaphone	SOO : zuh fohn	ˈsuzǝfon
souse	sows	saʊs
soutache	soo : TAHSH	suˈtaʃ
soutane	soo : TAHN	suˈtan
Southampton	sow THAMP tuhn	saʊˈθæmptǝn
southerly	SUH th : er li	ˈsʌðǝrlɪ
southern	SUH th : ern	ˈsʌðǝrn
Southey	SOW th : i	ˈsaʊðɪ
Southwark	SUH th : erk	ˈsʌðǝrk
Soutine	soo : TEEN	suˈtin
souvenir	soo : vuh NIR	suvǝˈnɪr
sou'wester, souwester	sow WE ster	saʊˈwɛstǝr
Souzay, Gérard	soo : ZAY, zhay RAHR	suˈze, ʒeˈrar
sovereign	SAHV rin	ˈsɑvrɪn
sovereignty	SAHV rin ti	ˈsɑvrɪntɪ
soviet, S-	SOH vi it	ˈsovɪɪt
sovietize	SOH vi uh tighz	ˈsovɪǝtaɪz
sow (pig)	sow	saʊ
sow (" plant ")	soh	so
sowar	soh WAHR	soˈwar
spa, S-	spah	spɑ
Spaak	spahk	spɑk
Spaatz	spahts	spɑts
Spaeth	spayth	speθ
spaghetti	spuh GE ti	spǝˈgɛtɪ
spahi, spahee	SPAH hee	ˈspɑhi

sing [ŋ] ; oh [o] ; oil [ɔɪ] ; foot [ʊ] ; foo :d [u] ; how [aʊ] ; pie [p] ; ray [r] ; so [s] ; shall [ʃ] ;
to [t] ; thin [θ] ; th :en [ð] ; above (uh BUHV) [ǝ, ˈʌ] ; vine [v] ; wine [w] ; whine [hw] ;
you [j] ; zoo [z] ; rouge (roo :zh) [ʒ].

Spain	spayn	spen
Spalato	SPAH lah taw	ˈspɑlɑtɔ
spaniel	SPA nyuhl	ˈspænjəl
spanner	SPA ner	ˈspænər
spar, S-, SPAR	spahr	spɑr
Spartacus	SPAHR tuh kuhs	ˈspɑrtəkəs
spasm	SPA zuhm	ˈspæzəm
spasmodic	spaz MAH dik	spæzˈmɑdɪk
spasmolytic	spaz muh LI tik	spæzməˈlɪtɪk
spastic	SPA stik	ˈspæstɪk
spatial	SPAY shuhl	ˈspeʃəl
spatiography	spay shi AH gruh fi	speʃɪˈɑgrəfɪ
spatiotemporal	SPAY shi oh TEM puh ruhl	ˈspeʃɪoˈtɛmpərəl
spatterdash	SPA ter dash	ˈspætərdæʃ
spatterdock	SPA ter dahk	ˈspætərdɑk
spatula	SPA chuh luh	ˈspætʃələ
spatulate (a)	SPA chuh lit	ˈspætʃəlɪt
spatulate (v)	SPA chuh layt	ˈspætʃəlet
spavin	SPA vin	ˈspævɪn
speciality	spe shi A luh ti	speʃɪˈælətɪ
specialty	SPE shuhl ti	ˈspeʃəltɪ
specie	SPEE shi	ˈspiʃɪ
species	SPEE shiz	ˈspiʃɪz
specific	spi SI fik	spɪˈsɪfɪk
specify	SPE suh figh	ˈspesəfaɪ
specimen	SPE suh muhn	ˈspesəmən
speciosity	spee shi AH suh ti	spiʃɪˈɑsətɪ
specious	SPEE shuhs	ˈspiʃəs
spectacle	SPEK tuh kuhl	ˈspɛktəkəl
spectacular	spek TA kyuh ler	spɛkˈtækjələr
spectator	SPEK tay ter	ˈspɛktetər
specter, spectre	SPEK ter	ˈspɛktər
spectral	SPEK truhl	ˈspɛktrəl
spectroscope	SPEK truh skohp	ˈspɛktrəskop
spectroscopic	spek truh SKAH pik	spɛktrəˈskɑpɪk
spectrum	SPEK truhm	ˈspɛktrəm
speculate	SPE kyuh layt	ˈspɛkjəlet
speculum	SPE kyuh luhm	ˈspɛkjələm
speedometer	spi DAH muh ter	spɪˈdɑmətər
Speicher	SPIGH ker	ˈspaɪkər
speiss	spighs	spaɪs
spelean, spelaean	spi LEE uhn	spɪˈliən
speleology	spee li AH luh ji	spilɪˈɑlədʒɪ
spelunker	spi LUHNG ker	spɪˈlʌŋkər
Spencerian	spen SI ri uhn	spɛnˈsɪrɪən
Spengler	SPENG ler	ˈspɛŋlər
Spenserian	spen SI ri uhn	spɛnˈsɪrɪən
sperm	sperm	spɝm
spermatozoon	sper muh tuh ZOH ahn	spɝmətəˈzoɑn
Spezia	SPET syah	ˈspɛtsjɑ
sphacelate	SFA suh layt	ˈsfæsəlet
sphagnum	SFAG nuhm	ˈsfægnəm

at [æ] ; *ah* [ɑ] ; *air* [ɛ] ; *awful* [ɔ] ; *say* [e] ; *back* [b] ; *chair* [tʃ] ; *do* [d] ; *elm* [ɛ] ; *eel* [i] ;
server [ˈɝ, ər] ; *f*it [f] ; *go* [g] ; *hurt* [h] ; *is* [ɪ] ; *high* [aɪ] ; *jet* [dʒ] ; *kiss* [k] ; *lamb* [l] ; *my* [m] ;
nice [n] ;

sphenic	SFEE nik	ˈsfinɪk
sphenography	sfi NAH gruh fi	sfɪˈnɑgrəfɪ
sphere	sfir	sfɪr
spherical	SFAI ri kuhl	ˈsfɛrɪkəl
sphericity	sfi RI suh ti	sfɪˈrɪsətɪ
spheroid	SFAI roid	ˈsfɛrɔɪd
sphincter	SFINGK ter	ˈsfɪŋktər
sphinx, S-	sfingks	sfɪŋks
sphragistics	sfruh JI stiks	sfrəˈdʒɪstɪks
sphygmic	SFIG mik	ˈsfɪgmɪk
sphygmograph	SFIG muh graf	ˈsfɪgməgræf
sphygmomanometer	SFIG moh muh NAH muh ter	ˈsfɪgmoməˈnɑmətər
sphygmus	SFIG muhs	ˈsfɪgməs
spica, S-	SPIGH kuh	ˈspaɪkə
spiccato	spi KAH toh	spɪˈkɑto
spicule	SPI kyoo : l	ˈspɪkjul
spiegel	SPEE guhl	ˈspigəl
spiegeleisen	SPEE guhl IGH zuhn	ˈspigəlˈaɪzən
spiel	speel	spil
spigot	SPI guht	ˈspɪgət
spikenard	SPIGHK nerd	ˈspaɪknərd
spilikin	SPI li kin	ˈspɪlɪkɪn
spinach	SPI nich	ˈspɪnɪtʃ
spinal	SPIGH nuhl	ˈspaɪnəl
spindly	SPIND li	ˈspɪndlɪ
spinel	spi NEL	spɪˈnɛl
spinescent	spigh NE suhnt	spaɪˈnɛsənt
spinet	SPI nit	ˈspɪnɪt
spinnaker	SPI nuh ker	ˈspɪnəkər
Spinoza	spi NOH zuh	spɪˈnozə
Spinozism	spi NOH zi zuhm	spɪˈnozɪzəm
spiracle	SPIGH ruh kuhl	ˈspaɪrəkəl
spiraea, spirea	spigh REE uh	spaɪˈriə
spiral	SPIGH ruhl	ˈspaɪrəl
spirant	SPIGH ruhnt	ˈspaɪrənt
spirit	SPI rit	ˈspɪrɪt
spiritoso	spi ri TOH soh	spɪrɪˈtoso
spiritual	SPI ri choo uhl	ˈspɪrɪtʃuəl
spirituous	SPI ri choo uhs	ˈspɪrɪtʃuəs
spiritus	SPI ri tuhs	ˈspɪrɪtəs
spirochete, spirochaete	SPIGH ruh keet	ˈspaɪrəkit
Spitsbergen	SPITS ber guhn	ˈspɪtsbɚgən
spittoon	spi TOO : N	spɪˈtun
spitz	spits	spɪts
spitzenburg, spitzenberg, S-	SPIT suhn berg	ˈspɪtsənbɚg
spiv	spiv	spɪv
splanchnic	SPLANGK nik	ˈsplæŋknɪk
splanchnology	splangk NAH luh ji	splæŋkˈnɑlədʒɪ
spleen	spleen	splin
splendor	SPLEN der	ˈsplɛndər
splenetic	spli NE tik	splɪˈnɛtɪk

splenius	SPLEE ni uhs	ˈsplinɪəs
Split	spleet	split
splurge	splerj	splɝdʒ
Spode, s-	spohd	spod
spodumene	SPAH joo meen	ˈspɑdʒʊmin
Spokane	spoh KAN	spoˈkæn
Spoleto	spoh LE toh	spoˈlɛto
spoliate	SPOH li ayt	ˈspolɪet
spoliation	spoh li AY shuhn	spolɪˈeʃən
spoliative	SPOH li ay tiv	ˈspolɪetɪv
spondaic	spahn DAY ik	spɑnˈdeɪk
spondee	SPAHN dee	ˈspɑndi
spondylitis	spahn duh LIGH tis	spɑndəˈlaɪtɪs
sponsion	SPAHN shuhn	ˈspɑnʃən
sponson	SPAHN suhn	ˈspɑnsən
spontaneity	spahn tuh NEE uh ti	spɑntəˈniətɪ
spontaneous	spahn TAY ni uhs	spɑnˈtenɪəs
spoonerism	SPOO: nuh ri zuhm	ˈspunərɪzəm
spoor	spoor	spʊr
Sporades	SPAW ruh deez	ˈspɔrədiz
sporadic	spaw RA dik	spɔˈrædɪk
sporran	SPAH ruhn	ˈspɑrən
Spotsylvania	spaht sil VAY ni uh	spɑtsɪlˈvenɪə
springbok	SPRING bahk	ˈsprɪŋbɑk
springe	sprinj	sprɪndʒ
sprue	sproo:	spru
spume	spyoo: m	spjum
spumescent	spyoo ME suhnt	spjʊˈmɛsənt
spumoni, spumone	spuh MOH ni	spəˈmonɪ
spumous	SPYOO: muhs	ˈspjuməs
spurious	SPYOO ri uhs	ˈspjʊrɪəs
sputnik, sputnick, S-	SPUHT nik	ˈspʌtnɪk
sputum	SPYOO: tuhm	ˈspjutəm
Spuyten Duyvil	SPIGH tuhn DIGH vuhl	ˈspaɪtən ˈdaɪvəl
squab	skwahb	skwɑb
squad	skwahd	skwɑd
squadron	SKWAH druhn	ˈskwɑdrən
squalid	SKWAH lid	ˈskwɑlɪd
squall	skwawl	skwɔl
squalor	SKWAH ler	ˈskwɑlər
squama	SKWAY muh	ˈskwemə
squander	SKWAHN der	ˈskwɑndər
squash	skwahsh	skwɑʃ
squeegee	SKWEE jee	ˈskwidʒi
squeteague	skwee TEEG	skwiˈtig
squirearchy	SKWIGH rahr ki	ˈskwaɪrɑrkɪ
squirrel	SKWER uhl	ˈskwɝəl
sri	shree	ʃri
Srinagar	sree NUH ger	sriˈnʌgər
Stabat Mater	STAH baht MAH ter	ˈstɑbɑt ˈmɑtər
stabile	STAY bil	ˈstebɪl
stabilize	STAY buh lighz	ˈstebəlaɪz

at [æ]; *ah* [ɑ]; *air* [ɛ]; *aw*ful [ɔ]; s*ay* [e]; *b*ack [b]; *ch*air [tʃ]; *d*o [d]; *e*lm [ɛ]; *ee*l [i]; *server* [ˈɝ, ər]; *f*it [f]; *g*o [g]; *h*urt [h]; *i*s [ɪ]; h*igh* [aɪ]; *j*et [dʒ]; *k*iss [k]; *l*amb [l]; *m*y [m]; *n*ice [n];

staccato	stuh KAH toh	stəˈkɑto
stacte	STAK tee	ˈstækti
Stader	STAY der	ˈstedər
stadholder	STAD hohl der	ˈstædholdər
stadia	STAY di uh	ˈstedɪə
stadiometer	stay di AH muh ter	stedɪˈɑmətər
stadium	STAY di uhm	ˈstedɪəm
stadtholder	STAT hohl der	ˈstætholdər
Staël, de	STAHL, duh	ˈstɑl, də
Stagirite	STA juh right	ˈstædʒərait
stagnant	STAG nuhnt	ˈstægnənt
staid	stayd	sted
Stakhanovism	stuh KAH nuh vi zuhm	stəˈkɑnəvizəm
Stakhanovite	stuh KAH nuh vight	stəˈkɑnəvait
stalactite	stuh LAK tight	stəˈlæktait
stalag	STA lag	ˈstælæg
stalagmite	stuh LAG might	stəˈlægmait
Stalin	STAH lin	ˈstɑlɪn
Stalinabad	STAH li nah BAHT	ˈstɑlɪnɑˈbɑt
Stalingrad	STAH lin grad	ˈstɑlɪngræd
Stalino	STAH li naw	ˈstɑlɪnɔ
Stalinsk	STAH linsk	ˈstɑlɪnsk
stalk	stawk	stɔk
stallion	STA lyuhn	ˈstæljən
stalwart	STAWL wert	ˈstɔlwərt
Stamboul, Stambul	stahm BOO : L	stɑmˈbul
stamen	STAY muhn	ˈstemən
stamina	STA muh nuh	ˈstæmənə
stammel	STA muhl	ˈstæməl
stampede	stam PEED	stæmˈpid
stanch	stahnch	stɑntʃ
stanchion	STAN shuhn	ˈstænʃən
Standish	STAN dish	ˈstændɪʃ
Stanhope, s-	STA nuhp	ˈstænəp
stanine	STAY nighn	ˈstenain
Stanislav	stah ni SLAHF	stɑnɪˈslɑf
Stanislavsky	sta ni SLAHF ski	stænɪˈslɑfskɪ
Stanley	STAN li	ˈstænlɪ
stannum	STA nuhm	ˈstænəm
Stanovoi	stah naw VOI	stɑnɔˈvɔɪ
Stanton	STAN tuhn	ˈstæntən
stanza	STAN zuh	ˈstænzə
stanzaic	stan ZAY ik	stænˈzeɪk
stapes	STAY peez	ˈstepiz
staphylococci	sta fi luh KAHK sigh	stæfɪləˈkɑksai
staphylococcic	sta fi luh KAHK sik	stæfɪləˈkɑksɪk
staphylococcus	sta fi luh KAH kuhs	stæfɪləˈkɑkəs
staphyloplasty	STA fi luh pla sti	ˈstæfɪləplæstɪ
staphylorrhaphy	sta fuh LAW ruh fi	stæfəˈlɔrəfɪ
Staraya Russa	STAH rah yah ROO : sah	ˈstɑrɑjɑ ˈrusɑ
stasis	STAY sis	ˈstesɪs
Stassen	STA suhn	ˈstæsən

sing [ŋ] ; *oh* [o] ; *oil* [ɔɪ] ; *foot* [ʊ] ; *foo*:*d* [u] ; *how* [aʊ] ; *pie* [p] ; *ray* [r] ; *so* [s] ; *shall* [ʃ] ;
to [t] ; *thin* [θ] ; *th*:*en* [ð] ; *above* (*uh* B*U*HV) [ə, ˈʌ] ; *vine* [v] ; *wine* [w] ; *whine* [hw] ;
*y*ou [j] ; *z*oo [z] ; *rouge* (roo:*zh*) [ʒ].

Staten	STA tuhn	ˈstætən
static	STA tik	ˈstætɪk
stationary, stationery	STAY shuh nai ri	ˈsteʃənɛrɪ
statism	STAY ti zuhm	ˈstetɪzəm
statist	STAY tist	ˈstetɪst
statistic	stuh TI stik	stəˈtɪstɪk
statistician	sta ti STI shuhn	stætɪˈstɪʃən
Statius	STAY shi uhs	ˈsteʃɪəs
statocyst	STA tuh sist	ˈstætəsɪst
stator	STAY ter	ˈstetər
statoscope	STA tuh skohp	ˈstætəskop
statuary	STA choo ai ri	ˈstætʃʊɛrɪ
statue	STA choo	ˈstætʃʊ
statuesque	sta choo ESK	stætʃuˈɛsk
statuette	sta choo ET	stætʃuˈɛt
stature	STA cher	ˈstætʃər
status	STAY tuhs	ˈstetəs
status quo	STAY tuhs KWOH	ˈstetəs ˈkwo
status quo ante	STAY tuhs kwoh AN ti	ˈstetəs kwo ˈæntɪ
statute	STA choot	ˈstætʃut
statutory	STA choo taw ri	ˈstætʃutɔrɪ
staunch	stawnch	stɔntʃ
Stavanger	stah VANG er	staˈvæŋər
stave	stayv	stev
stealth	stelth	stɛlθ
stealthy	STEL thi	ˈstɛlθɪ
steapsin	sti AP sin	stɪˈæpsɪn
stearic	sti A rik	stɪˈærɪk
Stearns	sternz	stɜnz
steatite	STEE uh tight	ˈstiətaɪt
steatopygia	stee uh toh PIGH ji uh	stiətoˈpaɪdʒɪə
steatopygous	stee uh toh PIGH guhs	stiətoˈpaɪgəs
steatorrhea	stee uh tuh REE uh	stiətəˈriə
Steber	STEE ber	ˈstibər
steelyard	STEEL yahrd	ˈstiljard
Steen, Jan	stayn, yahn	sten, jɑn
steenbok	STEEN bahk	ˈstinbɑk
Stefansson	STE fuhn suhn	ˈstɛfənsən
Steffens	STE fuhnz	ˈstɛfənz
stegosaurus	ste guh SAW ruhs	stɛgəˈsɔrəs
Steichen	STIGH kuhn	ˈstaɪkən
stein, S-	stighn	staɪn
Steinbeck	STIGHN bek	ˈstaɪnbɛk
steinbok	STIGHN bahk	ˈstaɪnbɑk
Steinmetz	STIGHN mets	ˈstaɪnmɛts
Steinway	STIGHN way	ˈstaɪnwe
stele	STEE li	ˈstilɪ
Sten	sten	stɛn
Stendahl	stahn DAHL	stɑnˈdɑl
stenograph	STE nuh graf	ˈstɛnəgræf
stenographic	ste nuh GRA fik	stɛnəˈgræfɪk
stenosis	sti NOH sis	stɪˈnosɪs

at [æ]; *ah* [ɑ]; *air* [ɛ]; *aw*ful [ɔ]; *say* [e]; *b*ack [b]; *ch*air [tʃ]; *do* [d]; *e*lm [ɛ]; *ee*l [i];
server [ˈɜ, ər]; *f*it [f]; *go* [g]; *h*urt [h]; *is* [ɪ]; *high* [aɪ]; *j*et [dʒ]; *k*iss [k]; *l*amb [l]; *my* [m];
*n*ice [n];

stenotype	STE nuh tighp	ˈstɛnətaɪp
Stentor, s-	STEN tawr	ˈstɛntɔr
stentorian	sten TAW ri uhn	stɛnˈtɔrɪən
steppe	step	stɛp
stercoraceous	ster kuh RAY shuhs	stɝkəˈreʃəs
stereo	STAI ri oh	ˈstɛrɪo
stereophonic	stai ri uh FAH nik	stɛrɪəˈfɑnɪk
stereopticon	stai ri AHP ti kuhn	stɛrɪˈɑptɪkən
stereoscope	STAI ri uh skohp	ˈstɛrɪəskop
stereotype	STAI ri uh tighp	ˈstɛrɪətaɪp
sterile	STAI ruhl	ˈstɛrəl
sterility	stuh RI luh ti	stəˈrɪlətɪ
sterilize	STAI ruh lighz	ˈstɛrəlaɪz
sternum	STER nuhm	ˈstɝnəm
steroid	STAI roid	ˈstɛrɔɪd
sterol	STAI rohl	ˈstɛrol
stertor	STER ter	ˈstɝtər
stertorous	STER tuh ruhs	ˈstɝtərəs
stet	stet	stɛt
stethoscope	STE thuh skohp	ˈstɛθəskop
Stettin	STE tin	ˈstɛtɪn
Stettinius	stuh TI ni uhs	stəˈtɪnɪəs
Steuben	STYOO : bin	ˈstjubɪn
stevedore	STEE vuh dawr	ˈstivədɔr
stew	stoo :	stu
steward, S-	STOO : erd	ˈstuərd
stewardess	STOO : er dis	ˈstuərdɪs
Stewart	STOO : ert	ˈstuərt
sthenia	sthi NEE uh	sθɪˈniə
sthenic	STHE nik	ˈsθɛnɪk
stiacciato	styah CHAH toh	stjaˈtʃɑto
stibium	STI bi uhm	ˈstɪbɪəm
stibnite	STIB night	ˈstɪbnaɪt
stichic	STI kik	ˈstɪkɪk
stichometry	sti KAH muh tri	stɪˈkɑmətrɪ
stichomythia	sti kuh MI thi uh	stɪkəˈmɪθɪə
Stieglitz	STEEG lits	ˈstiglɪts
stifle	STIGH fuhl	ˈstaɪfəl
stigma	STIG muh	ˈstɪgmə
stigmata	STIG muh tuh	ˈstɪgmətə
stigmatic	stig MA tik	stɪgˈmætɪk
stigmatism	STIG muh ti zuhm	ˈstɪgmətɪzəm
stigmatize	STIG muh tighz	ˈstɪgmətaɪz
stiletto	sti LE toh	stɪˈlɛto
Stilton	STIL tuhn	ˈstɪltən
Stilwell	STIL wel	ˈstɪlwɛl
Stimson	STIM suhn	ˈstɪmsən
stimulant	STI myuh luhnt	ˈstɪmjələnt
stimulus	STI myuh luhs	ˈstɪmjələs
stipend	STIGH pend	ˈstaɪpend
stipulation	sti pyuh LAY shuhn	stɪpjəˈleʃən
stirpiculture	STER pi kuhl cher	ˈstɝpɪkʌltʃər

---

si*ng* [ŋ] ; *oh* [o] ; *oil* [ɔɪ] ; *foot* [ʊ] ; *foo:*d [u] ; *how* [aʊ] ; *p*ie [p] ; *r*ay [r] ; *s*o [s] ; *sh*all [ʃ] ;
*t*o [t] ; *th*in [θ] ; *th:*en [ð] ; above (*uh* B*UH*V) [ə, ˈʌ] ; *v*ine [v] ; *w*ine [w] ; *wh*ine [hw] ;
*y*ou [j] ; *z*oo [z] ; rouge (roo:*zh*) [ʒ].

stirps	sterps	stɝps
stirrup	STER uhp	ˈstɝəp
stoa	STOH uh	ˈstoə
stoat	stoht	stot
stockade	stah KAYD	stɑˈked
Stockholm	STAHK hohm	ˈstɑkhom
stockinet	stah ki NET	stɑkɪˈnɛt
stodgy	STAH ji	ˈstɑdʒɪ
stogie, stogy	STOH gi	ˈstogɪ
Stoic, s-	STOH ik	ˈstoɪk
stoichiometry	stoi ki AH muh tri	stɔɪkɪˈɑmətrɪ
Stoicism, s-	STOH i si zuhm	ˈstoɪsɪzəm
Stokowski	stuh KAWF ski	stəˈkɔfskɪ
stolid	STAH lid	ˈstɑlɪd
stolidity	stuh LI duh ti	stəˈlɪdətɪ
stolon	STOH lahn	ˈstolɑn
stoma	STOH muh	ˈstomə
stomach	STUH muhk	ˈstʌmək
stomacher	STUH muh ker	ˈstʌməkər
stomachic	stoh MA kik	stoˈmækɪk
stomatic	stoh MA tik	stoˈmætɪk
stomatitis	stoh muh TIGH tis	stoməˈtaɪtɪs
stomatolalia	stoh muh tuh LAY li uh	stomətəˈleliə
Stonehenge	STOHN henj	ˈstonhɛndʒ
stony	STOH ni	ˈstonɪ
Storting, Storthing	STAWR ting	ˈstɔrtɪŋ
Stouffer	STOH fer	ˈstofər
stoup	stoo : p	stup
Stowe	stoh	sto
strabismus	struh BIZ muhs	strəˈbɪzməs
Strabo	STRAY boh	ˈstrebo
strabotomy	struh BAH tuh mi	strəˈbatəmɪ
Strachey	STRAY chi	ˈstretʃɪ
Stradivari	strah dee VAH ree	strɑdiˈvɑri
Stradivarius	stra duh VAI ri uhs	strædəˈvɛriəs
strafe	strayf	stref
Strafford	STRA ferd	ˈstræfərd
strait	strayt	stret
stramonium	struh MOH ni uhm	strəˈmonɪəm
strappado	struh PAY doh	strəˈpedo
Strasbourg	STRAS berg	ˈstræsbərg
strata	STRAY tuh	ˈstretə
stratagem	STRA tuh juhm	ˈstrætədʒəm
strategic	struh TEE jik	strəˈtidʒɪk
strategist	STRA tuh jist	ˈstrætədʒɪst
strategy	STRA tuh ji	ˈstrætədʒɪ
Stratford-on-Avon	STRAT ferd ahn AY vuhn	ˈstrætfərd ɑn ˈevən
strathspey	strath SPAY	stræθˈspe
stratification	stra tuh fi KAY shuhn	strætəfɪˈkeʃən
stratocracy	struh TAH kruh si	strəˈtakrəsɪ
strato-cumulus	STRAY toh KYOO : myuh luhs	ˈstreto ˈkjumjələs

---

at [æ]; *ah* [ɑ]; *air* [ɛ]; *aw*ful [ɔ]; *say* [e]; *b*ack [b]; *ch*air [tʃ]; *d*o [d]; *el*m [ɛ]; *ee*l [i]; *ser*ver [ɝ, ər]; *f*it [f]; *g*o [g]; *h*urt [h]; *is* [ɪ]; *high* [aɪ]; *j*et [dʒ]; *k*iss [k]; *l*amb [l]; *m*y [m]; *n*ice [n];

stratosphere	STRA tuh sfir	ˈstrætəsfɪr
stratum	STRAY tuhm	ˈstretəm
stratus	STRAY tuhs	ˈstretəs
Straus, -s	strows	strɑʊs
Straus, -s (German)	shtrows	ʃtrɑʊs
Stravinsky	struh VIN ski	strəˈvɪnskɪ
Streit	strayt	stret
strength	strength	strɛŋθ
strenuous	STRE nyoo uhs	ˈstrɛnjʊəs
streptococcal	strep tuh KAH kuhl	strɛptəˈkɑkəl
streptococci	strep tuh KAHK sigh	strɛptəˈkɑksaɪ
streptococcus	strep tuh KAH kuhs	strɛptəˈkɑkəs
streptomycin	strep tuh MIGH sin	strɛptəˈmaɪsɪn
streptothricin	strep tuh THRIGH sin	strɛptəˈθraɪsɪn
stretto	STRE toh	ˈstrɛto
stria	STRIGH uh	ˈstraɪə
striated	STRIGH ay tid	ˈstraɪetɪd
stricture	STRIK cher	ˈstrɪktʃər
stroboscope	STRAH buh skohp	ˈstrɑbəskop
strobotron	STRAH buh trahn	ˈstrɑbətrɑn
Stromboli	STRAWM baw lee	ˈstrɔmbɔli
stronger	STRAWNG ger	ˈstrɔŋgər
strongest	STRAWNG gist	ˈstrɔŋgɪst
strongyl, -e	STRAHN jil	ˈstrɑndʒɪl
strontium	STRAHN shi uhm	ˈstrɑnʃɪəm
strophe	STROH fi	ˈstrofɪ
strophic	STRAH fik	ˈstrɑfɪk
Strozzi	STRAHT see	ˈstrɑtsi
structure	STRUHK cher	ˈstrʌktʃər
strudel	STROO : duhl	ˈstrudəl
struma	STROO : muh	ˈstrumə
strychnin, -e	STRIK nin	ˈstrɪknɪn
stubborn	STUH bern	ˈstʌbərn
stucco	STUH koh	ˈstʌko
stud	stuhd	stʌd
studding	STUH ding	ˈstʌdɪŋ
studdingsail (nautical)	STUHN suhl	ˈstʌnsəl
student	STOO : duhnt	ˈstudənt
studio	STOO : di oh	ˈstudɪo
studious	STOO : di uhs	ˈstudɪəs
Stuka	STOO : kuh	ˈstukə
stultification	stuhl tuh fi KAY shuhn	stʌltəfɪˈkeʃən
stultify	STUHL tuh figh	ˈstʌltəfaɪ
stum	stuhm	stʌm
stupa	STOO : puh	ˈstupə
stupe	stoo : p	stup
stupefacient	stoo : puh FAY shuhnt	stupəˈfeʃənt
stupefaction	stoo : puh FAK shuhn	stupəˈfækʃən
stupefy	STOO : puh figh	ˈstupəfaɪ
stupendous	stoo : PEN duhs	stuˈpɛndəs
stupid	STO : pid	ˈstupɪd
stupor	STOO : per	ˈstupər

sing [ŋ]; *oh* [o]; *oil* [ɔɪ]; *foot* [ʊ]; *foo:*d [u]; *how* [ɑʊ]; *p*ie [p]; *ray* [r]; *so* [s]; *sh*all [ʃ];
to [t]; *thin* [θ]; *th:*en [ð]; *above (uh BUHV)* [ə, ˈʌ]; *v*ine [v]; *w*ine [w]; *wh*ine [hw];
ou [j]; *zoo* [z]; *rouge (roo:zh)* [ʒ].

sturgeon	STER juhn	ˈstɝdʒən
Sturges	STER juhs	ˈstɝdʒəs
Sturmabteilung	SHTOORM ahp tigh loong	ˈʃtʊrmɑptaɪluŋ
Sturm und Drang	SHTOORM oont DRAHNG	ˈʃtʊrm ʊnt ˈdrɑŋ
Stuttgart	STUHT gahrt	ˈstʌtgɑrt
Stuyvesant	STIGH vuh suhnt	ˈstaɪvəsənt
sty, -e	stigh	staɪ
Stygian, s-	STI ji uhn	ˈstɪdʒɪən
stylet	STIGH lit	ˈstaɪlɪt
stylite	STIGH light	ˈstaɪlaɪt
stylograph	STIGH luh graf	ˈstaɪləgræf
stylus	STIGH luhs	ˈstaɪləs
stymie, stymy	STIGH mi	ˈstaɪmɪ
styptic	STIP tik	ˈstɪptɪk
Styr	stir	stɪr
styrene	STIGH reen	ˈstaɪrin
Styx	stiks	stɪks
Suakin	SWAH kin	ˈswɑkɪn
suave	swahv	swɑv
suavity	SWAH vuh ti	ˈswɑvətɪ
subaltern	suhb AWL tern	səbˈɔltərn
subdue	suhb DOO :	səbˈdu
subito	SOO : bi toh	ˈsubɪto
subject (a, n)	SUHB jikt	ˈsʌbdʒɪkt
subject (v)	suhb JEKT	səbˈdʒɛkt
subjective	suhb JEK tiv	səbˈdʒɛktɪv
sub judice	suhb JOO : di si	sʌb ˈdʒudɪsɪ
subjugate	SUHB juh gayt	ˈsʌbdʒəget
sublimate (a, n)	SUH bluh mit	ˈsʌbləmɪt
sublimate (v)	SUH bluh mayt	ˈsʌbləmet
subliminal	suhb LI muh nuhl	sʌbˈlɪmənəl
submontane	suhb MAHN tayn	sʌbˈmɑnten
subordinate (a, n)	suh BAWR duh nit	səˈbɔrdənit
subordinate (v)	suh BAWR duh nayt	səˈbɔrdənet
suborn	suh BAWRN	səˈbɔrn
Subotica, Subotitsa	SOO : baw tit sah	ˈsubɔtɪtsɑ
subpoena, subpena	suh PEE nuh	səˈpinə
sub rosa	suhb ROH zuh	sʌb ˈrozə
subsequent	SUHB si kwuhnt	ˈsʌbsɪkwənt
subsidence	suhb SIGH duhns	səbˈsaɪdəns
subsidiary	suhb SI di ai ri	səbˈsɪdɪɛrɪ
subsidy	SUHB suh di	ˈsʌbsədɪ
sub specie	suhb SPEE shi ee	sʌb ˈspiʃɪi
substance	SUHB stuhns	ˈsʌbstəns
substantiate	suhb STAN shi ayt	səbˈstænʃɪet
substantiation	suhb stan shi AY shuhn	səbstænʃɪˈeʃən
substantive	SUHB stuhn tiv	ˈsʌbstəntɪv
subterranean	suhb tuh RAY ni uhn	sʌbtəˈrenɪən
subtile	SUH tuhl	ˈsʌtəl
subtle	SUH tuhl	ˈsʌtəl
subtlety	SUH tuhl ti	ˈsʌtəltɪ
suburb	SUH berb	ˈsʌbərb

at [æ] ; ah [ɑ] ; air [ɛ] ; awful [ɔ] ; say [e] ; back [b] ; chair [tʃ] ; do [d] ; elm [ɛ] ; eel [i] ;
server [ˈɝ, ər] ; fit [f] ; go [g] ; hurt [h] ; is [ɪ] ; high [aɪ] ; jet [dʒ] ; kiss [k] ; lamb [l] ; my [m] ;
nice [n] ;

suburban	suh BER buhn	sə'bɚbən
suburbanite	suh BER buh night	sə'bɚbənaɪt
sub verbo	suhb VER boh	sʌb 'vɚbo
subversion	suhb VER zhuhn	səb'vɚʒən
succedaneum	suhk si DAY ni uhm	sʌksɪ'denɪəm
succeed	suhk SEED	sək'sid
success	suhk SES	sək'sɛs
succinct	suhk SINGKT	sək'sɪŋkt
succor	SUH ker	'sʌkər
succotash	SUH kuh tash	'sʌkətæʃ
succubus	SUH kyuh buhs	'sʌkjəbəs
succulent	SUH kyuh luhnt	'sʌkjələnt
succumb	suh KUHM	sə'kʌm
Suceava	soo CHAH vah	su'tʃavɑ
such	suhch	sʌtʃ
Sucre, s-	SOO : kre	'sukrɛ
sucrose	SOO : krohs	'sukros
Sudan	soo : DAN	su'dæn
Sudanese	soo : duh NEEZ	sudə'niz
Sudanic	soo : DA nik	su'dænɪk
sudarium	soo : DAI ri uhm	su'dɛrɪəm
sudatory	SOO : duh taw ri	'sudətɔrɪ
Sudermann	SOO : der muhn	'sudərmən
Sudeten	soo : DAY tuhn	su'detən
Sudetes	soo : DEE teez	su'ditiz
sudorific	soo : duh RI fik	sudə'rɪfɪk
sue, S-	soo :	su
suede	swayd	swed
suet	SOO : it	'suɪt
Suetonius	swi TOH ni uhs	swɪ'tonɪəs
Suez	soo : EZ	su'ɛz
suffice	suh FIGHS	sə'faɪs
sufficient	suh FI shuhnt	sə'fɪʃənt
suffix (n)	SUH fiks	'sʌfɪks
suffix (v)	suh FIKS	sə'fɪks
Suffolk	SUH fuhk	'sʌfək
suffragan	SUH fruh guhn	'sʌfrəgən
suffrage	SUH frij	'sʌfrɪdʒ
suffragette	suh fruh JET	sʌfrə'dʒɛt
suffuse	suh FYOO : Z	sə'fjuz
Sufism	SOO : fi zuhm	'sufɪzəm
suggest	suhg JEST	səg'dʒɛst
suggestion	suhg JES chuhn	səg'dʒɛstʃən
suicidal	soo : uh SIGH duhl	suə'saɪdəl
suicide	SOO : uh sighd	'suəsaɪd
sui generis	SOO : i JE nuh ris	'suɪ 'dʒɛnərɪs
sui juris	SOO : i JOO ris	'suɪ 'dʒurɪs
suisse, S-	swees	swis
suit	soo : t	sut
suitable	SOO : tuh buhl	'sutəbəl
suite	sweet	swit
suitor	SOO : ter	'sutər

sing [ŋ] ; oh [o] ; oil [ɔɪ] ; foot [ʊ] ; foo:d [u] ; how [aʊ] ; pie [p] ; ray [r] ; so [s] ; shall [ʃ] ; to [t] ; thin [θ] ; th:en [ð] ; above (uh BUHV) [ə, 'ʌ] ; vine [v] ; wine [w] ; whine [hw] ; you [j] ; zoo [z] ; rouge (roo:zh) [ʒ].

Suiyuan	SWAY yoo AHN	ˈswe juˈɑn
Sukabumi	soo : kah BOO : mee	sukaˈbumi
Sukarno	soo : KAHR noh	suˈkɑrno
sukiyaki	SOO : ki YAH ki	ˈsukɪˈjɑkɪ
Sukkoth	soo KOHTH	suˈkoθ
sulcus	SUHL kuhs	ˈsʌlkəs
Suleiman	soo : lay MAHN	suleˈmɑn
sulfa	SUHL fuh	ˈsʌlfə
sulfadiazine	suhl fuh DIGH uh zeen	sʌlfəˈdaɪəzin
sulfaguanidine	suhl fuh GWA nuh deen	sʌlfəˈgwænədin
sulfamerazine	suhl fuh ME ruh zeen	sʌlfəˈmɛrəzin
sulfamethazine	suhl fuh ME thuh zeen	sʌlfəˈmɛθəzin
sulfamethylthiazole	suhl fuh me thuhl THIGH uh zohl	sʌlfəmɛθəlˈθaɪəzol
sulfanilamide	suhl fuh NI luh mighd	sʌlfəˈnɪləmaɪd
sulfapyrazine	suhl fuh PI ruh zeen	sʌlfəˈpɪrəzin
sulfapyridine	suhl fuh PI ruh deen	sʌlfəˈpɪrədin
sulfaquinoxaline	suhl fuh kwi NAHK suh leen	sʌlfəkwɪˈnɑksəlin
sulfarsenide	suhl FAHR suh nighd	səlˈfɑrsənaɪd
sulfasuxidine	suhl fuh SUHK suh deen	sʌlfəˈsʌksədin
sulfate	SUHL fayt	ˈsʌlfet
sulfathiazole	suhl fuh THIGH uh zohl	sʌlfəˈθaɪəzol
sulfide	SUHL fighd	ˈsʌlfaɪd
sulfonal	SUHL fuh nal	ˈsʌlfənæl
sulfonamide	suhl FAH nuh mighd	səlˈfɑnəmaɪd
sulfonate	SUHL fuh nayt	ˈsʌlfənet
sulfone	SUHL fohn	ˈsʌlfon
sulfonic	suhl FAH nik	səlˈfɑnɪk
sulfonium	suhl FOH ni uhm	səlˈfonɪəm
sulfonmethane	suhl fohn ME thayn	sʌlfonˈmɛθen
sulfonyl	SUHL fuh nil	ˈsʌlfənɪl
sulfur	SUHL fer	ˈsʌlfər
sulfureous	suhl FYOO ri uhs	səlˈfjurɪəs
sulfuric	suhl FYOO rik	səlˈfjurɪk
sulfurous	suhl FYOO ruhs	səlˈfjurəs
Sulla	SUH luh	ˈsʌlə
sullen	SUH luhn	ˈsʌlən
Sully, s-	SUH li	ˈsʌlɪ
sulphur	SUHL fer	ˈsʌlfər
sulphurous (chemistry)	suhl FYOO ruhs	səlˈfjurəs
sulphurous (" infernal ; fiery ")	SUHL fuh ruhs	ˈsʌlfərəs
sultan, S-	SUHL tuhn	ˈsʌltən
sultana	suhl TA nuh	səlˈtænə
sultanate	SUHL tuh nit	ˈsʌltənɪt
Sulu	SOO : loo :	ˈsulu
sumac, -h	SHOO : mak	ˈʃumæk
Sumatra	soo MAH truh	suˈmɑtrə
Sumba	SOO : M bah	ˈsumbɑ
Sumbawa	soo : m BAH wah	sumˈbɑwɑ
Sumer	SOO : mer	ˈsumər

at [æ]; *ah* [ɑ]; *air* [ɛ]; *awful* [ɔ]; *say* [e]; *back* [b]; *chair* [tʃ]; *do* [d]; *elm* [ɛ]; *eel* [i]; *server* [ˈɝ, ər]; *f*it [f]; *go* [g]; *h*urt [h]; *is* [ɪ]; *high* [aɪ]; *jet* [dʒ]; *kiss* [k]; *lamb* [l]; *my* [m]; *nice* [n];

Sumerian, Sumirian	soo : MI ri uhn	suˈmɪrɪən
summa cum laude	SUH muh kuhm LAW di	ˈsʌmə kʌm ˈlɔdɪ
summary	SUH muh ri	ˈsʌmərɪ
summation	suh MAY shuhn	səˈmeʃən
summersault	SUH mer sawlt	ˈsʌmərsɔlt
summum bonum	SUH muhm BOH nuhm	ˈsʌməm ˈbonəm
sumptuary	SUHMP choo ai ri	ˈsʌmptʃuɛrɪ
sumptuous	SUHMP choo uhs	ˈsʌmptʃuəs
Sunda	SUHN duh	ˈsʌndə
sundae	SUHN di	ˈsʌndɪ
Sunday	SUHN di	ˈsʌndɪ
Sunde	SOON duh	ˈsundə
sundry	SUHN dri	ˈsʌndrɪ
Sung	soong	suŋ
Sunna, -h	SOO nuh	ˈsunə
Sunnite	SOO night	ˈsunaɪt
Sun Yatsen	soon yaht sen	sun yɑtsɛn
Suomenlinna	soo AW men li nah	suˈɔmɛnlɪnɑ
Suomi	soo AW mi	suˈɔmɪ
super	SOO : per	ˈsupər
superb	soo PERB	suˈpɝb
supercilious	soo : per SI li uhs	supərˈsɪlɪəs
superficial	soo : per FI shuhl	supərˈfɪʃəl
superfluity	soo : per FLOO : uh ti	supərˈfluətɪ
superfluous	suh PER floo uhs	səˈpɝfluəs
superheterodyne	soo : per HE tuh ruh dighn	supərˈhɛtərədaɪn
superior, S-	suh PI ri er	səˈpɪrɪər
superiority	suh pi ri AW ruh ti	səpɪrɪˈɔrətɪ
superlative	suh PER luh tiv	səˈpɝlətɪv
supernal	soo : PER nuhl	suˈpɝnəl
supernova	soo : per NOH vuh	supərˈnovə
supernumerary	soo : per NOO : muh rai ri	supərˈnumərɛrɪ
supersonic	soo : per SAH nik	supərˈsɑnɪk
superstition	soo : per STI shuhn	supərˈstɪʃən
superstitious	soo : per STI shuhs	supərˈstɪʃəs
supine (a)	soo : PIGHN	suˈpaɪn
supine (n)	SOO : pighn	ˈsupaɪn
supple	SUH puhl	ˈsʌpəl
supplement (n)	SUH pluh muhnt	ˈsʌpləmənt
supplement (v)	SUH pluh ment	ˈsʌpləmɛnt
supplementary	suh pluh MEN tuh ri	səpləˈmɛntərɪ
suppletion	suh PLEE shuhn	səˈpliʃən
suppletive	SUH pluh tiv	ˈsʌplətɪv
suppliant	SUH pli uhnt	ˈsʌplɪənt
supplicant	SUH pluh kuhnt	ˈsʌpləkənt
supposition	suh puh ZI shuhn	səpəˈzɪʃən
suppository	suh PAH zuh taw ri	səˈpɑzətɔrɪ
suppurate	SUH pyuh rayt	ˈsʌpjəret
supralapsarian	soo : pruh lap SAI ri uhn	suprəlæpˈsɛrɪən
supremacy	suh PRE muh si	səˈprɛməsɪ
suprematism	suh PRE muh ti zuhm	səˈprɛmətɪzəm
supreme	suh PREEM	səˈprim

sing [ŋ] ; oh [o] ; oil [ɔɪ] ; foot [ʊ] ; foo:d [u] ; how [aʊ] ; pie [p] ; ray [r] ; so [s] ; shall [ʃ] ; to [t] ; thin [θ] ; th:en [ð] ; above (uh BUHV) [ə, ˈʌ] ; vine [v] ; wine [w] ; whine [hw] ; you [j] ; zoo [z] ; rouge (roo:zh) [ʒ].

sura	SOO ruh	ˈsʊrə
Surabaya	soo : rah BAH yah	suraˈbɑjɑ
surah	SOO ruh	ˈsʊrə
Surakarta	soo : rah KAHR tah	suraˈkɑrtɑ
Surat	soo RAT	suˈræt
surcease	ser SEES	sərˈsis
surcingle	SER sing guhl	ˈsɝsɪŋgəl
surcoat	SER koht	ˈsɝkot
surd	serd	sɝd
sure	shoor	ʃʊr
surely	SHOOR li	ˈʃʊrlɪ
surety	SHOOR ti	ˈʃʊrtɪ
surface	SER fis	ˈsɝfɪs
surfactant	ser FAK tuhnt	sərˈfæktənt
surfeit	SER fit	ˈsɝfɪt
surgeon	SER juhn	ˈsɝdʒən
surgery	SER juh ri	ˈsɝdʒərɪ
Suribachi	soo ruh BAH chi	surəˈbɑtʃɪ
Surinach	SOO : ri nahk	ˈsurɪnɑk
Surinam	soo ri NAHM	surɪˈnɑm
surly	SER li	ˈsɝlɪ
surmise	ser MIGHZ	sərˈmaɪz
surmount	ser MOWNT	sərˈmaʊnt
surpass	ser PAS	sərˈpæs
surplice	SER plis	ˈsɝplɪs
surprise	ser PRIGHZ	sərˈpraɪz
surrealism	suh REE uh li zuhm	səˈriəlɪzəm
surrealist	suh REE uh list	səˈriəlɪst
surreptitious	suh ruhp TI shuhs	sərəpˈtɪʃəs
surrey, S-	SER i	ˈsɝɪ
surrogate (a, n)	SER uh git	ˈsɝəgɪt
surrogate (v)	SER uh gayt	ˈsɝəget
sursum corda	SER suhm KAWR duh	ˈsɝsəm ˈkɔrdə
surtax	SER taks	ˈsɝtæks
surtout	ser TOO : T	sərˈtut
surveillance	ser VAY luhns	sərˈveləns
survey (n)	SER vay	ˈsɝve
survey (v)	ser VAY	sərˈve
surveyor	ser VAY er	sərˈveər
Susa	SOO : sah	ˈsusɑ
susceptible	suh SEP tuh buhl	səˈsɛptəbəl
suslik	SUH slik	ˈsʌslɪk
suspect (a, n)	SUH spekt	ˈsʌspɛkt
suspect (v)	suh SPEKT	səˈspɛkt
suspire	suh SPIGHR	səˈspaɪr
Susquehanna	suh skwi HA nuh	səskwɪˈhænə
Sussex	SUH siks	ˈsʌsɪks
sustain	suh STAYN	səˈsten
sustenance	SUH stuh nuhns	ˈsʌstənəns
susurrant	soo SER uhnt	suˈsɝənt
susurration	soo : suh RAY shuhn	susəˈreʃən
Sutherland	SUH th : er luhnd	ˈsʌðərlənd

---

at [æ] ; *ah* [ɑ] ; *air* [ɛ] ; *awful* [ɔ] ; *say* [e] ; *back* [b] ; *chair* [tʃ] ; *do* [d] ; *elm* [ɛ] ; *eel* [i] ; *server* [ˈɝ, ər] ; *f*it [f] ; *go* [g] ; *h*urt [h] ; *is* [ɪ] ; *high* [aɪ] ; *jet* [dʒ] ; *kiss* [k] ; *l*amb [l] ; *my* [m] ; *nice* [n] ;

sutler	SUHT ler	ˈsʌtlər
sutra	SOO: truh	ˈsutrə
suttee	suh TEE	səˈti
Sutter	SUH ter	ˈsʌtər
suture	SOO: cher	ˈsutʃər
suum cuique	SOO: uhm KWIGH kwee	ˈsuəm ˈkwaɪkwi
Suva	SOO: vah	ˈsuvɑ
Suvorov	soo VAW rawf	suˈvɔrɔf
Suwannee	suh WAW ni	səˈwɔnɪ
Suwon	soo: wahn	suwɑn
suzerain	SOO: zuh rin	ˈsuzərɪn
suzerainty	SOO: zuh rin ti	ˈsuzərɪntɪ
Svalbard	SVAHL bahr	ˈsvɑlbɑr
svelte	svelt	svɛlt
Svenska	SVEN skah	ˈsvɛnskɑ
Sverdlovsk	sverd LAWFSK	svɛrdˈlɔfsk
Svoboda	svah BAW dah	svɑˈbɔdɑ
swab	swahb	swɑb
Swabia	SWAY bi uh	ˈswebɪə
swaddle	SWAH duhl	ˈswɑdəl
Swadeshi, s-	swuh DAY shi	swəˈdeʃɪ
Swahili	swah HEE li	swɑˈhilɪ
swami	SWAH mi	ˈswɑmɪ
swamp	swahmp	swɑmp
Swanee	SWAW ni	ˈswɔnɪ
swank	swangk	swæŋk
Swansea	SWAHN si	ˈswɑnsɪ
swaraj, S-	swuh RAHJ	swəˈrɑdʒ
sward	swawrd	swɔrd
swart	swawrt	swɔrt
Swarthout	SWAHR thowt	ˈswɑrθaʊt
swarthy	SWAWR th:i	ˈswɔrðɪ
swastika, swastica	SWAH sti kuh	ˈswɑstɪkə
Swat, s-	swaht	swɑt
swatch	swahch	swɑtʃ
swath	swahth	swɑθ
swathe	swayth:	sweð
Swazi	SWAH zi	ˈswɑzɪ
Swaziland	SWAH zee land	ˈswɑzilænd
Sweden	SWEE duhn	ˈswidən
Swedenborg	SWEE duhn bawrg	ˈswidənbɔrg
sweetbread	SWEET bred	ˈswitbrɛd
Swinburne	SWIN bern	ˈswɪnbərn
Swithin, Swithun	SWI th:uhn	ˈswɪðən
Switzerland	SWIT ser luhnd	ˈswɪtsərlənd
swob	swahb	swɑb
sword	sawrd	sɔrd
Sybarite, s-	SI buh right	ˈsɪbəraɪt
Sybaritic, s-	si buh RI tik	sɪbəˈrɪtɪk
Sybil	SI buhl	ˈsɪbəl
sycamore	SI kuh mawr	ˈsɪkəmɔr
sycophant	SI kuh fuhnt	ˈsɪkəfənt

---

sing [ŋ]; oh [o]; oil [ɔɪ]; foot [ʊ]; foo:d [u]; how [aʊ]; pie [p]; ray [r]; so [s]; shall [ʃ]; to [t]; thin [θ]; th:en [ð]; above (uh BUHV) [ə, ˈʌ]; vine [v]; wine [w]; whine [hw]; you [j]; zoo [z]; rouge (roo:zh) [ʒ].

sycophantic	si kih FAN tik	sɪkəˈfæntɪk
sycosis	sigh KOH sis	saɪˈkosɪs
Sydney	SID ni	ˈsɪdnɪ
syllabary	SI luh bai ri	ˈsɪləbɛrɪ
syllabic	si LA bik	sɪˈlæbɪk
syllabus	SI luh buhs	ˈsɪləbəs
syllepsis	si LEP sis	sɪˈlɛpsɪs
syllogism	SI luh ji zuhm	ˈsɪlədʒɪzəm
sylph	silf	sɪlf
sylphid	SIL fid	ˈsɪlfɪd
sylvan	SIL vuhn	ˈsɪlvən
sylvatic	sil VA tik	sɪlˈvætɪk
sylvite	SIL vight	ˈsɪlvaɪt
symbiosis	sim bigh OH sis	sɪmbaɪˈosɪs
symbiotic	sim bigh AH tik	sɪmbaɪˈɑtɪk
symbol	SIM buhl	ˈsɪmbəl
Symington	SIGH ming tuhn	ˈsaɪmɪŋtən
symmetrical	si ME tri kuhl	sɪˈmɛtrɪkəl
symmetry	SI muh tri	ˈsɪmətrɪ
sympatholytic	sim puh thuh LI tik	sɪmpəθəˈlɪtɪk
symphonious	sim FOH ni uhs	sɪmˈfonɪəs
symposium	sim POH zi uhm	sɪmˈpozɪəm
symptom	SIMP tuhm	ˈsɪmptəm
symptomatic	simp tuh MA tik	sɪmptəˈmætɪk
synagog, -ue	SIN uh gawg	ˈsɪnəgɔg
synagogical	si nuh GAH ji kuhl	sɪnəˈgɑdʒɪkəl
synaloepha, synalepha	si nuh LEE fuh	sɪnəˈlifə
synapse	si NAPS	sɪˈnæps
synapsis	si NAP sis	sɪˈnæpsɪs
synchronic	sin KRAH nik	sɪnˈkrɑnɪk
synchronism	SING kruh ni zuhm	ˈsɪŋkrənɪzəm
synchronize	SING kruh nighz	ˈsɪŋkrənaɪz
synchronous	SING kruh nuhs	ˈsɪŋkrənəs
synchrotron	SING kruh trahn	ˈsɪŋkrətrɑn
synclinal	sin KLIGH nuhl	sɪnˈklaɪnəl
syncline	SING klighn	ˈsɪŋklaɪn
syncopate	SING kuh payt	ˈsɪŋkəpet
syncope	SING kuh pi	ˈsɪŋkəpɪ
syncretism	SING kruh ti zuhm	ˈsɪŋkrətɪzəm
syncrisis	SING kruh sis	ˈsɪŋkrəsɪs
syndactyl	sin DAK til	sɪnˈdæktɪl
syndetic	sin DE tik	sɪnˈdɛtɪk
syndic	SIN dik	ˈsɪndɪk
syndicalism	SIN di kuh li zuhm	ˈsɪndɪkəlɪzəm
syndicate (a, n)	SIN di kit	ˈsɪndɪkɪt
syndicate (v)	SIN di kayt	ˈsɪndɪket
syndrome	SIN drohm	ˈsɪndrom
synecdoche	si NEK duh ki	sɪˈnɛkdəkɪ
syneresis, synaeresis	si NAI ruh sis	sɪˈnɛrəsɪs
synergism	SI ner ji zuhm	ˈsɪnərdʒɪzəm
synergy	SI ner ji	ˈsɪnərdʒɪ
synesis	SI nuh sis	ˈsɪnəsɪs

at [æ] ; ah [ɑ] ; air [ɛ] ; awful [ɔ] ; say [e] ; back [b] ; chair [tʃ] ; do [d] ; elm [ɛ] ; eel [i] ;
server [ˈɜ, ər] ; fit [f] ; go [g] ; hurt [h] ; is [ɪ] ; high [aɪ] ; jet [dʒ] ; kiss [k] ; lamb [l] ; my [m] ;
nice [n] ;

Synge	sing	sıŋ
syngenesis	sin JE nuh sis	sın'dʒɛnəsıs
synizesis	si nuh ZEE sis	sınə'zisıs
synod	SI nuhd	'sınəd
synodical	si NAH di kuhl	sı'nɑdıkəl
synonymity	si nuh NI muh ti	sınə'nımətı
synonymous	si NAH nuh muhs	sı'nɑnəməs
synopses	si NAHP seez	sı'nɑpsiz
synopsis	si NAHP sis	sı'nɑpsıs
syntheses	SIN thuh seez	'sınθəsiz
synthesis	SIN thuh sis	'sınθəsıs
synthesize	SIN thuh sighz	'sınθəsaız
synthetic	sin THE tik	sın'θɛtık
syntonize	SIN tuh nighz	'sıntənaız
syntony	SIN tuh ni	'sıntənı
synusia	si NYOO : zi uh	sı'njuzıə
syphilis	SI fuh lis	'sıfəlıs
syphilitic	si fuh LI tik	sıfə'lıtık
Syracuse	SI ruh kyoo : s	'sırəkjus
Syr Darya	sir DAHR yah	sır 'dɑrjɑ
syrette, S-	si RET	sı'rɛt
Syria	SI ri uh	'sırıə
Syriac	SI ri ak	'sırıæk
syringa	suh RING guh	sə'rıŋgə
syringe (n)	SI rinj	'sırındʒ
syringe (v)	suh RINJ	sə'rındʒ
syringomyelia	suh RING goh migh EE li uh	sə'rıŋgomaı'ilıə
syrinx, S-	SI ringks	'sırıŋks
syrup	SI ruhp	'sırəp
systaltic	si STAL tik	sı'stæltık
systematist	SI stuh muh tist	'sıstəmətıst
systemic	si STE mik	sı'stɛmık
systole	SI stuh lee	'sıstəli
systolic	si STAH lik	sı'stɑlık
syzygy	SI zuh ji	'sızədʒı
Szamos	SAH mawsh	'sɑmɔʃ
Szechwan, Szech'wan	se chwahn	sɛ tʃwɑn
Szeged	SE ged	'sɛgɛd
Szekesfehervar	SAY kesh FE hayr vahr	'sekɛʃ'fɛhervɑr
Szell	sel	sɛl
Szepes	SE pesh	'sɛpɛʃ
Szigeti	si GE ti	sı'gɛtı
Szolnok	SAWL nawk	'sɔlnɔk
Szombathely	SAWM baht hay	'sɔmbɑthe
Szulc	shoolts	'ʃʊlts
Szydlowiec	shid LAW vyets	ʃɪd'lɔvjɛts

---

sing [ŋ] ; oh [o] ; oil [ɔı] ; foot [ʊ] ; foo:d [u] ; how [aʊ] ; pie [p] ; ray [r] ; so [s] ; shall [ʃ] ; to [t] ; thin [θ] ; th:en [ð] ; above (uh BUHV) [ə, 'ʌ] ; vine [v] ; wine [w] ; whine [hw] ; you [j] ; zoo [z] ; rouge (roo:zh) [ʒ].

T

Taal	tahl	tɑl
tabard	TA berd	ˈtæbərd
tabaret	TA buh rit	ˈtæbərɪt
tabasco, T-	tuh BA skoh	təˈbæsko
tabes	TAY beez	ˈtebiz
Tabitha	TA buh thuh	ˈtæbəθə
tablature	TA bluh cher	ˈtæblətʃər
tableau	TA bloh	ˈtæblo
tableau vivant	tah BLOH vee VAHN	tɑˈblo viˈvɑn
table d'hôte	TAH buhl DOHT	ˈtɑbəl ˈdot
taboo	tuh BOO :	təˈbu
tabor, tabour	TAY ber	ˈtebər
taboret, tabouret	TA buh rit	ˈtæbərɪt
taborin, -e	ta buh REEN	tæbəˈrin
Tabriz	tah BREEZ	tɑˈbriz
tabular	TA byuh ler	ˈtæbjələr
tabula rasa	TA byoo : luh RAY suh	ˈtæbjulə ˈresə
tacet	TAY set	ˈtesɛt
tachistoscope	tuh KI stuh skohp	təˈkɪstəskop
tachometer	tuh KAH muh ter	təˈkɑmətər
tachycardia	ta ki KAHR di uh	tækɪˈkɑrdɪə
tachygraphy	ta KI gruh fi	tæˈkɪgrəfɪ
tachylalia	ta ki LAY li uh	tækɪˈlelɪə
tacit	TA sit	ˈtæsɪt
taciturn	TA suh tern	ˈtæsətərn
Tacitus	TA suh tuhs	ˈtæsətəs
tackle	TA kuhl	ˈtækəl
Tacna	TAK nuh	ˈtæknə
Tacoma	tuh KOH muh	təˈkomə
taconite	TA kuh night	ˈtækənaɪt
tactical	TAK ti kuhl	ˈtæktɪkəl
tactician	tak TI shuhn	tækˈtɪʃən
tactile	TAK tuhl	ˈtæktəl
Tacubaya	tah koo : BAH yah	tɑkuˈbɑjɑ
Tadzhik, Tadjik	tah JEEK	tɑˈdʒik
taenia, tenia	TEE ni uh	ˈtinɪə
taffeta	TA fi tuh	ˈtæfɪtə
taffrail	TAF rayl	ˈtæfrel
tafia	TA fi uh	ˈtæfə
Tafti	TAF ti	ˈtæftɪ
Tag (German)	tahk	tɑk
Tagal	tah GAHL	tɑˈgɑl
Tagalog	tah GAH lahg	tɑˈgɑlɑg
Taganrog	tah gahn RAWK	tɑgɑnˈrɔk
Taggard	TA gerd	ˈtægərd
Tagliavini	tah lyah VEE nee	tɑljɑˈvini
Tagore, Rabindranath	tuh GAWR, ruh BIN druh naht	təˈgɔr, rəˈbɪndrənɑt

---

at [æ] ; *ah* [ɑ] ; *air* [ɛ] ; *awful* [ɔ] ; *say* [e] ; *back* [b] ; *chair* [tʃ] ; *do* [d] ; *elm* [ɛ] ; *eel* [i] ; *server* [ˈɝ, ər] ; *f* it [f] ; *go* [g] ; *hurt* [h] ; *is* [ɪ] ; *high* [aɪ] ; *jet* [dʒ] ; *kiss* [k] ; *lamb* [l] ; *my* [m] ; *nice* [n] ;

Tagus	TAY guhs	ˈtegəs
Tahiti	tah HEE ti	tɑˈhitɪ
Tahitian	tuh HEE shuhn	təˈhiʃən
Tahoe	TAH hoh	ˈtɑho
Taihoku	tigh HOH koo :	taɪˈhoku
taille	tayl	tel
Taimyr, Taimir	tigh MIR	taɪˈmɪr
Tainan	tigh nahn	taɪnɑn
Taine	tayn	ten
Taipeh, Taipei	tigh pe	taɪpɛ
Taiping	tigh ping	taɪpɪŋ
Taisho	tigh shoh	taɪʃo
Taiwan	tigh wahn	taɪwɑn
Taiyuan	TIGH yoo AHN	ˈtaɪjuˈɑn
Taiz	tah EEZ	tɑˈiz
Taj Mahal	TAHZH muh HAHL	ˈtɑʒ məˈhɑl
talapoin	TA luh poin	ˈtæləpɔɪn
talaria	tuh LAI ri uh	təˈlɛrɪə
Talbot	TAWL buht	ˈtɔlbət
tales (jury)	TAY leez	ˈteliz
talesman	TAYLZ muhn	ˈtelzmən
talion	TA li uhn	ˈtælɪən
taliped	TA luh ped	ˈtæləpɛd
talipes	TA luh peez	ˈtæləpiz
talipot	TA li paht	ˈtælɪpɑt
talisman	TA lis muhn	ˈtælɪsmən
talk	tawk	tɔk
talkathon	TAW kuh thahn	ˈtɔkəθɑn
Talkeetna	tal KEET nuh	tælˈkitnə
Tallahassee	ta luh HA si	tæləˈhæsɪ
Tallchief	TAWL cheef	ˈtɔltʃif
Talleyrand	TA li rand	ˈtælɪrænd
Tallinn	TAH lin	ˈtɑlɪn
tallith	TA lith	ˈtælɪθ
Talmud	TAL muhd	ˈtælməd
Talmudic	tal MUH dik	tælˈmʌdɪk
talon	TA luhn	ˈtælən
Talos	TAY lahs	ˈtelɑs
talus	TAY luhs	ˈteləs
tamale	tuh MAH li	təˈmɑlɪ
Tamar	TAY mer	ˈtemər
tamarack	TA muh rak	ˈtæməræk
tamarind	TA muh rind	ˈtæmərɪnd
tamarisk	TA muh risk	ˈtæmərɪsk
tamasha	tuh MAH shuh	təˈmɑʃə
Tamatave	tah mah TAHV	tɑmɑˈtɑv
Tamaulipas	tah mah oo LEE pahs	tɑmɑuˈlipɑs
Tambora	TAHM baw rah	ˈtɑmbɔrɑ
tambour	TAM boor	ˈtæmbʊr
tambourin	TAM boo rin	ˈtæmbʊrɪn
tambourine	tam buh REEN	tæmbəˈrin
Tambov	tahm BAWF	tɑmˈbɔf

sing [ŋ] ; *oh* [o] ; *oil* [ɔɪ] ; *foot* [ʊ] ; *foo*:d [u] ; *how* [aʊ] ; *p*ie [p] ; *r*ay [r] ; *s*o [s] ; *sh*all [ʃ] ;
*t*o [t] ; *th*in [θ] ; *th*:en [ð] ; above (*uh* B*UH*V) [ə, ˈʌ] ; *v*ine [v] ; *w*ine [w] ; *wh*ine [hw] ;
*y*ou [j] ; *z*oo [z] ; rouge (roo:*zh*) [ʒ].

Tamerlane	TA mer layn	ˈtæmərlen
Tamil	TA mil	ˈtæmɪl
Tammany	TA muh ni	ˈtæmənɪ
Tammuz	TAH mooz	ˈtɑmʊz
Tampa	TAM puh	ˈtæmpə
tampala	tam PA luh	tæmˈpælə
Tampere	TAHM per re	ˈtɑmpɛrɛ
Tampico	tam PEE koh	tæmˈpiko
tampion	TAM pi uhn	ˈtæmpɪən
tampon	TAM pahn	ˈtæmpɑn
Tana	TAH nah	ˈtɑnɑ
tanager	TA nuh jer	ˈtænədʒər
Tanana	ta nuh NAH	tænəˈnɑ
Tananarive	tah nah nah REEV	tɑnɑnɑˈriv
Tancred	TANG krid	ˈtæŋkrɪd
tandem	TAN duhm	ˈtændəm
Tanganyika	tang gan YEE kuh	tæŋgænˈjikə
tangelo	TAN juh loh	ˈtændʒəlo
tangent	TAN juhnt	ˈtændʒənt
tangential	tan JEN shuhl	tænˈdʒɛnʃəl
tangerine	TAN juh reen	ˈtændʒərin
tangible	TAN juh buhl	ˈtændʒəbəl
Tangier	tan JIR	tænˈdʒɪr
tangle	TANG guhl	ˈtæŋgəl
tango	TANG goh	ˈtæŋgo
Tanis	TAY nis	ˈtenɪs
Tannhäuser	TAHN hoi zer	ˈtɑnhɔɪzər
Tannu Tuva	TAH noo too VAH	ˈtɑnʊ tuˈvɑ
tantalum	TAN tuh luhm	ˈtæntələm
Tantalus, t-	TAN tuh luhs	ˈtæntələs
tantamount	TAN tuh mownt	ˈtæntəmaʊnt
tant mieux	tahn MYER	tɑn ˈmjɚ
tanto	TAHN taw	ˈtɑntɔ
tant pis	tahn PEE	tɑn ˈpi
tantrum	TAN truhm	ˈtæntrəm
Taoism	TOW i zuhm	ˈtaʊɪzəm
Taos	tows	taʊs
Tapajoz	tah puh ZHAWS	tɑpəˈʒɔs
taper	TAY per	ˈtepər
tapestry	TA pi stri	ˈtæpɪstrɪ
tapioca	ta pi OH kuh	tæpɪˈokə
tapir	TAY per	ˈtepər
tapis	TA pee	ˈtæpi
Tapuyan	tah POO : yuhn	tɑˈpujən
tarantas, -s	tah rahn TAHS	tɑrɑnˈtɑs
tarantella	ta ruhn TE luh	tærənˈtɛlə
Taranto	tuh RAN toh	təˈrænto
tarantula	tuh RAN chuh luh	təˈræntʃələ
Tarawa	tah RAH wah	tɑˈrɑwɑ
tarboosh	tahr BOO : SH	tɑrˈbuʃ
Tardieu	tahr DYER	tɑrˈdjɚ
tardo	TAHR daw	ˈtɑrdɔ

at [æ] ; *ah* [ɑ] ; *air* [ɛ] ; *aw*ful [ɔ] ; *say* [e] ; *b*ack [b] ; *ch*air [tʃ] ; *d*o [d] ; *e*lm [ɛ] ; *ee*l [i] ; *ser*ver [ˈɚ, ər] ; *f*it [f] ; *g*o [g] ; *h*urt [h] ; *is* [ɪ] ; *high* [aɪ] ; *j*et [dʒ] ; *k*iss [k] ; *l*amb [l] ; *m*y [m] ; *n*ice [n] ;

tare	tair	tɛr
Targoviste	TER goh VESH te	ˈtɝgoˈvɛʃtɛ
Targu-Jiu	TER goo ZHEE oo	ˈtɝgu ˈʒiu
Targu-Mures	TER goo MOO resh	ˈtɝgu ˈmurɛʃ
Tarim	tah REEM	tɑˈrim
tarlatan, tarletan	TAHR luh tuhn	ˈtɑrlətən
Tarnowskie Gory	tahr NAWF skye GOO ri	tɑrˈnɔfskjɛ ˈgurɪ
taro	TAH roh	ˈtɑro
tarpaulin	tahr PAW lin	tɑrˈpɔlɪn
Tarpeia	tahr PEE uh	tɑrˈpiə
tarpon	TAHR pahn	ˈtɑrpɑn
Tarquin	TAHR kwin	ˈtɑrkwɪn
tarragon	TA ruh gahn	ˈtærəgɑn
tarry (a)	TAH ri	ˈtɑrɪ
tarry (v)	TA ri	ˈtærɪ
Tarshish	TAHR shish	ˈtɑrʃɪʃ
tarsier	TAHR si er	ˈtɑrsɪər
Tarsus, t-	TAHR suhs	ˈtɑrsəs
tartan	TAHR tuhn	ˈtɑrtən
Tartar, t-, -e	TAHR ter	ˈtɑrtər
Tartarus	TAHR tuh ruhs	ˈtɑrtərəs
Tartini	tahr TEE nee	tɑrˈtini
Tartu	TAHR too :	ˈtɑrtu
Tartufe, Tartuffe, t-	tahr TOO: F	tɑrˈtuf
Tashkent, Tashkend	tahsh KENT	tɑʃˈkɛnt
task	task	tæsk
Tasman	TAZ muhn	ˈtæzmən
Tasmania	taz MAY ni uh	tæzˈmenɪə
Tass	tahs	tɑs
tassel	TA suhl	ˈtæsəl
Tasso	TA soh	ˈtæso
taste	tayst	test
Tatar	TAH ter	ˈtɑtər
tatbeb	TAT beb	ˈtætbɛb
Tatra	TAH trah	ˈtɑtrɑ
tatterdemalion	TA ter di MAY lyuhn	ˈtætərdɪˈmeljən
tattersall	TA ter sawl	ˈtætərsɔl
tattoo	ta TOO:	tæˈtu
Tatungkow	tah toong kow	tɑtuŋkɑu
tau	taw	tɔ
Tauchnitz	TOWK nits	ˈtaʊknɪts
taunt	tawnt	tɔnt
taupe	tohp	top
Taurus	TAW ruhs	ˈtɔrəs
Taussig	TOW sig	ˈtaʊsɪg
taut	tawt	tɔt
tautology	taw TAH luh ji	tɔˈtɑlədʒɪ
taxeme	TAK seem	ˈtæksim
taxidermy	TAK si der mi	ˈtæksɪdərmɪ
taxonomy	tak SAH nuh mi	tækˈsɑnəmɪ
Taygeta	tay I ji tuh	teˈɪdʒɪtə
Tchaikovsky	chigh KAWF ski	tʃaɪˈkɔfskɪ

sing [ŋ] ; oh [o] ; oil [ɔɪ] ; foot [ʊ] ; foo:d [u] ; how [aʊ] ; pie [p] ; ray [r] ; so [s] ; shall [ʃ] ;
to [t] ; thin [θ] ; th:en [ð] ; above (uh BUHV) [ə, ˈʌ] ; vine [v] ; wine [w] ; whine [hw] ;
you [j] ; zoo [z] ; rouge (roo:zh) [ʒ].

Tchekhov	CHE kawf	ˈtʃɛkɔf
Tchelitchew, Tchelitsheff	CHUH lee chef	ˈtʃʌlitʃɛf
Tczew	chef	tʃɛf
tear ("weep")	tir	tɪr
tear ("rend")	tair	tɛr
Tebaldi, Renata	tuh BAHL dee, ruh NAH tuh	təˈbɑldi, rəˈnɑtə
technetium	tek NEE shi uhm	tɛkˈniʃɪəm
technique	tek NEEK	tɛkˈnik
tectonic	tek TAH nik	tɛkˈtɑnɪk
Tecuci	te KOOCH	tɛˈkʊtʃ
Tecumseh	ti KUHM suh	tɪˈkʌmsə
tedesca	te DE skah	tɛˈdɛskɑ
Te Deum	TEE DEE uhm	ˈti ˈdiəm
tedious	TEE di uhs	ˈtidɪəs
tedium	TEE di uhm	ˈtidɪəm
teeth	teeth	tiθ
teethe	teeth :	tið
teetotaler	tee TOH tuh ler	tiˈtotələr
Tegal	te GAHL	tɛˈgɑl
Tegucigalpa	te GOO : see GAHL pah	tɛˈgusiˈgɑlpɑ
tegument	TE gyuh muhnt	ˈtɛgjəmənt
Teheran	te uh RAHN	tɛəˈrɑn
Tehuantepec	te WAHN tuh PEK	tɛˈwɑntəˈpɛk
Tehuelche	te WEL che	tɛˈwɛltʃɛ
te igitur	tee I juh ter	ti ˈɪdʒətər
Telamon, t-	TE luh mahn	ˈtɛləmɑn
telangiectasis	te lan ji EK tuh sis	tɛlændʒɪˈɛktəsɪs
telautograph	tel AW tuh graf	tɛlˈɔtəgræf
Tel Aviv	TEL ah VEEV	ˈtɛl ɑˈviv
telecast	TE luh kast	ˈtɛləkæst
telega	te LE gah	tɛˈlɛgɑ
telegenic	te luh JE nik	tɛləˈdʒɛnɪk
telegony	tuh LE guh ni	təˈlɛgənɪ
telegraph	TE luh graf	ˈtɛləgræf
telegrapher	tuh LE gruh fer	təˈlɛgrəfər
telegraphy	tuh LE gruh fi	təˈlɛgrəfɪ
Telegu	TE luh goo :	ˈtɛləgu
Telemachus	tuh LE muh kuhs	təˈlɛməkəs
Telemark	TE luh mahrk	ˈtɛləmɑrk
telemechanics	te luh mʹuh KA niks	tɛləməˈkænɪks
telemeter	tuh LE muh ter	təˈlɛmətər
telemetry	tuh LE muh tri	təˈlɛmətrɪ
teleology	te li AH luh ji	tɛlɪˈɑlədʒɪ
telepathic	te luh PA thik	tɛləˈpæθɪk
telepathy	tuh LE puh thi	təˈlɛpəθɪ
telephonic	te luh FAH nik	tɛləˈfɑnɪk
telephony	tuh LE fuh ni	təˈlɛfənɪ
telephote	TE luh foht	ˈtɛləfot
telephoto	te luh FOH toh	tɛləˈfoto
teleprompter, T-	TE luh prahmp ter	ˈtɛləprɑmptər
teleran	TE luh ran	ˈtɛləræn

at [æ] ; ah [ɑ] ; air [ɛ] ; awful [ɔ] ; say [e] ; back [b] ; chair [tʃ] ; do [d] ; elm [ɛ] ; eel [i] ; server [ˈɜ, ər] ; fit [f] ; go [g] ; hurt [h] ; is [ɪ] ; high [aɪ] ; jet [dʒ] ; kiss [k] ; lamb [l] ; my [m] ; nice [n] ;

telescopic	te luh SKAH pik	tɛləˈskɑpɪk
Telescopium	te luh SKOH pi uhm	tɛləˈskopɪəm
telescopy	tuh LE skuh pi	təˈlɛskəpɪ
telesthesia	te luhs THEE zhuh	tɛləsˈθiʒə
telestic, -h	tuh LE stik	təˈlɛstɪk
telethon	TE luh thahn	ˈtɛləθɑn
televise	TE luh vighz	ˈtɛləvaɪz
television	TE luh vi zhuhn	ˈtɛləvɪʒən
telic	TE lik	ˈtɛlɪk
Téllez	TE lyeth	ˈtɛljɛθ
tellurian	te LOO ri uhn	tɛˈlʊrɪən
tellurium	te LOO ri uhm	tɛˈlʊrɪəm
Tellus	TE luhs	ˈtɛləs
telpherage	TEL fuh rij	ˈtɛlfərɪdʒ
Telugu	TE loo goo:	ˈtɛlugu
temblor	tem BLAWR	tɛmˈblɔr
temerarious	te muh RAI ri uhs	tɛməˈrɛrɪəs
temerity	tuh MAI ruh ti	təˈmɛrətɪ
Tempe	TEM pi	ˈtɛmpɪ
tempera	TEM puh ruh	ˈtɛmpərə
temperament	TEM pruh muhnt	ˈtɛmprəmənt
temperamental	tem pruh MEN tuhl	tɛmprəˈmɛntəl
temperance	TEM pruhns	ˈtɛmprəns
temperate	TEM prit	ˈtɛmprɪt
temperature	TEM pruh cher	ˈtɛmprətʃər
tempestuous	tem PES choo uhs	tɛmˈpɛstʃʊəs
Templar, t-	TEM pler	ˈtɛmplər
template	TEM plit	ˈtɛmplɪt
tempo	TEM poh	ˈtɛmpo
temporal	TEM puh ruhl	ˈtɛmpərəl
temporarily	TEM puh rai ruh li	ˈtɛmpərɛrəlɪ
temporize	TEM puh righz	ˈtɛmpəraɪz
tempus fugit	TEM puhs FYOO: jit	ˈtɛmpəs ˈfjudʒɪt
tenable	TE nuh buhl	ˈtɛnəbəl
tenacious	ti NAY shuhs	tɪˈneʃəs
tenacity	ti NA suh ti	tɪˈnæsətɪ
Tenafly	TE nuh fligh	ˈtɛnəflaɪ
tenant	TE nuhnt	ˈtɛnənt
tendentious, tendencious	ten DEN shuhs	tɛnˈdɛnʃəs
tendon	TEN duhn	ˈtɛndən
Tenebrae	TE nuh bree	ˈtɛnəbri
tenebrous	TE nuh bruhs	ˈtɛnəbrəs
Tenedos	TE nuh dahs	ˈtɛnədɑs
Tenerife, Teneriffe	te nuh RIF	tɛnəˈrif
tenet	TE nit	ˈtɛnɪt
Tengri Khan	TENG gri KAHN	ˈtɛŋgrɪ ˈkɑn
Tengyueh	TUHNG yoo E	ˈtʌŋjuˈɛ
Teniers	TE nyerz	ˈtɛnjərz
Tenniel	TE nyuhl	ˈtɛnjəl
Tennysonian	te nuh SOH ni uhn	tɛnəˈsonɪən
tenon	TE nuhn	ˈtɛnən
tenonitis	te nuh NIGH tis	tɛnəˈnaɪtɪs

---

sing [ŋ]; *oh* [o]; *oil* [ɔɪ]; *foot* [ʊ]; *foo:d* [u]; *how* [aʊ]; *pie* [p]; *ray* [r]; *so* [s]; *shall* [ʃ];
to [t]; *thin* [θ]; *th:en* [ð]; *above* (*uh* B*U*HV) [ə, ˈʌ]; *vine* [v]; *wine* [w]; *whine* [hw];
you [j]; *zoo* [z]; *rouge* (roo:zh) [ʒ].

tenor	TE ner	ˈtɛnər
tenorrhaphy	tuh NAW ruh fi	təˈnɔrəfɪ
tensile	TEN suhl	ˈtɛnsəl
tension	TEN shuhn	ˈtɛnʃən
tentacle	TEN tuh kuhl	ˈtɛntəkəl
tentative	TEN tuh tiv	ˈtɛntətɪv
tenuis	TE nyoo : is	ˈtɛnjuɪs
tenuity	te NYOO : uh ti	tɛˈnjuətɪ
tenuous	TE nyoo uhs	ˈtɛnjuəs
tenure	TE nyer	ˈtɛnjər
tenuto	te NOO : taw	tɛˈnutɔ
teocalli	tee uh KA li	tiəˈkælɪ
tepee	TEE pee	ˈtipi
tepid	TE pid	ˈtɛpɪd
tepidarium	te puh DAI ri uhm	tɛpəˈdɛrɪəm
tequila	ti KEE lah	tɪˈkilɑ
Terah	TEE ruh	ˈtirə
teraphim	TAI ruh fim	ˈtɛrəfɪm
teratism	TAI ruh ti zuhm	ˈtɛrətɪzəm
teratology	tai ruh TAH luh ji	tɛrəˈtɑlədʒɪ
terbium	TER bi uhm	ˈtɜbɪəm
Ter Borch, Terborch	ter BAWRK	tərˈbɔrk
Terceira	tair SAY ruh	tɛrˈserə
tercel	TER suhl	ˈtɜsəl
tercentenary	ter SEN tuh nai ri	tərˈsɛntənɛrɪ
tercet	TER sit	ˈtɜsɪt
teredo	tai RAY doh	tɛˈredo
tergiversate	TER ji ver sayt	ˈtɜdʒɪvərset
tergiversation	ter ji ver SAY shuhn	tɜdʒɪvərˈseʃən
tergum	TER guhm	ˈtɜgəm
Terhune	ter HYOO : N	tərˈhjun
termagant	TER muh guhnt	ˈtɜməgənt
terminative	TER muh nay tiv	ˈtɜmənetɪv
terminology	ter muh NAH luh ji	tɜrməˈnɑlədʒɪ
terminus	TER muh nuhs	ˈtɜmənəs
Ternate	ter NAH te	tərˈnɑtɛ
terneplate	TERN playt	ˈtɜnplet
Terpsichore	terp SI kuh ree	tərpˈsɪkəri
terpsichorean, T-	terp si kuh REE uhn	tɜpsɪkəˈriən
terra, T-	TAI ruh	ˈtɛrə
terrace	TAI ris	ˈtɛrɪs
terra cotta	TAI ruh KAH tuh	ˈtɛrə ˈkɑtə
terra firma	TAI ruh FER muh	ˈtɛrə ˈfɜmə
terrain	tuh RAYN	təˈren
terra incognita	TAI ruh in KAHG ni tuh	ˈtɛrə ɪnˈkɑgnɪtə
terramycin	tai ruh MIGH sin	tɛrəˈmaɪsɪn
terrapin	TAI ruh pin	ˈtɛrəpɪn
terrarium	te RAI ri uhm	tɛˈrɛrɪəm
terrazzo	te RAHT saw	tɛˈratsɔ
Terre Haute	TAI ruh HOHT	ˈtɛrə ˈhot
terrene	te REEN	tɛˈrin
terreplein	TAIR playn	ˈtɛrplen

at [æ] ; ah [ɑ] ; air [ɛ] ; awful [ɔ] ; say [e] ; back [b] ; chair [tʃ] ; do [d] ; elm [ɛ] ; eel [i] ; server [ˈɜ, ər] ; fit [f] ; go [g] ; hurt [h] ; is [ɪ] ; high [aɪ] ; jet [dʒ] ; kiss [k] ; lamb [l] ; my [m] ; nice [n] ;

terrestrial	tuh RE stri uhl	təˈrɛstrɪəl
terrible	TAI ruh buhl	ˈtɛrəbəl
terrify	TAI ruh figh	ˈtɛrəfaɪ
terrigenous	te RI jin nuhs	tɛˈrɪdʒɪnəs
territorial	tai ruh TAW ri uhl	tɛrəˈtɔrɪəl
territory	TAI ruh taw ri	ˈtɛrətɔrɪ
terror	TAI rer	ˈtɛrər
terrorist	TAI ruh rist	ˈtɛrərɪst
terrorize	TAI ruh righz	ˈtɛrəraɪz
terry, T-	TAI ri	ˈtɛrɪ
tertiary, T-	TER shi ai ri	ˈtɝʃɪɛrɪ
Tertullian	ter TUH li uhn	tərˈtʌlɪən
terza rima	TERT suh REE muh	ˈtɝtsə ˈrimə
Terzin	TAIR zin	ˈtɛrzɪn
Tesla	TE sluh	ˈtɛslə
tessellate (a)	TE suh lit	ˈtɛsəlɪt
tessellate (v)	TE suh layt	ˈtɛsəlet
tessera	TE suh ruh	ˈtɛsərə
testate	TE stayt	ˈtɛstet
testator	TE stay ter	ˈtɛstetər
testes	TE steez	ˈtɛstiz
testicle	TE sti kuhl	ˈtɛstɪkəl
testimonial	te stuh MOH ni uhl	tɛstəˈmonɪəl
testimony	TE stuh moh ni	ˈtɛstəmonɪ
testis	TE stis	ˈtɛstɪs
testosterone	te STAH stuh rohn	tɛˈstɑstəron
testudo	te STOO : doh	tɛˈstudo
tetanic	ti TA nik	tɪˈtænɪk
tetanus	TE tuh nuhs	ˈtɛtənəs
tetany	TE tuh ni	ˈtɛtənɪ
tête-à-tête	TAY tuh TAYT	ˈtetəˈtet
tether	TE th : er	ˈtɛðər
Tethys	TEE this	ˈtiθɪs
tetra	TE truh	ˈtɛtrə
tetrachloride	te truh KLAW righd	tɛtrəˈklɔraɪd
tetrachord	TE truh kawrd	ˈtɛtrəkɔrd
tetraethyl	te truh E thuhl	tɛtrəˈɛθəl
Tetragrammaton	te truh GRA muh tahn	tɛtrəˈgræmətɑn
tetrahedron	te truh HEE druhn	tɛtrəˈhidrən
tetralogy	te TRA luh ji	tɛˈtrælədʒɪ
tetrameter	te TRA muh ter	tɛˈtræmətər
tetrarch	TE trahrk	ˈtɛtrɑrk
tetrarchy	TE trahr ki	ˈtɛtrɑrkɪ
tetrastich	TE truh stik	ˈtɛtrəstɪk
Tetrazzini	te truh ZEE ni	tɛtrəˈzinɪ
tetrode	TE trohd	ˈtɛtrod
tetter	TE ter	ˈtɛtər
Tetuán	te TWAHN	tɛˈtwɑn
Teufelsdröckh, Teufelsdroeckh	TOI fuhlz drek	ˈtɔɪfəlzdrɛk
Teuton	TOO : tuhn	ˈtutən
Teutonic	too : TAH nik	tuˈtɑnɪk

---

sing [ŋ] ; oh [o] ; oil [ɔɪ] ; foot [ʊ] ; foo:d [u] ; how [aʊ] ; pie [p] ; ray [r] ; so [s] ; shall [ʃ] ; to [t] ; thin [θ] ; th:en [ð] ; above (uh BUHV) [ə, ˈʌ] ; vine [v] ; wine [w] ; whine [hw] ; you [j] ; zoo [z] ; rouge (roo:zh) [ʒ].

Tewkesbury	TOO : KS bai ri	ˈtuksbɛrɪ
Texarkana	tek sahr KA nuh	tɛksɑrˈkænə
textile	TEK stuhl	ˈtɛkstəl
textual	TEKS choo uhl	ˈtɛkstʃʊəl
texture	TEKS cher	ˈtɛkstʃər
Teyde, Teide	TAY th : e	ˈteðɛ
Teyte	tayt	tet
Thaddeus, Thadeus	THA di uhs	ˈθædɪəs
Thai	tigh	taɪ
Thais	THAY is	ˈθeɪs
Thais (opera)	tah EES	tɑˈis
thalamotomy	tha luh MAH tuh mi	θæləˈmɑtəmɪ
thalamus	THA luh muhs	ˈθæləməs
thalassic	thuh LA sik	θəˈlæsɪk
Thalia (feminine name)	THAY li uh	ˈθelɪə
Thalia (Muse)	thuh LIGH uh	θəˈlaɪə
thalidomide	thuh LI dʊh mighd	θəˈlɪdəmɑɪd
thallium	THA li uhm	ˈθælɪəm
thallus	THA luhs	ˈθæləs
Thames (Connecticut)	thaymz	θemz
Thames (England, Canada)	temz	tɛmz
thanatophobia	tha nuh tuh FOH bi uh	θænətəˈfobɪə
thanatopsis	tha nuh TAHP sis	θænəˈtɑpsɪs
Thanatos	THA nuh tahs	ˈθænətɑs
thane	thayn	θen
Thapsus	THAP suhs	ˈθæpsəs
Thar	ter	tɝ
Thasos	THAH saws	ˈθɑsɔs
thaumatology	thaw muh TAH luh ji	θɔməˈtɑlədʒɪ
thaumaturge	THAW muh terj	ˈθɔmətərdʒ
thaumaturgy	THAW muh ter ji	ˈθɔmətərdʒɪ
theanthropic	thee an THRAH pik	θiænˈθrɑpɪk
theanthropism	thi AN thruh pi zuhm	θɪˈænθrəpɪzəm
thearchy	THEE ahr ki	ˈθiɑrkɪ
theater, theatre	THEE uh ter	ˈθiətər
theatrical	thi A tri kuhl	θɪˈætrɪkəl
Thebaid	THEE buh id	ˈθibəɪd
Theban	THEE buhn	ˈθibən
Thebes	theebz	θibz
Thebom	THEE bahm	ˈθibɑm
thé dansant	tay dahn SAHN	te dɑnˈsɑn
theelin	THEE lin	ˈθilɪn
thein, -e	THEE in	ˈθiɪn
their	th : air	ðɛr
theism	THEE i zuhm	ˈθiɪzəm
theistic	thee I stik	θiˈɪstɪk
thematic	thee MA tik	θiˈmætɪk
Themis	THEE mis	ˈθimɪs
Themistocles	thuh MI stuh kleez	θəˈmɪstəkliz
thence	th : ens	ðɛns
Theobald (Lewis)	TI buhld	ˈtɪbəld

at [æ]; *ah* [ɑ]; *air* [ɛ]; *awful* [ɔ]; *say* [e]; *back* [b]; *chair* [tʃ]; *do* [d]; *elm* [ɛ]; *eel* [i]; *server* [ˈɝ, ər]; *f*it [f]; *go* [g]; *hurt* [h]; *is* [ɪ]; *high* [aɪ]; *jet* [dʒ]; *kiss* [k]; *lamb* [l]; *my* [m]; *nice* [n];

Theobald	THEE uh bawld	ˈθiəbɔld
theocracy, theocrasy	thee AH kruh si	θiˈɑkrəsɪ
Theocritus	thee AH kri tuhs	θiˈɑkritəs
Theodoric	thee AH duh rik	θiˈɑdərɪk
Theodosius	thee uh DOH shi uhs	θiəˈdoʃɪəs
theogony	thee AH guh ni	θiˈɑgənɪ
theologian	thee uh LOH juhn	θiəˈlodʒən
theology	thee AH luh ji	θiˈɑlədʒɪ
theophany	thee AH fuh ni	θiˈɑfənɪ
Theophilus	thee AH fuh luhs	θiˈɑfələs
Theophrastus	thee uh FRA stuhs	θiəˈfræstəs
theoretician	thee uh ruh TI shuhn	θiərəˈtɪʃən
theosophy	thee AH suh fi	θiˈɑsəfɪ
therapeutic	the ruh PYOO : tik	θɛrəˈpjutɪk
therapist	THE ruh pist	ˈθɛrəpɪst
therapy	THE ruh pi	ˈθɛrəpɪ
there	th : air	ðɛr
theremin, T-	THE ruh min	ˈθɛrəmɪn
therianthropic	thi ri an THRAH pik	θɪrɪænˈθrɑpɪk
theriomorphic	thi ri uh MAWR fik	θɪrɪəˈmɔrfɪk
thermae	THER mee	ˈθɝmi
thermal	THER muhl	ˈθɝməl
thermion	THER migh uhn	ˈθɝmaɪən
thermistor	ther MI ster	θərˈmɪstər
thermodynamic	ther moh digh NA mik	θɝmodaɪˈnæmɪk
thermolysis	ther MAH luh sis	θərˈmɑləsɪs
thermometer	ther MAH muh ter	θərˈmɑmətər
thermonuclear	ther moh NOO : kli er	θɝmoˈnuklɪər
Thermopylae	ther MAH puh li	θərˈmɑpəlɪ
thermos, T-	THER muhs	ˈθɝməs
thermostat	THER muh stat	ˈθɝməstæt
Thersites	ther SIGH teez	θərˈsaɪtiz
thesaurus	thi SAW ruhs	θɪˈsɔrəs
Theseus	THEE soo : s	ˈθisus
Thespian	THE spi uhn	ˈθɛspɪən
Thespis	THE spis	ˈθɛspɪs
Thessalonica	the suh LAH ni kuh	θɛsəˈlɑnɪkə
Thessaly	THE suh li	ˈθɛsəlɪ
theta	THAY tuh	ˈθetə
Thetis	THEE tis	ˈθitɪs
theurgy	THEE er ji	ˈθiərdʒɪ
thew	thyoo :	θju
thiamine	THIGH uh meen	ˈθaɪəmin
thiazine	THIGH uh zeen	ˈθaɪəzin
thiazole	THIGH uh zohl	ˈθaɪəzol
Thibet	ti BET	tɪˈbɛt
Thiers	tyair	tjɛr
thine	th : ighn	ðaɪn
thiol	THIGH ohl	ˈθaɪol
thionic	thigh AH nik	θaɪˈɑnɪk
thionine	THIGH uh neen	ˈθaɪənin
this	th : is	ðɪs

sing [ŋ] ; *oh* [o] ; *oil* [ɔi] ; *foot* [ʊ] ; *foo*:d [u] ; *how* [aʊ] ; *pie* [p] ; *ray* [r] ; *so* [s] ; *shall* [ʃ] ; *to* [t] ; *thin* [θ] ; *th*:en [ð] ; above (*uh* B*UH*V) [ə, ˈʌ] ; *vine* [v] ; *wine* [w] ; *whine* [hw] ; *you* [j] ; *zoo* [z] ; rouge (roo:*zh*) [ʒ].

Thisbe	THIZ bi	ˈθɪzbɪ
thistle	THI suhl	θɪsəl
thither	THI th : er	ˈθɪðər
Thomism	TOH mi zuhm	ˈtomɪzəm
Thor	thawr	θɔr
thoracic	thaw RA sik	θɔˈræsɪk
thorax	THAW raks	ˈθɔræks
Thoreau	THAW roh	ˈθɔro
thorium	THAW ri uhm	ˈθɔrɪəm
thoron	THAW rahn	ˈθɔrɑn
thorough	THER oh	ˈθɝˑo
Thorshavn	tawrs HOWN	tɔrsˈhaʊn
Thoth	thohth	θoθ
thou	th : ow	ðaʊ
though	th : oh	ðo
Thracian	THRAY shuhn	ˈθreʃən
thr ʌl	thrawl	θrɔl
threepence	THRI puhns	ˈθrɪpəns
threnody	THRE nuh di	ˈθrɛnədɪ
threshold	THRE shohld	ˈθrɛʃold
thrombin	THRAHM bin	ˈθrɑmbɪn
thrombosis	thrahm BOH sis	θrɑmˈbosɪs
thrombotic	thrahm BAH tik	θrɑmˈbɑtɪk
thrombus	THRAHM buhs	ˈθrɑmbəs
throstle	THRAH suhl	ˈθrɑsəl
Thucydides	thoo : SI duh deez	θuˈsɪdədiz
thug	thuhg	θʌg
Thule	THOO : li	ˈθulɪ
thulium	THOO : li uhm	ˈθulɪəm
Thummim	THUH mim	ˈθʌmɪm
Thun	too : n	tun
Thurber	THER ber	ˈθɝbər
Thuringia	thoo RIN ji uh	θuˈrɪndʒɪə
Thursday	THERZ di	ˈθɝzdɪ
Thyestes	thigh E steez	θaɪˈɛstiz
thylacine	THIGH luh sign	ˈθaɪləsaɪn
thyme	tighm	taɪm
thymus	THIGH muhs	ˈθaɪməs
thyroid	THIGH roid	ˈθaɪrɔɪd
thyrsus	THER suhs	ˈθɝsəs
tiara	ti AI ruh	tɪˈɛrə
Tiberias, Tiberius	tigh BI ri uhs	taɪˈbɪrɪəs
Tibet	ti BET	tɪˈbɛt
Tibetan	ti BE tuhn	tɪˈbɛtən
tibia	TI bi uh	ˈtɪbɪə
Tibullus	ti BUH luhs	tɪˈbʌləs
Tichy	TI shi	ˈtɪʃɪ
Ticino	tee CHEE naw	tiˈtʃinɔ
Ticonderoga	tigh kahn duh ROH guh	taɪkɑndəˈrogə
tiemannite	TEE muh night	ˈtimənaɪt
Tien Shan	tyen shahn	tjɛn ʃɑn
Tientsin	tint sin	tɪntsɪn

at [æ] ; ah [ɑ] ; air [ɛ] ; awful [ɔ] ; say [e] ; back [b] ; chair [tʃ] ; do [d] ; elm [ɛ] ; eel [i] ;
server [ˈɝ, ər] ; fit [f] ; go [g] ; hurt [h] ; is [ɪ] ; high [aɪ] ; jet [dʒ] ; kiss [k] ; lamb [l] ; my [m] ;
nice [n] ;

Tiepolo	TYE paw law	ˈtjɛpɔlɔ
tierce	tirs	tɪrs
Tierra del Fuego	ti E ruh del foo : AY goh	tɪˈɛrə dɛl fuˈego
tiffany, T-	TI fuh ni	ˈtɪfənɪ
Tiflis	TI flis	ˈtɪflɪs
Tiglath-pileser	TIG lath puh LEE zer	ˈtɪglæθpəˈlizər
Tigris	TIGH gris	ˈtaɪgrɪs
tilde	TIL duh	ˈtɪldə
Tilsit	TIL zit	ˈtɪlzɪt
timarau	tee muh ROW	timəˈrau
timbal, -e	TIM buhl	ˈtɪmbəl
timber, timbre	TIM ber	ˈtɪmbər
Timbuktu	tim BUHK too :	tɪmˈbʌktu
Timisoara	tee mee SHWAH rah	timiˈʃwarɑ
timocracy	tigh MAH kruh si	taɪˈmɑkrəsɪ
Timon	TIGH muhn	ˈtaɪmən
Timor	TEE mawr	ˈtimɔr
timorous	TI muh ruhs	ˈtɪmərəs
Timoshenko	ti muh SHENG koh	tɪməˈʃɛŋko
Timotheus	ti MOH thi uhs	tɪˈmoθɪəs
timpani	TIM puh ni	ˈtɪmpənɪ
timpanist	TIM puh nist	ˈtɪmpənɪst
tinamou	TI nuh moo :	ˈtɪnəmu
tincture	TINGK cher	ˈtɪŋktʃər
tinea	TI ni uh	ˈtɪnɪə
tinnitus	ti NIGH tuhs	tɪˈnaɪtəs
Tintagel	tin TA juhl	tɪnˈtædʒəl
tintinnabulation	tin ti na byuh LAY shuhn	tɪntɪnæbjəˈleʃən
Tintoretto	tin tuh RE toh	tɪntəˈrɛto
tiny	TIGH ni	ˈtaɪnɪ
Tippecanoe	TI pi kuh NOO :	ˈtɪpɪkəˈnu
Tipperary	ti puh RAI ri	tɪpəˈrɛrɪ
tirade	TIGH rayd	ˈtaɪred
tirailleur	tee rah YER	tirɑˈjɚ
Tirana, Tiranë	tee RAH nuh	tiˈranə
Tiresias	tuh RE si uhs	təˈrɛsɪəs
Tirich Mir	TEE ruhch MIR	ˈtirətʃ ˈmɪr
Tiros	TIGH rohs	ˈtaɪros
Tirpitz	TIR pits	ˈtɪrpɪts
Tirzah	TER zuh	ˈtɝzə
tisane	ti ZAN	tɪˈzæn
Tishah b'Ab	TI shah BAWV	ˈtɪʃɑ ˈbɔv
Tishbite	TISH bight	ˈtɪʃbaɪt
Tisiphone	ti SI fuh nee	tɪˈsɪfəni
tissue	TI shoo	ˈtɪʃu
Tisza	TEE sah	ˈtisɑ
titan, T-	TIGH tuhn	ˈtaɪtən
Titania	ti TAY ni uh	tɪˈtenɪə
Titanic, t-	tigh TA nik	taɪˈtænɪk
titanium	tigh TAY ni uhm	taɪˈtenɪəm
tithe	tighth :	taɪð
tithing	TIGH th : ing	ˈtaɪðɪŋ

sing [ŋ] ; oh [o] ; oil [ɔɪ] ; foot [ʊ] ; foo :d [u] ; how [aʊ] ; pie [p] ; ray [r] ; so [s] ; shall [ʃ] ;
to [t] ; thin [θ] ; th :en [ð] ; above (uh BUHV) [ə, ˈʌ] ; vine [v] ; wine [w] ; whine [hw] ;
you [j] ; zoo [z] ; rouge (roo :zh) [ʒ].

Tithonus	ti THOH nuhs	tɪˈθonəs
Titian	TI shuhn	ˈtɪʃən
Titicaca	ti ti KAH kuh	tɪtɪˈkakə
titilate	TI tuh layt	ˈtɪtəlet
Tito	TEE toh	ˈtito
Titov, Gherman	ti TAWF, hair MAHN	tɪˈtɔf, hɛrˈman
titubation	ti choo BAY shuhn	tɪtʃuˈbeʃən
titular	TI chuh ler	ˈtɪtʃələr
Titus	TIGH tuhs	ˈtaɪtəs
Tivoli	TI vuh li	ˈtɪvəlɪ
tizzy	TI zi	ˈtɪzɪ
tmesis	MEE sis	ˈmisɪs
tobacco	tuh BA koh	təˈbæko
Tobago	toh BAY goh	toˈbego
Tobiah	toh BIGH uh	toˈbaɪə
Tobias	toh BIGH uhs	toˈbaɪəs
Tobit	TOH bit	ˈtobɪt
toboggan	tuh BAH guhn	təˈbagən
Toby	TOH bi	ˈtobɪ
Tocantins	taw kahn TEENS	tɔkanˈtins
toccata	tuh KAH tuh	təˈkatə
Tocharian	toh KAI ri uhn	toˈkɛrɪən
tocology	toh KAH luh ji	toˈkalədʒɪ
tocopherol	toh KAH fuh rohl	toˈkafərol
Tocqueville, de	tawk VEEL, duh	tɔkˈvil, də
tocsin	TAHK sin	ˈtaksɪn
today	tuh DAY	təˈde
toffee, toffy	TAW fi	ˈtɔfɪ
Togo	TOH goh	ˈtogo
toile	twahl	twal
Tojo	TOH joh	ˈtodʒo
Tokay, t-	toh KAY	toˈke
Tokharian	toh KAI ri uhn	toˈkɛrɪən
Tokio, Tokyo	TOH ki oh	ˈtokɪo
tole, tôle	tohl	tol
Tolima	taw LEE mah	tɔˈlima
toll	tohl	tol
Toller	TOH ler	ˈtolər
Tolstoy, Tolstoi	TAHL stoi	ˈtalstɔɪ
Toltec	TAHL tek	ˈtaltɛk
Toluca	tuh LOO : kuh	təˈlukə
toluene	TAH lyoo een	ˈtaljuin
tomato	tuh MAY toh	təˈmeto
Tombigbee	tahm BIG bee	tamˈbɪgbi
tome	tohm	tom
tomography	tuh MAH gruh fi	təˈmagrəfɪ
tomorrow	tuh MAH roh	təˈmaro
Tomsk	tawmsk	tɔmsk
tonality	toh NA luh ti	toˈnælətɪ
tonetic	toh NE tik	toˈnɛtɪk
Tonga, t-	TAHNG guh	ˈtaŋgə
tongue	tuhng	tʌŋ

at [æ] ; ah [ɑ] ; air [ɛ] ; awful [ɔ] ; say [e] ; back [b] ; chair [tʃ] ; do [d] ; elm [ɛ] ; eel [i] ; server [ˈɝ, ər] ; fit [f] ; go [g] ; hurt [h] ; is [ɪ] ; high [aɪ] ; jet [dʒ] ; kiss [k] ; lamb [l] ; my [m] ; nice [n] ;

tonight	tuh NIGHT	təˈnaɪt
tonite	TOH night	ˈtonaɪt
Tonkin, t-	tahn kin	tɑnkɪn
Tonle Sap	TAHN lay SAHP	ˈtɑnle ˈsɑp
tonneau	tuh NOH	təˈno
Tonsberg	TUHNS bair	ˈtʌnsbɛr
tonsil	TAHN suhl	ˈtɑnsəl
tonsillectomy	tahn suh LEK tuh mi	tɑnsəˈlɛktəmɪ
tonsillitis	tahn suh LIGH tis	tɑnsəˈlaɪtɪs
tonsorial	tahn SAW ri uhl	tɑnˈsɔrɪəl
tonsure	TAHN sher	ˈtɑnʃər
tontine	TAHN teen	ˈtɑntin
tonus	TOH nuhs	ˈtonəs
topaz	TOH paz	ˈtopæz
topectomy	tuh PEK tuh mi	təˈpɛktəmɪ
topee	toh PEE	toˈpi
Topeka	tuh PEE kuh	təˈpikə
Tophet, -h	TOH fit	ˈtofɪt
tophus	TOH fuhs	ˈtofəs
topiary	TOH pi ai ri	ˈtopɪɛrɪ
topography	tuh PAH gruh fi	təˈpɑgrəfɪ
toponym	TAH puh nim	ˈtɑpənɪm
toponymy	tuh PAH nuh mi	təˈpɑnəmɪ
topsail	TAHP suhl	ˈtɑpsəl
toque	tohk	tok
tor	tawr	tɔr
Tora, -h, t-	TOH ruh	ˈtorə
torchier, -e	tawr SHIR	tɔrˈʃɪr
torchon	TAWR shahn	ˈtɔrʃɑn
Tordesillas	tawr th : e SEE lyahs	tɔrðeˈsiljɑs
toreador	TAW ri uh dawr	ˈtɔrɪədɔr
torero	taw RE raw	tɔˈrɛrɔ
toreutic	tuh ROO : tik	təˈrutɪk
torii	TOH ri ee	ˈtorii
torment (n)	TAWR ment	ˈtɔrmɛnt
torment (v)	tawr MENT	tɔrˈmɛnt
tornadic	tawr NA dik	tɔrˈnædɪk
tornado	tawr NAY doh	tɔrˈnedo
Tornio	TAWR nee aw	ˈtɔrnɪɔ
Toronto	tuh RAHN toh	təˈrɑnto
torpedo	tawr PEE doh	tɔrˈpido
torpor	TAWR per	ˈtɔrpər
torque	tawrk	tɔrk
Torquemada	tawr ki MAH duh	tɔrkɪˈmɑdə
torrefy	TAW ruh figh	ˈtɔrəfaɪ
Torrens	TAW ruhnz	ˈtɔrənz
torrent	TAW ruhnt	ˈtɔrənt
Torrente	taw REN tay	tɔˈrɛnte
torrential	taw REN shuhl	tɔˈrɛnʃəl
Torricelli	taw ri CHE li	tɔrɪˈtʃɛlɪ
torrid	TAW rid	ˈtɔrɪd
torridity	taw RI duh ti	tɔˈrɪdətɪ

sing [ŋ] ; oh [o] ; oil [ɔɪ] ; foot [ʊ] ; foo:d [u] ; how [aʊ] ; pie [p] ; ray [r] ; so [s] ; shall [ʃ] ; to [t] ; thin [θ] ; th:en [ð] ; above (uh BUHV) [ə, ˈʌ] ; vine [v] ; wine [w] ; whine [hw] ; you [j] ; zoo [z] ; rouge (roo:zh) [ʒ].

torsade	tawr SAYD	tɔrˈsed
torsion	TAWR shuhn	ˈtɔrʃən
torso	TAWR soh	ˈtɔrso
tort, -e	tawrt	tɔrt
torticollis	tawr ti KAH lis	tɔrtɪˈkɑlɪs
tortilla	tawr TEE yah	tɔrˈtijɑ
tortoise	TAWR tuhs	ˈtɔrtəs
Tortuga	tawr TOO : guh	tɔrˈtugə
tortuous	TAWR choo uhs	ˈtɔrtʃʊəs
torture	TAWR cher	ˈtɔrtʃər
torturous	TAWR chuh ruhs	ˈtɔrtʃərəs
torulin	TAW roo lin	ˈtɔrulɪn
torus	TAW ruhs	ˈtɔrəs
Toscanini	tah skuh NEE ni	tɑskəˈnini
totalitarian	toh ta luh TAI ri uhn	totæləˈtɛriən
totaquine	TOH tuh kween	ˈtotəkwin
totem	TOH tuhm	ˈtotəm
Tottenham	TAH tuh nuhm	ˈtatənəm
toucan	TOO : kan	ˈtukæn
touché	too : SHAY	tuˈʃe
Toulon	too : LAHN	tuˈlɑn
Toulouse	too : LOO : Z	tuˈluz
Toulouse-Lautrec	too : LOO : Z loh TREK	tuˈluz loˈtrɛk
Toungoo	towng goo :	taʊŋgu
toupee	too : PAY	tuˈpe
tour	toor	tʊr
touraco	too : rah KOH	turɑˈko
Touraine	too : RAYN	tuˈren
tourbillion	toor BI lyuhn	tʊrˈbɪljən
tour de force	toor duh FAWRS	tʊr də ˈfɔrs
Tourel	too : REL	tuˈrɛl
tournament	TOOR nuh muhnt	ˈtʊrnəmənt
tourney	TOOR ni	ˈtʊrnɪ
tourniquet	TOOR ni ket	ˈtʊrnɪket
Tours	too : r	tur
Toussaint L'Ouverture	too : SAN loo : vair TOOR	tuˈsæn luverˈtʊr
tout	towt	taʊt
tout à fait	too : ta FE	tutæˈfɛ
tout à vous	too : ta VOO :	tutæˈvu
tout de suite	too : t SWEET	tut ˈswit
tout ensemble	too : tahn SAHN bluh	tutɑnˈsɑnblə
tout le monde	too : luh MOHND	tu lə ˈmond
tovarisch	toh VAH rish	toˈvɑrɪʃ
tow	toh	to
toward	tawrd	tɔrd
towards	tawrdz	tɔrdz
towel	tow uhl	ˈtaʊəl
towhead	TOH hed	ˈtohɛd
towline	TOH lighn	ˈtolaɪn
toxaphene	TAHK suh feen	ˈtɑksəfin
toxemia	tahk SEE mi uh	tɑkˈsimɪə
toxicosis	tahk si KOH sis	tɑksɪˈkosɪs

at [æ] ; ah [ɑ] ; air [ɛ] ; awful [ɔ] ; say [e] ; back [b] ; chair [tʃ] ; do [d] ; elm [ɛ] ; eel [i] ; server [ˈɝ, ər] ; fit [f] ; go [g] ; hurt [h] ; is [ɪ] ; high [aɪ] ; jet [dʒ] ; kiss [k] ; lamb [l] ; my [m] ; nice [n] ;

toxin, -e	TAHK sin	ˈtɑksɪn
toxophilite	tahk SAH fuh light	tɑkˈsɑfəlaɪt
toxoplasmosis	tahk soh plaz MOH sis	tɑksoplæzˈmosɪs
Toynbee	TOIN bi	ˈtɔɪnbɪ
Toyohashi	TAW yaw HAH shee	ˈtɔjɔˈhɑʃi
Tozzi, Giorgio	TOH tsee, JAWR joh	ˈtotsi, ˈdʒɔrdʒo
trachea	TRAY ki uh	ˈtrekɪə
tracheal	TRAY ki uhl	ˈtrekɪəl
tracheitis	tray ki IGH tis	trekɪˈaɪtɪs
tracheotomy	tray ki AH tuh mi	trekɪˈɑtəmɪ
trachoma	truh KOH muh	trəˈkomə
tract	trakt	trækt
tractable	TRAK tuh buhl	ˈtræktəbəl
tractile	TRAK tuhl	ˈtræktəl
traduce	truh DOO : S	trəˈdus
Trafalgar	truh FAL ger	trəˈfælgər
tragedian	truh JEE di uhn	trəˈdʒidɪən
tragedienne	truh jee di EN	trədʒidɪˈɛn
tragicomedy	tra ji KAH muh di	trædʒɪˈkɑmədɪ
traipse	trayps	treps
trait	trayt	tret
traitorous	TRAY tuh ruhs	ˈtretərəs
Trajan	TRAY juhn	ˈtredʒən
trajectory	truh JEK tuh ri	trəˈdʒɛktərɪ
Tralee	truh LEE	trəˈli
trammel	TRA muhl	ˈtræməl
tramontane	truh MAHN tayn	trəˈmɑnten
trampolin, -e	TRAM puh lin	ˈtræmpəlɪn
tramway	TRAM way	ˈtræmwe
tranquil	TRANG kwil	ˈtræŋkwɪl
tranquilizer, tranquillizer	TRANG kwuh ligh zer	ˈtræŋkwəlaɪzer
tranquillity	trang KWI luh ti	træŋˈkwɪlətɪ
Transcaucasia	trans kaw KAY zhuh	trænskɔˈkeʒə
transcendent	tran SEN duhnt	trænˈsɛndənt
transcendental	tran sen DEN tuhl	trænsɛnˈdɛntəl
transducer	trans DOO : ser	trænsˈdusər
transept	TRAN sept	ˈtrænsɛpt
transeunt	TRAN si uhnt	ˈtrænsɪənt
transfer (n)	TRANS fer	ˈtrænsfər
transfer (v)	trans FER	trænsˈfɚ
transferable	trans FER uh buhl	trænsˈfɚəbəl
transference	trans FER uhns	trænsˈfɚəns
transfiguration	trans fi gyuh RAY shuhn	trænsfɪgjəˈreʃən
transfix	trans FIKS	trænsˈfɪks
transform (n)	TRANS fawrm	ˈtrænsfɔrm
transform (v)	trans FAWRM	trænsˈfɔrm
transience	TRAN shuhns	ˈtrænʃəns
transient	TRAN shuhnt	ˈtrænʃənt
transistor	tran ZI ster	trænˈzɪstər
transit	TRAN sit	ˈtrænsɪt
transition	tran ZI shuhn	trænˈzɪʃən
transitive	TRAN suh tiv	ˈtrænsətɪv

sing [ŋ] ; oh [o] ; oil [ɔɪ] ; foot [ʊ] ; foo:d [u] ; how [aʊ] ; pie [p] ; ray [r] ; so [s] ; shall [ʃ] ;
to [t] ; thin [θ] ; th:en [ð] ; above (uh BUHV) [ə, ˈʌ] ; vine [v] ; wine [w] ; whine [hw] ;
you [j] ; zoo [z] ; rouge (roo:zh) [ʒ].

transitory	TRAN suh taw ri	ˈtrænsətɔrɪ
Trans-Jordan	trans JAWR duhn	trænsˈdʒɔrdən
Transjordania	trans jawr DAY ni uh	trænsdʒɔrˈdenɪə
translucent	trans LOO : suhnt	trænsˈlusənt
transmigration	trans migh GRAY shuhn	trænsmaɪˈgreʃən
transmission	trans MI shuhn	trænsˈmɪʃən
transmitter	trans MI ter	trænsˈmɪtər
transmogrification	trans MAH gruh fi KAY shuhn	trænsˈmɑgrəfɪˈkeʃən
transmontane	trans MAHN tayn	trænsˈmɑnten
transmundane	trans MUHN dayn	trænsˈmʌnden
transmutation	trans myoo : TAY shuhn	trænsmjuˈteʃən
transonic, transsonic	tran SAH nik	trænˈsɑnɪk
transport (n)	TRANS pawrt	ˈtrænsport
transport (v)	trans PAWRT	trænsˈport
transubstantiation	tran suhb stan shi AY shuhn	trænsəbstænʃɪˈeʃən
Transvaal	trans VAHL	trænsˈvɑl
transverse	trans VERS	trænsˈvɝs
transvestite	trans VE stight	trænsˈvɛstaɪt
Transylvania	tran sil VAY ni uh	trænsɪlˈvenɪə
Trapani	TRAH pah nee	ˈtrɑpɑni
trapeze	truh PEEZ	trəˈpiz
trapezium	truh PEE zi uhm	trəˈpizɪəm
trapezoid	TRA puh zoid	ˈtræpəzɔɪd
Trappist	TRA pist	ˈtræpɪst
trapunto	truh POON toh	trəˈpʊnto
Traubel	TROW buhl	ˈtraʊbəl
trauma	TRAW muh	ˈtrɔmə
traumatic	traw MA tik	trɔˈmætɪk
Träumerei	TROI muh righ	ˈtrɔɪməraɪ
travail	TRA vayl	ˈtrævel
travelog, -ue	TRA vuh lawg	ˈtrævəlɔg
traverse, T-	TRA vers	ˈtrævərs
travesty	TRA vi sti	ˈtrævɪstɪ
Traviata, La	trah VYAH tah, la	trɑˈvjɑtɑ, læ
treacherous	TRE chuh ruhs	ˈtrɛtʃərəs
treachery	TRE chuh ri	ˈtrɛtʃɔrɪ
treacle	TREE kuhl	ˈtrikəl
treadle	TRE duhl	ˈtrɛdəl
treasure	TRE zher	ˈtrɛʒər
Trebizond	TRE bi zahnd	ˈtrɛbɪzɑnd
treble	TRE buhl	ˈtrɛbəl
Treblinka	tre BLEENG kah	trɛˈbliŋkɑ
trecento	tre CHEN taw	trɛˈtʃɛntɔ
trefoil	TREE foil	ˈtrifɔɪl
Treitschke	TRIGHCH kuh	ˈtraɪtʃkə
trek	trek	trɛk
tremendous	tri MEN duhs	trɪˈmɛndəs
tremolo	TRE muh loh	ˈtrɛməlo
tremor	TRE mer	ˈtrɛmər
tremulous	TRE myuh luhs	ˈtrɛmjələs

at [æ] ; ah [ɑ] ; air [ɛ] ; awful [ɔ] ; say [e] ; back [b] ; chair [tʃ] ; do [d] ; elm [ɛ] ; eel [i] ; server [ˈɝ, ər] ; fit [f] ; go [g] ; hurt [h] ; is [ɪ] ; high [aɪ] ; jet [dʒ] ; kiss [k] ; lamb [l] ; my [m] ; nice [n] ;

trenchant	TREN chuhnt	ˈtrɛntʃənt
Trenet, Charles	truh NAY, shahrl	trəˈne, ʃɑrl
Trengganu	treng GAH noo :	trɛŋˈgɑnu
Trentino	tren TEE naw	trɛnˈtinɔ
trepan	tri PAN	trɪˈpæn
trephine	tri FIGHN	trɪˈfaɪn
trepidation	tre puh DAY shuhn	trɛpəˈdeʃən
treponema	tre puh NEE muh	trɛpəˈnimə
trespass	TRE spuhs	ˈtrɛspəs
trestle	TRE suhl	ˈtrɛsəl
Trevelyan	tri VE lyuhn	trɪˈvɛljən
trey	tray	tre
triad	TRIGH ad	ˈtraɪæd
trial	TRIGH uhl	ˈtraɪəl
triangle	TRIGH ang guhl	ˈtraɪæŋgəl
triangulation	trigh ang gyuh LAY shuhn	traɪæŋgjəˈleʃən
Triangulum	trigh ANG gyuh luhm	traɪˈæŋgjələm
triarchy	TRIGH ahr ki	ˈtraɪɑrkɪ
Trias	TRIGH uhs	ˈtraɪəs
triassic	trigh A sik	traɪˈæsɪk
tribal	TRIGH buhl	ˈtraɪbəl
tribrach	TRIGH brak	ˈtraɪbræk
tribulation	tri byuh LAY shuhn	trɪbjəˈleʃən
tribunal	tri BYOO : nuhl	trɪˈbjunəl
tribune	TRI byoo : n	ˈtrɪbjun
tributary	TRI byuh tai ri	ˈtrɪbjətɛrɪ
tribute	TRI byoo : t	ˈtrɪbjut
trichiasis	tri KIGH uh sis	trɪˈkaɪəsɪs
trichinosis	tri kuh NOH sis	trɪkəˈnosɪs
trichoma	tri KOH muh	trɪˈkomə
trichotomy	trigh KAH tuh mi	traɪˈkɑtəmɪ
triclinium	trigh KLI ni uhm	traɪˈklɪnɪəm
tricot	TREE koh	ˈtriko
tricotine	tri kuh TEEN	trɪkəˈtin
tricycle	TRIGH si kuhl	ˈtraɪsɪkəl
trident, T-	TRIGH duhnt	ˈtraɪdənt
triennial	trigh E ni uhl	traɪˈɛnɪəl
Trieste	tri EST	trɪˈɛst
trifle	TRIGH fuhl	ˈtraɪfəl
Trigère	tree ZHAIR	triˈʒɛər
trigon	TRIGH gahn	ˈtraɪgɑn
trigonometric	tri guh nuh ME trik	trɪgənəˈmɛtrɪk
trigonometry	tri guh NAH muh tri	trɪgəˈnɑmətrɪ
trihedron	trigh HEE druhn	traɪˈhidrən
trilingual	trigh LING gwuhl	traɪˈlɪŋgwəl
trillium	TRI li uhm	ˈtrɪlɪəm
trilobite	TRIGH luh bight	ˈtraɪləbaɪt
trilogy	TRI luh ji	ˈtrɪlədʒɪ
trimester	trigh ME ster	traɪˈmɛstər
trimeter	TRI muh ter	ˈtrɪmətər
trimetric	trigh ME trik	traɪˈmɛtrɪk
trimetrogon	trigh ME truh gahn	traɪˈmɛtrəgɑn

sing [ŋ] ; *oh* [o] ; *oil* [ɔɪ] ; *foot* [ʊ] ; *foo*:d [u] ; *how* [aʊ] ; *pie* [p] ; *ray* [r] ; *so* [s] ; *shall* [ʃ] ; *to* [t] ; *thin* [θ] ; *th*:en [ð] ; *above* (*uh BUHV*) [ə, ˈʌ] ; *vine* [v] ; *wine* [w] ; *whine* [hw] ; *you* [j] ; *zoo* [z] ; *rouge* (*roo*:*zh*) [ʒ].

Trimurti	tri MOOR ti	trɪˈmʊrtɪ
trinal	TRIGH nuhl	ˈtraɪnəl
Tringcomalee	tring kuh muh LEE	trɪŋkəməˈli
Trinidad	TRI nuh dad	ˈtrɪnədæd
trinitrotoluene	trigh NIGH troh TAH lyoo een	traɪˈnaɪtroˈtɑljʊin
trinomial	trigh NOH mi uhl	traɪˈnomɪəl
trio	TREE oh	ˈtrio
triode	TRIGH ohd	ˈtraɪod
triolet	TRIGH uh lit	ˈtraɪəlɪt
tripartite	trigh PAHR tight	traɪˈpɑrtaɪt
tripe	trighp	traɪp
triphibian	trigh FI bi uhn	traɪˈfɪbɪən
triphthong	TRIF thawng	ˈtrɪfθɔŋ
triplicate (a, n)	TRI pli kit	ˈtrɪplɪkɪt
triplicate (v)	TRI pli kayt	ˈtrɪplɪket
tripod	TRIGH pahd	ˈtraɪpɑd
tripody	TRI puh di	ˈtrɪpədɪ
Tripoli	TRI puh li	ˈtrɪpəlɪ
Tripolitania	tri pah li TAY ni uh	trɪpɑlɪˈtenɪə
tripos	TRIGH pahs	ˈtraɪpɑs
Trippe	trip	trɪp
triptane	TRIP tayn	ˈtrɪpten
tripterous	TRIP tuh ruhs	ˈtrɪptərəs
Triptolemus, Triptolemos	trip TAH li muhs	trɪpˈtɑlɪmʌs
triptych	TRIP tik	ˈtrɪptɪk
Tripura	TRI poo rah	ˈtrɪpʊrɑ
trireme	TRIGH reem	ˈtraɪrim
triskelion	tri SKE li ahn	trɪˈskɛlɪɑn
Trismegistus	tris muh JI stuhs	trɪsməˈdʒɪstəs
trismus	TRIZ muhs	ˈtrɪzməs
trisoctahedron	tri sahk tuh HEE druhn	trɪsɑktəˈhidrən
Tristan da Cunha	TRI stan duh KOO : nyuh	ˈtrɪstæn də ˈkunjə
triste	treest	trist
tristesse	tree STES	triˈstɛs
tristich	TRI stik	ˈtrɪstɪk
Tristram	TRI struhm	ˈtrɪstrəm
tritheism	TRIGH thee i zuhm	ˈtraɪθiɪzəm
triton, T-	TRIGH tuhn	ˈtraɪtən
triumvir	trigh UHM vir	traɪˈʌmvɪr
triumvirate	trigh UHM vi rit	traɪˈʌmvɪrɪt
Trivandrum	tri VAN druhm	trɪˈvændrəm
trivia	TRI vi uh	ˈtrɪvɪə
trivial	TRI vi uhl	ˈtrɪvɪəl
trivium	TRI vi uhm	ˈtrɪvɪəm
Trnava	TER nah vah	ˈtɜnɑvɑ
Trnovac	TER naw vahts	ˈtɜnɔvɑts
Troas	TROH as	ˈtroæs
trochaic	troh KAY ik	troˈkeɪk
trochee	TROH kee	ˈtroki
troglodyte	TRAH gluh dight	ˈtrɑglədaɪt
troika	TROI kuh	ˈtrɔɪkə

at [æ] ; ah [ɑ] ; air [ɛ] ; awful [ɔ] ; say [e] ; back [b] ; chair [tʃ] ; do [d] ; elm [ɛ] ; eel [i] ; server [ˈɜ, ər] ; fit [f] ; go [g] ; hurt [h] ; is [ɪ] ; high [aɪ] ; jet [dʒ] ; kiss [k] ; lamb [l] ; my [m] ; nice [n] ;

Troilus	TROI luhs	ˈtrɔɪləs
Trojan	TROH juhn	ˈtrodʒən
troll	trohl	trol
trollop, -e, T-	TRAH luhp	ˈtrɑləp
trombone	TRAHM bohn	ˈtrɑmbon
Tromsö	TROOM ser	ˈtrʊmsər
Trondheim	TRAWN haym	ˈtrɔnhem
tropaeolum	truh PEE uh luhm	trəˈpiələm
trope	trohp	trop
trophy	TROH fi	ˈtrofɪ
tropism	TROH pi zuhm	ˈtropɪzəm
tropology	troh PAH luh ji	troˈpɑlədʒɪ
troposphere	TRAH puh sfir	ˈtrɑpəsfɪr
troppo	TRAH poh	ˈtrɑpo
Trossachs	TRAH suhks	ˈtrɑsəks
troth	trawth	trɔθ
Trotsky	TRAHT ski	ˈtrɑtskɪ
troubadour	TROO : buh dawr	ˈtrubədɔr
trough	trawf	trɔf
troupe	troo : p	trup
trousseau	troo : SOH	truˈso
Trovatore	troh vah TOH ray	trovɑˈtore
trouvère	troo : VAIR	truˈvɛr
trow	troh	tro
trowel	TROW uhl	ˈtrauəl
truant	TROO : uhnt	ˈtruənt
Trucial Oman	TROO : shuhl oh MAHN	ˈtruʃəl oˈmɑn
truculence	TRUH kyuh luhns	ˈtrʌkjələns
truculent	TRUH kyuh luhnt	ˈtrʌkjələnt
Trud	troo : d	trud
true	troo :	tru
truffle	TRUH fuhl	ˈtrʌfəl
Trujillo	troo : HEE yoh	truˈhijo
Truk	truhk	trʌk
Trumbull	TRUHM buhl	ˈtrʌmbəl
truncheon	TRUHN chuhn	ˈtrʌntʃən
trypanosomiasis	tri puh noh soh MIGH uh sis	trɪpənosoˈmaɪəsɪs
trypsin	TRIP sin	ˈtrɪpsɪn
tryst	trist	trɪst
tsar	sahr	sɑr
Tschaikovsky, Tschaikowsky	chigh KAWF ski	tʃaɪˈkɔfskɪ
tsetse	SET si	ˈsɛtsɪ
Tshombe, Moise	CHAHM bay, maw EES	ˈtʃɑmbe, mɔˈis
Tsinling Shan	sin ling shahn	sɪnlɪŋʃɑn
Tsouderos	soo : th : e RAWS	suðɛˈrɔs
Tsushima	soo : shee mah	suʃimɑ
Tuamotu	TOO : ah MAW too :	ˈtuɑˈmɔtu
Tuapse	too : ahp SE	tuɑpˈsɛ
Tuareg	TWAH reg	ˈtwɑrɛg
tubal, T-	TOO : buhl	ˈtubəl

sing [ŋ] ; oh [o] ; oil [ɔɪ] ; foot [ʊ] ; foo:d [u] ; how [aʊ] ; pie [p] ; ray [r] ; so [s] ; shall [ʃ] ;
to [t] ; thin [θ] ; th:en [ð] ; above (uh BUHV) [ə, ˈʌ] ; vine [v] ; wine [w] ; whine [hw] ;
you [j] ; zoo [z] ; rouge (roo:zh) [ʒ].

tube	too : b	tub
tubercle	TOO : ber kuhl	ˈtubərkəl
tubercular	too : BER kyuh ler	tuˈbɜ˞kjələr
tuberculin	too : BER kyuh lin	tuˈbɜ˞kjəlɪn
tuberculosis	too : ber kyuh LOH sis	tubərkjəˈlosɪs
tubular	TOO : byuh ler	ˈtubjələr
tubule	TOO : byoo : l	ˈtubjul
Tucana	too : KAY nuh	tuˈkenə
Tucson	too : SAHN	tuˈsɑn
Tudor	TOO : der	ˈtudər
Tuesday	TOO : Z di	ˈtuzdɪ
tufa	TOO : fuh	ˈtufə
Tuguegarao	too : ge gah ROW	tugɛgɑˈrau
Tuileries	TWEE luh riz	ˈtwilərɪz
Tukums	TOO kooms	ˈtukʊms
Tula	TOO : lah	ˈtulɑ
Tulagi	too : LAH gee	tuˈlɑgi
tularemia, tularaemia	too : luh REE mi uh	tuləˈrimɪə
tulip	TOO : lip	ˈtulɪp
tulle	too : l	tul
Tully	TUH li	ˈtʌlɪ
tumbrel, tumbril	TUHM bruhl	ˈtʌmbrəl
tumefacient	too : muh FAY shuhnt	tuməˈfeʃənt
tumescent	too : ME suhnt	tuˈmɛsənt
tumor	TOO : mer	ˈtumər
tumult	TOO : muhlt	ˈtuməlt
tumultuous	too : MUHL choo uhs	tuˈmʌltʃuəs
tumulus	TOO : myuh luhs	ˈtumjələs
tuna	TOO : nuh	ˈtunə
tundra	TUHN druh	ˈtʌndrə
tune	too : n	tun
tung	tuhng	tʌŋ
Tungliao	too : ng lyow	tuŋljau
tungsten	TUHNG stuhn	ˈtʌŋstən
Tungting	toong ting	tʊŋtɪŋ
Tungus	toon GOOZ	tʊnˈguz
tunic	TOO : nik	ˈtunɪk
Tunis	TOO : nis	ˈtunɪs
Tunisia	too : NI shi uh	tuˈnɪʃɪə
Tunney	TUH ni	ˈtʌnɪ
tunny	TUH ni	ˈtʌnɪ
tupelo	TOO : pi loh	ˈtupɪlo
Tupi	too : PEE	tuˈpi
tu quoque	too : KWOH kwi	tuˈkwokwɪ
Turandot	too : ruhn DOH	turənˈdo
Turanian	too RAY ni uhn	tuˈrenɪən
turban	TER buhn	ˈtɜ˞bən
turbid	TER bid	ˈtɜ˞bɪd
turbine	TER bighn	ˈtɜ˞baɪn
turbojet	TER boh JET	ˈtɜ˞boˈdʒɛt
turbot	TER buht	ˈtɜ˞bət
turbulence	TER byuh luhns	ˈtɜ˞bjələns

at [æ] ; *ah* [ɑ] ; *air* [ɛ] ; *awful* [ɔ] ; *say* [e] ; *back* [b] ; *chair* [tʃ] ; *do* [d] ; *elm* [ɛ] ; *eel* [i] ;
server [ɜ, ər] ; *fit* [f] ; *go* [g] ; *hurt* [h] ; *is* [ɪ] ; *high* [aɪ] ; *jet* [dʒ] ; *kiss* [k] ; *lamb* [l] ; *my* [m] ;
nice [n] ;

turbulent	TER byuh luhnt	ˈtɜˑbjələnt
Turco	TER koh	ˈtɜˑko
tureen	too REEN	tuˈrin
Turenne	too REN	tuˈrɛn
turf	terf	tɜˑf
Turgenev, Turgenieff,	toor GE nyif	turˈgɛnjɪf
Turgeniev		
turgid	TER jid	ˈtɜˑdʒɪd
Turgot	toor GOH	turˈgo
Turin	TOO rin	ˈturɪn
Turkestan	ter ki STAN	tərkɪˈstæn
Turkey, t-	TER ki	ˈtɜˑkɪ
Turki	TOOR kee	ˈturki
Turkmen (U.S.S.R.)	TERK men	ˈtɜˑkmɛn
Turku	TOOR koo	ˈturku
turmeric	TER muh rik	ˈtɜˑmərɪk
turnip	TER nip	ˈtɜˑnɪp
Turnverein	TOORN fe righn	ˈturnfɛraɪn
turpentine	TER puhn tighn	ˈtɜˑpəntaɪn
turpitude	TER puh too : d	ˈtɜˑpətud
turquoise	TER koiz	ˈtɜˑkɔɪz
turret	TER it	ˈtɜˑɪt
Tuscaloosa	tuh skuh LOO : suh	tʌskəˈlusə
Tuscan	TUH skuhn	ˈtʌskən
Tuscany	TUH skuh ni	ˈtʌskənɪ
Tuscarora	tuh skuh RAW ruh	tʌskəˈrɔrə
Tuskegee	tuh SKEE gi	təˈskigɪ
Tussaud	too : SOH	tuˈso
tussive	TUH siv	ˈtʌsɪv
Tutankhamen	too : t ahngk AH muhn	tutaŋkˈamən
tutelage	TOO : tuh lij	ˈtutəlɪdʒ
tutelary	TOO : tuh lai ri	ˈtutəlɛrɪ
tutor	TOO : ter	ˈtutər
tutorial	too : TAW ri uhl	tuˈtɔrɪəl
tutti	TOO : ti	ˈtutɪ
tutti-frutti	TOO : ti FROO : ti	ˈtutɪ ˈfrutɪ
tutu	TOO : too :	ˈtutu
Tutuila	too: too: EE lah	tutuˈilɑ
Tuva	TOO: vah	ˈtuvɑ
tuxedo, T-	tuhk SEE doh	təkˈsido
Tweedsmuir	TWEEDZ myoor	ˈtwidzmjur
Twickenham	TWI kuh nuhm	ˈtwɪkənəm
twopence	TUH puhns	ˈtʌpəns
Tyburn	TIGH bern	ˈtaɪbərn
Tyche	TIGH ki	ˈtaɪkɪ
tycoon	tigh KOO : N	taɪˈkun
tympani	TIM puh ni	ˈtɪmpənɪ
tympanist	TIM puh nist	ˈtɪmpənɪst
tympanites	tim puh NIGH teez	tɪmpəˈnaɪtiz
tympanum	TIM puh nuhm	ˈtɪmpənəm
Tyndale, Tyndall	TIN duhl	ˈtɪndəl
Tyndareus	tin DAI ri uhs	tɪnˈdɛrɪəs

sing [ŋ] ; *oh* [o] ; *oil* [ɔɪ] ; *foot* [ʊ] ; *foo:d* [u] ; *how* [aʊ] ; *pie* [p] ; *ray* [r] ; *so* [s] ; *shall* [ʃ] ;
to [t] ; *thin* [θ] ; *th:en* [ð] ; *above* (*uh* B*UH*V) [ə, ˈʌ] ; *vine* [v] ; *wine* [w] ; *whine* [hw] ;
you [j] ; *zoo* [z] ; *rouge* (roo:*zh*) [ʒ].

Tyne	tighn	taɪn
Tynemouth	TIGHN muhth	ˈtaɪnməθ
type	tighp	taɪp
typhlosis	ti FLOH sis	tɪˈflosɪs
typhoid	TIGH foid	ˈtaɪfɔɪd
Typhon	TIGH fahn	ˈtaɪfɑn
typhoon	tigh FOO : N	taɪˈfun
typhus	TIGH fuhs	ˈtaɪfəs
typical	TI pi kuhl	ˈtɪpɪkəl
typography	tigh PAH gruh fi	taɪˈpɑgrəfɪ
typology	tigh PAH luh ji	taɪˈpɑlədʒɪ
Tyr	tir	tɪr
tyrannical	ti RA ni kuhl	tɪˈrænɪkəl
tyrannize	TI ruh nighz	ˈtɪrənaɪz
tyrannosaur	ti RA nuh sawr	tɪˈrænəsɔr
tyrannous	TI ruh nuhs	ˈtɪrənəs
tyranny	TI ruh ni	ˈtɪrənɪ
tyrant	TIGH ruhnt	ˈtaɪrənt
Tyre	tighr	taɪr
Tyrian	TI ri uhn	ˈtɪrɪən
tyro	TIGH roh	ˈtaɪro
Tyrol	TI rahl	ˈtɪrɑl
Tyrolean	ti ROH li uhn	tɪˈrolɪən
Tyrolese	ti ruh LEEZ	tɪrəˈliz
Tyrone	ti ROHN	tɪˈron
tyrothricin	tigh ruh THRIGH sin	taɪrəˈθraɪsɪn
Tyrrhenian	ti REE ni uhn	tɪˈrinɪən

U

Ubangi	oo : BAHNG gi	uˈbɑŋgɪ
Ubangi-Shari	oo : BAHNG gi SHAH ri	uˈbɑŋgɪ ˈʃarɪ
Ubeda	OO : be th : ah	ˈubɛða
ubiety	yoo : BIGH uh ti	juˈbaɪətɪ
ubique	yoo : BIGH kwi	juˈbaɪkwɪ
ubiquitous	yoo : BI kwuh tuhs	juˈbɪkwətəs
Ucayali	oo : kah YAH li	ukɑˈjɑlɪ
Udall, Udale	YOO : duhl	ˈjudəl
Udmurt	oo : d MOORT	udˈmurt
udometer	yoo : DAH muh ter	juˈdɑmətər
Uele	WAY luh	ˈwelə
Ufa	oo : FAH	uˈfa
Uffizi	oo : FEET see	uˈfitsi
Uganda	oo : GAHN dah	uˈgɑndɑ
Ugrian	OO : gri uhn	ˈugrɪən
Ugric	OO : grik	ˈugrɪk
uhlan	OO : lahn	ˈulɑn
Uigur	WEE goor	ˈwigur

at [æ]; *ah* [ɑ]; *air* [ɛ]; *awful* [ɔ]; *say* [e]; *back* [b]; *chair* [tʃ]; *do* [d]; *elm* [ɛ]; *eel* [i]; *server* [ˈɜ, ər]; *f*it [f]; *go* [g]; *hurt* [h]; *is* [ɪ]; *high* [aɪ]; *jet* [dʒ]; *kiss* [k]; *lamb* [l]; *my* [m]; *nice* [n];

Uinta	yoo: IN tuh	juˈɪntə
uitlander, U-	IGHT lan der	ˈaɪtlændər
Ujiji	oo: JEE ji	uˈdʒidʒɪ
Ujpest	OO: i pesht	ˈʊɪpeʃt
ukase	YOO: kays	ˈjukes
Ukraine	YOO: krayn	ˈjukren
Ukrainian	yoo: KRAY ni uhn	juˈkrenɪən
ukulele	yoo: kuh LAY li	jukəˈlelɪ
Ulan Bator Khoto	OO: lahn BAH tawr KOH toh	ˈulɑn ˈbɑtɔr ˈkoto
Ulbricht	OOL brikt	ˈʊlbrɪkt
ulcer	UHL ser	ˈʌlsər
ulema	oo: luh MAH	uləˈmɑ
Ulfilas	UHL fi luhs	ˈʌlfɪləs
Ulm	oolm	ʊlm
ulmus, U-	UHL muhs	ˈʌlməs
Ulotrichi	yoo: LAH tri kigh	juˈlɑtrɪkaɪ
Ulrica	UHL ri kuh	ˈʌlrɪkə
Ulster, u-	UHL ster	ˈʌlstər
ulterior	uhl TI ri er	ʌlˈtɪrɪər
ultimate	UHL tuh mit	ˈʌltəmɪt
ultima Thule	UHL tuh muh THOO: li	ˈʌltəmə ˈθulɪ
ultimatum	uhl tuh MAY tuhm	ʌltəˈmetəm
ultimo	UHL tuh moh	ˈʌltəmo
ultra	UHL truh	ˈʌltrə
ultramontane	uhl truh MAHN tayn	ʌltrəˈmɑnten
ultramundane	uhl truh MUHN dayn	ʌltrəˈmʌnden
ultraviolet	uhl truh VIGH uh lit	ʌltrəˈvaɪəlɪt
ultra vires	UHL truh VIGH reez	ˈʌltrə ˈvaɪriz
ululate	YOO: luh layt	ˈjuləlet
Ulysses	yoo LI seez	jʊˈlɪsiz
umber	UHM ber	ˈʌmbər
umbilical	uhm BI li kuhl	ʌmˈbɪlɪkəl
umbilicus	uhm BI li kuhs	ʌmˈbɪlɪkəs
umbra	UHM bruh	ˈʌmbrə
umbrage	UHM brij	ˈʌmbrɪdʒ
umbrageous	uhm BRAY juhs	ʌmˈbredʒəs
umbrella	uhm BRE luh	ʌmˈbrɛlə
Umbria	UHM bri uh	ˈʌmbrɪə
Umbriel	UHM bri uhl	ˈʌmbrɪəl
umiak, umiack	OO: mi ak	ˈumɪæk
umlaut	OOM lowt	ˈumlaut
umpire	UHM pighr	ˈʌmpaɪr
Unalaska	oo: nuh LA skuh	unəˈlæskə
Unamuno	oo: nah MOO: naw	unɑˈmunɔ
unanimity	yoo: nuh NI muh ti	junəˈnɪmətɪ
unanimous	yoo NA nuh muhs	jʊˈnænəməs
unbiased	uhn BIGH uhst	ʌnˈbaɪəst
uncial	UHN shi uhl	ˈʌnʃɪəl
unconscionable	uhn KAHN shuh nuh buhl	ʌnˈkɑnʃənəbəl
uncouth	uhn KOO: TH	ʌnˈkuθ
unction	UHNGK shuhn	ˈʌŋkʃən

sing [ŋ]; oh [o]; oil [ɔɪ]; foot [ʊ]; foo:d [u]; how [au]; pie [p]; ray [r]; so [s]; shall [ʃ]; to [t]; thin [θ]; th:en [ð]; above (uh BUHV) [ə, ˈʌ]; vine [v]; wine [w]; whine [hw]; you [j]; zoo [z]; rouge (roo:zh) [ʒ].

unctuous	UHNGK choo uhs	ˈʌŋktʃʊəs
undine, U-	uhn DEEN	ʌnˈdin
undoubtedly	uhn DOW tid li	ʌnˈdaʊtɪdlɪ
Undset, Sigrid	OON set, SI grid	ˈʊnsɛt, ˈsɪgrɪd
und so weiter	oont zoh VIGH ter	ʊnt zo ˈvaɪtər
undulant	UHN juh luhnt	ˈʌndʒələnt
undulate (a)	UHN juh lit	ˈʌndʒəlɪt
undulate (v)	UHN juh layt	ˈʌndʒəlet
undulatory	UHN juh luh taw ri	ˈʌndʒələtɔrɪ
unequivocal	uh ni KWI vuh kuhl	ʌnɪˈkwɪvəkəl
unerring	uhn ER ing	ʌnˈɝɪŋ
unfrequented	uhn fri KWEN tid	ʌnfrɪˈkwɛntɪd
ungual	UHNG gwuhl	ˈʌŋgwəl
unguent	UHNG gwuhnt	ˈʌŋgwənt
Unguentine	UHNG gwuhn teen	ˈʌŋgwəntin
ungulate	UHNG gyuh lit	ˈʌŋgjəlɪt
Uniat	YOO: ni at	ˈjunɪæt
unicameral	yoo: ni KA muh ruhl	junɪˈkæmərəl
unicorn, U-	YOO: nuh kawrn	ˈjunəkɔrn
unicycle	YOO: ni sigh kuhl	ˈjunɪsaɪkəl
union	YOO: nyuhn	ˈjunjən
unique	yoo: NEEK	juˈnik
unison	YOO: nuh suhn	ˈjunəsən
unit	YOO: nit	ˈjunɪt
Unitarian	yoo: nuh TAI ri uhn	junəˈtɛrɪən
unite	yoo NIGHT	jʊˈnaɪt
united	yoo NIGH tid	jʊˈnaɪtɪd
unity	YOO: nuh ti	ˈjunətɪ
universal	yoo: nuh VER suhl	junəˈvɝsəl
universality	yoo: nuh ver SA luh ti	junəvɝˈsælətɪ
universe	YOO: nuh vers	ˈjunəvɝs
unmitigated	uhn MI tuh gay tid	ʌnˈmɪtəgetɪd
unprecedented	uhn PRE suh den tid	ʌnˈprɛsədɛntɪd
unrighteous	uhn RIGH chuhs	ʌnˈraɪtʃəs
unruly	uhn ROO: li	ʌnˈrulɪ
unsavory, unsavoury	uhn SAY vuh ri	ʌnˈsevərɪ
Unter den Linden	OON ter den LIN duhn	ˈʊntər dɛn ˈlɪndən
Untermeyer	UHN ter migh er	ˈʌntərmaɪər
Unterseeboot	oon ter ZAY boht	ʊntərˈzebot
untoward	uhn TAWRD	ʌnˈtɔrd
U Nu	oo: noo:	u nu
unwonted	uhn WUHN tid	ʌnˈwʌntɪd
Upanishad	oo: PA ni shad	uˈpænɪʃæd
upas	YOO: puhs	ˈjupəs
Upolu	oo: POH loo:	uˈpolu
Uppsala, Upsala	UHP sah luh	ˈʌpsɑlə
uproarious	uhp RAW ri uhs	ʌpˈrɔrɪəs
upset (a, n)	UHP set	ˈʌpsɛt
upset (v)	uhp SET	ʌpˈsɛt
upsilon	YOO: P suh lahn	ˈjupsəlɑn
Ur	er	ɝ
uraeus	yoo REE uhs	jʊˈriəs

---

at [æ]; *ah* [ɑ]; *air* [ɛ]; *awful* [ɔ]; *say* [e]; *back* [b]; *chair* [tʃ]; *do* [d]; *elm* [ɛ]; *eel* [i]; *server* [ˈɝ, ər]; *f*it [f]; *go* [g]; *h*urt [h]; *is* [ɪ]; *high* [aɪ]; *jet* [dʒ]; *kiss* [k]; *l*amb [l]; *my* [m]; *n*ice [n];

Ural	YOO ruhl	ˈjʊrəl
Uralic	yoo RAY lik	jʊˈrelɪk
Urania	yoo RAY ni uh	jʊˈrenɪə
uranic	yoo RA nik	jʊˈrænɪk
uraninite	yoo RA nuh night	jʊˈrænənaɪt
uranium	yoo RAY ni uhm	jʊˈrenɪəm
Uranus	YOO ruh nuhs	ˈjʊrənəs
urban, U-	ER buhn	ˈɝbən
Urbana	er BA nuh	ɝˈbænə
urbane	er BAYN	ɝˈben
urbanity	er BA nuh ti	ɝˈbænətɪ
urchin	ER chin	ˈɝtʃɪn
Urdu	OOR doo :	ˈʊrdu
urea	yoo REE uh	jʊˈriə
uremia	yoo REE mi uh	jʊˈrimɪə
ureter	yoo REE ter	jʊˈritər
urethra	yoo REE thruh	jʊˈriθrə
uretic	yoo RE tik	jʊˈrɛtɪk
Urey	YOO ri	ˈjʊrɪ
Urfa	oor FAH	urˈfɑ
Urga	OOR gah	ˈʊrgɑ
Uriah	yoo RIGH uh	jʊˈraɪə
Uriel	YOO ri uhl	ˈjʊrɪəl
Urim	YOO rim	ˈjʊrɪm
urinal	YOO ruh nuhl	ˈjʊrənəl
urinalysis	yoo ruh NA luh sis	jʊrəˈnæləsɪs
Uris	YOO ris	ˈjʊrɪs
Urmia	OOR mi uh	ˈʊrmɪə
urn	ern	ɝn
urology	yoo RAH luh ji	jʊˈrɑlədʒɪ
Urquhart	ER kert	ˈɝkərt
Ursa	ER suh	ˈɝsə
ursine	ER sign	ˈɝsaɪn
Ursprache	OOR sprah kuh	ˈʊrsprɑkə
Ursuline	ER syoo lin	ˈɝsjʊlɪn
urticaria	er tuh KAI ri uh	ɝtəˈkɛrɪə
Uruguay	YOO ruh gway	ˈjʊrəgwe
Urundi	oo ROON di	uˈrʊndɪ
urus	YOO ruhs	ˈjʊrəs
usage	YOO : sij	ˈjusɪdʒ
use (n)	yoo : s	jus
use (v)	yoo : z	juz
Ushant	UH shuhnt	ˈʌʃənt
Ushas	OO shuhs	ˈuʃəs
Usk	uhsk	ʌsk
Uspallata	oo : spah YAH tah	uspɑˈjɑtɑ
usquebaugh	UH skwi baw	ˈʌskwɪbɔ
Ussachevsky, Vladimir	oo : sah CHEF skee, VLAH duh meer	usɑˈtʃɛfski, ˈvlɑdəmir
Ussuri	oo : SOO : ri	uˈsurɪ
usual	YOO : zhoo uhl	ˈjuʒʊəl
usufruct	YOO : zyoo fruhkt	ˈjuzjʊfrʌkt

---

sing [ŋ] ; *oh* [o] ; *oil* [ɔɪ] ; *foot* [ʊ] ; *foo :*d [u] ; *how* [aʊ] ; *pie* [p] ; *ray* [r] ; *so* [s] ; *shall* [ʃ] ;
to [t] ; *thin* [θ] ; *th :*en [ð] ; above (*uh* B*UH*V) [ə, ˈʌ] ; *vine* [v] ; *wine* [w] ; *whine* [hw] ;
you [j] ; *zoo* [z] ; *rouge* (roo :*zh*) [ʒ].

usurer	YOO : zhuh rer	ˈjuʒərər
usurious	yoo : ZHOO ri uhs	juˈʒʊriəs
usurp	yoo ZERP	jʊˈzɝp
usurpation	yoo : zer PAY shuhn	juzərˈpeʃən
usury	YOO : zhuh ri	ˈjuʒəri
Utah	YOO : taw	ˈjutɔ
Ute	yoo : t	jut
utensil	joo : TEN suhl	juˈtɛnsəl
uterine	YOO : tuh rin	ˈjutərɪn
uterus	YOO : tuh ruhs	ˈjutərəs
Uther	YOO : ther	ˈjuθər
Utica	YOO : ti kuh	ˈjutɪkə
utilitarian	yoo ti luh TAI ri uhn	jutɪləˈtɛriən
utility	yoo : TI luh ti	juˈtɪləti
utilize, utilise	YOO : tuh lighz	ˈjutəlaɪz
ut infra	uht IN fruh	ʌt ˈɪnfrə
uti possidetis	YOO : ti pah suh DEE tis	ˈjuti pɑsəˈditɪs
Uto-Aztecan	YOO : toh AZ tek uhn	ˈjuto ˈæztɛkən
Utopia	yoo : TOH pi uh	juˈtopɪə
Utrecht	YOO : trekt	ˈjutrɛkt
ut supra	uht SOO : pruh	ʌt ˈsuprə
Uttar Pradesh	UH ter PRAH desh	ˈʌtər ˈprɑdɛʃ
utterance	UH tuh ruhns	ˈʌtərəns
Uusikaupunki	OO : see KOW poong kee	ˈusiˈkaʊpʊŋki
uvea	YOO : vi uh	ˈjuvɪə
uvula	YOO : vyuh luh	ˈjuvjələ
Uxmal	oo : z MAHL	uzˈmɑl
uxoricide	uhk SAW ruh sighd	ʌkˈsɔrəsaɪd
uxorious	uhk SAW ri uhs	ʌkˈsɔriəs
Uzbek	UHZ bek	ˈʌzbɛk
Uzhorod	OO : ZH haw rawt	ˈuʒhɔrɔt
Uzice	OO : zhit se	ˈuʒɪtsɛ

V

Vaal	vahl	vɑl
Vaasa	VAH sah	ˈvɑsɑ
vacate	VAY kayt	ˈveket
vacation	vuh KAY shuhn	vəˈkeʃən
vaccinate	VAK suh nayt	ˈvæksənet
vaccine	VAK seen	ˈvæksin
Vachel	VAY chuhl	ˈvetʃəl
vacillate	VA suh layt	ˈvæsəlet
vacuity	va KYOO : uh ti	væˈkjuəti
vacuole	VA kyoo ohl	ˈvækjuol
vacuous	VA kyoo uhs	ˈvækjuəs
vacuum	VA kyoo uhm	ˈvækjuəm
vade mecum	VAY di MEE kuhm	ˈvedi ˈmikəm

at [æ] ; *ah* [ɑ] ; *air* [ɛ] ; *aw*ful [ɔ] ; *say* [e] ; *b*ack [b] ; *ch*air [tʃ] ; *do* [d] ; *e*lm [ɛ] ; *ee*l [i] ; *serv*er [ˈɝ, ər] ; *f*it [f] ; *go* [g] ; *h*urt [h] ; *is* [ɪ] ; *high* [aɪ] ; *j*et [dʒ] ; *k*iss [k] ; *l*amb [l] ; *m*y [m] ; *n*ice [n] ;

Vaduz	VAH doots	ˈvɑdʊts
vae victis	VEE VIK tis	ˈvi ˈvɪktɪs
vagary	vuh GAI ri	vəˈgɛrɪ
vagina	vuh JIGH nuh	vəˈdʒaɪnə
vagrancy	VAY gruhn si	ˈvegrənsɪ
vagrant	VAY gruhnt	ˈvegrənt
vair	vair	vɛr
valance	VA luhns	ˈvæləns
Valdai	vahl DIGH	vɑlˈdaɪ
Valdepeñas	vahl de PE nyahs	vɑldɛˈpɛnjɑs
vale (" farewell ")	VAY li	ˈvelɪ
valediction	va luh DIK shuhn	væləˈdɪkʃən
valedictory	va luh DIK tuh ri	væləˈdɪktərɪ
valence	VAY luhns	ˈveləns
Valencia	vuh LEN shi uh	vəˈlɛnʃɪə
Valenciennes	vuh len si ENZ	vəlɛnsɪˈɛnz
Valera, de	vuh LAI ruh, duh	vəˈlɛrə, də
valerian, V-	vuh LI ri uhn	vəˈlɪrɪən
valeric	vuh LAI rik	vəˈlɛrɪk
Valéry	vah lay REE	vɑleˈri
valet	VA lit	ˈvælɪt
valetudinarian	va luh too : duh NAI ri uhn	vælətudəˈnɛrɪən
Valga	VAHL gah	ˈvɑlgɑ
Valhalla	val HA luh	vælˈhælə
valiant	VA lyuhnt	ˈvæljənt
valid	VA lid	ˈvælɪd
valise	vuh LEES	vəˈlis
Valka	VAHL kah	ˈvɑlkɑ
Valkyrie	val KI ri	vælˈkɪrɪ
Valladolid	va luh DOH lid	væləˈdolɪd
Vallejo	va LAY hoh	væˈleho
Valletta	vah LE tah	vɑˈlɛtɑ
Vallombrosa	va luhm BROH suh	væləmˈbrosə
Vallone, Raf	vah LOH ne, rahf	vɑˈlone, rɑf
Valmiera	VAHL mye rah	ˈvɑlmjɛrɑ
Valois	val WAH	vælˈwɑ
Valparaiso	val puh RIGH soh	vælpəˈraɪso
valse	vahls	vɑls
valuable	VA lyuh buhl	ˈvæljəbəl
valvulitis	val vyuh LIGH tis	vælvjəˈlaɪtɪs
valvulotomy	val vyuh LAH tuh mi	vælvjəˈlɑtəmɪ
vanadium	vuh NAY di uhm	vəˈnedɪəm
van Beinum, Eduard	fahn BAY nuhm, AY dwart	fɑn ˈbenəm, ˈedwɑrt
Vanbrugh	van BROO :	vænˈbru
Van Buren	van BYOO ruhn	væn ˈbjʊrən
Vancouver	van KOO : ver	vænˈkuvər
vandal, V-	VAN duhl	ˈvændəl
Van Devanter	van di VAN ter	væn dɪˈvæntər
Van Doren	van DAW ruhn	væn ˈdorən
Van Druten	van DROO : tuhn	væn ˈdrutən
Van Dyck, Vandyke	van DIGHK	væn ˈdaɪk
Vaner	VE ner	ˈvenər

sing [ŋ]; oh [o]; oil [ɔɪ]; foot [ʊ]; foo:d [u]; how [aʊ]; pie [p]; ray [r]; so [s]; shall [ʃ]; to [t]; thin [θ]; th:en [ð]; above (uh BUHV) [ə, ˈʌ]; vine [v]; wine [w]; whine [hw]; you [j]; zoo [z]; rouge (roo:zh) [ʒ].

Van Eyck	van IGHK	væn ˈaɪk
van Gogh	van GOH	væn ˈgo
vanguard	VAN gahrd	ˈvængɑrd
Vanir	VAH nir	ˈvɑnɪr
Van Loon	van LOHN	væn ˈlon
vanquish	VANG kwish	ˈvæŋkwɪʃ
Van Rensselaer	van REN suh ler	væn ˈrɛnsələr
Vansittart	van SI tert	væn ˈsɪtərt
Vanua Levu	vah NOO : ah LE voo :	vɑˈnuɑ ˈlɛvu
Vanzetti	van ZE ti	væn ˈzɛtɪ
vapid	VA pid	ˈvæpɪd
vapor	VAY per	ˈvepər
vaporous	VAY puh ruhs	ˈvepərəs
vaquero	vah KAI roh	vɑˈkɛro
Varangian	vuh RAN ji uhn	vəˈrændʒɪən
Varazdin	vah RAHZH din	vɑˈrɑʒdɪn
Vardar	VAHR dahr	ˈvɑrdɑr
Vargas	VAHR guhs	ˈvɑrgəs
variable	VAI ri uh buhl	ˈvɛrɪəbəl
variation	vai ri AY shuhn	vɛrɪˈeʃən
varicose	VA ruh kohs	ˈværəkos
variegate	VAI ri uh gayt	ˈvɛrɪəget
variety	vuh RIGH uh ti	vəˈraɪətɪ
Varig	VA rig	ˈværɪg
variola	vuh RIGH uh luh	vəˈraɪələ
variorum	vai ri AW ruhm	vɛrɪˈɔrəm
Varna	VAHR nah	ˈvɑrnɑ
Varro	VA roh	ˈværo
Varuna	VA roo nuh	ˈværʊnə
vary	VAI ri	ˈvɛrɪ
vas	vas	væs
Vasari	vah ZAH ree	vɑˈzɑri
Vasco da Gama	VA skoh duh GA muh	ˈvæsko də ˈgæmə
vascular	VA skyuh ler	ˈvæskjələr
vaseline, V-	VA suh leen	ˈvæsəlin
Vashti	VASH tigh	ˈvæʃtaɪ
vasomotor	va soh MOH ter	væso ˈmotər
vassal	VA suhl	ˈvæsəl
vassalage	VA suh lij	ˈvæsəlɪdʒ
Vassilevsky	vah si LEF ski	vɑsɪˈlɛfskɪ
vast	vast	væst
Vaterland	FAH ter lahnt	ˈfɑtərlɑnt
Vatican	VA ti kuhn	ˈvætɪkən
vaudeville	VOHD vil	ˈvodvɪl
Vaudois	voh DWAH	voˈdwɑ
Vaughan	vawn	vɔn
vault	vawlt	vɔlt
vaunt	vawnt	vɔnt
Vauxhall	vahks hawl	vɑkshɔl
Veblen	VE bluhn	ˈvɛblən
vector	VEK ter	ˈvɛktər
Veda	VAY duh	ˈvedə

at [æ] ; *ah* [ɑ] ; *air* [ɛ] ; *awful* [ɔ] ; *say* [e] ; *back* [b] ; *chair* [tʃ] ; *do* [d] ; *elm* [ɛ] ; *eel* [i] ;
server [ˈɜ, ər] ; *fit* [f] ; *go* [g] ; *hurt* [h] ; *is* [ɪ] ; *high* [aɪ] ; *jet* [dʒ] ; *kiss* [k] ; *lamb* [l] ; *my* [m] ;
nice [n] ;

Vedanta	vi DAHN tuh	vɪˈdɑntə
vedette	vi DET	vɪˈdɛt
Vedic	VAY dik	ˈvedɪk
Vega (star)	VEE guh	ˈvigə
Vega, de	VE gah, de	ˈvɛgɑ, dɛ
vegetable	VEJ tuh buhl	ˈvɛdʒtəbəl
vegetarian	ve juh TAI ri uhn	vɛdʒəˈtɛrɪən
vehemence	VEE uh muhns	ˈviəməns
vehement	VEE uh muhnt	ˈviəmənt
vehicle	VEE uh kuhl	ˈviəkəl
vehicular	vee HI kyuh ler	viˈhɪkjələr
vein	vayn	ven
Vela	VEE luh	ˈvilə
Velasco	ve LAH skaw	vɛˈlɑskɔ
Velásquez, Velázquez	vuh LA skwiz	vəˈlæskwɪz
veld, veldt	velt	vɛlt
velleity	vuh LEE uh ti	vəˈliətɪ
vellum	VE luhm	ˈvɛləm
velocipede	vuh LAH suh peed	vəˈlɑsəpid
velocity	vuh LAH suh ti	vəˈlɑsətɪ
velour, velours	vuh LOOR	vəˈlʊr
velouté	vuh loo : TAY	vəluˈte
velum	VEE luhm	ˈviləm
velure	vuh LOOR	vəˈlʊr
velveteen	vel vuh TEEN	vɛlvəˈtin
vena cava	VEE nuh KAY vuh	ˈvinə ˈkevə
venal	VEE nuhl	ˈvinəl
venality	vee NA luh ti	viˈnælətɪ
vendetta	ven DE tuh	vɛnˈdɛtə
Vendôme	vahn DOHM	vɑnˈdom
vendor	VEN der	ˈvɛndər
vendue	ven DOO :	vɛnˈdu
veneer	vuh NIR	vəˈnɪr
venereal	vuh NI ri uhl	vəˈnɪrɪəl
Venetian	vuh NEE shuhn	vəˈniʃən
Venezia	ve NET syah	vɛˈnɛtsjɑ
Venezuela	ve nuh ZWAY luh	vɛnəˈzwelə
vengeance	VEN juhns	ˈvɛndʒəns
venial	VEE ni uhl	ˈvinɪəl
Venice	VE nis	ˈvɛnɪs
venire	vi NIGH ree	vɪˈnaɪri
venison	VE ni zuhn	ˈvɛnɪzən
Venite	vi NIGH tee	vɪˈnaɪti
veni, vidi, vici	VEE nigh, VIGH digh, VIGH sigh	ˈvinaɪ, ˈvaɪdaɪ, ˈvaɪsaɪ
Venizelos	ve ni ZAY lahs	vɛnɪˈzelɑs
venom	VE nuhm	ˈvɛnəm
venous	VEE nuhs	ˈvinəs
Venta	VEN tah	ˈvɛntɑ
ventral	VEN truhl	ˈvɛntrəl
ventricle	VEN tri kuhl	ˈvɛntrɪkəl
ventricular	ven TRI kyuh ler	vɛnˈtrɪkjələr

sing [ŋ]; *oh* [o]; *oil* [ɔɪ]; *foot* [ʊ]; *foo:*d [u]; *how* [aʊ]; *p*ie [p]; *r*ay [r]; *s*o [s]; *sh*all [ʃ]; *t*o [t]; *th*in [θ]; *th:*en [ð]; *above* (*uh B*U*H*V) [ə, ˈʌ]; *v*ine [v]; *w*ine [w]; *wh*ine [hw]; *y*ou [j]; *z*oo [z]; *rouge* (roo:*zh*) [ʒ].

H.P.—2 C

ventriloquist	ven TRI luh kwist	vɛnˈtrɪləkwɪst
Ventspils	VENTS peels	ˈvɛntspils
venture	VEN cher	ˈvɛntʃər
venturous	VEN chuh ruhs	ˈvɛntʃərəs
venue	VE nyoo :	ˈvɛnju
Venus	VEE nuhs	ˈvinəs
veracious	vuh RAY shuhs	vəˈreʃəs
veracity	vuh RA suh ti	vəˈræsətɪ
Veracruz	VE ruh KROO : Z	ˈvɛrəˈkruz
veranda, -h	vuh RAN duh	vəˈrændə
verbatim	ver BAY tim	vərˈbetɪm
verbena	ver BEE nuh	vərˈbinə
verbiage	VER bi ij	ˈvɜˈbɪɪdʒ
verbose	ver BOHS	vərˈbos
verbosity	ver BAH suh ti	vərˈbɑsətɪ
verboten	fer BOH tuhn	fərˈbotən
Vercingetorix	ver sin JE tuh riks	vɜˈsɪnˈdʒɛtərɪks
verdant	VER duhnt	ˈvɜˈdənt
Verde (cape)	verd	vɜˈd
Verdi	VAIR dee	ˈvɛrdi
verdigris	VER di grees	ˈvɜˈdɪgris
Verdun	vair DUHN	vɛrˈdʌn
verdure	VER jer	ˈvɜˈdʒər
Verein	fai RIGHN	fɛˈraɪn
verisimilitude	vai ruh si MI luh too : d	vɛrəsɪˈmɪlətud
veritable	VAI ri tuh buhl	ˈvɛrɪtəbəl
Verlaine	vair LEN	vɛrˈlɛn
Vermeer	ver MIR	vərˈmɪr
vermeil	VER mil	ˈvɜˈmɪl
vermicelli	ver muh CHE li	vərməˈtʃɛlɪ
vermicular	ver MI kyuh ler	vərˈmɪkjələr
vermiform	VER muh fawrm	ˈvɜˈməfɔrm
vermifuge	VER muh fyoo : j	ˈvɜˈməfjudʒ
vermilion	ver MI lyuhn	vərˈmɪljən
vermin	VER min	ˈvɜˈmɪn
Vermont	ver MAHNT	vərˈmɑnt
vermouth	ver MOO : TH	vərˈmuθ
vernacular	ver NA kyuh ler	vərˈnækjələr
vernal	VER nuhl	ˈvɜˈnəl
Verne	vern	vɜˈn
Verner	VER ner	ˈvɜˈnər
Vernier, v-	VER ni er	ˈvɜˈnɪər
Vernon	VER nuhn	ˈvɜˈnən
Verona	vuh ROH nuh	vəˈronə
veronal, V-	VAI ruh nuhl	ˈvɛrənəl
Veronese	vai ruh NEEZ	vɛrəˈniz
veronica, V-	vuh RAH ni kuh	vəˈrɑnɪkə
Verrazano	vai raht SAH naw	vɛrɑtˈsɑnɔ
Verrocchio	vai RAW kyaw	vɛˈrɔkjɔ
verruca	vai ROO : kuh	vɛˈrukə
Versailles	ver SIGH	vərˈsaɪ
versatile	VER suh tuhl	ˈvɜˈsətəl

at [æ] ; *ah* [ɑ] ; *air* [ɛ] ; *awful* [ɔ] ; *say* [e] ; *back* [b] ; *chair* [tʃ] ; *do* [d] ; *elm* [ɛ] ; *eel* [i] ; *server* [ˈɜˈ, ər] ; *f*it [f] ; *go* [g] ; *hurt* [h] ; *is* [ɪ] ; *high* [aɪ] ; *jet* [dʒ] ; *kiss* [k] ; *lamb* [l] ; *my* [m] ; *nice* [n] ;

vers de société	VAIR duh saw syay TAY	ˈvɛr də sɔsjeˈte
version	VER zhuhn	ˈvɝʒən
vers libre	vair LEE bruh	vɛr ˈlibrə
verso	VER soh	ˈvɝso
versus	VER suhs	ˈvɝsəs
vertebra	VER tuh bruh	ˈvɝtəbrə
vertebral	VER tuh bruhl	ˈvɝtəbrəl
vertebrate	VER tuh brit	ˈvɝtəbrɪt
vertiginous	ver TI juh nuhs	vərˈtɪdʒənəs
vertigo	VER tuh goh	ˈvɝtəgo
Vertumnus	ver TUHM nuhs	vərˈtʌmnəs
Verulam	VAI roo luhm	ˈvɛrʊləm
Verulamium	vai roo LAY mi uhm	vɛrʊˈlemɪəm
vervain	VER vayn	ˈvɝven
very	VAI ri	ˈvɛrɪ
vesicle	VE si kuhl	ˈvɛsɪkəl
Vespasian	ve SPAY zhi uhn	vɛˈspeʒɪən
vesper	VE sper	ˈvɛspər
Vespucci, Amerigo	ve SPOO : chee, ah me REE gaw	vɛˈsputʃi, ɑmɛˈrigɔ
Vesta	VES tuh	ˈvɛstə
Vest-Agder	VEST ahg der	ˈvɛst ɑgdər
Vestfold	VEST fawl	ˈvɛstfɔl
vestibule	VE stuh byoo : l	ˈvɛstəbjul
vestige	VE stij	ˈvɛstɪdʒ
vestigial	ve STI ji uhl	vɛˈstɪdʒɪəl
vesture	VES cher	ˈvɛstʃər
Vesuvius	vuh SOO : vi uhs	vəˈsuvɪəs
veterinarian	ve tuh ruh NAI ri uhn	vɛtərəˈnɛrɪən
veterinary	VE tuh ruh nai ri	ˈvɛtərənɛrɪ
via	VIGH uh	ˈvaɪə
viaduct	VIGH uh duhkt	ˈvaɪədʌkt
vial	VIGH uhl	ˈvaɪəl
viand	VIGH uhnd	ˈvaɪənd
Via Veneto	VEE ah ve NAY toh	ˈviɑ vɛˈneto
Viborg	VEE bawr	ˈvibɔr
vibrant	VIGH bruhnt	ˈvaɪbrənt
vibrato	vi BRAH toh	vɪˈbrɑto
vibronic	vigh BRAH nik	vaɪˈbrɑnɪk
viburnum	vigh BER nuhm	vaɪˈbɝnəm
vicar	VI ker	ˈvɪkər
vicarious	vigh KAI ri uhs	vaɪˈkɛrɪəs
vicegerent	vighs JI ruhnt	vaɪsˈdʒɪrənt
vicennial	vigh SE ni uhl	vaɪˈsɛnɪəl
vice-regent	vighs REE juhnt	vaɪsˈridʒənt
vicereine	VIGHS rayn	ˈvaɪsren
viceroy	VIGHS roi	ˈvaɪsrɔɪ
vice versa	VIGH si VER suh	ˈvaɪsɪ ˈvɝsə
Vichy	VI shi	ˈvɪʃɪ
Vichyssoise, v-	vee shee SWAHZ	viʃiˈswɑz
vicinity	vuh SI nuh ti	vəˈsɪnətɪ
vicious	VI shuhs	ˈvɪʃəs

---

sing [ŋ]; *oh* [o]; *oil* [ɔɪ]; *foot* [ʊ]; *foo*:d [u]; *how* [aʊ]; *pie* [p]; *ray* [r]; *so* [s]; *shall* [ʃ];
to [t]; *thin* [θ]; *th*:en [ð]; *above* (*uh* BU*H*V) [ə, ˈʌ]; *vine* [v]; *wine* [w]; *whine* [hw];
you [j]; *zoo* [z]; *rouge* (roo:*zh*) [ʒ].

vicissitude	vi SI suh too : d	vɪˈsɪsətud
Victoria, v-	vik TAW ri uh	vɪkˈtɔrɪə
victual	VI tuhl	ˈvɪtəl
victualer, victualler	VI tuh ler	ˈvɪtələr
vicuña	vi KOO : nyuh	vɪˈkunjə
Vidal, Gore	vee DAHL, GAWR	viˈdɑl, ˈgɔr
vide	VIGH di	ˈvaɪdɪ
videlicet	vi DE luh sit	vɪˈdɛləsɪt
Vidzeme	VEED ze me	ˈvidzɛmɛ
vie (French)	vee	vi
Vienna	vi E nuh	vɪˈɛnə
Vientiane	vyan TYAHN	vjænˈtjɑn
Viereck	FEE rek	ˈfirɛk
Vietcong	vee ET KAHNG	viˈɛtˈkɑŋ
Vietminh	VEE uht MIN	ˈviətˈmɪn
Viet-Nam, Vietnam	VEE uht NAHM	ˈviət ˈnɑm
Vietor	VEE uh tawr	ˈviətɔr
view	vyoo :	vju
Vigan	VEE gahn	ˈvigɑn
vigesimal	vigh JE suh muhl	vaɪˈdʒɛsəməl
vigil	VI juhl	ˈvɪdʒəl
vigilant	VI juh luhnt	ˈvɪdʒələnt
vigilante	vi juh LAN ti	vɪdʒəˈlæntɪ
vignette	vin YET	vɪnˈjɛt
Vigny	vee NYEE	viˈnji
vigor	VI ger	ˈvɪgər
vigoroso	vee gaw RAW saw	vigɔˈrɔsɔ
Viipuri	VEE poo ree	ˈvipuri
viking	VIGH king	ˈvaɪkɪŋ
Vila	VEE lah	ˈvilɑ
vilify	VI luh figh	ˈvɪləfaɪ
Viljandi	VIL yahn di	ˈvɪljɑndɪ
Villa, Pancho	VEE yah, PAHN choh	ˈvijɑ, ˈpɑntʃo
village	VI lij	ˈvɪlɪdʒ
villain	VI luhn	ˈvɪlən
Villa-Lobos, Heitor	VEE lah LAW boosh, AY toor	ˈvilɑ ˈlɔbuʃ, ˈetur
Villamor	vee lyah MAWR	viljɑˈmɔr
Villard	vi LAHRD	vɪˈlɑrd
Villarroel	vee LYAH raw EL	viˈljɑrɔˈɛl
Villiers	VI lerz	ˈvɪlərz
Villon	vee YOHN	viˈjon
Vilna	VIL nuh	ˈvɪlnə
vinaigrette	vi nuh GRET	vɪnəˈgrɛt
Vincennes (France)	van SEN	vænˈsɛn
Vincennes (Indiana)	vin SENZ	vɪnˈsɛnz
Vinci, da	VIN chi, duh	ˈvɪntʃɪ, də
Vindhya	VIND yah	ˈvɪndjɑ
vindicative	VIN duh kay tiv	ˈvɪndəketɪv
vindictive	vin DIK tiv	vɪnˈdɪktɪv
vineyard	VIN yerd	ˈvɪnjərd
viniculture	VI ni kuhl cher	ˈvɪnɪkʌltʃər

at [æ] ; ah [ɑ] ; air [ɛ] ; awful [ɔ] ; say [e] ; back [b] ; chair [tʃ] ; do [d] ; elm [ɛ] ; eel [i] ; server [ˈɝ, ər] ; fit [f] ; go [g] ; hurt [h] ; is [ɪ] ; high [aɪ] ; jet [dʒ] ; kiss [k] ; lamb [l] ; my [m] ; nice [n] ;

vin ordinaire	van awr dee NAIR	væn ɔrdiˈnɛr
vinous	VIGH nuhs	ˈvaɪnəs
vintage	VIN tij	ˈvɪntɪdʒ
vinyl	VIGH nil	ˈvaɪnɪl
vinylite	VIGH ni light	ˈvaɪnɪlaɪt
viola	vi OH luh	vɪˈolə
violate	VIGH uh layt	ˈvaɪəlet
violet, V-	VIGH uh lit	ˈvaɪəlɪt
violin	vigh uh LIN	vaɪəˈlɪn
violoncello	vee uh lahn CHE loh	viələnˈtʃɛlo
viosterol	vigh AH stuh rohl	vaɪˈɑstərol
virago	vi RAY goh	vɪˈrego
virelay	VI ruh lay	ˈvɪrəle
vireo	VI ri oh	ˈvɪrɪo
Virgil	VER juhl	ˈvɝdʒəl
Virgilian	ver JI li uhn	vərˈdʒɪlɪən
virginal	VER ji nuhl	ˈvɝdʒɪnəl
Virgo	VER goh	ˈvɝgo
Virile	VI ruhl	ˈvɪrəl
virility	vi RI luh ti	vɪˈrɪlətɪ
virosis	vigh ROH sis	vaɪˈrosɪs
virtu	ver TOO :	vərˈtu
virtual	VER choo uhl	ˈvɝtʃuəl
virtue	VER choo	ˈvɝtʃu
Virtuosi di Roma	veer too : OH zee di ROH mah	virtuˈozi dɪ ˈromɑ
virtuosity	ver choo AH suh ti	vɝtʃuˈɑsətɪ
virtuoso	ver choo OH soh	vɝtʃuˈoso
virtuous	VER choo uhs	ˈvɝtʃuəs
virulent	VI ryuh luhnt	ˈvɪrjələnt
virus	VIGH ruhs	ˈvaɪrəs
visa	VEE zuh	ˈvizə
visage	VI zij	ˈvɪzɪdʒ
vis-à-vis	vee zuh VEE	vizəˈvi
Visayan	vee SAH yuhn	viˈsɑjən
viscera	VI suh ruh	ˈvɪsərə
viscid	VI sid	ˈvɪsɪd
viscosity	vi SKAH suh ti	vɪˈskɑsətɪ
viscount	VIGH kownt	ˈvaɪkaʊnt
viscous	VI skuhs	ˈvɪskəs
visé	VEE zay	ˈvize
Vishinsky	vi SHIN ski	vɪˈʃɪnskɪ
Visigoth	VI zi gahth	ˈvɪzɪgɑθ
vision	VI zhuhn	ˈvɪʒən
visionary	VI zhuh nai ri	ˈvɪʒənɛrɪ
vis major	vis MAY jer	vɪs ˈmedʒər
visor	VIGH zer	ˈvaɪzər
Vistula	VIS choo luh	ˈvɪstʃʊlə
visual	VI zhoo uhl	ˈvɪʒuəl
Vitalis	vigh TA lis	vaɪˈtælɪs
vitamer	VIGH tuh mer	ˈvaɪtəmər
vitamin	VIGH tuh min	ˈvaɪtəmɪn

---

sing [ŋ] ; *oh* [o] ; *oil* [ɔɪ] ; *foot* [ʊ] ; *foo*:d [u] ; *how* [aʊ] ; *pie* [p] ; *ray* [r] ; *so* [s] ; *shall* [ʃ] ;
to [t] ; *thin* [θ] ; *th*:en [ð] ; *above* (*uh* BUHV) [ə, ˈʌ] ; *vine* [v] ; *wine* [w] ; *whine* [hw] ;
you [j] ; *zoo* [z] ; rouge (roo:*zh*) [ʒ].

Vitebsk	VEE tepsk	ˈvitɛpsk
vitiate	VI shi ayt	ˈvɪʃiet
viticulture	VI ti kuhl cher	ˈvɪtɪkʌltʃər
Viti Levu	VEE tee LE voo:	ˈviti ˈlɛvu
vitiligo	vi ti LIGH goh	vɪtɪˈlaɪgo
vitreous	VI tri uhs	ˈvɪtrɪəs
vitriol	VI tri uhl	ˈvɪtrɪəl
vitriolic	vi tri AH lik	vɪtrɪˈɑlɪk
Vittorio	vi TAW ree oh	vɪˈtɔrio
vituperation	vigh too: puh RAY shuhn	vaɪtupəˈreʃən
vituperative	vigh TOO: puh ray tiv	vaɪˈtupəretɪv
viva	VEE vah	ˈvivɑ
vivace	vee VAH che	viˈvatʃɛ
vivacious	vi VAY shuhs	vɪˈveʃəs
vivacity	vi VA suh ti	vɪˈvæsətɪ
Vivaldi	vi VAHL di	vɪˈvaldɪ
vivarium	vigh VAI ri uhm	vaɪˈvɛrɪəm
viva voce	VIGH vuh VOH si	ˈvaɪvə ˈvosɪ
vivax	VIGH vaks	ˈvaɪvæks
vive	veev	viv
viviparous	vigh VI puh ruhs	vaɪˈvɪpərəs
vivisection	vi vuh SEK shuhn	vɪvəˈsɛkʃən
vixen	VIK suhn	ˈvɪksən
vizier, vizir	vi ZIR	vɪˈzɪr
vizor	VIGH zer	ˈvaɪzər
Vladimir	VLA duh mir	ˈvlædəmɪr
Vladivostok	vla di VAH stahk	vlædɪˈvastɑk
vocalic	voh KA lik	voˈkælɪk
vocative	VAH kuh tiv	ˈvɑkətɪv
vocalize	VOH kuh lighz	ˈvokəlaɪz
vociferous	voh SI fuh ruhs	voˈsɪfərəs
vodka	VAHD kuh	ˈvadkə
Vogul	VOH gool	ˈvogʊl
voilà	vwah LAH	vwɑˈlɑ
voile	voil	vɔɪl
Volans	VOH lanz	ˈvolænz
volant	VOH luhnt	ˈvolənt
Volapuk	VAH luh pook	ˈvaləpʊk
volatile	VAH luh tuhl	ˈvalətəl
vol-au-vent	vaw law VAHN	vɔlɔˈvan
volcanic	vahl KA nik	valˈkænɪk
volcano, V-	vahl KAY noh	valˈkeno
volé	voh LAY	voˈle
Volga	VAHL guh	ˈvalgə
volition	voh LI shuhn	voˈlɪʃən
volitive	VAH luh tiv	ˈvalətɪv
Volk (German)	fawlk	fɔlk
Volkswagen	FOHLKS vah guhn	ˈfolksvagən
Vologda	VAW lawg dah	ˈvɔlɔgda
volplane	VAHL playn	ˈvalplen
Volpone	vahl POH ni	valˈponɪ
Volsci	VAHL sigh	ˈvalsaɪ

---

at [æ] ; *ah* [ɑ] ; *air* [ɛ] ; *aw*ful [ɔ] ; *say* [e] ; *b*ack [b] ; *ch*air [tʃ] ; *do* [d] ; *e*lm [ɛ] ; *ee*l [i] ; *server* [ˈɝ, ər] ; *f*it [f] ; *go* [g] ; *h*urt [h] ; *is* [ɪ] ; *high* [aɪ] ; *j*et [dʒ] ; *k*iss [k] ; *l*amb [l] ; *m*y [m] ; *n*ice [n] ;

Volsunga	VAHL soong guh	ˈvɑlsʊŋgə
volt	vohlt	volt
Volta, v-	VAHL tuh	ˈvɑltə
voltaic	vahl TAY ik	vɑlˈteɪk
Voltaire	vahl TAIR	vɑlˈtɛr
volte-face	VAHLT fahs	ˈvɑltfɑs
Volturno	vawl TOOR naw	vɔlˈtʊrnɔ
voluble	VAH lyuh buhl	ˈvɑljəbəl
volume	VAH lyuhm	ˈvɑljəm
voluminous	vuh LOO: muh nuhs	vəˈlumənəs
voluptuary	vuh LUHP choo ai ri	vəˈlʌptʃuɛrɪ
voluptuous	vuh LUHP choo uhs	vəˈlʌptʃuəs
von, V- (German)	fawn	fɔn
voodoo	VOO: doo:	ˈvudu
voracious	vaw RAY shuhs	vɔˈreʃəs
voracity	vaw RA suh ti	vɔˈræsətɪ
Vorhees, Vorhis	VOH reez	ˈvoriz
Voronezh	vaw RAW nesh	vɔˈrɔnɛʃ
Voroshilov	vaw ruh SHEE lahv	vɔrəˈʃilɑv
vortex	VAWR teks	ˈvɔrtɛks
Vosges	vohzh	voʒ
vostra salute	VAW strah sa LOO: te	ˈvɔstrɑ sæˈlutɛ
votary	VOH tuh ri	ˈvotərɪ
Votyak	vaw TYAHK	vɔˈtjɑk
vouchsafe	vowch SAYF	vautʃˈsef
vox populi, vox Dei	VAKS PAH pyoo ligh, VAKS DEE igh	ˈvɑks ˈpɑpjʊlaɪ, ˈvɑks ˈdiaɪ
voyage	VOI ij	ˈvɔɪdʒ
voyager	VOI i jer	ˈvɔɪdʒər
voyageur	vwah yah ZHER	vwɑjɑˈʒɝ
voyeur	vwah YER	vwɑˈjɝ
voyeurism	vwah YER i zuhm	vwɑˈjɝɪzəm
vraisemblance	vray sahn BLAHNS	vresɑnˈblɑns
Vries	vrees	vris
Vrsac	VER shahts	ˈvɝʃɑts
Vuelta Abajo	VWEL taw ah BAH haw	ˈvwɛltɔ ɑˈbɑhɔ
Vulcan	VUHL kuhn	ˈvʌlkən
vulgarian	vuhl GAI ri uhn	vʌlˈgɛrɪən
Vulgate	VUHL gayt	ˈvʌlget
vulnerable	VUHL nuh ruh buhl	ˈvʌlnərəbəl
Vulpecula	vuhl PE kyoo luh	vʌlˈpɛkjʊlə
vulpine	VUHL pighn	ˈvʌlpaɪn
vulva	VUHL vuh	ˈvʌlvə
Vyatka	VYAHT kah	ˈvjɑtkɑ
Vyazma	VYAHZ mah	ˈvjɑzmɑ

W

Waal	wahl	wɑl
Waals	vahls	vɑls

sing [ŋ]; oh [o]; oil [ɔɪ]; foot [ʊ]; foo:d [u]; how [aʊ]; pie [p]; ray [r]; so [s]; shall [ʃ];
to [t]; thin [θ]; th:en [ð]; above (uh BUHV) [ə, ʌ]; vine [v]; wine [w]; whine [hw];
you [j]; zoo [z]; rouge (roo:zh) [ʒ].

Wabash	WAW bash	ˈwɔbæʃ
Wace	ways	wes
Wachuku, Jaja	WAH choo: koo:, JAH jah	ˈwatʃuku, ˈdʒadʒa
Waco	WAY koh	ˈweko
Wadai	wah DIGH	waˈdaɪ
wadi	WAH di	ˈwadɪ
Wafd, Wafd'	wahft	waft
waft	waft	wæft
Wagner, Richard	VAHG ner, RI kahrt	ˈvagnər, ˈrɪkart
Wagnerian	vahg NI ri uhn	vagˈnɪrɪən
wagoner, W-	WA guh ner	ˈwægənər
wagon-lit	vah gohn LEE	vagonˈli
Wahabi, Wahabee	wah HAH bee	waˈhabi
Waichow	WIGH chow	ˈwaɪtʃaʊ
waif	wayf	wef
Waikiki	WIGH kee kee	ˈwaɪkiki
wainscot	WAYN skuht	ˈwenskət
wainwright, W-	WAYN right	ˈwenraɪt
waistcoat	WAYST koht	ˈwestkot
waiter	WAY ter	ˈwetər
Wakayama	WAH kah YAH mah	ˈwakaˈjama
Waksman	WAKS muhn	ˈwæksmən
Walachia, Wallachia	wah LAY ki uh	waˈlekɪə
Waldenses	wahl DEN seez	walˈdɛnsiz
Waldorf	WAWL dawrf	ˈwɔldɔrf
walk	wawk	wɔk
Walküre, Die	vahl KI ruh, dee	valˈkɪrə, di
wallah	WAH lah	ˈwala
wallaroo	wah luh ROO:	walaˈru
Wallenstein	WAW luhn stighn	ˈwɔlənstaɪn
Walloon	wah LOO:N	waˈlun
wallow	WAH loh	ˈwalo
Walpurgis	vahl POOR gis	valˈpurgɪs
Walsingham	WAWL sing uhm	ˈwɔlsɪŋəm
Waltari, Mika	VAHL tuh ree, MI kah	ˈval təri, ˈmɪka
Walter, Bruno	VAHL ter, BROO: noh	ˈvaltər, ˈbruno
waltz	wawlts	wɔlts
Walvis	WAWL vis	ˈwɔlvɪs
Wampanoag	wahm puh NOH ag	wampəˈnoæg
wamus	WAW muhs	ˈwɔməs
wan	wahn	wan
Wanamaker	WAH nuh may ker	ˈwanəmekər
wander	WAHN der	ˈwandər
Wanderjahr	VAHN der yahr	ˈvandərjar
wanderlust	WAHN der luhst	ˈwandərlʌst
wannish	WAH nish	ˈwanɪʃ
want	wahnt	want
wanton	WAHN tuhn	ˈwantən
wapentake	WAH puhn tayk	ˈwapəntek
war	wawr	wɔr
Warburton	WAWR ber tuhn	ˈwɔrbərtən
warlock	WAWR lahk	ˈwɔrlak

---

at [æ]; ah [ɑ]; air [ɛ]; awful [ɔ]; say [e]; back [b]; chair [tʃ]; do [d]; elm [ɛ]; eel [i]; server [ˈɝ, ər]; fit [f]; go [g]; hurt [h]; is [ɪ]; high [aɪ]; jet [dʒ]; kiss [k]; lamb [l]; my [m]; nice [n];

warrant	WAW ruhnt	ˈwɔrənt
warranty	WAW ruhn ti	ˈwɔrəntɪ
warrior	WAW ri er	ˈwɔrɪər
Warsaw	WAWR saw	ˈwɔrsɔ
Warszawa	vahr SHAH vah	vɑrˈʃɑvɑ
Warwick	WAW rik	ˈwɔrɪk
wary	WAI ri	ˈwɛrɪ
Wasatch	WAW sach	ˈwɔsætʃ
Wasell	wah SEL	wɑˈsɛl
wash	wahsh	wɑʃ
Washington	WAH shing tuhn	ˈwɑʃɪŋtən
wassail	WAH suhl	ˈwɑsəl
Wassermann	WAH ser muhn	ˈwɑsərmən
wastrel	WAY struhl	ˈwestrəl
watch	wahch	wɑtʃ
water	WAW ter	ˈwɔtər
Waterbury	WAW ter bai ri	ˈwɔtərbɛrɪ
Waterloo	waw ter LOO:	wɔtərˈlu
Watling	WAHT ling	ˈwɑtlɪŋ
watt, W-	waht	wɑt
Watteau	wah TOH	wɑˈto
Waugh	waw	wɔ
Waukegan	waw KEE guhn	wɔˈkigən
Wavell	WAY vuhl	ˈwevəl
Waziristan	wah zi ri STAHN	wɑzɪrɪˈstɑn
weal	weel	wil
weald, W-	weeld	wild
wear	wair	wɛr
weary	WI ri	ˈwɪrɪ
Weber (German)	VAY ber	ˈvebər
Wechsler	WEKS ler	ˈwɛkslər
Weddell	WE duhl	ˈwɛdəl
wedgie, W-	WE ji	ˈwɛdʒɪ
Wedgwood	WEJ wood	ˈwɛdʒwʊd
Wednesday	WENZ di	ˈwɛnzdɪ
Wehrmacht	VAYR mahkt	ˈvermɑkt
weigela	wigh JEE luh	waɪˈdʒilə
Weimar	VIGH mahr	ˈvaɪmɑr
Weingartner	VIGHN gahrt ner	ˈvaɪngɑrtnər
Weintraub	WIGHN trowb	ˈwaɪntraʊb
weir	wir	wɪr
weird	wird	wɪrd
Weismann, Weissmann (German)	VIGHS mahn	ˈvaɪsmɑn
Weizmann, Chaim	WIGHTS muhn, KIGH yim	ˈwaɪtzmən, ˈkaɪjɪm
weka	WAY kah	ˈwekɑ
well	wel	wɛl
Welland	WE luhnd	ˈwɛlənd
Wellesley	WELZ li	ˈwɛlzlɪ
Wellington	WE ling tuhn	ˈwɛlɪŋtən
Welsbach	WELZ bak	ˈwɛlzbæk
Welsh, w-	welsh	wɛlʃ

sing [ŋ] ; oh [o] ; oil [ɔɪ] ; foot [ʊ] ; foo:d [u] ; how [aʊ] ; pie [p] ; ray [r] ; so [s] ; shall [ʃ] ;
to [t] ; thin [θ] ; th:en [ð] ; above (uh BUHV) [ə, ˈʌ] ; vine [v] ; wine [w] ; whine [hw] ;
you [j] ; zoo [z] ; rouge (roo:zh) [ʒ].

Weltanschauung	VELT ahn show oong	ˈvɛltɑnʃauuŋ
Weltansicht	VELT ahn zikt	ˈvɛltɑnzɪkt
Weltpolitik	VELT paw li TEEK	ˈvɛltpɔlɪˈtik
Weltschmerz	VELT shmairts	ˈvɛltʃmɛrts
Wemyss, -s	weemz	wimz
Wenceslaus	WEN suh slaws	ˈwɛnsəslɔs
Wenchow	wen chow	wɛntʃau
Wend, w-	wend	wɛnd
Werfel, Franz	VAIR fuhl, FRAHNTS	ˈvɛrfəl, ˈfrɑnts
Werther (German)	VAIR ter	ˈvɛrtər
Weser	VAY zer	ˈvezər
Wesley	WE sli	ˈwɛslɪ
western	WE stern	ˈwɛstərn
Westminster	WEST min ster	ˈwɛstmɪnstər
Westphalia	west FAY li uh	wɛstˈfelɪə
Wetterhorn	VE ter hawrn	ˈvɛtərhɔrn
Weygand	vay GAHN	veˈgɑn
wharf	hwawrf	hwɔrf
wharfinger	HWAWR fin jer	ˈhwɔrfɪndʒər
Wharton	HWAWR tuhn	ˈhwɔrtən
what	hwuht	hwʌt
whatever	hwuht E ver	hwətˈɛvər
wheat	hweet	hwit
when	hwen	hwɛn
whence	hwens	hwɛns
whenever	hwen E ver	hwɛnˈɛvər
where	hwair	hwɛr
whereof	hwair UHV	hwɛrˈʌv
wherever	hwair E ver	hwɛrˈɛvər
wherewith	hwair WITH	hwɛrˈwɪθ
whether	HWE th : er	ˈhwɛðər
whew	hwyoo :	hwju
Whewell	HYOO : uhl	ˈhjuəl
which	hwich	hwɪtʃ
whidah	HWI duh	ˈhwɪdə
whiffenpoof	HWI fuhn poo : f	ˈhwɪfənpuf
while	hwighl	hwaɪl
whilom	HWIGH luhm	ˈhwaɪləm
whimsy, whimsey	HWIM zi	ˈhwɪmzɪ
whippet	HWI pit	ˈhwɪpɪt
whippoorwill	hwi per WIL	hwɪpərˈwɪl
whir	hwer	hwɝ
whisper	HWI sper	ˈhwɪspər
whistle	HWI suhl	ˈhwɪsəl
white	hwight	hwaɪt
whither	HWI th : er	ˈhwɪðər
Whittaker	HWI tuh ker	ˈhwɪtəkər
Whittier	HWI ti er	ˈhwɪtɪər
who	hoo :	hu
whoa	hwoh	hwo
whole	hohl	hol
wholly	HOH li	ˈholɪ

at [æ] ; *ah* [ɑ] ; *air* [ɛ] ; *awful* [ɔ] ; *say* [e] ; *back* [b] ; *chair* [tʃ] ; *do* [d] ; *elm* [ɛ] ; *eel* [i] ;
server [ˈɝ, ər] ; *fit* [f] ; *go* [g] ; *hurt* [h] ; *is* [ɪ] ; *high* [aɪ] ; *jet* [dʒ] ; *kiss* [k] ; *lamb* [l] ; *my* [m] ;
nice [n] ;

whom	hoo : m	hum
whoop	hoo : p	hup
whortleberry	HWER tuhl bai ri	ˈhwɝtəlbɛrɪ
whose	hoo : z	huz
why	hwigh	hwaɪ
Wichita	WI chuh taw	ˈwɪtʃətɔ
widgeon	WI juhn	ˈwɪdʒən
wieder (German)	VEE der	ˈvidər
wie geht's	vee GAYTS	vi ˈgets
Wieland	VEE lahnt	ˈvilɑnt
Wieler	WEE ler	ˈwilər
Wien (German)	veen	vin
wiener	WEE ner	ˈwinər
Wiener schnitzel, w-	VEE ner SHNIT suhl	ˈvinər ˈʃnɪtsəl
Wiesbaden	VEES bah duhn	ˈvisbɑdən
wiggle	WI guhl	ˈwɪgəl
wight, W-	wight	waɪt
wildebeest	WIL duh beest	ˈwɪldəbist
Wilder	WIGHL der	ˈwaɪldər
wilderness	WIL der nis	ˈwɪldərnɪs
Wilhelmina	wil hel MEE nuh	wɪlhɛlˈminə
Wilhelm Meister	VIL helm MIGH ster	ˈvɪlhɛlm ˈmaɪstər
Wilhelmshaven	VIL helms HAH fuhn	ˈvɪlhɛlmsˈhɑfən
Wilhelmstrasse	VIL helm SHTRAH suh	ˈvɪlhɛlmʃtrɑsə
Wilkes	wilks	wɪlks
Wilkes-Barre	WILKS ba ri	ˈwɪlksbærɪ
Willamette	wi LA mit	wɪˈlæmɪt
Willemstad	WI luhm staht	ˈwɪləmstɑt
Willesden	WILZ duhn	ˈwɪlzdən
Wiltshire	WILT shir	ˈwɪltʃɪr
wily	WIGH li	ˈwaɪlɪ
Wimbledon	WIM buhl duhn	ˈwɪmbəldən
Winckelmann	VING kuhl mahn	ˈvɪŋkəlmɑn
Windermere	WIN der mir	ˈwɪndərmɪr
Windhoek	VINT hook	ˈvɪnthʊk
windlass	WIND luhs	ˈwɪndləs
window	WIN doh	ˈwɪndo
Windsor	WIN zer	ˈwɪnzər
windward, W-	WIND werd	ˈwɪndwərd
Winnebago	wi nuh BAY goh	wɪnəˈbego
Winnepesaukee	wi nuh puh SAW ki	wɪnəpəˈsɔkɪ
Winnipeg	WI nuh peg	ˈwɪnəpɛg
Winnipegosis	wi ni puh GOH sis	wɪnɪpəˈgosɪs
Winslow	WINZ loh	ˈwɪnzlo
Winston-Salem	WIN stuhn SAY luhm	ˈwɪnstən ˈseləm
Winthrop	WIN thruhp	ˈwɪnθrəp
wisdom	WIZ duhm	ˈwɪzdəm
wish	wish	wɪʃ
Wisla	VEE slah	ˈvislɑ
wistaria	wi STAI ri uh	wɪˈstɛrɪə
wisteria	wi STI ri uh	wɪˈstɪrɪə
with	with :	wɪð

sing [ŋ] ; oh [o] ; oil [ɔɪ] ; foot [ʊ] ; foo:d [u] ; how [aʊ] ; pie [p] ; ray [r] ; so [s] ; shall [ʃ] ; to [t] ; thin [θ] ; th:en [ð] ; above (uh BUHV) [ə, ˈʌ] ; vine [v] ; wine [w] ; whine [hw] ; you [j] ; zoo [z] ; rouge (roo:zh) [ʒ].

wither	WI th : er	ˈwɪðər
withy	WI th : i	ˈwɪðɪ
Wittenberg	WI tuhn berg	ˈwɪtənbərg
wivern	WIGH vern	ˈwaɪvərn
wizard	WI zerd	ˈwɪzərd
wizen	WI zuhn	ˈwɪzən
Wodehouse	WOOD hows	ˈwʊdhaʊs
Woden, Wodan	WOH duhn	ˈwodən
wog	wahg	wɑg
Wolf, Hugo	VAWLF, HOO : goh	ˈvɔlf, ˈhugo
wolfram	WOOL fruhm	ˈwʊlfrəm
Wolfram von Eschenbach	VAWL frahm fawn E shuhn bahk	ˈvɔlfrɑm fɔn ˈɛʃənbɑk
Wollstonecraft	WOOL stuhn kraft	ˈwʊlstənkræft
Wolseley	WOOLZ li	ˈwʊlzlɪ
Wolsey	WOOL zi	ˈwʊlzɪ
wombat	WAHM bat	ˈwɑmbæt
wonder	WUHN der	ˈwʌndər
wont	wuhnt	wʌnt
won't	wohnt	wont
wonted	WUHN tid	ˈwʌntɪd
woof	woo : f	wuf
woofer	WOO fer	ˈwʊfər
Woolf	woolf	wʊlf
Woollcott	WOOL kuht	ˈwʊlkət
Woolwich	WOO lij	ˈwʊlɪdʒ
Woolworth	WOOL werth	ˈwʊlwərθ
Woonsocket	woo : n SAH kit	wunˈsɑkɪt
Woosung	woo : soong	wusuŋ
Worcester	WOO ster	ˈwʊstər
Worcestershire	WOO ster shir	ˈwʊstərʃɪr
Worms	wermz	wɝmz
worsted (yarn)	WOO stid	ˈwʊstɪd
Wotton	WOO tuhn	ˈwʊtən
Wouk	wohk	wok
Wozzeck	VAW tsek	ˈvɔtsɛk
wraith	rayth	reθ
Wrangel, -l	RANG guhl	ˈræŋgəl
wrasse	ras	ræs
wrath	rath	ræθ
wreath	reeth	riθ
wreathe	reeth :	rið
wrestle	RE suhl	ˈrɛsəl
writhe	righth :	raɪð
wrong	rawng	rɔŋ
wroth	rawth	rɔθ
wrought	rawt	rɔt
Wuchang	woo : chahng	wutʃɑŋ
Wuhan	woo : hahn	wuhɑn
Wundt, Wilhem	VOONT, VIL helm	ˈvʊnt, ˈvɪlhɛlm
Württemberg	WER tuhm berg	ˈwɝtəmbərg
Würzburg	WERTS berg	ˈwɝtsbərg

at [æ] ; *ah* [ɑ] ; *air* [ɛ] ; *awful* [ɔ] ; *say* [e] ; *back* [b] ; *chair* [tʃ] ; *do* [d] ; *elm* [ɛ] ; *eel* [i] ; *server* [ˈɝ, ər] ; *f*it [f] ; *go* [g] ; *hurt* [h] ; *is* [ɪ] ; *high* [aɪ] ; *jet* [dʒ] ; *kiss* [k] ; *lamb* [l] ; *my* [m] ; *nice* [n] ;

Wyandot, -te	WIGH uhn daht	ˈwaɪəndɑt
Wyatt	WIGH uht	ˈwaɪət
Wycherley	WI cher li	ˈwɪtʃərlɪ
Wyclif, -fe	WI klif	ˈwɪklɪf
wynd	wighnd	waɪnd
Wyoming	wigh OH ming	waɪˈomɪŋ

X

Xanadu	ZA nuh doo:	ˈzænədu
xanthic	ZAN thik	ˈzænθɪk
Xanthippe, Xantippe	zan TI pi	zænˈtɪpɪ
Xavier	ZAY vi er	ˈzevɪər
Xavier (Spanish)	hah VYAIR	hɑˈvjɛr
xebec	ZEE bek	ˈzibɛk
Xenocrates	zi NAH kruh teez	zɪˈnɑkrətiz
xenon	ZEE nahn	ˈzinɑn
xenophobia	ze nuh FOH bi uh	zɛnəˈfobɪə
Xenophon	ZE nuh fuhn	ˈzɛnəfɑn
xeric	ZEE rik	ˈzɪrɪk
xeroderma	zi ruh DER muh	zɪrəˈdɝmə
xerography	zi RAH gruh fi	zɪˈrɑgrəfɪ
xerophilous	zi RAH fuh luhs	zɪˈrɑfələs
xerophthalmia	zi rahf THAL mi uh	zɪrɑfˈθælmɪə
xerosis	zi ROH sis	zɪˈrosɪs
Xerxes	ZERK seez	ˈzɝksiz
xi	zigh	zaɪ
Xingú	shing GOO:	ʃɪŋˈgu
xiphoid	ZI foid	ˈzɪfɔɪd
xylene	ZIGH leen	ˈzaɪlin
xylography	zigh LAH gruh fi	zaɪˈlɑgrəfɪ
xylol	ZIGH lohl	ˈzaɪlol
xylophone	ZIGH luh fohn	ˈzaɪləfon
xyster	ZI ster	ˈzɪstər

Y

Yablonoi	yah blaw NOI	jɑbloˈnɔɪ
yacht	yaht	jɑt
Yadkin	YAD kin	ˈjædkɪn
yagi	YAH gi	ˈjɑgɪ
Yakima	YA kuh muh	ˈjækəmə
Yahoo	YAH hoo:	ˈjɑhu
Yahwe, -h	YAH we	ˈjɑwɛ

sing [ŋ]; *oh* [o]; *oi*l [ɔɪ]; *foot* [ʊ]; *foo*:d [u]; *how* [aʊ]; *p*ie [p]; *ray* [r]; *so* [s]; *sh*all [ʃ];
to [t]; *thin* [θ]; *th*:en [ð]; above (*uh* B*UH*V) [ə, ˈʌ]; *v*ine [v]; *w*ine [w]; *wh*ine [hw];
*y*ou [j]; *z*oo [z]; rouge (roo:*zh*) [ʒ].

yak	yak	jæk
Yakut	yah KOOT	jɑˈkʊt
Yalta	YAHL tuh	ˈjɑltə
Yalu	yah loo	jɑlu
Yangtze	yang see	jæŋsi
Yaoundé	yah oo : n DAY	jɑunˈde
Yap	yahp	jɑp
Yaqui	YAH kee	ˈjɑki
yare	yair	jɛr
Yarmouth	YAHR muhth	ˈjɑrməθ
Yaroslavl	yah raw SLAH vuhl	jarɔˈslavəl
yaupon	YAW puhn	ˈjɔpən
yaw	yaw	jɔ
yawn	yawn	jɔn
yea	yay	je
yearling	YIR ling	ˈjɪrlɪŋ
yeast	yeest	jist
Yeats	yayts	jets
yellow	YE loh	ˈjɛlo
Yemen	YE muhn	ˈjɛmən
Yenangyaung	yay nahn JOWNG	jenɑnˈdʒauŋ
Yenisei	ye ni SAY	jɛnɪˈse
yeoman	YOH muhn	ˈjomən
Yerba Buena	YAIR buh BWAY nuh	ˈjɛrbə ˈbwenə
yes	yes	jɛs
Yeshiva	yuh SHEE vuh	jəˈʃivə
Yggdrasill	IG druh sil	ˈɪgdrəsɪl
Yiddish	YI dish	ˈjɪdɪʃ
Ymir	EE mir	ˈimɪr
yoga	YOH guh	ˈjogə
yogi	YOH gi	ˈjogɪ
yogurt, yoghurt	YOH goort	ˈjogurt
Yoknapatawpha	YAHK nuh puh TAW fuh	ˈjɑknəpəˈtɔfə
Yokohama	yoh kuh HAH muh	jokəˈhɑmə
yolk	yohk	jok
Yom Kippur	yahm KI per	jɑm ˈkɪpər
Yorkshire	YAWRK shir	ˈjɔrkʃɪr
Yoruba	YOH roo bah	ˈjoruba
Yosemite	yoh SE muh ti	joˈsɛmətɪ
Yoshihito	YAW shee HEE taw	ˈjɔʃiˈhitɔ
youth	yoo : th	juθ
Ypres	EE pruh	ˈiprə
Ypsilanti	ip suh LAN ti	ɪpsəˈlæntɪ
Yquem	ee KEM	iˈkɛm
Yseult	i SOO : LT	ɪˈsult
ytterbium	i TER bi uhm	ɪˈtɚbɪəm
yttrium	I tri uhm	ˈɪtrɪəm
Yucatan	yoo : kuh TAN	jukəˈtæn
yucca	YUH kuh	ˈjʌkə
Yuen	yoo : EN	juˈɛn
Yuga	YOO guh	ˈjugə
Yugoslavia	yoo : goh SLAH vi uh	jugoˈslɑvɪə

---

at [æ] ; *ah* [ɑ] ; *air* [ɛ] ; *awful* [ɔ] ; *say* [e] ; *back* [b] ; *chair* [tʃ] ; *do* [d] ; *elm* [ɛ] ; *eel* [i] ;
server [ˈɝ, ər] ; *f*it [f] ; *go* [g] ; *hurt* [h] ; *is* [ɪ] ; *high* [aɪ] ; *jet* [dʒ] ; *kiss* [k] ; *lamb* [l] ; *my* [m] ;
nice [n] ;

Yukon	YOO : kahn	ˈjukɑn
Yuma	YOO : muh	ˈjumə
Yunnan	yoo nahn	jʊnɑn

Z

Zabulon	ZA byuh luhn	ˈzæbjələn
Zacatecas	sah kah TE kahs	sɑkɑˈtɛkɑs
Zachariah	za kuh RIGH uh	zækəˈraɪə
Zacharias	za kuh RIGH uhs	zækəˈraɪəs
Zagazig	zah gah ZEEG	zɑgɑˈzig
Zagreb	ZAH greb	ˈzɑgrɛb
zaibatsu	zigh BAHT soo :	zaɪˈbɑtsu
Zambezi, Zambesi	zam BEE zi	zæmˈbizɪ
Zangwill	ZANG gwil	ˈzæŋgwɪl
Zanuck	ZA nuhk	ˈzænək
Zanzibar	ZAN zuh bahr	ˈzænzəbɑr
Zaporozhe	zah paw RAWZH ye	zɑpəˈrɔʒjɛ
Zapotocky, Antonin	zah poh TOHT skee, ahn TOH nyeen	zɑpoˈtotski, ɑnˈtonjin
Zarathustra	za ruh THOO : struh	zærəˈθustrə
zareba, zareeba	zuh REE buh	zəˈribə
zarf	zahrf	zɑrf
Zarubin	zah ROO : bin	zɑˈrubɪn
Zatec	ZHAH tets	ˈʒɑtɛts
zealot	ZE luht	ˈzɛlət
zealous	ZE luhs	ˈzɛləs
zebra	ZEE bruh	ˈzibrə
zebu	ZEE byoo :	ˈzibju
Zeebrugge	ZEE broo guh	ˈzibrʊgə
Zeitgeist	SIGHT gighst	ˈsaɪtgaɪst
Zeitschrift	SIGHT shrift	ˈsaɪtʃrɪft
Zeitung	SIGH toong	ˈsaɪtʊŋ
Zellerbach	ZEL er bak	ˈzɛlərbæk
Zemgale	ZEM gah le	ˈzɛmgɑlɛ
Zen	zen	zɛn
zenana	ze NAH nuh	zɛˈnɑnə
Zend	zend	zɛnd
Zend-Avesta	ZEN duh VE stuh	ˈzɛndəˈvɛstə
zenith	ZEE nith	ˈzinɪθ
Zeno	ZEE noh	ˈzino
zephyr	ZE fer	ˈzɛfər
Zephyrus	ZE fuh ruhs	ˈzɛfərəs
zeppelin, Z-	ZE puh lin	ˈzɛpəlɪn
zero	ZI roh	ˈzɪro
zeugma	ZOO : G muh	ˈzugmə
Zeus	zoo : s	zus
Zhdanov	zhuh DAH nawf	ʒəˈdɑnɔf

---

sing [ŋ] ; oh [o] ; oil [ɔɪ] ; foot [ʊ] ; foo:d [u] ; how [aʊ] ; pie [p] ; ray [r] ; so [s] ; shall [ʃ] ; to [t] ; thin [θ] ; th:en [ð] ; above (uh BUHV) [ə, ˈʌ] ; vine [v] ; wine [w] ; whine [hw] ; you [j] ; zoo [z] ; rouge (roo:zh) [ʒ].

Zhukov	ZHOO : kawf	ˈʒukɔf
Ziegfeld	ZIG feld	ˈzɪgfɛld
ziggurat	ZI goo rat	ˈzɪgʊræt
Zimbalist	ZIM buh list	ˈzɪmbəlɪst
zingara	SIN gah rah	ˈsɪngɑrɑ
zinnia	ZI ni uh	ˈzɪnɪə
zircon	ZER kahn	ˈzɝkɑn
zloty	ZLAW ti	ˈzlɔtɪ
zoanthropy	zoh AN thruh pi	zoˈænθrəpɪ
zodiac	ZOH di ak	ˈzodɪæk
zodiacal	zoh DIGH uh kuhl	zoˈdaɪəkəl
Zola	ZOH luh	ˈzolə
Zollverein	SAWL fuh righn	ˈsɔlfəraɪn
Zolotov	ZAW law tawf	ˈzɔlɔtɔf
zombi, -e	ZAHM bi	ˈzɑmbɪ
zone	zohn	zon
Zonta	ZAHN tuh	ˈzɑntə
zoo	zoo :	zu
zooerastia	zoh uh i RA sti uh	zoəɪˈræstɪə
zoolatry	zoh AH luh tri	zoˈɑlətrɪ
zoological	zoh uh LAH ji kuhl	zoəˈlɑdʒɪkəl
zoology	zoh AH luh ji	zoˈɑlədʒɪ
Zoomar, z-	ZOO : mahr	ˈzumɑr
zoomorphism	zoh uh MAWR fi zuhm	zoəˈmɔrfɪzəm
zoophyte	ZOH uh fight	ˈzoəfaɪt
zoot	zoo : t	zut
zoppa	SAW pah	ˈsɔpɑ
Zorin, Valerian	ZAW rin, vah lair ee AHN	ˈzɔrɪn, vɑleəriˈɑn
Zorina	zaw REE nuh	zɔˈrinə
Zorn	sawrn	sɔrn
Zoroaster	zoh roh A ster	zoroˈæstər
zoster	ZAH ster	ˈzɑstər
Zouave	zoo : AHV	zuˈɑv
zucchini	zoo : KEE ni	zuˈkinɪ
Zuider Zee	ZIGH der ZEE	ˈzaɪdər ˈzi
Zuleta-Angel	soo LE tah ahn HEL	suˈlɛta ɑnˈhɛl
zum Beispiel	soom BIGH shpeel	sʊm ˈbaɪʃpil
zuñi	ZOO : nyi	ˈzunjɪ
Zurich	ZOO rik	ˈzurɪk
Zweig	swighg	swaɪg
zwieback	SWIGH bak	ˈswaɪbæk
Zwingli	ZWING gli	ˈzwɪŋglɪ
zygote	ZIGH goht	ˈzaɪgot
zyme	zighm	zaɪm
zymurgy	ZIGH mer ji	ˈzaɪmərdʒɪ

---

at [æ] ; ah [ɑ] ; air [ɛ] ; awful [ɔ] ; say [e] ; back [b] ; chair [tʃ] ; do [d] ; elm [ɛ] ; eel [i] ; server [ˈɝ, ər] ; fit [f] ; go [g] ; hurt [h] ; is [ɪ] ; high [aɪ] ; jet [dʒ] ; kiss [k] ; lamb [l] ; my [m] ; nice [n] ; sing [ŋ] ; oh [o] ; oil [ɔɪ] ; foot [ʊ] ; foo:d [u] ; how [aʊ] ; pie [p] ; ray [r] ; so [s] ; shall [ʃ] ; to [t] ; thin [θ] ; th:en [ð] ; above (uh BUHV) [ə, ˈʌ] ; vine [v] ; wine [w] ; whine [hw] ; you [j] ; zoo [z] ; rouge (roo:zh) [ʒ].

NAMES IN THE NEWS

Names in the News is a compilation of difficult-to-pronounce names of persons from all walks of life—United Nations' delegates, ambassadors, political figures, artists, playwrights, actors, musicians, and sports figures—whose importance has been established for Americans within the last decade. Other contemporaries whose names recur frequently in news accounts, but whose fame has been established for many years, will be found in the main portion of the book.

A

Abboud, Ibrahim	ah BOO : D, ee brah HEEM	aˈbud, ibraˈhim
Adebo	ah DAY baw	aˈdebɔ
Adeel, Omar Abdel	ah DEEL, OH mahr AHB duhl	aˈdil, ˈomar ˈabdəl
Adoula, Cyrille	a DOO : lah, SI ril	æˈdula, ˈsɪrɪl
Adzhubei, Alexei	ahd zhoo : BAY, ah LEK see	adʒuˈbe, aˈlɛksi
Ahidjo, Ahmadou	ah HEE dyoh, ah MAH doo :	aˈhidjo, aˈmadu
Aidit	igh DEET	aɪˈdit
Aiken	AY kin	ˈekɪn
Aimée, Anouk	e MAY, ah NOO : K	ɛˈme, aˈnuk
Akakpo, André	ah KAH boh, ahn DRAY	aˈkabo, anˈdre
Al-Aini, Muhsin Ahmad	ahl IGH nee, MUH sin AH mahd	al ˈaɪni, ˈmʌsɪn ˈamad
Albee	AWL bee	ˈɔlbi
Alberghetti	al ber GE tee	ælbərˈgɛti
Alemann, Roberto	ah lay MAHN, roh BAIR toh	aleˈman, roˈbɛərto
Alessandri, Jorge	ah le SAHN dree, HAWR hay	alɛˈsandri, ˈhɔrhe
Allers, Franz	AH lers, frahnz	ˈalərs, franz
Alou, Felipe	ah LOO :, fuh LEEP	aˈlu, fəˈlip
Alphand, Hervé	ahl FAHN, air VAY	alˈfan, ɛərˈve
al-Sallal	ahl SAH lahl	alˈsalal
al-Tall, Wasfi	ahl TUHL, WAHS fee	alˈtʌl, ˈwasfi
Alvarez Vidaurre	AHL vah rez vee TH : OWR ray	ˈalvarez viˈðaurre
Angeli, Pier	AHN juh lee, pee AIR	ˈandʒəli, piˈɛər
Anuman-Rajadhon, Somchai	ah noo : MAHN-rah jah TOHN, soom CHIGH	anuˈman-radʒaˈton, sʊmˈtʃaɪ
Arosemena Monroy	ah roh say MAY nah MOHN roy	aroseˈmena ˈmonrɔɪ
Arruza, Carlos	ah ROO : zuh, KAHR lohs	aˈruza, ˈkarlos
Asakai, Koichiro	ah sah KIGH, koh ee CHEE roh	asaˈkaɪ, koiˈtʃiro
Asgeirsson, Asgeir	AHS geer suhn, AHS geer	ˈasgirsən ˈasgir
Aspromonte	a sproh MAHN tee	æsproˈmanti
Astapenko, Pavel	ah STAH peng koh, PAH vyel	aˈstapɛŋko, ˈpavjɛl
Auguste, Carlet	oh GOO : ST, kahr LAY	oˈgust, karˈle
Awolowo, Obafemi	a woh LAW waw, aw BAH fe mee	æwoˈlɔwɔ, ɔˈbafɛmi
Ayub Kahn	igh YOO : B KAHN	aɪˈjub ˈkan

at [æ]; ah [ɑ]; air [ɛ]; awful [ɔ]; say [e]; back [b]; chair [tʃ]; do [d]; elm [ɛ]; eel [i];
server [ˈɝ, ər]; fit [f]; go [g]; hurt [h]; is [ɪ]; high [aɪ]; jet [dʒ]; kiss [k]; lamb [l]; my [m];
nice [n]; sing [ŋ]; oh [o]; oil [ɔɪ]; foot [ʊ]; foo:d [u]; how [aʊ]; pie [p]; ray [r]; so [s];
shall [ʃ]; to [t]; thin [θ]; th:en [ð]; above (uh BUHV) [ə, ʌ]; vine [v]; wine [w]; whine
[hw]; you [j]; zoo [z]; rouge (roo:zh) [ʒ].

| Azikiwe, Nnamdi | a zee kee WE, nahm DEE | æziki'wɛ, nɑm'di |
| Azuma, Tokuho | ahd zoo MAH, toh koo : HOH | ɑdzʊ'mɑ, tokʊ'ho |

B

Baddeley, Hermione	BA di lee, her MIGH uh nee	'bædɪli, hɝ'maɪəni
Baez (Joan)	bigh EZ	baɪ'ɛz
Bagaya	bah GAH yah	bɑ'gɑjɑ
Balaguer, Joaquín	bah lah GAIR, hoh ah KEEN	bɑlɑ'gɛɑr, hoɑ'kin
Balewa, Abubakar Tafawa	ba LAY wah, a BOO : ba kahr ta FAH wah	bæ'lewɑ, æ'bubækɑr, tæ'fawɑ
Banda	BAHN dah	'bɑndɑ
Bandaranaike, Mrs. Sirimavo	buhn druh NIGH uhk, see ruh MAH voh	bʌndrə'naɪək, sirə'mɑvo
Bastida	bahs TEE th : ah	bɑs'tiðɑ
Baumann	BOW muhn	'baʊmən
Bayh, Birch	bah, berch	bɑ, bɝtʃ
Behan, Brendan	BEE uhn, BREN duhn	'biən, 'brɛndən
Beliveau, Jean	be li VOH, zhahn	bɛlɪ'vo, ʒɑn
Belmondo, Jean-Paul	bel mohn DOH, zhahn-pawl	bɛlmon'do, ʒɑn-pɔl
Ben Bella	ben BE luh	bɛn 'bɛlə
Benhima, Ahmed Taibi	ben HEE mah, AH met tah ee BEE	bɛn'himɑ, 'amɛt tɑi'bi
Benites, Leopoldo	be NEE tes, lay oh POHL doh	bɛ'nitɛs, leo'poldo
Ben Khedda, Benyoussef	ben KAY duh, ben YOO : suhf	bɛn 'kedə, bɛn'jusəf
Berganza	ber GAHN zuh	bɝ'gɑnzə
Bergonzi, Carlo	bair GOHN dzee, KAHR loh	bɛɑr'gondzi, 'kɑrlo
Berhanyer, Elio	BAIR hah nyer, AY lyoh	'bɛɑrhanjər, 'eljo
Besoyan	buh SOI yuhn	bə'sɔɪjən
Bettis, Valerie	BE tis, VA luh rce	'bɛtɪs, 'væləri
Bhumibol, Adulyadej	POO : mee pohn, a DOO : n ded	'pumipon, æ'dundɛd
Biely, Andrey	bee e LEE, AHN dray	biɛ'li, 'ɑndre
Bikel	bi KEL	bɪ'kɛl
Bindzi, Benoit	BIND zee, BEN wah	'bɪndzi, 'bɛnwɑ
Bitsios, Dimitri	BEET see ohs, dee MEE tree	'bitsios, di'mitri
Blasingame	BLA sing gaym	'blæsiŋgem
Blough	blow	blaʊ
Bogarde, Dirk	BOH gahrd, derk	'bogɑrd, dɝk
Bohan, Marc	boh AHN, mahrk	bo'ɑn, mɑrk
Bomboko	buhm BOH koh	bʌm'boko
Bonnelly, Rafael	boh NE lee, rah fah EL	bo'nɛli, rɑfɑ'ɛl
Bonynge	BAH ning	'bɑnɪŋ

at [æ] ; *ah* [ɑ] ; *air* [ɛ] ; *aw*ful [ɔ] ; *say* [e] ; *back* [b] ; *chair* [tʃ] ; *do* [d] ; *elm* [ɛ] ; *eel* [i] ; *server* ['ɝ, ər] ; *f*it [f] ; *go* [g] ; *h*urt [h] ; *is* [ɪ] ; *high* [aɪ] ; *jet* [dʒ] ; *kiss* [k] ; *lamb* [l] ; *my* [m] ; *n*ice [n] ;

Borja, Jacinto Castel	BAWR hah, hah SEEN toh kah STEL	ˈbɔrhɑ, hɑˈsinto kɑˈstɛl
Bosch, Juan	bohsh, hwahn	boʃ, huɑn
Bosley	BAHZ lee	ˈbɑzli
Botha, Matthys	BOH tuh, mah TAYS	ˈbotə, mɑˈtes
Bourguiba, Habib	boo : r GEE bah, hah BEEB	burˈgibɑ, hɑˈbib
Boyd, Aquilino	boyd, ah kee LEE noh	bɔɪd, ɑkiˈlino
Brazzi, Rossano	BRAH tsee, roh SAH noh	ˈbrɑtsi, roˈsɑno
Brentano	bren TAH noh	brɛnˈtɑno
Bressoud	bre SOO : D	brɛˈsud
Brezhnev, Leonid	BREZH nyef, LAY oh nid	ˈbreʒnjɛf, ˈleonɪd
Broglio	BROH lee oh	ˈbrolio
Brumel, Valery	BROO : mil, vah LAI ree	ˈbrumɪl, vɑˈleəri
Bubiriza, Pascal	boo : bee REE zah, PAH skahl	bubiˈrizɑ, ˈpɑskɑl
Buchholz, Horst	BUHK hohlts, hawrst	ˈbʌkholts, hɔrst
Buchwald	BOOK wawld	ˈbʊkwɔld
Bucyk	BYOO : sik	ˈbjusɪk
Budo, Halim	BOO : doh, HAH leem	ˈbudo, ˈhɑlim
Bustamente	boo : stah MEN tay	bustɑˈmɛnte
Butor, Michel	boo : TAWR, mee SHEL	buˈtɔr, miˈʃɛl

C

Caballero Tamayo, Jaime	kah bah YAIR oh tah MAH yoh, HIGH may	kabɑˈjeəro tɑˈmɑjo, ˈhaɪme
Capucci	kah POO : chee	kɑˈputʃi
Capucine	ka pyoo : SEEN	kæpjuˈsin
Cárdenas, Lázaro	KAR day nahs, LAH sah roh	ˈkɑrdenɑs, ˈlasɑro
Cardinale, Claudia	kahr dee NAH le, KLOW dee ah	kardiˈnɑlɛ, ˈklaʊdiɑ
Cardoso, Mario	kahr DOH soh, MAH ree oh	karˈdoso, ˈmario
Carreon, Camilio	kah ray OHN, kah MEE lyoh	kareˈon, kɑˈmiljo
Carrillo Flores, Antonio	kah REEL yoh FLAW res, ahn TOH nyo	ˈkariljo ˈflɔrɛs, ɑnˈtonjo
Cartier-Bresson, Henri	kahr TYAY-bray SOHN, ahn REE	karˈtje-breˈson, ɑnˈri
Carvalho Silos, Geraldo de	ker VAH lyoo : SEE loo : sh, zhuh RAHL doo : duh	kərˈvɑlju ˈsiluʃ, ʒəˈrɑldu də
Cassel, Jean-Pierre	kah SEL, zhahn-pyair	kɑˈsɛl, ʒɑn-pjɛər
Celebrezze	se luh BREE zee	sɛləˈbrizi
Cepeda, Orlando	suh PAY duh, awr LAHN doh	səˈpedɑ, ɔrˈlɑndo
Chakiris	chah KEE ris	tʃɑˈkirɪs
Chakravarty	chah krah vahr TEE	tʃɑkrɑvɑrˈti
Chanderli, Abdelkader	chahn der LEE, ahb duhl KAH der	tʃɑndərˈli, ɑbdəlˈkɑdər

sing [ŋ] ; oh [o] ; oil [ɔɪ] ; foot [ʊ] ; foo :d [u] ; how [aʊ] ; pie [p] ; ray [r] ; so [s] ; shall [ʃ] ; to [t] ; thin [θ] ; th:en [ð] ; above (uh BUHV) [ə, ˈʌ] ; vine [v] ; wine [w] ; whine [hw] ; you [j] ; zoo [z] ; rouge (roo:zh) [ʒ].

Chaudet	shoh DAY	ʃoˈde
Chehab, Fuad	shuh HAB, FOO : ahd	ʃəˈhæb, ˈfuɑd
Chen Cheng	chen cheng	tʃɛn tʃɛŋ
Chenoweth	CHEN oh weth	ˈtʃɛnoweθ
Chiari	kee AH ree	kiˈɑri
Chicheri, Caruncho	chee CHAIR ee, kah ROO : N choh	tʃiˈtʃɛəri, kaˈruntʃo
Chookasian, Lili	choo : KAH syahn, LEE lee	tʃuˈkɑsjɑn, ˈlili
Cimoli, Gino	si MOH lee, JEE noh	sɪˈmoli, ˈdʒino
Colavito	kah luh VEE toh	kɑləˈvito
Collier, Gershon	KAH lyuhr, GER shuhn	ˈkɑljər, ˈgɝʃən
Colzani, Anselmo	kohlt SAH nee, ahn SEL moh	koltˈsɑni, ɑnˈsɛlmo
Comay	koh MIGH	koˈmaɪ
Corner	KAWR nuhr	ˈkɔrnər
Coulibaly, Sori	koo : lee BUH lee, SAW ree	kuliˈbʌli, ˈsɔri
Cousy	KOO : zee	ˈkuzi
Coutts	koo : ts	kuts
Crespin, Régine	kres PAN, ray ZHEEN	krɛsˈpæn, reˈʒin
Csatorday, Karoly	CHAH tohr digh, KAH raw lyi	ˈtʃɑtordaɪ, ˈkɑrɔljɪ
Cvejic, Biserka	TSVAY ich, BI ser kah	ˈtsveɪtʃ, ˈbɪsərkɑ
Cyrankiewicz, Jozef	tsee rahn KAY vich, YOO : zef	tsirɑnˈkevɪtʃ, ˈjuzɛf

D

Dacko, David	DAH koh, DAY vid	ˈdɑko, ˈdevɪd
Daddah, Moktar O.	DAH dah, MOHK tahr oo :	ˈdɑdɑ, ˈmoktɑr u
Dadet, Emmanuel	dah DAY, uh mahn yoo : EL	dɑˈde, əmɑnjuˈɛl
Dalhousie	dahl HOO : see	dɑlˈhusi
Dar es Salaam	DAHR ES sah LAHM	ˈdɑr ˈɛs sɑˈlɑm
Darian	DA ree uhn	ˈdæriɑn
Darvas, Lili	DAHR vuhs, LI lee	ˈdɑrvɔs, ˈlɪli
Dawalibi, Maarouf	dah wah LEE bee, mah ROO : F	dɑwɑˈlibi, mɑˈruf
de Barentzen	duh bah rend ZEN	də bɑrɛndˈzɛn
Delock	duh LAHK	dəˈlɑk
Delon, Alain	duh LOHN, ah LAN	dəˈlon, ɑˈlæn
De Los Angeles, Victoria	day lohs AHN je lez, vik TAW ree uh	de los ˈɑndʒɛlɛz, vɪkˈtɔriɑ
Delvecchio	del VE kee oh	dɛlˈvɛkio
De Oliveira, Campos, Roberto	duh oh lee VAIR uh KAHMP uhsh ruh BAIR too :	də oliˈveərə ˈkɑmpəʃ, rəˈbeərtu
de Quay, Jan	duh KWIGH, yahn	də ˈkwaɪ, jɑn
Derounian	de ROO : nee uhn	deˈruniɑn
Dessès	duh SE	dəˈsɛ

---

at [æ] ; *ah* [ɑ] ; *air* [ɛ] ; *aw*ful [ɔ] ; *say* [e] ; *b*ack [b] ; *ch*air [tʃ] ; *d*o [d] ; *e*lm [ɛ] ; *ee*l [i] ; *s*erver [ˈɝ, ər] ; *f*it [f] ; *g*o [g] ; *h*urt [h] ; *is* [ɪ] ; *high* [aɪ] ; *j*et [dʒ] ; *k*iss [k] ; *l*amb [l] ; *m*y [m] ; *n*ice [n] ;

de Wilde	duh WIL duh	də ˈwɪldə
Diallo Telli	dee AH loh TE lee	diˈɑlo ˈtɛli
Diop, Ousmane Soce	dyahp, oo : s MAHN soh SAY	djɑp, usˈmɑn soˈse
Diori, Hamani	dee AW ree, HAH mah nee	diˈɔri, ˈhɑmɑni
Diroc	di RAHK	dɪˈrɑk
Dischinger	DI shing ger	ˈdɪʃɪŋgər
Dobi, Istvan	DOH bee, ISH tvahn	ˈdobi, ˈɪʃtvɑn
Dobrynin, Anatoliy	doh BREE nyin, ah nah TOH lee	doˈbrinjɪn, ɑnɑˈtoli
Dolukhanova, Zara	doh loo : KAH noh vah, ZAH rah	doluˈkɑnovɑ, ˈzɑrɑ
Drozniak	DRUHZH nyak	ˈdrʌʒnjæk
Dudintsev, Vladimir	doo : DEENT sef, VLAH duh meer	duˈdintsɛf, ˈvlɑdəmir
Dullea, Keir	duh LAY, keer	dəˈle, kir
Dupas	doo : PAH	duˈpɑ
Dürrenmatt, Friedrich	DOO : ruhn maht, FREE drish	ˈdurənmɑt, ˈfridrɪʃ
Dussault, Nancy	DOO : sawlt, NAN see	ˈdusɔlt, ˈnænsi
Duvalier, François	doo : vah LYAY, frahn SWAH	duvɑˈlje, franˈswɑ

E

el-Kodsi, Nazem	ahl KOH tsee, NAH zem	ɑlˈkotsi, ˈnɑzɛm
Elmi, Hassan Nur	EL mee, HAH suhn noo : r	ˈɛlmi, ˈhɑsən nur
Enckell	ENG kel	ˈɛŋkɛl
Entezam, Nasrollah	en tuh ZAHM, nahs ROH lah	ɛntəˈzɑm, nɑsˈrolɑ
Erhard, Ludwig	AIR hahrt, LOOT vig	ˈɛərhɑrt, ˈlutvɪg
Erlander, Tage	er LAHN dair, TAH gi	ɝrˈlɑndɛər, ˈtɑgɪ
Essegian	uh SEE juhn	əˈsidʒən
Eyskens, Gaston	AY skinz, gah STOHN	ˈeskɪnz, gɑˈston

F

Fabiani	fah bee AH nee	fɑbiˈɑni
Fabray, Nanette	fa BRAY, nuh NET	fæˈbre, nəˈnɛt
Facio, Gonzalo	fah SEE oh, gohn ZAH loh	fɑˈsio, gonˈzɑlo
Fanfani, Amintore	fahn FAH nee, ah MIN taw re	fanˈfɑni, ɑˈmɪntɔrɛ
Fascell	fay SEL	feˈsɛl
Fassi, Allal El	FAH see, ah LAHL el	ˈfɑsi, ɑˈlɑl ɛl
Fedorenko, Nikolai	fe daw RENG koh, nee koh LIGH	fɛdɔˈrɛŋko, nikoˈlaɪ

---

sing [ŋ] ; oh [o] ; oil [ɔɪ] ; foot [ʊ] ; foo:d [u] ; how [aʊ] ; pie [p] ; ray [r] ; so [s] ; shall [ʃ] ; to [t] ; thin [θ] ; th:en [ð] ; above (uh BUHV) [ə, ˈʌ] ; vine [v] ; wine [w] ; whine [hw] ; you [j] ; zoo [z] ; rouge (roo:zh) [ʒ].

Fekini, Mohieddine	fe KEE nee, moh hye DEEN	fɛˈkini, mohjeˈdin
Fenoaltea, Sergio	fe noh AHL tay ah, SAIR jee oh	fɛnoˈɑltea, ˈsɛərdzio
Fernós-Isern, Antonio	fayr NOHS-EE sern, ahn TOH nyoh	ferˈnos-ˈisərn, ɑnˈtonjo
Ffrangcon-Davies	FRANG kin DAY veez	ˈfræŋkɪn ˈdeviz
Fino	FEE noh	ˈfino
Fischer-Dieskau	FI sher DEE skow	ˈfɪʃər ˈdiskɑʊ
Flon, Suzanne	flohn, soo : ZAHN	flon, suˈzɑn
Flores Avendaño, Guillermo	FLAW res ah ben TH : AH nyoh, gee LYAIR moh	ˈflɔrɛs ɑbɛnˈðɑnjo, giˈljɛrmo
Foo Hsing	foo : shing	fu ʃɪŋ
Forquet	fawr KAY	fɔrˈke
Frelinghuysen	FREE ling HIGH zuhn	ˈfrilɪŋˈhaɪzən
Frisch, Max	frish, mahks	frɪʃ, mɑks

G

Gagarin	gah GAH rin	gɑˈgɑrɪn
Galitzine	gah leed ZIN	gɑlidˈzɪn
Gallanos	guh LAH nohs	gəˈlɑnos
Gallin-Douathe, Michel	gah LAN doh WAHT, mee SHEL	gɑˈlæn doˈwat, miˈʃɛl
Ganev, Dimiter	GAH nef, DI mi tuhr	ˈgɑnɛf, ˈdɪmɪtər
Garcia del Solar, Lucio	gahr SEE ah del soh LAHR, LOO : see oh	gɑrˈsia dɛl soˈlɑr, ˈlusio
Garin, Vasco Vieira	gah RAN, VAHSH koh vee AY ruh	gɑˈræn ˈvɑʃko viˈerə
Garrigues	gah REE ges	gɑˈrigɛs
Gazzara	guh ZA ruh	gəˈzærə
Gbenye, Christophe	guh BENG yay, KREE stawf	gəˈbɛŋje, ˈkristɔf
Gebre-Egzy, Tesfaye	GAB ruh EG zee, tahs FIGH ay	ˈgæbrə ˈɛgzi, tɑsˈfaɪe
Genêt, Jean	zhuh NAY, zhahn	ʒəˈne, ʒɑn
Gentile (Jim)	jen TEEL	dʒɛnˈtil
Geoffrion	JE free uhn	ˈdʒɛfriən
Gerhardsen, Einar	ge RAHRD sen, IGH nahr	gɛˈrardsɛn, ˈaɪnɑr
Gheorghiu-Dej, Georghe	dyawr DYOO : -dezh, DYAWR dyay	djɔrˈdju-dɛʒ, ˈdjɔrdje
Giaimo	JIGH moh	ˈdʒaɪmo
Giaiotti, Bonaldo	jigh OH tee, boh NAHL doh	dʒaɪˈoti, boˈnɑldo
Gill, Geula	gil, ge OO : lah	gɪl, gɛˈulɑ
Gizenga, Antoine	gi ZENG guh, ahn TWAHN	gɪˈzɛŋgə, ɑnˈtwɑn
Goldhaber, Maurice	GOHLD hay ber, maw REES	ˈgoldhebər, mɔˈris
Golembiewski	gah luhm BYOO : skee	gɑləmˈbjuski
Golovanov	guh lah VAH nuhf	gəlɑˈvɑnəf
Goma	GOH muh	ˈgomə

at [æ]; *ah* [ɑ]; *air* [ɛ]; *awful* [ɔ]; *say* [e]; *back* [b]; *chair* [tʃ]; *do* [d]; *elm* [ɛ]; *eel* [i]; *server* [ˈɜ, ər]; *fit* [f]; *go* [g]; *hurt* [h]; *is* [ɪ]; *high* [aɪ]; *jet* [dʒ]; *kiss* [k]; *lamb* [l]; *my* [m]; *nice* [n];

Gopallawa	goh pah LAH wah	gopaˈlɑwɑ
Gorbach, Alfons	GAWR bahk, AHL fuhns	ˈgɔrbɑk, ˈɑlfəns
Gotay	goh TIGH	goˈtaɪ
Goulart, João	GOO : lahr, zhoo : OW	ˈgulɑr, ʒuˈaʊ
Gruening	GROO : ning	ˈgrunɪŋ
Gubner	GOO : B ner	ˈgubnər
Gubser	GOO : B ser	ˈgubsər
Guerin	GAIR in	ˈgɛərɪn
Guido, José María	GEE doh, hoh SAY mah REE ah	ˈgido, hoˈse mɑˈriɑ
Gursel, Cemal	guhr SEL, ke MAHL	gərˈsɛl, kɛˈmɑl

H

Hajek, Jiri	HAH yek, YEE ree	ˈhɑjɛk, ˈjiri
Hakim, Georges	hah KEEM, zhawrzh	hɑˈkim, ʒɔrʒ
Harada, Masahiko	HAH rah dah, mah SAH hee koh	ˈhɑrɑdɑ mɑˈsɑhiko
Haseganu, Mihail	hah say GAH noo :, mi hah EEL	hɑseˈgɑnu, mɪhɑˈil
Hayakawa, Sessue	hah yah KAH wah, SAY shoo :	hɑjɑˈkɑwɑ ˈseʃu
Hayashi, Teru	hah yah SHEE, TE roo :	hɑjɑʃi, ˈtɛru
Hébert	ay BAIR	eˈbɛər
Hechler	HE kler	ˈhɛklər
Heilbroner	HIGHL broh ner	ˈhaɪlbronər
Heinsohn	HIGHN sohn	ˈhaɪnson
Hessellund-Jensen, Aage	HE se luhn YEN sen, Oh uh	ˈhɛsɛlʌn-ˈjɛnsɛn, ˈoə
Hochoy, Solomon	hoh CHOI, SAH luh muhn	hoˈtʃɔɪ, ˈsɑləmən
Hoeven	HOH vuhn	ˈhovən
Hofstadter	HAHF sta der	ˈhɑfstædər
Holyoake	HOH lee yohk	ˈholijok
Home, earls of	hyoo : m	hjum
Horszowski, Mieczyslaw	hawr SHUHF skee, mye CHI swahf	hɔrˈʃʌfski, mjɛˈtʃɪswɑf
Hosmer	HAWZ mer	ˈhɔzmər
Houphouet-Boigny, Felix	OO : fwet BWAH nyee, fe LEE	ˈufwɛt ˈbwɑnji, fɛˈli
Hoxha, Enver	HOHK sah, EN vair	ˈhoksɑ, ˈɛnvɛər

I

Idris Senussi	i DREES se NOO : see	ɪˈdris sɛˈnusi
Idzumbuir, Theodore	id zoom BWEER, tay oh DAWR	ɪdzʊmˈbwir, teoˈdɔr

---

siŋg [ŋ] ; oh [o] ; oil [ɔɪ] ; foot [ʊ] ; foo : d [u] ; how [aʊ] ; pie [p] ; ray [r] ; so [s] ; shall [ʃ] ; to [t] ; thin [θ] ; th : en [ð] ; above (uh BUHV) [ə, ˈʌ] ; vine [v] ; wine [w] ; whine [hw] ; you [j] ; zoo [z] ; rouge (roo : zh) [ʒ].

Ignacio-Pinto, Louis	ig NAH see oh-PEEN toh, lwees	ɪgˈnɑsio-ˈpinto, ˈlwis
Ikeda, Hayato	ee kay DAH, hah yah TOH	ikeˈdɑ, hɑjɑˈto
Ileo	i LAY oh	ɪˈleo
Inge	inj	ɪndʒ
Inouye	i NOY ay	ɪˈnɔɪe
Issembe, Aristide	EE sem bay, A ris teed	ˈisɛmbe, ˈærɪstid

J

Jagan, Cheddi	HAH gahn, CHE dee	ˈhɑgɑn, ˈtʃɛdi
Jargalsaikhan, Bayaryn	jahr GAHL sigh hahn, BIGH ah rin	dʒɑrˈgɑlsaɪhɑn, ˈbaɪɑrɪn
Javier	hah vee AIR	hɑviˈɛər
Jeanmaire	zhahn MAIR	ʒɑnˈmɛər
Jens, Salome	jenz, SAL oh may	dʒɛnz, ˈsælome
Jigme Dorji Wanchuk	DYIG me DAWR jee VANG choo : k	ˈdjɪgmɛ ˈdɔrdʒi ˈvæŋtʃuk
Johansson, Ingemar	joh HAN suhn, ING guh mahr	dʒoˈhænsən, ˈɪŋgəmɑr

K

Kaat	kat	kæt
Kabaiwanska	kah BIGH ee VAHN skuh	kɑˈbaɪiˈvɑnskə
Kabore, John Boureima	kah buh REE, jahn boo : RAY muh	kɑbəˈri, dʒɑn buˈremə
Kaline	KAY lighn	ˈke laɪn
Kalonji	kah LOHN jee	kɑˈlondʒi
Karamanlis, Constantin	kah rah MAHN lis, KAHN stuhn teen	kɑrɑˈmɑnlɪs, ˈkɑnstəntin
Karame, Rashid	KAH ruh may, rah SHEED	ˈkɑrəme, rɑˈʃid
Karjalainen, Ahti	KAHR yuh ligh nuhn, AH tee	ˈkɑrjəlaɪnən, ˈɑti
Kartawidjaja, Djuanda	kahr tah wee JIGH uh, JOO : ahn doh	kɑrtɑwiˈdʒaɪə, ˈdʒuɑndo
Kasavubu	kah sah VOO : boo :	kɑsɑˈvubu
Kastenmeier	KAH sten migh uhr	ˈkɑstɛnmaɪər
Kayibanda, Gregoire	kah yee BAHN dah, gre GWAHR	kɑjiˈbɑndɑ grɛˈgwɑr
Keita, Modibo	KAY tah, moh DEE boh	ˈketɑ, moˈdibo
Kekkonen, Urho	KE koh nen, OO : R hoh	ˈkɛkonɛn, ˈurho
Kenyatta	ken YAH tah	kɛnˈjɑtɑ
Keough	KEE oh	ˈkio
Khan, Muhammad Zafrulla	KAHN, muh HAH muhd ZAH fruh lah	ˈkɑn, məˈhɑməd ˈzɑfrəlɑ
Kigeri	kee GAI ree	kiˈgɛəri
Kim Du-bong	kim doo : bohng	kɪm du boŋ

at [æ]; *ah* [ɑ]; *a*ir [ɛ]; *aw*ful [ɔ]; s*ay* [e]; *b*ack [b]; *ch*air [tʃ]; *d*o [d]; *e*lm [ɛ]; *ee*l [i]; s*er*ver [ˈɝ, ər]; *f*it [f]; *g*o [g]; *h*urt [h]; *i*s [ɪ]; h*igh* [aɪ]; *j*et [dʒ]; *k*iss [k]; *l*amb [l]; *m*y [m]; *n*ice [n];

Kim Il-sung	kim eel suhng	kɪm il sʌŋ
Kimny, Nong	KIM nee, nahng	ˈkɪmni, naŋ
Kironde, Apollo	kee RAHN day, ah POH loh	kiˈrande, aˈpolo
Kishi, Nobusuke	KEE shee, noh BOO ske	ˈkiʃi, noˈbuskɛ
Kizya, Luka	KEE zhah, loo꞉ KAH	ˈkiʒa, luˈka
Koht	koo꞉t	kut
Koirala, Matrika Prasad	kaw RAH lah, MAH tri kah prah SAHD	kɔˈrala, ˈmatrɪka praˈsad
Kónya, Sándor	KAWN yah, SHAHN dawr	ˈkɔnja, ˈʃandɔr
Kopit	KOH pit	ˈkopɪt
Kornegay, Horace	KAWRN gay, HAW ris	ˈkɔrnge, ˈhɔrɪs
Krag, Jens Otto	krow, yens AH toh	krau, jɛns ato
Kuchel	KEE kuhl	ˈkikəl
Kuchta	KOO꞉SH tah	ˈkuʃta
Kuenn	keen	ˈkin
Kural, Adnan	koo꞉RAHL, ahd NAHN	kuˈral adˈnan
Kusch, Polycarp	koosh, PAH lee kahrp	kuʃ, ˈpalikarp
Kuwatly, Shukri Al	koo꞉WAHT lee, SHOO꞉ kree ahl	kuˈwatli, ˈʃukri al

L

Laroche	lah ROHSH	laˈroʃ
Lausche	LOW shee	ˈlauʃi
Laver	LAY ver	ˈlevər
Lechuga, Carlos	lay CHOO꞉ gah KAHR lohs	leˈtʃuga ˈkarlos
Lemass, Sean	luh MAHS, shawn	ləˈmas, ʃɔn
Lewandowski, Bohdan	le vahn DOHV skee, BOHG dahn	lɛvanˈdovski, ˈbogdan
Lieshi, Haxhi	LEE shee, HAHK si	ˈliʃi, ˈhaksi
Liu Chieh	loo꞉ chah	lu tʃa
Liu Shao-chi	loo꞉ shaw-chee	lu ʃɔ-tʃi
Lopez Mateos, Adolfo	LOH pez mah TAY ohs, ah DAWL foh	ˈlopɛz maˈteos, aˈdɔlfo
Loren, Sophia	LAW ren, soh FEE ah	ˈlɔrɛn, soˈfia
Loridan	law ree DAHN	lɔriˈdan
Loudon	LOW duhn	ˈlaudən
Løvberg, Aase	LOOV berg, AWS se	ˈluvbɚg, ˈɔssɛ
Lübke, Heinrich	LOO꞉P kuh, HIGHN rish	ˈlupkə, ˈhaɪnrɪʃ
Luthuli	loo꞉ THOO꞉ lee	luˈθuli

M

Maazel, Lorin	muh ZEL, LAW rin	məˈzɛl, ˈlɔrɪn
Macapagal, Diosdado	mah kah pah GAHL, dee ohs DAH doh	makapaˈgal, diosˈdado
MacDiarmid	muhk DIGHR mid	məkˈdaɪrmɪd

---

sing [ŋ]; oh [o]; oil [ɔɪ]; foot [ʊ]; foo꞉d [u]; how [aʊ]; pie [p]; ray [r]; so [s]; shall [ʃ]; to [t]; thin [θ]; th꞉en [ð]; above (uh BUHV) [ə, ˈʌ]; vine [v]; wine [w]; whine [hw]; you [j]; zoo [z]; rouge (roo꞉zh) [ʒ].

Mackehenie, Carlos	mah KE nee, KAHR lohs	mɑˈkɛni, ˈkɑrlos
Maga, Hubert	MAH gah, yoo : BAIRT	ˈmɑgɑ, juˈbɛərt
Mahendra Bir Bikram Shah Deva	muh HEN drah beer bee KRUHM shah dee VAH	məˈhɛndrɑ bir biˈkrʌm ʃɑ diˈvɑ
Mahovlich	mah HAHV lich	mɑˈhɑvlɪtʃ
Mailliard	MIGH yard	ˈmaɪjɑrd
Malalasekera, Gunapala Piyasena	mah lah lah SAY kuh ruh, goo : nuh PAH luh pee yuh SAY nuh	mɑlɑlɑˈsekərə, gunəˈpɑlə pijəˈsenə
Malamud	MA luh moo : d	ˈmæləmud
Malzone (Frank)	mal ZOHN	mælˈzon
Mangano, Silvana	mahn GAH noh, seel VAH nah	mɑnˈgɑno, silˈvɑnɑ
Mannes, Marya	MA nis, MAR ee uh	ˈmænɪs, ˈmæriə
Marceau, Marcel	mahr SOH, mahr SEL	mɑrˈso, mɑrˈsɛl
Margolin	MAHR guh lin	ˈmɑrgəlɪn
Marichal, Juan	MAH ri shahl, hwahn	ˈmɑrɪʃɑl, hwɑn
Mastroianni, Marcello	mah stroh YAH nee, mahr CHE loh	mɑstrɔˈjɑni, mɑrˈtʃɛlo
Matsas	MAHT sahs	ˈmɑtsɑs
Matsch, Franz	mahtch, frahns	mɑtʃ, frɑns
Matsunaga	mat soo : NAH gah	mætsuˈnɑgɑ
Maurer, Ion	MOW rair, yahn	ˈmaʊrɛər, jɑn
Mayakovsky, Vladimir	migh ah KUHV skee, VLAH duh meer	maɪɑˈkʌvski, ˈvlɑdəmir
M'Ba, Leon	m BAH, lee AHN	mˈbɑ, liˈɑn
Mboya	muh BOI ah	məˈbɔɪə
Mehta, Ved	MEH tuh, ved	ˈmɛtə, vɛd
Mejias, Roman	muh HEE uhs, roh MAHN	məˈhiəs, roˈmɑn
Menshikov, Mikhail	MEN shi kuhf, mi KIGHL	ˈmɛnʃɪkəf, mɪˈkaɪl
Menzies	MEN zeez	ˈmɛnziz
Mercouri, Melina	mer KOO : ree, muh LEE nuh	mərˈkuri, məˈlinə
Mifune, Toshiro	MEE foo ne, toh shee ROH	ˈmifune, toʃiˈro
Mikita	muh KEE tuh	məˈkitə
Milla Bermudez	MEE lyah bair MOO : dez	ˈmiljə bɛərˈmudɛz
Mimieux, Yvette	mee MYOO, ee VET	miˈmjʊ, iˈvɛt
Mineo, Sal	MI nee oh, sal	ˈmɪnio, ˈsæl
Minow	MI noh	ˈmɪno
Miró Cardona	mee ROH kahr DOH nuh	miˈro kɑrˈdonə
Mirvish	MER vish	ˈmɚvɪʃ
Mobutu	moh BOO : too :	moˈbutu
Mohammed Da'ud	moh HAM uhd dah OO : D	moˈhæməd dɑˈud
Mohammed Na'im	moh HAM uhd nah EEM	moˈhæməd nɑˈim
Mohammed Zahir Shah	moh HAM uhd zah EER shaw	moˈhæməd zɑˈir ʃɔ
Mohyeddin, Zia	moi YE din, TSEE ah	mɔɪˈjɛdɪn, ˈtsiɑ
Monbouquette	mohn boo : KET	monbuˈket
Montand, Yves	mohn TAHN, eev	monˈtɑn, ˈiv
Moreno (Rita)	muh REE noh	məˈrino
Moscoso	mohs KOH zoh	mosˈkozo
Mössbauer, Rudolf	MAHS bow uhr, ROO : dohlf	ˈmɑsbaʊər, ˈrudolf

---

*a*t [æ] ; *ah* [ɑ] ; *air* [ɛ] ; *aw*ful [ɔ] ; *s*ay [e] ; *b*ack [b] ; *ch*air [tʃ] ; *d*o [d] ; *e*lm [ɛ] ; *ee*l [i] ; *s*erver [ˈɝ, ər] ; *f*it [f] ; *g*o [g] ; *h*urt [h] ; *i*s [ɪ] ; *h*igh [aɪ] ; *j*et [dʒ] ; *k*iss [k] ; *l*amb [l] ; *m*y [m] ; *n*ice [n] ;

Mwambutsa, Mwami	mwahm BOO : tsah, MWAH mee	mwɑmˈbutsɑ, ˈmwɑmi
Mydans	MIGH danz	ˈmaɪdænz

N

Nabokov, Vladimir	NAH boh kuhf, VLAH duh meer	ˈnɑbokʌf, ˈvlɑdəmir
Na Champassak, Sisouk	nah shahm PAH sahk, see SOO : K	nɑ ʃɑmˈpɑsɑk, siˈsuk
Narasimhan	nah rah sim HAHN	nɑrɑsɪmˈhɑn
Narayan	na RIGH an	næˈraɪæn
Nehru, Braj Kumar	NAY roo :, brahj koo : MAHR	ˈneru, brɑdʒ kuˈmɑr
Ne Win	nay win	ne wɪn
Ngo Dinh Diem	uhng O DIN zi EM	əŋˈo ˈdɪn zɪˈɛm
Nielsen, Sivert	NEEL sen, SEE vert	ˈnilsɛn, ˈsivərt
Nikula, Pentti	NI koo : lah, PEN tee	ˈnɪkulɑ, ˈpɛnti
Nilsson, Birgit	NEEL sohn, BEER git	ˈnilson, ˈbirgɪt
Nkrumah, Kwame	uhn KROO : mah, KWAH me	ənˈkrumɑ, ˈkwɑmɛ
Nosavan, Phoumi	noh sah VAHN, POO : mee	nosɑˈvɑn, ˈpumi
Novotny, Antonin	nah VUHT nee, ahn TOH neen	nɑˈvʌtni, ɑnˈtonin
Nuyen, France	noo : YEN, frans	nuˈjɛn, fræns
Nyerere	nyuh RAI ray	njəˈrɛəre
Nygaard, Hjalmar	NI gawrd, YAHL mahr	ˈnɪgɔrd, ˈjɑlmɑr

O

Okazaki, Katsuo	oh KAH zah kee, KAHT soo : oh	oˈkɑzɑki, ˈkɑtsuo
Ollenauer, Erich	AW luhn ow uhr, AIR ish	ˈɔlənaʊər, ˈɛərɪʃ
Olmedo	ohl MAY doh	olˈmedo
Ong Yoke Lin, Dató	ohng yoh KAY leen, dah TOH	oŋ yoˈke lin, dɑˈto
Ordoñez, Antonio	awr DO nyez, ahn TOH ni oh	ɔrˈdonjɛz, ɑnˈtonɪo
Orlich	awr LEECH	ɔrˈlitʃ
Ormsby-Gore	AWRMZ bee-gawr	ˈɔrmzbi-gɔr
Ortiz, Carlos	awr TEES, KAHR lohs	ɔrˈtis, ˈkɑrlos
Osman, Aden Abdulla	OHS muhn, AH duhn ahb DOO : luh	ˈosmən, ˈɑdən ɑbˈdulə
Osuna, Rafael	oh SOO : nuh, ra figh EL	oˈsunə, rɑfaɪˈɛl

sing [ŋ] ; oh [o] ; oil [ɔɪ] ; foot [ʊ] ; foo:d [u] ; how [aʊ] ; pie [p] ; ray [r] ; so [s] ; shall [ʃ] ; to [t] ; thin [θ] ; th:en [ð] ; above (uh BUHV) [ə, ˈʌ] ; vine [v] ; wine [w] ; whine [hw] ; you [j] ; zoo [z] ; rouge (roo:zh) [ʒ].

P

Pachachi, Adnan	puh SHAH shee, ahd NAHN	pə'ʃaʃi, ad'nɑn
Padilla Nervo, Luis	pah DEEL yah NAIR vo, loo : EES	pa'dilja 'nɛərvo, lu'is
Pagan, José	pah GAHN, hoh ZAY	pa'gɑn, ho'ze
Pagliaroni	pa glee uh ROH nee	pægliə'roni
Palafox, Antonio	PA luh fahks, an TOH nee oh	'pæləfɑks, æn'tonio
Palar, Lambertus Nicodemus	pah LAHR, lahm BER tuhs nee koh DEE moo : s	pa'lɑr, lam'bɜrtəs niko'dimus
Papas	PA puhs	'pæpəs
Park, Chung Hee	pahrk, choong hee	pɑrk tʃʊŋ hi
Pastore	pah STAW re	pa'stɔre
Patachou	pah tah SHOO :	pata'ʃu
Pavicevic, Miso	pah VI chay vich, MEE shoh	pa'vɪtʃevɪtʃ, 'miʃo
Paz Estenssoro	pahs es ten SAW roh	pɑs ɛstɛn'sɔro
Pazhwak, Abdul Rahman	pazh WAWK, ahb DOOL rah MAHN	pæʒ'wɔk, ɑb'dʊl rɑ'mɑn
Pellegrin, Raymond	PEL gran, RAY mohn	'pɛlgræn, 'remon
Perlis	per LIS	pər'lɪs
Petrides, Avra	pe TREE th : is, AH vrah	pɛ'tridɪs, 'ɑvrɑ
Pham Van Dong	fahm vahn dahng	fɑm vɑn dɑŋ
Pilote, Pierre	pee LAHT, pyair	pi'lɑt, pjɛər
Plate, Juan	PLAH tay, hwahn	'plate, hwɑn
Platzer, Wilfried	PLAHT suhr, VIL freet	'plɑtsər, 'vɪlfrit
Plimsoll	PLIM sohl	'plɪmsol
Plisetskaya, Maya	plee SETS kigh uh, MIGH uh	pli'sɛtskaɪə, 'maɪə
Plowright	PLOW right	'plaʊraɪt
Poage	pohg	pog
Podres	PAH drez	'pɑdrɛz
Poitier	PWAH tee ay	'pwɑtie
Pompidou, Georges	pohm pee DOO :, zhawrzh	pompi'du, ʒɔrʒ
Porumbeanu	paw ruhm bee AH noo :	pərəmbi'ɑnu
Price, Leontyne	prighs, Lee uhn teen	praɪs, 'liəntin
Prochnik	PRAHCH nik	'prɑtʃnɪk
Pucci, Emilio	POO : chee, ay MEE lyoh	'putʃi, e'miljo

Q

Quadros, Jânio	KWAH drohsh, ZHA nee oh	'kwɑdroʃ, 'ʒænio
Quaison-Sackey, Alex	KWE suhn SA kay, A leks	'kwɛsən 'sæke, 'ælɛks

R

Radhakrishnan	rah dah KRISH nuhn	rɑda'krɪʃnən
Radványi, János	ROHD vah nyee, YAH nohsh	'rodvɑnji, 'jɑnoʃ

at [æ]; *ah* [ɑ]; *air* [ɛ]; *awful* [ɔ]; *say* [e]; *back* [b]; *chair* [tʃ]; *do* [d]; *elm* [ɛ]; *eel* [i]; *server* ['ɝ, ər]; *f* it [f]; *go* [g]; *hurt* [h]; *is* [ɪ]; *high* [aɪ]; *jet* [dʒ]; *kiss* [k]; *lamb* [l]; *my* [m]; *nice* [n];

Radziwill	RAD zi wil	ˈrædzɪwɪl
Rakotomalala, Louis	rah koh toh MAH lahl, loo : EE	rɑkotoˈmɑlɑl, luˈi
Rama Rau, Santha	RAH mah row, SAHN tuh	ˈrɑmɑ rɑʊ, ˈsɑntə
Ramirez Pane, Ruben	rah MEER ez, PAH nay, ROO : ben	rɑˈmirɛz ˈpɑne, ˈrubɛn
Rapacki, Adam	rah PAHT skee, ah DAHM	rɑˈpɑtski, ɑˈdɑm
Reifel	RIGH fuhl	ˈraɪfəl
Renais, Alain	ruh NAY, ah LAN	rəˈne, ɑˈlæn
Reuss	rois	rɔɪs
Riad, Mahmoud	ree AHD, MAH moo : d	riˈɑd, ˈmɑmud
Richard, Henri	ree SHAHR, AHN ree	riˈʃɑr, ˈɑnri
Rifaʻi, Abdul Monem	ree FIGH, AHB duhl moh NEM	riˈfaɪ, ˈɑbdəl moˈnɛm
Rikhoff	RIK hawf	ˈrɪkhɔf
Robbe-Grillet, Alain	rohb gree YAY, ah LAN	rob-griˈje, ɑˈlæn
Roebling	ROH bling	ˈroblɪŋ
Roncalli, Angelo Giuseppe	rohn KAH lee, AHN juh loh juh ZE pee	ronˈkɑli, ˈɑndʒəlo dʒəˈzɛpi
Rossel, Agda	RUH sel, AHG dah	ˈrʌsɛl, ˈɑgdɑ
Rossides, Zenon	roh SEE th : ees, ZEE noon	roˈsiðis, ˈzinʊn
Rossi-Drago	ROH see-DRAH goh	ˈrosi-ˈdrɑgo
Rouleau, Raymond	ROO : loh, ray MOHN	ˈrulo, reˈmon

S

Salinger (Pierre, and J. D.)	SA lin jer	ˈsælɪndʒər
Sandys, Duncan	sandz, DUHNG kuhn	ˈsændz, ˈdʌŋkən
Sarrante, Nathalie	sah RAHNT, nah tah LEE	sɑˈrɑnt, nɑtɑˈli
Savalas, Telly	suh VAH luhs, TE lee	səˈvɑləs, ˈtɛli
Savang Vatthana	sah VAHNG vah TAH nah	sɑˈvɑŋ vɑˈtɑnɑ
Scaasi	SKAH see	ˈskɑsi
Schell, Maximilian	shel, mahk suh MEE lyahn	ʃɛl, mɑksəˈmiljɑn
Scheyven	SHI vin	ˈʃɪvɪn
Schiaffino, Rosanna	shah FEE no, roh ZAH nah	ʃɑˈfino, roˈzɑnɑ
Schurmann	SHER mahn	ˈʃɝmɑn
Schwengel	SHWENG guhl	ˈʃwɛŋgəl
Scofield	SKOH feeld	ˈskofild
Sebrell	se BREL	sɛˈbrɛl
Secrest	SEE kruhst	ˈsi krəst
Segni, Antonio	SAY nyee, ahn TOH nyoh	ˈsenji, ɑnˈtonjo
Segré, Emilio	say GRAY, ay MEE lyoh	seˈgre, eˈmiljo
Senghor, Leopold	seng GAWR, lee oh POHLD	sɛŋˈgɔr, lioˈpold
Seppälä	SE pa la	ˈsɛpælæ
Sevilla-Sacasa, Guillermo	say VEEL yah sah KAH sah, gi LYAIR mo	seˈviljɑ sɑˈkɑsɑ, gɪˈljeərmo
Seydoux, Roger	say DOO :, roh ZHAY	seˈdu, roˈʒe
Shaerf, Adolph	shairf, AH dawlf	ʃeərf, ˈɑdolf

sing [ŋ] ; oh [o] ; oil [ɔɪ] ; foot [ʊ] ; foo :d [u] ; how [aʊ] ; pie [p] ; ray [r] ; so [s] ; shall [ʃ] ; to [t] ; thin [θ] ; th :en [ð] ; above (uh BUHV) [ə, ˈʌ] ; vine [v] ; wine [w] ; whine [hw] ; you [j] ; zoo [z] ; rouge (roo :zh) [ʒ].

Shehu, Mehmet	SHAY hoo :, ME met	ˈʃehu, ˈmɛmɛt
Shevtsova, Ludmila	sheft SOH vah, loo :d MEE luh	ʃeft'sova, lud'milə
Shriver	SHRIGH ver	ˈʃraɪvər
Shukairy, Ahmed	shoo : KIGH ree, AH med	ʃu'kaɪri, 'amɛd
Sidikou, Abdou	see dee KOO :, AHB doo :	sidi'ku, 'abdu
Signoret, Simone	see nyaw RAY, see MOHN	sinjɔ're, si'mon
Sihanouk, Norodom	see hah NOHK, naw roh DOHM	siha'nok, nɔro'dom
Simonetta	see moh NE tah	simo'nɛtɑ
Simonov, Konstantin	SEE muh nuhv, kahn stahn TEEN	'simənʌv, kɑnstɑn'tin
Siroky, Viliam	shee ROH kee, VEE lyahm	ʃi'roki, 'viljɑm
Slim, Mongi	suh LEEM, MOHN jee	sə'lim, 'mondʒi
Slim, Taïeb	suh LEEM, TIGH yib	sə'lim, 'taɪjɪb
Solzhenitsyn	sohl zhe NEET zin	solʒe'nitzɪn
Sosa-Rodriguez	SOH sah roh DREE gez	'sosɑ ro'drigɛz
Soulat, Robert	SOO : lah, roh BAIR	'sula, ro'bɛər
Souleymane Ould Cheikh Sidya	soo : lay MAHN, OO : LT chayk SEE dyah	sule'man, 'ult tʃek 'sidjɑ
Souphanouvong	soo FAH noo : vawng	su'fɑnuvɔŋ
Souvanna Phouma	soo VAH nuh FOO : muh	su'vɑnə 'fumə
Souvannavong	soo vah nuh VAWNG	suvɑnə'vɔŋ
Sow, Adam Malick	SOH, uh DAHM MA leek	so, ə'dɑm 'mælik
Spiegel, Der	SHPEE guhl, dair	'ʃpigəl, 'dɛər
Staebler	STAY bluhr	'steblər
Stasiuk	STAY see uhk	'stesiək
Stikker, Dirk	STIK uhr, derk	'stɪkər, dɝk
Streich	shtrighk	'ʃtraɪk
Streisand	STRIGH suhnd	'straɪsənd
Stroessner, Alfredo	STROHS nair, ahl FRAY th : oh	'strosnɛər, al'freðo
Strudwick	STRUHD wik	'strʌdwɪk
Styne	stighn	staɪn
Swai, (A. Z.) Nsilo	swigh, uhn SEE loh	swaɪ, ən'silo
Swart	swahrt	'swɑrt

T

Tanner, Väinö	TAH nair, VIGH nuh	'tɑnɛər, 'vaɪnə
Tarazi, Salah El Dine	TAH rah zee, sah LAHK uhl DEEN	'tɑrazi, sɑl'lɑk ə'din
Tcherina, Ludmila	CHE ree nah, loo : d MEE luh	'tʃerinɑ, lud'milə
Tchobanov, Yordan	choh BAH nawf, YAWR dahn	tʃo'bɑnɔf, 'jɔrdɑn
Ter-Ovanesyan, Igor	ter ah ven yes YAHN, EE gawr	ter ɑvenjes'jɑn, 'igɔr
Tertz, Abram	terts, uh BRAHM	tɝts, ə'brɑm

at [æ] ; ah [ɑ] ; air [ɛ] ; awful [ɔ] ; say [e] ; back [b] ; chair [tʃ] ; do [d] ; elm [ɛ] ; eel [i] ; server [ˈɝ, ər] ; fit [f] ; go [g] ; hurt [h] ; is [ɪ] ; high [aɪ] ; jet [dʒ] ; kiss [k] ; lamb [l] ; my [m] ; nice [n] ;

Thanarat, Sarit	tah nah RAHT, sah REET	tɑnɑˈrɑt, sɑˈrit
Thant, U	TAHNT, OO :	ˈtɑnt, ˈu
Thors, Thor	tawrz, tawr	tɔrz, tɔr
Tomalbaye, François	toh mahl BIGH, frahn SWAH	tomɑlˈbaɪ, frɑnˈswɑ
Tomaz, Americo	TOO : mahsh, uh ME ri koo :	ˈtumɑʃ, əˈmɛrɪku
Toppazzini	tah puh SEE nee	tɑpəˈsini
Touré, Sekou	too : RAY, se KOO :	tuˈre, sɛˈku
Tremblay	truhm BLAY	trəmˈble
Tsarapkin, Semyon	tse RAHP kin, sem YOHN	tsɛˈrɑpkɪn, sɛmˈjon
Tsiang, Tingfu	chang, ting foo :	tʃæŋ, tɪŋ fu
Tsiranana, Philibert	tsee RUH nuhn, pi lee BAIR	tsiˈrʌnən, pɪliˈbɛər
Tynan	TIGH nin	ˈtaɪnɪn

U

Uelses	YOOL sis	ˈjʊlsɪs
Umeki, Myoshi	oo : ME kee, MEE oh shee	uˈmɛki, ˈmioʃi
Usher, Arsène Assouan	OO : shee, AHR sen a SOO : ah	ˈuʃi, ˈɑrsɛn æˈsuɑ
Ustinov	YOO : sti nawf	ˈjustɪnɔf
Utt	uht	ʌt
U Win Maung	oo : win mowng	u wɪn mauŋ
Uzamugura	oo : zah moo : GOO : rah	uzɑmuˈgurɑ

V

Vakil, Mehdi	va KEEL, meh DEE	væˈkil, mɛˈdi
Valencia, Guillermo León	vah LEN see uh, gee LYAIR mo lay OHN	vɑˈlɛnsiə, giˈljɛrmo leˈon
Van Deerlin	van DEER lin	væn ˈdirlɪn
Vanier	va NYAY	væˈnje
Velázquez, Guaroa	bay LAHS kez, gwah ROH ah	beˈlɑskɛz, gwɑˈroɑ
Venet	vuh NAY	vəˈne
Verwoerd, Hendrik	fair FOOT, HEN drik	fɛərˈfʊt, ˈhɛndrɪk
Villeda Morales, Ramón	vee LYAY th : ah moh RAH les, rah MOHN	viˈljeðɑ moˈrɑlɛs, rɑˈmon
Vishnevskaya, Galina	veesh NYEV skigh uh, gah LEE nuh	viʃˈnjɛvskaɪə, gɑˈlinə
Vitti	VEE tee	ˈviti
Volio Jiménez, Fernando	voh LEE oh hee MAY nez, fair NAHN doh	voˈlio hiˈmenɛz, fɛərˈnɑndo
von Hassel, Kai-Uwe	fuhn HAH suhl, kigh OO : vuh	fən ˈhɑsəl, kaɪ ˈuvə

---

sing [ŋ] ; *oh* [o] ; *oil* [ɔɪ] ; *foot* [ʊ] ; *foo* :d [u] ; *how* [au] ; *pie* [p] ; *ray* [r] ; *so* [s] ; *shall* [ʃ] ; *to* [t] ; *thin* [θ] ; *th* :en [ð] ; *above* (*uh* BUHV) [ə, ˈʌ] ; *vine* [v] ; *wine* [w] ; *whine* [hw] ; *you* [j] ; *zoo* [z] ; *rouge* (roo :zh) [ʒ].

Voznesensky, Andrei   vohz nyuh SEN skee, AHN   voznjə'sɛnski, 'andre
                        dray

W

Wallhauser   WAWL how zuhr   'wɔlhaʊzər
Weede   WEE dee   'widi
Wickersham   WI ker sham   'wɪkərʃæm
Wirtz   werts   'wɜ˞ts
Wynyard   WIN yerd   'wɪnjərd

Y

Yameogo, Maurice   yah may OH goh, maw   jɑme'ogo, mɔ'ris
                        REES
Yarborough   YAHR buh roh   'jɑrbəro
Ydígoras Fuentes,   ee DEE gaw rahs FWEN   i'digɔrɑs 'fwɛntɛs,
    Miguel   tes, mee GEL   mi'gɛl
Yesenin-Volpin   ye SAY nyin VOHL pin   jɛ'senjɪn 'volpɪn
Yevtushenko, Yevgeni   yev too: SHENG koh, yev   jɛvtu'ʃɛŋko, jɛv'geni
                        GAY nee
Youlou, Abbe   YOO: loo, AH be   'julu, 'abɛ
Yugov, Anton   YOO: gawf, AHN tohn   'jugɔf, 'anton

Z

Zea, German   SAY ah, her MAHN   'seɑ, hər'mɑn
Zetterling, Mai   ZE ter ling, migh   'zɛtərlɪŋ, maɪ
Zhivkov, Totor   ZHEEV kawf, TOH tawr   'ʒivkɔf, 'totɔr
Zoppi, Vittorio   DZOH pee, vee TAW ree oh   'dzopi, vi'tɔrio

---

at [æ] ; *ah* [ɑ] ; *air* [ɛ] ; *aw*ful [ɔ] ; s*ay* [e] ; *b*ack [b] ; *ch*air [tʃ] ; *d*o [d] ; *e*lm [ɛ] ; *ee*l [i] ;
s*er*v*er* ['ɝ, ər] ; *f*it [f] ; *g*o [g] ; *h*urt [h] ; *i*s [ɪ] ; h*igh* [aɪ] ; *j*et [dʒ] ; *k*iss [k] ; *l*amb [l] ; *m*y [m] ;
*n*ice [n] ; si*ng* [ŋ] ; *oh* [o] ; *oi*l [ɔɪ] ; *f*oot [ʊ] ; *f*oo:d [u] ; h*ow* [aʊ] ; *p*ie [p] ; *r*ay [r] ; *s*o [s] ;
*sh*all [ʃ] ; *t*o [t] ; *th*in [θ] ; *th*:en [ð] ; ab*o*ve (*uh* B*UH*V) [ə, 'ʌ] ; *v*ine [v] ; *w*ine [w] ; *wh*ine
[hw] ; *y*ou [j] ; *z*oo [z] ; rou*g*e (roo:*zh*) [ʒ].